Visual Basic 6
from the Ground Up

Gary Cornell

Osborne/**McGraw-Hill**

Berkeley New York St. Louis San Francisco
Auckland Bogotá Hamburg London Madrid
Mexico City Milan Montreal New Delhi Panama City
Paris São Paulo Singapore Sydney
Tokyo Toronto

Osborne/**McGraw-Hill**
2600 Tenth Street
Berkeley, California 94710
U.S.A.

For information on translations or book distributors outside the U.S.A., or to arrange bulk purchase discounts for sales promotions, premiums, or fund-raisers, please contact Osborne/**McGraw-Hill** at the above address.

Visual Basic 6 from the Ground Up

1234567890 AGM AGM 901987654321098

ISBN 0-07-882508-3

Publisher	**Proofreader**
Brandon A. Nordin	Pat Mannion
Editor-in-Chief	**Indexer**
Scott Rogers	David Heiret
Acquisitions Editor	**Computer Designers**
Wendy Rinaldi	Ann Sellers
	Jani Beckwith
Project Editor	
Janet Walden	**Illustrator**
	Lance Ravella
Editorial Assistant	
Marlene Vasilieff	**Series Design**
	Peter Hancik
Technical Editor	
Dave Jezak	**Cover Design**
	John Nedwidek
Copy Editor	
Andy Carroll	

For my family and friends who provide an anchor for my far
too hectic life

About the Author . . .

Gary Cornell is today's top-selling programming author and a noted expert on Visual Basic, Java, and Delphi. His *CORE JAVA* led the market last year as the #1 programming title. His best-selling *The Visual Basic 4 for Windows 95 Handbook* received the Readers' Choice Award from *Visual Basic Programmer's Journal*. A professional programmer and a professor at the University of Connecticut, Gary is in charge of the university's "Modern Visual Programming" curriculum and holds a Ph.D. from Brown University.

Contents at a Glance

Contents

Contents

Contents

Acknowledgments

One of the best parts of writing a book is when the author gets to thank those who have helped him or her, for rarely (and certainly not in this case) is a book by one author truly produced alone. First and foremost, I have to thank the team at Osborne/McGraw-Hill who got this book out under quite stressful conditions! Without this dedicated team you wouldn't have the book you see in your hands. I want to especially thank Andy Carroll: he went far beyond what I could have expected or hoped to have from a developmental/copy editor. Next, I have to thank those people at Microsoft (whose names I unfortunately don't know) who created Visual Basic and have now made it so much better in version 6.

I also want to single out my sometimes co-author, sometime tech reviewer, and always friend Dave Jezak: I have learned an immense amount about Visual Basic from him. I also want to thank Mike Lang, who has helped me with my seminars in which I teach VB programming to professionals. He also helped with the tech review of many of the chapters in this book. Finally, thanks to all my family and friends who put up with my strange ways and my occasionally short temper for lo, so many months.

Introduction

When Visual Basic 1.0 was released, Bill Gates, Chairman and CEO of Microsoft, described it as "awesome." Steve Gibson of *InfoWorld* said Visual Basic is a "stunning new miracle" and will "dramatically change the way people feel about and use [Microsoft] Windows." Stewart Alsop was quoted in the *New York Times* as saying Visual Basic is "the perfect programming environment for the 1990s."

It has been nearly 10 years and six versions of Visual Basic, and Visual Basic is far and away the most popular programming language in the world today. So what was the hype all about and why is VB the most popular language on the planet today? Exactly what is Visual Basic, and what can it do for you?

Well, Bill Gates describes Visual Basic as an "easy yet powerful tool for developing Windows applications in Basic." This may not seem like enough to justify all the hoopla until you realize that Microsoft Windows is used by tens of millions of people, and that developing a Microsoft Windows application formerly required an expert C/C++ programmer supplied with about 20 pounds worth of documentation for the needed C/C++ compiler and the essential add-ons. As Charles Petzold (author of one of the standard books on Windows programming in C) put it in the *New York Times*: "For those of us who make our living explaining the complexities of Windows programming to programmers, Visual Basic poses a real threat to our livelihood."

Visual Basic 2.0 was faster, more powerful and even easier to use than Visual Basic 1.0. Visual Basic 3.0 added simple ways to control the most powerful databases available. Visual Basic 4.0 added support for 32-bit development and began the process of turning Visual Basic into a fully object oriented programming language. Visual Basic 5.0 added the ability to create true executables and even the ability to make your own controls. Visual Basic 6.0 has added some long desired language features, even more Internet power and even more powerful database features. It's the slickest and most powerful Visual Basic yet. So welcome to the latest and best version of Visual Basic, the programming tool not only of the 90's but also of the twenty-first century!

About This Book

This tutorial is a comprehensive, hands-on guide to Visual Basic 6 programming—but one that doesn't assume you've programmed before. (People familiar with earlier versions of Visual Basic or another structured programming language will, of course, have an easier time and can move through the early chapters quickly.)

Soon, you'll be writing sophisticated Windows programs that take full advantage of Visual Basic's exciting and powerful event-driven nature. You'll start at the beginning, and when you have finished this book, you will have moved far along the road to VB mastery. I have tried hard to cover at the least the fundamentals of every technique that a professional VB developer will need to master. I know what techniques these are, as I have taught hundreds of professional programmers VB in intensive courses that used the previous version of this book.

I've also tried hard to stress the new ways of thinking needed to master Visual Basic programming, so even experts in more traditional programming languages can benefit from this book. I've taken this approach because trying to force Visual Basic into the framework of older programming languages is ultimately self-defeating—you can't take advantage of its power if you continue to think within an older paradigm.

To make this book even more useful, there are extensive discussions of important topics left out of most other introductory books. There's a whole chapter on objects, including non-trivial examples of building your own objects with Visual Basic. When I teach you debugging techniques, I show you how to use them to debug object-based programs as well as the more traditional style VB programs. There's a chapter on building your own custom controls. There's even a whole chapter on recursion. There are methods of keeping file information secret and ways to add protection to programs you may want to distribute. There are two chapters devoted to VB and the Internet and lots of examples in other chapters about how to adapt VB to the world of the Web. The book also includes an extensive discussion of sorting and searching techniques and lots of tips and tricks. In sum, unlike many of the introductory books out there, I not only want to introduce you to a topic, but I go into it in enough depth that you can actually use the techniques for writing practical programs.

Now a confession: My original goal was to make this book a "one-stop resource," but, realistically, Visual Basic has gotten far too big and is far too powerful for any one book to do this. Nonetheless, if you finish this book, I truly believe that you will be in a position to begin writing commercial-quality Visual Basic programs! True mastery will take longer: I have tried to give you suggestions about books that can take you to the next level.

Finally, because most users of Visual Basic have (or eventually will have) the higher-end versions ("Visual Basic Professional Edition" or "Visual Basic Enterprise Edition"), I cover many of the special features of these higher-end products in the text itself, rather than relegating them to an appendix.

How This Book Is Organized

This book can be used in a variety of ways, depending on your background and needs. People familiar with structured programming techniques can skim the complete discussions of the programming constructs such as loops and Sub and Function procedures in Visual Basic. These appear in Chapters 5 through 12. Beginners will want to work through this material more carefully, but experienced programmers can move quickly through this information. From Chapter 12 on, most readers will find lots of new information!

Here are short descriptions of the chapters:

Chapters 1 and 2 introduce you to Visual Basic and help you become familiar with the Visual Basic environment.

Chapters 3 and 4 start you right off with the notion of a customizable window (called a form) that is the heart of every Microsoft Windows (and thus, Visual Basic) application. You'll see how to add the basic controls—such as command buttons, text boxes, and labels—to your forms.

Chapters 5 through 12 discuss the core programming techniques needed to release Visual Basic's powers. You'll see how to take full advantage of Visual Basic's various data types and control structures, as well as its many built-in functions. You'll also learn how to add your own functions. You'll see how to sort and search through data, use the grid control, and use modular programming techniques to make your programs more flexible, powerful, and easier to debug. You'll see how to build multiform projects and format information for a professional-looking application.

Chapter 13 is a comprehensive introduction to Visual Basic's implementation of part of the object oriented programming paradigm—including how to build your own reuseable objects with Visual Basic.

Chapter 14 takes up the user interface again and takes you through most of the rest of the controls you can add to your forms. I cover both the standard controls and those found in the Professional and Enterprise editions as well as some sophisticated techniques for building interfaces that are independent of the resolution of the user's screen.

Chapter 15 shows you the powerful debugging tools in Visual Basic. You'll learn how to isolate bugs (programming errors) and then eradicate them. I even cover a topic stinted in most introductory books: how to debug object oriented programs.

Chapter 16 introduces you to the world of graphics. Because Microsoft Windows is a graphically based environment, the powers of Visual Basic in this arena are pretty spectacular.

Chapter 17 shows you how to analyze the way a user is manipulating his or her mouse.

Chapter 18 shows you how to handle files in Visual Basic, including sophisticated methods for encrypting (that is, keeping the contents of files safe from casual probes).

Chapter 19 introduces you to the file system controls and the really neat file system objects that were added to VB6.

Chapter 20 shows you how to communicate with other Windows applications from Visual Basic. This includes an introduction to COM/OLE, Microsoft's common object model for making reusable objects. I even show you how to use the amazing power of OLE "drag and drop" to allow users to drag files of Windows Explorer into VB programs.

Chapter 21 is an extensive treatment of recursion. Recursion is one of the most powerful programming tools available, and it's too often slighted in introductory books. In addition to discussing powerful methods for handling disks and sorting data, this chapter gives you a short introduction to recursive graphics, or fractals. Fractals are one of the most powerful tools in graphics—for example, they were used in the Genesis sequence in *Star Trek II: The Wrath of Khan*.

Chapter 22 is an introduction to the world of database development with Visual Basic. You'll see how to access information from powerful databases with only a few lines of code using the data controls as well as get a start on database programming with the various database objects.

Chapter 23 is an introduction to writing your own custom controls. You'll see how to build a special-purpose text box for the very common task of entering only numeric information.

Chapter 24 is an introduction to the WebBrowser and WebTransfer control. You'll see how to use this amazing control to build your own special-purpose browser.

Chapter 25 introduces you to VBScript and Dynamic HTML.

Chapter 26 shows you how to use the new Package and Deployment Wizard that makes distributing your files a breeze.

Conventions Used in This Book

Keys and keystrokes are set in small capital letters in the text. For example, keys such as CTRL and HOME appear as shown here. Arrow and other direction keys are spelled out and also appear in small capital letters. For example, if you need to press the right arrow key, you'll see, "Press RIGHT ARROW."

When you need to use a combination of keys to activate a menu item, the first two keys will be separated by a plus sign and the entire key combination will appear in small capital letters. For example, "Press CTRL A+B" indicates that you should hold down the key marked CTRL on your keyboard while holding down the A and the B keys. On the other hand, ALT F, P means press the ALT key, then the F key, and then the P key—you don't have to hold down the ALT key.

Microsoft Windows 95, 98, and Windows NT 3.51 or later are referred to collectively as simply Windows most of the time. Earlier versions of Windows are called Windows 3.*x* when they need to be referred to specifically. Keywords in Visual Basic appear with the first letter of each word capitalized: for example, Print, AutoRedraw, BorderStyle, and so on.

The syntax for a command in Visual Basic is set in ordinary type except that items the programmer can change appear in italics. For example, the Name command used to rename a file appears as

Name *OldFileName* As *NewFileName*

Also, programs are set in a monospaced font, as shown here:

```
Private Sub Form_Click()
  Print "Hello world!"
End Sub
```

and lines of code that should appear on one line when you program, but which for typographic reasons need to be on more than one line in this book, will be broken with an underscore. (Visual Basic has a line continuation character—the underscore—which you can use whenever you are not inside quotes and I will use it whenever possible.) Here's an example:

```
M$ = "This line is also too long but it has an " + _
underscore so it will be regarded as one line by VB"
```

Menu choices are indicated by writing the menu name, followed by a bar (|), followed by the menu item; for example, "choose File|Open" means open the File menu and then choose the Open option.

Finally, Osborne-McGraw Hill maintains a web site (http://www.osborne.com) from which you can download all the non-trivial pieces of code. I expect we will keep the errata list here as well. And, most importantly if you have any suggestions for improvements or comments, I hope you will not hesitate to e-mail me (gary@theCornells.com). I can't guarantee to answer every e-mail (though I try) but I do promise to read every one.

CHAPTER 1

Getting Started

This chapter gives you an overview of Microsoft's Visual Basic Version 6.0. (Usually I'll just call it Visual Basic, or simply VB. To distinguish the current version from earlier ones, I'll use VB5, VB4, and so on.) There are three commercial editions of Visual Basic 6 available (Learning, Pro, and Enterprise). They differ in their features (and price!) considerably. This particular chapter takes a very high-level view of what VB is about and therefore applies to all the editions. I hope, therefore, it is useful to users of all versions.

NOTE: Since I am assuming you are not a naive user of Windows, this chapter (and book) spends only a short time on how to install Visual Basic, or start it, and no time at all on how to manipulate windows within the Windows 95/98 NT4 environment. (I'll often say "Windows" for these three similar environments.) However, I am not assuming any expertise in Visual Basic, or in any programming language for that matter.

Why Windows and Why Visual Basic?

Graphical user interfaces, or *GUIs* (pronounced "gooies"), have revolutionized the microcomputer industry. They demonstrate that the proverb, "A picture is worth a thousand words," hasn't lost its truth to most computer users. Instead of the cryptic C:> prompt that DOS users have long seen (and some have long feared), you are presented with a desktop filled with icons and with programs that use mice and menus.

Perhaps even more important than the *look* of Microsoft Windows applications is the *feel* that the applications developed for Windows have. Windows applications generally have a consistent user interface. This means that users can spend more time mastering the application and less time worrying about which keystrokes do what within menus and dialog boxes. (Of course, Windows 95/98 and Windows NT 4 applications look a bit different than Windows 3.1 applications did: the consistency is *within* versions of Windows, not *between* versions of Windows.) Luckily, Microsoft is going to a uniform "look and feel" on all its products, so users will eventually have to learn a single interface.

While programmers have long had mixed feelings about GUIs, beginning users like them, and so Windows programs are expected to be based on the GUI model (and to have the right look and feel). Therefore, if you need to develop programs for any version of Windows, you'll want a tool to develop GUI-based applications efficiently.

For a long time there were few such tools for developing Windows applications. Before Visual Basic was introduced in 1991, developing Windows applications was *much* harder than developing DOS applications. Programmers had too much to worry about, such as what the mouse was doing, where the user was inside a menu, and whether he or she was clicking or double-clicking at a given place. Developing a Windows application required expert C programmers and hundreds of lines of code for the simplest task. Even the experts had trouble. (The Microsoft Windows Software

Development Kit that was required at that time—in addition to a C compiler—weighed in at nine and a half pounds.)

This is why, when Visual Basic 1.0 was released, Bill Gates, chairman and CEO of Microsoft, described it as "awesome." Steve Gibson in *InfoWorld* said Visual Basic is a "stunning new miracle" and will "dramatically change the way people feel about and use Microsoft Windows." Stewart Alsop was quoted in the *New York Times* as saying Visual Basic is "the perfect programming environment for the 1990s." And as Charles Petzold, author of one of the standard books on Windows programming in C, put it in the *New York Times*: "For those of us who make our living explaining the complexities of Windows programming to programmers, Visual Basic poses a real threat to our livelihood." The latest version of Visual Basic continues this tradition: sophisticated Windows 95/98 and Windows NT applications can now be developed in a fraction of the time previously needed. Programming errors (bugs) don't happen as often as they did, and if they do, they're a lot easier to detect and fix. Simply put: *with Visual Basic, programming for Windows has become not only more efficient but it has become fun* (well, most of the time, at least).

NOTE: Version 6 of Visual Basic is Windows 95/98 and Windows NT specific; it cannot run in or build Windows 3.1 applications.

In particular, Visual Basic lets you add menus, text boxes, command buttons, option buttons (for making exclusive choices), check boxes (for nonexclusive choices), list boxes, scroll bars, and file and directory boxes to blank windows. You can use grids to handle tabular data. You can communicate with other Windows applications, and, perhaps most importantly, you'll have an easy method to let users control and access databases. (By the way, in Visual Basic, components like these are usually called *controls*.)

You can have multiple windows on a screen. These windows have full access to the clipboard and to the information in most other Windows applications running at the same time. You can use Visual Basic to communicate with other applications running under Windows, using the most modern version of Microsoft's COM/OLE technology (see Chapter 20).

However, the earlier versions of Visual Basic (especially VB5) could do most, if not all, of what I just described. What's so special about the newest version of Visual Basic? In a nutshell, the answer is that Visual Basic 6 offers you more: more Internet features, better support for database development, more language features to make your programming jobs easier, more Wizards, more, more, more.

What You Need to Run Visual Basic

All versions of Visual Basic are sophisticated and powerful and therefore require a machine to match. Realistically, even the Learning edition of VB requires around

50MB of free hard disk space, a fast Pentium class chip (166MHz or better), and at least 16MB of RAM (and 32MB is *really* want you want as a minimum). A full installation of the most powerful version of Visual Basic, the Enterprise edition, could require more than 300MB of hard disk space!

NOTE: The commercial editions of Visual Basic come with all the tutorials and (usually) other documentation supplied in printed form (or they are available by sending in a coupon and paying a small fee). But they all come with the documentation available online. You can install this information on your hard disk to speed up access to it (see the next chapter). This requires a fair amount of extra hard disk space (say another 50MB, at least).

Setting Up Visual Basic

Visual Basic 6 comes only on CDs; it is also available as part of the larger "Visual Studio" product. (There are at least two CDs—one for the program and one for the documentation. The full Visual Studio comes on five(!) CDs.) If you purchase VB6, I'd suggest sending in the registration card or registering by modem. It's true that you'll get a certain amount of junk mail as a result, but it also will be easier to get support and notices of upgrades from Microsoft.

Running the Setup Program

The first CD that comes with Visual Basic or Visual Studio contains an automated Setup program to install Visual Basic. If it doesn't activate itself automatically when you put the CD in your machine, look for a program called Setup.exe on the CD. All editions require Windows 95/98 or Windows NT 3.51 or later. I won't bother going into the details of using an automated setup program. I assume, by now, that you have installed lots of programs under the Windows environment.

You can run the Setup program as many times as you want, which means you are not tied to the options you choose the first time. (It's usually a good idea for first-time users to use the default options.) The first time you set up Visual Basic, the Setup program asks for your name and the name of the company that bought the copy of Visual Basic. It keeps track of this information and uses it to remind you to whom the program is licensed—every time you start Visual Basic.

After you've completed the installation procedure, Visual Basic is installed in its own program group on the Start menu or under a program group called Visual Studio (depending on whether you bought VB as part of the Visual Studio package or not). You can use standard Windows 95/98 or NT Explorer techniques to move it to a different place on your Start menu. Consult the documentation that came with your Windows package or a standard book to see how to do this.

If there are any corrections or additions to the documentation, you'll find them in a bunch of HTML files on the CD.

NOTE: You don't have to explicitly set up a printer for Visual Basic. Visual Basic uses whatever printer information Windows is currently using.

Starting Visual Basic

The easiest way to run Visual Basic under Windows 95/98 or NT 4 is to use the Program option on the Start menu. (The Setup program automatically adds it.) There are, of course, lots of other ways to run Visual Basic. You can also start Visual Basic from the Microsoft Windows desktop by moving to the directory that contains it through Explorer or My Computer and then double-clicking on the Visual Basic icon. Or you can start Visual Basic by opening the Run dialog box and entering the path to Visual Basic. (Under Windows 95/98 or NT 4.0 the list of ways to start Visual Basic goes on and on.)

When you start Visual Basic, you see a copyright screen telling you to whom the copy of Visual Basic is licensed. After that, you see a screen like the one in Figure 1-1. (What exactly you see in this dialog box depends on the edition of Visual Basic you have. I am using the Enterprise edition to write this book, so Figure 1-1 shows more options than you might see in another edition of VB.) This New Project dialog box lets you start to build all the different types of Visual Basic applications. In this chapter we will only get started on making what VB calls a Standard EXE—shorthand for an ordinary stand-alone program.

NOTE: The reason this box is titled "New Project" rather than "New Program" is that the designers of VB want to stress that a lot more goes into a VB application than simply code. Thus, they coined the word "Project" to describe all the pieces that will go into your VB application. (Luckily, VB manages all the pieces of your application—especially the visual pieces—quite well. You rarely have to worry about them yourself.)

Working with Visual Basic

In this section we will build two Visual Basic applications. The first, which we'll build totally by hand, will simply be a resizeable window with the usual maximize, minimize, and exit buttons. For the second application we will use the Application Wizard supplied with Visual Basic to build the framework for a highly nontrivial application. These kinds of applications are called MDI (multiple document interface) applications. Much like the default environment supplied with Visual Basic, they let you add multiple windows inside a single parent window. The application will also have all the menus that you have grown to expect: File, Help, and so on. The Application Wizard generates an amazing amount of useful code automatically.

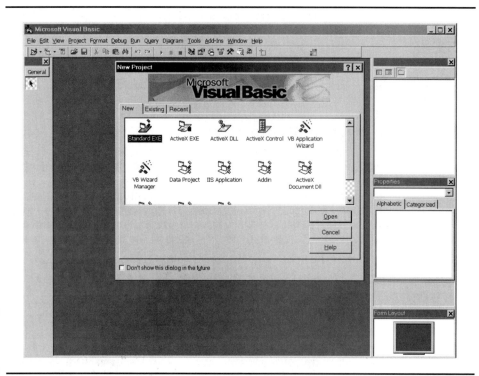

The New Project
dialog box
Figure 1-1.

Then you will only need to add relatively little additional code to make all the automatically generated features come completely alive.

NOTE: Of course, knowing what code you need to add or which automatically generated code you need to modify isn't that easy. In all honesty, working effectively with the code automatically generated by the Application Wizard requires knowing quite a lot about how to program with Visual Basic. The Application Wizard, powerful as it is, is an aid to your programming knowledge; it will not substitute for it. I actually think that if you try to use it at the beginning of your journey to VB mastery, you'll be slowed down. Trying to understand what is sometimes hundreds of lines of automatically generated code is not going to be helpful to a beginner who is trying to master the basics!

A Simple Handcrafted Application

As mentioned before, when you start Visual Basic, your initial screen will look something like the one in Figure 1-1. In the New Project dialog box shown in Figure

1-1, double-click on the Standard EXE icon (the first one). (Or, if it is highlighted, like it is in Figure 1-1, simply click on the Open button or press ENTER.)

Once you do, you will be immediately taken to a screen like the one in Figure 1-2. This is called the VB *IDE*—which stands for *Integrated Development Environment* (because you do all your Visual Basic development inside this environment).

Note the blank window named Project1-Form1 (Form) in the center of Figure 1-2. Inside it is another window called simply Form1, which has a grid of dots. This is the *form* that you will customize by placing controls on it. You use the grid to align controls, such as command buttons and list boxes that you place on the form. (You'll learn more about how to do this in Chapters 3 and 4.)

When you run your project (or compile it so that it can be run independently of the Visual Basic development environment), forms like Form1 become the windows that users see. At the top of the blank form is the title bar with its caption. (*Caption* is the Visual Basic term for what appears in the title bar of the form.) Currently, this form is titled Form1, which is the default caption that Visual Basic gives to a form when you start working on a new project.

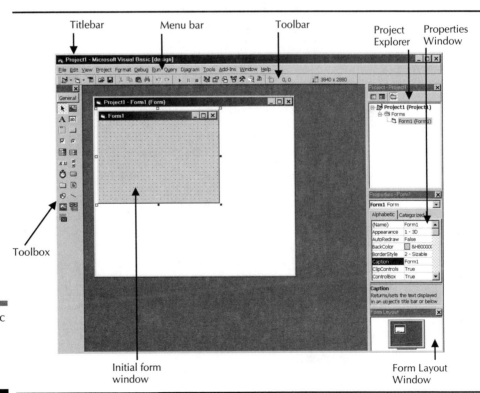

The Visual Basic
IDE (Integrated
Development
Environment)

Figure 1-2.

To the left of the Form1 window in Figure 1-2 is the toolbox, where you find the controls you will place on the form. (As I mentioned earlier in this chapter, *control* is the term used in Visual Basic for the objects you place on the windows you are designing. You'll see how to use the toolbox and manipulate controls in Chapter 4.) To the right of the form window are three other windows. The top one is called the Project Explorer; we will have a lot more to say about this window in Chapter 9. Immediately below it is the Properties window, which you use to customize the form and the various controls you place on the form. (You'll see how to use the Properties window in Chapters 3 and 4.) To the bottom right is the Form Layout window that you'll learn about shortly.

For now, concentrate on the central window called Project1-Form1 (Form) and the extra window inside it named Form1. In many Visual Basic applications, the size and location of the form at the time you finish the design (usually called *design time*) are the size and shape that the user sees at *run time*. This is not to say that Visual Basic doesn't let you change the size and location of forms as a project runs (see Chapter 4); in fact, an essential feature of Visual Basic is its ability to make dynamic changes in response to user events.

Let's make the Project1 window bigger, so we will have more room to work with the Form inside it. To do this, simply click on the maximize button in the title bar that says

Project1 – Form1 (Form)

(and not the Maximize button of the Form itself). The result looks like Figure 1-3.

Now that we have more room to work with Form1, let's try to resize it. One way to resize a form that is common to all Microsoft Windows applications is to first click inside the form so that it is active. (You can always tell when a window is active because the title bar is highlighted.) Then move the mouse to any part of the border of the form. The mouse pointer changes to a double-headed arrow when you're at a hot spot. At this point, you can drag the form to change its size or shape.

To start developing the first sample application, simply do the following:

1. Change the form's default size and shape by manipulating it at some of the hot spots.
2. Run the project by pressing F5 or choosing Start from the Run menu (ALT+R, S).

Notice that what you see is an ordinary-looking Windows window with the same size and shape that you left the form in at design time. Next, notice that when you run this new project, the window that pops up has standard Windows features, such as resizable borders, a control box (in the upper-left corner), and maximum, minimum, and exit buttons (in the upper-right corner). This shows one of the most important features of Visual Basic: your forms become windows that already behave as they should under the version of Windows you are using, without your having to do anything!

Return to the development environment by pressing ALT+F4, double-clicking on the control box for the Form1 form, or clicking on the exit button in the Form1 form.

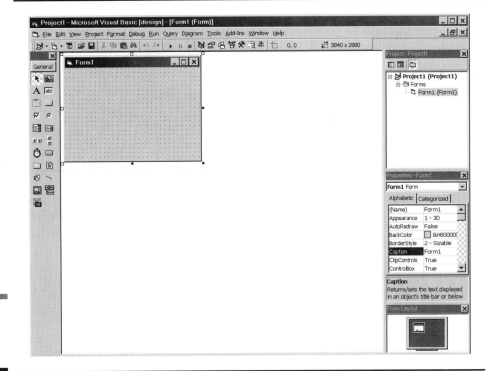

VB IDE with
Form window
maximized
Figure 1-3.

Notice that your application automatically responds to these standard ways of closing a Windows application. This illustrates the important point that, in many cases, Visual Basic applications behave as Windows users expect, without requiring any special intervention by the programmer (or the user).

NOTE: What you just did (without any code!) may not seem like much, but it turns out that building a window that behaves the way the user expects so that he or she can resize it, minimize it, or close it would require a hundred lines of complicated code in a language like C!

Next let's change the location where the user initially sees the running form. For this, move to the Form Layout window on the bottom right of your screen. Notice the image of a little form inside the Form Layout window. Here's a blowup of what you will see:

Simply drag the form inside the Form Layout window to a new location. Now rerun the application by pressing F5. You will see that the initial form appears where you placed it inside the Form Layout window.

NOTE: The size, shape, and location of your form are examples of what are called its *properties*. As you have seen, they can be set by direct manipulation. They can also be set by working with the Properties window—you'll see how to do this in Chapters 3 and 4.

Using the Application Wizard

Next, I want to run through a session using the powerful VB Application Wizard that comes with all editions of VB. To get this started, again choose File|New Project and, from the screen shown in Figure 1-1, choose the VB Application Wizard. If you do, then after a short delay, you are taken to a screen like Figure 1-4.

Since you haven't used VB and won't have made a "Profile" of your custom settings for application, click on the Next button to move forward with the Application Wizard. The next window you see looks like Figure 1-5. This is where you choose the type of "look" you want your applications to have. Notice that this window describes in both words and pictures what the interface looks like.

To see this at work, temporarily, click on the Explorer Style button. Notice that the screen changes to look like Figure 1-6. This shows you that for the Application Wizard, "Explorer Style" is a tree structure like the one used in Windows Explorer, not Internet Explorer.

For now, though, let's use the first (default) option in the Interface Type window (Figure 1-5), Multiple Document Interface (MDI). Make sure this option is chosen, as in the window shown in Figure 1-5. (Multiple Document Interface is a fancy term for a program like VB itself, where all the windows sit inside a big parent window. In the Single Document Interface (SDI), each window in your program exists independently of its cousin.)

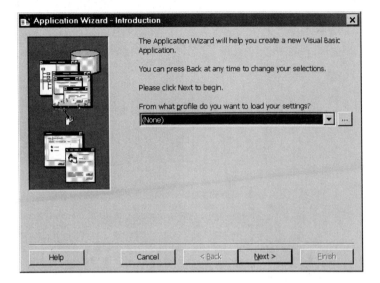

The initial
window in the
Application
Wizard
Figure 1-4.

Click Next. You will see a window like the one shown in Figure 1-7, which lets you choose what type of menus you want.

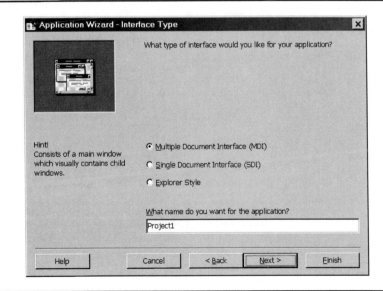

Choosing the
Interface Type in
the Application
Wizard
Figure 1-5.

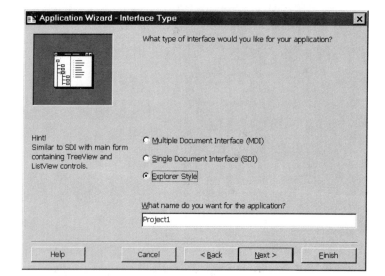

The Explorer Style Interface Type in the Application Wizard

Figure 1-6.

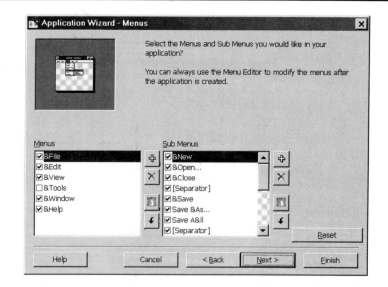

Choosing menus in the Application Wizard

Figure 1-7.

Again, accept the defaults and click Next. This displays a window, like the one in Figure 1-8, that is used for choosing what tools you would like to have on your toolbar. (Or even if you want to have a toolbar at all.)

Again, accept the defaults and click Next. This displays a window for choosing *resources*. This is an advanced feature that we won't cover in this book. (For those who are curious, *resource files,* as the wizard tells you, make it easy to change the names of things like captions and menu items to be appropriate in a different language.) Click Next again to go to the window shown in Figure 1-9.

These settings will be useful when you know more about how Visual Basic works with the Internet (see Chapters 24 and 25). For now just click the Next button to get to a window that allows you to add some extra forms for things like a startup screen or an About box. Click Next again. You will see a window that allows you to connect your application to a database. I'll have a lot more to say about databases in Chapter 22; for now, again just click the Next button. That's it—you're at the Finished window shown in Figure 1-10. Click on Finish and the wizard generates the code for your application.

You can click on the View Report button to see a summary of what the Application Wizard did. Part of the summary report for what we just built is shown in Figure 1-11.

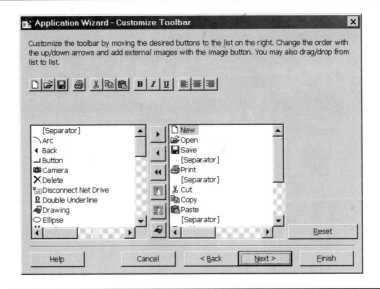

Choosing tools for a toolbar in the Application Wizard

Figure 1-8.

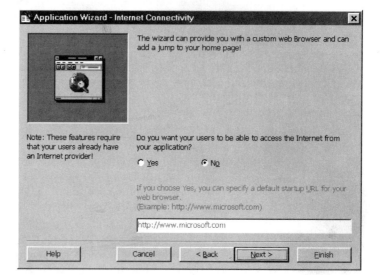

Getting Internet
access in the
Application
Wizard
Figure 1-9.

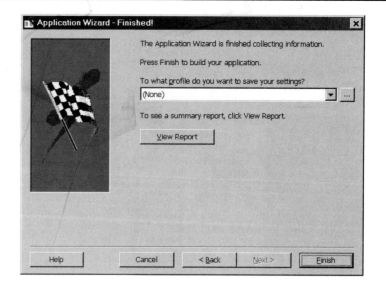

The Finished!
window in the
Application
Wizard
Figure 1-10.

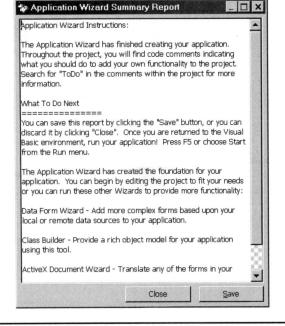

Report window
in the
Application
Wizard
Figure 1-11.

Finally, you'll see a window like the one shown in Figure 1-12. After you click on OK, the wizard goes off and generates literally hundreds of lines of code, two windows, and a lot more. The resulting VB IDE is shown in Figure 1-13—I've moved things around so you can see some of what the wizard did. (As you can imagine, it will take some time before you can figure out everything the wizard did!)

Overview of How You Develop a Visual Basic Application

I want to end this chapter by giving you an overview of how you develop a Visual Basic application. Some of these steps may seem unclear now, but very shortly they will all become second nature.

The *first* step in developing a Visual Basic application is to plan what the user will see—in other words, to design the screens. What menus do you want? How large a window should the application use? How many windows should there be? Should the user be able to resize the windows? Where will you place the command buttons that the user will click on to activate the applications? Will the applications have places (*text boxes)* in which to enter text? What sort of controls do you need to accomplish what you want? Are those controls part of your version of Visual Basic or will you need to buy or build them?

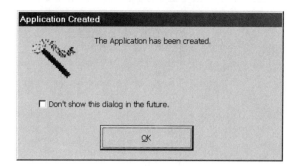

The number of controls you have at your disposal depends on the edition of Visual Basic you are using and, ultimately, the state of your wallet or the amount of time you have available to build special-purpose controls. The standard edition has more than 20 controls, the Professional and Enterprise editions, more than 50. Moreover, since

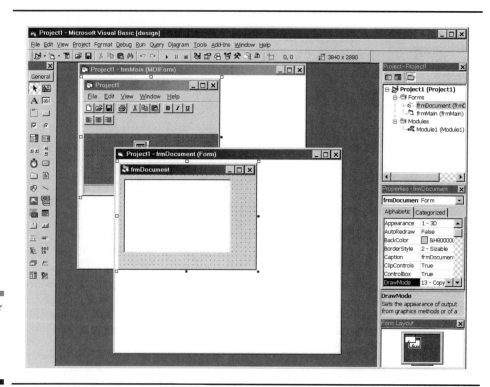

Visual Basic has inspired third-party vendors to create a large number of controls for specialized tasks, you can almost always find a custom control for a specialized task. (Microsoft estimates there are more than 3,000 commercial controls and literally countless shareware and free controls.) Finally, I can't emphasize enough: you can use the new power built into VB6 to build your own controls by either extending an existing control or building one from scratch. (The latter is, in all honesty, quite unlikely.)

You haven't seen much of this at work yet, but I want to repeat that ultimately what makes Visual Basic different from almost any other programming tool is how easy it is to design the user interface and then activate the user interface with code. You can literally *draw* the user interface, much like using a paint program. When you're finished drawing the interface, the command buttons, text boxes, and other controls that you have placed in a blank window will automatically recognize user actions, such as mouse movements and button clicks. Visual Basic also comes with a menu design feature that makes creating both ordinary and pop-up menus a snap.

Only after you design the interface does anything like traditional programming occur. This leads to the *second* step in building a Visual Basic application: writing the code to activate the visual interface you built in step one. The point is, objects in Visual Basic *will* recognize events like mouse clicks; how the objects respond to them depends on the code you write. You will almost always need to write code in order to make controls respond to events. This makes Visual Basic programming fundamentally different from conventional programming.

Programs in conventional programming languages run from the top, down. For older programming languages, execution starts from the first line and moves with the flow of the program to different parts as needed. A Visual Basic program works completely differently. The core of a Visual Basic program is a set of independent pieces of code that are *activated* by, and so respond to, only the events they have been told to recognize. This is a fundamental shift. Now instead of designing a program to do what the programmer thinks should happen, the user is in control.

Much of the programming code in Visual Basic that tells your program how to respond to events such as mouse clicks occurs in what Visual Basic calls *event procedures*. An event procedure is nothing more than the code needed to tell Visual Basic how to respond to an event. Essentially, everything executable in a Visual Basic program is either in an event procedure or is used by an event procedure to help the procedure carry out its job. The *third* and *fourth* steps are—of course, and unfortunately—finding the errors in the code (*debugging* in programmer jargon) and then fixing them.

Here's a summary of the steps you take to design a Visual Basic application:

1. Customize the windows that the user sees.
2. Decide what events the controls on the window should recognize.
3. Write the event procedures for those events (and the subsidiary procedures that make those event procedures work).

Here is what happens when the application is running:

1. Visual Basic monitors the windows and the controls in each window for *all* the events that each control can recognize (mouse movements, clicks, keystrokes, and so on).
2. When Visual Basic detects an event, if there isn't a built-in response to the event, Visual Basic examines the application to see if you've written an event procedure for that event.
3. If you have written an event procedure, Visual Basic executes the code that makes up that event procedure and goes back to step 1.
4. If you have not written an event procedure, Visual Basic does nothing and goes back to step 1.

These steps cycle continuously until the application ends. Usually, an event must happen before Visual Basic will do anything. Thus event-driven programs are more *reactive* than *active*—and that makes them more user-friendly.

A final word before we get into the details of the program: since Visual Basic's programming language is based on a modern structured version of BASIC, it's easy to build large programs by using modern modular and object-oriented techniques. (It is not at all like the condemned BASICs of long ago.) Visual Basic also provides sophisticated error handling for the all-too-common task of preventing users from bombing an application. The Visual Basic compiler is fast, and even lets you do background compilation or compile only the code that is needed to start the application. This means that any changes needed to correct the routine programming and typographical errors that are so common when you begin building an application are a snap. In addition, VB has an extensive online help system for quick reference while you're developing an application.

CHAPTER 2

The Visual Basic Environment and Help System

W hat I want to do in this chapter is show you the menus and windows that make up the Visual Basic environment. Given the power of Visual Basic, with its rich set of tools, detailed menus, and many windows, it's easy to be overwhelmed at first. The key point to remember is that the online help system gives you a quick way to understand almost everything in the Visual Basic environment with a simple keystroke (when in doubt press F1!). For this reason, you might find it easier to simply move directly to Chapter 3 after learning how to use the online help system, returning to this chapter only when you need to.

T IP: In any case, I don't suggest trying to memorize all the information in this chapter! I have found when I teach professional programmers, the way they deal with the myriad of options available in the VB IDE that are detailed in this chapter is that they simply study the first two sections (finishing the section on the online help, including the part on running some of the samples that come with VB) and then they skim the rest of this chapter. In fact, many people find that a good way to become familiar with a program as complicated as the VB IDE is to first look at the menus (much like looking at the table of contents of a book). Then they look through all the preferences/settings that the program allows you to set. This doesn't really teach you how to do anything, but the possible preferences/settings can usually give you a good sense of what the program can do, and how you can interact with it.

One point always worth keeping in mind is that if you are not completely comfortable with the look and feel of Microsoft Windows 95/98/NT 4.0 applications, then studying VB's environment and this chapter will help. After all, Visual Basic is itself a well-designed Windows application, and the way its menus and windows respond is typical of Windows programs. (For example, Visual Basic pops up context-sensitive menus when you click the right mouse button.)

N OTE: One of the main reasons for spending the time getting comfortable with the "look and feel" of the environment is that, unless you are familiar with how a Windows application should look and feel, you can't take full advantage of the power of Visual Basic.

Of course, if you are developing an application with Visual Basic for your personal use, having your program conform to the Windows standard is not essential. However, if others will be using your application, following the Windows standard essentially eliminates the learning curve for using your application. For example, Windows 95/98/NT 4.0 users expect a single click with a mouse to select an item and a double-click to activate it (in spite of Microsoft's move to a Web-style "single-click" approach on their "Active Desktop"). Users will want Exit buttons on the far right of the title bar, context menus to be available with a right mouse click, and so on.

As you saw in Chapter 1, the default settings built into the design process of a Visual Basic application make it easy to conform to the Windows guidelines. (Remember, I'll be calling the Windows 95/98/NT group of operating systems simply "Windows" most of the time.) For example, the windows you build default to having the usual buttons located where users would expect to find them. In particular, any window you design defaults to having an Exit button on the far right of the title bar along with the usual maximize and minimize buttons, and windows can also be moved and resized as users expect. Similarly, menus respond the way users expect. Of course, Visual Basic doesn't lock you into these defaults, but it is not a good idea to make changes casually.

 NOTE: I used the Enterprise edition of Visual Basic for the screen shots in this book. If you have another edition of Visual Basic, your screens will be slightly different. In particular, you may have fewer items on some of the menus and even the main menu bar may be slightly different. The main menu bar is the same for the two most common editions of VB: the Enterprise and the Professional.

Getting Started

As I mentioned in Chapter 1, when you start Visual Basic, you are presented with a copyright screen indicating to whom the copy of the program is licensed. After a short delay, you will see Visual Basic's New Project dialog box. It looks like Figure 2-1 in the Enterprise edition. (The New Project dialog box looks the same in all editions; you will simply have fewer choices for the kinds of projects that you can work with.). To get started, simply click on the kind of project you want to work with. You already saw in Chapter 1 that the Standard EXE option gives you an ordinary Windows application and that the Application Wizard option can generate hundreds of lines of code in a "paint by the numbers" approach to a program. In most cases in this book we will be working either with the Standard EXE choice or the ActiveX Control choice from the New Project dialog box.

 TIP: Once you are more familiar with coding, you'll certainly want to explore the possible projects that can be generated by the Application Wizard. Tweaking the code it generates is a good way to move to the next level of Visual Basic mastery.

The ActiveX Control choice in Figure 2-1 is covered in Chapter 23. As you will see there, this choice allows you to build your own controls that work just like the ones supplied with Visual Basic. Finally, I'll briefly cover the ActiveX DLL option in Chapter 20.

As their names suggest, the three tabs on the New Project dialog box are your gateway to:

◆ Starting a specific kind of project from scratch

◆ Working with an existing project

◆ Working with an existing project that you were recently working on

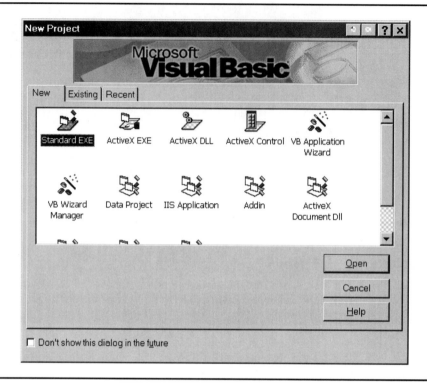

The New Project
dialog box
Figure 2-1.

The Existing tab leads to a standard File Open dialog box, an example of which is shown in Figure 2-2. The Recent tab leads to a dialog box containing a list of your most recent projects, as the example shown in Figure 2-3 indicates. If you look closely at Figure 2-2, you can see that Visual Basic stores the information needed for its projects in files with three possible extensions: .vbp, .mak, and .vbg. All of these files are special "bookkeeping" files (or *project* files) that keep track of all the different files that make up your project. The most common are .vbp files, which, naturally enough, stand for Visual Basic project. (Project files with the extension .mak were built using earlier versions of Visual Basic. Project files with .vbg (Visual Basic group) are mostly used when building controls—you'll see them in Chapter 23.)

The Initial Visual Basic Screen

For now, I'll assume that you choose the Standard EXE option from the New Project dialog box. This drops you into a screen that looks like Figure 2-4. As you can see, there are lots of elements in the main screen of the Visual Basic IDE (integrated development environment).

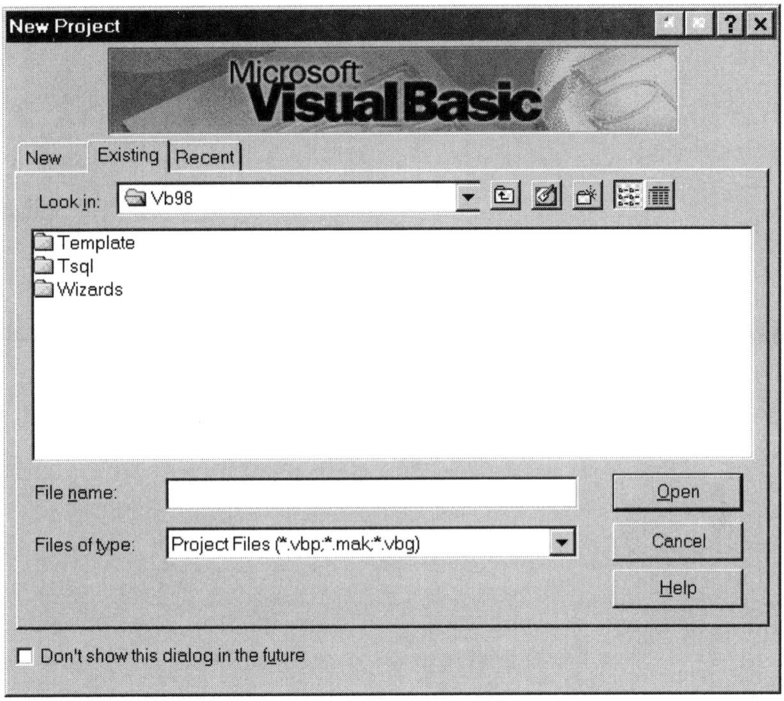

The Existing tab
in the New
Project dialog
box

Figure 2-2.

NOTE: Visual Basic remembers your last screen arrangement and reuses it. For this reason, your screen may look different from Figure 2-4.

The screen is certainly crowded. The Properties window is used when customizing a form or control and is discussed at length in Chapters 3 and 4. A few other windows show up when you are running or debugging a program; for these see Chapter 15.

What follows in this section is a description of the other parts of the main screen. Subsequent sections of this chapter cover the most commonly used parts of the menus.

Title Bar

The *title bar* is the horizontal bar located at the top of the screen; it gives the name of the application and is common to all Windows applications. Interactions between the

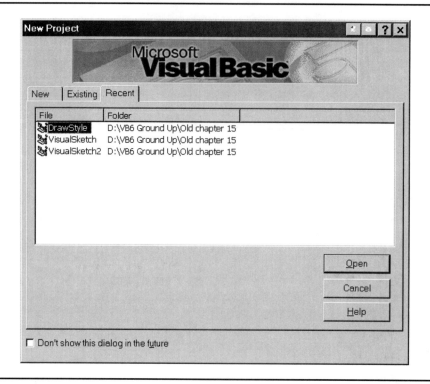

user and the title bar are handled by Windows, not by the application. Everything below the title and menu bars in a Windows application is called the *client area*. Your application is completely responsible for the look, feel, and response of the objects you place in this area.

In Visual Basic, the title bar starts out by displaying:

Project1 - Microsoft Visual Basic [design]

This is typical of Windows applications: in sophisticated programs (such as Visual Basic) that have multiple states, the title bar changes to indicate important information. For example, Project1 is the default name for a project—it is not necessarily the same as the name you saved the project under. As you will see, you can change this using the Project|Properties dialog box. As another example of how the title bar changes, when you are running a program within the Visual Basic environment, the title bar switches so that it say something like

Project1 - Microsoft Visual Basic [run]

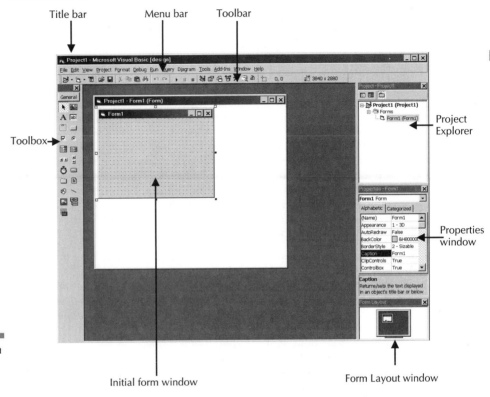

Title bar   Menu bar   Toolbar

Toolbox →

Project Explorer

Properties window

The main screen in the Visual Basic IDE

Figure 2-4.

Initial form window   Form Layout window

and when you are debugging (having temporarily stopped the program—see Chapter 15 for how to do this), the title bar switches to:

Project1 - Microsoft Visual Basic [break]

Overview of the Menu Bar

Selecting items from the pull-down menus listed on a *menu bar* is one of the most common ways to unleash the power of a Windows application. The same is true of Visual Basic itself. For Visual Basic, the menu bar gives you the tools needed to develop, test, and save your application. The File menu contains the commands for working with the files that go into your application. The Edit menu contains many of the editing tools that will help you write the code that activates the interface you design for your application, including the search-and-replace editing tools. The View menu gives you fast access to the different parts of your program and to the different parts of the Visual Basic environment. The Project menu gives you access for inserting external files or new Visual Basic objects into your projects. The Format menu gives you a way to specify the look of controls that you place on your forms. The Debug menu contains the tools used to correct (debug) problems, or *bugs,* in your code. (Chapter 15 offers a detailed discussion of debugging techniques.) The Run menu gives you the tools needed to stop and start your program while in the development environment. The Query and Diagram menus are mostly used in advanced database development; we won't touch on them in this book. The Tools menu gives you access to ways of adding procedures and menus to your programs (Chapters 9 and 14) and is also how you get to the important tabbed Options dialog box that lets you control Visual Basic's environment. The Add-Ins menu gives you access to tools that can be added to the Visual Basic environment. (How many add-ins you start out with depends on your version of Visual Basic. All versions, for example, have an add-in for building sophisticated controls called the Control Interface Wizard (see Chapter 23) and for working with databases (Chapter 22). The Window menu lets you control how the windows that make up the Visual Basic environment are arranged. Finally, you use the Help menu to gain access to the detailed online help system provided with VB. I'll talk more about this help system in the next section.

Notice that all the menus have one letter underlined. Pressing ALT and the underlined letter opens that menu. Another way to access the menu is to press ALT alone to activate the menu bar. When you do, notice that the File menu item is highlighted and looks like a raised button. You can now use the arrow keys to move around the menu bar. Press ENTER or DOWN ARROW to open the menu. Once a menu is open, all you need is a single *accelerator key* (also called an *access* or *hot key*) to select a menu option. For example, if the Help menu is open, pressing W brings up a submenu which contains links to different web sites. These sites contain lots of useful information about Microsoft (and VB)—http://www.microsoft.com/vbasic is the basic address to keep in mind.

TIP: Accelerator keys are not case-sensitive.

Some menu items have *shortcut keys*. A shortcut key is usually a combination of keys the user can press to perform an action without opening a menu. For example, as is common in Windows applications, pressing CTRL+P will bring up the Print dialog box and ALT+F4 exits Visual Basic without going through the File menu.

NOTE: Remember, I will describe choosing an item from a menu by using the pipe symbol (|). For example, "Choose File|Open Project" means pull down the File menu, and then choose the Open Project item.

The SDI (Single Document Interface) Environment

The environment I just described is the default MDI (or multiple document interface) environment. MDI style interfaces mean that all the windows are part of a larger whole. You can move them around only within the larger parent window. Visual Basic 6 also lets you use the older SDI environment that was used in earlier versions of Visual Basic. In this environment, shown in Figure 2-5 with the same windows available as in the default MDI environment, you can move all the different windows around independently, and (usually) part of your desktop shows through as it does in Figure 2-5. Note that in this case each of the windows in the Visual Basic environment is completely independent of the others. If you wanted to, you could even move the title bar to the bottom of your screen!

To switch to the SDI environment:

1. Choose Tools|Options.
2. Click on the Advanced tab.
3. Select the SDI Development Environment check box.

The SDI environment will be available the next time you start Visual Basic.

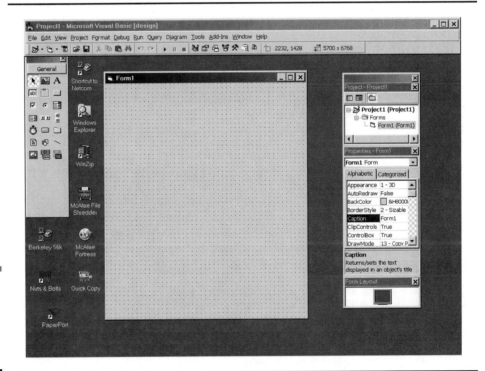

The SDI (single document interface) version of the VB IDE

Figure 2-5.

NOTE: I will not be using the SDI environment in any of the screen shots from this point on. However, if you are running Visual Basic on a screen with anything less than 800 X 600 resolution, you will probably find the SDI environment easier to work with.

The Help System

The online help system that comes with VB contains an incredible amount of useful information. For example, there are hundreds of sample programs and dozens of useful tables. You can even use the help system to gain access to all the documentation that would otherwise take up hundreds of pages of printed manuals. Depending on which version of VB you have, you may have two (!) CD-ROMs full of information that form the current version of the MSDN (Microsoft Developers Network) Library.

TIP: The latest version of the MSDN is always available free online; it's worth registering at http://www.microsoft.com/msdn in order to take advantage of it.

NOTE: Visual Studio 6 (of which Visual Basic is a part) is the first Microsoft product to extensively use the new HTML (Internet style) help. I'll be quite honest—though this new approach is potentially very powerful, not all the bugs are ironed out of it yet. Don't be surprised if the HTML-based online Help in Visual Basic behaves strangely at times!

The online help system contains a very useful feature: it is context-sensitive. This means that you can press F1 and bypass the help menus to go directly to the needed information (most of the time—occasionally the context-sensitive help fails for no good reason). You can get information about any keyword in the Visual Basic programming language, about an error message, or about the parts of the Visual Basic environment. For example, the screen in Figure 2-6 shows what you get if you press F1 when the focus is in the Project Explorer.

TIP: Having so much information available is certainly a mixed blessing. If you have a hundred or so megabytes of extra hard disk space, I strongly suggest choosing the Custom install option during the setup of the MSDN Library. Once you do, check the boxes labeled "VB Documentation," "VB Product Samples," and "VS Shared Documentation." If you don't (or can't) do this, you may need to swap CDs to access the context-sensitive help.

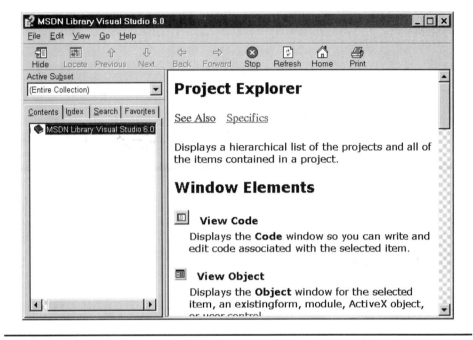

Context-sensitive
help for the
Project Explorer
Figure 2-6.

You use the help windows pretty much the same way you use Internet Explorer or
other browsers—many people (including myself) refer to the screen you see in Figure
2-6 as the "Help browser" for this reason. Once you start the help system, you can
move the Help browser window anywhere you want. You can resize it or shrink it to
an icon, as needed, or close it when you are through with it.

T IP: If you have enough memory to keep it running, shrinking the help system
to an icon on the Windows task bar makes it quicker to get at the help files.

Drilling Down to the VB Documentation

If you look at the left hand side of Figure 2-6, you'll see the little book sign in front of
the line marked "MSDN Visual Studio 6.0". If you double-click on this icon, your
screen will look like Figure 2-7.

Start clicking on the + signs next to the Visual Basic documentation titles. If you keep
on doing this, you can see all the information that comes free with your version of
VB. Figure 2-8 shows you some of what you may have available; I have highlighted

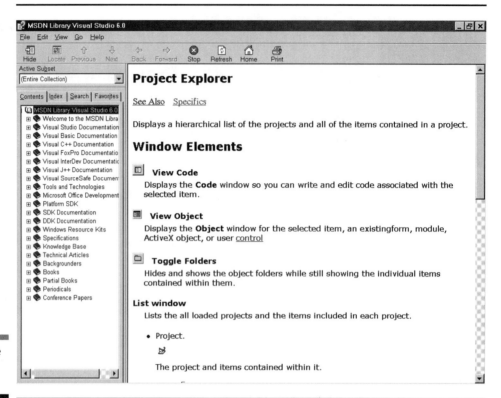

The parts of the
MSDN Library
Figure 2-7.

the "What's New in Visual Basic 6.0" page in order to see it in the right-hand pane of
the Help browser.

You can move through the documentation the same way you move through the
World Wide Web in a browser: anything underlined is a hyperlink. If you click on
one, you go to that page.

T IP: As in Windows Explorer, you can change the amount of space given to
each pane in the Help browser by dragging the dividing bar with your mouse.

Printing the Documentation

Having all this information online is certainly convenient, but there are times when
you want to have a printed version. Printed versions of all the documentation are
published by Microsoft Press and there are coupons in some editions of VB that let

2

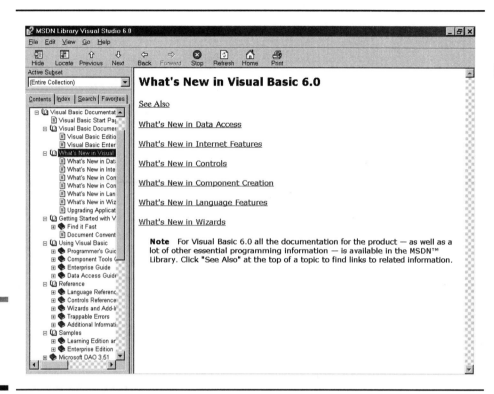

The VB
documentation
in the MSDN
Library
Figure 2-8.

you buy it for less than list price. Nonetheless, there will be times when you want to print one or more help topics. If you want to print a single topic:

1. Open it up so it shows in the right-hand pane of the Help browser.
2. Choose File|Print from the menu bar in the Help browser.

But suppose you want to print all the topics in a certain "book" more than one topic at once. Here is a useful technique that is not as well documented as it should be:

1. Move to the line that contains the book icon for those topics.
2. Right-click and choose Print from the pop-up menu. This will pop up a Print Topics dialog box with the following options: "Print the selected topic" and "Print the selected heading and all subtopics." Choose "Print the selected heading and all subtopics" and then click OK.

The Find Page in the Help Browser
If you look at the left-hand (Explorer) pane of the Help browser, you'll see four tabs. The Index tab is the most common place to look for information. It has what is often called an "Incremental search" feature. As you can see in the following

illustration, when I typed "hi", I was taken to the first of the indexed topics that begin with those letters:

The Search tab in the Explorer pane lets you find all topics that contain a keyword. I entered "Print", clicked on the List Topics button, and widened the pane in order to see more about the topics—you can see the result in Figure 2-9.

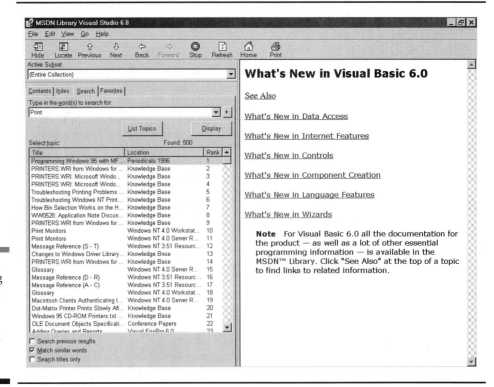

Searching instead of using the Index tab usually leads to an embarrassment of riches

Figure 2-9.

Running a Supplied Sample Program

The Help browser is also your pathway to the hundreds of sample programs supplied with Visual Basic. To see a list and description of these programs:

1. Open up the Samples item in the Visual Basic documentation book.
2. Drill down to the version of VB whose samples you want to explore. (Figure 2-10 shows you the samples supplied with the Learning and Professional Edition.)
3. Click on the sample you want to work with in order to see a description of that sample.

2

The actual samples are on the MSDN CD in the \Samples\VB98 directory. If you have room, you should certainly install them on your hard disk. You can do this by selecting "VB Product Samples" in the Custom dialog box when you install MSDN, as shown in Figure 2-11.

Once you have installed the sample applications using the default names for the directories, then the sample projects will probably be in the rather intimidating subdirectory named:

\Program Files\Microsoft Visual Studio\MSDN98\98VS\1033\samples\VB98\

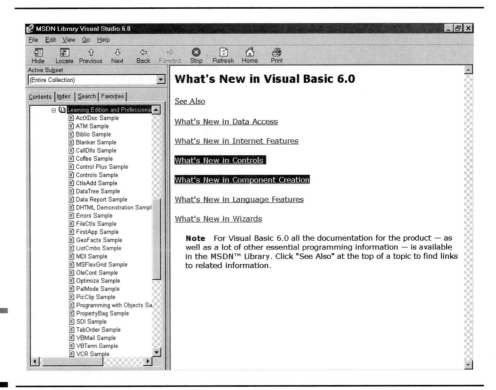

The samples
supplied with
VB

Figure 2-10.

as shown here in the Existing tab of the New Project dialog box—I dropped down the arrow to show you the directory tree.

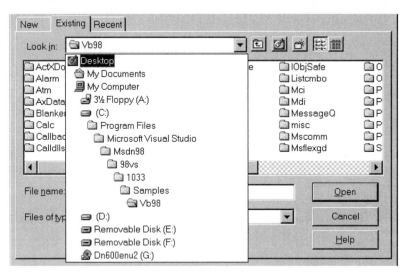

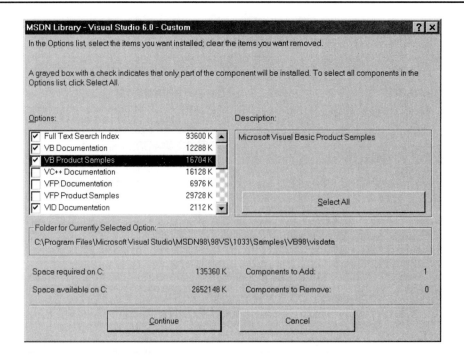

Installing the sample code supplied with the MSDN CD

Figure 2-11.

Once you have loaded a project into VB, simply press F5 to see it run.

Toolbars

Visual Basic, like many Windows applications, has multiple toolbars available. They are customizable, so you can easily build your own toolbar to suit your needs (see the section "Customizing a Toolbar" a little later in the chapter). Of course, almost every tool has a keyboard equivalent, so most of the time you don't need to use toolbars if you don't want to.

The four built-in toolbars are Standard, Edit, Debug, and Form Editor. By default, the Standard toolbar appears immediately below the menu bar. If you can't remember what a tool on the toolbar means, Microsoft has added ToolTips that give you a textual description of what the tool does. These tips pop up when you rest the cursor on a tool. They are on by default. If you don't see them, see the section "Using the Tools Menu," near the end of the chapter, for information on turning them on. (Makes one wonder, doesn't it: is the next trend in icons to replace pictures with buttons that have words on them? In fact, as you will soon see, Visual Basic 6 *does* in fact allow you to replace the icons with words!)

Standard Toolbar

Table 2-1 lists the tools in the Standard toolbar (reading from left to right) and what they do.

Icon	Name	Purpose
	Add Standard EXE	Lets you build a new executable. If you click on the down arrow, you can choose to add the other types of Windows executables that Visual Basic can build.
	Add Form	Lets you add a new form to your project. If you click on the down arrow, you can choose to add the other possible pieces of a full-scale Visual Basic application.
	Menu Editor	Lets you design menus (see Chapter 14). Same as Tools|Menu Editor or the shortcut key combination of CTRL+E.
	Open Project	Lets you open an existing Visual Basic project. Same as File|Open.
	Save Project	Lets you save your Visual Basic project. Same as File|Save Project.

Standard
Toolbar Icons
Table 2-1.

Icon	Name	Purpose
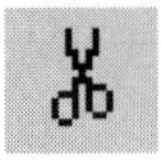	Cut	Cuts the selected text or object. (As usual, CTRL+X is the shortcut.)
	Copy	Copies the selected text or object into the clipboard (CTRL+C).
	Paste	Pastes the selected text or object (CTRL+V).
	Find	Brings up the Find dialog box.
	Undo	Undoes the last action if possible.
	Redo	Redoes the last action if possible.
	Start	Lets you run the application. After you design an application, this is the same as choosing Run|Start.
	Break	Pauses a running program. (Programs can usually be continued by using the Run tool or SHIFT+F5.) Same as Run|Break or the CTRL+BREAK combination. (Mostly used as a debugging tool—see Chapter 15.)
	End	Ends the running program. Same as choosing Run|End.
	Project Explorer	Makes the Project Explorer visible if it is not and moves the focus there.
	Properties Window	Brings up the window that lets you modify the default size, shape, and color of your Visual Basic objects (see Chapters 3 and 4). This is the same as pressing the F4 shortcut key or choosing View|Properties Window.

Standard
Toolbar Icons
(*continued*)
Table 2-1.

Icon	Name	Purpose
	Form Layout Window	Lets you control the initial positioning of your form (see Chapter 3).
	Object Browser	Opens the Object Browser dialog box. Same as View|Object Browser. The shortcut is F2. (The Object Browser is discussed in Chapters 5, 9, and 13.)
	Toolbox	Brings up the toolbox if it is hidden.
	Data View Window	Brings up the Data View window for managing database development visually.
	Visual Component Manager	Brings up the Visual Component Manager— a tool used for organizing the pieces of a complex application.

Standard
Toolbar Icons
(*continued*)
Table 2-1.

Edit Toolbar

The Edit toolbar is explained in detail in Chapter 5. Table 2-2 lists the buttons and what they do, for a quick reference.

Icon	Name	Purpose
	List Properties/ Methods	Displays a pop-up list of the properties and methods for the properties of the object preceding the period. CTRL+J is the keyboard shortcut.
	List Constants	Displays a pop-up list of the valid constants after you type an = sign. CTRL+SHIFT+J is the keyboard equivalent.
	Quick Info	Gives the syntax for the procedure or method. CTRL+I is the keyboard equivalent.
	Info Parameter	Gives a short description of the item if one is available. CTRL+SHIFT+I is the keyboard equivalent.

Edit Toolbar
Icons
Table 2-2.

Icon	Name	Purpose
A+.	Complete Word	Completes the keyword or object when enough information is given. CTRL+SPACEBAR is the keyboard equivalent.
	Indent	Indents the selected text one tab stop. TAB is the keyboard equivalent.
	Outdent	Moves the selected text back one tab stop. SHIFT+TAB is the keyboard equivalent.
	Toggle Breakpoint	Used for debugging (see Chapter 14). F9 is the keyboard shortcut.
	Comment Block	See Chapter 4 for more information on comments.
	Uncomment Block	There is no default keyboard equivalent for this tool.
	Toggle Bookmark	Bookmarks allow easier navigation between parts of your code.
	Next Bookmark	Jumps to the next saved bookmark.
	Previous Bookmark	Jumps to the previously saved bookmark.
	Clear All Bookmarks	Clears all bookmarks currently saved. Bookmarks do not persist when you exit the IDE, so they will be cleared then, as well.

Edit Toolbar
Icons
(*continued*)
Table 2-2.

Debug Toolbar

Although you will see a lot more about these tools in Chapter 15, and some of the words may not even be familiar yet, I decided to give you a table of them here so that you could turn to it for a quick reference. Reading from left to right on the toolbar, Table 2-3 describes what the tools on this toolbar do.

2

Icon	Name	Purpose
▶	Start	Runs the current project. Same as Run|Start or F5.
‖	Break	Puts the current project into break mode. Same as Run|Break or CTRL+BREAK.
■	End	Stops the current project. Same as Run|End.
✋	Toggle Breakpoint	Toggles the breakpoint on the current line on or off. Same as Debug|Toggle Breakpoint or F9.
	Step Into	Executes the next line of code while in break mode, and steps into a subprogram if one is called. Same as Debug|Step Into or F8.
	Step Over	Executes the next line of code while in break mode, and steps over a subprogram if one is called. Same as Debug|Step Over or SHIFT+F8.
	Step Out	Steps out of a subprogram that you entered with Step Into or stepped into as a result of a break. Same as Debug|Step Out or CTRL+SHIFT+F8.
	Local Window	Displays the local window and sets the focus to it. Same as View|Local Window.
	Immediate Window	Displays the immediate window and sets the focus to it. Same as View|Immediate Window or CTRL+G.
	Watch Window	Same as View|Watch Window. This window is explained in detail in Chapter 15.
👓	Quick Watch	Displays the value of the currently highlighted text in a Code window. Same as Debug|Quick Watch or SHIFT+F9.
	Call Stack	Displays the value of the current call stack (how the procedure was invoked). Same as View|Call Stack or CTRL+L.

Debug Toolbar Icons
Table 2-3.

Icon	Name	Purpose
	Bring to Front	Sets the ZOrder of the currently selected control to 0. This makes it display on top of the other controls. (See Chapter 14 for more on ZOrder.) Same as Format|Order|Bring to Front or CTRL+J.
	Send to Back	Sets the ZOrder of the currently selected control to 1. This makes it go behind any controls that reside in the same area. Same as Format|Order|Send to Back or CTRL+K.
	Align	Allows you to align a group of controls to the Left, Center, Right, Top, Middle, Bottom, or to the Grid. Same as Format|Align.
	Center	Allows you to center a group of selected controls horizontally or vertically. Same as Format|Center.
	Make Same	Allows you to make the selected controls the same Height, Width, or Both. Same as Format|Make Same Size.
	Lock Controls	Locks or unlocks the controls on a form.

Form Editor
Toolbar Icons
Table 2-4.

Form Editor Toolbar

You use the Form Editor toolbar when you are designing forms (see Chapters 3 and 4). Reading from left to right in the toolbar, Table 2-4 (above) describes what the tools on this toolbar do. The tools with little down arrows are actually two tools combined into one. For example, the Center tool that you see is for centering controls horizontally; if you click on the down arrow, you'll see the tool for centering vertically.

Customizing a Toolbar

You can build your own custom toolbars or modify the display on any existing toolbar. For example, suppose you decide that icons are confusing and you want to go to (or add) a text description of a specific tool. Here's what you need to do:

1. Right-click inside the toolbar you want to customize.
2. From the context menu that pops up choose Customize. This opens the Customize dialog box, Toolbars tab, shown in Figure 2-12.
3. While the Customize dialog box shown in Figure 2-12 is open, right-click on the button you want to customize. This displays a pop-up menu, an example of which is shown here:

2

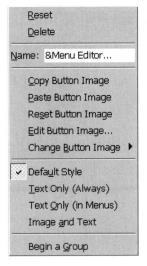

4. Choose Text Only (or Image and Text) from this pop-up menu.

Now let's suppose you want to build a toolbar from scratch. Here's what you need to do:

1. Right-click inside a toolbar and choose Customize.
2. Choose New.
3. Give a name to your new toolbar in the dialog box that pops up and click on OK.

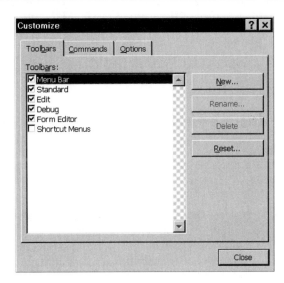

Toolbars tab of
the Customize
dialog box
Figure 2-12.

Your screen will now look like this:

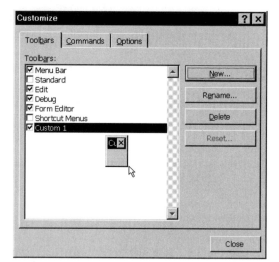

Notice the tiny new toolbar pointed to here in the center of the Customize dialog box. All you have to do is drag items from the Commands pane (in the Commands tab) of this dialog box to the new toolbar.

The Toolbox and Custom Controls and Components

The *toolbox* is located at the left of the screen in Figure 2-4, just below the toolbar, and it contains the controls you use to build the interface for your application. How many controls you have available depends on which version of Visual Basic you have (and which controls you have bought from third-party vendors or built yourself).

To add new components to your toolbox that are already registered with Windows (registering is usually done automatically when you install the control), follow these steps:

1. Choose Project|Components.
2. From the dialog box that pops up (an example of which is shown in Figure 2-13), choose which controls you want to add by clicking in the box that marks the appropriate component. (Hitting the SPACEBAR works also.)
3. Click on OK.

Note that you can add multiple tabs to the toolbox in order to make it easier to see what components you have available. To add another tab, do this:

1. Right-click in the toolbar.
2. Choose Add Tab from the Context menu that pops up.

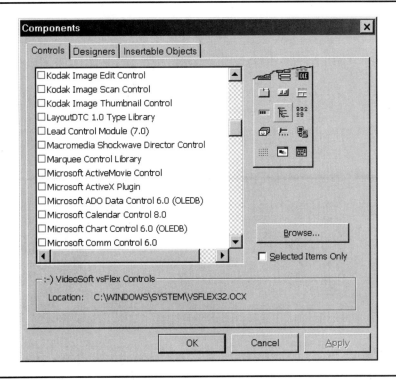

The Project|
Components
dialog box
Figure 2-13.

3. Give the new tab a name.

To actually add the controls, you can either

◆ Drag the control from an existing tab, or

◆ Click on the tab in order to make it active, and then add the new component via
the Components dialog box shown in Figure 2-13.

The Initial Form Window

The initial *Form* window, shown in the following illustration, takes up part of the
center of the screen. (Recall that the Visual Basic documentation uses the term *form*
for a customizable window.) You customize the Form window by adding controls and
changing its size; the result is what users will see. See Chapter 3 for more details on
the initial Form window.

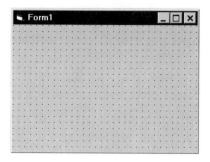

Project Explorer

Since it is quite common for Visual Basic applications to share code or previously customized forms, Visual Basic organizes applications into what it calls *projects*. Each project can have multiple forms, and the code that activates the controls on a form is stored with the form in separate files. General programming code shared by all the forms in your application can be divided into different modules, which are also stored separately. (These are called *Standard* or *code* modules and are described in Chapter 12.) The Project Explorer is usually located at the far right of the screen (see Figure 2-4). It contains a Windows Explorer–like tree view of all the customizable forms and general code (modules) that make up your application. Here's what the initial Project Explorer window looks like:

Notice the three tools in the top of the Project Explorer. They are described in the following table.

Tool	Name	Description
	View Code	Shows you the Code window (see Chapters 3, 4, and 5).
	View Object	Shows you the Form window (see Chapter 3) or current object.
	Toggle Folders	Views or hides the folders in the Project Explorer.

(The functions of the tools for the Project Explorer window are also items on the context menu for the Project Explorer—see the next section.)

Notice that one item is already listed in the Project Explorer window. This is the initial form on which you will build an application. If you can click on the View Form button, you bring the highlighted form to the forefront. (Or more generally, the button will be named View Object rather than View Form since what it really does is show you the current *object*.) Clicking on the View Code button will take you to the code associated with that form or object.

Although Visual Basic stores all the files that go into making up the project separately, it does keep track of where they are. As mentioned earlier, it creates a file, called the *project file*, that has a .vbp extension that tells it (and you, if you look at the file) where the individual files that make up a project are located. Visual Basic creates the project file whenever you choose Save Project from the File menu (or equivalently, the Save Project tool from the toolbar). It creates a different project file whenever you choose Save Project As. You can (I think you should) use a long filename to give a descriptive name to your project; Visual Basic will add the .vbp extension to your filename regardless of the length of the other part of the name. So if you name a project "My first VB thing", its project file will be named "My first VB thing.vbp" automatically.

NOTE: Visual Basic 6 allows you to have multiple projects open in the IDE at the same time in what is called a project group. Project groups are especially important in building controls, so they are discussed in Chapter 23. As mentioned before, these have the extension .vbg.

Shortcut (Pop-up) Menus

Although you can't see them in Figure 2-4, Visual Basic, like all Windows 95/98/NT 4.0–compliant programs, has context-sensitive pop-up menus available in most of the parts of the IDE. You can gain access to them by clicking (usually) the right mouse button. (If you have swapped your mouse buttons because you are left-handed, then, of course, you get the shortcut menu by clicking the left mouse button.) These pop-up menus give you another way of getting at common tasks. For reference, this section gives you the pop-up menus available in each of the various windows.

Toolbox
The following illustration shows you the context menu for the toolbox:

The Components item leads to a dialog box that was shown in Figure 2-13. The Add Tab item, as mentioned earlier, lets you add a new tab to the toolbox when you have too many controls to fit easily.

Toolbar

If you right-click in the toolbar, you will see a context menu similar to this,

which lists all the toolbars that are available. (The checked ones are the ones that are visible.) Click on any toolbar in the context menu to display or hide it. As you have seen, you can click on the Customize option in order to add your own toolbars or to customize an existing toolbar.

Form Designer and Code Window

Here is the context menu for the form designer:

The options on this menu are discussed in Chapter 3. The following illustration shows the context menu for the Code window. The options on this menu are discussed in Chapter 5.

Project Explorer

There are actually two context menus available for the Project Explorer window: one for right-clicking on a project or one of the objects, such as a form, and one for building a user control (Chapter 23). The functionality of both context menus is similar. The following illustration shows the context menu when you click on a form:

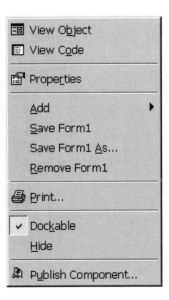

Using the File Menu

You will need to use the main File menu to work with the files that make up your project. This menu includes commands for saving, loading, and printing files. They are covered briefly here, and you'll learn more about them in Chapter 3. The File menu also lets you exit Visual Basic. As you've seen, the other way to exit Visual Basic is to use ALT+F4 when the focus is on the main menu bar, and like any Windows application, you can also open the control box on the menu bar and choose Close or double-click on the control box.

NOTE: Under Windows 95/98 and NT 4.0, the control box appears as an icon.

Most of the items on the main File menu, shown here, are useful only when you've started developing your own applications, as discussed in the later chapters of this book. What follows is a brief look at the items you will use most, which should help you orient yourself.

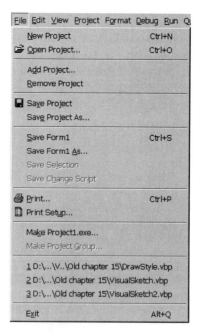

New Project   This option unloads the current project before bringing up the New Project dialog box that you saw in Figure 2-1. If you've made any changes to a project since you last saved it, a dialog box like the following pops up, asking if you want to save your work:

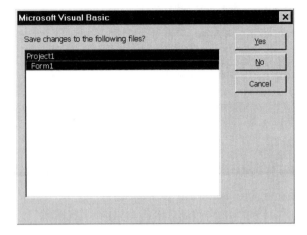

If you answer Yes by pressing ENTER or ALT+Y, you are led to another dialog box for saving files.

Open Project   This option opens a dialog box as shown here:

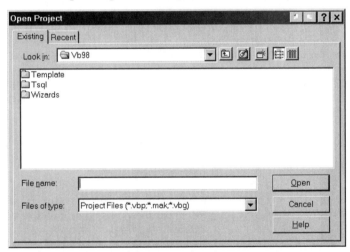

As you can see, it duplicates the functionality found in the two right-hand tabs of the New Project dialog box. As before, the Existing tab lets you work with any Visual Basic project, and the Recent tab gives you a list of your most recent projects.

Add/Remove Project   These two items are used when you have a project group. See Chapter 23 for an example of when you will need one.

Save Project   This item saves all the files in the current project and creates the project file if one doesn't yet exist. (Recall that a project file is a list of all the files used in the project plus some other information used by Visual Basic.) The first time you choose this option, the program opens a dialog box identical to the one for the Save Project As option.

Save Project As   This option pops up a dialog box that lets you save all the files that make up the current project with a new name. It does this by creating a new project file and saving the files with their current names. You can also use this option to keep backup copies of the project on a different disk or to save different versions of the project.

NOTE: The Save Project As option only makes a new project (.vbp) file; it does not make new copies of all the files in your project. Use the next items on the File menu (Save Form and Save Form As) on each file in your project before you choose Save Project As if your intention is to make a whole new version of a project with new filenames for all the files in it.

Save Form   This option lets you save a copy of the form. The name of this item actually changes to reflect the active object. For example, for a class module (see Chapter 13), it becomes Save Class. The first time you choose this option, Visual Basic opens a dialog box identical to the one for the Save Form As option discussed next. After the first time you use this, Visual Basic simply saves the file using the previous name. Note that *no backup of the previous version is kept.* You will need to make backups yourself by using the Save Form As option described next.

Save Form As   This option pops up a dialog box that lets you save the active form. (As with Save Form, the name of this item changes to reflect what object you are trying to save.) Use this option to keep backup copies of a specific piece of a project on a different disk or to save different versions. You also use this option when part of your current application will be useful in other projects. (In that case, once you have the New Project open, you would use items on the Project menu to add the saved file to a different project.)

Print   This lets you print either the current form, code in the form, module (code) that you are working with, or all forms and modules in your application. Choosing it opens a dialog box that looks like this:

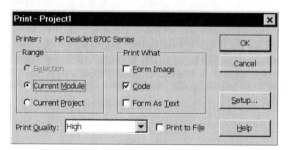

The option (radio) buttons (Selection, Current Module, and Current Project) determine whether you'll be printing from the part of the application you're currently working with or printing the entire application.

The three check boxes (Form Image, Code, and Form As Text) determine whether you print the forms that make up all or part of the application (what the user sees) or the code that activates the interface (see Chapter 3).

Print Setup   This brings up a standard Windows Print Setup dialog box that lets you select the printer and set both the paper and the orientation for printing.

Make .exe File   The Make .exe File option opens a dialog box that lets you create Visual Basic applications that can run in the Windows environment independent of Visual Basic. Standalone Visual Basic applications require dynamic link library (DLL) files and possibly custom control files (see Chapter 23). Due to Visual Basic's ability to create OLE applications and to use custom controls, it is best to use the Package and Deployment Wizard discussed in Chapter 26, as well as in the chapter in the *Programmer's Guide* called "Distributing Your Application," rather than trying to determine the correct files that your application needs. (For more on this option, see Chapters 3, 12, and 26.)

Make Project Group   This item (grayed in the illustration of the File menu shown at the beginning of this section) is mostly used with user controls (see Chapter 23).

The Most Recently Used (MRU) List   This keeps track of the four most recently opened Visual Basic projects. If you click on one of the files listed here, Visual Basic automatically loads the project. This makes returning to work in progress easy.

Exit   Clicking on the Exit button at the right of the title bar is the usual way to leave Visual Basic, but choosing this option is totally equivalent to clicking on that button. If you've made any changes to the current project, Visual Basic asks if you want to save them before ending the session.

Editing

Visual Basic comes with a full-screen program editor. Since it is a program editor, it lacks features such as word wrap and print formatting that even a primitive word processor, such as Write, has. On the other hand, it does add features such as syntax checking, which can spot certain common programming typos. The Visual Basic program editor also color-codes the various parts of your code. For example, Visual Basic commands can be one color and comments another. The colors used are customizable via the Editor Format page from the Tools|Options dialog box. The Visual Basic program editor is activated whenever you are writing or viewing code. The font used in the editor can be changed to suit your needs. (For more on this, see the discussion of the Editor Format tab under "Using the Tools Menu" later in this chapter.)

Edit Menu

The Edit menu contains more than 20 items. Here are brief descriptions of the ones you will use most.

Undo, Redo   The Undo command reverses the last edit you made. Redo reverses the last editing action that you undid. The shortcut for Undo is CTRL+Z.

Cut, Copy, Paste   You use Cut, Copy, and Paste after you select text. Cut deletes text and places it in the Windows clipboard, Copy places a copy of selected text in the clipboard, and Paste takes whatever is in the clipboard and pastes it into your Visual Basic application. You can use these techniques to exchange information (text or graphics) between another Windows application and Visual Basic. The usual Windows shortcuts apply: CTRL+X (or SHIFT+DEL) for Cut, CTRL+C (or CTRL+INS) for Copy, CTRL+V (or SHIFT+INS) for Paste.

Paste Link   This is used in exchanging information dynamically between Windows applications.

Delete   The Delete command removes the selected information but does not place a copy in the clipboard. (It's usually easier just to press DEL when text is highlighted.)

Select All   This is equivalent to CTRL+A and gives you another way to select all the text (or objects) in the situation you are working with.

Find, Find Next   Choosing the Find option displays a dialog box in which you enter the text (string) you want Visual Basic to search for. Visual Basic searches the entire project for the string. The shortcut is CTRL+F. (After you have used the Find dialog box, you can use the F3 (Find Next) and SHIFT+F3 (Find Previous) shortcuts to search for the same text again.)

If a search is successful, the Find dialog box closes and Visual Basic places you at the location in the code where the first occurrence of the text was found. It also selects the text. If no match is found, Visual Basic displays a message stating that the text was not found. Here's a picture of what the Find dialog box looks like:

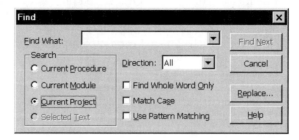

As you can see, this dialog box has a text box where you can enter or paste the text to search for and it also has several options. You can decide whether to search all or part of your code, what kind of search it should be (case-sensitive, whole words only), and whether you want to search everything or just from the current insertion point. The pattern-matching button allows you to use the normal wildcards: an asterisk (*) to match any character and a question mark (?) to match one character, for example.

Replace   The Replace option opens a dialog box with two text boxes, but it is otherwise similar to the dialog box for Find. It is shown here:

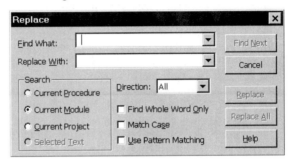

The first of the two text boxes is for the text to be found, and the second is for what should replace it. CTRL+H is the shortcut.

NOTE: When you click on the Replace button in the Find dialog box, you are taken to the Replace dialog box.

Indent, Outdent   Reading code is a lot easier if you keep a consistent indentation pattern. These two commands are one way to do it. (Although, in my opinion, they are kind of superfluous, since they are simply the TAB and SHIFT+TAB key combinations.)

Insert File   This command lets you place a file at the current cursor position in the Code window. Choosing this item brings up a standard Open File dialog box.

List Properties/Methods, ...,Complete Word   These items are part of Microsoft's new IntelliSense feature, which eliminates certain routine typing. These features and options are discussed in Chapter 5.

Bookmark   Use the Bookmark command to navigate more quickly when you have a lot of code in your project. A *bookmark*, as its name suggests, is a marker you place at a specific location in your code. Choosing this item opens up another menu that lets you move among your bookmarks, make new bookmarks, or clear old bookmarks.

Using the View Menu

The View menu lets you display or hide features of the Visual Basic environment. You also use it to manipulate the objects and controls that make up your application. Here are brief descriptions of the items on this menu that we will use in this book.

Code   You use the Code item to view the program code for the form or module that has the focus. The shortcut is F7.

Object   You use the Object item to view the form or other object associated with the code that you are working with. The shortcut is SHIFT+F7.

Definition   This option displays the code for the procedure that the cursor is on. The shortcut is SHIFT+F2. See Chapter 9 for more on procedures.

Last Position   You use the Last Position item to jump to your previous position in a Code window. The shortcut is CTRL+SHIFT+F2.

Object Browser   This option displays the Object Browser window. With the Object Browser, you can see information about your project and the pieces of Visual Basic. (See Chapters 5, 9, and 13 for more on the Object Browser.) The shortcut is F2.

Immediate Window, Local Window, Watch Window, Call Stack   These items are all connected with debugging. See Chapter 15 for more on them.

Project Explorer   This moves the focus to the Project Explorer. Use the Explorer window to view what files make up your application. The shortcut is CTRL+R.

Properties Window   You use the Properties option to display or bring to the front the Properties window. The shortcut is F4, or click on the Properties tool.

Form Layout Window   As you saw in Chapter 1, this determines the initial position of the form when your application runs. See Chapter 3 for more on forms.

Properties Pages   Certain objects have properties that can be set via a dialog box. This item would bring up this custom dialog box. The shortcut is SHIFT+F4. (See Chapter 14 for more on Custom dialog boxes.)

Toolbox   You use the Toolbox option to display the toolbox or bring it to the front.

Color Palette   You use the Color Palette option to display or bring to the front the Color Palette window, which lets you change the colors of Visual Basic objects. (See Chapter 3 for how to use the color palette.)

Toolbars   You use the Toolbars option to choose which toolbars you want visible or to customize a new or existing toolbar. This item is equivalent to the context menu for the toolbar.

Using the Project Menu

The Project menu, shown in the following illustration, contains items that let you insert various procedures, windows, code, modules, and so on, into your projects.

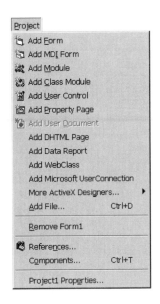

Here are brief descriptions of the items on this menu that we will use in this book.

Add Form   You use the Add Form item to add multiple windows to your application. See Chapter 12 for more on this option.

Add MDI Form   You use the MDI (multiple document interface) Form to make windows act as child windows to a main window. These kinds of forms are discussed in Chapter 14.

Add Module   You use the Add Module option to add programming code that you'll want to share amongst all the parts of the application you develop. These are usually called *code modules*. In Visual Basic, code is attached to a specific window (form) unless you place it in a module. Code modules are discussed in Chapter 12.

Add Class Module   You use the Add Class Module option to add a module containing the definition of a class that you'll want to share among all the parts of the application you develop. See Chapter 13 for more on class modules, which let you use object-oriented design principles in your Visual Basic projects.

Add User Control   You use Add User Control to add the *code* for a user control. This lets you modify the control. Please note that this is different from using Project|Components, which lets you add instances of the control to your form.

More ActiveX Designers   *Designer* is the term Visual Basic uses for the environment in which you build a project. For example, Visual Basic's default environment is technically called the Form designer. All versions of Visual Basic come with other designers, such as the User Control designer discussed in Chapter 23 for building user controls and the Dynamic HTML designer which lets you build Dynamic HTML projects. One point of having this menu is that third-party vendors are free to come up with their own designers, and they can be made as much a part of the Visual Basic environment as the built-in designers.

Add File You use Add File to insert code from another file into the current code module at the point where the cursor is located.

Remove Form1 The name of this item changes to reflect the current active object. In this case it lets you remove the initial form.

References This lets you add functions contained in a library of compiled code to Visual Basic.

Components This brings up the Components dialog box (Figure 2-13), which you have already seen. The shortcut is CTRL+T.

Project Properties This brings up the very useful tabbed dialog box shown in Figure 2-14. At this point, you can think of this dialog box as being where you keep "bookkeeping" information about the project. For example, the Make tab of this dialog box lets you do version control. (For more on the Compile tab, see Chapter 12.)

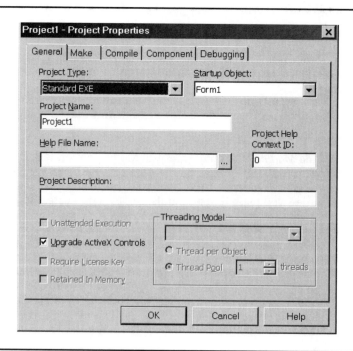

Project
Properties
dialog box

Figure 2-14.

The Format Menu

This menu, shown in the following illustration, is used to make it easier to position controls where you want them. The tools are described in Chapter 4.

The Run and Debug Menus

Most of the items on these two menus are used when debugging (see Chapter 15). However, a few items on the Run menu that you need to know about now are described here.

Start This runs your project (although most people either use the completely equivalent Run tool on the toolbar or press F5). This menu item is only available at design time; when you are actually running a project, this item disappears from the Run menu and becomes the Break command (used in debugging).

Start with Full Compile To save time, Visual Basic only compiles the part of your code it needs to get the project off and running. If you choose this option, Visual Basic will compile all the code in your project before starting. (You will only notice a substantial difference with projects involving multiple forms and/or thousands of lines of code.)

End This ends the program and reclaims all resources used by Visual Basic while running your program. Most people prefer to use the End tool on the toolbar, which is completely equivalent, but as you will see when we start coding, closing down the main form by clicking on its exit button is the preferred way to close a VB application down—even while developing in the IDE.

Using the Tools Menu

The Add Procedure item on the Tools menu is used when you add code (see Chapter 9 especially). The Procedure Attributes item pops open a specialized dialog box that we don't discuss in this book. The Menu Editor lets you add menus to your Visual Basic projects. It is also discussed in Chapter 14. (If you have the Enterprise edition of VB, you may see an option on this menu for the Source Safe "version control" system. Source Safe lets groups of programmers work on the same application, checking code in and out as needed from a central source.)

The item that you need to be familiar with now is the Options item, which opens the dialog box shown in Figure 2-15. What follows is a short discussion of this important dialog box, which you use to control the Visual Basic environment.

Editor Tab This is the tab that is visible in the Options dialog box in its default form. Only one item is unchecked—Require Variable Declaration—which is discussed in Chapter 5. I usually change the Tab setting to 2 in order to have the maximum room for code while still allowing an indentation level. (As you will see in Chapters 5 through 8, indenting code in certain situations makes it much more readable.)

Editor Format Tab This tab, shown in the following illustration, controls how your code appears. The various drop-down list boxes let you adjust the color of the parts of your code, the font used, and the size.

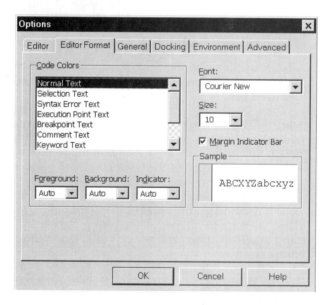

General Tab The items on this tab, shown next, let you control a wide variety of options that are used at different times in the development process. For example, you use the grid options when working with controls (see Chapter 4) and the error trapping options when working with error trapping (see Chapter 12).

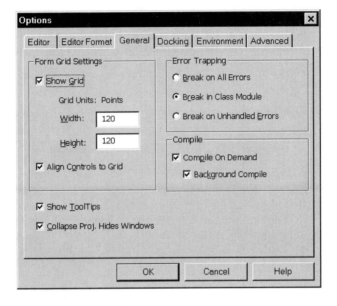

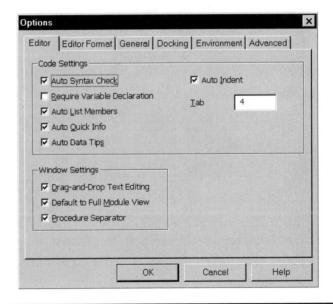

The
Tools|Options
dialog box
Figure 2-15.

Docking Tab   This tab controls which windows are "dockable," which is Windows-speak for automatically moving to a position at one or more edges of the screen. I usually just leave the defaults as they are.

T ....
IP: If you hold down the CTRL key while dragging, Windows won't dock regardless of how this tab is set.

Environment Tab   This tab, shown in the following illustration, controls the Visual Basic environment itself. Most of the items will be described when coding techniques are discussed. However, the various Save options are worth noting more than once! Experienced programmers know by bitter experience that occasionally they will write some code that locks up their machine. If you forget to save the code before this happens, you may lose hours of work. For this reason, I strongly recommend that you check off either the Save Changes or Prompt To Save Changes item in the "When a program starts" frame.

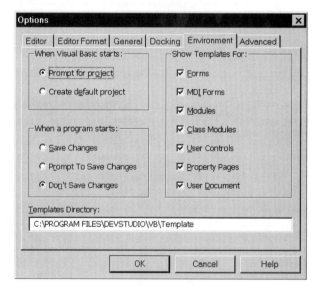

Advanced Tab   Except for the SDI Environment setting, which was discussed earlier, it is best not to change any of the settings on this page.

2

Using the Add-Ins Menu

The Add-Ins menu gives you access to separate tools that can be seamlessly integrated into Visual Basic. You just check off the item you want to add, and Visual Basic does the rest. You use the Add-In Manager option to open up a dialog box like the one shown here that lets you add and remove add-ins from the Add-In menu.

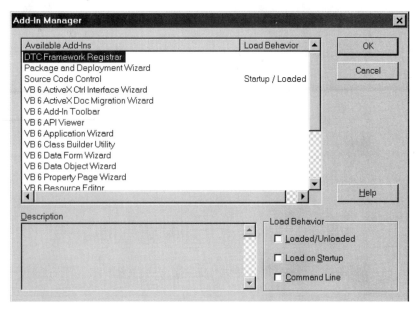

Microsoft expects add-ins to become much more important in Visual Basic 6. The idea is that third-party vendors will be supplying lots of cool add-ins to make you more productive.

Using the Window Menu

The Window menu is common to most Windows applications. It lets you control how the windows in your screen appear. For example, Figure 2-16 shows the use of the Tile Horizontally option in order to have the Form window and Code window on the screen simultaneously. (If you have a big enough screen, running at a high enough resolution, you could have even more windows visible at the same time.)

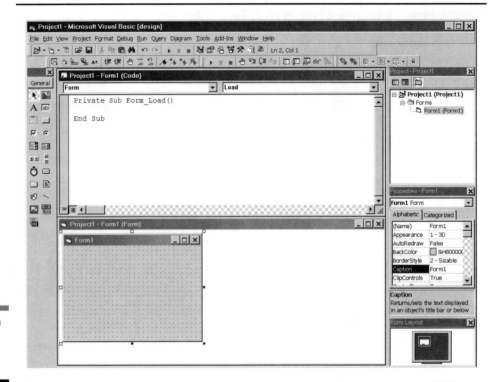

Code and Form
windows tiled
horizontally

Figure 2-16.

CHAPTER 3

Customizing a Form and Writing Simple Programs

As you will soon see, Visual Basic makes it easy for you to build an application with all the features that Windows users demand. Menus and other user-friendly controls, such as list boxes, dialog boxes, and command buttons, are a snap to add to your forms. (Recall that *form* is the term Visual Basic uses for a customizable window, and *controls* are the widgets you place on a form.) You can even use Visual Basic to extend existing controls in order to make them more useful for your needs (see Chapter 23 for more details on how to do this).

Of course, you already saw in Chapter 1 how the VB Application Wizard can almost effortlessly build a lot of the infrastructure needed for a very sophisticated program. Still, in spite of its power, the Application Wizard can hardly do it all. The results of a wizard—no matter how sophisticated—almost invariably require some hand-tweaking in order to get things "just right." The purpose of this chapter is to start you on the road to knowing how to get it "just right."

So, what I first want to do in this chapter is to get you comfortable using Visual Basic to customize a blank form. For example, you'll see how to design forms with a given size, shape, or location on the screen. You'll also learn how to display text in a form and how to print an image of a form on your printer. And then, most importantly for moving further with VB, *you'll see how to make a form respond to events such as a mouse click or double-click in the form.* (As you saw in Chapter 1, the event-driven nature of Visual Basic is the primary reason it is both extraordinarily powerful and easy to use.)

Starting a New Project

When you start Visual Basic, it assumes you want to work with a new project (*project* being the name Visual Basic uses for an application that is being developed). A project may be a Standard EXE, as we will build in this chapter, or an ActiveX control you are building from scratch (see Chapter 23) as one of the many other types available from the New Project dialog box. The opening screen for the New Project dialog box (an example of which is shown in Figure 3-1) lets you pick the type of project or whether you want to use one of the supplied wizards. (Note that different versions of VB may have fewer or more items in this dialog box than you see in Figure 3-1.)

At this point we want to work with the first item shown in Figure 3-1—a *standard EXE*. This means a standard "executable"—a program that can be run by double-clicking on its name in Windows Explorer, for example.

NOTE: As you saw in Chapter 2, you can also start Visual Basic by opening an existing project (which you can do from the File menu, the Existing tab in the dialog box shown in Figure 3-1, the toolbar, or from Explorer by double-clicking the name of the project file).

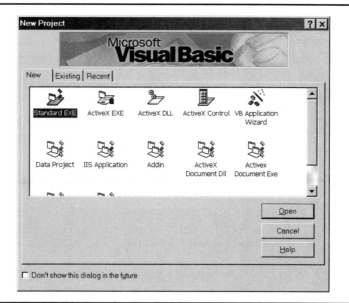

The New Project
screen
Figure 3-1.

TIP: To make working with an existing project easier, Visual Basic keeps a list of
the most recent projects on its File menu. If the File menu is open, you can click on
that item to work on that project (or press its number). You can even click on the
Recent tab shown in Figure 3-1 to see a much larger list of your recent projects. This
tab usually gives you a much larger list of recent projects than will normally be
available on the File menu.

Any time you want or need to throw away your work and start a new project, you can
always open the File menu and click the New Project item (CTRL+N is the shortcut).
This will again bring up a New Project dialog box similar to the one shown in Figure
3-1. If you do choose to start a new Project, you'll be given an opourtunity to save
your existing Project. (Starting up a New Project removes the current one.)

Anyway, click on the item marked Standard EXE in the New Project window. Then,
after a short delay, your screen will look something like the one shown in Figure 3-2.
Eight elements are shown in Figure 3-2. If any are missing, you can make them visible
by opening the View menu and clicking on the name of the item. For example, if you
don't see the toolbox on the far left, you can choose View|Toolbox. (There are usually

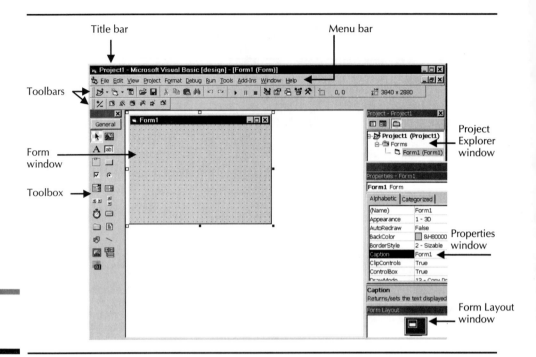

The opening
screen
Figure 3-2.

icons available for the items on the View menu. As you saw in Chapter 2, the icon for
the toolbox is a hammer and a wrench crossed.)

Next, note the blank window in the upper-left corner of the center window, which
has a grid of dots. This is the *form* that you will customize by adding controls such as
command buttons and list boxes to it. You can then use the grid to align the controls
that you will place on the form. (You'll learn more about the grid in Chapter 4.)

At the top of the blank form is the title bar with its *caption. Caption* is the term used
in Visual Basic for what appears in the title bar of the form. You'll see how to
customize the caption shortly. This will let you give meaningful titles to your forms.
Notice that currently, this form is titled Form1, which is the default name that Visual
Basic gives to a form when you start working on a new project—it isn't particularly
meaningful!

To the left of the Form1 window is the toolbox. (If it is not available, use ALT+V, X, its
tool on the toolbar, or click on the Toolbox item in the View menu to reveal it.) The
toolbox contains icons for the various controls, such as command buttons and text
boxes, that you can use to customize a form. (The controls on the toolbox are
discussed extensively in later chapters of this book. In particular, see Chapters 4, 6, 11
and 14.) Near the top-right of your screen is the Project Explorer window that you'll
learn more about in Chapter 11. Also on the right is the Properties window, which
you will read about in a moment.

Altering a Form

For now, concentrate on the form named Form1 in the middle window. You should be completely comfortable with the methods for changing the size and location of this form before you move on. One reason is that in many Visual Basic applications, the size and location of the form at the time you finish the design (usually called *design time*) are the size and shape that the user initially sees at run time. Although how you set the form's location and size is important this doesn't mean that this is fixed forever. Visual Basic lets you (via the code you write) change the size and location of forms while the program is running or even when it starts up. After all, an *essential* feature of Visual Basic is its ability to make dynamic changes in response to user events. Even more is true: unless you explicitly prevent it, users can always resize or move a form while your program is running.

Okay, how can you resize a form at design time? One way to resize a form is common to all Microsoft Windows applications: move the mouse to one of the hot spots of the form. In a form, the hot spots are the sides or corners of the form. The mouse pointer changes to a double-headed arrow when you're at a hot spot. At this point, you can hold the mouse button down and drag the form to change its size or shape. (This is also how the user of your form will change its size while the program is running.)

Moving the form at design time so that it will show up at a different location when the program starts up is a little trickier. To change where the form will appear at run time, you need to work with the Form Layout window, which is in the lower-right corner of your screen. This window looks like a blank monitor, as shown here (on your screen it may look a little smaller, and you may not be able to see the name of the form inside the icon).

To change the position of a form at run time, follow these steps:

1. Move the cursor to the Form Layout window. (The cursor will change to a four-headed arrow.)
2. Drag the form to the position in which you want it to appear when the user starts your program.

NOTE: Changes you make in the Form Layout window are run-time changes only. The position of the form in the design window in the center of your screen doesn't reflect your changes.

Finally, like most of the windows in the Visual Basic environment, you can resize or move the Form Layout window around. (Remember to hold down the CTRL key while dragging if you want to prevent a window from docking.) This allows you to change its size or location if VB's defaults don't suit you.

The Properties Window

You just saw how to change the size of a form or its location using "click and drag" techniques. The size and location of a form are actually examples of what Visual Basic calls the *properties* of the form. Although you can change some properties by working with the various windows on your screen, shown in Figure 3-2, you'll have more control if you change them using the *Properties window*, which is usually located above the Form Layout window on the right-hand side of the VB environment. If the Properties window is hidden for some reason, you can make it visible by pressing F4, clicking on the Properties tool, or simply choosing View|Properties. The Properties window looks like this when you enlarge it a bit to make its contents clearer:

Notice that the title bar of the Properties window says you are working with the properties of Form1. The line below the title bar also tells you what object you are working with; in this case it reads "Form1 Form". This line always tells you the name of the object you are working with (Form1) and what type of object it is (a form). (When you have other controls on your forms, you can click the down arrow at the far right of this line to see a list of these controls; you'll see more about this in Chapter 4.)

Next, notice the highlighted line that reads "Caption" in the first column and "Form1" in the second column. (If it isn't highlighted on your screen, click on this line to make it so.) The second column of the Properties window always indicates the current *setting* of the property. (The right-hand column of the Properties window is sometimes called the Settings box for this reason.) Once you've highlighted a line in the Properties window, you will be able to change the current setting.

The Settings box mostly works like an ordinary Windows text box as far as how you enter or edit information. For example, if you click the mouse inside text shown as a setting, you can make changes at that location. The DEL and INS keys work as you would expect, and so on. The key point to keep in mind is that whatever you enter in the Caption Settings box becomes the new caption for the form. For example, if you double-click in the right-hand column of the Properties window, the whole Caption line will be selected. That way you can change it completely—for example, if you double-clicked in the right side of the Caption line, and then typed **First Window App** in the Settings box for the Caption property. If you only single-clicked in the line, the cursor will be at the beginning of the box and you'll end up with a caption on your form that says: "First Window AppForm1"—probably not what you wanted. In any case, notice as you enter characters for the setting of the Caption property, that the caption on the form changes instantly to reflect what you've typed.

TIP: If the short description of the property at the bottom of the Properties window isn't enough, you can use Visual Basic's context-sensitive help. All you need to do is press F1 when the focus is at a specific line in the Properties window; this will usually bring up the help file for that property.

Since the right-hand column is working like an ordinary text box, there's another method for changing the setting for a property, which some people prefer:

1. Move the mouse until the mouse pointer is in the right column of the correct line in the Properties window.
2. Click at the location where you want to insert the text.
3. Enter the text you want to insert.

Note that this method inserts text; it doesn't replace the text originally there. To replace part of the text, you first have to select the text you want to replace. Double-clicking in the column selects all of the text; holding down the mouse button and dragging the pointer across the text or using a SHIFT+arrow key combination lets you select part of the text.

Finally, the default arrangement in the Properties window is alphabetical. If you want the properties to be listed by functionality, simply click on the Categorized tab at the top of the Properties window. This rearranges the properties by what they do. As you can see here, there are categories for the appearance of the form, its behavior, and so on.

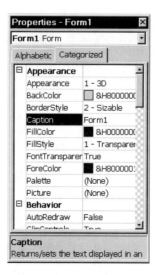

Moving Through the Properties Window

In general, you'll need to move through the Properties window until you get to the line containing the property you want to change. You can use the arrow keys or the mouse to scroll through the Properties window. As you can see, you can set a large number of properties (over 40) for a form. Although you won't learn about them all in this chapter, later sections discuss the most useful ones.

While it is true that, as with any Windows list box, you can scroll through the Properties window by repeatedly clicking an arrow in the scroll bars, the standard Microsoft Windows shortcut for moving through a list box *doesn't* work here. (You can't press the first letter of an item to move to the item because anything you type goes into the Settings box!)

T IP: To quickly move through the properties in the Properties window, use SHIFT+CTRL+letter key. This moves you to the first property that begins with that letter. Subsequent uses of this combination move to succeeding properties that begin with the letter.

An Example of Setting a Nontrivial Property

Move through the Properties window to the item marked MaxButton (for example, by pressing SHIFT+CTRL+M once). Notice that MaxButton replaces Caption in the left-hand column, and True appears in the right-hand column.

When the value of the MaxButton property is at its default value of True, the form you are designing will have the normal Windows maximize button. (Recall that a maximize button appears in the upper-right corner of a window and lets you maximize the window by clicking the mouse on it once.)

As an experiment for your first application, change this property to False. There are three ways to do this:

◆ Once you have highlighted this line in the Properties window, the simplest way to do this is just to press F. The MaxButton property changes from True to False.

◆ The second way is to double-click in the right-hand column.

◆ The third way is to click the arrow immediately to the right of the Settings box where True appears. A list box drops down with the two options, True and False, as shown here:

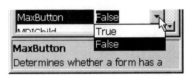

You can select the False option by pressing DOWN ARROW and then pressing ENTER, or by clicking the word False. A general feature in Visual Basic is that whenever a property has a fixed number of options, you'll see an arrow in the line of the Properties window. This indicates that a drop-down list box is available. You can see the list of options by clicking on the arrow.

Now pick your favorite method from the three I just showed you to change the MinButton property to False. With both of these properties set to False, let's run this application and see what happens.

You have three ways to run a Visual Basic application:

◆ Select the Start option from the toolbar by clicking the forward arrow (it's usually the twelfth tool).

◆ Select the Start option from the Run menu by using the mouse or by pressing ALT+R, S.

◆ Press the F5 shortcut.

After a short delay, the form will pop up super-imposed on the Visual Basic IDE and looking like the one in Figure 3-3. Notice that this form has neither a minimize nor a maximize button and is located relative to the screen as was indicated in the Form Layout window. Notice also that, unlike when you changed the caption, the changes to the Max and Min button properties show up only at run time (that is, when you run the application).

To return to developing an application, you can click on the exit (X) button on the form, or open the Run menu and click the End option, or use the End tool (the tool that looks like a stop button on a cassette recorder).

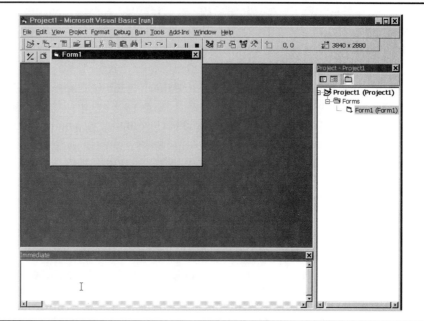

Form without maximize or minimize button

Figure 3-3.

NOTE: The exit button is the best choice. I only use one of the other methods if this doesn't seem to work—see the section on multiple form applications in Chapter 12 for more on potential problems in shutting down a VB application.

Anyway, in all three cases VB brings you back to the design environment for the application you've just developed.

Designing a form that lacks both minimize and maximize buttons may not seem like much, but it does illustrate the absolutely essential process of changing the properties of a Visual Basic object and how those changes show up for the user of your program to see.

Summary of the Methods for Working with the Properties Window

Here is a summary of the methods for changing the properties of a Visual Basic form:

1. Display the Properties window by pressing F4 if it isn't visible.
2. Move to the Properties window and select an item from the properties in the list box.
3. Enter the new setting for the property.
4. Press ENTER to accept the new setting.

Here's a table that shows you the keyboard shortcuts for manipulating the Properties window when it has the focus.

Key	Action
SHIFT+CTRL+letter key	Moves to the first item beginning with that letter
DOWN ARROW	Moves to the next item in the Properties list box
UP ARROW	Moves to the previous item in the Properties list box
PAGE DOWN/END	Moves to the last item displayed in the Properties list box or to the last item
PAGE UP/HOME	Moves to the first item displayed in the Properties list box or to the first item
F4	Brings up the Properties window (you can also use the View menu or the tool for the Properties window)

After you enter a new setting, press ENTER, click the mouse, or press TAB to accept the changes.

Once you are working with a setting for a property, the usual Windows editing techniques work. Double-clicking selects all of the text, you can highlight text with SHIFT+arrow combinations, and the usual editing keys will work just as you expect: CTRL+Z or ALT+BACKSPACE undoes the last action, CTRL+C (or CTRL+INS) copies selected text to the clipboard, CTRL+V (or SHIFT+INS) pastes, and so on.

As you saw earlier, when Visual Basic can display a complete list of the settings for a specific property, you can click the down arrow that appears in the Settings column in order to see the list (or press F4 or ALT+DOWN ARROW, or ALT+UP ARROW). (Properties for which you can see the complete list are sometimes called *enumerated* properties.) Once you have dropped down the list, you can navigate through it using ordinary Windows techniques. For example, typing a character moves to the first item beginning with that character, PAGE DOWN moves to the last item shown, and so on.

Common Form Properties

In this section I want to give you short descriptions of some of the most common properties of forms. The next two sections discuss other form properties that need more extensive treatment. As you'll see in later chapters, a single property can pertain to many different objects. For example, you will want to set the Font property for text boxes, command buttons, and the like. I'll start with two properties that are sometimes confused, Caption and Name, and then go through the other basic properties of forms in alphabetical order.

Caption As you already know, the Caption property sets the title of the form. The caption is also the title that Microsoft Windows uses for the application icon when the user minimizes the application.

Name   This property is used only in code. It gives the name that you want to use to refer to the Form. The default value is, of course, a rather prosaic "Form1" and so its value starts out the same as the default value of the Caption property. Please note that this property is different than the Caption property, though, and once you change one or the other they will no longer be "in synch." This property is mostly used in larger projects (see Chapter 12).

Appearance   Determines whether the form (and controls on the form) will have a three-dimensional look. If you leave it at the default value of 1, the form will look three-dimensional. Change it to 0, and the form will appear flat. (Each control has its own appearance property.) Most people leave this at the default value of 1.

BorderStyle   Also offers only a small number of choices. Because of this, you'll see the arrow to the right of the property setting. Drop down the list and you can see the value and a description. You can choose among five values for this property. The default value, 2-Sizable, allows the user to size and shape the form via the hot spots located on the boundary of the form.

Change this setting to 1-Fixed Single, and the user will no longer be able to resize the window. All the user will be able to do is minimize or maximize the window (unless, of course, you turn off those options, as well, when you design the application).

Set the BorderStyle value to 0-None, and the application will show no border whatsoever, and therefore no minimize, maximize, or control box buttons. Because of this, a form created without a border cannot be moved, resized, or reshaped. This setting is useful for splash screens or when you don't want users to be able to alter your forms.

The third setting, 3-Fixed Double, is not often used for ordinary forms, but it is commonly used for dialog boxes. It gives a nonsizable (it has no hot spots) border that is twice as thick as normal.

The fourth setting, 4-Fixed ToolWindow, is not used very often. Under Windows 95/98 and NT 4, this displays the form with a Close button. (The text from the title bar will appear in a reduced size, and the form does not appear in the Windows 95/98 and NT 4 task bar, nor can the user change the size of the form.)

The fifth setting, 5-Sizable ToolWindow, works much like the Fixed ToolWindow setting. This will display the form with a Close button, and the text from the title bar will appear in a reduced size. The form does not appear in the Windows 95/98 and NT 4 task bar, but the user can change the size of the form.

 NOTE: These last two settings are used when you want to create toolbox-style windows similar to the one in VB itself.

ControlBox Changes to this property go into effect only when a user runs the application. As in any Microsoft Windows application, control boxes are located in the far left corner of the title bar. (They show up as an icon under Windows 95/98 and NT 4, and as a box under Windows NT 3.5.) Clicking the box displays a list of common window tasks, such as window minimizing, maximizing, and closing, along with keyboard equivalents when they exist.

You have only two choices: you can either have a control box or not. Because there are only two possible settings, the list box to the right of the settings area is enabled. Note that if your application doesn't have a control box, a user without a mouse is in trouble. He or she won't be able to minimize, maximize, or close the application. Control boxes are generally not a good thing to remove.

3

Enabled You do not want to change the Enabled property casually. If you set Enabled to False, the form cannot respond to any events such as the user clicking on the form. Usually you will use code to toggle this property back and forth in response to some user event, and thereby make your forms respond dynamically. It is a good idea to keep in mind that the Properties window is most often used for setting the static properties of your objects, and not dynamic properties like this one.

Font This is the first example you have seen of a property that is set from an ordinary Windows dialog box. If you move the focus to this item and then double-click on the three dots (usually called an *ellipsis*), you'll see a dialog box that looks something like this:

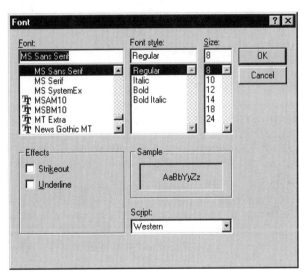

(What you see in this dialog box will depend on the fonts you have installed in your machine.) You can use this dialog box to change the font used to display information on the form.

NOTE: The changes you make in this dialog box will also set the default font for any controls placed on the form; however, you can change the font property of each control individually (see the next chapter).

Height, Width   Height and Width are interesting properties—and not only because they can be set two ways. They are examples of properties that default to using the Microsoft Windows twips scale to measure the sizes of the objects involved. There are 1,440 twips to an inch (567 to a centimeter). The term actually stands for one twentieth of a point. (Points are a common measure for printers; this book is set in 11-point type.)

CAUTION: Twips measure how large the object would be if it were printed; they do not correspond exactly to the size of the object on your screen. For example, on a 15-inch diagonal monitor, the default size of a form is approximately 4.5 inches. (See the section "An Example: The Screen and Printer Objects" in Chapter 6 for a discussion of how to adjust your Visual Basic projects for different-sized monitors.)

Look at the far right of the toolbar, as shown here:

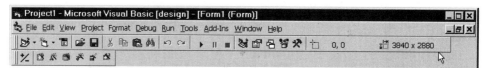

Notice the last box has the value 3840 X 2880. (The numbers you see will depend on your screen resolution.) This box always tells you the current value in twips for the width and height of the form. Now drag your form to change its width and height. Notice that when you change the size of the form by dragging, the value at the far right of the toolbar changes to reflect the new size. If you look in the Properties window, you'll see that the values for these properties change as well.

Of course, using the mouse and dragging to set the height and width is a less precise procedure than you may need. Luckily, since Height and Width are properties, you can change their values directly via the Properties window. To do this you just have to enter the value you want in the appropriate line in the right-hand column of the Properties window. For example, if I changed the width to 1920 twips, I would cut my window in half (at least as close to half as the screen can display).

Like the Caption property, any changes you make to the height and width of the form go into effect immediately—they do not wait until the application runs.

NOTE: Unless you disable the border by changing the BorderStyle property, a user can size and reshape the various forms in the application regardless of how you set them at design time.

Icon The Icon property is one you will use frequently. This property determines the icon your application will display when it is minimized on the toolbar or turned into a stand-alone application on the Windows desktop. (It is also the icon used for the control box under Windows 95/98 and NT 4.) Visual Basic comes with a large library of icons that you can use freely.

3

NOTE: The Professional and Enterprise editions of Visual Basic come with programs for creating and modifying icons and there are many good shareware ones available. (Check out http://www.hotfiles.com for example.)

To see how to choose an icon for your application, go to the Properties window and select the Icon property. Notice that to the right of the Settings box is the ellipsis indicating that a dialog box is available to help you select the value of the property. Click the box containing the three dots, and a dialog box appears like the following one:

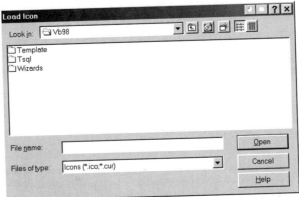

Assuming that you have installed Visual Basic in the ordinary way, you will find the icons supplied with Visual Basic in the subdirectories of the Icons directory, which is under the Graphics directory where Visual Basic is installed. (If you have Visual Studio it will be in the \Microsoft Visual Studio\Common\Graphics\Icons directory.) As always, there are many ways to get to this subdirectory; probably the fastest is to move the mouse pointer to the Icons subdirectory in the dialog box and double-click. Of course, you can type the full path name of the file in the File name text box or move the focus to the Directories list and select the name by keystrokes alone.

To see an example of how to set the Icon property, find the Icons subdirectory and move through the list of its subdirectories until you get to the one marked Misc; double-click this name. The Files list box now shows the more than 70 icon files in this directory as shown here.

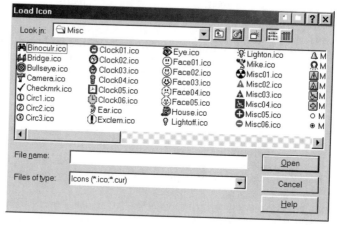

(Under Windows 95/98 and NT 4 you can actually see the icons.) To choose the FACE03 icon, double-click on it. To be sure that you really have changed the icon for the Form1 application, simply look at the control box.

Left, Top   These properties determine the distance between the left or top of the form and the screen. Set the value of the Top property to 0, and the form you're designing is flush with the top. Set the value of the Left property to 0, and it will be flush with the left side of the screen. Using the Form Layout window is, of course, another way to control these properties. These settings work in much the same way as the Height and Width properties.

MousePointer, MouseIcon   MousePointer is a useful property that lets you set the shape of the mouse pointer. The default value is 0, but as the pull-down list indicates, there are 17 other values. A setting of 4-Icon, for example, turns the mouse pointer into a rather pretty square within a square. The settings you will use most often are 0 (the default arrow shape) and a value of 11. Using a value of 11-Hourglass changes the mouse pointer to the usual hourglass, and as in other Microsoft Windows applications, this setting is useful for indicating to the user that he or she has to wait until the computer finishes what it is doing. Set the MousePointer property to a value of 99 and you will be able to use a custom icon. This is most commonly done using code when the cursor is over a specific control (see Chapter 17), but you can change it at design time by following these steps:

1. Set the MousePointer property to 99.

2. Pick the icon you want to be the custom mouse icon as the value of the MouseIcon property. Note that you cannot set the MouseIcon property until you set the MousePointer property to be 99. (Use the same techniques to select this custom mouse icon as were described for setting the Icon property.)

3

StartUpPosition   This neat property gives you another way to decide on the initial position of your form at run time. It is generally more precise than using the Form Layout window. You have four choices; the most common (besides the default value) is a setting of 2, which lets you center the form on the screen—no matter what resolution the user has set for his or her screen!

Visible   This is another property that is dangerous to change by mistake. Set the value of this property to False, and the form will no longer be visible (and is, therefore, somewhat difficult for the user to manipulate!). You usually will want to make a form invisible only when you are designing an application with multiple forms. Then you will often want to hide one or more of the forms by using the Visible property. Often, you will reset this property by using code and not at the time you design the application.

WindowState   This property determines how the form will look at run time. There are three possible settings. A setting of 1 reduces the form to an icon, and a setting of 2 maximizes the form. A setting of 0 is the normal default setting. This property is most often changed in code.

Scale Properties

You will often need to position objects or text in a form accurately. Some people are not comfortable thinking in terms of twips. To help you, Visual Basic provides five properties that affect the scale used in a form. (For more information on the scale properties, see Chapter 16.)

ScaleMode   ScaleMode allows you to change the units used in the form's internal coordinate system. Tired of twips? There are seven other possibilities. You can create your own units (the value of this setting is 0), keep the default twips (this value is 1), or use one of the six remaining choices. An interesting setting—especially for graphics—is 3. This uses one pixel (a picture element—the smallest unit of resolution on your monitor) as the scale. And of course, if you are more comfortable with them, you can choose inches (5), millimeters (6), or centimeters (7).

ScaleHeight, ScaleWidth   Use the ScaleHeight and ScaleWidth properties when you set up your own scale for the height and width of the form. Resetting these properties has the side effect of setting the value of the ScaleMode property back to 0. For example, if you set the value of each of these properties to 100, then the form uses a scale that has point 50,50 as its center. You will probably reset the values of these properties only when you are writing an application that uses graphics. (See Chapter 16 for more information on these properties.)

ScaleLeft, ScaleTop   These properties describe what value Visual Basic uses for the left or top corner of the form. The original (default) value for each of these properties is 0. Like ScaleHeight and ScaleWidth, these properties are most useful when you are working with graphics (Chapter 16). For example, if you are writing a program that works with a graph, you rarely want the top left corner to be at point 0,0.

Color Properties

The colors you use in an application have a dramatic effect on how easy and pleasurable the application is to use and, as a result, how well it is received. You can specify the background color (BackColor) and the foreground color (ForeColor) for text and graphics in the form.

NOTE: Visual Basic has many ways to change the colors of an application dynamically by using code. See Chapters 5 and 16 for more information on using code to do this.

The BackColor and ForeColor Properties via the Color Palette

Suppose you try to set the BackColor property. If you open the Properties window and select BackColor, you'll see the following setting,

&H8000000F&

which is rather cryptic, to say the least. In fact, Visual Basic describes color codes by using a hexadecimal code (base 16), which is described in the section "Bits, Bytes, and Hexidecimal (Base 16) Numbers in Visual Basic" in Chapter 5. In theory, using hexadecimal color codes allows you to set up to 16,777,216 different colors—usually finer control than one really needs.

The most common way for you to set colors is to choose one of the color properties and click the down arrow in the Settings box. This opens up a tabbed dialog box with two tabs, as shown here:

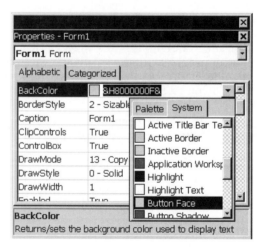

The System tab on this dialog box gives you a list of the colors currently used by Windows for its various elements. (For example, on my system the color for the Active Title Bar is dark blue.) If you click on the Palette tab, the color grid shown here pops up. (Although this illustration can't show the colors, the gray scale gives you an idea of what you will see.)

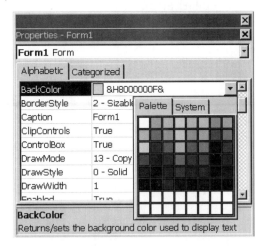

Click whatever color you like, and the color code for that color is placed in the Settings box. The background color of the form will automatically show your changes to the BackGround property. You won't see the effect of changing the ForeColor property until you do something like displaying text on the form.

Working with the Color Palette

You can also create your own colors by working with the color palette directly. Open the color palette by going to the View menu and choosing the color palette (ALT+V, L). Here's something like what you'll see:

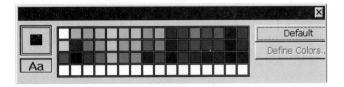

Notice, to the left of the palette, a dark box enclosed in a lighter box. The inner box displays the current foreground color, and the outer box displays the current background color.

You can change the foreground color by clicking the inner box and then clicking any of the colored boxes displayed. To change the background color, click the outer box and then click any of the colored boxes displayed.

The text box in the lower-left corner of the color palette displays the foreground and background colors for any text in the form or control you've selected. To go back to the default colors specified in the Windows control panel, click the Default command button at the right.

You can also create your own colors for the color palette. Each of the blank boxes on the bottom of the color palette represents a possible custom color. To make one, follow these steps:

1. Click one of these blank boxes, and then click the Define Colors command button (which is now enabled). This opens the Define Color dialog box, shown here:

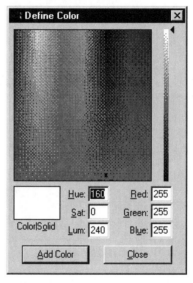

2. Change the amount of red, green, or blue; color; hue; saturation; or luminosity of the color to suit your needs by adjusting the controls in the dialog box.

3. Press the Add Color button to create the custom color or the Close button to cancel.

To make the color palette go away, double-click on its control box or use the ALT+F4 shortcut when the palette has the focus.

Making a Form Responsive

By now, you should be comfortable with designing Visual Basic forms. But making a form in the right size, shape, and having the right background color is hardly what Windows programming is all about. The essence of a Microsoft Windows program (and, therefore, of Visual Basic) is to make your forms *respond* to user actions.

Visual Basic objects can recognize many different events. For example, if a user clicks an area on the screen, you may want to display a message; if the user clicks a command button, you may want to perform a specific action, such as displaying an image. Making something happen is where the programming comes in!

The point (and it hardly can be stressed enough) is that although Visual Basic objects can recognize many different events, the objects will basically sit there inert unless you've written code to tell them what to do when the event happens. This means that for any event to which you want a Visual Basic object to respond, you must write an *event procedure* telling Visual Basic what to do. Event procedures are nothing more than the lines of programming code that tell Visual Basic how to respond to a given event.

3

The Code Window and Writing a Simple Event Procedure

In this section I want to show you how to make your form respond to a mouse click. Double-click in any blank part of Form1 (your form may have a different name if you were experimenting, of course). Your screen now looks something like the one in Figure 3-4. Double-clicking the form opens the *Code window* (you can also choose View | Code or press F7. This window is where you will enter the code to tell Visual Basic how to respond to the event.

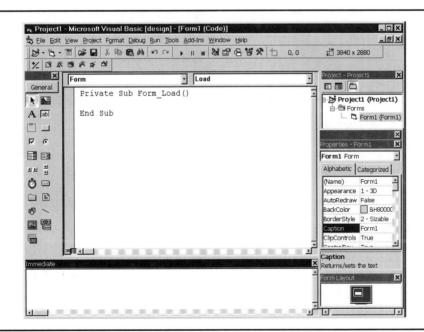

The Visual Basic IDE with a Code window

Figure 3-4.

Notice the two drop-down list boxes in the top part of the screen. If you click the arrow in the right-hand box, you pull down a list of all the events a form can recognize, as shown here:

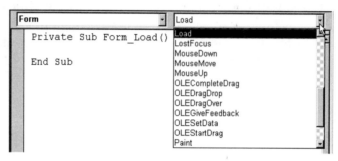

(A form can recognize 31 events (!), so this box actually has 31 items in it. You might want to scroll through it just to get a sense of the power you will soon have in your hands.)

If you pull down the left-hand box in the Code window, you will see a list of the controls on your form. Since you have yet to put any text boxes, command buttons, or other controls on this form, no objects except the form itself (and an object called General, which is discussed in Chapter 5) are listed in this box.

In Figure 3-4, you see the following code:

```
Private Sub Form_Load ()

End Sub
```

This code is an example of an *event procedure template*. Like any template, it gives you a framework in which you'll work. Note that the Form_Load event is triggered when Visual Basic loads a form in memory. As you'll see shortly it is one of the first events that is triggered for a form. You will often write code in this event in order to set the initial properties of forms via code. (You'll learn more about the Load and its related events in Chapter 5.) For example, if you make the Form_Load event procedure read:

```
Private Sub Form_Load ()
  BackColor = vbRed
End Sub
```

and run the program you'll see that the background color of the form indeed changes to red.

Note that you can use all the normal Windows editing keys to enter code. For example, you can switch between insert and overstrike modes when you type. You can select text and then copy or cut it. It is worth noting, however, that the IntelliSense features of Visual Basic cut down dramatically on the amount of routine typing needed to enter code. (See Chapter 5 for more on IntelliSense.)

Working with the Form_Click Event

Let's start up a new Project (Standard EXE type) to show off this event procedure. What we want to do is trigger some code being processed in response to the user clicking on the form. To do this, you have to bring up the template for the Form_Click event procedure. For this, make sure you are in the code window and then:

1. Move to the event drop-down list box on the right and click the down arrow.
2. Move through the box until you get to the Click item. Notice that items in the Event list box are listed in "shorthand form"—that's why you see Click rather than Form_Click. You have to look at the left drop-down list box to see what object you are working with in order to conclude that this is really the Form_Click event.
3. Click on it.

Then Visual Basic does the following:

◆ Gives you a new event procedure template for the Form_Click event procedure

◆ Adds a dotted line between the Form_Load event and the Click event

◆ Moves the cursor to the blank line before the End Sub line in the Click event procedure template as shown in Figure 3-5

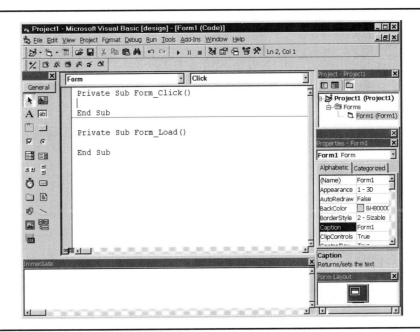

Code window when working with Click event procedure

Figure 3-5.

TIP: As in any list or combo box, you can quickly go to a specific event procedure by pressing the first letter of the item. For example, pressing C will quickly take you to the Click procedure.

Suppose you want to write the code necessary for Visual Basic to respond to a mouse click with a message. If the cursor is not at the blank line before the End Sub in the Form_Click template, move it there by scrolling through the Code window and clicking on the blank line. Press the TAB key once or the SPACEBAR a few times (this indentation will improve readability) and type **Print "You clicked the mouse once."** Your Code window will look like this:

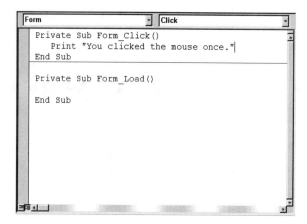

Now press F5 to run the application. As soon as the form pops up, move the mouse until the pointer is inside the form and click once. You'll see something like this:

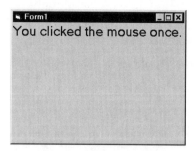

As you've probably guessed, the Print command sends the exact text found between the quotation marks directly to the form. It uses whatever values you have currently set for the Font property and the ForeColor property. In the preceding illustration, I changed the Font property so the font size for the form would be 14 points—this makes a larger "splash" than the default size of 8 points. Notice that the default starting position for displaying text is the upper-left corner of the screen; you'll see how to change this in Chapter 6.

More General Event Procedures

In general, no matter what event you want the form to respond to, the code for an event procedure for a form in Visual Basic begins with something that looks like this:

```
Private Sub Form_NameOfTheEvent ( )
```

3

The following table gives you some of the most common examples of event procedures that are user driven and when you will want to use them. (Some events like the Form_Load are not really ones that user action commonly triggers.)

Event Procedure	Tells the Form
Private Sub Form_Click( )	To respond to a click
Private Sub Form_DblClick( )	To respond to a double-click
Private Sub Form_Resize( )	To respond when the user resizes the form

Monitoring Multiple Events

Visual Basic is always monitoring your computer for events, but unless you write code for the event, nothing happens. For example, you can add more code to the previous little program to monitor (and print) something when the user double-clicks.

To do this, end the previous program by clicking on the exit button (or by going to the Run menu and clicking End, or by clicking the End tool—the one that looks like the stop button on a cassette recorder). Now open the Code window (if it is not already open) by double-clicking in a blank part of the form. Notice that Visual Basic now displays the code for the Click event. We want to add some code to the existing project in the Double-click event. For this, move the mouse to the arrow that drops down the list box for event procedures and go to the Double-click procedure. (DblClick is its name in the drop-down box.)

TIP: Notice that the Click event procedure is now listed in bold in the Event procedure list box—this is how Visual Basic indicates that an event procedure already exists for a particular event.

VB now will add a new event template for the Double-click event to your Code window. Just as before, you need to type between the beginning and ending lines of this event template in order to enter the code. For example, type **Print "I said to click once, not twice!"** The Code window will look like this:

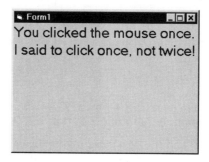

```
Form                          ▾   DblClick                          ▾
    Private Sub Form_Click()
        Print "You clicked the mouse once."
    End Sub

    Private Sub Form_DblClick()
        Print "I said to click once, not twice!"
    End Sub
```

Now run the application and double-click. You'll see something like this:

```
Form1                              _ □ ✕
You clicked the mouse once.
I said to click once, not twice!
```

Notice that both lines of text appear on the screen. This is because in monitoring for a double-click, Visual Basic also detected the single click and activated the code for that event as well.

If all you want to do is clear the screen before displaying the second message, you need only make the first line of the Double-click procedure the Cls keyword. As its name suggests, this keyword clears any text and graphics in the form. Your Double-click event procedure now looks like this:

```
Private Sub Form_DblClick ()
  Cls
  Print "I said to click once, not twice!"
End Sub
```

By the way, the Print and Cls keywords are examples of what Visual Basic usually calls *methods* instead of commands. Roughly speaking, methods are Visual Basic statements that affect what Visual Basic objects do (as opposed to properties, which affect what they are).

You can use another syntax for the Print or Cls method, which is used for other Visual Basic objects. The general form is usually described as Object.Method. The idea is that when you leave off the name of the object VB just assumes you mean the form whose code is being processed, so you can get away (as I did) with a shorthand. On the other hand, many VB programmers like to always be clear about the object they are working with and thus use the longer form that would require the Form's name. The syntax for this more explicit way of giving a method or a property is to use the name of the object, followed by a period, followed by the method or property, followed (if applicable) by what the method should do or the property should be:

ObjectName.Method WhatToDo

The default name for the first form created in a Visual Basic project is Form1, so the Double-click procedure in this syntax could be written as follows:

```
Sub Form_DblClick ()
  Form1.Cls
  Form1.Print "I said to click once, not twice!"
End Sub
```

You will often need to use the longer version when your projects involve more than one form, because this version makes it clear which form to apply the method to. (You'll see more about the *Object.Method* notation in Chapter 4.)

TIP: Many programmers like to use the reserved object name of Me instead of the form's name. The Me keyword always refers to whatever object (the form in this case) the code is attached to. Thus, a line of code such as Me.Cls in an event procedure that is attached to a form will always clear the screen in that form. I usually use the Me object name.

Printing a Visual Representation of a Form

Visual Basic relies on the underlying Windows program to handle its printing needs. For this reason, you should make sure you have configured Windows with the name of your printer. Most of the time you won't need to get involved with the Windows Print Manager; Visual Basic takes care of the interface pretty well. It uses whatever printer information is contained in the Microsoft Windows environment control panel. (However, you can use VB to control or even change the current printer; see Chapter 6 for how to do this.)

However, getting an image of the form, including whatever is currently displayed on the form, to the printer requires only a single command: PrintForm. Notice that since this also affects what the form does, as opposed to what it is, it is another example of a Visual Basic method. The PrintForm method tries to send to your printer a dot-for-dot image of the entire form. As an example, add the line PrintForm to the Double-click procedure before the End Sub line. Then double-click and see what happens.

3

Typos

Nobody types completely accurately all the time. Visual Basic can point out many typing errors when you enter a line of code, and it will even correct some (such as leaving off a closing quote). All this happens even before you try to run your program.

But few programmers enter code without typos. So to see what might happen, let's suppose you made a typo when you were writing the Click event procedure presented earlier, and you misspelled the command word Print by typing Printf instead.

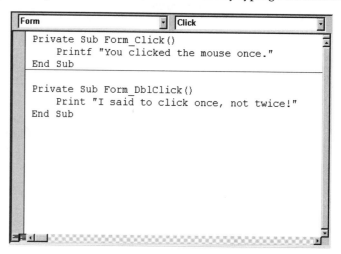

Notice that on your screen the word Printf should be in a different color than it was when it was correctly spelled (probably red or black instead of blue). If you don't notice the color change and try to run the program and click in the form, Visual Basic will immediately respond with an error message box, and your screen will look something like Figure 3-6. Notice that the offending word is highlighted, and the message box tells you, "Sub or Function not defined"—what you entered isn't recognizable to Visual Basic. As you'll see in Chapters 8 and 9, Visual Basic lets you define your own functions and Subs (like the event procedure ones) that extend its powers. In this case, Visual Basic thinks you mean one of these user-defined gadgets.

If you press ENTER or click the OK command button, the offending word remains highlighted, and you can either type the correct replacement or move the mouse pointer to the "f" and press DEL. After you make the correction, the program will run as before.

Another common typo with the Print method is to forget it completely—you just type the text and run the program. To see what happens when you do this, delete the keyword Print and run the program again. This time Visual Basic responds with a box saying it can't compile the line of code. If you need some help determining what is causing the error, press F1 for context-sensitive help when the error message is on the screen. Visual Basic opens the Help window and gives you some general information on the error. For example, the help screen for a syntax error looks like Figure 3-7.

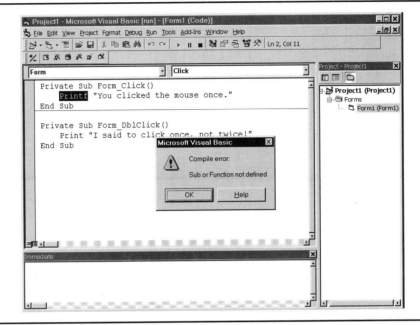

Effects of a typo
when coding
Figure 3-6.

Visual Basic can even find some syntax errors after you finish typing a line. To make sure this feature is on (or to turn it on, if it is off), choose Tools|Options and then go to the Environment page. Move to the item marked Auto Syntax Check and make sure that it is checked (on).

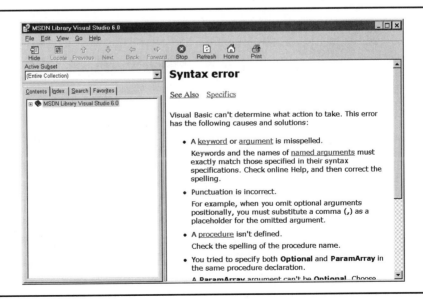

Help screen
explaining what
a syntax error is
Figure 3-7.

Saving Your Work

You should get into the habit of saving your work frequently and, in fact, Visual Basic will not let you exit the program or start a new project without asking whether you want to save your work. Even more is true: Visual Basic lets you set its options so that it will automatically save your work before a project runs. This minimizes the dire effects of system crashes, because you can't save a project while it is running or when you are in break mode. To activate this feature:

1. Choose Tools|Options and go to the Environment page.

2. In the "When a program starts" box, change the "Don't Save Changes" to either one of the two other options. (I always choose the "Save changes, don't prompt" option.)

In any case, most of the ways of saving your work are done by working with the File menu, so they are explained next.

Saving from the File Menu

The following sections describe the four save methods that are listed on the File menu.

Save Form This item shows you the name of the form that you are currently working on. (For example, if you use the default name of a form, it would show up as Save Form1 on the menu bar.) Use this item to save the specific form you are working on. To use this option, press CTRL+S (or use ALT+F, S). The default extension for form files is .frm. The first time you choose this option, Visual Basic pops up a dialog box like the one shown in Figure 3-8. Subsequent uses do not pop up a dialog box—the saving occurs almost without your being aware of it.

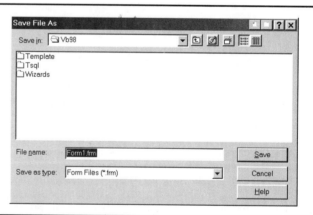

Save File As
dialog box for
saving a form

Figure 3-8.

NOTE: When you save a form again by using the Save Form option, Visual Basic does not keep a backup copy of the previous version.

Save Form As This option also uses the actual name of the form. Choosing this item opens the same dialog box you saw in Figure 3-8. This box allows you to rename the current form (.frm) file and is the only way to make a backup copy or store a copy of the current form on another disk. To select this option, press CTRL+A (or ALT+F, A). The next time you save the project (see the next topic), Visual Basic will update the file it uses for bookkeeping purposes to reflect the new name. (These bookkeeping files are usually called project files and have the extension .vbp.)

3

Save Project Choose this option in order to save the entire project. To select this option, press ALT+F, V or use the Save Project tool. When you first try to save a project by clicking this option, Visual Basic opens a dialog box similar to the one shown in Figure 3-8 for saving the forms in your project. It also gives the project a suggested name (a rather prosaic Project1.vbp). The Project file is how VB keeps track of all the pieces of a project. (For more on Project files, please see Chapter 12.) What you enter into the Save Project dialog box becomes the name of the Project or .vbp file as it is sometimes called (since .vbp is the extension). When you choose save Project (or save Project As) VB pops up individual dialog boxes for saving all the other files in the project if they haven't been saved already. When you create a stand-alone application, Visual Basic combines all the files in the project by looking for them where the .vbp file tells it to.

If you use the Save Project option to save revised versions of the same project during the course of developing and improving it, Visual Basic no longer provides you with a dialog box; it assumes you want to use the same project name every time.

NOTE: When you save a project using the Save Project option, Visual Basic does not keep a backup copy of the previous version. To save a backup copy of a project, do the following:

1. Save each of the files on the project with a new name.
2. Choose the Save Project As option and give the project file (.vbp) a new (path) name.

(You can also use standard Windows 95/98 or NT 4 techniques to work with the Explorer in order to save these files while still in Visual Basic.)

Save Project As The final save option pops up the same sort of dialog box as you see when you first use the Save Project option, but it asks only for the new name of the .vbp (Project) file.

CAUTION: Save Project As does not make a backup copy of
the unchanged files in the project. It simply saves a new .vbp file with the
current filenames.

Creating Stand-Alone Windows Programs

One of the most exciting features of Visual Basic is the ability to change your projects
into stand-alone Microsoft Windows programs. These will be files that users can
simply double-click on in Explorer in order to run them. Users won't need to have a
copy of VB on their systems at all!

NOTE: In this section I want to introduce you to the procedure for making
stand-alone VB programs; for more on making stand-alone VB applications, please see
the online help and Chapter 26.

To make a stand-alone VB application, simply go to the File menu and choose the
Make Project EXE File option (ALT+F, K). This opens a dialog box that looks like Figure
3-9. For now, notice that the default name for the .exe version of your file is the
project name (the name of the .vbp file with an .exe extension). For the stand-alone
program, the Windows desktop uses the same icon that Visual Basic uses for the
executable version of the project.

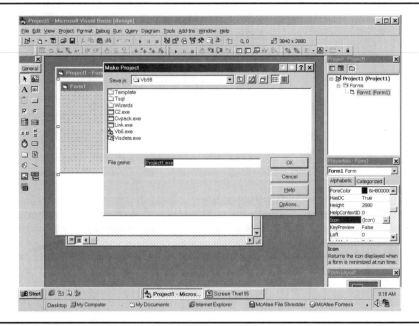

Make Project
dialog box
Figure 3-9.

When you distribute a Visual Basic program, it is also necessary to supply one or more dynamic link libraries (*DLLs for* short) to the user. Dynamic link libraries are the cornerstone of Windows programming; among other features, they allow many programs to use the same code simultaneously. The largest one of these dynamic link libraries (and one you will always need) is the one that contains the VB library itself. It's around 1.4 megabytes. The VB DLL file contains various support routines that a Visual Basic program needs to handle the screens, numbers, and other parts of the application. Microsoft freely allows you to distribute the needed DLLs. Note that if you use the Package and Deployment Wizard (see the last chapter in this book) the needed files will automatically be added to the distribution disks you make.

3

Luckily, because DLLs can be shared, no matter how many different stand-alone Visual Basic applications users have, they need only one copy of the 1.4 megabyte VB DLL in a directory accessible to Windows. They will also need only one copy of any custom control files used by your Visual Basic application. The directory containing the system files for Windows itself (Windows\System) is the usual place to put all these files.

CHAPTER 4

First Steps in Building the User Interface

In Chapter 3 you saw how to customize a blank form and how to write simple, event driven programs. In particular, you saw how to use the Properties window to make a form more visually appealing, and you encountered the key notion of an *event* procedure, where you write the code to make a form respond.

What I want to do in this chapter is show you the basic methods for adding controls to a form. After that, you'll see how to use the most common of the 20 controls that are part of the basic toolbox. Then it's on to more in-depth coverage of the most common controls. The controls I'll cover in this chapter are:

◆ command buttons, which initiate actions

◆ text boxes, which accept or display data

◆ labels, which identify controls and data

◆ image controls, which display pictures

After you see the most common properties of these basic controls, it's on to the most common events they respond to. Then we'll write a few programs by placing code in the associated event procedures for these common events.

Keep in mind that, just as with forms, controls remain essentially inert until you write the code in the event procedures that tells them how to respond. Moreover, the techniques for writing event procedures for controls are similar to those you use for writing a form. For example, to make a click on a command button initiate an action requires writing an event procedure almost identical to the one that makes a blank form respond to a click. Finally, you'll see how message boxes can make applications more friendly by, for example, warning users of irreversible steps they may be taking.

NOTE: The purpose of this chapter is to give you just enough information about how to manipulate controls so that you can write some basic applications. This, in turn, will get you started on the road to mastering the underlying programming language used in Visual Basic.

Before I begin the chapter proper, a reminder: the techniques described in Chapter 3 for using the Properties window will appear again and again; it's a good idea to make sure you are completely comfortable with the techniques for setting properties before you continue. For example, the SHIFT+CTRL+letter combination for moving through the Properties window of a form works for properties of controls as well.

Finally, keep in mind that while the controls discussed in this chapter are among the most commonly used ones for Visual Basic applications, a polished and professional Visual Basic application will likely need the controls that are discussed in Chapters 6, 11 and 14. Visual Basic is amazingly powerful—there are more controls with more properties than you'll ever want to keep in your head. But, if you master the basic controls and their properties first, you can learn about the other controls and their properties when you need them. (The on-line help is great for this.)

The Toolbox

You can think of the toolbox as containing a set of tools you use to embellish a blank form. However, its name is a bit of a misnomer actually. The tools for working with a form are found on the menus; the toolbox itself contains the icons representing the controls you can add to your forms. The standard edition of Visual Basic comes with more than 20 different controls; the Professional and Enterprise editions add many many more.

T IP: One of the more exciting features of Visual Basic is its extendability by what are called custom controls. Chapter 2 showed you how to add custom controls to your projects. You can buy custom tools from third-party developers that can extend Visual Basic in even more dramatic ways. There are also many free and shareware controls available on the Web. (A good place to start is the Microsoft VB Owner's site (http://www.microsoft.com/vbasic/owners/) and CNet's ActiveX site (http://www.activex.com).

Figure 4-1 shows the toolbox supplied with the default installation of Visual Basic. The toolbox is usually located on the far left of the Visual Basic screen, but it need not be visible at all times. If the toolbox isn't visible, you must make it visible in order to work with a control. To open the toolbox, use the Toolbox tool or go to the View menu and choose Toolbox (ALT+V, X). You can move the toolbox to another location

4

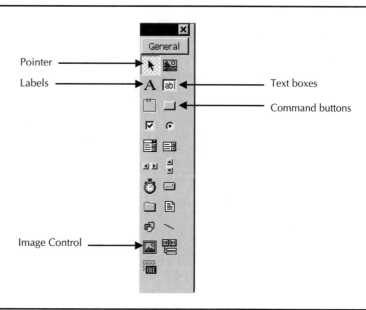

The toolbox
Figure 4-1.

on your screen using ordinary Windows drag-and-drop techniques. Here are brief descriptions of the tools covered in this chapter.

The Pointer   The first item on the toolbox is not a control but is used to manipulate controls after you create them. Click the pointer when you want to select, resize, or move an existing control. The pointer is automatically activated after you place a control on a form.

Command Buttons   Sometimes called push buttons, the idea behind these controls is that when the user moves the mouse to the command button and clicks, something interesting should happen. (And it will, *once* you write the event procedure that tells Visual Basic how to respond to the mouse click.) When you click a command button, it gives the illusion of being pressed. This optical illusion comes from the shading used by Visual Basic for command buttons, and it is inherited from the Windows operating system.

Image Controls   These are one of the two types of standard controls that you can use to display pictures. Image controls use the fewest Windows resources for displaying images. (Picture boxes—see Chapters 6 and 15—can do more but use more resources.) Since image controls also recognize the Click event, you can use them as graphical replacements for command buttons. However, in Visual Basic 6, ordinary command buttons can also display pictures (see the section on Command Buttons later in this chapter), so using image controls for this purpose is less common nowadays. Note that unlike command buttons, image controls do not give the user any feedback when they've been pressed, unless you program them to do so.

Text Boxes   You use text boxes (sometimes called edit fields) to display text or to accept user input. Most of the code you write for text boxes is to process the information users enter into them. Text boxes can wordwrap automatically or display multiple lines of text. All the ordinary Windows editing tools, such as cutting and pasting, are available when you enter information in a text box. This means users can automatically use such shortcuts as CTRL+X to cut, CTRL+C to copy, and CTRL+V to paste. Text boxes can word wrap and may have scroll bars for moving through the text. (Scroll bars are occasionally vital because text boxes can accept large amounts of text.) The usual limit for a text box is approximately 32,000 characters.

TIP: The Professional and Enterprise editions come with a RichTextBox control that goes way beyond what an ordinary text box can do. RichTextBoxes are discussed further in Chapter 6.

Labels   Use labels for information that users shouldn't be able to change. Labels identify objects and occasionally you might want to use them to display output. You have almost complete control over how the label displays information—whether the text is boldfaced, what size it is, and so forth. (You cannot mix fonts, however.) Although labels do respond to 12 events, usually they are used passively—for display purposes only.

Creating Controls

You can always get a control on a form by double clicking on its icon in the toolbox. This gives you the control in its default size and shape in the middle of the form. This is certainly one way to proceed. (See the sections on resizing and moving controls later in this chapter if you choose to use this technique extensively.)

Many of the more sophisticated methods for using the toolbox are similar to those used in a paint program, such as Microsoft Paint, which comes with Windows. You can use a combination of pointing, clicking, and dragging to manipulate the toolbox. For example, to draw an item from the toolbox on a form at a specific location with a specific size:

4

1. Move the mouse pointer to the tool you want to use and click. The background of the tool changes color when you've successfully selected it. (It also looks pressed in.) You can at this point, for example, hit F1 to go to the online help for this control.
2. Move the mouse pointer to the form. Think of this as the paint area in which you will draw the control. Notice that the mouse pointer has changed from an arrow to a shape like a crosshair.
3. Hold the mouse button down and drag the mouse to create the object. As you drag the mouse pointer, an outline of the control appears on the form.

One corner of the control is determined by where you press the mouse button in step 3, and the other is determined by where you release the button.

Notice as well that when you release the mouse button, the control has eight little boxes, called *sizing handles*, jutting out. (Line controls are one-dimensional and have only two sizing handles.) As you will soon see, you can use these handles to move and resize a control after you've created it. The pointer control is automatically highlighted when you release the left mouse button as well.

Next, notice that as you manipulate the control, it seems to move or enlarge in fits and starts, not smoothly. As the old computer joke goes, this is not a bug in Visual Basic, it really is a feature. The position of controls on a form in Visual Basic default so that they are located only at grid points. If you are willing to have a control appear off the grid, you can smooth out the motion of the controls. However, doing this makes it more difficult to align the controls on a form. If you want to do this, the section called "The Grid" at the end of this chapter shows you how. That section also shows you how to make the design grid even finer, which is often preferable to removing the design grid completely.

T IP: The dotted design grid can help you accurately position your controls.

There are two reasons why the feature of locating controls only at grid points—called *aligning to the grid* or *snapping to the grid*—makes positioning controls in Visual Basic a snap. First, the corners and sides of any control will always end up on a grid mark. Second, you have a small amount of leeway when you move the crosshair. Only when the vertical line of the crosshair hits a grid mark does the object move left or right. Similarly, only when the horizontal line of the crosshair hits a grid mark does the object move up or down.

Working with a Control Already on a Form

Let's suppose you've used the techniques described in the previous section to create a command button on a blank form. (When you create a command button, it appears with a centered caption: Command1, Command2, and so on. As you'll soon see, you can easily change these captions via the Properties window.)

The techniques in the previous section let you create a control and place it anywhere you like on a form. However, in Visual Basic you are never forced to keep a control at its original size or at its original location, and the techniques needed for moving or resizing controls are the same for all Visual Basic controls. You can also cut and paste controls by cutting out the control and using the Copy item on the Edit menu. (Chapter 11 describes the effect of copying an existing control.) When you paste a control that you cut out of a form, it always appears in the top left-hand corner of the form.

To work with an existing control, you must first select it (remember the buzzword for this is "giving it the focus"). You do this by moving the mouse pointer until it is inside the control and then clicking. (Or, you can press the TAB key until the focus is at the control. You can tell which control has the focus by looking for the sizing handles.)

Resizing an Existing Control

Suppose you've created a command button but aren't happy with its size. To change the size of an existing command button at design time, you can either:

◆ Use the Properties window to adjust the Width and Height properties, or

◆ Work with the sizing handles (as discussed next)

Figure 4-2 shows a command button with its eight sizing handles on an otherwise blank form. If the sizing handles aren't showing up, it means the control doesn't have the focus. Simply click inside the control by moving the mouse pointer to the control and clicking once. When the sizing handles are visible, you know the control is selected.

The four corner handles let you change the height and width at the same time. The mouse pointer changes to a double-sided diagonal arrow when you move the pointer to one of the corner sizing handles. The four side handles let you change the size in one direction only. At these handles, the mouse pointer changes to a straight double-sided arrow.

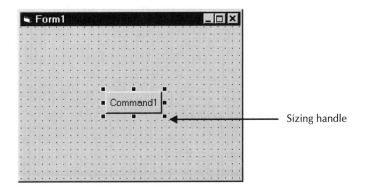

Sizing handle

Command
button with
sizing handles
Figure 4-2.

Try resizing a control with the sizing handles by following these steps:

1. Move the mouse pointer to a sizing handle and click and hold down the left mouse button.
2. Drag the mouse until the control is the size you want.

For example, if you want to shrink a control button from the left side while keeping the right side fixed, move the mouse pointer to the sizing handle in the center of the left side, click, and drag the mouse over to the right. You get more feedback on the size and position of the control by looking at the far right of the toolbar, which gives the current size of the control that has the focus. This is especially useful for adjustments you make using the Properties window.

Moving an Existing Control
In order to move an existing control with the mouse, the focus must be at that control. Notice that when you move the mouse so that the mouse pointer is inside a form or a control, its shape returns to the form of an arrow. The crosshair shows up only when you are creating a new control. Now, to move an existing control:

1. Move the pointer anywhere inside the control, click the left mouse button, and hold it down.
2. Drag the mouse until the control is at the location you want it to be, and then release the left button.

For finer control over the movement of controls:

1. Select the control.
2. Use CTRL+an arrow key to move the control one grid mark at a time.
3. Or, you can directly adjust the Left and Top properties in the Properties window.

Using the Double-Click Shortcut for Creating Controls

Now that you know how to move controls, you may prefer to use the double-click method to quickly create them. As you know, if you double-click on any of the toolbox icons, the matching control appears in the center of the screen. The more controls you double-click on, the higher they get stacked. You then can use the techniques from the previous section for moving controls to reposition and resize the controls on the stack.

For example, suppose you want to create an application with five command buttons symmetrically dispersed, as shown in Figure 4-3. The easiest way to do this is to double-click on the Command Button icon five times. This stacks five command buttons in the center of the form. Then you can easily use the method given in the previous section to move the buttons to the locations shown in Figure 4-3. (See the next section for other ways to align groups of controls.)

You may have noticed that the captions are more informative than the usual Command1, Command2, and so on. As with a form, you can change the captions by adjusting the Caption property of the command buttons via the Properties window.

NOTE: See Chapter 14 for another method of creating multiple controls at design time. See Chapters 11 and 13 for the methods for creating controls at run time.

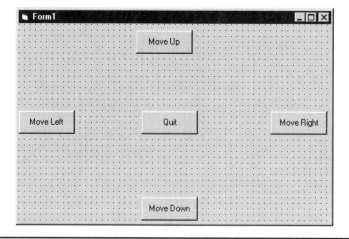

Form with multiple command buttons

Figure 4-3.

Working with Multiple Controls

Occasionally, you'll want to move a group of controls in the same direction. For example, you may have three command buttons lined up and want to keep them aligned but move them all up a couple of grid marks. To work with multiple controls as a single unit, you must first tell Visual Basic that you wish the controls to be temporarily treated as a unit. There are two ways to do this. Here are the steps for the "dragging" method to select multiple controls:

1. Imagine a rectangle that surrounds only those controls you want to select. Move to one corner of this imagined rectangle and click the left mouse button.
2. Hold the left mouse button down and drag the dotted rectangle until it covers all (and only) the controls you want to select. Then release the mouse button.

4

The grouped controls *all* show sizing handles now. Note that all but one of the sizing handles are grayed. This is how you know a group has been successfully selected.

Once you have selected a group of controls, when you move any control in the group, Visual Basic moves the other controls in a similar way. For example, if you move one control that is part of a selected group down two grid marks, all the other controls move down two grid marks.

The dragging method of selecting mutiple controls only works when the controls to be moved can be placed in a rectangular "lasso" that excludes any other controls. If the controls are widely scattered on the form, you'll need this next method:

◆ Select each control by moving the mouse pointer to it and holding down the left mouse button while pressing CTRL.

Regardless of what method you choose, if you move the mouse pointer to any one of the controls you've selected and drag it to a new location, the other controls move along with it in the same direction.

When you are done treating a group of controls as one unit, you'll need to tell VB that they should no longer be treated as a group. To take controls out of their temporary grouping and treat them individually again:

◆ Move the mouse pointer to any place outside the selected controls and click.

When you have a group of controls selected, you can do more than just move them as a group. The Tools|Format menu shown in the following illustration has multiple submenus that let you resize and reshape a group of controls. For example, the

Format|Align submenu lets you align controls so that their left edges match, their centers are aligned, and so on:

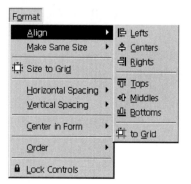

NOTE: The alignment used for a group of controls is determined by the control in the group with the black sizing handles. This is the *last* control that you selected in the group. For example, in the illustration shown here, if you choose Format|Align Lefts, all the control would move to match up with the middle text box (the one with "Text2") because that is the one with the black sizing handles.

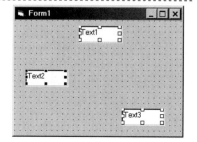

Similarly, the Format|Make Same Size menu lets you make a group of controls all the same width, height, or both:

Locking Controls

Once you are happy with the position of the controls on your form, you may want to use Visual Basic's *locking* feature. By choosing Format|Lock Controls or the Lock Control tool from the toolbar, you can prevent yourself from inadvertently moving a properly positioned control. Since this item is a toggle, choosing it again frees up controls so that you can move them again.

Deleting Controls

You may end up with too many controls on your form—especially if you use the double-click method a lot. To delete a control:

1. Move the mouse pointer until it is inside the control, and click the left mouse button to select it.
2. Press DEL, or open the Edit menu and choose the Delete option by pressing ALT+E, D.

The methods for selecting multiple controls so you can move them as a unit (discussed in the previous section) are also used when you want to delete many controls at once. Once you've selected the controls as a unit, the DEL key or Delete menu option works on all the controls in the group. You can also use the ordinary Windows editing shortcut keys such as CTRL+X to cut a group of controls out of a form.

4

The Name (Control Name) Property

This property determines the name Visual Basic uses for the event procedures you write to make the control respond to the user. Note that, as important as the Name property is for forms, the Name property for a control is even more important. While you can avoid using the Name of a form (or even better, use the Me keyword) in your code because VB knows the form that the code is attached to, *you can't avoid using the name of the control in your code.* That is, if you say either

    Height = 5000

or

    Me.Height = 5000

then Visual Basic will always assume you mean to change the height of the current form. On the other hand, if you wanted to change the height of a command button whose Name property is MyCommandButton, you must say:

    MyCommandButton.Height = 500

Picking meaningful names for your controls goes a long way toward making the inevitable debugging of your application easier. For example, suppose you are writing the code to make a form move to the left when you click a command button—code that could go with the Move Left command button in the form in Figure 4-3. When you have five command buttons in an application, writing code that looks like this

```
Private Sub Command4_Click ()

End Sub
```

to make a form move left is a lot more confusing than writing it like this:

```
Private Sub LeftButton_Click ()

End Sub
```

Actually, Microsoft suggests using a prefix to start the name of any control. For command buttons the prefix is *cmd*. Thus, the most common way to name such a command button would be cmdLeft. This in turn leads to an event procedure that looks like this:

```
Private Sub cmdLeft_Click ()

End Sub
```

Don't go overboard; the setting you use for a control's name should be meaningful but not ridiculous; you have to type the names of the controls in your code, after all. The limits on a control name are the same as for form names:

◆ The name must begin with a letter.

◆ After that, you can use any combination of letters, digits, and underscores. (Thus, no spaces are allowed in a control's name.)

◆ The name cannot be longer than 40 characters.

NOTE: Microsoft's convention for naming controls (see Chapter 3 of the *Programmer's Guide*) is to use an abbreviation for the type of control followed by the meaningful part, as indicated by the cmdLeft name used above. This book uses Microsoft's convention for naming controls most of the time, because most (but not all) people have decided to conform to the rainy kingdom's "suggestions". I actually prefer control names like LeftButton rather than cmdLeft—since it is easier for me to read. The trend—helped along by Microsoft of course—is against this, so I bowed to the inevitable. Whatever you do, however, follow some convention for your control names, or else your code may be unreadable soon after you've written it!

Properties of Command Buttons

Just as you use the Properties window to customize the size and shape of blank forms, you can use it to customize controls. For example, if you don't like the default value for a control's property, simply open the Properties window and change it.

The next few sections take you through what are the most useful properties of command buttons. But you also may want to scroll through the list of properties that show up in the Properties window and use the online help for any property that has a name that intrigues you, even if that property is not covered in this chapter.

The Caption Property

As you know, the Caption property of a form determines the name that shows in the title bar. Similarly, the Caption property on a command button determines what the user sees on the face of the button. Unlike the Name property, the Caption property can use just about any symbols available in a single font (see the Font property below). If you chose the Symbol font for the font in a control, you could, for example, have the caption on your button read: ευρεκα!

Any text you use for the caption on a command button is automatically centered within the button. However, command buttons aren't resized to fit the caption you set—you have to do that yourself.

4

Command buttons always start out with captions like Command1, Command2, reflecting the default value of the Name property. The number indicates the order in which the buttons were created. Let's create a simple command button like the one shown in Figure 4-4. The name shown in the button will not fit inside the default size of a command button. Luckily, you can create the caption for the button first via the Properties window and then resize the control to fit it.

Let's suppose that you want to change the Caption property of the command button as indicated in Figure 4-4. Double-click on the Command Button icon to create the button in the center of the screen. The Properties window should be visible (if not, use the F4 shortcut to make it appear). If for some reason the Caption property isn't showing up on the Properties window for the command button, the method to get to it is similar to the one you learned in Chapter 3:

1. Move to the Properties window.
2. Go to the Caption property by using the mouse or the UP ARROW and DOWN ARROW keys. (SHIFT+CTRL+C will get you there a whole lot quicker of course.)

Now you can type the new setting for the Caption property. If you need to replace the old setting (or part of it), hold down the left mouse button and drag it until all the

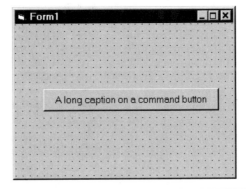

A long caption
on a command
button

Figure 4-4.

text you want to replace is highlighted. Overwrite the old setting or fill in the blank area by typing the phrase **A long caption on a command button**.

You should see something like Figure 4-5. Now you can resize the command button to fit the new caption. More of the message shows up as you enlarge the control, so it's easy to judge when to stop.

NOTE: In Chapter 6, I'll show you how to use code to figure out the exact size of text. This will enable you to resize controls so that text fits perfectly.

Other Useful Properties for Command Buttons

You can set 31 properties for a command button from the Properties window. Many of them are similar to the ones you saw for a form in Chapter 3. For example, command buttons have BackColor, Left, Top, Height, and Width properties. What follows is a short discussion of the most basic ones.

Visible This property determines whether the command button is visible or not. It's quite common to have your code alternately make a command button visible and invisible, depending on the situation. Like the Visible property for forms, this property can only be set to True or False.

Enabled This property determines whether the button can respond to any event whatsoever. If you set this property to False, Visual Basic will not respond to any event concerning that button. Unlike the Visible property, the button remains on the form but is inert. Changing this property also changes the appearance of an item, usually by graying out the text. The Enabled property is more often temporarily

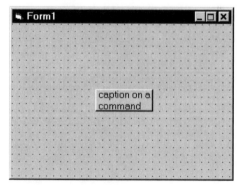

Designing a long caption

Figure 4-5.

toggled on or off via code than set in the Properties window, thus maintaining flexibility in your program.

Font   This property controls which font is used for the caption of the button. You can only use one font at a time. When you open up the Font dialog box, all the font characteristics—Bold, Italic, Font Name, and so on—can be set independently for each command button.

Height, Width   These properties define the height and width of the command button. Note that the units used are the ones set by the scale properties for the surrounding *container*. Usually the container is the form, but as you'll see in Chapters 12 and 14, you can block out regions within a form by using controls such as frames or picture boxes. This means the default measurement for the height and width of a command button is expressed in twips (1/20 of a printer's point, or 1/1440 of an inch). On the other hand, if you set the ScaleMode property of the surrounding form to 4 (inches), the Height and Width properties for command buttons will also be measured in inches.

4

You can change the settings for these properties directly from the Properties window or by using the sizing handles. As with a form, once you select a button, the current values for the size of the command button are displayed at the far right of the toolbar.

Left, Top   These properties determine the distance between the command button and the left edge and top of the container (again, usually the form), respectively. As with the Height and Width properties, these properties use the scale determined by the surrounding form. You can also change them by dragging and, as with forms, the values are displayed to the right on the toolbar.

MousePointer   Setting the MousePointer to something different than the usual arrow is a good way to give a user feedback that he or she has moved the focus to the command button. (Recall that "having the focus" is the standard phrase in Microsoft Windows to describe that a control is primed to receive input.) The same 17 settings that are available for the mouse pointer on a form are available for a command button—including the ability to make custom cursors by the method discussed in Chapter 3.

DisabledPicture, DownPicture, Picture, Style   Visual Basic gives command buttons the ability to display graphics. In addition to giving a command button a picture in its normal state, you can set a special picture when the control is disabled or when it is clicked. Note that while you can use all the standard picture types (bitmaps, icons, jpegs, gifs, Window metafiles—see the section on the Image control a little later in this chapter for more information on these standard picture types), the command button won't resize itself to fit the image—you'll need to do that by hand.

To make a command button display a picture, you first need to set the Style property to 1. After that, you need only specify the picture to be used as the value of the other three properties.

Shortcuts for Setting Properties

Suppose you want to set the Caption property for all the command buttons on your form. If you set it for one command button and immediately select another command button, the Caption property for the new control is highlighted in the Properties window. In general then, Visual Basic remembers the property just set for a control and, if possible, brings up the same property in the Properties window for the next control you select. (But you still have to change the property.)

Similarly, if you select a group of controls, the Properties window will show only the common properties that the controls in the group share. Change one of them and all of them change.

TIP: The easiest way to work with the different controls on a form is to click the down arrow to the right of the first line of the Properties window (below the title bar). This gives you a list of all the objects on the form. Here's an example of what you'll see:

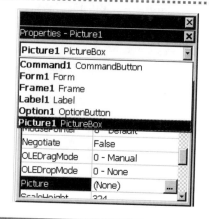

Simple Event Procedures for Command Buttons

Writing an event procedure for a command button is similar to writing one for a form. Whenever you double-click a control or use the F7 shortcut, Visual Basic opens the Code window. Visual Basic presents you with a template for the most common event procedure (usually the Click event) for that object.

Suppose you set up a command button with the caption "Click here for help!" Moreover, suppose you set the control's name (the Name property) to the more meaningful cmdHelp. Figure 4-6 shows what you will see in the Code window. Notice that the event procedure template has a form similar to the ones you saw in Chapter 3. The only difference is that the control name for the object is used, followed by an underscore, followed by the name of the event. This is the general form for the event procedure template for controls:

```
Private Sub ControlName_EventName( )

End Sub
```

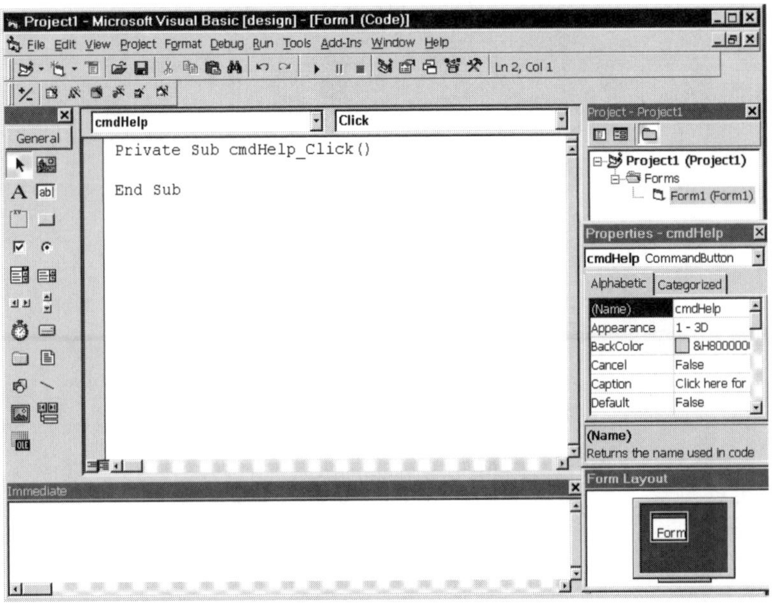

Code window
for setting up a
command
button
Figure 4-6.

Click the down arrow to the right of cmdHelp in the Properties window. Your Code window should look like the one in Figure 4-7. Notice that the list of objects in the Object list box has grown to include one named cmdHelp. Visual Basic always keeps track of all the objects in your project, and you can write event procedures for any of them by opening the Code window, moving through the Object list box, and selecting the object that interests you.

Let's add a simple Print statement to this event procedure, as shown here:

```
Private Sub cmdHelp_Click ()
  Print "No Help is yet available. Sorry."
End Sub
```

Now if you run this program (by pressing F5) and click the form (or the button), you should see something like what is shown in Figure 4-8.

In general, you have to be aware of the problems of using Print statements with a form that already has controls on it. If a control is located where the text is supposed to appear, the information printed to the form appears behind the control. Figure 4-9 shows an example of this.

The usual way to handle help information (or any other information you don't want obscured) is to use a context-sensitive help system or occasionally a separate form or message box. Also, you should be aware that if you iconize a window or move another window so that it temporarily covers a form with text on it, the text will disappear. You can overcome this by setting the AutoRedraw property of the form to True. (See

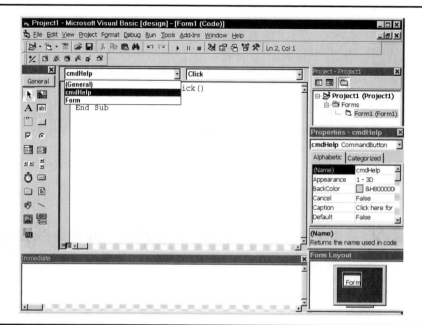

Pull-down list
showing objects
in a project
Figure 4-7.

the section "The AutoRedraw Property for Forms," later in this chapter, and Chapter 16, for more on this important property.) Another possibility is to rewrite the text as needed. The Paint event procedure is the usual place to do this. This is because Visual Basic generates the Paint event whenever a form is moved, enlarged, or uncovered when AutoRedraw is False. (See Chapter 16 for more on these events.)

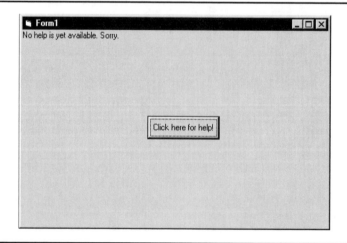

Results of
clicking on the
help button
Figure 4-8.

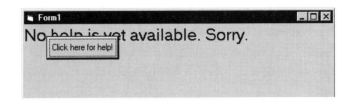

Text obscured
by an existing
control
Figure 4-9.

Other Events for Command Buttons

4

Command buttons can respond to 12 events, but clicking is by far the most common. Two others you may find useful are GotFocus and LostFocus. Naive users are often inattentive to just where the focus is and may get confused if what they type or click seems to be having no effect. Controls in Visual Basic can monitor whether the person has inadvertently moved the focus. You can then remind users that they've moved the focus and ask if they really want to do that. An event procedure that looks like this

```
Private Sub cmdButton_LostFocus

End Sub
```

lets you write the code to respond to users moving the focus away from that button—for example, by asking them if they really want to.

Similarly, code like this

```
Private Sub cmdButton_GotFocus

End Sub
```

might include code to generate help about that command button.

Command buttons can also respond to a user's pressing specific keys (see Chapter 7) and to mouse events (see Chapter 17).

Some Final Points on Command Buttons

Usually, the user of the application you develop chooses a command button by moving the mouse pointer to the button and clicking. However, sometimes you will want more flexibility. One other method for activating a command button is common to all Windows applications: move the focus by pressing TAB, and then press the SPACEBAR when the focus is where you want it to be. (The user knows a button has received the focus when it gives the appearance of being three-dimensional. What actually happens is Visual Basic draws a thinly dashed box around the text in the button and a fine rectangle around the button itself.) Both clicking and using the Tab/SpaceBar combination tell Visual Basic to activate the Click event procedure if you wrote one for that control.

NOTE: As you'll see in Chapter 5, you can also activate a Click event procedure (or any other event procedure for that matter) for a control via code.

In addition, you will often want to give people an *escape* button for a form that asks the user to do something. (Much like ordinary Windows dialog boxes work.) A user can activate an escape command button (only one for each form) by pressing ESC on the keyboard. Use an escape button to allow users to cancel an action or otherwise extricate themselves from some sort of situation they don't want to be in. (Note, a command button that does this is also called a *cancel button* in the Visual Basic manuals.)

How do you make a command button an escape button? Well, if you have scrolled through the list of properties available for a command button, you may have noticed the Cancel property. (Because the Cancel button doesn't normally change as the program runs, you usually use the Properties window to make a command button the escape (cancel) button. However, you can use code as well.)

As its name suggests, if you set the Cancel property to True, you will make that button an escape button. Setting the Cancel property to True for one button automatically sets it to False for all the other command buttons on the form, since you can have only one escape (cancel) button per form. Once you set this property, you'll need to keep in mind that when the user presses ESC, VB will trigger the Click event procedure for this button, *regardless* of where the focus is.

Another possibility you may want to consider—but one that has its problems for novice users—is to set up a *default command button* for the form. The way a default command button works is that VB will trigger the Click event procedure for the chosen (default) button whenever the user presses ENTER unless the focus is at another button.

Why is this a potential problem for naive users? Well, unsophisticated Windows users are apt to press ENTER at the strangest times, such as in a text box when they are done. In any case, if you want to have a default command button, set the *Default* property of the button to True. Also, as with a cancel button, you can have one default command button to a form, at most.

TIP: You can combine the default and cancel buttons into a default cancel button. This feature is especially useful if you feel the user is about to take an irreversible action.

Access Keys

Many Windows applications allow pressing ALT and one other key, the *access key*, to quickly activate a control or a menu item—Visual Basic itself, for example. These access keys are underlined in the caption of the control or name of the menu item.

Visual Basic makes it easy to set up an access key for any object that has a Caption property. When you set the caption, all you have to do is place an ampersand (&) in front of the letter you want to be the access key. For example, look at Figure 4-10. Notice that the *C* in the caption is underlined. When the application is running, you can activate this button either by pressing the ALT+C combination or by clicking on the button.

Although it is possible to have the same access key for more than one control on a form, doing so is unusual. What happens in this situation is that the focus moves to the next control with the same access key, but that control is not activated until you click the mouse or press the SPACEBAR.

4

Image Controls

Image controls hold pictures. They can also be used to create toolboxes if you don't have the Professional edition (see Chapter 14). The toolbox icon for an image control is the sun over a mountain (look back to Figure 4-1). Image controls can be used to

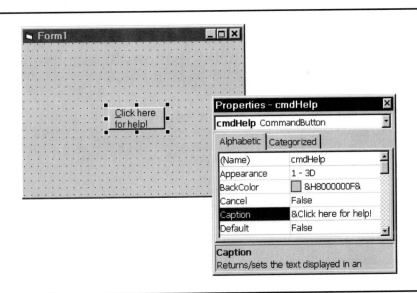

Caption
allowing access
key for control

Figure 4-10.

display icons or pictures created with a program such as Microsoft Paintbrush. They can also hold Windows metafiles or Jpegs or Gifs (the most common formats for the Internet). Jpeg format is also the common format used by most digital cameras. Here are typical examples of image controls at work:

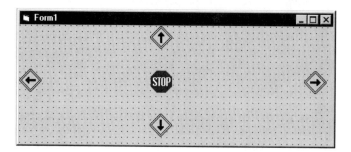

Since image controls respond to the Click event, you can use these images (taken from the Traffic icon directory) to substitute for the command buttons in Figure 4-3.

You load a picture into an image control by resetting the value of the Picture property. If you choose the Picture property for the image control, this opens up a dialog box that lets you choose what image file to load.

You can also reset the Picture property directly by copying an image from a graphics program to the Windows clipboard and then using the Copy command on the Edit menu to paste the image into the image control. Visual Basic will attach the graphic to the project when you save it. Finally, you can also change this property via code, as you'll see in Chapter 14.

Properties of Image Controls

Many of the properties of image controls are similar to those for command buttons. For example, you can set the Left and Top properties to control where the image control is located relative to its container. However, unlike forms, the BorderStyle property for an image control has only two possible settings: you can either have no border (setting = 0) or a fixed single border (setting = 1).

 NOTE: Microsoft's suggested prefix for the Name property of an image control is img.

The most important property of an image control that you haven't yet seen is the *Stretch* property. This determines whether the image control adjusts to fit the picture, or the picture adjusts to fit the control. If the Stretch property is left at the default value of False, the control resizes itself to fit the picture. If you change it to True, the picture resizes (as best it can) to fit the control. As a general rule, only Windows metafiles—which essentially store directions for drawing pictures rather than actual bitmaps—can be enlarged without great loss of detail. To see this, start a new project and place two large image controls on the form. Set the Stretch property to True for one of them, and leave the default for the other. Load the TRFFC07 "slippery road" icon. Notice that the detail in the enlarged image is greatly reduced (Stretch property = True), as shown here:

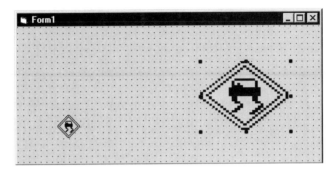

4

Text Boxes

Text boxes (and RichTextBoxes if you have them in your Professional edition—see Chapter 6 for more on them) are the primary method for accepting input and displaying output in Visual Basic. In fact, printing too many lines of text to a form will often lead to a run-time error and, in any case, you can't scroll back through the form to see lines that may have slipped off the top. (The icon in the toolbox for a text box shows the letters *ab*, as shown in Figure 4-1.)

T IP: Use a text box (or a RichTextBox) for all but the simplest textual displays on a form.

Text boxes never treat what a user types in as a number; this means that getting numeric information to a Visual Basic program requires transforming a string of digits into a number by using a built-in function or Visual Basic's built-in automatic conversions (see Chapter 5).

Standard Properties of Text Boxes

There are around 50 properties for text boxes (39 can be set at design time via the Properties window). Many of them should be familiar to you. As before, the Name property is used only for the code you write; the user never sees it. (Microsoft's prefix for the Name property of a text box is *txt*, by the way.)

NOTE: You can set the font properties via the Font dialog box available from the Properties window, but you can only use one font per text box. A RichTextBox, on the other hand, allows you to mix fonts so that you can (as its name suggests!) have the richest possible display of text. (See Chapter 6 for more on RichTextBoxes.)

Since users can move the focus to a text box and type information there, the font properties also affect what the user sees when he or she enters information inside the text box. As with command buttons, the Height, Width, Left, and Top properties use the scale determined by the surrounding container.

Unlike command buttons (but like forms), you can set both the BackColor and ForeColor properties for a text box. The ForeColor property affects the color of the text that is displayed. BackColor affects the rest of the text box. Both of these can be set independently of the surrounding container. It is easiest to set them using the color palette from the Properties window. (To control colors directly via the color codes, see the section on color codes and hexadecimal notation in Chapter 5.)

As with command buttons, the Enabled property affects whether the text box will respond to events. In particular, if a text box is disabled, the user cannot enter text inside it. When a text box is disabled, it is grayed. Also, as before, it is quite common to toggle the Visible property between True and False with code, in order to make a text box appear and disappear. The MousePointer property has the same 17 possible settings as for forms; you often change this property to dramatize that the focus is now within the control.

Some Special Properties for Text Boxes

There are a few properties for text boxes you have not seen before, and the BorderStyle property works differently than for forms. This section covers these important properties.

NOTE: Because text boxes do not have a Caption property, you will need a trick to give the user an access key for them. You'll see how to do this shortly, in the section on Labels.

Text   The Text property in text boxes is the analog of the Caption property for a command button or a form; it controls the text the user sees. When you create a text box, the default value for this property is set to Text1, Text2, and so on. If you want a text box to be empty when the application starts, select the Text property and blank out the original setting.

Alignment   This property controls how text is displayed. The default value is 0, which leaves the text left-aligned. Use a value of 1 and text is right-aligned. Use a value of 2 and text is centered.

MultiLine This property determines whether a text box can accept more than one line of text when the user runs the application, and it is usually combined with resetting the value of the ScrollBars property. In any case, if you set this to True, a user can always use the standard methods in Windows to move through the text box: the arrow keys, HOME, CTRL+HOME, END, and CTRL+END.

Visual Basic automatically word-wraps when a user types more than one line of information into a multiline text box—unless you've added horizontal scroll bars to the text box. Also, users can use the ENTER key to separate lines, unless you've added a default command button to the form (yet another reason to be careful of adding one). If you have a default command button, the user has to press CTRL+ENTER to break lines.

Since forms can only display a limited amount of text and they do not scroll, multiline text boxes are the usual method for displaying large amounts of text in Visual Basic. The limit for a multiline text box is approximately 32,000 characters.

ScrollBars This property determines whether a text box has horizontal or vertical scroll bars. These are useful, because Visual Basic allows you to accept long or multiple lines of data from a single text box; roughly 32,000 characters is the limit for a multiline text box. Without scroll bars, it becomes much harder for the user to move through the data contained in the text box, thus making editing the information that much more difficult.

The following table lists the four possible settings for the ScrollBars property.

Value	Meaning
0	This is the default value. The text box lacks both vertical and horizontal scroll bars.
1	The text box has horizontal scroll bars only (limits text inside the box to a total of 255 characters).
2	The text box has vertical scroll bars only.
3	The text box has both horizontal and vertical scroll bars.

BorderStyle As with the image control, there are only two possible settings for the BorderStyle property for a text box. The default value is 1, which gives you a single-width border, called a *fixed single*. If you change the value of this property to 0, the border disappears.

MaxLength This property determines the maximum number of characters the text box will accept. The default value is 0, which (somewhat counter-intuitively) means there is no maximum other than the (roughly) 32,000-character limit for multiline text boxes. Any setting other than 0 will limit the user's ability to enter data into that text box to that number of characters.

PasswordChar As you might expect from the name, the PasswordChar property lets you limit what the text box displays (although all characters are accepted and stored). The convention is to use an asterisk (*) for the password character. Once you set this property, all the user sees is a row of asterisks. This property is often combined with the MaxLength property to add a password feature to your programs (see Chapter 7).

Locked   This True/False property lets you prevent users from changing the contents of the text box. Users can scroll and highlight text but won't be able to change it. (Because users can highlight text, they will still be able to use ordinary Windows techniques to copy information from the text box—they just won't be able to change it. This property is most commonly toggled on or off via code.) Its advantage over setting the Enabled property to False is that the box isn't grayed.

Event Procedures for Text Boxes

Text boxes can recognize 23 events. Events such as GotFocus and LostFocus work exactly as you saw before. Three others—KeyDown, KeyUp, and KeyPress—are for monitoring exactly what the user types. This type of data processing requires a fair amount of code, which you'll see in Chapter 7.

Although the Change event lacks the flexibility of the key events you'll see in Chapter 7, you may find it very useful. Visual Basic monitors the text box and calls the Change event procedure whenever a user makes any changes in the text box. No matter what the user types or pastes into the text box, Visual Basic will trigger the Change event procedure. One of the most common uses of the Change event procedure is to warn people that they should not be entering data in a specific text box at this moment. You can then set the Text property back to what it was, blanking out what they typed. (See Chapter 7 for how to do this as well.)

Labels

Use labels to display information you don't want the user to be able to change. Probably the most common use for labels is to identify a text box or other control by describing its contents. Another common use is to display help information. The icon for a label is the bold, capital letter *A*, and Microsoft's suggested prefix for the Name property of labels is *lbl*.

Labels have 34 possible properties (30 are displayed in the Properties window). Most of them overlap with the properties for text boxes and forms, and many of them should be familiar to you by now. Like forms (but unlike text boxes), labels have a Caption property that determines what they display, the Font being set via the Font property. The Caption property is originally set to be the same as the default Name property: Label1 for the first label on your form, Label2 for the second, and so on. At design time you can have one line of text, at most, as the caption for a label. With code (see Chapter 5) you can add blank lines of text to a caption. As before, the Name property for the control is used only for the code you write; the user never sees it.

As with command buttons, the Height, Width, Left, and Top properties use the scale determined by the surrounding container.

Also, as with text boxes, you can set the BackColor and ForeColor properties for a label. The ForeColor property affects the color of the text that is displayed. BackColor affects the rest of the label. Both of these can be set independently of the surrounding container.

The Enabled property is not often used for labels. Its primary role is to determine whether the user can move the focus to the control that follows the label in tab order (see the section a little later in this chapter called "Assigning Access Keys for Text Boxes"). As before, it is quite common to have code toggle the Visible property between True and False to make a label appear and disappear.

4

The MousePointer property uses the same 17 possible settings. This is rarely changed for labels, but one possibility is to change the icon when the user moves from the label to the control that is being labeled.

Useful Properties for Labels

There are five especially useful properties for labels, one of which you have not seen before: AutoSize. Another property, WordWrap, works slightly differently than it does for text boxes. For example, you can only use the WordWrap property after you set the AutoSize property to True. Also, the BorderStyle property has one neat use that can give more polish to your applications.

Alignment The Alignment property for a label has three possible settings. The usual (default) value is 0, which means the text in the label is left-justified (flush left). Set the value of this property to 1, and the text inside the label will be right-justified; set the value to 2, and the text is centered.

BorderStyle, BackStyle The BorderStyle property has the same two possible values as text boxes do. The difference is that the default value is 0, so labels do not start out with a border. Set the value to 1, and the label resembles a text box. This is occasionally useful when your program displays results. Using labels with a BorderStyle property value of 1 for displaying output avoids the problem of text boxes being changed by the user. Your form will have a control that looks like a text box, but it will not be responsive to the user. The BackStyle property determines whether the label is transparent or opaque.

AutoSize, WordWrap Unlike command buttons, labels can be made to grow automatically in a horizontal direction to encompass the text you place in them. This is a function of the AutoSize property. The default value for this property, though, is set to False, and you need to change it to True to take advantage of this neat feature. (Be careful though, you'll want to make sure the label doesn't grow so big as to be hidden by another control or to hide it.) If you also set the WordWrap property to

True, the label will grow in the vertical direction to encompass its contents, but the horizontal size will stay the same. In addition, the words will be wrapped so that they are never broken, as indicated next:

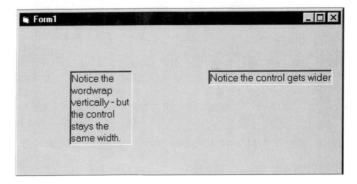

The labels in this example have the BorderStyle set to 1 so that you can see them more easily, and each started out at the same width.

Event Procedures for Labels

Labels respond to 18 events. For example, they can respond to clicking, double-clicking, or the Change event. The most common event procedures for a label are mouse events (see Chapter 17). You can use a click of the right mouse button to provide context-sensitive help or pop up a menu, for example. One problem is that labels do not respond to key events or detect whether the user has shifted the focus. This dramatically restricts the use of event procedures for labels. Labels in Visual Basic remain primarily descriptive and not responsive.

Navigating Between Controls

Using the mouse is the most common way to move from control to control in a Windows application, but your applications have to allow for using the TAB key as well. *Tab order* is the term used in a Windows application for the sequence of controls that pressing TAB moves you through. In a Visual Basic application, the order in which you create the controls is the order used for the tab order. The first control you create at design time is the one that receives the focus when the application starts. If you press TAB once when the application is running, you move to the second control you created at design time, and so on. If you press TAB when the focus is at the last control you've created, the focus moves back to the first control. (Disabled controls are skipped.)

It's possible to change the setting for the tab order via the Properties window or by writing code. The property you need to set is the TabIndex property. If you set this value to 0 for a control, this control automatically becomes the first control in tab order, and all the other controls move upward in tab order. What used to be the first control in tab order is now the second, the second is now the third, and so on. If you change a control with a higher tab index, then only controls with larger tab indexes are affected. If you create a control and set the TabIndex property at design time, the settings for the TabIndex property are moved higher to make way for the new control. You can also change the TabIndex property via code (see Chapter 5).

NOTE: There is also a true/false property called TabStop that controls whether the user can tab to the control. For example, if you set the TabStop property of a command button to False, the user can directly click on it but wouldn't be able to tab to it and press the SPACEBAR to activate it.

Assigning Access Keys for Text Boxes

4

Text boxes lack a Caption property, so you need a trick to allow users to move the focus to them quickly via an access key. The trick works like this: labels have captions, so you can set an access key for them by using the ampersand (&) in front of the letter you want as the access key. However, labels do not respond to the GotFocus or LostFocus event. So what happens when you use the access key?

If the user presses the access key for a control, such as a label, that does not respond to focus events, the focus moves to the next control that will accept it in tab order.

This makes it easy to give an access key for a text box.

1. Create a label for the text box.
2. Set up the access key for the label.
3. Then create the text box.

Actually, the point of step 3 is to ensure that the text box follows the label in tab order. If you are willing to change the TabOrder property of the text box after the fact, you can create the text box whenever you want.

TIP: If you need to use an ampersand in a label but don't want to create an access key, set the UseMnemonic property to False or use a double ampersand (&&) instead of the single ampersand.

Message Boxes

Message boxes display information in a dialog box superimposed on the form. They wait for the user to choose a button before returning to the application. Users cannot switch to another form in your application as long as Visual Basic is displaying a message box. Message boxes should be used for short messages or to give transient feedback. For example, you would not generally use them to provide a help screen unless you wanted to say something as simple as "Hey, don't do that." A good example of where an application might display a message box is when the user moves the focus away from a text box before placing information inside it. The simplest form of the message box command looks like this:

```
MsgBox "The message goes in quotes"
```

Message boxes can hold a maximum of 1,024 characters, and Visual Basic automatically breaks the lines at the right side of the dialog box. You can set line breaks yourself, using the techniques you will see in Chapter 5.

For example, suppose you wrote an application and thought the user needed to be reminded that nothing would happen until he or she clicked a command button. You might add a LostFocus event procedure that looks something like this:

```
Private Sub cmdMyButton_LostFocus ()
   MsgBox "You have to click the button for anything to happen!"
End Sub
```

When you run this application and move the focus away from the command button, you will see a screen like the one shown in Figure 4-11. Notice in Figure 4-11 that the title bar for the message box isn't particularly informative. You can add your own, more informative, title to a message box. For this, you have to use the full form of the message box statement by adding two options to it. Here is the complete syntax for the MsgBox command:

MsgBox *MessageInBox*, *TypeOfBox*, *TitleOfBox*

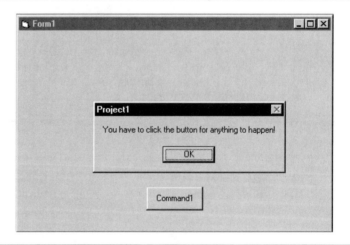

Message box
demonstration
Figure 4-11.

4

You combine three different groups of built-in integer constants to specify the kind of message box. The first number controls what kind of buttons appear. The following table summarizes this information.

Symbolic Constant	Value	Meaning
vbOKOnly	0	Display OK button only
vbOKCancel	1	Display OK and Cancel buttons
vbAbortRetryIgnore	2	Display Abort, Retry, and Ignore buttons
vbYesNoCancel	3	Display Yes, No, and Cancel buttons
vbYesNo	4	Display Yes and No buttons
vbRetryCancel	5	Display Retry and Cancel buttons
vbCritical	16	Display Critical Message icon
vbQuestion	32	Display Warning Query icon
vbExclamation	48	Display Warning Message icon
vbInformation	64	Display Information Message icon

For example, the following statement

```
MsgBox("Will have Yes and No buttons", vbYesNo)
```

gives you a message box like this:

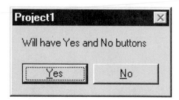

The next group of numbers controls which button is the default button for the box. This is summarized in the following table.

Symbolic Constant	Value	Meaning
vbDefaultButton1	0	First button is default
vbDefaultButton2	256	Second button is default
vbDefaultButton3	512	Third button is default

You can combine these options by adding the constants or values together. For example, the statement

```
MsgBox "Examples of buttons", vbOKCancel + vbExclamation + _
vbDefaultButton2, "Test Message Box"
```

displays a message box that looks like this:

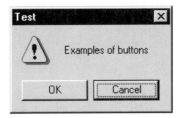

This box contains an exclamation mark icon with OK and Cancel buttons, and the second button, Cancel, would be the default button for this form. The title bar of the message box would show Test Message Box.

Although message boxes do not have event procedures associated with them, it is possible to determine which button was pressed by assigning the value of MsgBox to a variable and reading off the value, as you will see in Chapter 7.

The Grid

Since the grid is so important for accurately positioning controls, mastering it will help you give your applications a finished, professional look. In order to control the grid, choose Tools|Options (ALT+T, O), and then go to the General page on the Options dialog box, as shown in Figure 4-12. The four properties you can control are described next.

Show Grid   You can turn the grid on or off by changing the Show Grid setting. The default setting is on. There is usually little reason to turn the grid off.

Grid Width, Grid Height Boxes   The Width and Height text boxes let you set the distance (in twips) between grid marks. The default is 120 twips. Change these both to 60, and the grid becomes twice as fine.

Align Controls to Grid   The Align Controls to Grid check box determines whether controls automatically move to the next grid mark or whether they can be placed between grid marks. Usually you are better off changing the grid spacing to match your design requirements than turning this option off.

It's possible to align an item to the grid even if you've chosen to turn this option off. To do this, select the control by clicking it once (the sizing handles show up) and choosing Format|Align|to Grid (or using the right-click menu).

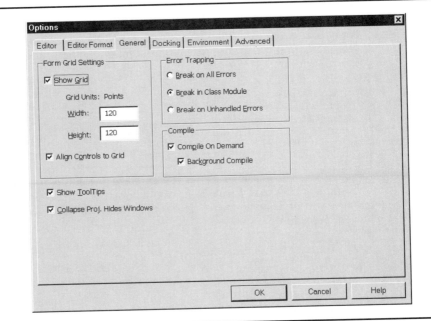

General page in
the Options
dialog box
Figure 4-12.

What Happens When a Visual Basic Application Runs

When the user runs an application developed with Visual Basic, he or she usually sees the initial form that you've designed. (See Chapter 12 for multiple form applications.) However, a lot needs to happen in the background before the user actually sees the form. For example, before the form is visible to the user, Visual Basic checks whether you've written an event procedure for initializing the state of the form. This event procedure has a mnemonic name—it's called the Form_Initialize procedure. The most common use of this event procedure is to initialize form-level variables (see Chapter 5) and change the property settings for controls and the form itself.

The Initialize procedure occurs prior to the Form_Load procedure, which was the first procedure that versions of Visual Basic prior to VB5 used for initialization. Some people still prefer to use the Form_Load procedure to set the initial properties for a form. In any case, you may find it easier to initialize the properties of the form and its controls by using code in the Form_Initialize and Form_Load procedures, rather than using the Properties window. (See the section "Setting Properties with Code" in Chapter 5 for more information.)

Since the Form_Load procedure is the default event procedure for a form, all you usually have to do is double-click in any blank area of the form to get to the Form_Load event procedure template. You will have to explicitly choose the Initialize procedure from the Event procedure list box on the right of the Code window in order to work with it.

```
Private Sub Form_Initialize ()
  'Initialize form level variables
  'Initialize properties
  ' etc.
End Sub
```

Right after Visual Basic processes the Initialize procedure, it calls the Form_Load procedure. After that, Visual Basic calls a bunch of other event procedures—if you've written code for them. Here is the order that Visual Basic invokes these event procedures:

◆ Form_Initialize procedure

◆ Form_Load procedure

◆ Form_Resize procedure

◆ Form_Activate procedure

◆ Form_GotFocus procedure (only if no controls on the form are enabled)

◆ Form_Paint procedure (only if the AutoRedraw property, discussed shortly, is False)

Generally speaking, initial information you want printed to the form should be handled by placing Print statements in one of the other event procedures, rather than in the Form_Initialize or Form_Load procedure. This is because, unless you first use the Show method or set the AutoRedraw property to True, nothing will show up on the form!

These events can be confused because they are triggered under similar circumstances. It is important that you keep in mind the order in which they are triggered by Visual Basic, so I want to spend a bit of time on them.

Form_Initialize Event   The Initialize event is triggered first and only once: Visual Basic triggers this event when the form is first created. *The Initialize event occurs before the Load event.* As its name suggests, the Initialize event is where you can place code that sets the initial properties of the form.

Form_Load Event   The Load event is triggered when a form is loaded into memory and occurs after the Initialize event. Usually this code is triggered once only. (However, using code, it is possible to unload and then reload a form, as discussed in Chapter 12, so one can have this event triggered more than once.) When you start a program with a single form, it will generally be loaded automatically—thus triggering this event. (See Chapter 5 for dealing with multiple form applications.)

Form_Resize Event Visual Basic triggers the Form_Resize event whenever the user resizes a form, or minimizes and then restores the form. For this reason, the most common use of this event procedure is to recalculate (and rescale if necessary) the size and position of any objects on your form. For example, suppose you spent a lot of time positioning controls symmetrically on a form. Without repositioning them in the Form_Resize procedure, a user can, all too easily, spoil your hard work! (See Chapter 14 for an example of how to use this procedure to prevent your carefully positioned controls from getting messed up.)

Form_Activate Event Visual Basic triggers the Form_Activate event procedure whenever a form becomes active (that is, when the user moves the focus to it). However, if you move to a different application running under Windows and then return to the form, Visual Basic does not call the Form_Activate event procedure again. For this reason, the Form_Activate event procedure is usually used only in multiple form applications.

4

Form_GotFocus Event After the Activate event is triggered, Visual Basic will trigger the GotFocus event for the form *only if all visible controls on it are disabled.* (For this reason, people rarely use the GetFocus event for a form.)

Form_Paint Event The Form_Paint procedure is where you put Print methods when the AutoRedraw property is set to False. Visual Basic calls this event whenever the form is moved, enlarged, or newly uncovered. You then use this event procedure to redraw the information on the form. However, when the AutoRedraw property is set to True, this event is *not* called, and you'll need to use the Refresh method directly (see the section on this method later in this chapter).

NOTE: Visual Basic also generates events when someone tries to close an application by closing the last form. See Chapters 7 and 12 for how to work with the Unload, Query_Unload, and Terminate events.

The Display in Visual Basic

After Visual Basic processes any statement that affects the display, it calls on Windows to do the work. Windows, in turn, tells the display adapter how to display the image. When someone installs any version of Windows, the installation program checks (or you tell it) what hardware and software you have. Then the Windows installation program installs the necessary screen and print drivers. If you are writing a Visual Basic program for other users, you can safely assume the user has all this information set up to work at least reasonably well.

NOTE: One exception to the assumption that all is as it should be is when it comes to printers. When the user has multiple printers available, you may want to reset the default Printer via Visual Basic code. See Chapter 6 for more on how to take advantage of this power in VB.

Since Windows is a graphical environment, this does mean that what you can do with Visual Basic depends on the driver programs that Windows uses for controlling the screen and printer. A nice plus to this approach is that using these driver programs is automatic. You do not have to worry about all the possible combinations of hardware a user may have.

NOTE: If need be, you can always check (via code) what the resolution of the user's screen is. You may want to write the code to adjust your forms to different screen resolutions (see Chapter 14). This is because a form designed for 640 X 480 resolution will appear rather strange in 1280 X 1040!

Nothing comes for free, however. Windows has to do a lot to manage a graphics environment, and this forces trade-offs. For example, the Visual Basic default is that when you move a form or temporarily hide it, or when one form covers another and moves away, the original text and graphics will probably disappear. This will happen even if the window that covers your form comes from a completely different Windows application. You can arrange for Visual Basic to have *persistent graphics*, but the cost is that Visual Basic must keep a pixel-by-pixel copy of the object in memory. This is called a *bitmap of the screen*. Since many machines will not have enough available memory to store more than a couple of screens, Windows may use your hard disk for temporary storage, slowing down reaction time dramatically.

The AutoRedraw Property for Forms

As you'd expect, persistent graphics are determined by a Boolean (True or False) property of forms (this also applies to picture boxes—see Chapter 14). Like most properties, you can set this at design or run time. Once you set the AutoRedraw property to True, Visual Basic saves a copy of the object in memory. Set it to False, and you will have to manage the redrawing of graphics yourself.

For a resizable form, when AutoRedraw is True, Visual Basic saves a screen representation of the window. In particular, this means that when you enlarge the form, or when it is covered by another form, no text displayed on the form (and no graphics information—see Chapter 14) is lost. This setting for AutoRedraw requires by far the most memory.

NOTE: People sometimes can't believe what the fuss about memory constraints is. The reason is that the amount of memory needed for even a simple form can be mind boggling. For example, a computer running with 1024 X 768 resolution with a good video card would use around 2 megabytes of memory for each form! If your user doesn't have a lot of physical RAM, setting AutoRedraw to True will slow their system down to a crawl.

There is one other problem you must be aware of when you set AutoRedraw to True. When AutoRedraw is True, Visual Basic draws the complete image to memory before displaying it on the screen. Only when the bitmap is complete and Visual Basic is in *idle time* (not responding to a specific event—see Chapter 12) will the image finally show up on your screen. On the other hand, you can use the Refresh method to display the image at different stages. However, each time Visual Basic processes a Refresh statement, it redraws every dot in the image from scratch. This can be painfully slow.

4

Whenever the AutoRedraw property is False, Visual Basic activates the Paint event each time a part of the form is newly exposed. This often happens when the user moves or enlarges the form. You can write the necessary code in the Paint procedure whenever you want to redraw part of a form (or picture box—see Chapter 14). Therefore, the least memory-intensive way to handle the problem of text or graphics disappearing when a user covers a form is to:

1. Set AutoRedraw to False
2. Redraw the information on the form or picture box in the Paint or resize event procedure.

This again shows the constant trade-off in programming between memory-intensive and CPU-intensive activities. Set AutoRedraw to True, and you use up real memory (if you have it), so this, potentially, can speed up the program. (But of course if the user doesn't have a lot of RAM, their hard disk will whirl constantly while Windows uses the hard disk to make up for the lack of RAM ("Virtual Memory" as it is called in the jargon). Using the Paint event procedure (or the hard disk, if you don't have enough memory) uses up time. You have to choose what's best for the application. At the extremes, the choice is easy: If the amount of drawing to be done is minimal, using the Paint event procedure is better. In any case, Visual Basic calls the Paint procedure for the object only if the AutoRedraw property of the object is set to False.

CAUTION: Do not put any statements that move or resize the object inside the Paint or ReSize event procedures. This is because Visual Basic will just call the Paint event procedure again and again, and you will be stuck in an infinite regression.

The Refresh Method

The other method you need in order to get started with Visual Basic programming is the Refresh method which I mentioned briefly above. This method applies to forms and controls. It forces an immediate refresh of the form or control and, as mentioned previously, will let you see an image develop even when AutoRedraw is True. If you use the Refresh method, Visual Basic will also call any Paint event procedure you have written for the object. It is quite common to use this method inside the Form_Resize procedure in order to redisplay any graphics that are calculated in the Paint event procedure. Also, although Visual Basic handles refreshing the screen during idle time, occasionally you will want to take control of this yourself. Whenever Visual Basic processes an *Object*.Refresh statement, it will redraw the object immediately and generate the Paint event if the object supports this.

The ASCII Representation of Forms

All the information about the controls and your form is stored in text format that you can read (and change), using your favorite text editor or word processor. (Be sure to save the file back into text format if you do change it!) Using the text representation of a program makes it easy to check that the properties of the various controls and forms are exactly what you want. To see what the ASCII representation of a form looks like, do the following:

1. Start a new Standard EXE project.
2. Set the caption of the form to "Form description as saved example".
3. Add a command button in the default size, in the default location, and using the default name of Command1 by double-clicking on the Command Button tool.
4. Add a Click procedure to the command button with the single line of code:

```
Private Sub Command1_Click
  Print "You clicked me"
End Sub
```

5. Save the form with the name ASCII.frm. (Use the Save Form1 As option on the File menu.)

Now, if you examine the file in another word processor, such as Windows WordPad, or in a text editor, such as Windows Notepad, here's what you will see. (Don't be intimidated by the length of the following listing; the pieces will be described step by step. Also, note that the values for height and width and such will depend on your machine.)

NOTE: You may be wondering why a VB6 projecy says "VERSION 5.00." The reason is that the formats of the .frm files are the same for both VB5 and VB6. If you don't use any of the new features of FB6, you should be able to run the proejct in VB5!

4

```
VERSION 5.00
Begin VB.Form Form1
    Caption         =   "Form description as saved example"
    ClientHeight    =   2544
    ClientLeft      =   48
    ClientTop       =   288
    ClientWidth     =   3744
    LinkTopic       =   "Form1"
    ScaleHeight     =   2544
    ScaleWidth      =   3744
    Begin VB.CommandButton Command1
        Caption     =   "Command1"
        Height      =   372
        Left        =   1440
        TabIndex    =   0
        Top         =   1080
        Width       =   972
    End
End
Attribute VB_Name = "Form1"
Attribute VB_GlobalNameSpace = False
Attribute VB_Creatable = False
Attribute VB_PredeclaredId = True
Attribute VB_Exposed = False
Private Sub Command1_Click()
    Print "You clicked me"
End Sub
```

The idea of the ASCII form representation is simple: It contains a textual description of the form's properties. The listing begins with the file version used (as the previous Note indicated, VB5 and VB6 share the same file format), followed by the name of the form. Then come the current settings of all the properties associated with the form. For example, the new caption for the form is reflected by the line of code that looks like this

```
Caption         =   "Form description as saved example"
```

because this is what we reset the Caption property to be. The Client properties describe the form's position in relation to the desktop. After the properties of the form come the various controls on the form in the same format, indented slightly for readability. The ASCII format for most Visual Basic controls starts out like the following:

```
Begin VB.ControlType ControlName
```

In the example, this is the line:

```
Begin VB.CommandButton Command1
```

Then come the properties of the control. For example, since we didn't change the control name or any of the other properties, the preceding listing does not show the default values for the other properties of a command button. Finally, whatever code is attached to the form is listed after an Attribute section that describes properties of the form. (For more on the ASCII representation of a form, consult the *Programmer's Guide* that comes with most versions of Visual Basic.)

TIP: You can use a word processor to modify the ASCII representation of the form; then reload the project into Visual Basic and see the changes you've made. Using the various sophisticated search and replace functions available in modern word processors or program editors is occasionally the most efficient method of making wholesale changes to control names or properties. But be careful and make a backup first! Any mistakes you make in the textual description of a form may prevent your form from loading back into Visual Basic.

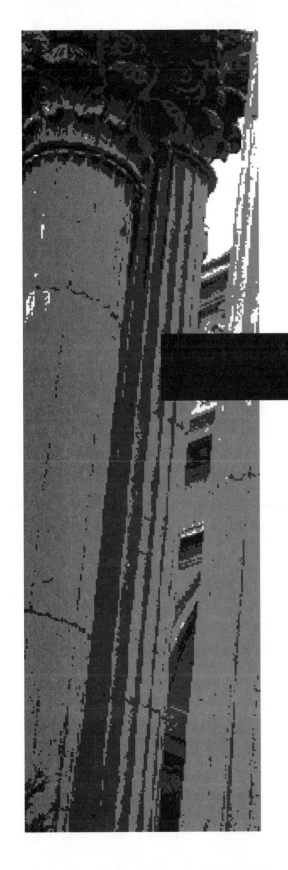

CHAPTER 5

First Steps in Programming

By now I hope you have a feel for what a Visual Basic application looks like. I've shown you how to customize forms by adding controls, and you've started writing the event procedures that are the backbone of a Visual Basic application. But, as you've probably realized, the event procedures covered so far haven't done much, so the applications you wrote couldn't do much either. To make your programs more useful, you must become comfortable with the sophisticated programming language built into Visual Basic—this is what I'll cover in the next five chapters.

If you are familiar with QuickBASIC, Pascal, C, or even QBASIC, you'll have an easier time of it, and the next five chapters will go pretty quickly. If you are familiar only with HTML, or a scripting language like JavaScript, or the older interpreted BASIC found on pre-Windows PCs (GW-BASIC, BASICA), or, for that matter, have never programmed before, you'll want to read these chapters carefully. In any case, there are subtle differences between Visual Basic programming and conventional programming that can trip up even experienced programmers, so you probably won't want to skip these chapters.

Anatomy of a Visual Basic Application

I can't stress enough that the key to Visual Basic programming is recognizing that Visual Basic generally processes code only in response to events. If you think of a Visual Basic application as a set of independent pieces that "wake up" only in response to events they have been told to recognize, you won't go far wrong, but if you think of the program as having a starting line and an ending line and moving from top to bottom, you will. In fact, unlike many programming languages, executable lines in Visual Basic must be inside procedures or functions. Isolated executable lines of code don't work.

CAUTION: For illustration purposes, I may show you fragments of a program, but they are not meant to work independently (nor can they).

Basically, even if you know a more traditional programming language well, you shouldn't try to force your Visual Basic programs into its framework. If you impose programming habits learned from older programming languages on your Visual Basic programs, you're likely to run into problems.

The Code Window

You write your code in what the designers of Visual Basic naturally decided to call a *Code window*. (When you are dealing with multiple forms or more complicated code, you can have multiple Code windows open at the same time.) Figure 5-1 shows the Code window for the sample calculator application that comes with Visual Basic. As you have seen, the Code window opens whenever you double-click a control or form. You

```
  Calculator                                                    _ | ⊟ | ✕
Object:  (General)                  ▼    Proc:  (declarations)              ▼
'  --------------------------------------------------------------------    ◄─── Split bar
'                    Copyright (C) 1994 Microsoft Corporation
'
'  You have a royalty-free right to use, modify, reproduce and distribute
'  the Sample Application Files (and/or any modified version) in any way
'  you find useful, provided that you agree that Microsoft has no warranty,
'  obligations or liability for any Sample Application Files.
'  --------------------------------------------------------------------
Option Explicit
Dim Op1, Op2                  ' Previously input operand.
Dim DecimalFlag As Integer    ' Decimal point present yet?
Dim NumOps As Integer         ' Number of operands.
Dim LastInput                 ' Indicate type of last keypress event.
Dim OpFlag                    ' Indicate pending operation.
Dim TempReadout
────────────────────────────────────────────────────────────────────────
' Click event procedure for C (cancel) key.
' Reset the display and initializes variables.
Private Sub Cancel_Click()
    ReadOut = Format(0, "0.")
    Op1 = 0
    Op2 = 0
    Form_Load
End Sub
```

Code window
for Calculator
project

Figure 5-1.

can also click View Code from the Project window or View menu, or press F7, to open the Code window.

The Code window has a caption that lists the name of the form, which is the current value of the Name property of the form. (It is Calculator in Figure 5-1.) It also has two list boxes and an area for editing your code. All the code attached to a form in Visual Basic defaults to being displayed in one continuous stream in the same Code windows—just the way it would appear if you looked at the text version (review Chapter 4) in another word processor. This continuous stream approach to your code is usually called *full module view*. The default is that each procedure in full module view is separated from the next by a dotted line.

TIP: To remove the dotted separator in full module view, choose Tools|Options and go to the Editor Options page. Then uncheck the Procedure Separator box. (See below for more on this important page.)

All the usual Windows editing techniques are available to you when you enter code (as discussed in Chapter 2), and the ones for the default editor setting in full module view are summarized in Table 5-1. (Some of these keys are shortcuts for techniques described in later chapters—don't worry if you don't know what something means yet.)

5

Description	Shortcut Keys
View Code window	View Form	F7/SHIFT F7
Find	CTRL+F
Replace	CTRL+H
Find next	F3
Find previous	SHIFT+F3
Move one word to right	CTRL+RIGHT ARROW
Move one word to left	CTRL+LEFT ARROW
Move to end of line	END
Move to beginning of line	HOME
Insert new line	CTRL+N
Delete current line	CTRL+Y
Delete to end of word	CTRL+DEL
Indent	TAB or CTRL+M
Remove indent	SHIFT+TAB or CTRL+SHIFT+M
Shift one screen down (Go to bottom of current screen)	CTRL+PAGE DOWN
Shift one screen up (Go to top of current screen)	CTRL+PAGE UP
Go to last position	CTRL+SHIFT+F2
Go to beginning of Code window (module)	CTRL+HOME
Go to end of Code window (module)	CTRL+END
Clear all breakpoints	CTRL+SHIFT+F9
Move focus to Object list box	CTRL+F2
View Object Browser	F2

Code Window
Shortcut Keys
Table 5-1.

T IP: The shortcut menu (click the right mouse button) lets you copy, cut, and paste while in the Code window.

The Split Bar

As indicated in Figure 5-1, the Code window has a *split bar* located below the title bar at the top of the vertical scroll bar. The idea is that as your code gets more complicated, you may want to see two different parts of your code in the Code window at once. If you drag this bar down, Visual Basic splits the Code window into two horizontal panes. (What you see in the Object box and Procedure box depends on which pane has the focus.) You can then scroll separately through the panes as needed. Dragging the split bar to the top of the window closes the top pane. If you drag the split bar to the top it closes the top pane, and if you drag it to the bottom it closes the bottom pane.

The Object List Box

The left drop-down list box in the Code window, called the *Object box,* lists all the objects on the form. This includes all the controls on the form, plus an object called General that holds common code that can be used by all the procedures attached to the form. You'll see more about this kind of code in the sections of this chapter titled "Requiring Variable Declaration" and "Constants." When you drop down the list box and click on any item in it, the editor takes you to the first piece of code written for that object (if one exists).

5

The Procedure List Box

The right-hand drop-down list box in the Code window is usually called the *Procedure list box* (sometimes it's called the *Proc box*). As you have seen, this list box gives all the events recognized by the object you have selected in the Object list box. If you have already written an event procedure, it shows up in bold in the Procedure list box. If you click on any event listed in this box, Visual Basic displays the event procedure or event procedure template in the Code window and moves the cursor to it.

IntelliSense

Microsoft's sophisticated completion technology, IntelliSense, is really neat; it can save you a lot of typing and it often lets you avoid looking up stuff in the online help. In fact, you have probably seen this technology at work already if you have experimented with writing any code on your own.

What IntelliSense does is pop up little list boxes with helpful information about the object you are working with. It has three components, which I'll describe next.

NOTE: If you have IntelliSense turned off, its features are part of the right-click menu in the Code window.

QuickInfo   You get information about the syntax for a Visual Basic operator from QuickInfo. Whenever you enter a keyword followed by a space or opening parenthesis, a tip appears and gives the syntax for that element. Here's an example of this QuickInfo feature at work for the MsgBox statement, which pops up a simple message box. (Don't worry about what all these cryptic things mean—we will cover them later in this chapter.)

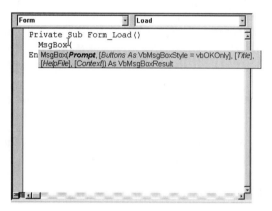

 T IP: You can turn QuickInfo off by using the Editor page on the Options dialog box. If it's turned off, you can still use CTRL+I to access QuickInfo for a specific procedure or method.

List Properties/Methods   This IntelliSense feature gives you a list of the properties and methods of an object right after you type the period. For example, if you have a Label named Label1 on your form and you type

```
Label1.
```

then, immediately after you type the period you will see something like this:

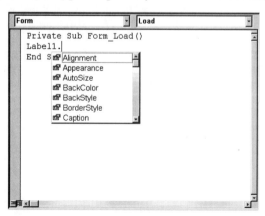

Select the item you want by scrolling through the list. Then press TAB to insert the item. (If you turn List Properties/Methods off, CRTL+J is the keyboard shortcut for this IntelliSense feature.)

Available Constants   The final nifty IntelliSense feature gives you a list of available constants. For example, if you had a label named Label1 on your form and you entered

```
Label1.Visible =
```

you would see a pop-up box listing True or False. (Again, select the one you want and press TAB to complete it.)

NOTE: Pressing ENTER also works in IntelliSense to accept a suggestion. The potential downside to doing this is that this adds a carriage return to your code so that you will be taken to the next line.

Visual Basic's Editing Tools

Good programming builds on code that is easy to read, and since version 5 of Visual Basic you have been able to control the size, font, and even the color of different pieces of your code. VB also makes it easy to use a consistent indentation pattern for your code. Indenting lines, as you will soon see, makes your code a lot easier to understand. All these features are controlled by the editor pages in the Options dialog box and the Edit toolbar.

The Editor Format Page

To get to the Options dialog box, choose Tools|Options (ALT+T, O) and click on the Editor Format tab (see Figure 5-2). Let's go over the items in this important dialog box one by one.

First off, the Code Colors frame contains a list of the possible objects you can change. For example, as Figure 5-2 shows, you can change Normal Text, Comment Text, and so on. The bottom of this frame has three boxes currently set to Auto, which means VB is in control of the color choices. Here are some short descriptions of the other elements in this dialog box.

Font List Box   Click on the down arrow in the Font drop-down list box to see the complete list of fonts that your system knows about. If you don't like the default Courier New font, choose another one by clicking on the font name when the list is dropped down.

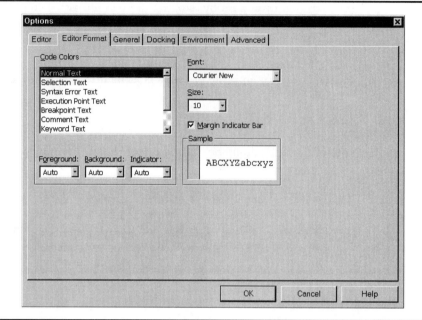

The Editor
Format page in
the Options
dialog box
Figure 5-2.

Size List Box   You can type a point size for the font directly in the Size list box or choose a size by clicking on the down arrow and then clicking on the size. This lets you change the font size if you are working with a laptop or if you have trouble seeing smaller print.

Foreground, Background, and Indicator List Boxes   The three Code Colors boxes determine the foreground and background colors used for each type of code as well as for the text used for indicators in the margin, such as bookmarks. For example, the default is that comments are green and syntax errors are highlighted in red. If you don't like the defaults, change them by following these steps:

1. Click on the code element you want to work with in the Code Colors list box.
2. Click on the arrow in the Foreground drop-down list.
3. Click on the color you like, and choose OK.

(Changing the background color is less common but works the same way.)

Sample Box   This box lets you see a sample of text in the font, size, and color settings that are currently set.

NOTE: If you decide to close the Editor Format page without making any changes, click on Cancel or press the ESC key. To have whatever changes you made go into effect, choose OK.

The Editor Page

The other page in the Options dialog box that you will want to work with to take complete control of your editing environment is the Editor page, shown in Figure 5-3. Three of the items on this page control whether the IntelliSense features you have already read about are on. Obviously I suggest leaving those boxes checked (Auto List Members, Auto Quick Info, and Auto Data Tips). What follows are short discussions of the most important remaining options on this page.

5

Auto Syntax Check   Visual Basic can automatically check your code when you press ENTER and thereby detect certain kinds of mistakes immediately. If you like to have immediate notification of problems, like certain kinds of typos, leave this box checked, if not, uncheck it.

Require Variable Declaration   I'll have a lot to say about why you will want to have this option checked a little later in this chapter (see the section on "Requiring

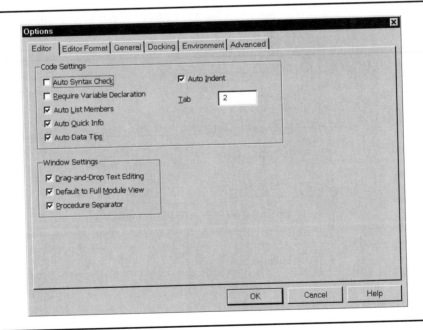

The Editor page
in the Options
dialog box
Figure 5-3.

Declaration of Variables," but for now, just trust me that it is a good idea to keep this box checked!

Tab Width Box   Use the Tab width box to set the number of spaces you get when you press the TAB key. This can be anything from 1 to 32 spaces; the default is 4 spaces. (As you can see in Figure 5-3, I have it set to 2 spaces to save real estate in my Code window. As you start writing more sophisticated code, you want to have the least amount of white space in your code consistent with readability as possible.)

TIP: Remember, if you have selected text, pressing TAB shifts it all forward one tab stop. Pressing SHIFT+TAB shifts it all back one tab stop.

Auto Indent Check Box   If the Auto Indent box is checked, pressing ENTER after you use the TAB key to indent a line makes the subsequent line start at the same place as the line above it. Indentation is one of the best ways to make programming structures clearer. (This option defaults to being on, probably for the reason I just mentioned!)

Drag-and-Drop Text Editing Check Box   If you like Word's style of dragging text around, keep this option checked. If not, leave it unchecked.

Default to Full Module View Check Box   When this option is checked (the default), you see all the code as one unit in the Code window. You can then scroll through the code with the arrow keys, PAGE UP/PAGE DOWN keys, and so on. If you uncheck this option, you go back to the older (Visual Basic 3 and earlier) way of looking at code: In this model each piece (procedure) of code pops up in a separate window, and you need to use CTRL+UP ARROW and CTRL+DOWN ARROW to cycle through the different pieces of code.

Procedure Separator Check Box   As I mentioned earlier, use this check box in conjunction with full module view. If you leave this checked, you will see separator bars between the pieces of code in the Code window.

The Edit Toolbar

Many useful editing features have button equivalents on the Edit toolbar. Unfortunately, some of them do *not* have keyboard equivalents. For this reason you might want to choose View | Toolbars and add the Edit toolbar to your environment. (The Edit toolbar is yet another way to get at the IntelliSense features if you have disabled them from automatically popping up.) Table 5-2 summarizes the tools available on this toolbar.

Tool	Function	Keyboard Equivalent	Description
	List properties/ methods	CTRL+J	Displays a pop-up list box with the properties and methods for the object preceding the period.
	List constants	CTRL+SHIFT+J	Displays a pop-up list box with the valid constants.
	QuickInfo	CTRL+I	Gives the syntax for the procedure or method.
	Parameter info	CTRL+SHIFT+I	Provides the parameter list for the current function call (see Chapter 8).
	Complete word	CTRL+SPACEBAR	Completes the keyword or object when enough information is there (for example, msg would complete to MsgBox).
	Indent	TAB	Indents the selected text one tab stop. (Use the Editor page on the Tools|Options dialog box to change the number of spaces.)
	Outdent	SHIFT+TAB	Moves the selected text back one tab stop.
	Toggle breakpoint	F9 (Left-clicking in the left margin next to a line of code also toggles the breakpoint.)	Used for debugging (see Chapter 15).
	Comment block	None	See the following section "Comments" for more information on comments.

Tools on the Edit
Toolbar
Table 5-2.

Tool	Function	Keyboard Equivalent	Description
	Uncomment block	None	See the following section, "Comments" for more information on comments.
	Toggle bookmark	None	The editor allows you to put bookmarks at specific places in your code. You can jump from bookmark to bookmark to more easily navigate between parts of your code.
	Next bookmark	None	Move to next bookmark.
	Previous bookmark	None	Move to previous bookmark
	Clear all bookmarks	None	

Tools on the Edit
Toolbar
(*continued*)
Table 5-2.

Statements in Visual Basic

First off, let me remind you that a good way to think of a statement in a programming language is to think of it as a complete sentence—a complete thought. When you enter a statement in Visual Basic and have the Auto Syntax option that I just discussed turned on, the intelligent editor built into VB analyzes what you typed. This happens immediately after you press ENTER. VB checks to see that what you entered makes sense. It is amazing how Visual Basic can detect many typos at this stage, but *only* if you have Auto Syntax Check turned on in the Editor page of the Options dialog box. Sometimes VB can even fix the error: for example it will add a closing quote if you left it out. If a statement you entered can't be analyzed, though, a message box pops up and can often help you find out what caused the problem.

T IP: Remember the context-sensitive help feature of Visual Basic. If you need help on the syntax for functions, statements, properties, events, or methods in the Code window, move the cursor to (or type) the keyword or the property, event, or method name, and press F1. You can also select an event name in the Procedure box and press F1 for information about that event.

Visual Basic ignores case and spacing, except within quotation marks. Nonetheless, the language does try to impose its own conventions. It capitalizes the first letter of command words and often adds extra spaces for readability. For example, no matter how you capitalize the command word Print—PRint, Print, print, and so on—pressing ENTER will change it to Print. It's a good idea to stick to a standard method of spacing and capitalization in your code.

Statements in Visual Basic rarely use line numbers, and each statement generally occurs on its own line. Lines are limited to 1,023 characters but a statement can be extended to the next line by using the underscore character (_) preceded by a space at the end of the line. (Make sure the underscore doesn't appear inside quotation marks though.) However, *unless* a line ends with an underscore, pressing ENTER indicates to VB that the line is done. If you use a line with more characters than can fit in the window, Visual Basic scrolls the window toward the right as needed. Given the line continuation character, you should only rarely need to have lines that are longer than the width of the screen. Finally, you can combine statements on one line by placing a colon (:) between the statements.

Sometimes in this book you'll see lines that easily fit on a screen (and certainly fit within the 1,023 character limit) but are longer than can fit on one line of a printed page. When this happens, I will usually use the underscore line continuation character. However, if the split has to take place inside quotation marks, we can't use the underscore in the actual code. In this case, the succeeding line will be outdented, and the double quotation marks or parentheses will be closed on that succeeding line. Here are some examples of these conventions:

```
MsgBox "Please click a button so something  will happen" _
vbOKOnly, "Test Button"
    Print "This is an example of a line that won't fit on a
single line of the page, so I outdented it."
```

If you were entering these lines in Visual Basic, in the first example you could either omit the underscore and continue typing on one line, or you could use the underscore and press ENTER after it. In the second example you would have to continue on one line until you reached the closing quote.

Comments

Comment statements are statements that help explain your code to people (including yourself!) down the road. They are not processed by Visual Basic and so they won't make the compiled version of your code any bigger. Although it may seem hard to believe at this stage—especially if you have never programmed before—it can be hard to figure out what your code is doing six months after you wrote it. It is even harder to maintain and modify code written by someone else. The horrid process of scratching your head and saying "What did I (or he or she) mean by that line of code" is all too common, unless the code is well commented!

In fact, many programming shops have a standard format for comments. For example, the beginning of any code might list who wrote the code, when it was last modified, what those modifications are, and so forth.

You have two ways to indicate a comment. The most common method is to use a single quotation mark (')—not the backward apostrophe found below the tilde (~) but the one usually found below the double quotation mark ("). Here are some examples:

```
Private Sub Command1_Click ()
  'A comment describing the procedure could go here
  'and here

End Sub
```

As usual, I indented the programming lines to improve readability.

Here are the kind of comment lines that might precede any procedures in your code:

```
'This program was written by Gary Cornell on April 1, 1998
'it is designed to change ordinary English into pig Latin
'it was last modified on May 1, 1998 by Emma Cornell
```

You can also use the older Rem keyword for a comment (comments are sometimes called *remark* statements for this reason):

```
Private Sub Command1_Click ()
  Rem    Comments describing the procedure would go here
  Rem

End Sub
```

If you want to add comments to the ends of lines, it is easier to use the single quotation mark because the Rem form requires a colon before it. For example:

```
PrintForm    'Dump the current window
PrintForm    :Rem A bit more cumbersome
```

Everything on a line following a comment symbol or the Rem keyword is ignored, *regardless* of whether it is an executable Visual Basic statement or not. In fact, although Visual Basic has some sophisticated features for debugging, commenting out executable statements is still one of the most common techniques used in debugging programs. (This is especially true since VB now has the neat comment/uncomment block feature on the Edit toolbar.)

The End Statement

When Visual Basic processes an End statement, the program stops. If you are developing a program, you are dumped back into the development environment. The effect is exactly the same as choosing the End option on the Run menu. In a stand-alone program, after the End statement, all windows opened by the program are closed and the program is cleared from memory. You can have as many End statements within a Visual Basic program as you want, but it is good programming practice to restrict the number of events that end a program.

Many professional programmers prefer to use only one End statement in their code. They place this End statement in the QueryUnload event for the main form. (One advantage to doing this is that you can then use the QueryUnload event to execute any code needed for cleaning up.) If you choose to write your programs this way, replace any End statements in other places with an Unload Me statement. This calls the QueryUnload event for that form. (See the section in Chapter 12 called "Applications That Look Like They Are Over—But Aren't" for more on how to use the QueryUnload event.)

Variables

Variables in Visual Basic hold information (values). Whenever you use a variable, Visual Basic sets up an area in the computer's memory to store the information. Variable names in Visual Basic can be up to 255 characters long and, provided the first character is a letter, can include any combination of letters, numerals, and underscores. The case of the letters in the variable name is irrelevant. The following table lists some possible variable names and indicates whether they are acceptable.

Base1_Ball	Acceptable
1Base_Ball	Not acceptable—first character is not a letter
Base.1	Not acceptable—uses a period
Base&1	Not acceptable—includes & inside the name
ThisIsLongButOK	Acceptable—only 15 characters long

All characters in a variable name are significant, but case is irrelevant. BASE is the same variable as base. On the other hand, Base is a different variable from Base1, and both are different from Base_1. However, Visual Basic always changes the form of the names of your variables to reflect the capitalization pattern you used when you "Dimmed" the variable. (See the section on "Declaring the Types of Variables" later in the chapter for more on this feature.)

TIP: Visual Basic's capitalization feature is often useful for detecting typos in variable names, especially after you've dimmed the variable. If you suspect that a misspelled variable name is causing a problem, change one occurrence to use random case (like vARiaBLENaME), move off the line, and then see if that occurrence of the variable name was changed. If you find one that wasn't changed, you will know that it contains a typo. Correct the error and then change the variable name back to the form you want; all occurrences of the name will change again as well. For another way to help detect typos and variable names, see the section "Requiring Declaration of Variables" later in this chapter.

Choosing meaningful variable names helps document your program and makes the inevitable debugging process easier. For example, don't use IR for a variable that is meant to hold an interest rate; use InterestRate (or IRate at the very least). A line of code like:

```
InterestEarned = Total*InterestRate
```

is pretty much self-documenting, whereas

```
IE = T*IR
```

is a whole lot more confusing. (Programmers coming from older languages that only allowed shorter variable names tend to code in the latter style. Try to break the habit. VB doesn't care if you use a longer, and so more meaningful, name!)

The one other restriction on variable names is that you can't use names reserved by Visual Basic; for example, Print is not acceptable as a variable name. However, you can embed reserved words within a variable's name. For example, PrintIt is a perfectly acceptable variable name. Visual Basic will present an error message if you try to use a reserved word as a variable name—usually immediately after you press ENTER.

One of the most common conventions for styling variable names is the one I used above: Use capitals only at the beginning of the words that make up the parts of it (for example, InterestRate, not Interestrate). This convention is called *mixed case variable names*. This is the convention used in this book, as most people find it easy to read. Some people add underscores as well (for example, Interest_Rate)—I don't like this style and so I won't use it in this book.

Variable Assignment Statements

Assignment statements are what you use to give a Visual Basic variable a (new) value. Another way is to think about assignment statements as a means of copying information from a source to a destination. In any case, giving values to variables is one of the most common tasks in Visual Basic code. Visual Basic uses an equal sign for this operation; for example

```
InterestRate = .05
```

sets the value of a variable named InterestRate to be .05. The variable name always appears on the left of the equality sign, and the value always appears on the right. Visual Basic *must* be able to obtain a value from the right side of an assignment statement, and it will do any processing needed to make this happen. For example:

```
NewRate = .05+.1
```

would make the variable NewRate have the value .15. This is because VB would do the addition first, and then store the result in the variable.

NOTE: You can also use the older Let notation for an assignment:

```
Let InterestRate = .05
```

Setting Properties with Code

Just as variable assignments use the equal sign, so too does the code for resetting properties. If you want to change a property setting for a Visual Basic object with code, place the object's name followed by a period and then the name of the property on the left side of the equal sign, and put the new value on the right-hand side:

```
object.property = value
```

For example, suppose you have a text button (control name of Text1) and want to blank it out in code rather than use the Properties window. You need only have a line like this in an event procedure:

```
Text1.Text = ""
```

Since there is nothing between the quotation marks, the text assigned to this property is blank. Similarly, a line like

```
Text1.Text = "This is the new text."
```

in an event procedure changes the setting for the text property to the text in the quotation marks.

You can change the setting of a property via code as often as necessary. For example, if you wanted to change the caption on a command button called Command1, you would place a line like this in an event procedure:

```
Command1.Caption = "Put new caption here."
```

Similarly, if you wanted to set a button called Command5 to be the first button in tab order, you would add a line like this to an event procedure:

```
Command5.TabIndex = 0
```

Now suppose you want a form called Form1 to move around when various command buttons are clicked. Here is an example of one of the event procedures you would need:

```
Private Sub LeftButton_Click ()
   Form1.Left = Form1.Left - 75
End Sub
```

Let's look at the key line: Form1.Left = Form1.Left - 75. On the left-hand side of the assignment statement is the property that gets the value, but it seems that the property occurs on the right-hand side as well. How can this work? Doesn't VB get confused on which is the new value and which is the old value? The answer is no; Visual Basic always analyzes the right-hand side of *any* assignment first, to extract a value from it. In this case it looks at the *current* position of the left side of the form and calculates the number of twips it is from the left side of the screen. It then subtracts 75 from this number. Only after it has done this does it look to the left side of the assignment. Visual Basic then changes the old value of the "Left" property to the new calculated value.

All this can be a little confusing. Some people find it helpful to remember that right-hand sides of assignment statements are there only for the values they yield, and only the left-hand side gets changed. So if you just keep in mind the rule that VB always tries to evaluate the right-hand side before making either a property or a variable assignment, you should be okay.

Default Properties

Every Visual Basic object has a default property (for example, text boxes have the Text property). When referring to the default property, you don't need to use the property name. For example, you can enter

```
Text1 = "This is new text"
```

to change the Text property of a text box. Most Visual Basic programmers avoid using the default property because they feel it makes their code less readable. (If you want to know which default properties are assigned to which controls, see the *Programmer's Guide* in the online help.) I can never remember what the default properties are in most cases anyway so I will almost never use them in this book (nor do I use them in code that I write professionally).

Boolean Properties

Properties that take only the value True or False are called *Boolean properties,* after the English logician George Boole. You have already seen many Boolean properties. For example, the Visible property of a control is a Boolean property. Thus Boolean properties specify whether a command button is visible, is enabled, or is the default cancel or command button. More generally, Boolean properties are commonly used whenever you have an "on/off" situation. Visual Basic has built-in constants for these important property values, called True and False, naturally enough. A statement such as

```
Command1.Visible = False
```

in an event procedure hides the command button by resetting the Visible property to be False. The control stays hidden until Visual Basic processes the statement

```
Command1.Visible = True
```

As another example, if you want the TAB key to skip a control while a program is running, change the TabStop property to False:

```
Control.TabStop = False
```

TIP: Another example of a Boolean property is the Value property of command buttons. Setting this property to True in code has the same effect as the user clicking the button. This feature is useful for self-running demonstrations when combined with the SetFocus method to move the focus to the correct control.

The Not Operator and Boolean Properties

5

The usual way to toggle (change from on to off, and vice versa) Boolean properties is with the Not operator. Suppose you have a statement such as

```
Command1.Visible = Not(Command1.Visible)
```

in an event procedure. This statement works as follows: Visual Basic finds the current value of Command1.Visible, and then the Not operator reverses this value; that is, if the value was True, it changes to False, and vice versa.

NOTE: Internally, Visual Basic uses the values 0 for False and -1 for True (actually, any nonzero value will work for True). As you will soon see, the ability to use numbers for True/False values is convenient but, alas, is also sometimes a source of obscure bugs. For example, for the Not operator to work properly in toggling a Boolean property between on and off, you must use the built-in True constant or a value of -1 for True.

(For more information on the Not operator, see the section "Bit-Twiddling Functions" in Chapter 8.)

Data Types

Programmers use the word *type* as the buzzword for what might better be called *flavor*. Just as ice cream come in flavors, so too does data come in types. There are various kinds of numeric data types, the string data type, and even a Boolean data type. In fact, Visual Basic handles 14 standard types of data. (It is also possible to define your own data types; you will see how in Chapter 10.) This section describes the data types you will use in most of your VB code. Later sections of this chapter will go into their features in more detail.

NOTE: There are actually many types of numeric data. For example, Visual Basic thinks of integers (1, 2, 3 ...) as being of a different type than numbers that have a decimal point.

String

The string data type holds characters. You can have a single character in a string or many. A variable holding a string is called, naturally enough, a string variable. One method of identifying variables of this type is to place a dollar sign ($) at the end of the variable name:

```
AStringVariable$.
```

Once you add the dollar sign, that variable can only hold strings. String variables can theoretically hold about 2 billion characters. On a specific computer, though, the variable may hold less, due to memory constraints, overhead requirements for Windows, or the number of strings used in the form.

One of the most common uses of string variables is to pick up the information contained in a text box. For example, if you have a text box named Text1, then

```
ContentOfText1$ = Text1.Text
```

assigns the string contained in the text box to the variable named ContentOfText1$ on the left-hand side of the assignment.

Integer

Integer variables hold relatively small integer values (between -32,768 and +32,767). Integer arithmetic is very fast but is restricted to these ranges or you'll get an error message. One way to make sure that a variable will only be capable of holding integers is to use the percent sign (%) at the end of the variable name:

```
AnIntegerVariable% = 3
```

Long Integer

The long integer variable holds integers between -2,147,483,648 and +2,147,483,647. The identifier you can use for your variables is the ampersand (&). Long integer arithmetic is also fast, and there is very little (if any) performance penalty on modern machines. They do take up twice as much memory per variable as the smaller Integers however.

```
ALongIntegerVariable& = 123456789
```

Single Precision

Just as there are two integer types for different size values, numbers with decimal points have different variable types depending on how large and how accurate you want them to be.

The least accurate is called single precision. They have a decimal point, but you can be sure of the accuracy of only seven digits. This means that if an answer comes out as 12,345,678.97, the 8.97 may or may not be accurate. The answer could just as well be 12,345,670.01. Although the accuracy is limited, the size (range) of these numbers is up to 38 digits. I need to stress: *Calculations will always be approximate for these types of variables; exact answers are impossible to guarantee.*

Moreover, arithmetic with these numbers is slower than with integer or long integer variables. For single-precision numbers, the identifier you can use to make sure a variable will only hold a single precision number is an exclamation point (!).

5

```
ASinglePrecisionVariable! = 12.345
```

Double Precision

The double-precision data type is used when you need numbers with up to 16 places of accuracy; they will also allow you more than 300 digits. Calculations are also approximate for these variables. You can rely only on the first 16 digits. Furthermore, calculations are relatively slow with double-precision numbers. Double-precision variables are mainly used in scientific calculations in Visual Basic. The identifier used for double-precision variables is a pound sign (#). You should also use the # sign at the end of the actual number—especially if you have relatively few digits because otherwise VB will assume you meant to use the variable with only the limited precision of a single precision number. More precisely, if you wrote

```
ADoublePrecisionVariable# = 12.345#
```

then VB assumes you mean

12.34500000000000

which is much more accurate than

12.345000

which is what VB would assume if you left off the #.

Currency

Currency variables are a type that will be new to even experienced programmers. They are designed to avoid certain problems inherent in switching from binary fractions to decimal fractions. (It's impossible to make 1/10 out of the binary combinations of 1/2, 1/4, 1/8, 1/16, and so on that modern computers use for calculations.)

The currency type can have 4 digits to the right of the decimal place and up to 15 to the left of the decimal point. Arithmetic will be exact within this range. The identifier is an "at" sign (@)—*not* the dollar sign, which, recall, identifies strings. While calculations other than addition and subtraction are about as slow as for double-precision numbers, this is the preferred variable type to use for financial calculations of any reasonable size. (For those who are interested, this type uses 19-digit integers, which are then scaled by a factor of 10,000. This gives you 15 places to the left of the decimal point and 4 places to the right.)

```
ACurrencyVariable@ = 12.345@
```

Date

The date data type gives you a convenient way to store both date and time information for any time between midnight on January 1, 100, to midnight on December 31, 9999. You need to surround any assignment to date variables with two #'s, for example:

```
Millennium = #January 1, 2000#
Millennium = #Jan 1, 2000#
Millennium = #1/1/2000#
```

As you can see in the above examples, VB is quite forgiving of the form you use to describe the date. If you do not include a time in a date, Visual Basic assumes it is midnight. You can use ordinary AM/PM for time or a 24-hour clock as in the following examples:

```
PreMillennium = #December 31, 1999 11:59 PM#
PreMillennium = #December 31, 1999 23:59#
```

Byte

The byte type was added to Visual Basic 5; it can hold integers between 0 and 255. This is a great convenience when you need to save space, and it makes certain arrays (see Chapter 10) much smaller than they would have been in earlier versions of Visual Basic. It is also needed for handling binary files in versions of Visual Basic after version 5.

Boolean

Use the Boolean type when you need data to be either True or False. It is considered good programming practice to use this data type rather than integers for True/False values.

Variant

The variant data type was added to Visual Basic way back in version 2. The variant data type is designed to store all the different possible Visual Basic data received in one place. If you don't tell Visual Basic what type of information a variable holds, it will use this data type. It doesn't matter whether the information is numeric, date/time, or string; the variant type can hold it all. Visual Basic automatically performs conversions of data stored in variants to data of another type, so you often don't have to worry about what type of data is being stored in the variant data type.

But I'll be honest, the variant data type is a mixed blessing. It certainly *seems* convenient to have a variable that can hold any type of data. The trouble is that you can't always rely on VB to convert the data stored in a variant in the way you expect. In addition, many programmers feel that relying on automatic type conversions leads to sloppy programming because it makes their programs potentially buggy. As you will soon see, relying on VB to do conversions can lead to some weird behavior in your programs. Using a variant variable rather than a specific type is also slower, because of the conversions needed, and it takes up more memory. Most importantly, programmers have learned from bitter experience that their programs will be more "bug resistant", if:

◆ They insist that variables hold data of only one type for the duration of the program

◆ They don't try to have a variable that holds strings in one part of the program and numbers in another

NOTE: I agree with the above and therefore use variants only when their special properties are needed. I feel strongly that the programmer should always be in control of the form that the data is taking and should rarely, if ever, rely on automatic conversions from the variant data type. If you control any conversions made for data, you are more likely to be aware of any strange consequences (such as loss of accuracy). Thus, this book uses the variant data type rarely.

Declaring the Type of Variables

Many people prefer not to use the suffix identifiers like ! and % to specify the type of a variable (and, in any case, variables such as date variables have no distinguishing identifier). Instead, they use a new keyword, *Dim*, to specify the type of a variable. The technical term for these kinds of statements is *declarations*, but many people simply call them "Dim statements" and talk about "dimming a variable." Declaring the types of variables used in an event procedure before using them—and commenting the code as needed, of course—is a good programming habit. It can even make your programs more readable. Here's an example:

```
Private Sub cmdCalculate_Click
    ' This procedure calculates mortgage interest
    'it uses two integer variables, three currency variables,
    'and one string variable

    Dim Years As Integer
    Dim Rate As Currency
    Dim Amount As Currency
    Dim I As Integer
    Dim TextBox As String
```

```
    Dim Interest As Currency
End Sub
```

You can combine declarations on a single line, for example:

```
Dim Year As Integer, Rate As Currency, Name As String
```

CAUTION: Although you can declare multiple variables on the same line, a common mistake is to use something like

```
Dim X, Y, Z As Integer
```

and assume that all three variables will be integer variables. In fact, in this code, X and Y default to be variants and only Z is an integer variable. You must use the type identifier each time. (You can also write: `Dim Years%, Rate@, Name$`, and so on, if you prefer using a type identifier.)

If you declare a variable in a Dim statement, then trying to use variables with the same name but a different type identifier at the end of the variable will make VB give you a "duplicate definition" error when the program is run. For example, if you use the statement

```
Dim Count As Integer
```

to declare the integer variable Count, then you can't use the variables Count$, Count!, Count#, and Count@. You could use Count% however, and it is recognized by Visual Basic as just another way of denoting the variable Count.

To give a variable the variant data type, just use the Dim statement without any As clause or identifier:

```
Dim Foo      'makes Foo have the variant data type
```

You can also use

```
Dim Foo As Variant 'more explicit, easier to read
```

which I think is the better strategy.

Finally, there is always the question of where to declare variables. There are two schools of thought and both have good arguments in their favor. The first school says declare all variables at the beginning of a procedure, the second says declare them right before you use them for the first time. I was trained using the first model, but many people prefer the second. You'll have to decide which you are most comfortable with.

"Hungarian" Notation

Some programmers like to use the convention of adding a lowercase prefix to variables to indicate what type they are. For example, sngInterestRate and intCount would be a single precision variable and an integer, respectively. This is usually called "Hungarian Notation." (It's so named because its chief proponent at Microsoft, a master programmer named Charles Simonyi, is from Hungary.) I don't use Hungarian notation for variables in my code, preferring code that reads more easily as English. I simply find sngInterestRate to be a less appealing name than InterestRate. You (or your boss!) will have to come to your own conclusion as to whether Hungarian notation makes your programs more maintainable. Certainly, almost everybody uses "Hungarian style" prefixes for the names of controls, as you saw in Chapter 4: txtFirstName, for example, as the name of a text box. The following table summarizes the Hungarian prefixes for the basic data types:

Type	Prefix
String	str
Boolean	bln
Integer	int
Long	lng
Single	sng
Double	dbl
Currency	cur
Variant	vnt

5

TIP: For more on naming conventions, please see the appendix "Visual Basic Coding Conventions" in the online help.

Requiring Declaration of Variables

One of the most common bugs in programs is the misspelled variable name. Unless you take precautions when you start writing your program, you are likely to encounter this problem in your Visual Basic code. The problem is that Visual Basic allows you to create variables "on the fly" by merely using a variable name in any line in a program. Misspell the name for a variable that already exists in your program and Visual Basic will just create a new variable that has nothing to do with the one you wanted to work with—giving it a default value that will inevitably cause bugs. VB's gung-ho attitude to implicit variable creation makes it very difficult to track down bugs, because you have to *find* the misspelled variable name in a morass of other names that probably look very similar. In fact, most experienced programmers think that one of the stupidest "features" of VB is having the default setting of VB be to create a variable without declaring it!

The easiest way to avoid these problems is to *force* all variables to be declared. Then, VB will notify you if a variable name is spelled incorrectly in a procedure. The designers of Visual Basic give you this option, but do not force you to use it. The statement you need for this is:

```
Option Explicit
```

The Option Explicit statement is the first example you have seen of a statement that you do not (and in fact cannot) put within an event procedure. A good way to remember why this must be so is that you use Option Explicit to change defaults. You would not bother doing this unless you wanted the change to be true for more than one event procedure.

Thus, you have to put the Option Explicit statement in the (General) section of your Code window. Here's how:

1. Open the Code window.
2. Select the (General) object from the list of objects presented in the Object list box.
3. Select (Declarations) from the Procedure list box.
4. Type **Option Explicit**.

NOTE: You will often need to place form-level variable declarations in the (General) section when you experiment with the example code found in the help system. In fact, any information that you want to be usable by all the event procedures attached to a form is placed in the (General) section of the form.

After Visual Basic processes an Option Explicit command, it will no longer allow you to use a variable unless you declare it first. If you try to use a variable without declaring it, VB will pop up an error message, like the one shown here:

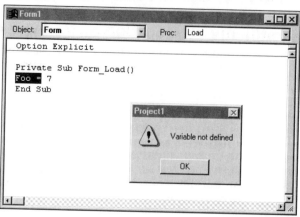

TIP: You can also choose Tools|Options and then go to the Editor page in order to require variable declaration. In fact, I (and every other serious Visual Basic programmer that I know!) always have this check box set. Once you set this option, then from that point on VB inserts an Option Explicit command automatically into the (General) section of all your forms and other code modules (Chapter 12) whenever you start a new program.

Subtleties of Variable Data Types

Unlike many other versions of BASIC, in Visual Basic you cannot use variables such as A% and A!, which differ only in the type identifier, in the same program. Using them produces a "duplicate definition" error when you try to run your program.

The first time you use a variant variable, Visual Basic temporarily assigns it a default value of "empty" and gives it the variant type. The "empty" value disappears the moment you assign a value to the variable. Every other type of variable also has a default value. For string variables, this is the null (empty) string—the one you get by assigning "" to a string variable. For numeric variables, the default value is zero. One good rule of thumb is to only rely on the default value of a variable if you document this (with a Remark statement, for example) in your program. Otherwise, you risk creating hard-to-find bugs since you haven't made it clear that you really wanted to use the default value: Did you mean for it to start out with a value of 37 and forget—and that's what caused the bug? It is therefore quite common to use the first few statements in an event procedure to initialize variables after you declare them.

5

NOTE: Unlike many programming languages, you can't initialize a variable in VB when you declare it. This may be the reason why some VB programmers like the convention of declaring (and therefore initializing) a variable right before they use the variable for the first time.

Changing the Default for the Type of a Variable

When you use a statement like the following with Visual Basic set to its default settings, you automatically make I, J, and K variants:

```
Dim I, J, K
```

You will sometimes have a program in which you know it will only (or primarily) use integer variables. In cases like this it is sometimes convenient to change the defaults built into Visual Basic so that variables declared without a type specification identifier are no longer variants. You can change the default variable types with what is called a DefType statement. The following table gives some examples:

DefType Statement	What It Does
DefInt A-Z	Changes the default—all variables default to being integer variables.
DefInt I-J	All variables beginning with I and J default to being integer variables.
DefStr S-Z	All variables beginning with the letters S through Z default to being string variables.

In particular, you can, if you want, establish the convention that all variables that begin with an *I* will be integer variables by adding a DefInt I statement. After this, Dim I will always give you an integer variable. The general forms of the various DefType statements you can use are:

```
DefLng letter range (for long integers)
DefSng letter range (for single precision)
DefDbl letter range (for double precision)
DefCur letter range (for currency)
DefStr letter range (for strings)
DefVar letter range (for variants)
DefBool letter range (for Booleans)
DefByte letter range (for bytes)
DefDate letter range (for dates)
```

The letters in the ranges need not be capitals: DefStr s-Z and DefStr S-Z work equally well. Also, you can always override the default settings by using an identifier or a Dim statement for a specific variable. DefType statements get put in the (General) section of the code—just as you would (preferably) put the Option Explicit command there.

Working with Variables

Although variables seem pretty straightforward on the surface, there are some subtleties that can trip you up. The point to keep in mind is that when you assign one variable to another you lose what was there before. Here's an example of this that comes up a lot: consider the common task of "swapping" the contents of two variables. Surprisingly, the designers of Visual Basic left out the Swap command that QuickBASIC has for this. So, suppose you have two variables, *x* and *y*, and you try the following code to swap variables within an event procedure:

```
x = y
y = x
```

This doesn't work, and it is important that you understand why. What goes wrong is that the first assignment gives the current value of *y* to the variable *x*, *but it wipes out the previous value of x*. The result is that the second statement merely copies the original value of *y*, which is what it was originally anyway. The solution is to use a temporary variable:

```
temp = x       ' copy old value of x to temp
x = y          ' x now has old value of y
y = temp       ' retrieve original value of x, give to y
```

Scope of Variables

Imagine for a second that, every time (and without you controlling it), changing the value of a variable named Total in one event procedure would affect the value of a *different* variable named Total in *another* event procedure. Imagine tracking down a bug caused by such cross contamination! In older programming languages, where *all* variables were available to *all* parts of the program, keeping variable names straight and isolated from each other was always a problem. VB lets you make your programs more bug proof by making it easy to avoid cross contamination.

NOTE: Programmers refer to the *scope* of variables when they want to talk about whether a variable used in one part of the program can be used (and potentially changed) in other parts of the program.

The solution in modern programming languages, such as Visual Basic, is to allow you to isolate variables within procedures. Unless you specifically arrange it, changing the value of a variable named Total in one procedure will *not* affect another variable with the same name in another procedure. Thus, variables are *local* to procedures unless specified otherwise—making the default for variables be to have *local scope* is the buzzword for this way of limiting cross contamination. In VB an event procedure will normally not have access to the value of a variable in another event procedure. As always, it is not a good programming practice to rely on defaults since, as you'll see in Chapter 12, somebody working on another part of a program could make a variable default to *not* having local scope when it first appears in *your* part of the program. If you want to be sure that a variable is local within an event procedure, use the Dim statement inside the event procedure to declare the variable there.

Sharing Values Across All Code Procedures

Occasionally, you will want to share the values of variables across various parts of a program—such as across multiple event procedures. For example, if an application is designed to perform a calculation involving one interest rate at a time, you might want to make that rate available to all the procedures in a form. Variables in a form that allow such sharing are called *form-level* or *module-level variables*. Figure 5-4 shows the scope of variables for a Visual Basic project with a single form.

Just as with the Option Explicit statement, you put the declaration statements for form-level variables in the Declarations section. For example, if you open the Code window, select (Declarations) for the (General) object, and enter

```
Private InterestRate As Currency 'private in lower-case is OK too
```

◆ The value of the variable named InterestRate will be visible to all the procedures attached to the form.

◆ Any changes made to this variable in one event procedure will persist so that the changes will still be there when the variable is accessed from another event procedure.

Obviously, the last point means you have to be careful when assigning values to form-level variables. Any information passed between event procedures is a breeding ground for programming bugs. Moreover, these errors are often hard to pinpoint.

NOTE: There is also a Public keyword. Variables that you declare with the Public keyword can actually be seen by code in other forms or other parts of your program. I'll have more to say about this keyword in Chapter 12. (Yes, I agree the terminology is stupid: Private is not all that private, since for VB, Private = form-level. The idea was to distinguish form-level variables from the Public variables discussed in Chapter 12.) Also, you should be aware that some people use the Dim keyword instead of using the Private keyword for form-level variables. This is a carryover from earlier versions of Visual Basic, and Microsoft discourages you from using this older form.

Although most programmers don't think it is a good idea, you can use the same variable name as both a local and a form-level variable. Any Dim statements contained in a procedure take precedence over form-level declarations—they create a new variable with the same name as the (possibly) already existing form-level variable but one that has *nothing* to do with the form level variable. Therefore, if you do declare a variable inside a procedure with the same name as a form-level variable, you lose the ability to use the information contained in the form-level variable of the same name. Duplicating the names makes the form-level variable invisible to the procedure. (The buzzword for this is to say that the variable inside the procedure *shadows* the form-level variable.) Unfortunately, Visual Basic doesn't warn you if you

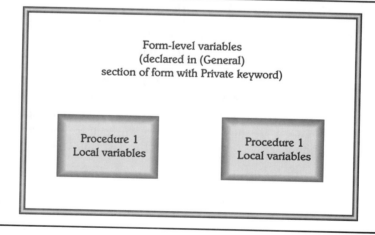

Scope of
variables

Figure 5-4.

are shadowing a form-level variable—it will never tell you if you declare a form-level variable with the same name as a local variable. This is one more reason to make sure that variables you want to be local really are local by dimensioning them inside the procedure. This forces the variable to be local to that procedure.

T **IP:** Almost all programmers (regardless of their feelings about Hungarian notation) like to prefix form-level variables with the letter f (for example, fInterest) or m (for module level—mInterest) and global variables with the letter g (for example, gInterest). This makes it easier to identify them at a glance—and since they are the most common source of bugs, you do want to be able to identify them at a glance. See Chapter 12 for more on global variables.

Having Values Persist

5

When Visual Basic reinvokes an event procedure, the old values of local variables are wiped out. All the values of all the variables potentially go back to their default values (0 for numbers, "" for strings, and so on). (Of course, as I mentioned before, you are often better off if you wrote code to initialize their values. In this case they will at least be reinitialized.)

Variables that are constantly reset to their initial state are called *dynamic variables*. However, dynamic variables are not suitable for all programming situations. For example, suppose you need to keep track of how many times a command button has been clicked. If the counter is always set back to zero every time you leave the Click event procedure, you're in trouble. You *could* have the values persist by using a form-level variable, but this is generally considered a poor programming practice. Why? Well, always keep in mind that the wider the scope of a variable, the more easily it can cause contamination— and therefore bugs—in your program. It really is a good idea to reserve form-level variables only for sharing information. Most experienced programmers would choose a form-level variable for a counter in an event procedure only if other procedures needed access to the counter information.

The solution is to use what are called *static variables* in Visual Basic. Static variables are *not* reinitialized each time Visual Basic invokes the procedure. Besides being ideal for counters, they are ideal for making controls alternately visible or invisible (or for switching between any Boolean properties, for that matter) and as a debugging tool. To make a variable static within a procedure, replace the keyword Dim with the keyword Static:

```
Static Counter As Integer, IsVisible As Integer
```

this makes both Counter and Is Visible static variables.

To see this at work, start up a new project, add a command button to the form and write the following in the Click event procedure for the command button. This procedure uses a static variable to count the number of times that button is clicked and then displays that number on the form:

```
Private Sub Command1_Click()
   'This procedure uses a static variable to count clicks
   Static Counter As Integer    ' Counter starts at 0
   Counter = Counter + 1
   Print Counter
End Sub
```

The first time you click on the button, the counter starts out with its default value of zero. Visual Basic then adds 1 to it and prints the result. Notice that by placing the Print statement after the addition, you are not off by 1 in the count. And because Counter was declared as a static variable, every time you click again VB will add one to the previous count so that it always displays the correct answer.

Occasionally, you will want all local variables within a procedure to be static. To do this, add the keyword Static before the words "Private Sub" that start the procedure:

```
Static Private Sub Command1_Click()
```

More on Strings

As you saw earlier, a string is simply a bunch of characters surrounded by double quotes. When people enter information into a text box, Visual Basic stores that information as a string. Thus, even if you have a text box meant to hold an amount, it starts out as a string. (Don't worry, it is very easy to convert a string of digits to a number so that you can do arithmetic on it.)

Probably the most common operation done with strings is to put two strings together (*concatenate* is the buzzword). To concatenate two strings, use the ampersand (&). For example:

```
Title$ = "Queen "
Name$ = "Elizabeth "
Numeral$ = "I"
' gives Queen Elizabeth I
FirstElizabeth = Title$ & Name$ & Numeral$
' gives Queen Elizabeth II
CurrentQueen = Title$ & Name$ & Numeral$ & Numeral$
```

The & joins the strings in the order in which you present them. Thus, unlike when you add numbers together, the order is important when using the & sign to join strings together.

Finally, it is quite common to build up a long string with the & sign before using it in a message box. For example:

```
Message = "This program was created by "
Message = Message & "Gary Cornell"
MsgBox Message
```

(or use the underscore).

You can also use the & in the MsgBox itself:

```
Message = "This program was created by "
MyName = "Gary Cornell"
MsgBox Message & MyName
```

Evil Type Conversions I: Beware of the + Sign for Strings

Many programming languages (including early versions of Visual Basic) use a + sign to join together strings. Although the + still works in VB to join strings together, don't use it; it can lead to incredibly hard-to-find bugs. This is because of Visual Basic's equally incredible and unbelievably annoying habit of converting strings to numbers when *it thinks it makes sense.* Experienced VB programmers hate this so much that they came up with a special name for it—they call it "the problem of evil type coercion." (Coercion being the programmer's buzzword for a conversion of data from one type to another.) Evil type coercions are especially likely to happen if you make sloppy use of variant variables. To see evil type coercion at work, start up a new project and try the following simple code:

```
Private Sub Form_Load
   'zip+4 doesn't work if you use a + and make a typo!
   Dim Zip As String
   Dim Plus4   'oops, meant to make this a string variable
   Zip = "12345"
   Plus4 = 6789   'oops, meant to use quotes but I goofed
   MsgBox Zip + Plus4
End Sub
```

If you run this code, here's what happens:

◆ VB assumes you want Plus4 to be a number (not so crazy).

◆ Then, VB *stupidly* and *blindly* assumes that since you used the + sign with a string and a number that was stored in a variant, you meant the result to be a number.

◆ Based on its silly assumption, it added them together!

Every serious programmer that I know would prefer that VB warn you that the types of variables don't match, instead of converting them willy nilly!

The & sign, on the other hand, always does what you expect. For example, even in the above code, `MsgBox Zip & Plus4` would work correctly.

ASCII/ANSI Codes

A computer doesn't have one kind of memory for text and another for numbers. Anything stored in a computer's memory is actually stored as a number (actually, as a binary representation of a number). The program keeps track of whether the memory patterns are codes for text or not. Usually, the code for translating text to numbers is called the ASCII code (American Standard Code for Information Interchange). The

ASCII code associates with each number from 0 through 255 a displayable or control character, although Windows cannot display all 255 ASCII characters and uses a more limited set of characters called the ANSI (American National Standards Institute) character set. The control characters, and such special keys as TAB and line feed, have numbers less than 32.

The value of the function Chr(*n*) is the string consisting of the character of ASCII value *n*. The statement

```
Print Chr(n)
```

either displays the character numbered *n* in the ASCII sequence *for the font currently in use* or produces the specified effect that the control code will have on your screen—or both. For example, the statement

```
Print Chr(227)
```

prints the Greek letter pi (π) on the screen if you have previously set the FontType to be MS LineDraw by using the Properties window or via code.

The following code uses the ASCII/ANSI value for the quotation mark, 34, to display a sentence surrounded with quotation marks.

```
Print Chr(34);
Print "Quoth the raven, nevermore.";
Print Chr(34)
```

TIP: The Chr function returns a string stored in a variant. You can still use the older Chr$ if you want. Chr$ gives you a string value directly.

The output of these lines is

```
"Quoth the raven, nevermore."
```

NOTE: The preceding output also can be produced by the statement

```
Print """Quoth the raven, nevermore.""";
```

since Visual Basic—unlike many programming languages—interprets two consecutive quotation marks as a literal quotation mark inside Print statements and string assignments.

Visual Basic also has a function that takes a string expression and returns the ASCII/ANSI value of the first character: it is Asc. If the string is empty (the null string), using this function generates a run-time error.

As you'll see in Chapter 7, ASCII/ANSI order is what Visual Basic uses by default to compare strings when you use relational operators such as < or >. The most important use of the ASCII/ANSI codes is for the KeyPress event procedure, which is also covered in Chapter 7.

NOTE: Internally, Visual Basic uses Unicode—a system designed for generating all possible languages. It has more than 65,000 possible character codes. For more on Visual Basic's use of Unicode, see the appendix to the Programmer's Guide. Except for some special situations involving binary files (discussed in Chapter 18), the switch from ASCII/ANSI to Unicode is transparent to the programmer.

5

Built-in String Constants

In early versions of Visual Basic, one of the most important uses of the Chr function was to set up a newline code for use in your programs. If you wanted to place separate lines in a multiline text box or add breaks in a message box, you needed this code for a new line. As in an old-fashioned typewriter, new lines are made up of two parts: a carriage return to bring the cursor to the first column and the line feed to move it to the next line. In terms of the Chr function, the newline code is

```
vbCrLf = Chr(13) & Chr(10)
```

Now, though, you can just use the built-in constant vbCrLf.

For example, suppose you want to add line breaks in message boxes or multiline text boxes. The fastest way to do this is to first set up a string variable that includes the newline character:

```
TextString$ = "Visual Basic For Windows" & vbCrLf
TextString$ = TextString$ & "Osborne/McGraw-Hill"$+ vbCrLf
TextString$ = TextString$ & "Berkeley, CA"
Text1.Text = TextString$
```

TIP: If you neglect to set the multiline property of a text box to True and try to use a newline character, you'll see two funny-looking vertical bars in your text box.

By the way, you might be wondering why I built the string up first and then assigned it to the Text property. This is a general way to speed up a Visual Basic program. It is worth repeating:

TIP: It is much faster to build up the string first and then change the Text property once than to change the Text property repeatedly.

Similarly, you can force a break in a message box by setting up the message string using the vbCrLf built-in constant:

```
Message$ = "This will be on line 1."
Message = Message$ & vbCrLf & "This will be on line 2."
MsgBox Message$
```

Besides the vbCrLf constant for the carriage return/line feed combination, you might find the following built-in constants for various characters useful.

Character	Symbolic Constant
Null character	vbNullChar = Chr$(0)
Carriage return	vbCr = Chr$(13)
Line feed	vbLf = Chr$(10)
Backspace	vbBack = Chr$(8)
Tab	vbTab = Chr$(9)
Vertical tab	vbVerticalTab = Chr$(11)
Form feed	vbFormFeed = Chr$(12)

TIP: VB also comes with a constant called vbNullString that you can use instead of "" for the empty string. (There is no Chr equivalent of the empty string, Chr(0) is not "".) Using vbNullString is actually safer than using "" because if you inadvertently put a space between the quotes, your programs would have a very hard-to-detect bug. (Trust me, it is hard to tell the difference between " " and "" when searching hundreds of lines of code for an elusive bug.)

Fixed-Length Strings

A fixed-length string is a special type of string that plays an important role in later chapters (Chapters 9 and 18). These variables are also created with a Dim statement. Here is an example:

```
Dim ShortString As String * 10
Dim strShort As String * 10
```

Both of these statements set up string variables (in spite of not using the identifier). However, this variable will always hold strings of length 10. If you assign a longer string to ShortString, as shown here,

```
ShortString = "antidisestablishment"
```

what you get is the same thing as:

```
ShortString = "antidisest"
```

As you can see, the variable contains only the left ten characters of the value. Similarly, if you assign a shorter string to ShortString, like this,

```
ShortString = "a"
```

you still get a string of length 10, only this time the contents of the variable are padded on the right so that the string is really stored in the same way as:

```
ShortString = "a         "
```

Thus, fixed-length strings are "right padded" if necessary.

NOTE: Chapter 18 explains how fixed-length strings are used with random-access files. People whose only experience is with the clumsy method of handling random-access files in interpreted BASIC are in for a very pleasant surprise.

More on Numbers

When you write code to assign a value to a numeric variable in Visual Basic, you can't use a comma to delineate thousands. VB will not let you enter code like:

```
Dim I As Integer
I = 1,234
```

You *can* use a decimal point, but if you assign such a number to an integer or long integer variable, it will automatically be rounded to an integer value. If you assign a number larger than the limits for the given variable, Visual Basic will give you an error message at run time.

Here are some examples:

Number	Acceptable in an assignment to a numeric variable?
3001	Okay for all numeric variables
3000001	Okay for all but short integer variables

Number	Acceptable in an assignment to a numeric variable?
30000.01	Okay for all but integer variables (rounded off for them and for long integer variables)
3,001	Illegal because it uses a comma

The Numeric Operators

The following table gives you the symbols for the five fundamental arithmetic operations.

Operator	Operation
+	Addition
-	Subtraction (and used to denote negative numbers)
/	Division
*	Multiplication
^	Exponentiation

For integers and long integers, there is one symbol and one keyword for the arithmetic operations unique to numbers of these types:

Operator	Operation
\	Integer division (this symbol is a backslash)
Mod	The remainder after integer division

The ordinary division symbol (/) gives you a value that is a single-precision, double-precision, or currency answer, depending on the objects involved. The backslash (\), on the other hand, throws away the remainder in order to give you an integer. For example, 7\3 = 2. Since a / gives either a single- or double-precision answer, use a \ or the Mod operator if you really want to work with integers or long integers.

The Mod operator is the other half of integer division—it gives you the remainder after integer division. For example, 7 Mod 3 = 1. When one integer perfectly divides another, there is no remainder, so the Mod operator gives zero: 8 Mod 4 = 0.

The usual term for a combination of numbers, variables, and operators from which Visual Basic can extract a value is a *numeric expression*.

Parentheses and Precedence

When you do calculations, you have two ways to indicate the order in which you want operations to occur. The first way is by using parentheses, and you may well prefer this method. Parentheses let you easily specify the order in which operations occur. Something like 3 + (4 * 5) gives 23 because Visual Basic does the operation within the parentheses first (4 times 5), and only then adds the 3. On the other hand, (3 + 4) * 5 gives 35 because Visual Basic adds the 3 and the 4 first to get 7, and only then multiplies by 5.

Here's another example:

  ((6 * 5) + 4) * 3

gives 102 since VB works within the parentheses.

Visual Basic allows you to avoid parentheses, provided you carefully follow rules that determine the precedence of the mathematical operations. For example, multiplication has higher precedence than addition. This means 3 + 4 * 5 is 23 rather than 35 because the multiplication (4 * 5) is done before the addition.

The following list gives the order (hierarchy) of operations:

  Exponentiation (^)
  Negation (making a number negative)
  Multiplication and division
  Integer division
  The remainder (Mod) function
  Addition and subtraction

For example, -4 ^ 2 gives -16 because Visual Basic first does the exponentiation (4 ^ 2 = 4 * 4 = 16) and only then makes the number negative.

Think of these as levels. Operations on the same level are done from left to right, so 96 / 4 * 2 is 48. Because division and multiplication are on the same level, first the division is done, giving 24, and then the multiplication is done. On the other hand, 96 / 4 ^ 2 is 6. This is because the exponentiation is done first, yielding 16, and only then is the division done.

To show you how obscure using the hierarchy of operations can make your programs, try to figure out what Visual Basic would do with this:

  4 * 2 + 16 / 8 + 2 ^ 3 ^ 4

Here's what happens: first the exponents (level 1) are computed left to right (2 ^ 3 = 8; 8 ^ 4 = 8 * 8 * 8 * 8 = 4096), then the multiplication and division from left to right (4 * 2 = 8, 16 / 8 = 2), and then the addition (8 + 2 + 4096 = 4106).

Examples like this one should convince you that a judicious use of parentheses will make your programs clearer and your life easier as a result.

Arithmetic on Date Variables
Visual Basic makes it easy to do calculations with date variables. If you subtract or add an integer, you subtract or add that many days. Adding a fraction changes the time within a day. For example,

```
Dim foo As Date
foo = Now 'Now gives you the current day and time
Print foo
Print foo - 1000
```

prints today's date and time and then prints the day and time 1,000 days ago. (See Chapter 8 for more on the functions that Visual Basic has for dealing with dates.)

Arithmetic on Variant Variables
You can, of course, store numeric information in variant variables. You can then use the ordinary arithmetic operations on these variant variables. This trusts Visual Basic to make the right kind of conversion and not get confused—something most programmers won't do. As always, I recommend avoiding variant variables whenever possible.

Scientific Notation
If you've tried any calculations involving large numbers in Visual Basic, you've probably discovered that the program often doesn't bother printing out large numbers. Instead, it uses a variant on *scientific notation*. For example, if you ask Visual Basic to print a number consisting of a 1 followed by 25 zeros by using a statement such as Print 10 ^ 25, what you will see is 1E+25. If you are not familiar with this notation, think of the E+ as meaning: Move the decimal place to the right, adding zeros if necessary. The number of places the decimal place is moved is exactly the number following the E. If a negative number follows the E, the decimal point is moved to the left. For example, 2.1E-5 gives you .000021. You can enter a number using the E notation if it's convenient; Visual Basic doesn't care whether you enter 1000, 1E3, or 1E+3. (If you want the number stored as a double-precision number, use a D instead of an E.)

How VB Treats Numbers of Different Data Types
When you assign a variable or value of one type to a variable of a different type, Visual Basic does a type conversion if it can. If it cannot figure out a way to do this that makes sense, it generates an error at run time. For example, you can't do the following

```
Dim I As Integer, L As Long
L = 1234567
I = L
```

because the information in L is too big to fit into an integer variable. (You'll get a message box reporting what VB calls an "Overflow" error.) This code, however, will run fine:

```
Dim I As Integer, L As Long
L = 123
I = L
```

When you use numbers in your program and do not assign them to a variable of the variant type, Visual Basic assumes the following:

◆ If a number has no decimal point and is in the range -32,768 to 32,767, it's an integer.

◆ If a number has no decimal point and is in the range for a long integer (-2,147,483,648 to 2,147,483,647), it's a long integer.

◆ If a number has a decimal point and is in the range for a single-precision number, it is assumed to be single precision.

◆ If a number has a decimal point and is outside the range for a single-precision number, it is assumed to be double precision.

These built-in assumptions occasionally lead to problems. This is because the realm in which an answer lives is determined by where the question lives. If you start out with two integers, Visual Basic assumes the answer is also an integer. For example, a statement such as

```
Print 12345*6789
```

starts with two integers, so VB assumes the answer will also be an integer. But the answer is too large for an integer, so you would get an overflow error. The solution is to add the appropriate identifier to at least one of the numbers. Use the statement

```
Print 12345&*6789
```

which tells VB to consider 12345 as a long, so the whole result will be a long.

CAUTION: If you assign the value of a single-precision variable to a double-precision variable, you do not suddenly increase its accuracy. The number may have more (or even different) digits, but only the first six or seven can be trusted.

Type Conversions

You can always use a built-in function to force a type conversion from one variable to another—if the values stored are compatible. Actually, even more is true; these really neat functions allow you to convert a string that looks like a number *even if it has commas in it or a leading $ sign* (or the equivalent currency symbol for the country where your code is running). For example, if you apply one of these conversion functions to 1,234, you'll be able to use the number correctly. If the user enters $123.45 and you use one of these conversion function, VB will change this to the number 123.45.

NOTE: VB allows the user to use whatever symbols for the thousands separator or the currency symbol are stored by the operating system. British Windows users should be able to use the pound symbol (£), for example.

5

Of course, Visual Basic will only do a conversion to a numeric type if the result will be in the permitted range for the target type or if the string is really a number represented in numerals. (You can use one of these conversion functions to convert "30Something" but not "thirtysomething".)

If a conversion won't work, Visual Basic generates an error message. Using the numeric conversion functions between numeric variables has the same effect as assigning the numeric expression to a variable of the type specified. The following table summarizes these functions, which you can use to convert either a string of numerals to a number or to convert from one type of variable to another.

Conversion Function	What It Does
CInt	Converts to an integer
CLng	Converts to a long integer
CSng	Converts to single precision
CDbl	Converts to double precision
CCur	Converts to the currency type

The Val Function

VB has a function called Val that is a catch-all converter, and so VB programmers still often use Val to convert a numeric string to a number. It turns out that Val is a mixed blessing, just like the variant data type. On the one hand, Val is far more forgiving of input errors than the 'C' conversion functions. Val simply reads through the string until it encounters a non-numeric character (or a second period). The number you get from it is determined by where it stopped searching. For example:

```
Val ("30Something") = 30
```

Or,

```
Val(7.5%) = 7.5
```

But, because of its forgiving nature, your program could be accepting something you really didn't want it to accept. A truly professional program would not accept 12#$ since the user probably meant 1234. Unfortunately, a program that uses Val would simply report what the user entered as 12. I think your programs will be more reliable

♦   *If* you use one of the more precise "C" conversion functions

♦   *After* you check that what the user entered makes sense (See Chapter 7 for how to do this.)

Converting Numbers Back to Strings

VB also lets you convert a number to a string. The simplest way of doing this is with the Str function. (The Str function returns a variant that holds a string; its cousin the

Str$ function returns a pure string.) The Str and Str$ functions convert numbers to strings but don't clean them up in any way.

Str(123)	= "123"
Str(123.4567)	= "123.4567"
Str(-987654321)	= "-987654321"

T IP: To polish the display, the Str function is often replaced by the Format function. (See the section "The Format Function" in Chapter 6.) The Format function is very versatile. Among its many features, it lets you cut off extraneous digits and display a (large) number with commas or a leading dollar sign.

5

Of course if you use the & function with numbers, they will automatically be converted to a string. To see this at work, start up a new program and use the following code in the Form_Load:

```
Private Sub Form_Load()
  Dim X As Integer, Y As Integer
  Dim Message As String
  X = 3: Y = 4
  Message = "See how the & converts numbers to strings "
  Message = Message & "because you'll see:"
  Message = Message & X & Y
  MsgBox Message
  End
End Sub
```

Evil Type Conversions II
Conversion from strings of numerals to numbers is great when you are in control, but, unfortunately, VB's evil type coercion facility occasionally makes this neat feature dangerous. Start up a new form and add a command button to it. Put the following code in the Command_Click procedure:

```
Dim I As Integer, S As String
I = 2
S = "1,234"
I = I*S  'bug--never should I multiply a string by a number!
Print I
```

Guess what? VB assumes that you meant the string to be a number and converts it for you—you will see 2468! As I said, this is clearly a bug, and most other programming languages would simply not compile this kind of code. That way you would be aware that you introduced a bug into your code. (You probably meant I = I&S.)

Bits, Bytes, and Hexadecimal (Base 16) Numbers in Visual Basic

You may have wondered what cryptic notations such as &HFFFFFF meant for a color code when you looked at the Properties window. It turns out that to set colors directly from the Properties window, you'll need to know a bit about counting in *binary* (base 2) and *hexadecimal* (base 16) formats. (This information is also useful in various other contexts in Visual Basic; although you may want to skip this section now, you will probably want to return to it later.)

Roughly speaking, a computer is ultimately a giant collection of on-off switches, and a disk is a collection of particles that can either be magnetized or not. Think of each memory location in your PC as being made up of eight on-off switches. This affects the internal representation of numbers inside a PC. For example, when you write 255, you ordinarily think two hundreds, five tens, and five ones. These digits are arranged in decimal notation, or base-10 notation, with each position holding numbers 10 times as large as the position to the right. However, your computer thinks in binary notation (base-2 notation) and stores the number 255 in a single memory location as 11111111, meaning one 128, one 64, one 32, one 16, one 8, one 4, one 2, and one 1 (all of which adds up to 255). Each of the eight switches just mentioned represents a *bit* (for *binary digit*). When a switch stores a 1, the bit is said to be on, and the value stored in that position is twice the value of the digit in the place to the right (instead of 10 times the value, as in decimal notation). Eight bits form a *byte* (which is one memory location), and half a byte forms a *nibble*.

The following table shows you how to count to 15 in binary notation.

Binary	Decimal
0	0
1	1
10	2
11	3
100	4
101	5
110	6
111	7
1000	8
1001	9
1010	10
1011	11

Binary	Decimal
1100	12
1101	13
1110	14
1111	15

Fifteen is the largest number that can be stored in a single nibble, and 255 is the largest number that can be stored in a byte. Bits are numbered with the leftmost bit called the *most significant* and the rightmost bit called the *least significant*. (The rightmost bit is sometimes called the *zeroth bit*.)

Binary numbers are difficult for most people to handle. Hexadecimal numbers (base 16) are much easier. Each place in a hexadecimal numbering scheme is 16 times the place to the right. So instead of saying "1's place, 10's place, 100's place," as you learned in grade school (for decimal notation), in hexadecimal (hex) notation you say, "1's place, 16's place, 256's place," and so on. For example, hexadecimal 10 is decimal 16. Hexadecimal notation uses A for decimal 10, B for decimal 11, C for decimal 12, D for decimal 13, E for decimal 14, and F for decimal 15. In Visual Basic programs, you prefix a number with &H to indicate that it is a hexadecimal number. Thus, you would write decimal 49 as &H31. Each hexadecimal digit represents four binary digits, or one nibble.

5

To convert binary numbers to hexadecimal format, group the digits from right to left in groups of four and convert. For example, 11010111 (1101 0111, in two groups of four) is hexadecimal D7: 1101 is 13 in decimal format and D in hexadecimal format, and 0111 is 7 in both decimal and hexadecimal formats.

How Color Works in Visual Basic

The settings for the color properties are indicated by hexadecimal coding. Every color code in Visual Basic is made up of six hexadecimal digits, from &H000000& (0) to &HFFFFFF& (16,777,215). This might seem awkward, but the code actually is fairly simple to use—if you understand hexadecimal notation.

Finally, it's a good idea to get into the habit of adding another ampersand to the end of a color code—for example: &HFFFFFF&. This tells Visual Basic to treat the color code as a long integer. As you have seen, long integers are integers greater than 32,767 or less than -32,768, and color codes are usually outside these limits. Forgetting the identifier doesn't usually cause problems, but it's best not to take chances.

To understand the code, think of RGB (red, green, and blue) color monitors as being told to send out a specific amount of redness, greenness, and blueness. The combination of these primary colors gives you all the remaining ones. In the coding used by Visual Basic, the last two hexadecimal digits give you the amount of redness, the middle two give you the amount of greenness, and the first two, the most significant, give you the amount of blueness. Here are a few examples of hexadecimal color codes and the colors they produce:

Hex Color Code	Color
&H0000FF&	Maximum red (no green or blue)
&H00FF00&	Maximum green (no red or blue)
&HFF0000&	Maximum blue (no red or green)
&H000000&	Black (no color)
&HFFFFFF&	White (all colors)
&H00FFFF&	Yellow (red and green)
&H808080&	Gray (equal mixtures of all colors)

The reason that &H808080& is an equal mixture of all colors is that half of &HFF& is about &H80&, because half of 255 is about 128; 128 is equal to 8 *16, which is equal to &H80&.

NOTE: Some people find it convenient to think of the color code as &HBBGGRR& (B for blue, G for green, and R for red). Also, if you are familiar with HTML page color coding please be aware that this is the exact opposite as is used on Web pages. There the code is RRGGBB!

Now you can change color settings directly:

1. Move to the Properties window, and select BackColor or ForeColor.
2. Decide how much red, green, and blue you want.
3. Enter the appropriate hexadecimal code.

Example Program: A Mortgage Calculator

At this point you are probably itching to do something other than run toy examples that illustrate programming concepts. Well, you have certainly seen enough of Visual Basic to write a few useful programs. The one I'll show you here is a basic mortgage calculator. At this stage, what you can make such a program do is:

◆   Allow a user to enter the amount of the mortgage, the interest rate, and the term in years in three text boxes.

◆   Calculate the monthly mortgage payment from scratch, using a standard formula.

◆   Display the result.

NOTE: Visual Basic actually has many financial functions available. These functions are discussed in Chapter 8. In particular, there's a function for doing calculations that not only includes mortgage analysis but can do far more.

The first thing to do is design the form. Figure 5-5 shows the form with the caption not yet changed. This form has two command buttons, four labels, and four text boxes. It uses the default sizes for all the controls. This lets you use the double-click method for generating them. You then use the sizing handles to move the controls around until you are happy with the locations. Table 5-3 lists the controls in this project, following the tab order.

As you can see in Figure 5-5 or by looking at the ampersands in Table 5-3, this form has many access keys for the controls. There are even access keys for the labels. As you learned in Chapter 4, this gives quick access to the controls that follow them in tab order. For this to work, though, the text box must follow the label in tab order when you design the form. The TabStop property for the MortgagePayment text box has been changed to False since there is no reason in this application to allow the user to move the focus to this box. The Locked property is also changed to True, since you don't want the user to be able to change the contents of this box. (Other possibilities are using a bordered label or setting the Enabled property to False, although this has the side effect of dimming the box.)

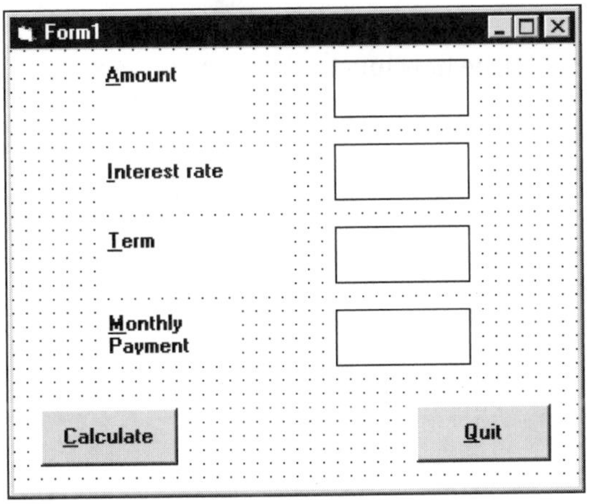

Form for the
mortgage
calculator
Figure 5-5.

Control	Control Name	Caption (or Text)
Form		Mortgage Calculator
1st label	Label1	&Amount
1st text box	txtMortgageAmount	
2nd label	Label2	&Interest Rate
2nd text box	txtInterestRate	
3rd label	Label3	&Term
3rd text box	txtMortgageTerm	
4th label	Label4	&Monthly Payment
4th text box	txtMortgagePayment	
Left command button	cmdCalculate	&Calculate
Right command button	cmdQuit	&Quit

Controls for the Mortgage Calculator Program in Tab Order **Table 5-3.**

Let's go over one way to code this application. All the code is attached to the two command buttons. The code for the Quit button is simple:

```
Private Sub cmdQuit_Click ()
   End
End Sub
```

The code to actually calculate the mortgage payment is a little more involved. First, you need a formula for mortgage payments. The formula for monthly mortgage payments is a bit complicated. It is

$$Principal*MonthInt/(1-(1/(1+MonthInt))^\wedge(Years *12))$$

where *MonthInt* is the annual interest rate divided by 12. Since entering this formula is prone to error, we break it up into a numerator and denominator in the following code sample.

```
Private Sub cmdCalculate_Click ()
  'This calculates the mortgage
  'Using the formula
  'Principal*MonthInt/(1-(1/(1+MonthInt))^(Years*12))

  Dim Years As Integer, Payment As Currency
  Dim MonthInt As Single, Amount As Currency
  Dim Percent As Single, Principal As Currency
  Dim Numerator As Currency, Denominator As Currency
  ' Get info
  Years = CInt(txtMortgageTerm.Text)
```

```
Principal = CCur(txtMortgageAmount.Text)
Percent = CSng(txtInterestRate.Text) / 100
MonthInt = Percent/12

Numerator = Principal * MonthInt
Denominator = 1 - (1 / (1 + MonthInt))^ (Years * 12)
Payment = Numerator/Denominator
txtMortgagePayment.Text = Str$(Payment)
End Sub
```

For more accuracy, this program keeps the years in an integer variable, the interest rate and percent as a single-precision number, and all the others as currency variables. (The program will run a little more quickly if it uses single-precision variables instead of currency variables.) The next point to remember is that text boxes do not give numbers; it is good programming to convert the data inside them by using the correct conversion function (CInt, CSng) instead of relying on variants. This program assumes that the user enters the interest rate as a percentage. Because the CSng function assumes the user entered something in the form of a number, this program is not as crash-proof (*robust* is the buzzword by the way) as I would like. (See Chapter 7 for how to check input so as to make your programs more robust.) To make the logic of the program clearer, there is a separate calculation for the monthly interest, and the formula is separated into its numerator and denominator.

Finally, the program uses the Str$ function to convert the data back to a string in order to assign it to the text property of the text box named txtMortgagePayment instead of using the automatic conversion provided by variants.

Improvements to the Mortgage Calculator

There are lots of ways to improve the mortgage calculator program. As I just said, probably the most important would be to make the program more "bulletproof." Inexperienced users often make typos when entering information and the conversion functions will not allow this. In Chapter 7 you'll see how to write the code either to allow or prevent this, as you see fit.

For now, though, suppose you want to add two command buttons that either increase or decrease the interest rate (say by 1/8% = .00125) and then redo the calculations. Here's a simple way to write the code for a button to increase the interest rate:

```
Sub cmdIncrease_Click()
  Dim NewRate As Single

  Percent = CSng(txtInterestRate.Text) / 100
  NewRate = (Percent + .00125)*100
  txtInterestRate.Text = Str$(NewRate)
  cmdCalculate_Click
End Sub
```

Before getting to the question of why this program may not be the best solution, take a look at the key statement, cmdCalculate_Click. This is the first example you've seen of one event procedure using (the technical term is *calling*) another event procedure. As your programs get more sophisticated, event procedures become more and more interrelated. (Chapter 9 discusses this topic in depth.) What happens here is that when Visual Basic calls the Click procedure you wrote earlier, it uses the current contents of the text boxes. Because the line

```
txtInterestRate.Text = Str$(NewRate)
```

changes the contents of the text box directly, the Click procedure has new data to work with.

NOTE: As this example indicates, you call an event procedure by entering its name. More complicated event procedures (those having arguments) are still called by using their names—you just need to supply the required arguments.

Inefficiencies in the Mortgage Calculator Example

Now why would some people think this version of the mortgage program is not the most efficient programming solution? The offending line is

```
Percent = CSng(txtInterestRate.Text) / 100
```

What this line does is recalculate something that has been calculated once already. While not a mistake, it is inefficient. In a more complicated program, these inefficiencies might grow until they really put a drag on the performance of your application. The problem is that in Visual Basic there is no way to pass information to an event procedure *except through form-level variables.* So some programmers would advocate making all the numeric information derived from the text boxes in this example the values of form-level variables.

If you want to make the information from the text boxes be form-level variables, you can do this by adding one of the following to the (Declarations) section of the form and removing the corresponding declarations from the event procedures:

```
Private Principal As Single, Percent as Single
Private Years As Integer, Payment As Currency
```

Unfortunately, form-level variables are also a breeding ground for bugs, so many programmers prefer to use them only when they have to. (And they would not be needed in this example once you have mastered Visual Basic!) At this point, given what we have covered so far about Visual Basic, there is no good solution. (Once you have seen how to use non-event procedures (Chapter 9), there will be quite a few possible solutions.)

The moral is that inefficiencies and bug breeding are common when you modify an old program for new uses. You can end up forcing the original program into a frame in which it was never supposed to appear. You're likely to introduce bugs as well. Often, you're better off rewriting the program from scratch—unless you have designed the program well in the first place.

In any case, debugging a program will always be necessary, but it will never be fun. Programs rarely run perfectly the first time. One way to cut down on debugging time is to get into the habit of "thinking first and coding later" (sometimes described as "the sooner you start coding, the longer it takes"). If you think through the possibilities carefully first—for example, deciding which variables should be global and which should be local—you'll go a long way toward "bug proofing" your programs.

Constants

A program is easiest to debug when it's readable. Try to prevent the MEGO ("my eyes glaze over") syndrome that is all too common when a program has lots of mysterious numbers sprinkled about. It's a lot easier to read a line of code such as

```
Calculate.Visible = True
```

than if you use

5

```
Calculate.Visible = -1
```

even though both will have the same effect.

More generally, Visual Basic's *named constant* feature allows you to create and then use mnemonic names for values that never change. Constants are declared just like variables, and the rules for their names are also the same: 255 characters, first character a letter, and then any combination of letters, underscores, and numerals. The older convention was to use all capitals for constants; now the manuals suggest going to the same mixed-case format that is being used for variables. Just as some people like to use a prefix for the variable type, some people who are into Hungarian notation in a big way like to use the prefix "con" for constants. (I particularly don't like this convention for constants, because something like PI (3.14159...) seems to make a lot more sense than conPi!)

If you have only one form or want the constants visible to the event procedures for only one form, put them in the (Declarations) section for the (General) object, just as you did with the definers that change Visual Basic's default types or for form-level variables. Some people like to use the Private keyword for form-level constants that you saw for form-level variables as well—although it is not needed. Finally, you can also define a constant within a procedure, but this is less common, and only that procedure would have access to the constant.

Set up a constant by using the keyword Const followed by the name of the constant, an equal sign, and then the value:

```
Const Pie = 3.14159
```

You can also set up string constants:

```
Const UserName = "Bill Smith"
Const Language = "Visual Basic Version 6.0"
```

You can even use numeric expressions for constants—or define new constants in terms of previously defined constants:

```
Const PieOver2 = Pie/2
```

What you can't do is define a constant in terms of Visual Basic's built-in functions or the exponentiation operator. For example, if you need the square root of ten in a program, you need to calculate it before you can write

```
Const SquareRootOfTen = 3.16227766016838
```

TIP: The Immediate window is a great help for these kinds of constants. For the above example you could enter 10^.5 in the Immediate window and then paste the result into your code.

Visual Basic uses the simplest type it can for a constant, but you can override this by adding a type identifier to a constant. For example:

```
Const ThisWillBeALongInteger& = 37
```

As mentioned, the convention is to use mixed case for constants, but this is not required. Moreover, references to constants don't depend on the case.

The Supplied Constant File

Visual Basic comes with hundreds (maybe thousands—I don't know anyone who has actually counted them) of useful constants for working with the built-in functions, objects, and methods. Many of them show up because of the IntelliSense feature described earlier.

You have seen a few constants already: for example, the vbCrLf constant that replaces the older Chr(13) + Chr(10). The built-in constants are available for pasting into the Code window from the Object Browser. The Object Browser pops up when you press F2 or choose Object Browser from the View menu (ALT+V+O). It is shown in Figure 5-6 with some of the Constants highlighted.

Each different component of Visual Basic, such as the database features or the features coming from Visual Basic for Applications, has its own built-in constants that are available from the Object Browser—many controls have their own as well. Scroll down the left pane until you get to what you want. Moreover, you can paste these constants into your code and they will automatically be recognized. In general, Visual Basic constants begin with a "vb", database constants (Chapter 22) with a "db", and so on. As you can see in Figure 5-6, constants show up in the browser with a little box next to them.

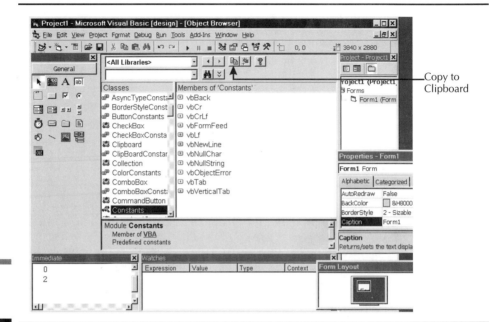

— Copy to Clipboard

The Object
Browser
Figure 5-6.

To paste a constant into your code from the Object Browser:

1. Make sure the cursor is where you want the constant to appear in the Code window.
2. Click on the Copy to Clipboard button in the Object Browser (the third button on the first line).
3. Go to where you want the constant in your code and press CTRL+V.

T ....
IP: If you are unsure of what constants you need, and IntelliSense isn't enough, the online help system will tell you which one you need for a specific function, action, or method.

Input Boxes

I want to end this chapter by discussing input boxes, which are an alternative way of getting information from the user. Now, it is true that text boxes are the most common way for a Visual Basic application to accept data, but the InputBox function displays a *modal* dialog box on the screen—just like the MsgBox function. (Recall that modality is the buzzword for something that must be closed before the user can continue using the program.) Modality is the principal advantage of input boxes; you sometimes need to insist that a user supply some necessary data before letting him or her move on in the application. The disadvantages are that the dimensions of the input box are fixed beforehand, and you lose the flexibility that text boxes provide. Here is an example of an input box:

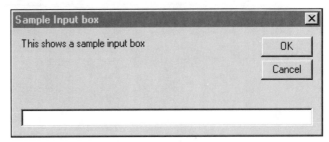

As you can see, input boxes have a title bar that you can set (see below for how). There is also a prompt; in the example above it simply is "This shows a sample input box." There are always two command buttons labeled OK and Cancel. Finally, there is a text area at the bottom. Visual Basic always places the focus in this text area when it processes a statement containing an InputBox function. The simplest syntax for the InputBox function as shown in the Quick Info IntelliSense feature is

>   *StringVariable* = InputBox(*PromptString*)

This form uses the name of the project in the title bar of the input box. The full syntax for the InputBox function is

>   VariableName = InputBox(*prompt*[, *title*][, *default*][, *xpos*][, *ypos*][, *helpfile, context*])

Here are short descriptions of these items (they are often called *parameters* or *arguments* in the jargon).

◆   The *prompt* parameter is a string or string variable whose value Visual Basic displays in the dialog box. It is limited to roughly 1,024 characters. The prompt doesn't wrap, and you have to explicitly add line separators using the vbCrLf character that was described earlier.

◆   The *title* parameter is optional and gives the caption used in the title bar. There is no default value; if you leave this out, the application's name is used in the title bar.

◆   The *default* parameter is also optional. It lets you display default text in the Edit box where the user will be entering information. If you omit this, the box starts out empty.

◆   Also optional, both *xpos* and *ypos* are integral numeric expressions. *xpos* is the distance in twips between the left edge of the input box and the left edge of the screen. *ypos* gives the distance in twips between the top of the box and the top of the screen. (If you omit *xpos*, the box is horizontally centered; if you omit *ypos*, it will show up around one-third of the way down the screen.)

◆   The two parameters *helpfile* and *context* are used together when you have a help message attached to the box (see Chapter 14).

Note that the notation presented in the syntax statement may seem cryptic at first, but it is a good idea to get used to it. It is the notation used in both the QuickInfo feature, the manuals, and the online documentation. With this notation, anything in brackets is optional. Notice that the parentheses are outside the square brackets so they are required. The commas separate the optional elements (the parameters or arguments) in this function. If you skip one of the arguments, you still have to use a comma as a separator. (How else would Visual Basic know which argument belongs where? For example,

```
My  = InputBox("Example", , "A default string", 100, 200)
```

leaves the title bar as the default value (the project name) but starts the box out with the string "A default string" inside of it.

 E: Please see the section "Advanced Uses of Procedures and Functions" in C. 9 for a way around having to use a lot of empty commas.

Regardless of which type of Input Box you use, the user can type whatever he or she wants in the text box. If he or she presses ENTER or clicks on the OK button, then VB takes whatever is in the text box and sets it as the value of the string variable. Pressing ESC or clicking the Cancel button causes Visual Basic to assign the null string to the variable.

CHAPTER 6

Displaying Information

Visual Basic gives you extraordinary control over the appearance of what you place on a form and what you print on a page. The purpose of this chapter is to introduce you to the methods, functions, and properties you use to display your data in a professional way. (Chapters 11, 14 and 16 will finish the job.)

First you'll work with data that you want to display on a form. Then you'll learn about picture boxes, which work in much the same way as forms and have the advantage over forms that text will not be obscured by any controls that might be on the form. Next, it's on to the RichTextBox control, which lets you display information in multiple fonts and multiple sizes. I'll end the chapter with a short introduction to using the printer.

Displaying Information on a Form

As you have seen, Visual Basic displays text on a form using the Print method. The general syntax for the Print method applied to a form is

   FormName.Print *expression*

where *expression* is any Visual Basic expression that VB can convert to a string. (You can use the Me keyword to identify the current form instead of using its name or simply leave it out for code attached to the current form.) Visual Basic uses whatever settings are current for the Font object for the current form in order to determine the font information to use when it prints.

 CAUTION: If you want to use Print statements in the Form_Load event to display information when the form starts up, you can't simply use a Print statement. You have two choices of how to make this happen. The first is to have VB process a Show statement before it processes any Print statements. The second is to set the AutoRedraw property to be True. Without one of these two extra steps, you won't see the text you were trying to print.

(The Show method forces a Form to be visible. If you place it before the Print statements, you'll know there is a form visible to Print on! AutoRedraw being True, as you saw earlier, simply tells VB to keep a copy of the information on the form in its memory at all times so when the form finally gets displayed the information is still there.)

In addition to the curable problem of not being able to put Print statements in the Form_Load without some extra work, there are a couple of more serious potential problems you have to be on the lookout for. In fact, you have already seen one problem with a naïve use of Print statements on a form way back in Chapter 4 (see Figure 4-9): *controls can obscure text.* Unfortunately, there are even more problems you need to be aware of; these problems will potentially occur when the form is either

◆   Minimized and then restored

◆   Covered by another window (not just a VB window)

◆   Enlarged or shrunk

Unless the AutoRedraw property of the form is set to True, the text will disappear. This seems so surprising at first that I recommend running the experiment. To do so:

1. Start up a new project.
2. Change the Font property so the Font size is, say, 18 points.
3. Put the following code in the Form_Load:

```
Private Sub Form_Load()
   Show
   Print "Hello world -- or is it goodbye world?"
End Sub
```

Now run the program. No problem so far, of course. Next, minimize the form and restore it. As you can see, the text has disappeared! (The buzzword is to say that with AutoRedraw set to False, the information is not *persistent*.)

Although the simplest solution to the problem is to set the AutoRedraw property of the form to be True, other solutions are often a better choice since, as you saw in Chapter 4, AutoRedraw carries a cost in increasing the memory required to make your program run efficiently. One simple method to fix this problem without using the AutoRedraw property is to simply move the above code to both the Form_Resize event and Form_Paint event procedures as in the following code. (Note the use of the Cls command to keep only one copy of the statement at the top of the screen.)

6

```
Private Sub Form_Paint()
  Cls
  Print "Hello world -- or is it goodbye world?"
End Sub

Private Sub Form_Resize()
  Cls
  Print "Hello world -- or is it goodbye world?"
End Sub
```

Since VB will always call these two events when the form is either hidden or changed in size, you know the information you want to display can never be lost no matter what the user does to the form! (You can also have the Resize event procedure simply call the Paint procedure.)

CurrentX and CurrentY

In many fonts, letters like "m" take up more space than letters like "i". Fonts in which all characters are the same width are called *non-proportionally spaced fonts*; fonts where characters may be of different widths are called *proportionally spaced* fonts. Courier New is the most common non-proportionally spaced font and Arial is a common proportionally spaced font, as the following examples show:

```
This is set in Courier New.
```

This is set in Arial.

Proportional spacing gives a more polished look to your type.

Since most fonts in Windows are proportional, this makes it more difficult to position text accurately compared to older text-based systems. You can't simply say "move 10 characters to the left" and have that be the same location for all fonts. Luckily, Visual Basic always reports the current position (where the next character would be typed) as the values of two properties of the form or picture box: CurrentX and CurrentY.

◆ CurrentX refers to the horizontal position where Visual Basic will display the information.

◆ CurrentY refers to the vertical position where it will display the information.

If you change the value of these properties, you change where the next Print statement will display its information. The units used for these properties are determined by the scale set via the various scale methods that you saw in Chapter 3. For example, if the scale mode is pixels, and before each Print statement you set the CurrentX position to be 100, then all text will start 100 pixels over from the left side of the form.

You set CurrentX and CurrentY the same way you'd set any property. For example, for a form:

> *FormName*.CurrentX = *Value*
> *FormName*.CurrentY = *Value*

The value may be any numeric expression from which Visual Basic can extract a single-precision value. (Of course, for code attached to the form you can leave out the *FormName* or, even better, use the Me keyword.)

Whenever you use the Cls method to clear a form, Visual Basic resets the CurrentX and CurrentY values to zero. After clearing the form using the Cls method, and then using the default setting for the various scale properties, the next Print statement puts information in the top left corner. If you have changed the scale (for example, by using the ScaleLeft and ScaleTop properties), Visual Basic will use whatever location on the form now represents 0,0. (For more information on the scale properties, see Chapter 16.)

Of course, resetting CurrentX and CurrentY won't be of much use if you don't know how much space a specific character or string is taking up. The key to doing this is two built-in methods: TextWidth and TextHeight. The syntax for the TextWidth method is

> *FormName*.TextWidth(*string*)

After processing this statement, Visual Basic returns the value for the width of the string inside the parentheses, using the current font and reporting the results in the current scale. Similarly, the syntax for the TextHeight method is

> *FormName*.TextHeight(*string*)

and this gives the height of the string inside the parentheses. In general, TextHeight is used to determine the amount of vertical space and TextWidth the amount of horizontal space you need to display a string.

Here is an example in which these methods are needed. Suppose you want to display information at the beginning of the tenth line of text as it would appear in the ordinary coordinate system (0,0 as the top left). All you need to do is use the following fragment:

```
CurrentY = Me.TextHeight("I") * 9
CurrentX = 0
```

I used a capital letter to take into account that TextHeight gives the height of the text used. You also have to multiply by 9 rather than 10 to take into account that Visual Basic starts with 0,0 for the top left corner.

NOTE: To position text inside a multiline text box or a rich text box, you need to insert spaces and newline characters (vbCrLf) as needed. Text boxes do not support direct positioning of text.

6

Finally, I want to end this section by again stressing that many Visual Basic programmers prefer to use picture boxes or RichTextBoxes (described later in this chapter) instead of printing directly to a form. (Even labels and ordinary text boxes can be preferable.) For example, information on a form can't be scrolled without a lot of work. Information in a text box can be made to scroll up and down or left and right with essentially no programming work by adding scroll bars at design time or run time.

Example: Centering Text Inside a Form

Suppose you want to display a message in the exact center of a form. This turns out to be not as easy as it sounds. As a first approximation, here is an outline of what you need to do to find the coordinates of the exact center of the form:

1. Find the current value of the ScaleHeight and ScaleWidth properties. These properties (unlike Height and Width) tell you how large the internal area of the form (without the borders and title bar) is.
2. Divide these values in half.
3. Find the values of the ScaleLeft and ScaleTop properties for the form.
4. Add the results from step 2 to the values from step 3. This gives you the coordinates of the exact center of the form.

The problem is that this doesn't quite finish the job. If you reset the values CurrentX and CurrentY to the results from step 5 of this outline, you would start printing at the center of the screen, but the message wouldn't be centered. What you also need to do is take into account the font size and the length of the message. Once you know this information, you then could shift left and up by half the length and width of the message. As I just mentioned, the key to doing this is the built-in methods TextWidth and TextHeight. So, to the preceding outline, you need to add:

5. Use the TextWidth method on the string you want to center.

6. Subtract half the value Visual Basic obtains from step 5 from the value in step 4, and make this the value of CurrentX.

7. Similarly, subtract half Me.TextHeight(*string*) from the value of CurrentY obtained in step 5.

To see this at work start up a new project and add the following code to the Form_Resize event. Note that by putting the code in the Form_Resize procedure we ensure that it works equally well no matter what size the form takes. (Well, not quite. Of course, if the form is too small, the text will be chopped off. In the next chapter, you'll see how to prevent the form from being shrunk too far.)

```
Private Sub Form_Resize()
  'this routine calculates the necessary fudge factors
  'so as to make text perfectly centered
  'and readjusts CurrentX, CurrentY accordingly
  Dim Message As String
  Dim WidthFudgefactor As Integer
  Dim HeightFudgefactor As Integer
  Dim LeftCoord As Integer, TopCoord As Integer

  Cls  'clear any text already there
  Message = "Welcome to Visual Basic!"
  LeftCoord = Me.ScaleWidth / 2
  TopCoord = Me.ScaleHeight / 2
  LeftCoord = Me.ScaleLeft + LeftCoord
  TopCoord = Me.ScaleTop + TopCoord
  WidthFudgefactor = Me.TextWidth(Message) / 2
  HeightFudgefactor = Me.TextHeight(Message) / 2
  CurrentX = LeftCoord - WidthFudgefactor
  CurrentY = TopCoord - HeightFudgefactor
  Print Message
End Sub
```

The results are shown in Figure 6-1 (in 18-point type).

The Font Properties in Code

Which fonts and font sizes you can use depends on what kind of hardware and software is available to the system that is running the application. Visual Basic lets you find out this information; Chapter 7 shows you how. To assign a font name in code, place the name in quotation marks on the right-hand side of an assignment statement using the Name property of the Font object:

ObjectName.Font.Name = "Courier New"
Object.Font.Name = "Arial"

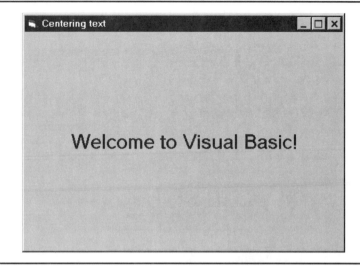

Centering text
Figure 6-1.

6

(If the target system doesn't have the font you select, it uses its best approximation.)

All objects that display text let you set the Name property of the Font object. These include forms, command buttons, labels, and the various kinds of text boxes. Of these, only forms, picture boxes, and RichTextBoxes let you combine different fonts. If you change these properties at run time for any other control, all the old text switches to the new font as well. The rule is that if text is specified by a property (for example, by the Caption property for command buttons), changing a font changes the previous text. On the other hand, if you display text by using the Print method, the changes are not retroactive and therefore go into effect only for subsequent Print statements.

You can change all the properties of the Font object via code. Except for Font.Size, they are all Boolean properties (True or False). As with Font.Name, any control that displays text lets you set the following:

```
ObjectName.Font.Size = 18                '18 point type
ObjectName.Font.Bold = True
ObjectName.Font.Italic = True
ObjectName.Font.Strikethru = False
ObjectName.Font.Underline = False
```

As with changing fonts, only forms, RichTextBoxes, and picture boxes let you mix these font properties.

Forms (and picture boxes) have one other font property you may occasionally find useful: FontTransparent. If you leave this at its default setting of True, background graphics and background text will show through the text displayed in the transparent font. Here's an example of this property at work:

You can combine the properties of the Font object almost any way you want. If your hardware and software support it, you can have 18-point bold italic script type in a control if that seems appropriate.

Displaying Tabular Data in a Non-Proportionally Spaced Font

Although the CurrentX and CurrentY properties give you absolute control over the placement of text in a form, often it will not be worth the trouble to use them for tabular data. When you want to display a table on a blank form, for example, you should probably use the grid control (see Chapter 11). On the other hand, if you just have lots of text and intend to use a non-proportionally spaced font, such as Courier, you might want to consider using the built-in *print zones* on a form. (In a non-proportionally spaced font, all characters have the same width.) Print zones are always set 14 columns apart, and Visual Basic recalculates this distance depending on the font characteristics in effect. Each column is the width of the average character in the font. This is why print zones do not work well for the majority of Windows fonts. Most fonts in Windows applications are proportional and what you type may not be "average."

Each time you use a comma in a Print method (statement), Visual Basic displays the data to the next print zone. For example, a statement like

```
Me.Print FirstName$, MiddleInit$, LastName$
```

tries to have the value of the string variable FirstName$ printed in the first zone, the value of the variable MiddleInit$ at the beginning of the second zone, and the value of the variable LastName$ printed at the beginning of the third zone. However, if a previous expression runs over into the next print zone, Visual Basic moves to the beginning of the next zone for the next Print statement.

The Tab and Spc Commands and Semicolons

Normally, after Visual Basic processes a statement involving the Print method, it moves to the next line. CurrentY increases by the height of the current font and CurrentX is set back to 0. You can also use an empty Print statement to add a blank line. If you want to suppress the automatic carriage return and line feed, place a semicolon at the end of the statement. For example start up a new project and then use the following Form_Load:

```
Sub Form_Load ()
  ' demonstrates the difference between using a ; and not
  Show
  Me.Font.Name = "Courier"
  Me.Print "This is a test"
  Me.Print "of the Print method"
  Me.Print                            'blank line

  Me.Print "This is a test";
  Me.Print "of the Print method"
  Me.Print                            'blank line
End Sub
```

The Tab function lets you move to a specific column (again using the average size of a character in the current font) and start printing there. Its syntax is

Print Tab(*ColumnNumber%*);

ColumnNumber% is an integral expression. If the current column position is greater than its value, Tab skips to this column on the next line. If the value is less than 1, Visual Basic moves to the first column. In theory, you can have values as large as 32,767 for the column. However, since Visual Basic doesn't wrap around to the next line, you wouldn't really want to do this.

The Spc function has a syntax similar to the Tab function:

Spc(*Integer%*)

This function inserts the specified number of spaces into a line, starting at the current print position and using spaces the width of an average character. The value inside the parentheses can't be negative.

The Format Function

If you've run the mortgage program from Chapter 5 or have been experimenting on your own, you have probably decided that the answers to simple calculations look strange. You may end up with 16 decimal digits when you really want the answer to look like 1.01, for example. You can overcome this problem by replacing the Str function with a new function called the Format function. This function works with a number and a template (also called a format string). The syntax is

Format(*NumericExpression,FormatString$*)

and this gives you a copy of the original expression in the form of a string that has the correct format. For example,

```
Me.Print Format(123.456789,"###.##")
```

yields a string "123.46" that will be printed on the form. When you use a format string like this, Visual Basic rounds the number off so there are only two digits after the decimal point. The Format function, unlike the Str function, does not leave room for an implied + sign in front of the number. This means that in a statement like

```
Me.Print "The interest rate is "&Format(Payment,"####.##")
```

the extra space after the word "is" is essential.

In general, a # is the placeholder for a digit, except that leading and trailing zeros are ignored. For example,

```
Me.Print Format(123.450,"###.###")
```

yields 123.45. Unlike with QuickBASIC, you don't have to worry about having too few #s before the decimal point in the format string. Visual Basic will print all the digits to the left of the decimal point. This way you can concentrate on deciding the number of decimals you want displayed and adjust the format string accordingly.

If you want to have Visual Basic display leading and trailing zeros, use a zero in place of the # in the format string. For example,

```
Me.Print Format(123.450,"000.000")
```

yields 123.450 or

```
Me.Print Format(123.450,"0000.000")
```

would give you 0123.450.

You may want to display numbers with commas every three digits. For this, place a comma between any two-digit placeholders. For example,

```
Me.Print Format(123456789.991,"#,#.##")
```

yields 123,456,789.99.

One subtle point about using the comma at the end of a format string. Each comma you use has the effect of eliminating three of the digits. This is occasionally useful in scaling numbers. For example, if your program deals with Japanese yen and you need to display one hundred million yen, you might want to write 100 million yen rather than 100,000,000 yen. To do this, you use the following statement:

```
Me.Print Format(100000000,"#00,,")&" million yen"
```

Combining the # with the two commas ensures that trailing zeros are suppressed. More generally, if you place multiple commas immediately to the left of the decimal point, Visual Basic interprets this to mean it should skip as many groups of three digits as fall between the comma and the decimal point (or between the commas).

If you need to display a symbol, such as -, +, $, (,), or a space, you use it in the format string exactly in the place you want it to occur. For example, if you want to have a dollar sign in front of a value, use this:

```
Me.Print Format(Amount,"$###.##")
```

You can use the Format function in any Visual Basic statement that expects a string—not only with the Print method. For example:

```
M$ = "Your balance is " & Format(CurrentBalance, "$###.##")
MsgBox M$
```

NOTE: VB has some simplified functions for formatting that don't use format strings. They are not as flexible as the tried and true Format function and were added primarily for compatibility with VBScript. For this reason, I'll describe them in Chapter 25 on VBScript.

6

Predefined Format Strings

Visual Basic makes it even easier to deal with the most common formatting situations by adding what are called *named formats* to the Format function. For example, you can use a statement like

```
Me.Print Format(Amount, "Currency")
```

instead of

```
Me.Print Format(Amount, "###,###.##")
```

and you will get the same results in the United States. This is because the Currency named format is (in the United States) defined to be the same as the ###,###.## format (that is, commas when needed and always two places to the right of the decimal point).

NOTE: One advantage to using named formats is that Visual Basic automatically adjusts things like the thousands separator and the currency symbol to reflect the country in which the program is being run.

In particular, using Format(*Amount*, "Currency") works better for products that are going to be used in more than one country!

The following table summarizes the predefined numeric formats. You simply have to use the name in the first column in quotes in the second position of the Format function.

Name of Format	Description
General Number	Gives you a string of digits with no thousands separator.
Currency	Uses the appropriate thousands separator and displays two digits to the right of the decimal point.
Fixed	Displays at least one digit to the left and two digits to the right of the decimal point.
Standard	Uses the appropriate thousands separator, and at least one digit to the left and two digits to the right of the decimal point.
Percent	Gives you the number in percentage form (that is, multiplied by 100 with a % sign after it). Always displays two digits to the right of the decimal point.
Scientific	Uses Visual Basic's version of scientific notation.
Yes/No	Displays No if the number is 0; otherwise, displays Yes.
True/False	Displays False if the number is 0; otherwise, displays True.
On/Off	Displays Off if the number is 0; otherwise, displays On.

NOTE: See Chapter 25 for the Format Number function that is occasionally useful.

The following table gives you the various formats for dates and times. Again, the advantage to using them is that Visual Basic will automatically adjust the format for the current locality.

Name of Format	Description
General Date	Displays a date and/or time. If there is no fractional part, you get a date. If there is no integer part, you get a time. If there are both, you get both.
Long Date	Displays a date using the format that Windows uses for full dates.

Name of Format	Description
Medium Date	Displays a date using the middle date format.
Short Date	Displays a date using the short date format.
Long Time	Displays a time with the hours, minutes, seconds.
Medium Time	Displays time in 12-hour format using only hours and minutes and AM/PM.
Short Time	Displays the time using a 24-hour clock.

If you start up a new project and use the following Form_Load event procedure in it, then when you run the program, you can see the various date and time formats at work, as shown in Figure 6-2. (Of course, since the demo program uses the Now function, what you see depends on when you run it.)

```
Private Sub Form_Load()
  Show
  Me.Font.Size = 12
  Me.Print Format(Now, "General Date")
  Me.Print Format(Now, "Long Date")
  Me.Print Format(Now, "Medium Date")
  Me.Print Format(Now, "Short Date")
  Me.Print Format(Now, "Long Time")
  Me.Print Format(Now, "Medium Time")
  Me.Print Format(Now, "Short Time")
End Sub
```

6

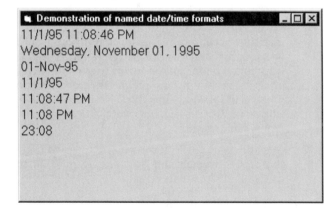

Demonstration
of named
date/time
formats
Figure 6-2.

In earlier versions of Visual Basic it was often useful to set up string constants for the various format strings. This is still useful if you have a custom format that is not one of the named formats. For example, when you have to format values repeatedly, it's worth first setting up a constant such as:

```
Const INFLATION_MONEY = "#00,,"
```

From that point on you can write

```
Format(Amount, INFLATION_MONEY)
```

which is far more readable and less prone to typos, and which will be easier to modify in the future.

Picture Boxes

You can use picture boxes in many different contexts, not just as passive containers for graphics or icons. The icon in the toolbox for picture boxes looks like a desert scene and is supposed to remind you that this control holds graphical images. Picture boxes, like image controls, can display icons, gifs, jpegs, bitmaps, and Windows metafiles. Here again are short descriptions of what these types of files are:

◆ Bitmaps are graphical images of the screen (or part of the screen). Each dot (or pixel) corresponds to one bit for black-and-white displays and many bits for color or gray-scale displays. Image controls are often used for bitmaps. When bitmaps are stored in a file, the convention is to use a .bmp extension for the filename. The Windows Paintbrush program generates bitmaps, so this is a convenient source of them.

◆ You already saw icon files in Chapters 3 and 4. The appendix to the *Programmer's Guide* supplied with the online help lists the 400 or so icons supplied with Visual Basic.

◆ Instead of a dot-by-dot description of the graphical image, think of Windows metafiles as containing descriptions of how and where to draw the object. Because they describe the picture in terms of circles, lines, and the like, they work much better than bitmaps when you need to shrink or enlarge a graphical image. Many publishing programs (such as Microsoft Publisher) come with libraries of Windows metafiles. No metafiles are supplied with the standard edition of Visual Basic, but over 80 are supplied with the Visual Basic Professional edition.

◆ Gifs and jpegs are both formats widely used on the Internet. Both are compressed formats and jpegs can be quite small (although, in this case, there will be some loss of information).

Note that because picture boxes respond to the Click and Double-click events, you can use them exactly as you would use a command button, although image controls would be a better choice if that is all you are doing with them. On the other hand, for the purposes of displaying information and containing controls, you might want to think of picture boxes as being "forms within forms." For example:

◆ Picture boxes have CurrentX and CurrentY properties, as well as the same Scale properties as forms, so you can accurately position text inside them.

◆ You can mix fonts and font sizes when you print to a picture box.

◆ You can add controls to a picture box by working with the toolbox in the same way that you would add controls to a form. (It is a little more difficult to attach a control to a picture box if it already was on the form. This requires cutting and pasting it into the Picture box at design time or setting the controls Container property to the name of the Picture box at run-time.)

The main difference between picture boxes and forms is that you use the Height and Width properties of the picture box rather than the ScaleHeight and ScaleWidth properties of the form. For example, the following line would let you vertically center a line of text in the current font by resetting the value of CurrentX correctly for the picture box.

```
Picture1.CurrentX = Picture1.Height/2 - TextHeight("A")/2
```

The main advantages to using a picture box rather than a form to display data are that

◆ Information displayed in a picture box will not be obscured by any controls on the form. For this reason they are preferred by experienced VB programmers for displaying information using the Print statement.

◆ Picture boxes are less memory-hungry.

◆ You can have more than one picture box on a single form (for example, this means you can display multiple images and also have multiple regions for text).

Working with Picture Boxes

Picture boxes have over 50 properties and respond to 19 events, and you can use any one of 22 methods for them. Many of the properties are already familiar to you: the font properties control how text appears, Visible and Enabled determine whether the control is responsive or even visible, and so on. One property, AutoSize, which you've seen for labels, is even more important for picture boxes. This is because the amount of the image your picture box will show depends on how large you make the picture box—unless you set the AutoSize property to True. If AutoSize is True, the picture box will automatically resize itself to fit the image. Of course, like text boxes, labels, and command buttons, you can also resize the picture box by manipulating the sizing handles when you select the control at design time.

6

The Cls method works in much the same way for picture boxes as it does for forms: it erases whatever image and text were placed in the picture box while the program was running and resets the CurrentX and CurrentY properties. (You will see shortly how to clear graphics that were placed in a picture box or form at design time by using the LoadPicture statement.)

The Move method lets you move the picture box around at run time. The TextHeight and TextWidth methods are used, as with forms, to accurately size text in order to position it better (using the Scale and CurrentX and CurrentY properties). For more on the methods for picture boxes that are used for graphics (Circle, Line, and so on) and to learn a few subtleties about how picture boxes work when AutoRedraw is on, see Chapter 16.

The picture box events that respond to mouse movements or clicks are covered in Chapter 17. All the remaining events are those like Click, Double-click, or the key events you've already seen.

There are two ways to display an image inside a picture box (or form) at design time. The first is to load a picture by setting the Picture property via the Properties window, just like you did for an image control. Another possibility is to paste a picture directly into the picture box (or form). For example, you may be enamored of a picture you just drew using Paintbrush and want to bring this image inside a Visual Basic project. You do this by using the clipboard. For example, if the picture box is the active control, copy the picture from Paintbrush to the clipboard. Then, in Visual Basic, choose Edit|Paste (ALT+E, P or CTRL+V). Visual Basic then attaches the bitmap to the picture box or form. In particular, when you save the Visual Basic project, the image is saved at the same time. Pictures added at design time do not need to be supplied as individual files, as they would if you wanted to load the picture while the project was running. This is because the information is stored in a file with the extension .frx that is compiled into your project.

Nonetheless, you will occasionally want to add (or allow the user to add) a picture while a Visual Basic project is running. There are also two ways to do this. The first requires you to have the picture already loaded in a form or a picture box on some form in the project. If you are in this situation, you only need to assign the Picture property of one object to the Picture property of the other. For example, suppose you have two picture boxes, Picture1 and Picture2, and Picture1 has an image attached to it and Picture2 does not. Then a line of code like

```
Picture2.Picture = Picture1.Picture
```

copies the image from the first picture box to the second.

More common, however, is using the LoadPicture function to attach a file containing a graphical image to a picture box at run time. The syntax for this function is

PictureBoxName.Picture = LoadPicture([*filename*])

or, for forms:

[*FormName*.]Picture = LoadPicture([*filename*])

If you leave out the optional filename, the current image is cleared from the form or picture box. The filename should include the full path name if the file isn't in the current directory. Unlike the Cls method, which clears images and text placed only while the project is running, the LoadPicture statement without a filename will also clear a picture that was added at design time.

RichTextBoxes

The RichTextBox control that is supplied with most versions of Visual Basic is one of the most useful controls in your toolchest. While it is, so to speak, in your toolchest because the RichTextBox control is a custom control, you will need to add it to the *toolbox* if it is not already there. To do this:

6

1. Choose Project|Components to open the Components dialog box.
2. Choose Microsoft RichTextBox Control 6.0.

The icon for the RichTextBox looks like this on your toolbox:

The RichTextBox control lets you display text with multiple fonts and sizes without having to go out and buy a third-party custom control. Moreover, the RichTextBox is not limited to 32K characters like an ordinary text box.

NOTE: See Chapter 18 for how to save (and retrieve) the information in a RichTextBox control to (and from) a file.

Important Properties for RichTextBoxes

Many of the properties of a RichTextBox are the same as those for the standard TextBox control, which were described in Chapter 4 (for example, MultiLine, ScrollBars, and the like). This section explains the other properties that you will need to manipulate with code in order to take full advantage of the RichTextBox.

The trick in using a RichTextBox control is that you must always remember that you first have to select text (or have the user select it) before you can format it. The three properties that tell you what text is selected are described in the following table.

Property	What It Does
SelLength	Returns or sets the number of characters selected.
SelStart	Returns or sets the starting point of the selected text. (It will tell you the current insertion point if no text is selected.)
SelText	Returns or sets a string equal to the currently selected text. (It gives you a "" if no characters are currently selected.)

For example, if the value of RichTextBox.SelLength is 0, then no text is selected. (See Chapter 20 for more on working with these properties.)

The properties described next all work with the selected text in a RichTextBox and thereby let you change its format. You can also use these properties to read off the format of the currently selected text if necessary. (For the properties of the RichTextBox not covered here, please see the online help.)

All these properties work the same way. They affect the currently selected text and *all text added after the current insertion point until they are changed.*

SelBold, SelItalic, SelStrikethru, SelUnderline   As you might expect, these properties let you control whether text is bold, italic, and so on. For example, to change the currently selected text to bold in a RichTextBox using the default name of RichTextBox1, you might use

```
RichTextBox1.SelBold = True
```

This would make all selected text (and all text added after the current insertion point) bold. And text would continue to be bold until the SelBold property was toggled off with the subsequent statement. (Make sure no text is selected before this statement is processed!)

```
RichtextBox1.SelBold = False
```

SelColor   This property sets the color of the currently selected text and of all text added after the current insertion point. For example:

```
RichText1.SelColor = vbRed
```

would change the color of the selected text to red. (You can also use the &HBBGGRR& codes you saw in Chapter 5.)

SelFontName   This property lets you change the font. For example,

```
RichText1.SelFontName = "Courier"
```

The next chapter shows you how to find out what fonts are available in
your system.

SelFontSize   This property lets you change the size of the currently selected text.
The syntax is

   object.SelFontSize = *Size*

The theoretical maximum value for SelFontSize is 2,160 points.

A RichTextBox Example

As an example of using a RichTextBox control, consider the code needed to activate
Figure 6-3. The idea is pretty simple: all you need to do is modify the currently
selected text. For example, to toggle italic text on and off, you need only a single line
of code:

```
RichTextBox1.SelItalic = Not (RichTextBox1.SelItalic)
```

One tricky feature comes from the fact that Visual Basic defaults to removing the
highlighting from selected text when the focus is removed from a control. (The text
still remains selected when the focus returns—you just can't see that it is still
selected.)

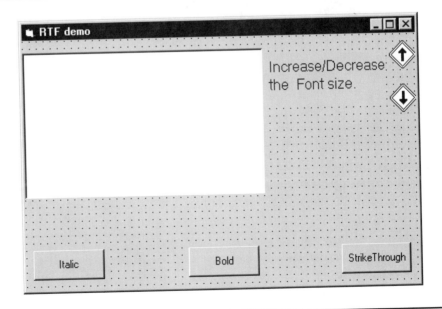

A sample
RichTextBox
project
Figure 6-3.

You can cure this by changing the design-time property called HideSelection to False from its default value of True. This property controls whether Visual Basic removes the highlighting from selected text when the focus shifts from the control.

NOTE: Moving the focus doesn't affect which text is selected; you just lose the highlighting (unless HideSelection is changed to False).

Here are the ASCII descriptions of the form, its controls, and the code needed to activate Figure 6-3. Notice that I simply need to put code in the various Click event procedures of the buttons to change the size/form of the selected text. (I also set the font in the RichTextBox to be Arial so that you can see the changes. Arial can show a change of as little as up one point or down one point—not every font can do this.)

```
VERSION 5.00
Object = "{3B7C8863-D78F-101B-B9B5-04021C009402}#1.1#0"; "RICHTX32.OCX"
Begin VB.Form Form1
    Caption         =   "RTF demo"
    ClientHeight    =   4380
    ClientLeft      =   1800
    ClientTop       =   1500
    ClientWidth     =   7248
    LinkTopic       =   "Form1"
    ScaleHeight     =   4380
    ScaleWidth      =   7248
    Begin RichTextLib.RichTextBox RichTextBox1
        Height      =   3012
        Left        =   240
        TabIndex    =   4
        Top         =   240
        Width       =   3612
        _ExtentX    =   6371
        _ExtentY    =   5313
        _Version    =   393217
        TextRTF     =   $"Rich text box example.frx":0000
        BeginProperty Font {0BE35203-8F91-11CE-9DE3-00AA004BB851}
            Name          =   "Arial"
            Size          =   7.8
            Charset       =   0
            Weight        =   400
            Underline     =   0       'False
            Italic        =   0       'False
            Strikethrough =   0       'False
        EndProperty
    End
    Begin VB.CommandButton cmdStrikeThru
        Caption         =   "StrikeThrough"
```

```
         Height          =     495
         Left            =     5640
         TabIndex        =     2
         Top             =     3720
         Width           =     1215
      End
      Begin VB.CommandButton cmdBold
         Caption         =     "Bold"
         Height          =     495
         Left            =     3000
         TabIndex        =     1
         Top             =     3720
         Width           =     1215
      End
      Begin VB.CommandButton cmdItalic
         Caption         =     "Italic"
         Height          =     495
         Left            =     360
         TabIndex        =     0
         Top             =     3720
         Width           =     1215
      End
      Begin VB.Label Label1
         Caption         =     "Increase/Decrease the  Font size."
         BeginProperty Font

            Name         =     "MS Sans Serif"
            Size         =     12
            Charset      =     0
            Weight       =     400
            Underline    =     0     'False
            Italic       =     0     'False
            Strikethrough =    0     'False
         EndProperty
         Height          =     735
         Left            =     4200
         TabIndex        =     3
         Top             =     360
         Width           =     2040
      End
      Begin VB.Image imgFontDecrease
         Height          =     384
         Left            =     6300
         Picture         =     "Rich text box example.frx":00CD
         Top             =     840
         Width           =     384
      End
      Begin VB.Image imgFontIncrease
         Height          =     384
         Left            =     6300
         Picture         =     "Rich text box example.frx":050F
         Top             =     120
```

```
      Width            =    384
   End
End
Attribute VB_Name = "Form1"
Attribute VB_GlobalNameSpace = False
Attribute VB_Creatable = False
Attribute VB_PredeclaredId = True
Attribute VB_Exposed = False

Option Explicit

Private Sub Form_Load()
  Dim Message As String
  Message = "You can select text after you type in the box and "
  Message = Message & "then click on one of the butttons to see the changes
  go into effect."
  MsgBox Message
End Sub
Private Sub Command1_Click()


  RichTextBox1.SelItalic = Not (RichTextBox1.SelItalic)
End Sub


Private Sub cmdBold_Click()
  RichTextBox1.SelBold = Not (RichTextBox1.SelBold)
End Sub


Private Sub cmdItalic_Click()
    RichTextBox1.SelItalic = Not (RichTextBox1.SelStrikeThru)
End Sub
Private Sub cmdStrikeThru_Click()
  RichTextBox1.SelStrikeThru = Not (RichTextBox1.SelStrikeThru)
End Sub


Private Sub imgFontIncrease_Click()
  RichTextBox1.SelFontSize = RichTextBox1.SelFontSize + 1
End Sub



Private Sub imgFontDecrease_Click()
  RichTextBox1.SelFontSize = RichTextBox1.SelFontSize - 1
End Sub


Private Sub Form_QueryUnload(Cancel As Integer, _
UnloadMode As Integer)
  Unload Me
  End
End Sub
```

The Printer Object

Visual Basic uses the printer that is currently set up as the default printer in the Control Panel. (See below for how to change the default printer from within a VB program.) Visual Basic makes it easy to use whatever resolution, font properties, and so on that the printer driver in Windows can coax from the printer.

First, you have already seen the PrintForm command, which sends a screen dump of a form to the printer. If your application has more than one form, then you have to use the form name in this command:

FormName.PrintForm

Because this command does a bit-by-bit dump of the whole form (including captions and borders), it lacks flexibility. Moreover, most printers have higher resolution than the screen.

Most of the printer commands in Visual Basic are page oriented. This means that Visual Basic calculates all the characters (actually dots) that will appear on a page before it sends the information to the printer. This allows you to have complete control over the appearance of the printed page.

6

The usual way to send information to a printer is the Print method applied to the Printer object. For example, because the Print method is page oriented, you can set the CurrentX and CurrentY properties to precisely position text or even dots on a page. The syntax used to send text to the printer is similar to that used for Forms or picture boxes:

Printer.Print *TextToPrint*

Semicolons and commas also work the same way they do for forms. The semicolon suppresses the automatic carriage return/line feed combination; the comma moves to the next free print zone (still 14 columns apart in the average character width of the current font). The Tab and Spc functions also work the same.

You control the font properties in the same way as for forms and picture boxes. For example:

```
Printer.Font.Name = "Script"          'Use script font
Printer.Font.Size = 18                '18 point type
```

As with printing to forms, font changes on a printer are not retroactive. They affect only text printed after Visual Basic processes the change.

Useful Properties and Methods for the Printer

If you check the online help, you'll see that there are 40 properties and 12 methods for the Printer object. Most of the ones that are unfamiliar to you, such as DrawMode, apply to graphics (see Chapter 16). The vast majority, however, should be familiar because you've seen them for forms. What follow are short descriptions of some printer properties and methods you will use most often. (Check the online help for the printer properties not covered here as well as for the symbolic constants you need to work with the various printer properties not discussed here.)

ColorMode   This property lets you determine whether a color printer prints in color or monochrome. The two possibilities are shown in the following table.

Symbolic Constant	Value	Description
vbPRCMMonochrome	1	Prints output in monochrome
vbPRCMColor	2	Prints output in color

Copies   This property lets you set the number of copies to be printed.

Height, Width   These properties give you the height and width of the paper in the printer as reported by Windows. This is measured in twips, regardless of how you set the scale properties. You can't change these at run time; they are read-only properties. One example of how you might use these properties is to make sure that someone has switched to wider paper before printing something that would not fit on the usual 8 1/2 × 11-inch paper. (For 8 1/2 × 11-inch paper, Visual Basic reports an available width of 12,288 twips and an available height of 15,744 twips.)

EndDoc   This method tells Windows that a document is finished. The syntax is

    Printer.EndDoc

This releases whatever information there is about the page or pages still in memory and sends it to the Windows Print Manager for printing.

NewPage   This method ends the current page and tells the printer to move to the next page. The syntax is

    Printer.NewPage

Page   This property keeps track of the number of pages printed in the current document. The counter starts over at 1 after Visual Basic processes a statement with EndDoc. It increases by 1 every time you use the NewPage method or when the information you send to the printer with the Print method didn't fit on the previous page. A common use of this property is to print a header at the top of each page.

PrintQuality   This property is used to set the quality of the printed output—if the printer driver supports it. The syntax is

    Printer.PrintQuality = *value*

where you can use four built-in constants, as described in the following table.

Constant	Value	Description
vbPRPQDraft	–1	Draft resolution
vbPRPQLow	–2	Low resolution
vbPRPQMedium	–3	Medium resolution
vbPRPQHigh	–4	High resolution

NOTE: You can also set the value to the number of dots per inch if the printer (and its driver) supports this.

6

The Printers Collection

The Printer object is defined to be the current default printer. The Printers collection, on the other hand, lets you access all the printer drivers stored in the system. (For example, there might be a fax driver installed.) The number of printers installed is

```
Printers.Count
```

The syntax for accessing an element of the Printers collection is simply,

Printers(*index*)

where *index* is a number from 0 to Printers.Count-1.

NOTE: You can actually change the default printer directly from Visual Basic. This is done with the Set command. For example, if you have WinFax 8.0 then the following line would let you use WinFax as the default printer (and thus actually fax documents).

```
Set Printer = "WinFax 8.0"
```

(You'll see more about the Set command in Chapter 13.)

As another example the following Form_Load uses the For-Next statement, which you will see in the next chapter, to find out if any of the printers in a user's system are set up to print in color. If one is, a message box pops up to notify the user of this fact. (Once you learn a few more commands, you could easily add the code necessary to allow the user to change the default printer to the color printer.)

```
Sub Form_Load()
For I = 1 To Printers.Count -1
    If Printers(I).ColorMode = vbPRCMColor Then
      MsgBox "At least one printer has a color mode"
    End If
Next I
End Sub
```

NOTE: You can only set the properties of the current default printer.

Printing Information in a RichTextBox

The SelPrint method of a RichTextBox lets you print the current *formatted* contents of a RichTextBox on the current printer. If the user has selected text in the RichTextBox control, then the SelPrint method sends only the selected text to the printer. If no text is selected, the entire contents of the RichTextBox are sent to the printer. The syntax is a little silly. You first have to print a null string to the Printer in order to "wake it up." You then have to use something called the *device context* of the current printer to tell Windows where to send the information. (A device context is just an integer that Windows uses to identify the object.)

The actual code you need looks like this:

```
Printer.Print ""
RichTextBox1.SelPrint(Printer.hDC)
```

(The hDC property of the Printer object gets its device context ID. It is needed here for some arcane reasons specific to Windows that aren't worth getting into.)

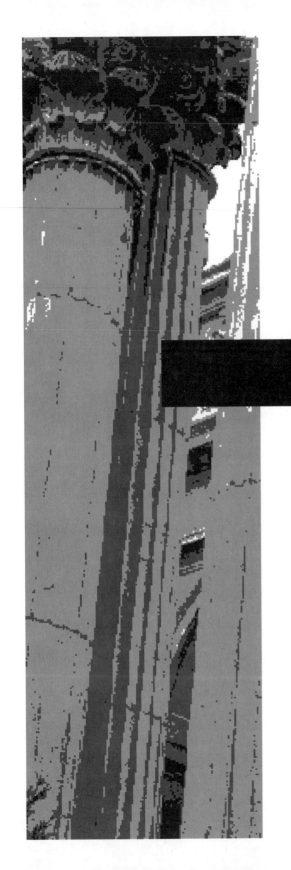

CHAPTER 7

Controlling
Program Flow

Computers derive part of their amazing power from their ability to repeat operations hundreds, thousands, or even millions of times. But they can do far more than repeat an operation a fixed number of times. You can easily write the code that tells the computer to continue repeating an operation *until* it reaches a target or *while* some condition is true (or false, for that matter),and this chapter will show you how to code all these possibilities.

The buzzword for code that repeats an operation is a *loop*. Thus, repeating an operation a fixed number of times is called a *determinate loop*. Continuing until you reach a predetermined specific goal or until certain initial conditions have finally changed is called an *indeterminate loop*. Visual Basic allows all three kinds of loops, so there are three different control structures in Visual Basic for repeating operations.

The other situation you will find yourself needing to frequently code is the programming equivalent of the "if this is true do X otherwise do Y". ("If-Then"s, for short.) The code for this is often called a *conditional* (*branching* is another word for the same action). This chapter also shows you how to program the standard conditionals used in Visual Basic.

 **N**OTE: The parts of a programming language that let you repeat operations or make decisions are often called *control structures*. If you see this term elsewhere, keep in mind that they have nothing to do with the controls you place on forms in Visual Basic.

Determinate Loops

Suppose you want to print the numbers 1 to 10 on the current form inside an event procedure. The simplest way to do this is to place the following lines of code inside the procedure:

```
Dim I As Integer
For I = 1 To 10
  Print I
Next I
```

In the preceding example, the line with the For and To keywords is shorthand for "for every value of I from 1 to 10." You can think of a For-Next loop as winding up a wheel inside the computer so the wheel will spin a fixed number of times. You can tell the computer what you want it to do during each spin of the wheel.

For and Next are keywords that must be used together. The statements between the For and the Next are usually called the body of the loop, and the whole control structure is called, naturally enough, a For-Next loop.

The keyword For sets up a counter variable, which can be a variable of any Visual Basic numeric type. In the preceding example, the counter is an integer variable: I.

Notice how the starting value for the counter in this example is set to 1. The ending value is set to 10. Having set the stage, here's what happens:

1. Visual Basic first sets the counter variable to the starting value.
2. Then it checks whether the value for the counter is less than or equal to the ending value.
3. If the value is greater than the ending value, it does nothing.
4. If the starting value is less than or equal to the ending value, Visual Basic processes all the subsequent statements until it comes to the keyword Next.
5. At that point it adds 1 to the counter variable and starts the process again.
6. This process continues until the counter variable is larger than the ending value. At that point, the loop is finished, and Visual Basic moves past it to the next statement after the keyword "Next".

Figure 7-1 shows a flow diagram for the For-Next loop.

T **IP:** Whenever possible (as I did), choose integer or, if necessary, long integer variables for the counter in a For-Next loop. This allows Visual Basic to spend as little time as possible on the arithmetic needed to change the counter and so speeds up the loop.

7

Finally, you may have noticed that I indented the body of the For-Next loop. As always, the purpose of spacing in a program is to make the program more readable for people and therefore easier to debug; Visual Basic doesn't care.

T **IP:** The designers of Visual Basic make it easy to consistently indent code. The Visual Basic editor defaults to remembering the indentation of the previous line, and every time you press ENTER, the cursor returns to the spot directly below the beginning of the previous line. To move the cursor to the left, you can use the LEFT ARROW key. Or if you get into the habit of using the TAB key to start each level of indentation, you can use the SHIFT+TAB combination to move backward one tab stop. In fact, if you use the TAB key to indent, you can undo the indentation pattern by selecting the block of text and then pressing SHIFT+TAB.

Off-by-One Errors
The most common type of error when using For-Next loops is the *off-by-one error*. When you have this kind of coding error, instead of performing an operation, say, 500 times as you had planned, the program seems to perform it 499 or 501 times.

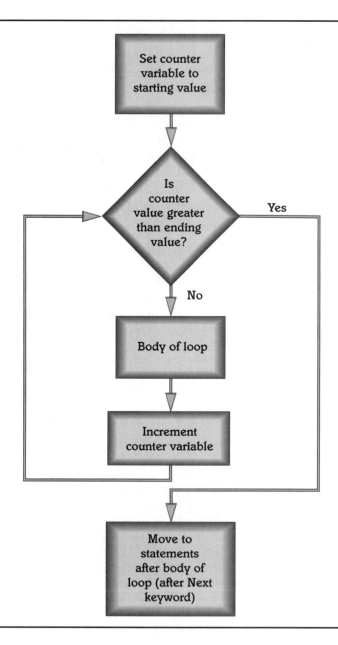

Flow diagram of
For-
Next loop
Figure 7-1.

NOTE: Off-by-one errors are sometimes called *fencepost* errors. This is because many people get the answer wrong if asked how many fenceposts (or how many shelves) are needed to build a fence (or a bookcase). For example, a five shelf bookcase actually needs *six* shelves because of the one for the top.

Here's an example of code that has a fencepost error in it. You want to calculate how much you will have if you start with $1,000 and save $1,000 a year for 10 years so you write.

```
For I = 1 To 10
  Savings = Savings + 1000
Next I
```

Do you see why this is "off by one"? The reason is that you forgot the initial amount—"year 0". Here's the correct code:

```
For I = 0 To 10
  Savings = Savings + 1000
Next I
```

Although this is a trivial example, surprisingly enough, forgetting "year 0" (or putting it in when you don't need it) is a common cause of off-by-one errors.

For more serious off-by-one errors, the debugging techniques in Chapter 15 can help you pinpoint the fault in the loop. Obviously, it's best to avoid off-by-one errors in the first place. One way to do this is to keep in mind that the loop starts at the counter and ends only when the counter *exceeds* (and not equals) the test value (that is, the range is inclusive).

Example: A Retirement Calculator

With a For-Next loop, you can compute many financial quantities without knowing any formulas or using the sophisticated functions built into VB (see Chapter 8 for these). For example, suppose you wanted to write a program that would allow users to enter the following:

◆ The fixed amount of money they think they can put away for retirement each year

◆ The interest rate they expect to get each year

◆ The number of years until retirement

The program would then tell them how much money they will have when they retire. There are sophisticated formulas involving geometric progressions for this sort of calculation, but common sense (and a very simple For-Next loop) suffices. What happens is that each year you get interest on the previous amount, and you add the new amount to it.

Assume that the interest is compounded annually. Then this program will need four text boxes, four labels, and two command buttons. The screen in Figure 7-2 shows the form.

The control names for the text controls in the program should be self-documenting: txtAmountPerYear, txtInterestRate, txtNumberOfYears, and txtNestEgg. Set the Locked property of the txtNestEgg button to True and the TabStop property to be False, since you don't want people to be able to edit the contents of this box. The

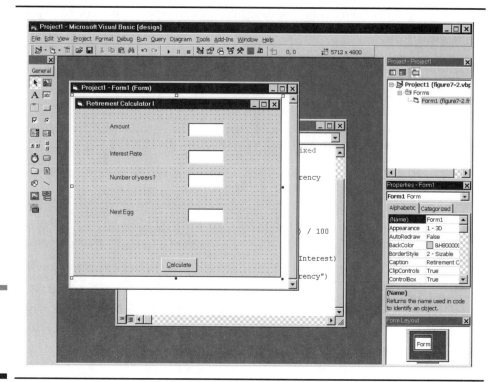

Form for
calculating
retirement
income
Figure 7-2.

command button should be named cmdCalculate with a Caption property of
&Calculate to allow for an access key.

Here is the cmdCalculate_Click procedure that does everything:

```
Private Sub cmdCalculate_Click()
'Calculate retirement value assuming fixed
'deposit and fixed interest rate

  Dim Amount As Currency, Total As Currency
  Dim Interest As Single
  Dim Years As Integer, I As Integer

  Total = 0
  Amount = CCur(txtAmountPerYear.Text)
  Interest = CSng(txtInterestRate.Text) / 100
  Years = CInt(txtNumberOfYears.Text)
  For I = 1 To Years
    Total = Amount + Total + (Total * Interest)
  Next I
  txtNestEgg.Text = Format(Total, "Currency")
End Sub
```

The new total is derived from the previous year by adding the interest earned to the previous total amount.

By the way, some people would say this loop has an off-by-one error. Try it for one year with $1,000 and 10% interest. You should see $1,000 as the answer! So, does this loop have an off-by-one error? The answer is no, it is simply not a well enough documented routine. My code (and I) assumes that you put your retirement money in on December 31 of the current year. If you do this, you would forgo any interest on the money you deposited for that year. (Which is why brokerage firms always advertise, "put your retirement money in your retirement plan on January 1 of the current year, not on April 15 of the following year"!) So, in this case what I should have done is change the comments (documentation) to show that I was aware of the possibility of confusion and that this was not a "bug" but rather a "feature." For example:

```
Private Sub cmdCalculate_Click()
'Calculate retirement value assuming fixed deposit
'and fixed interest rate. Assumes the deposit was
'made on December 31, so no interest was received
'in the year of the deposit
```

More on For-Next Loops

7

You don't always count by ones. Sometimes it's necessary to count by twos, by fractions, or backward. You do this by adding the Step keyword to a For-Next loop. The Step keyword tells Visual Basic to change the counter by the specified amount rather than by 1, as was done previously.

For example, a space simulation program would not be complete without the inclusion, somewhere in the program, of the fragment:

```
Dim I As Integer
For I = 10 To 1 Step -1
  Print "It's t minus " &  I &  " and counting."
Next I
Print "Blastoff!"
```

When you use a negative step, the body of the For-Next loop is bypassed if the starting value for the counter is smaller than the ending value, and it continues until the counter is less than the ending value.

CAUTION: Loops with fractional Step values will run more slowly than loops with integer Step values, as will loops with Variants for counters—even if they are integers.

Example: Improving the Mortgage Calculator

Here's a more serious example. Let's modify the mortgage program from Chapter 5 to add a multiline text box that can show a table with various interest rates 1 percent above and below the rate initially selected. (Let's name the command button cmdCalculate again.) This new form (see Figure 7-3) will contain a labeled, multiline text box with vertical scroll bars added at design time. Let's call this text box txtMortgageTable.

All the work is done in the cmdCalculate_Click procedure attached to the command button. The code for this example may seem long, but most of the complications relate to formatting the display nicely. Essentially, what you need to do is enclose the original formula in a For-Next loop with a step of 1/8% = 1/800 = .00125.

Ideally, this kind of application should be written using a grid control. You'll see how to do this in Chapter 11. Because you haven't seen the grid control yet, this program changes the font to a non-proportionally spaced font (Courier New) in order to make alignment look acceptable. I do that in the Form_Load.

```
Private Sub Form_Load()
  lblMortgageTable.Font.Name = "Courier New"
  txtMortgageTable.Font.Name = "Courier New"
  lblMortgageTable.Caption = "Interest Rate" & Space$(18) & "Payment"
End Sub
```

Here's the code for the cmdCalculate_Click procedure:

```
Private Sub cmdCalculate_Click()
  'Calculates a mortgage table using original amounts
  'but having the interest rate move up by 1/8%
  'local variables and constants
  Dim SpaceChar As String, T$
  Dim Years As Integer, Payment As Currency
  Dim MonthInt As Single, Principal As Currency
  Dim Percent As Single, Interest As Single
  Dim StartInterest As Single, EndInterest As Single
  Const DAMOUNT = "###.00"
  Const IRATE = "00.00%"

 'Get info
 Years = CInt(txtMortgageTerm.Text)
 Principal = CCur(txtMortgageAmount.Text)
 Percent = CInt(txtInterestRate.Text) / 100
 StartInterest = Percent - 0.01               '1% change
 EndInterest = Percent + 0.01

 For Interest = StartInterest To EndInterest Step 0.00125
   MonthInt = Interest / 12
   Payment = Principal * MonthInt / (1 - (1 / (1 + MonthInt)) _
^ (Years * 12))
```

```
    T$ = T$ & Format$(Interest, IRATE) & Space$(25) + _
Format$(Payment, DAMOUNT) & vbCrLf
  Next Interest
  txtMortgageTable.Text = T$
End Sub
```

The program starts with the Dim statements that declare the variables. Next come the string constants for the Format$ command; for example, the IRATE constant displays the interest rate as a two-place decimal percent. Next comes the code for extracting the information from the text boxes on the original form. Then, because it is much faster to build a string up rather than to change the text property of a text box repeatedly, the code inside the For-Next loop adds to the string T$. After the For-Next loop finishes, I change the text property of the multiline text box to T$.

Example: The Screen Object and the Printer Object

Another good example of a For-Next loop gives you a list of the fonts available to Windows. You can do this by using a simple For-Next loop to analyze a property of the Screen or Printer object. The Screen object is one that you will use frequently within Visual Basic. For example, it will let you manipulate forms by their placement on the screen. For our example you need two properties of the Screen object. The first

7

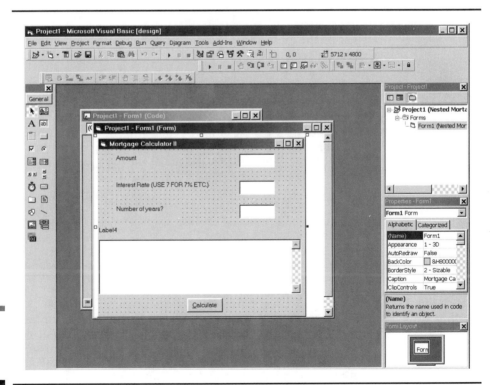

Form for mortgage calculator

Figure 7-3.

is the FontCount property, which gives you the number of available fonts that the printer or screen has available:

```
NumberOfScreenFonts = Screen.FontCount
NumberOfPrinterFonts = Printer.FontCount
```

The second property that you need is the Fonts property. Screen.Fonts(0) is the first font for your display, Screen.Fonts(1) is the second, and so on, up to Screen.Fonts(FontCount - 1), which is the last. All this information is determined by how Windows was set up and by the hardware and software you have.

To run this program, create a new project with a blank form. Add the Click procedure given here, press F5, and then click anywhere in the form.

```
Sub Form_Click()
  Dim I As Integer
  WindowState = 2
  Print "Here is a list of the fonts for your display."
  For I = 0 To Screen.FontCount - 1
    Font.Name = Screen.Fonts(I)
    Print "This is displayed in ";Screen.Fonts(I)
  Next I
End Sub
```

To report on the fonts that Windows can pull out of your printer, change the keyword Screen to the keyword Printer.

TIP: The Screen object also supports the Height and Width properties. These give you the height and width of the physical screen, in twips, as reported by Windows. You can use these properties to adjust the size of a window to fit the screen on which it is running. For example, use the following code if you want to have the Form_Load( ) procedure initialize the size of the form that Visual Basic is loading to be 50 percent of the full screen:

```
Sub Form_Load()
Me.Width = Screen.Width/2
  Me.Height = Screen.Height/2
End Sub
```

Nested For-Next Loops

Suppose you want to allow not only a range of interest rates in the mortgage table but also a range of dollar amounts, with horizontal scroll bars to move through the information. For each dollar amount, you want to run through an entire range of interest rates. This is a typical situation: you have an inner loop that does something interesting in a particular case, and you want to alter the situation to address a slightly different case. Placing one loop inside another is called *nesting* loops.

You'll see how to solve the mortgage problem a little later in this section. For now, though, let's look at a simpler example of a multiplication table. A fragment such as

```
For I% = 2 To 12
  Print 2*I%
Next I%
```

gives you the "twos table." To get an entire multiplication table, you need to enclose this loop with another one that changes the 2 to a 3, the 3 to a 4, and so on. The loop now looks like this:

```
For J% = 2 To 12
  For I% = 2 To 12
    Print I%*J%,
  Next I%
  Print
Next J%
```

Here's what is happening: The value of J% starts out at 2, and then Visual Basic enters the inner loop. The value of I% starts out at 2 as well. Now Visual Basic makes 11 passes through the loop before it finishes. Once it does this, it processes the extra Print statement before it processes the Next J% statement. At this point Visual Basic changes the value of J% to 3 and starts the process all over again.

7

Sometimes it's helpful to think of the inner loop in a nested For-Next loop as really doing one thing—that is, as a statement in Visual Basic a bit more complicated than the usual ones. If you keep in mind the idea of the inner loop of a nested For-Next loop as accomplishing one task, then outlining the nested loops needed to modify the mortgage program given in the previous section is easy. Here it is:

> For *Principal* = *StartingAmount* To *EndingAmount* Step 1000
>   The original loop with new display statements & principal modified
> Next *Principal*

Nested loops have a reputation for being hard to program, hard to understand, and a breeding ground for bugs. This need not be true. If you are careful about outlining the loops, they won't be hard to program. If you are careful about your indentation pattern, they won't be hard to read and understand (or, therefore, to debug).

The rule for nesting For-Next loops is simple: The inner loop must be completed before the Next statement for the outer loop is encountered. You can have triple-nested loops, quadruple-nested loops, or even more. You are limited only by how well you understand the logic of the program, not by Visual Basic.

The Mortgage Program Redone One More Time

Although we are certainly getting near the practical limits of a multiline text box and really should be using a grid control, here's the code for a version of the mortgage calculator program that wraps the previous code in a loop in the obvious way. All it does is add a changeable amount to the text window. The lines I needed to add and modify are in bold.

```
Private Sub cmdCalculate_Click()
  'Calculates a mortgage table using a band around the original
  'amounts and has the interest rate move up by 1/8%
  'local variables and constants
  Dim SpaceChar As String, T$
  Dim Years As Integer, Payment As Currency
  Dim MonthInt As Single, Principal As Currency
  Dim Percent As Single, Interest As Single
  Dim StartInterest As Single, EndInterest As Single
  Dim Amount As Currency, StartAmount As Currency
  Dim EndAmount As Currency

  Const DAMOUNT = "###.00"
  Const IRATE = "00.00%"

  'Get info
  Years = CInt(txtMortgageTerm.Text)
  Principal = CCur(txtMortgageAmount.Text)
  Percent = CInt(txtInterestRate.Text) / 100
  StartInterest = Percent - 0.01              '1% change
  EndInterest = Percent + 0.01
StartAmount = Principal - 25000
EndAmount = Principal + 25000
For Amount = StartAmount To EndAmount Step 5000
For Interest = StartInterest To EndInterest Step 0.00125
      MonthInt = Interest / 12
      Payment = Principal * MonthInt / (1 - (1 / (1 + MonthInt)) _
  ^ (Years * 12))
T$ = T$ & Format$(Interest, IRATE) & Space$(20) + _
"for " & Amount & " =" & Space$(7) & _
Format$(Payment, DAMOUNT) & vbCrLf
Next Interest
      txtMortgageTable.Text = T$
Next Amount
End Sub
```

As you can see, not many changes were necessary. (Obviously, a more professional program would let the user scroll horizontally through the amounts at a given interest rate. As I said at the beginning of this section, I'll show you how to do that in Chapter 11 when we cover the grid control.)

Indeterminate Loops

Let's go back to the retirement problem discussed earlier. Instead of asking how much money a person will have at the end of a specified number of years, let's ask how long until the person has $1,000,000—again assuming that the same amount of money is put in each year and that the interest rate doesn't change. You could use the previous program and try trial and error, but there is a more direct approach.

The modified retirement program offers a good example of a task that comes up repeatedly in programming. Loops must either keep on repeating an operation or not, depending on the results obtained within the loop. Such loops are indeterminate—that is, not executed a fixed number of times—by their very nature. You use the following pattern when you write this type of loop in Visual Basic:

    Do
        Visual Basic statements
    Until *condition is met*

Figure 7-4 shows what Visual Basic does in a Do loop.

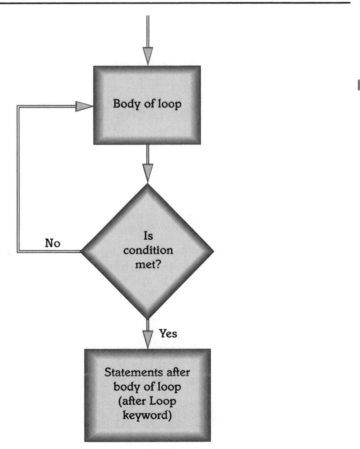

7

Flow diagram
for Do loop (test
at end)

Figure 7-4.

A simple example of this is a password fragment in a Form_Load procedure that starts an application. If you compiled a project to a stand-alone program with a Form_Load procedure that looked like this,

```
Sub Form_Load()
'Password protection
 Dim X$
  Do
    X$ = InputBox$("Password please?")
  Loop Until X$ = "Vanilla Orange"
End Sub
```

it would be more difficult for anyone who didn't know the password to use this program. (It would not be impossible, however; a very experienced programmer could find the password by carefully examining the .exe file, but it wouldn't be easy.)

It's important to remember that the test for equality is strict: typing **VANILLA ORANGE** would not work, nor would **Vanilla orange**. Another point worth keeping in mind is that the test is done only at the end of the loop, when Visual Basic processes the Until statement. If you change the fragment to

```
Sub Form_Load()
Dim X$
 Do
   X$ = "Vanilla Orange"
   X$ = InputBox$("Password please?")
 Loop Until X$ = "Vanilla Orange"
End Sub
```

then, whether you break out of the loop still depends on what the user types in the input box. Initializing the variable to the correct value is irrelevant.

When you write an indeterminate loop, something must change; otherwise the test will always fail and you'll be stuck in an infinite loop. To stop an infinite loop, you can use the CTRL+BREAK combination, or choose End from the Run menu, or use the toolbar. You can also close the application, of course.

Relational Operators

In more sophisticated programs, you need ways to check for something besides equality. You do this by means of the *relational* operators. Here's a table that lists the relational operators:

Symbol	Checks (Tests For)
<>	Not equal to
<	Less than
<=	Less than or equal to

Symbol	Checks (Tests For)
>	Greater than
>=	Greater than or equal to

For strings, these operators test for ANSI order. This means that "A" comes before "B," but "B" comes before "a" (and a space comes before any typewriter character). The string "aBCD" comes after the string "CDE" because uppercase letters come before lowercase letters. (The online help contains a complete ANSI table, which you can find by using the Search button and looking for the ANSI character set.) The ANSI codes from 0 to 31 are for control combinations and include the BACKSPACE and ENTER keys.

NOTE: You can set all comparisons in the code attached to a form to be insensitive to case by putting the statement Option Compare Text in the Declarations section of the form. The Option Compare Text statement uses an order determined by the country set when you install Windows. Use Option Compare Binary to return to the default method of comparing strings by ANSI order.

7

As another example, suppose you wanted to prevent a "divide-by-zero" error when a user enters data in a text box. Use a fragment like this:

```
Do
  N$ = InputBox$("Non-zero number? Please!")
  Number = Val(N$)
Loop Until Number <> 0
```

Or, to test that the first character of a string in a text box is not a space or a control code, use this:

```
Do
  Text$ = Text1.Text
Loop Until Text$ > Chr$(32)
```

These kinds of loops are the first steps for stopping a user from entering the wrong kind of data. Testing input data is one way to begin to bulletproof a program. In fact, a large part of bulletproofing programs (the jargon is "making them robust") requires making them tolerant of input errors. Instead of blowing up because of a typo, they check that the data entered is usable. If not, they warn the user. The more robust a program is, the less likely it is to behave strangely for an inexperienced user. (The section "Example: What Is It?" later in this chapter has more on checking input.)

You can even monitor keystrokes as they are made inside any control that accepts input. For this, see the section "Example: The KeyPress Procedure" later in this chapter.

Example: A "Be a Millionaire" Calculator

Suppose we wanted to write the code that activates the form shown in Figure 7-5. If we call the text boxes txtAmountPerYear and txtInterestRate and the command button cmdCalculate, then the code in the cmdCalculate_Click procedure will look like this:

```
Private Sub cmdCalculate_Click()
  '  Calculate retirement value assuming fixed
  ' deposit and fixed interest rate

  Dim Amount As Currency, Total As Currency
  Dim Interest As Single
  Dim Years As Integer,

  Amount = CCur(txtAmountPerYear.Text)
  Interest = CSng(txtInterestRate.Text) / 100
  Do
    Total = Amount + Total + (Total * Interest)
    Years = Years + 1
  Loop Until Total >= 1000000
  Dim Message As String
  Message = "You will be a millionaire in " & Years
  Message = Message & " years!"
  MsgBox Message
End Sub
```

The body of the loop is much like the one in the retirement program from the beginning of the chapter—figure the yearly change and add it to the previous total to get a new total. This time, however, another counter (Years) keeps track of the number of years. Finally, the loop continues as long as the value of the variable Total is less than 1,000,000. The moment the total equals or exceeds this target, the loop ends and Visual Basic reports the results via a message box.

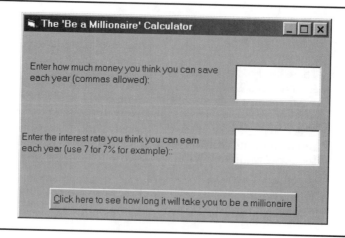

"Be a Millionaire" calculator
Figure 7-5.

A Common Source of Bugs in Indeterminate Loops

You should be aware of a problem that frequently occurs with these new kinds of loops that can lead to a hard-to-track-down bug. Consider this fragment:

```
Total = 0
PassNumber = 0
Do
   Total = Total + .1
   PassNumber = PassNumber + 1
   Print PassNumber, Total
Loop Until Total = 1
```

You might think this program would end after ten passes through the loop, but it doesn't. In fact, this fragment results in an infinite loop, and you need to press the CTRL+BREAK combination or use the toolbar to stop it. This infinite loop occurs for a subtle but important reason. In this fragment, by default, the variant variables get transformed into single-precision variables, and as discussed in Chapter 5, these numbers are only approximations. Visual Basic's internal characterization of .1 is off by a little in, say, the seventh decimal place. As Visual Basic adds .1 to the total, tiny errors accumulate, and the resulting total, although it comes very close to 1, never exactly equals 1. This rule is so important that I want to separate it out from the usual text:

7

> *In indeterminate loops, check only integer and long integer variables for equality!*

What is the cure? This program should be rewritten to allow for a tiny error by changing the test to read

```
Loop Until Total > .99999999
```

or, to be sure that the number is at least 1,

```
Loop Until Total >= 1
```

Changing the test to either case ensures that the program really will stop after ten passes through the loop. Single, double, or variant variables that can be transformed into one of these types, can be checked only to see if they are close (within a certain tolerance) to a number. At the risk of boring you, let me repeat it one more time. The only numeric types you should test for equality are the types that don't have a decimal point: integer, long, byte, and Boolean.

Finally, you may have noticed I left currency variables out of the above discussion. The problem here is that whether or not you can test them for equality depends on how you use them. As I said in Chapter 5, currency variables are completely accurate within their range (15 digits to the right and four to the left of the decimal place). Thus code like

```
Dim Total As Currency
Total = 0
```

```
Do
  Total = Total + 0.001
Loop Until Total = 9.95
```

will work fine (because there are only three digits after the decimal point in the number being added) but code like

```
Dim Total As Currency
Total = 0
Do
  Total = Total + 0.00001
Loop Until Total = 9.95
```

won't work at all (because there are five digits after the decimal point in the number being added).

Sophisticated Indeterminate Loops

A common task is reading a list of names until the last one is encountered (for example, reading names out of a file—see Chapter 18), keeping count all the while. Suppose you are looking through the dictionary and happen to notice that the last entry is the name of an insect: the zyzzyva. You decide you want to add up the number of different types of insects that occur in North America. You take out your entomology book and start running the following code:

```
InsectCount = 0
 Do
    InsectName$ = InputBox("The next insect name?")
    InsectCount = InsectCount + 1
 Loop Until InsectName$ = "zyzzyva"
Print "The number of different types of insects is ";InsectCount
```

Although this fragment may seem like a prototype for code that reads in a list of items until the last one is encountered, you won't always know what the last entry of the list is. It's only a coincidence that the last word in many dictionaries is the name of an American insect. In general, you won't know the last entry, so you're likely to use a group of strange characters (like "ZZZ") to act as a flag. Instead of testing for zyzzyva, you test for a flag.

It's easy to modify the "InsectCount" fragment to test for a flag. Here is a program that does this (but beware, it has a subtle bug):

```
NameCount = 0
Do
  Entry$ = InputBox$("Name - type ZZZ when done")
  NameCount = NameCount + 1
Loop Until Entry$ = "ZZZ"
Print "The total number of names is ";NameCount
```

The problem with this fragment is that it suffers from an off-by-one error! How can you figure this out? Imagine that the list consists of only one name besides the flag.

What happens? Let's work through this program by hand. The user types the first name and the count increases to 1. Next the user types **ZZZ**. However, because the test is only done at the end of the loop, the count increases to 2 before the test is done. Therefore, when the loop ends, the count is 2 when it ought to be 1. One possible cure is to subtract 1 from the count once the loop ends. The trouble with this type of ad hoc solution (in the jargon, a *kludge*—pronounced "klooge") is that the programmer is stuck with constantly figuring out how far off the results of the loops are when they finish, in order to move backward.

Moving backward is a bit silly when Visual Basic makes the cure for this so easy: move the test in the loop to the top. Consider this:

```
NameCount = 0
Entry$ = InputBox$("Name - ZZZ to end")
Do Until Entry$ = "ZZZ"
   NameCount = NameCount + 1
   Entry$ = InputBox$("Name - ZZZ to end")
Loop
```

Now the user types the first name before the loop starts. Once this is done, the program does an initial test. The loop is entered, and 1 starts being added to the counter only if this test fails. (Notice that this kind of loop also works if there is nothing in the list except the flag.) Figure 7-6 shows a picture of what Visual Basic does for this type of loop.

7

TIP: A good rule of thumb is that if you are going to use the flag, put the test at the end; if not, put the test at the beginning.

With the test at the end, the loop is always executed at least once; with the test at the beginning, the loop may not be executed at all. Also remember that when the test is at the top, you obviously must have something to test. Therefore, when the test is done at the beginning, initialize all variables to be tested before the loop starts. Finally, don't forget that you usually need two assignment statements when the test is at the top—the first before the test and the second (to keep the process going) inside the loop.

When nesting Do loops together or when nesting them with For-Next loops, you must follow a rule similar to the one you follow for nesting For-Next loops alone: Inner loops must be finished before the outer loops are tested. Choose a reasonable indenting pattern and you will not have any problems.

Keep in mind that Visual Basic is always asking a True-False question in a Do loop; it's just hidden sometimes. Luckily, all arithmetic operators are done first (they have higher precedence than the relational operators). Visual Basic has no trouble interpreting

```
Loop Until Number*5 > 10
```

as meaning first do the calculation and then do the test (but as always, parentheses make things clearer).

TIP: In situations where the user is entering data by using a click on a command button after each entry, you usually don't have to worry about off-by-one errors in the count at the end if you start the count at 0 before the first piece of data is entered.

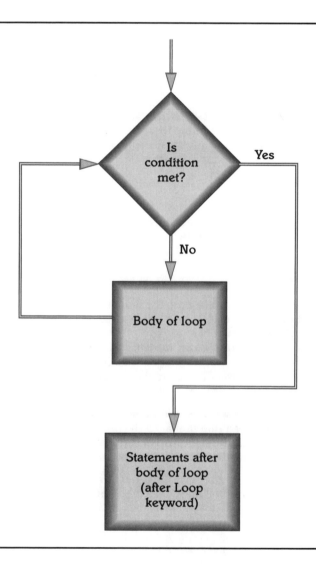

Flow diagram for Do loop (test at beginning)

Figure 7-6.

The Do While Loop

Visual Basic has other kinds of loops. These loops consist of replacing the keyword Until with the keyword While. This new loop may seem superfluous since you can always change a Do Until into a Do While by reversing the relational operator. For example,

```
Do
Loop Until X$ <>""
```

is the same as

```
Do
Loop While X$ = " "
```

and

```
Do
Loop Until Number > 5
```

is the same as

```
Do
Loop While Number <= 5
```

7

Given this, why bother learning this new type of loop? There are two reasons why the While loop isn't superfluous. The first is that, as much as possible, you want to write a program conforming to the way your mind works. Sometimes you will think of an operation as going on until something happens, while other times you think of it as continuing while, as the saying goes, "the status is quo." The richness of Visual Basic's programming language helps make a better fit between your thought patterns and the computer program you're trying to write. In fact, psychologists have found that tests with positive conditions are easier to understand. Do While Number = 0 is easier to process for most people than its counterpart, Do Until Number <> 0.

Do Loops with And, Or, Not

The previous section gave you one reason to use both Do Until and Do While loops, but this is not the only reason. Probably the best reason to use both kinds of loops comes when you have to combine conditions. This is most commonly done with the Or, Not, and And keywords. These three keywords work just like they do in English. You can continue a process as long as both conditions are True or stop it when one turns False. However, it becomes increasingly confusing to try to force combinations of the And, Or, and Not operators into loops that they don't seem to fit. For example, suppose you want to continue a process while a number is greater than zero and a text box is empty. It is much easier to say

```
Do While Number > 0 And Text1.Text = ""
```

than to say

```
Do Until Number <=0 Or Text1.Text <> ""
```

although they both mean the same thing.

The While/Wend Loop

There is one other loop possible in Visual Basic. To preserve compatibility with interpreted BASIC, Visual Basic allows a variant on the Do While loop (that is, the test at the top). Instead of saying

```
Do While X = 0

Loop
```

you can say

```
While X = 0

Wend
```

I don't recommend using a While/Wend though you may see it in code that you are maintaining. This form of a loop is not as flexible as the newer forms. For example, you can't leave a While/Wend loop as easily as you can a Do Loop. (See the section in this chapter called "Combining the If-Then with Loops" for how to do this with Do Loops.)

Making Decisions (Conditionals)

At this point, your programs can only decide whether to repeat a group of statements or not. They can't, as yet, change which statements are processed depending on what the program has already done or what it has just encountered. The next few sections take care of this. All the commands in these sections deal with turning an outline containing a phrase such as

If *condition* Then *do something else...*

into Visual Basic code. Visual Basic uses the If-Then statement in much the same way that you do in normal English. For example, to warn a user that a number must be positive, use a line like this:

```
If X < 0 Then MsgBox "Number must be positive!"
```

More generally, when Visual Basic encounters an If-Then statement, it checks whether the first clause (called, naturally enough, the If clause) is True. If that clause is True, the computer does whatever follows (called the Then clause). If the test fails, processing skips to the next statement.

Just as in the loops from the previous sections, you can use the If-Then statement to compare numbers or strings. For example, a statement such as

```
If A$ < B$  Then Print A$;" comes before ";B$;
```

tests for ANSI order (unless an Option Compare Text statement has been processed), and

```
If A <= B  Then Print A; " is no more than "; B
```

tests for numerical order if A and B are numeric variables.

Example: Using the If-Then with a Message Box

You can use an If-Then to determine which button was pressed in a message box. For instance, assign the value of the MsgBox function to a variable and then use If-Then to check the value. For example:

```
X% = MsgBox ("Yes/No?",vbYesNo)
If X% = vbYes Then Print "Yes button clicked."
```

7

Notice that you need to use parentheses when using MsgBox in this way. The following table lists the constants you might need for working with the return values from a message box.

Symbolic Constant	Value	Button Chosen
vbOK	1	OK
vbCancel	2	Cancel
vbAbort	3	Abort
vbRetry	4	Retry
vbIgnore	5	Ignore
vbYes	6	Yes
vbNo	7	No

The Else

Suppose you need to write a Social Security calculator. The way this tax works is that if you are not self-employed, you and your employer each pay 7.65 percent of your gross salary, up to a limit set by law. According to http://www.ssa.gov/pubs/10094.html, the current limit is $65,400. After that, whether you make $66,000 or $5,550,000 per year, you pay no more social security tax. To write code that would activate this type of calculator, you need to add an "otherwise" clause to your original If-Then. The keyword for this is, naturally enough, the "Else". For our example you'll need to write:

```
If Wages < 65400 Then STax=.0765*Wages Else STax=65400*.0765
```

When Visual Basic processes an If-Then-Else, if the test succeeds, Visual Basic processes the statement that follows the keyword Then (the Then clause). If the test fails, Visual Basic processes the statement that follows the keyword Else (called the Else clause). Figure 7-7 shows you what Visual Basic does with an If-Then-Else in flow-diagram style.

Combining Conditions in an If-Then

You can also use the keywords And, Or, and Not in an If-Then. These let you check two conditions at once. For example, suppose you have to check whether a number is between 0 and 9:

```
If Digit >= 0 And Digit <= 9 Then Print "Ok"
```

The ways of using the And operator should be pretty clear, but one word of caution. In both speaking and writing, we sometimes say, "If my average is greater than 80 and less than 90, then . . .". Translating this sentence construction directly into Visual Basic code won't work. You must repeat the variable each time you want to test something. To do the translation from English to Visual Basic, say, "If my average is greater than 80 and my average is less than 90, then . . . ".

A final note on using the And: you do not have to use the same variable. A statement such as

```
If (Grade4 > Grade3) And Average > 60 Then Print "Improving!"
```

is a perfectly good Visual Basic statement. (The parentheses are there only to improve readability; they are not necessary. As you saw earlier, Visual Basic calculates relational operators before worrying about the logical connectors such as And.)

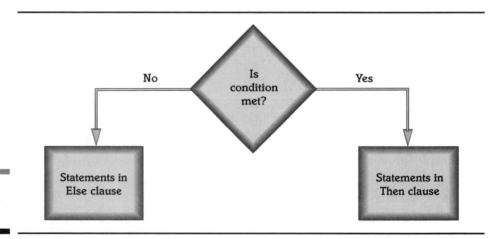

Flow diagram
for If-Then-Else

Figure 7-7.

Using the keyword Or in an If-Then is similar. The test is successful if either one of the conditions is True. Suppose you had to test whether at least one of two numbers was nonzero:

```
If A <> 0 Or B <> 0 Then ...
```

There are other, somewhat less common ways of combining tests. For example, you can use the Eqv (equivalence) operator. This test asks whether two conditions are both True or both False. For example,

```
If (X = True And Y = True) or (X = False And Y = False) ...
```

is the same as

```
If X Eqv Y ...
```

Another useful operator (especially for graphics and file security programs) is the Xor (exclusive Or). This corresponds to the English "if A or B but not both."

Similarly, there's the Not that you've already seen. Choosing to use this depends a lot on personal taste (like deciding between Do While and Do Until). Most people find it easier just to change the relational operators. For example,

7

```
If Not (A$ = "Big Blue")
```

is harder to write than

```
If A$ <> "Big Blue"
```

Similarly,

```
If Not (A > 50)
```

is exactly like

```
If A <= 50
```

If you prefer to use the Not, you'll need parentheses; without them your program is apt to be unreadable.

Since Visual Basic is really testing for a Boolean (True-False) relation in the If clause, you can actually have any Boolean property. For example, in the statement

```
If Text1.Enabled Then ...
```

Visual Basic processes the Then clause only when the Text1 box is enabled.

The Block If-Then

More often than not, you will want to process multiple statements if a condition is True or False. For this you need the most powerful form of the If-Then-Else, called the *block If-Then*. This lets you process as many statements as you like in response to a True condition, as in this example:

```
If I win the lottery Then
    I'm happy
    My family is happy
    And, the tax man is happy.
```

Here, there are three statements in response to something being True. To write this statement in Visual Basic, you use a slightly different format than the usual If-Then. The block If-Then looks like this:

If *thing to test* Then
    lots of statements
Else
    more statements
End If

Now, you do not put anything on the line following the keyword Then; press ENTER immediately after typing it. A bare "Then" is how Visual Basic knows it's beginning a block If-Then. The Else clause is optional; putting it there (again alone on a line) tells VB that another block will follow. It will be processed only if the If clause is False. However, whether the Else is there or not, the block If must end with the keywords End If.

For an example of this, let's modify the original mortgage program in Chapter 5 so the program checks whether the user wants to calculate the payment or the maximum he or she can borrow, depending on which text box is empty. The comments in the following program give the formula you need for this. (You have to do a little algebra on the original formula.)

```
Sub cmdCalculate_Click ()
  ' This calculates the mortgage
  ' Using the formula, Payment =
  ' Principal*MonthInt/(1-(1/(1+MonthInt))^(Years*12))
  ' Principal =
  ' Payment * (MonthInt / (1 - (1 / (1 + MonthInt))^_
  ' (Years * 12)))-1

  Dim Years As Integer, Payment As Currency
  Dim MonthInt As Single, Amount As Currency
  Dim Percent as Single

  ' Get info
  Years = CInt(txtMortgageTerm.Text)
  Principal = CCur(txtMortgageAmount.Text)
  Payment = CCur(txtMortgagePayment.Text)
```

```
   Percent = CSng(txtInterestRate.Text) / 100
   MonthInt = Percent/12
   If Payment = 0 Then
     Payment = Principal * MonthInt / (1 - (1 / (1 + _
     MonthInt))^ (Years * 12))
     txtMortgagePayment.Text = Format$(Payment,"###,###.##")
   Else
     Principal = Payment * (MonthInt / (1 - (1 / (1 + _
     MonthInt))^ (Years * 12)))^-1
     txtMortgageAmount.Text = Format$(Principal,"###,###.##")
   End If
End Sub
```

As usual, the indentation is there to make the program more readable; Visual Basic doesn't care.

Example: What Is It?

You can easily use If-Then to determine whether the user has entered a string in the form of a date or a number. The procedure depends on the variant data type combined with two new Boolean functions (functions that return either True or False). For example, the built-in function IsDate tells you whether an expression can be converted to a date. Consider the following code, which checks whether the contents of a text box are in the right form to be used as a date:

```
Dim DT     ' DT is a variant
DT = Text1.Text
If IsDate(DT) Then
  ' do whatever you want with the date
Else
  MsgBox "Please enter the text in the form of a date!"
End If
```

Similarly, you can use the IsNumeric function to determine whether a variable can be converted to a number. This gives you a quick way of checking for extraneous characters in a string of digits:

```
Dim NT     'NT is a variant
NT = Text1.Text
If IsNumeric(NT) Then
  ' do whatever you want with the number
Else
  MsgBox "Please enter the data in the box as a number!"
End If
```

NOTE: VB will, of course, allow the user to enter a comma or a decimal point and still report True as the value of IsNumeric.

7

Similarly, you can use the VarType function to determine what type of information is being stored in a variant variable (see the online help for more on this function if you will be using variants a lot).

Example: The Dir$ Command

Another good example of where you'll need an If-Then-Else is when, during a program, you have to find out whether a file or files exist with a specific extension. (You can also use a file list box—see Chapter 19.) The functions needed are

Dir$(*filespec*) or Dir(*filespec*)

The difference between the two is that Dir$ returns a string and Dir returns a string stored in a variant. *filespec* is a string expression that contains the filename or file pattern—it is not case sensitive. You can use the two DOS wildcards (? for a single character match and * to allow more characters). You can also include path name information. Each time Visual Basic encounters a Dir$ command with a *filespec*, it returns the first filename it finds that matches the pattern. When no filenames match, Visual Basic returns the empty string. To continue searching for the same pattern, you call the Dir$ function with no pattern.

Here is a program fragment that checks whether the current directory contains any .TXT files:

```
X$ = Dir$("*.TXT")
If X$ = ""  Then
  Print "No text files found"
Else
  Print "First file found is "; X$
End If
```

To find all the files with a .TXT extension, use this:

```
X$ = Dir$("*.TXT")
Do While X$ <> ""   'or While Len(X$)
  Print "Text File found is "; X$
  X$ = Dir$                      'Don't reuse the file spec
Loop
```

Example: The KeyPress Procedure

Almost all Visual Basic objects will recognize when a user presses and then releases a key. If the key that was pressed generates an ordinary ASCII/ANSI code, it triggers the KeyPress event procedure. Not only can this procedure detect what the user types, but you can also use it to change or restrict what the control will accept.

The syntax for this event procedure is a little different than all the event procedures you've seen up to now. The template for the KeyPress event procedure looks like this:

Private Sub ControlName_KeyPress(*KeyAscii* As Integer)

End Sub

Inside the parentheses is the first example of a parameter—the formal name for a placeholder. When Visual Basic detects the user pressing an ASCII key inside a control that recognizes this event, you get a call to this event procedure. Visual Basic replaces the parameter with the ASCII code of the key that generated the event.

For example, a form can detect the KeyPress event if all the controls on it are disabled or invisible, or if the form's KeyPreview property is set to True. If you start a new project with a blank form, change the KeyPreview property to True, and then attach the following event procedure to it,

```
Sub Form_KeyPress(KeyAscii As Integer)
  Cls
  Print "The ASCII code of the key you pressed is " &KeyAscii
  Print
  Print "The character itself is " & Chr$(KeyAscii)
End Sub
```

you'll be able to explore the ASCII codes for the characters you type until you end the program.

On the other hand, if you want to cancel a keystroke, you need only reassign the parameter KeyAscii in the KeyPress event to be zero. For example, use the following to force the user to type a digit between 0 and 9 into a text box:

7

```
Sub Text1_KeyPress(KeyAscii As Integer)
  If KeyAscii < Asc("0") Or KeyAscii > Asc("9") Then
    Beep
    KeyAscii = 0
  End If
End Sub
```

This event procedure absolutely prevents the user from typing anything but a digit inside the text box. The procedure blanks out any other character the user may have typed.

Since you can detect whether a user has typed a comma or more than one decimal point, you can use the KeyPress event procedure to check what he or she types in a text box. The next chapter shows you how to write a procedure that accepts a number but disregards commas, extraneous decimal points, and non-numeric characters.

Example: Working with the QueryUnload Event

One of the most common times you will combine the If-Then with a message box is inside the QueryUnload event. (Recall that this event is triggered whenever someone tries to unload a form. As mentioned in Chapter 5, especially with multiform applications, you will want to put cleanup code in this event.)

The syntax for this event is

Private Sub Form_QueryUnload(*cancel* As Integer, *unloadmode* As Integer)

If you set the *cancel* parameter to a nonzero integer, you prevent the form from closing. Thus, you will often need code like this:

```
Private Sub Form_QueryUnload(cancel As Integer, unloadmode _
As Integer)
Dim YesNo As Integer
YesNo = MsgBox("Are you sure you want to end the program?", vbYesNo)
If YesNo = vbNo Then
  cancel = True
 'cleanup code for resuming goes here
Else
  cancel = False
 'cleanup code for exiting can go here
End If
End Sub
```

The *unloadmode* parameter is used to tell you why the form is unloading. Its values are summarized in the following table.

Constant	Value	Description
vbFormControlMenu	0	The user chose the Close command from the Control menu on the form.
vbFormCode	1	The Unload statement is invoked from code.
vbAppWindows	2	Windows is ending.
vbAppTaskManager	3	The Task Manager is closing the application.
vbFormMDIForm	4	An MDI child form is closing because the MDI form is closing (see Chapter 14).

Combining the If-Then with Loops

Suppose you need to check that there is exactly one file with a .TXT extension in the current directory. To do this, you have to use the Dir$ function, but you need to allow two ways to leave the loop. Here is a fragment that does this:

```
NameOfFile$ = Dir$("*.TXT")
NumberOfFiles = 0
Do Until NameOfFile$ = vbNullString Or NumberOfFiles > 1
  NumberOfFiles = NumberOfFiles + 1
  NameOfFile$ = Dir$
Loop
If NumberOfFiles = 0 Then Print "No Files Found"
If NumberOfFiles > 1 Then Print "Too Many Files"
```

Notice that Visual Basic enters the loop only if it finds an example of the file. You have to allow for the loop never being entered at all. Once the loop is entered, you have Visual Basic add 1 to the file count.

These kinds of loops are so common that computer scientists gave them a special name, *Eureka loops*, after Archimedes' famous bathtub experience. You set up a loop to end if either one of two situations prevails. Then you follow the loop by a test for what actually took place.

Another example of this type of loop would occur if you modified the program that calculated how long it would take to build up a $1,000,000 nest egg to end either if the number of years until you retired was exceeded or you reached the $1,000,000 goal.

Exiting a Loop Prematurely

You can use the If-Then to give you a way to write a loop that "tests in the middle." For this, you combine the If-Then with a new command: the Exit Do. Whenever Visual Basic processes the Exit Do statement, it pops you out of the loop, directly to the statement following the keyword Loop.

More generally, Visual Basic allows you to set up a potentially infinite loop at any time; just leave off the tests in a Do loop (an unadorned Do at the top and an equally unadorned Loop at the bottom). Once you've done this, the loop will end only when Visual Basic processes an Exit Do statement. (During program development, you can always end the program prematurely from the Run menu, and you can also use the toolbar or CTRL+BREAK combination, of course.) There is a version of the Exit command for leaving a For-Next loop as well; in this case, it takes the form Exit For.

7

Visual Basic places no restriction on the number of Exit statements you place inside a loop, but loops that have 37 different ways to end are awfully hard to debug. As a general rule, most programmers aim for programs that have only "single entry/single exit" loops. They also find it easier to debug programs that have the loop test at the beginning or end of the loop. Most programmers use the Exit Do (or Exit For) only for abnormal exits from loops, such as when a program is about to divide by zero and it is better to leave the loop than generate a divide-by-zero error.

Select Case

Suppose you were designing a program to compute grades based on the average of four exams. If the average was 90 or higher, the person should get an A, 80 to 89, a B, and so on. This is such a common situation that Visual Basic has another control structure designed exactly for it. It's called the Select Case. For example, by using the Select Case control structure, instead of this:

```
If Grade > 90 Then YourGrade = "A"
If Grade > 80 and Grade < 90 then YourGrade = "B"
```

you can write this:

```
Select Case Grade
   Case Is > 90
     YourGrade = "A"
   Case Is >= 80
     YourGrade = "B"
End Select
```

(If you leave the Is off in a Select Case, VB will insert it automatically.) The Select Case command makes it clear that a program has reached a point with many branches; multiple If-Then's do not. (And the clearer a program is, the easier it is to debug.)

 NOTE: Only one clause of a Select Case can be activated in each Select Case.

That's why you could use the line Grade Is > 80 in the select case, whereas two consecutive If-Then lines, like this,

```
If Grade > 90 Then YourGrade = "A"
If Grade >= 80 Then YourGrade = "B"
```

won't work (since a score of 90 would activate both if-thens).

What follows the keywords Select Case is a variable or expression, and what Visual Basic is going to do depends on the value of the variable or expression. The keyword Case is shorthand for "In the case that the variable (expression) is," and you usually follow it with a relational operator. If you want to use a relational operator, use the Is keyword or let VB insert it automatically. Here's another example of using Is and a relational operator:

```
Case Is < "A"
  Print "Character is not a letter."
  Print "Meaningless question"
```

To eliminate all possible non-letter values, you have to consult an ASCII chart, available online via the Help menu. By looking at that, you can see that you also need to eliminate those characters whose ASCII codes are between 91 and 95. You do this as follows:

```
Case Chr$(91) To Chr$(95)
  Print "Character is not a letter."
  Print "Meaningless question"
```

Here, the keyword To allows you to give a range of values. Therefore, this statement is shorthand for, "In the case that the variable is in the range from Chr$(91) to Chr$(95) inclusive, do the following."

Having eliminated the case when the character was not a letter, you may want to print out the message that it is a consonant. You do this with the Case Else, which is shorthand for "Do this case if none of the other situations holds." (The Case Else should always be the last Case in a Select Case.)

```
Select Case Grade
   Case Is > 90
     YourGrade = "A"
   Case Is > 80
```

```
      YourGrade = "B"
   Case Is > 70
      YourGrade = "C"
   Case Else
      "Please retake the final."
 End Select
```

Finally, the Select Case control structure allows you to combine many tests for equality on one line. You could write, for example,

```
Case "A", "E", "I", "O", "U"
  Print "letter is a vowel"
```

instead of the obvious five different cases.

Nested If-Then's

The Select Case command allows you multiple branches but allows you to test only one expression—ultimately one number or string. Suppose you have two numbers, A and B, and your outline looks like this:

```
If A=B  Do ....
If A>B  Do ....
If A<B  Do ....
```

7

One way to program this is to set up a variable,

```
Difference = A - B
```

and then select whether the value of Difference was zero (when A = B), greater than zero (in which case A > B), or less than zero (A < B). But now suppose someone throws in one or two extra conditions:

```
If A > B And A < 2*B
If A > 2*B
```

Now it's no longer obvious how to use the Select Case command. You could write four block If-Then's corresponding to each of the different conditions in the outline, and most of the time this wouldn't cause any problems. Problems may happen if (as in the preceding example) you have to do something to A or B in one of the blocks. From that point on you're in trouble. All further tests are off.

Here's a more realistic example of what I mean. Suppose you are trying to write a program that calculates quotas for a sales force. The minimum quota per salesperson is 100,000. Here are the other rules:

1. If someone sells more than 150,000 they get a bonus *and* their next month's quota is reduced by whatever they sold over 150,000. (So if they sold 250,000 in one month they could take the next month off.)

2. If they sold between 100,000 and 150,000 they get no bonus but their quota for the next month remains at 100,000.

3. If they sold less than 100,000 in a given month they have to make it up next month—that is, they start "in the hole".

Here's a first attempt to code this outline:

```
If Sales > 150000 Then
  Bonus = True
  Sales = Sales - 150000
End If
If Sales > 100000 And Sales < 150000 Then Sales = 0
If Sales < 100000 Then Sales = Sales - 100000
```

Unfortunately, this code won't work. See what happens by playing computer for a salesperson selling 151,000. They would start 99,000 in the hole! This situation is similar to when you first used the Else command. You need to continue testing within the confines of the original If-Then. This is done with the keywords ElseIf-Then. Here is the correct translation of the outline:

```
If Sales > 150000 Then
  Sales = Sales - 150000
  Bonus = True
ElseIf Sales > 100000 And Sales < 150000 Then
  Sales = 0
Else
    Sales = Sales - 100000
End If
```

Now everything is tied together. And just like in the If-Then-Else or the Select command, Visual Basic activates, at most, one clause. In particular, if your salesperson did well, they wouldn't be penalized! (Visual Basic processes only the first clause.) And when Visual Basic is finished doing that, it bypasses any other ElseIf's that may be contained in the block; it goes immediately to the statement following the End If. A block If-Then can have as many ElseIf's as you like, but only one Else (as the last clause). The limits are determined by how much you can process rather than what Visual Basic can do. (That's why it's often preferable to use Select Case. Although any Select Case can be transformed into an If-Then-ElseIf, the latter can be much harder to read and hence to debug.)

The final point worth noting is that the block If-Then is extremely flexible. You can put any Visual Basic statement following the keyword Then—in particular, another If-Then-Else. Consider the following, which a teacher might use if he or she regarded the final exam as being not all-important:

```
If FinalExam < 65 Then
  Print "You failed the final exam."
```

```
   If Average > 70 Then
      Print "You pass because your average is"
      Print "high enough to overcome failing the final"
   Else
      Print "I'm sorry failing the final and a marginal ";
      Print " passing average means failing the course"
   End If
End If
```

Is it clear (forgetting the indentation pattern for a moment) that the Else belongs to the inner If-Then? The way to see this is to "play computer." For the Else to belong to the outer If-Then, the inner If-Then must have already finished. But it hasn't because, to that point, no End If has shown up. Therefore, the first End If finishes the inner If-Then and the second finishes the outer one, and so the Else must belong to the inner If-Then. Of course, you should, as in the preceding example, use a consistent indentation pattern to make it obvious at a glance where nested If-Then's belong.

The GoTo

Like most programming languages, Visual Basic retains the unconditional jump or GoTo. To paraphrase the old joke about split infinitives—modern programmers may be divided into three groups: those who neither know nor care about when they should use the GoTo, those who do not know but seem to care very much, and those who know *when* to use it.

Obviously, routine use of the GoTo leads to *spaghetti code*: code that is hard to read and harder to debug. On the other hand, there are times when using the GoTo actually makes your code cleaner and easier to understand. (In Visual Basic this situation typically comes up when you are deeply inside a nested loop and some condition forces you to leave all the loops simultaneously. You can't use the various forms of the Exit command because all that does is get you out of the loop you are currently in.)

To use a GoTo in Visual Basic, you must label a line. Labels must begin with a letter and end with a colon. They must also start in the *first* column. (Obviously, you should use as descriptive a label as possible.) Here's an example:

```
BadInput:
   'Code we want to process can GoTo here
```

For example, suppose you are using a nested For loop to input data and want to leave the loop if the user enters **ZZZ**.

```
For i = 1 to 10
   For j = 1 to 100
   GetData := InputBox("Data Input", "Enter data - ZZZ to end", "")
   If GetData =  "ZZZ" then
       GoTo BadInput
```

```
     Else
        'Process data
     End If;
Exit Sub
BadInput:
  MsgBox("Data entry ended at user request");
```

Notice how using the Exit For keywords would be cumbersome here. For example, it would require extra code in order to break completely out of the nested loop. Also notice the Exit Sub keywords that prevent you from "falling into" the labeled code.

CHAPTER 8

Built-In Functions

A built-in *function* is simply a prepackaged piece of code that accomplishes a single task. (The next chapter will show you how to write your own functions.) This chapter covers most of Visual Basic's built-in functions. Most of these functions were put into Visual Basic in order to let you to transform raw data into the form that you need. For example, there are functions that let you take strings apart as well as ones that put them together.

You'll also see how the pseudo-random number generator function lets you build an element of indeterminacy (chance) into your programs, a necessary tool for programming games of chance or simulations. There are also many functions for doing mathematical and financial analysis, and I'll survey them here as well.

Finally, you have to be prepared to check the online help about specific functions. The examples given there will complement and extend the ones I give in this chapter and there are many specialized functions that I will not be covering.

String Functions

Much of what you need to do in programming is analyze data. This can be as simple as splitting up a full name into the first and last names, or as sophisticated as writing the code needed to convert a file stored in one format into a file stored in another. All these kinds of manipulations will require mastering Visual Basic's powerful string -handling functions. (Which, by the way, are even more powerful in VB 6 than in previous versions.) In the next few sections you'll see the functions available in Visual Basic that let you examine the characters in a string one by one, take strings apart, replace part of one string with another, and a whole lot more.

NOTE: Because information in Visual Basic text boxes is usually kept as strings or strings contained in variants, string functions are far more important in Visual Basic than in many other programming languages. Keep in mind that relying on implicit conversions from the variant data type to the string or numeric types will occasionally lead to problems and in all cases is slower, so you should use an explicit function whenever possible.

Let's start with a bunch of simple examples to get us warmed up. In Chapter 5 you saw how two strings can be joined together (concatenated) using the ampersand (&). Suppose you needed a string variable that contains the lowercase alphabet. Just combine the & with a For-Next loop. If you start up a new project and use the following Form_Load, you can test this loop:

```
Private Sub Form_Load()
  Dim I As Integer, LowerCase$
  LowerCase$ = vbNullString
  For I% = Asc("a") To Asc("z")
    LowerCase$ = LowerCase$ & Chr$(I%)
  Next I%
```

```
    MsgBox "Here's a lowercase alphabet: " _
    & vbCrLf & LowerCase$
    End
End Sub
```

(You can also look up the ASCII/ANSI codes for "a" (97) and "z" (122) in the help files and change the loop counters; they would run from 97 to 122 if you chose this route or say Print Asc ("a") in the Immediate window.)

Next, you will often need to build up a string of spaces or a string of repeated characters. The function

```
Space(NumberOfSpaces)
```

gives you a string consisting of only spaces, with the number of spaces determined by the value inside the parentheses. The function

```
String(Number, StringExpression$)
```

gives you a string (in the form of a variant) of repeated characters. The character repeated is the first character of the string expression in the second position of the function (the *StringExpression*), and the number of times the characters are repeated is determined by the value in the first position (*Number*). You can also use the extended ASCII/ANSI code in the second position. The following examples all yield the same string of ten z's:

```
X$ = String(10,"z")
X$ = String(10,"zyzzyva")      'only first character is used
X$ = String(10,122)            '122 = Asc("z")
```

8

NOTE: From now on I'll be saying simply "ANSI" code rather than "ASCII/ANSI."

TIP: VB programmers are about equally divided between using the Space and String functions or their older Space$ and String$ counterparts, which return strings rather than variants. I prefer the Space$ and String$ forms that return actual strings rather than strings stored in variants, but code that you work with may use either form, so you need to be familiar with both versions.

One of the things you will always have to do is take care of extra spaces that users may have entered. Getting rid of extra spaces inside a string requires a little bit of work that you will see in the section on the Replace function a little later in this chapter. However, getting rid of them at either end of a string is trivial. To do this you use one of the Trim (Trim$), LTrim (LTrim$), RTrim (RTrim$) functions. For example, the Trim function (Trim$) removes spaces from both the left and right ends of a string. For example:

```
A$ = "    This has far too many spaces.
TrimmedVersion$ = Trim$(A$)
'TrimmedVersion$ = "This has far too many spaces." 'well not any more
```

Similarly, LTrim (LTrim$) removes spaces from the left end, and RTrim (RTrim$) removes spaces from the right.

The next common task you will need to do for string manipulations is to change the case of the letters. As you might expect from the name, the LCase (LCase$) function forces all the characters in a string to be lowercase. Similarly, UCase (UCase$) switches all the characters in a string to uppercase.

```
NormalEmphasis$ = "I am not shouting"
StrongEmphasis$ = UCase$("I am Shouting!")
'gives I AM SHOUTING!
```

Finding the Length of a String

Suppose you want to examine an expression, character by character. For example, you might want to check how many periods (decimal points) are in a string expression before you convert it to a number with the appropriate "C" function (CInt if there is no decimal point, CSng, CDbl, etc., if there is). This ability to analyze each character in a purported number gives you a lot more control than simply checking with the IsNumeric function that you saw in Chapter 7.

If you think about what you need to do for a second, then you will quickly realize that the code for this task calls for a For-Next loop that will let you move character by character through the string, *and* the ending value of the loop must be set to the length of the string. In Visual Basic, the function that tells you the length of a string is Len( ), where the parentheses following the function hold the string expression. This function counts all spaces and nonprinting characters that appear in the string. For example, the following little Form_Load procedure in a new project would let you test this kind of code:

```
Private Sub Form_Load()
  TheString = InputBox("Enter a string and I'll tell you how long it is")
  MsgBox "The string '" & TheString & "' is " & Len(TheString) _
  & " characters long."
  End
End Sub
```

(Notice that I used single quotes to surround the string the user entered when I reported the result in the message box—this is the simplest way to highlight the text.)

As you saw in Chapter 5, you can also use the triple quote or a Chr(34) to display actual quote marks around the strings.)

Checking Input in the KeyPress Event Procedure

Let's end this warm-up by using what you have already seen about the Chr and Asc functions in code that will check what the user enters and then disregard everything but numerals, commas, and the first decimal point. You should keep in mind that this kind of code, though somewhat boring to write, is probably the most important way to bulletproof a program. You really have to check user input before you start processing the data; don't wait until it's too late. This task was discussed to some extent in Chapter 7 (using the IsNumeric function), but now I want to go further. The check
for bad keyboarding is done in the KeyPress event procedure and is long but conceptually pretty simple. The outline for writing this type of code is as follows:

1. Examine a character.
2. If the character is a digit, place it on the right.
3. If the character is the first decimal point, accept that too and also place it on the right. Otherwise, disregard the character.
4. If the character is a comma, don't do anything to it.
5. All other characters are canceled (maybe with a beep to remind the user).

The following KeyPress event procedure stores the input (which is now guaranteed to be of the right form) as the contents of a form-level variable I called fNumeral$:

```
Private Sub Text1_KeyPress(KeyAscii As Integer)
   'This fragment accepts only numerals
   'we will store the information in a
   'form-level variable I called fNumeral$
   Static DecimalPointUsed As Boolean

   Select Case KeyAscii
     Case Asc("0") To Asc("9")
       fNumeral$ = fNumeral$ & Chr$(KeyAscii)
     Case Asc(".")
       If DecimalPointUsed Then
         KeyAscii = 0
         Beep
       Else
         DecimalPointUsed = True
         fNumeral$ = fNumeral$ & Chr$(KeyAscii)
       End If
     Case Asc(",")
        ' Comma - do nothing to fNumeral$
     Case Else
       KeyAscii = 0
       Beep
   End Select
End Sub
```

The key point is that the variable DecimalPointUsed is a *static* variable, which means the information in it is preserved by Visual Basic after the KeyPress event ends (when one key was pressed). This, in turn, means that during each subsequent call to the KeyPress event procedure, we still know whether the user has entered a decimal point or not. By keeping this *flag* (as the jargon usually calls such a variable) as a static variable, once it flips over, it stays flipped over.

Otherwise the code is pretty straightforward. If a character is in the range from 0 to 9, then it's a digit. Therefore, it's added at the right of the variable fNumeral$. Next, the fragment moves to the case that accepts a single decimal point in the number. However, entering a decimal point flips the DecimalPointUsed flag to True. The fragment leaves the commas intact in the display but doesn't add them to the fNumeral$ variable, although we even could have left them in, since the various 'C' conversion functions such as CSng disregard commas. The key point is that by setting KeyAscii to 0 for any other characters, we cancel them—the user won't even see them in the box. (The computer beeps to provide some feedback as well. You might use a message box here instead.)

NOTE: If you wanted to be able to reuse this routine so that users could reenter a new number in the text box, the code gets a bit more complicated. The problem (and it is a common problem with flags) is that you would have to have a way of setting the DecimalPointUsed flag back to False. One idea is to make the flag a form-level variable and reset it to False each time the text box was blank (for example, in the Text1_Change event procedure).

Finally, the above code doesn't completely eliminate the problem of the user entering bad data. He or she can always paste data from someplace else into the text box using the ordinary Windows shortcuts such as CTRL+V. The kind of code that analyzes an existing string will require tools that let us walk through the characters in the string. I'll show you these functions next.

Analyzing Strings with the Mid Function, Left and Right Functions

To do any kind of analysis of an existing string, we need to put a function in the body of the loop that will let us pull individual letters or larger chunks out of a string.

```
For I = 1 To Len(TheString)
'code to work with individual characters
Next I
```

Note that all string functions in VB count the first character as being in place one. (The jargon is to say the VB's string functions are "one-based." This is a pleasant change from other languages which often insist on saying that the first character is in position '0'.) The most important of these functions are the Mid function, which returns a string stored in a variant, and the Mid$ function, which returns an actual string. For all practical purposes you can use these two versions interchangeably. (I prefer the Mid$ form since, as you have probably realized already, I am not too fond of variants!) The syntax for these functions is:

PartOfString = Mid$(*string*, *start*[, *length*])

PartOfString = Mid(*string*, *start*[, *length*])

The first entry holds the string (or string expression) you want to cut up (*string*). Next comes the starting position (*start*) of the characters you want cut out of the string. As I mentioned all string functions are one based so if *start* is one you would be working from the first character. The optional last position (*length*) specifies the number of characters you want to pull out. These last two options can be either integers or long integers or an expression that Visual Basic can round off to lie in this range. Here are some examples of what this function would give:

```
FiveLetters = Mid$("Visual Basic", 1, 5)   '= "Visua"
SixLetters = Mid$("Visual Basic", 1, 6)    '= "Visual"
EndStuff = Mid("Visual Basic", 8, 5)       '= "Basic"
```

If you leave out the last entry (the one telling how many letters to pull out), Visual Basic retrieves a copy of the rest of the string—starting, of course, from the position determined by the second entry. The following two uses of the Mid command produce the same results:

8

```
Mid("Visual Basic", 8, 5)      '= "Basic"
Mid("Visual Basic", 8)         '= "Basic"
```

You will also get a copy of the rest of the string if the third entry is too large (greater than the number of characters remaining).

Programmers say that Mid is a function of three (or occasionally two) *arguments* or *parameters*. Both terms are borrowed from mathematics. Think of them as meaning "the number of pieces of information to be massaged." When using a Visual Basic function, each argument must be separated from the next by commas (a colon and an equal sign). As you have seen, the Mid function usually uses three pieces of information: a string in the first position and integers or long integers in the remaining two positions. (Of course, you can use expressions that evaluate to these as well.)

NOTE: The Mid function supports *named* arguments, so you can say Mid(TheString, start:=5; length:=4) for example. The idea behind named arguments, as you can see, is that you give the names of the parameter followed by a colon and an equal sign, followed by the value. Which functions take named arguments can be found in the online help.

The Mid function has two cousins that are occasionally useful; as with all string functions, they come in both unadorned and $ versions. The functions Left (Left$) and Right (Right$), as their names suggest, make copies of characters from the beginning of a word or the end. Of the two, Right is the more common. It avoids a subtraction operation inside the Mid function and can work a bit faster as a result. For example, the following lines of code all give the same string:

```
Mid(A$, Len(A$) - 3, 4)
Mid(A$, Len(A$) - 3)
Right(A$, 4)
```

Left works the same way but only saves you from putting a 1 in the second position in the Mid function. If you want the first five characters in a string, use one of the following:

```
FirstFiveCharacters = Mid(A$, 1, 5)
FirstFiveCharacters = Left(A$, 5)
```

Example: Counting the Number of Periods in a String

Let's write code that counts the number of periods in a string. You could use this to find the number of 'sentences' in a string, for example, or check that someone hasn't entered more than one decimal point. Here's one version that you can test in a new project by simply making it the Form_Load procedure as I did.

```
Private Sub Form_Load()
  Dim PeriodCount%, Length%, I%
  Dim StringExpression$
  StringExpression$ = InputBox("Enter a string expression
that may or may not contain periods.")
  PeriodCount% = 0
  Length% = Len(StringExpression$)
  For I% = 1 To Length%
    If Mid(StringExpression$, I%, 1) = "." Then
        PeriodCount% = PeriodCount% + 1
    End If
  Next I%
  MsgBox "You had " & PeriodCount% & " periods in that string"
End
End Sub
```

Notice that on each pass through the loop, the position (which is the value of I%) where the Mid function is currently working increases by one. Notice also that the third position, which governs how many characters Mid should pull out, always remains the same (one).

Mid as a Statement

So far we have just used Mid as a function. You can use it as a statement to make changes inside a string. For example, if

```
BestBasicForDos$ = "PowerBasic"
```

then the statement

```
Mid(BestBasicForDos$, 1, 5) = "Quick"
```

gives the string variable BestBasicForDos$ the value "QuickBasic". When you use Mid as a statement this way, the second position controls where the change will start, and the third position controls how many letters to pull out from the string on the right-hand side of the equals sign. These are the letters that will be switched into the original string. For example,

```
Mid(BestBasicForDos$, 1, 5) = "QuickBasic by Microsoft"
```

gives the same result as before. If the right-hand side has fewer characters than the number given in the third position of the left-hand side demands, Visual Basic changes as many characters as occur on the right-hand side. Therefore,

```
Mid(BestBasic$, 1, 5) = "VB"
```

gives BestBasicForDos$ the value "VBwerBasic".

Always keep in mind that the Mid statement makes changes within a string but *never* changes the length of the original string. (Changing the size of the string can be done with the new Replace function that I'll show you soon.) In particular, if the number in the third position is too large relative to the number in the second position—that is, greater than the remaining number of characters—then only the characters remaining can change. Finally, just as with the Mid function, you can leave out the last position. For example,

8

```
Mid("In the beginning ", 8) = "middle was"
```

changes the string to

```
"In the middle was"
```

In this case, there's just enough room to fit the string on the right-hand side into the string on the left, starting at the eighth position. Counting from the eighth position, there are ten characters left in the phrase "In the beginning ". (The space counts as a character.)

Evil Type Coercions: One More Time
Visual Basic is a great tool but its seemingly insane desire to try to read your mind sometimes defies polite descriptions. Consider the following code:

```
Dim Numeral As String
Dim ANumber As Long
AZipCode = 11224
Foo = Mid(AZipCode, 3)
```

```
MsgBox Foo
Foo = Mid(3, AZipCode)
MsgBox Foo
```

What does this code do? Well in the first call to the Mid function, VB changes the number to a string and extracts the last three digits. I would certainly prefer that VB not change my numbers to strings without asking me. But I suppose this is *conceivably* acceptable behavior. The second part, of course, is where most serious programmers take VB to task. What I did was reverse the positions of the arguments (a very common typo). As you will see if you run this code, VB accepts this version as well! That Visual Basic will allow this kind of absurd code to compile and run can lead to really hard to find bugs. It would be nice if VB insisted that arguments for functions be of the right type in order to help us with our common typos.

The InStr Function

Suppose you wanted to find out all the digits before the decimal point in a number. You could, of course, use Mid to search through the string version of the number, character by character, until you found the decimal point. That, however, is a lot of work and searching character by character is *much* slower for long strings than using a neat function called InStr that I'll describe in this section. In any case, programming with the Mid function would be a bit painful if you always had to go in and count characters in order to find the position of the character you wanted to deal with.

Like the Mid function, the InStr function ("instring") also works with three (and occasionally two) pieces of information; that is, it's a function of three (occasionally two) arguments.

The InStr function tells you whether a string is part of another string (the jargon is to say "is a substring of"). And, if it is, InStr tells you the position at which the substring starts. Here's an example:

```
Phrase$ = "QuickBASIC was Visual Basic's distant ancestor"
X% = InStr(1, Phrase$, "BASIC")
```

The value of X% is 6 because the string "BASIC" occurs in the phrase "QuickBASIC was Visual Basic's distant ancestor", starting at the sixth position.

What Visual Basic does is search the string (specified in the second position of the InStr function) starting from the first position until it finds the substring (specified in the third position). If it doesn't find the string, it gives back a value of 0. Therefore, the following line

```
X% =InStr(1, Phrase$, "basic")
```

would set the value of X% to 0, because "basic" isn't a substring of the phrase "QuickBASIC was Visual Basic's distant ancestor". Remember that case is important inside quotation marks; the InStr function defaults to being case sensitive.

CAUTION: The current setting for the Option Compare statement, which you may have set in the Declaration section of the form, determines the type of comparison for all code in the form. Thus, if you added an Option Compare Text in the general section of the form, then the value of X% =InStr(1, Phrase$, "basic") would also be 6 in the above example.

The usual form of the InStr function that you use is similar to the above examples, but it also lets you specify at what character to start the search. It looks like this:

InStr(*[where to start,] string to search, string to find*)

In this case, the optional first position specifies from which position to start the search. If you leave this entry out, the search automatically starts from the first position.

The full form of the function is even more powerful and lets you always make a case-sensitive or case-insensitive comparison *regardless* of the current setting of Option Compare. The syntax (using Microsoft's notation) is

InStr(*[start,]string1, string2[, compare]*)

where the *compare* parameter specifies the type of string comparison. If you set it to 0 (equal to the built-in constant vbBinaryCompare) then the comparison *is case sensitive* regardless of the current setting of Option Compare. If you use the built-in constant vbTextCompare, you get a case-insensitive comparison again, regardless of the setting of Option Compare. Thus,

8

```
X% =InStr(1, Phrase$, "basic", vbTextCompare)
```

will always give you the value 6.

Example: Finding the Number of Digits in a String of Numerals
For another example of using InStr, suppose you need to decide on the number of digits before the decimal point in a number. This is easy to do if you combine the Str command with the InStr command. Here's an outline for this program:

1. We take in the number as a string using an Input Box and then apply the Trim function in order to remove leading and trailing spaces.
2. We use the Instr function to find out if there is a decimal point in the string.
3. If the value returned by the InStr function from the previous step is 0, then there's no decimal point and the number of digits is the length of the (now trimmed) string of numerals.
4. If there is a decimal point then the number of digits in front of the decimal point is one less than the value returned by InStr—since this is where the decimal point was.

Here's a little Visual Basic program you can run to test the code that implements this outline. (As usual, to test the code, make it the Form_Load of a new project.):

```
Private Sub Form_Load()
  ' find the number of digits in a number before the decimal point
  Dim Numerals$, DecimalPointAt As Integer, NumOfDigits As Integer
  Numerals$ = InputBox("Enter a number and I'll tell you how many digits
                       before the decimal point it has.")
  Numerals$ = Trim(Numerals$)
  DecimalPointAt = InStr(Numerals$, ".")
  If DecimalPointAt <> 0 Then
    NumOfDigits = DecimalPointAt - 1
  Else
    NumOfDigits = Len(Numerals$)
  End If
  MsgBox "The number of digits before the decimal point " & _
  "in " & Numerals & " was " & NumOfDigits
  End
End Sub
```

Finally, you should be aware when you look at other people's code that a common idiom is to take advantage of the fact that 0 is False in VB and a non-zero value is True and write the code like this:

```
DecimalPointAt = InStr(Numerals$, ".")
If DecimalPointAt Then
   NumOfDigits = DecimalPointAt - 1
Else
  NumOfDigits = Len(Numerals$)
End If
```

Doing Repeated Searches with InStr

You often have to search repeatedly for the same character. You can do this by using the previous value obtained by InStr inside a loop in *another use of* InStr. The pattern looks like this:

```
Location = InStr(OriginalString, Substring)
Do Until Location = 0
   do whatever you need to do;
   Location = InStr(Location, OriginalString, Substring)
Loop
```

Note that the statement InStr(Location, *OriginalString, Substring*) tells VB to continue the search from the previously obtained location.

Note many people prefer to use a "Found" helper variable to make the code clearer so you may see this in code you maintain. In this case, the outline looks like this:

```
Found = InStr(OriginalString, Substring)
Do Until Not Found
```

```
        do whatever you need;
        then find next instance of substring
        Found = InStr(Found, OriginalString, Substring)
    Loop
```

The InStrRev Function

Visual Basic 6 adds an InStrRev function to your arsenal that starts searching from the back end of the string. Note that the syntax for the InStrRev function is slightly different than that of the InStr function (well, actually, it is almost the reverse—perhaps what one would expect from its name). It looks like this:

InStrRev(*OriginalString*, *Substring*[, *Start*[, *Compare*]])

The *Compare* parameter is exactly as before.

One common use of InStrRev would be to check the extension at the end of a filename that a user typed. The reason you really want to start from the end and look for the *last* period is that since Windows 95 debuted, filenames like *this.is.a.dumb.but.legal.filename* are now allowed. InStr would fail miserably on weird filenames like this (or you would have to write a lot of code to make sure you had found the last period!).

All you need to do to pull out the filename extension is to have InStrRev work with the Mid function. Here's some sample code that you can add to a new project to show off this neat new function.

8

```
Private Sub Form_Load()
  Dim TestFileName As String, Location As Long
  TestFileName = "Full.Extension.html"
  Location = InStrRev(TestFileName, ".")
  MsgBox "Your extension is " & Mid(TestFileName, Location)
  TestFileName = "ShorterExtension.htm"
  Location = InStrRev(A.Test.File.Name, ".")
  MsgBox "Your extension is " & Mid(TestFileName, Location)
End
End Sub
```

The Nifty (New) Replace Function

If you want to change the size of a string, the Mid statement is of little use without extra work. In fact, prior to Visual Basic 6 you needed to use it along with a procedure that was a bit like splicing tape. It wasn't hard but it was tedious. Although I'll describe this procedure shortly (since you may need to maintain programs that use this kind of code), the new Replace function makes this (and many other) common search and replacement tasks almost trivial. For example, suppose you want to change the string

"JavaScript is the best scripting language."

to read

"VBScript is the best scripting language".

Here's the (one line!) code fragment that will now do this in VB6:

```
TestString$ = "JavaScript is the best scripting language."

TestString$ = Replace(TestString$, "JavaScript", "VBScript")
```

As you can see, you usually use the Replace function by assigning its result to a variable. It can be the original variable, as in the fragment above. In this case you are changing the original string. You can also make up a new string by assigning the value obtained by using Replace to a new variable. For example, the following code keeps intact the variable SomePeoplesOpinionIs$ and only changes the variable MyOpinionIs$:

```
SomePeoplesOpinionIs$ = "Java is the best programming language."

MyOpinionIs$ = Replace(SomePeoplesOpinionIs$, "Java", "Visual Basic")
```

Other Uses for the Replace Function

The Replace function actually is amazingly powerful, so I'll go over all its features by using them in various kinds of examples in this section. First off, here's the full syntax for the Replace function:

Replace(*Expression, Find, ReplaceWith*[, *Start*[, *Count*[, *Compare*]]])

You have just seen examples of using the first three parameters. The optional *Start* parameter lets you tell VB the position at which to start looking for the string that needs to be replaced. The *Start* parameter is usually combined with the results of a use of the InStr function, which you already know about. If you omit the *Start* parameter, as I did in the examples above, the Replace function starts looking at the first character in the string.

Next, the optional *Count* parameter specifies the number of times you want to do the substitution if there are multiple copies of the same string inside the original string. If you omit this parameter (as I did above), the default behavior of Replace is to replace *all* occurrences of the string. For example, after VB processes the following code,

```
TestString = "AAAAAA"
TestString = Replace(TestString, "A", "Z", 1, 1)
```

you would end up with the string "ZAAAAA" since I set the Count parameter to 1.

Next, the optional *Compare* parameter works exactly as before and allows you to do case-insensitive replacements by using the constant vbCompareText.

Finally, if you use the empty string as your *ReplaceWith* value, you will remove the substring from the original string. (Of course, it is better to use the built-in constant vbNullString than the "" for this.) For example, the following line of code,

```
NoHyphens = Replace("1-800-555-1212","-",vbNullString)
```

gives

NoHyphens the value "18005551212".

The following table summarizes the results from this and other special situations in the Replace function:

If	The Resulting String Is
The original string (*Expression* parameter) is the empty string (vbNullString or "")	An empty string ("")
The string that you want to replace (*Find* parameter) is an empty string	The original string
The *Start* parameter is greater than the length of the original string	An empty string
The *Count* parameter is 0	The original string
The original string (*Expression* parameter) is Null	An error

8

Replacing Strings with Mid

As I mentioned at the beginning of the section on the Replace function, in earlier versions of Visual Basic (and hence in code that you may have to maintain) if you wanted to change the string

"Java is the best programming language"

to read

"Visual Basic is the best programming language"

you had to do some work. The problem is that since the string "Java" has 4 letters and the string "Visual Basic" has 12 (counting the space), you couldn't use the Mid statement, which was the only tool available in earlier versions of Visual Basic. You had to follow the splicing analogy as given in these steps:

1. Find the phrase "Java" and cut it out.
2. Hold the phrase "is the best programming language".
3. Splice in the phrase "Visual Basic" and reassemble.

Here's a fragment to do this for the strings I just mentioned:

```
Phrase$ = "Java is the best programming language"
Begin$ = "Visual Basic"
EndPhrase$ = Mid(Phrase$, 5)
Phrase$ = Begin$ & EndPhrase$
MsgBox Phrase$
```

The StrComp Function

This function can be used instead of the relational operators (such as < or >) to
compare strings. Unlike the relational operators, this function returns a value, so
you usually use it together with an assignment statement. For example, if you set X =
StrComp(A$, B$), then the value of X is -1 if A$ is less than B$, 0 if A$ equals B$, 1
if A$ is greater than B$, and it is the reserved constant NULL if one of the strings
is empty.

By adding a third argument to StrComp that is identical to the one you used for InStr,
you can control the case sensitivity of the comparison. If you use StrComp(A$, B$,
vbCompareText), then the comparison is not case sensitive; for StrComp(A$, B$,
vbBinaryCompare), it is. Using StrComp this way is sometimes preferable to using the
Option Compare Text feature that globally controls comparisons.

The Like Function and Fuzzy Searching

The Like function lets you compare strings using *wildcards*. For example, it can tell
you if there are digits inside a string or if a group of characters is not inside a string.
For non-null strings, this operator returns True if there is a match and False if not. The
case sensitivity of the Like function depends on the current setting of Option
Compare in the form or module. (Of course, you could program all these features
using the InStr function, but the Like function is faster and, of course, saves you
programming time.)

As with the Windows operating system (for example the Find dialog box), a question
mark (?) matches one character only and an asterisk (*) allows matches with zero, one,
or more characters. For example, an If-Then like this

```
If "Visual Basic" Like "*Basic" Then
  Print "a Basic language"
Else
  Print "not a Basic language"
End If
```

will print "a Basic language". But change the If clause to

```
If "Visual Basic" Like "?Basic" Then
```

then you'll see "not a Basic language".

The following table summarizes the possible patterns you can use with the Like function:

Pattern Character	Match
?	Any single character
*	Zero or more characters
#	Any single digit
[list of characters]	Any single character in the list
[!list of characters]	Any single character not in the list

For example, if X = ("###" Like "123"), then X is True; but if X = ("[ABC]" Like "123"), then X is False. But X = ("[!ABC]" Like "123") is True!

You can also use a hyphen inside the brackets to show an ascending range. For example,

```
If "[0-9]" Like A$
```

would tell you whether a digit occurred inside A$.

NOTE: To match a left bracket ([), question mark (?), number sign (#), or asterisk (*), enclose them in brackets. For example: *[?] would check for the occurrence of a question mark.

8

For example "*[?]" would check if the string had a question mark inside of it. So, these lines of code would display a message box.

```
T$ = "Yes? No!"
If (T$ Like "*?") Then MsgBox "The string ends with a question mark."
```

The Rnd Function

The Solitaire program provided with Windows shuffles a deck of cards whenever you ask it to. In card games and most other games, the play is unpredictable. This is exactly what is meant by a game of chance. On the other hand, computers are machines, and the behavior of machines should be predictable. To write a program in Visual Basic that allows you, for example, to simulate the throwing of a die, you need a function that makes the behavior of the computer seem random. You do this by means of the function Rnd. For example, add the following Form_Click procedure on a blank form in a new project:

```
Private Sub Form_Click()
  Cls
  Dim I As Integer
  For I = 1 To 5
    Print Rnd
  Next I
End Sub
```

When you click on the form, you will see something like the screen in Figure 8-1. As you can see, five numbers between 0 and 1, each having six or seven digits, roll down the screen. These numbers seem to follow no pattern: that's what is usually meant by random. They'll also have many, but not all, of the sophisticated statistical properties that scientists expect of random numbers.

NOTE: Without some changes, the results of naively using Rnd would not work well in certain kinds of simulation programs. See Chapter 10 for how to modify the built-in random number generator for simulations.

Each time your computer processes a line containing the statement "Print Rnd", it will print a different number between 0 and 1. In theory, the number can be 0 but can't ever be 1.

It's natural to wonder what a number with up to seven decimal places is good for. Well suppose, for example, you wanted to write a program that simulated a coin toss. There are three possibilities: it could be heads, it could be tails—or it could stand on

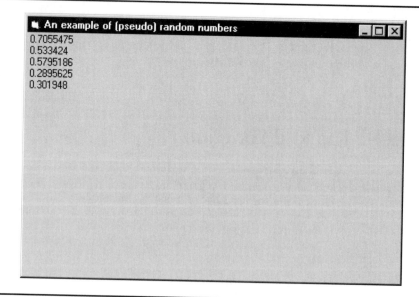

Demonstration
of (pseudo)
random
numbers
Figure 8-1.

edge (don't wait up for this to happen). A fragment to simulate a coin toss might look like this:

```
' A coin toss simulator

CoinToss = Rnd

Select Case CoinToss
  Case Is < .5
    Print "Heads"
  Case .5
    Print "Stood on edge!!!!"
  Case Else
    Print "Tails"
End Select
```

Next, suppose you incorporate this fragment into a Form_Click procedure for a new project:

```
Private Sub Form_Click ()
  ' A multiple coin toss simulator

  Dim Trials As Integer, NumOfHeads As Integer
  Dim NumOfTails As Integer, I As Integer
  Dim CoinToss As Single

  Trials = Val(InputBox$("How many trials?"))
  NumOfHeads = 0
  NumOfTails = 0
  Unbelievable = 0

  For I = 1 To Trials
    CoinToss = Rnd
    Select Case CoinToss
      Case Is < .5
        NumOfHeads = NumOfHeads + 1
      Case .5
        Print "Stood on edge!!!!"     'maybe in a couple of
                                       'zillion trials
        Beep: Beep
        Unbelievable = Unbelievable + 1
      Case Else
        NumOfTails = NumOfTails + 1
    End Select
  Next I
  Cls
  Print "Number of heads was"; NumOfHeads
  Print "Number of tails was"; NumOfTails
  If Unbelievable > 0 Then
    Print "The coin stood on edge!"
  End If
End Sub
```

8

Try this program with a large number of trials. You should get roughly the same number of heads as tails, and no "standing on edges." (For a large number of trials, it would be very unlikely that you'd get equal numbers of heads and tails. When I tried it with 4000 trials, I got 2012 heads and 1988 tails.)

OK, now end the program and run it again, using the *same* number of trials as you did before. If you do, you'll notice that you will get *exactly* the same number of heads and tails as you did before. This would certainly be unusual behavior for an honest coin! What is happening?

In fact, the numbers you get using the Rnd function are only "pseudo-random." Pseudo generally means false, and you've just seen one of the problems of pseudo-random numbers. Every time you start a program that uses pseudo-random numbers, you will get the same sequence of pseudo-random numbers. Our little sample program operates as if the computer's memory contains a book of these numbers, and after each program is over, the book gets turned back to page one. The book always starts at the same place and the numbers are always in the same order, therefore, the results are fixed. You need a way to "shuffle" the pages each time the program starts. The best way not to stack the cards at the outset is to use the exact time of the system clock to *reseed* the random number generator. (*Reseed* is the jargon for the process of starting a new sequence of random numbers.) Since the system clock is accurate to a small fraction of a second, it's quite unlikely that a program will start at exactly the same moment each time it is run.)

To reseed the random-number generator, simply insert the command "Randomize" before you use Rnd for the first time. For example, if you add the following line in bold to the previous code, at the beginning of the routine, and leave the rest of the code the same, you will almost certainly see different results each time you run the program.

```
Private Sub Form_Click ()
    ' A multiple coin toss simulator
    Randomize
```

NOTE: From this point on, I'll stop using the term "pseudo-random" and refer to the numbers coming from the Rnd function as being "random"; this follows the usual terminology in programming.

Getting Integers via the Rnd Function

Numbers between 0 and 1 may (with a little work) be good for imitating a coin toss, but the method used earlier would be cumbersome for, say, a dice simulation. The outline would have to be something like this:

◆   If the random number is less than 1/6, make it a 1.

◆   If more than 1/6 but less than 2/6 (= 1/3), make it a 2.

◆   If more than 2/6 but less than 3/6 (= 1/2), make it a 3, and so on.

This would certainly be tedious to implement. However, thinking about this outline leads to a simple trick called *scaling* that more or less automates this process. Suppose you take a number between 0 and 1 and multiply it by 6. If it was less than 1/6 to start with, it will now be less than 1; if it was between 1/6 and 2/6 (1/3), it will now be between 1 and 2; and so on. All you need to do then is multiply the number by 6 and move up to the next integer. In general, if the number was between 0 and 1 (but never quite getting to 1), the result of multiplying by 6 goes from 0 not quite up to 6.

Unfortunately, there's no command in Visual Basic to move *up* to the next integer. Instead, you can use the Fix function, which lets you throw away the decimal part of a number. For example:

Fix(3.456) = 3   Fix(-7.9998) = -7 Fix(8) = 8

The idea to make our dice simulation work is to add 1 to the result of "fixing" a positive number. By doing this we will, in effect, move to the next highest positive integer. For example, look at the following fragment:

```
' A dice simulation using Fix
Randomize
Cls
Die% = Fix(6 * Rnd) + 1
Print "I rolled a"; Die%
```

The key to the fragment is that the number inside the parentheses—6*Rnd—is always between 0 and 6, but it can't be 6 because Rnd is never 1. Applying the Fix function gives you an integer between 0 and 5 (that is, 0, 1, 2, 3, 4, or 5), and now you only have to add 1 to make it a proper-looking die.

8

More on the Rnd Function

By adding an argument to the Rnd function, you can change how it works. First, suppose you use the Rnd(0) command in your program by adding an argument of "0" to it. Then, you get the *last* random number generated. (You can use this trick in the Immediate window, for example.) This ability is very useful when trying to debug a program. Imagine trying to debug a program if an important number changes each time and you have no way of knowing its previous value! The Rnd(0) form gives you a way of checking which random number the machine just used.

Next, suppose there is a negative number inside the parentheses. (The number inside the parentheses is usually called the *seed*.) Each time you give the command

```
Rnd(negative number)    'example: Rnd(-5)
```

that is, you use a negative seed, you get the same sequences of pseudo-random numbers. This is another important debugging tool. It lets you rerun a program keeping the pseudo-random numbers temporarily stable. A good way to think about what a negative seed does is to imagine that there is a different list of pseudo-random numbers, each one corresponding to a different negative seed. You can think of the seed as the number from which the random numbers grow.

NOTE: For those who are interested, VB generates its random numbers using a method that is called the linear congruential method. This transforms the number using the Mod function. The easiest way to understand what Visual Basic is doing for its random number generator is to imagine you are working only with integers. The random number generator would then use the built-in Mod function to generate the next pseudo-random number roughly as follows:

NextNumber = (A*PreviousNumber + B) mod M

Here, A, B, and M are fixed integers and the PreviousNumber starts from the seed. This method is very fast. But because A, B, and M are fixed by Visual Basic designers, this method can be unreliable if you need many random numbers for a simulation program. If you need thousands of random numbers for such a program, see Chapter 10, which gives you one way of improving the built-in random number generator. The cost is that the program will run slightly more slowly and need slightly more memory.

Example: Writing a Jumble Program

Suppose you wanted to write a "jumble" program. This would take a string and shuffle the letters around. It's a prototype for many other types of operations—for example, shuffling a deck of cards. Here's an outline for one way to do it:

1. Start at the first character.
2. Swap it with a randomly chosen character.
3. Do the same for the second character until there are no more characters left.

The swapping can be done with the Mid statement, since you are never changing the size of the string. The screen in Figure 8-2 shows what the form might look like. Suppose the command button is given a control name of cmdJumbleIt, the top text box is called txtOriginal, and the destination text box is called txtJumbled. Then the Click procedure looks like this:

```
Private Sub cmdJumbleIt_Click()
  ' a Jumble program demonstrates Mid as a statement
  ' and the Rnd function

  Dim Phrase$, HoldChar$, I As Integer
  Dim LenPhrase As Integer, INum As Integer

  Randomize
  Phrase$ = txtOriginal.Text
  LenPhrase = Len(Phrase$)
  For I = 1 To LenPhrase
    INum = Int(LenPhrase * Rnd) + 1
```

```
    HoldChar$ = Mid(Phrase$, I, 1)
    Mid(Phrase$, I, 1) = Mid(Phrase, INum, 1)
    Mid(Phrase$, INum, 1) = HoldChar$
  Next I
  txtJumbled.Text = Phrase$
End Sub
```

Since values inside the string commands start at 1 and range up to the length of the string, you need to add 1 to the value of Int(LenPhrase*Rnd). Using this value gives you a random position within the string. Once you have the random character, you swap it with the current character in the string, as determined by the counter in the For-Next loop.

Next, since there is no Swap statement in Visual Basic that will just exchange the two characters, we need to remember both the old and new characters in order to program the interchange.

To make this program into a card shuffler, all you need to do is give Phrase$ the right value. You can do this by using the Chr command in a font that has the correct symbols.

Getting a Range of Random Integers

Up to this point, all the random integers you've used have started from 0 or 1. Sometimes it's convenient to have random integers that span a range. For example, take a random four-letter combination; how likely is it to be a word in English? To try this out, you need to generate four random letters and string them together. An obvious way to do this is to apply the Chr$ command to a random integer between

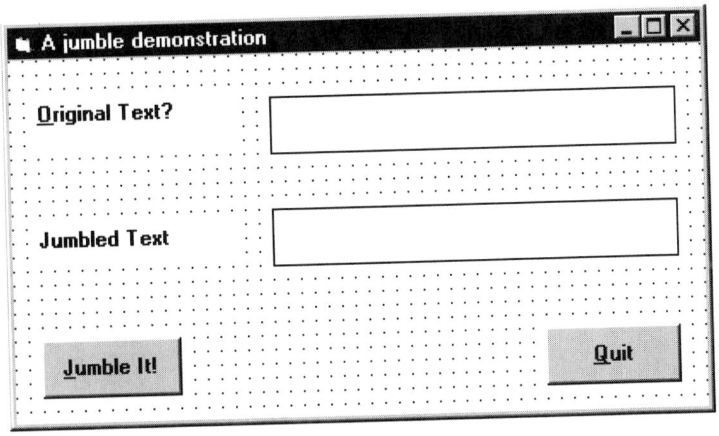

8

Form for a
Jumble program
Figure 8-2.

65 and 90 (the range of ANSII codes for the uppercase alphabet). To get a random integer in this range:

1. Generate a random integer between 0 and 25.
2. Add it to 65 to get the ANSII value of an uppercase letter.

Here is a translation of this into code:

```
CharNum = Int(26*Rnd) + 65
```

And here is a little Form_Click procedure you can add to a new project to generate 25 random four-letter combinations:

```
Private Sub Form_Click()
'25 Random 4 letter 'words'
' demonstrates Rnd for a range

  Dim I As Integer, J As Integer, CharNum As Integer
  Randomize
  Cls
  For J = 1 To 25
    Word$ = vbNullString
    For I = 1 To 4
      CharNum = Fix(26 * Rnd) + 65
      Word$ = Word$ &  Chr$(CharNum)
    Next I
    Print Word$
  Next
End Sub
```

The key, as explained in the outline for this program given previously, is the statement defining the value of CharNum that gives you a random integer in the correct range. The next statement turns it into a random uppercase letter. As usual, these two statements can be combined into one:

```
Word$ & Chr$(Fix(26*Rnd) + 65)
```

However, this code is less readable than the preceding code.

Bit-Twiddling Functions

Bit twiddling refers to looking at the individual bits that make up a number and possibly resetting them if necessary. You need to do this in order to use the KeyUp and KeyDown event procedures that let you detect the non-ASCII coded keys, such as the function and arrow keys. Knowing how the logical operators work on the bit level also makes it easy to program powerful systems for encrypting your data (see Chapter 18). This section builds on the section in Chapter 5 where you saw how binary arithmetic works. (Recall that this was needed to set the background and foreground colors via the Properties box.)

First, Visual Basic has built-in functions to convert a number to a string of hexadecimal (base 16) or octal (base 8) digits. They are

```
Hex ' for hexadecimal
Oct ' for octal
```

Surprisingly, Visual Basic does not have a built-in function for converting a number to binary. There are many ways to write such a program. As usual, it's best to take an example and work through it step-by-step. The easiest examples are, of course, 0 and 1, which are the same in decimal and binary. What about 3? This is 11 in binary (1 * 2 + 1). In general, the rightmost (least significant) binary digit is given by checking whether the number is even or odd. The built-in Mod function tells this. For example, the last binary digit is the number Mod 2.

To move to the next binary digit, you have to divide by 2 and throw away the remainder (which you just took into account by using the Mod function). You continue this process until there's nothing left to divide.

As a more serious example, suppose you want to convert the number 43 to binary:

Last binary digit = 43 Mod 2 = 1

Now you divide by 2, using the integer division function (the backslash), and continue the process:

8

Next binary digit = (43 \ 2) Mod 2 = 21 Mod 2 = 1

And then you continue this process:

Next binary digit = (21 \ 2) Mod 2 = 10 Mod 2 = 0
Next binary digit = (10 \ 2) Mod 2 = 5 Mod 2 = 1
Next binary digit = (5 \ 2) Mod 2 = 2 Mod 2 = 0
Next binary digit = (2 \ 2) Mod 2 = 1 Mod 2 = 1

Since 1 \ 2 is 0, you stop here. Stringing these digits together from bottom to top gives you 101011 (which is 43 in binary).

Here's a program that implements this outline, attached to a Click event procedure for the command button named cmdConvertToBinary. The program also assumes there are two text boxes—named txtNumber for the number to be converted and txtBinary for the string of binary digits.

```
Private Sub cmdConvertToBinary_Click()
   Dim Number As Integer
   Dim BinaryForm As String

   Number = Val(txtNumber.Text)
   BinaryForm = ""
   Do
      Digit = Number Mod 2
      If Digit = 0 Then
```

```
      BinaryForm = "0" + BinaryForm
    Else
      BinaryForm = "1" + BinaryForm
    End If
    Number = Number \ 2
  Loop Until Number = 0
  txtBinary.Text = BinaryForm
End Sub
```

Notice that we could use a Select Case statement inside the procedure, but with two options this seems like overkill. Finally, as the example shows, when integer division gives you zero, you stop. The next section shows you another way to write a binary conversion routine.

The And Operator at the Bit Level

You may think that Visual Basic's using 0 for False makes sense, but why -1 for True? To understand this, you have to know that all the logical operators (Not, And, Or, and so on) are really functions that work on the bit (binary digit) level. Suppose you are given two integers, X and Y. Then "X And Y" makes a binary digit 1 only if both binary digits are 1; otherwise, it is 0. For example, if

X = 7 in decimal	= 0111 in binary
Y = 12 in decimal	= 1100 in binary

then X And Y = 0100 in binary (4 in decimal) because only in the third position are both bits 1. Because And gives a 1 only if both digits are 1, using And with a number whose binary digit is a single 1 and whose remaining digits are all 0 lets you isolate that binary digit of any integer. For example:

X And 1	Tells you whether the least significant (rightmost) binary digit is on. You get a 0 if it is not on.
X And 2	Since 2 in decimal is 10 in binary, getting a 0 tells you that the next significant (second from the right) binary digit is off, a 1 if it's on.
X And 4	Since 4 in decimal is 100 in binary, this tells you whether the next significant (third from the right) binary digit is on or off.

This process is called *bit masking* (or simply *masking*) and is the key to using the KeyUp and KeyDown event procedures described in the next section and the Mouse event procedure described in Chapter 17.

Before I go on to the Key events, though, notice that you can also easily adapt the bit masking process to write another binary conversion routine as given here:

```
Private Sub cmdConvertToBinary_Click()
  Dim BitPattern, Number As Integer
```

```
Dim BinaryForm As String

Number = CInt(txtNumber.Text)
BinaryForm = ""
BitPattern = 1
Do
  Digit = Number And BitPattern
  If Digit = 0 Then
    BinaryForm = "0" + BinaryForm
  Else
    BinaryForm = "1" + BinaryForm
  End If
  BitPattern = BitPattern * 2    'next bit
Loop Until BitPattern > Number
  txtBinary.Text = BinaryForm
End Sub
```

Example: Working with KeyUp and KeyDown

The KeyPress event reports on which ASCII-coded key a user pressed. The two events described in this section report much-lower-level information. They will tell exactly what the user did to the keyboard. If you need to determine whether he or she pressed CTRL, a function key, or the like, these are the event procedures to use. For example, if you want your application to supply context-sensitive help when the user presses the F1 key, these event procedures can make it possible.

However, these event procedures are a bit more complicated to use than KeyPress because you must distinguish, for example, between lowercase and uppercase letters. The syntax for both of these event procedures is the same:

Private Sub Control_KeyUp(*KeyCode As Integer, Shift As Integer*)

Private Sub Control_KeyDown(*KeyCode As Integer, Shift As Integer*)

CAUTION: Only the control that has the focus can respond to keyboard events. The active form has the focus if no control on the form does, unless you set the KeyPreview property to True. In this case, the form's keyboard events take precedence.

First, you have to use bit masking on the *Shift* parameter to determine whether the SHIFT key, the CTRL key, or the ALT key (or some combination of the three) was pressed. The three constants that you can use are summarized in the following table:

Symbolic Constant	Value	Key
vbShiftMask	1	SHIFT key bit mask
vbCtrlMask	2	CTRL key bit mask
vbAltMask	4	ALT key bit mask

For example:

```
If Shift And vbShiftMask = vbShiftMask Then Print "Shift key pressed"
If Shift And vbCtrlMask = vbCtrlMask Then Print "Ctrl key pressed"
If Shift And vbAltMask = vbAltMask Then Print "Alt key pressed"
```

You can also use the numbers directly, of course:

```
If (Shift And 1) = 1 Then Print "Shift key pressed"
```

This means there are eight possibilities. For example, set up a blank form and add the following event procedure:

```
Private Sub Form_KeyDown(KeyCode As Integer, Shift As Integer)
  Select Case Shift
    Case 0
      Print "Neither Ctrl nor Alt nor Shift key pressed"
    Case vbShiftMask
      Print "Only Shift key pressed"
    Case vbCtrlMask
      Print "Only Ctrl key pressed"
    Case 3    'or vbShiftMask + vbCtrlMask
      Print "Shift + Ctrl keys pressed"
    Case 4    'or vbAltMask
      Print "Only Alt key pressed"
    Case 5
      Print "Alt + Shift keys pressed"
    Case 6
      Print "Alt + Ctrl keys pressed"
    Case 7
      Print "Alt, Shift, and Ctrl keys pressed"
  End Select
End Sub
```

(You can simply add the symbolic constants if you wish.)

This procedure assumes that only the first three bits of the *Shift* parameter are used. Since Microsoft reserves the right to use the higher order bits, it actually is preferable to start by setting up a new variable as in the following and using this new variable in the Select Case statement.

```
LowerThreeBits = Shift And 7        '7 = 0111 in binary
```

This works because, as the comment indicates, 7 is 0111 in binary, so we are using the right mask.

Next, the *KeyCode* integer parameter tells you what physical key was pressed. The code returned in the KeyUp and KeyDown events does *not* distinguish between a key and its shifted sibling. "A" and "a" or "1" and "!" have the same KeyCode parameter as its unshifted sibling. (The point being that the Shift parameter can (and needs to) be checked using the techniques you just saw!)

To make matters even more complicated, the key codes for the various possible characters follow the ASCII/ANSI codes only for A-Z, and hence a-z and 0-9 on the keyboard. For all the remaining codes, whether for the arrow keys, the function keys, or the numeric keypad, the needed constants are given in the library of constants supplied with Visual Basic. (Use the Object Browser to search the Visual Basic library for "Key code constants.") Most of the constants are pretty straightforward: they take the form vbKey*x*. For example, suppose you want to detect whether a user pressed F1. The code for this turns out to be given by the symbolic constant vbKeyF1. Therefore, a statement inside a KeyDown event procedure, such as

```
If KeyCode = vbKeyF1 Then          'easier then &H70!
    ' perhaps put a msg box with help information here
    ' or show a form until the F1 key is released
    ' check this with KeyUp!
End If
```

is all it takes. (You could use this to start context-sensitive help, for example.)

T ....
IP: Remember that if the KeyPreview property of the form is set to True, then the form receives the key events before VB will trigger the key events for any of the controls on the form. Set the KeyPreview property to True when you want to create a global keyboard handler. Also, the KeyDown and KeyUp events aren't triggered if someone presses ENTER when the form has a command-button control with the Default property set to True, or the ESC key when a form has a command-button control with the Cancel property set to True. It is never invoked for the user pressing the TAB key—there is no way strictly within Visual Basic to trap this key.

8

The Other Operator at the Bit Level

The Or operator, as opposed to the And operator, gives a 1 if either or both of the binary digits are 1. Therefore:

   7 Or 12 = 15 (= 0111 Or 1100 = 1111 in binary)

Use Or to make sure specific bits are 1's (the on state). For example, X Or 4 makes sure that the third bit is on, X Or 64, the seventh bit, and so on.

One of the most interesting operators on the bit level is Xor (exclusive Or—X or Y but not both). This gives a 1 in a specific position if exactly one of the bits is on. Here's an example:

   7 Xor 12 = 11 (= 0111 Xor 1100 = 1011 in binary)

Xor has the useful property that using Xor twice with the same number does nothing. For example,

   (7 Xor 12) Xor 12 = 11 Xor 12 = 7

or, on the bit level,

```
0111 Xor 1100 = 1011
1011 Xor 1100 = 0111
```

That using the Xor command twice brings you back to where you started from is the key to a popular animation technique. This is because you can restore the previous display exactly as it was before (see Chapter 16). This property of the Xor operator is also the key to a popular method of encrypting information (see Chapter 18).

There are three other logical operators: Imp, Eqv, and Not. X Imp Y gives 1 except when X is 1 and Y is 0. X Eqv Y is 1 only when both bits are the same—both 1 or both 0. The Not operator, on the other hand, works on a number by reversing the bits—a 1 becomes a 0 and a 0 becomes a 1.

Finally, for those who are curious, here's the answer to the question posed at the beginning of the section as to why -1 is True in Visual Basic. Each integer takes 16 bits. Not 0 is then

```
Not (0000 0000 0000 0000) = 1111 1111 1111 1111
```

You might expect this to be the largest integer that can be represented in 16 bits (65,535 in decimal), but Visual Basic uses the leftmost bit for the sign. A 1 there means the number is negative. However, Visual Basic uses what is called *two's-complement notation* for negative numbers. In two's-complement notation, to represent a negative number you do the following:

1. Apply Not to the 15 bits that represent the number.
2. Set the leftmost bit to 1.
3. Add 1 to the result.

Therefore, for –1, take the bit pattern for 1:

```
000 0000 0000 0001
```

Apply Not:

```
111 1111 1111 1110
```

Add the leftmost bit as a –1:

```
1111 1111 1111 1110
```

Now add 1:

```
1111 1111 1111 1111
```

The result is that Not(0) is –1!

For an explanation of why this system really is useful, consult any book on microcomputer architecture.

Numeric Functions

If you don't do a lot of scientific work, it's unlikely that you will use many of the functions in this section very much. (One surprising use of the numeric functions is to draw curves. Chapter 16 shows you how to do this.)

However, one numeric function that you will often see (and may use a lot) is a cousin of the Fix function called Int. Int gives the *floor* of a number—the first integer that's smaller than or equal to the number. It's usually called the *greatest integer function*. However, thinking of it as the floor function makes it easy to remember what happens for negative numbers. With negative numbers, you move down. For example, Int(-3.5) is -4, Int(-4.1) is -5, and so on. You can see that Fix and Int work the same way for positive numbers but are different for negative ones. Using Int and adding 1 always moves to the next largest integer.

The Int and Fix functions have other uses. For example, the post office rates for first-class mail are 32 cents for the first ounce and 23 cents for each additional ounce (or fraction thereof). Suppose an item weighed 3.4 ounces. Then the cost would be 32 cents for the first ounce and 69 (3*23) for the additional ounces, counting the fraction. The cost is

```
.32 + Int(3.4)*.23  '.32 + Fix(3.4)*.23  works as well
```

In general, it's given by the following fragment:

```
If Int(WeightOfObject) = WeightOfObject Then
   Cost = .32 + .23*(WeightOfObject - 1)
Else
   Cost = .32 + .23*(Int(WeightOfObject))
EndIf
```

8

The (New) Round Function

One of the pains in previous versions of Visual Basic was the contortions you had to go through to round off a number. In VB6 all this pain is eliminated by using the nifty new Round function whose syntax is

Round(*expression* [,*NumberOfDecimalPlaces*])

where the optional second parameter allows you to round past the decimal point. If you leave it off, you get an integer. For example:

Round(3.7) = 4

Round(3.76, 1) = 3.76

Round(3.786, 2) = 3.79

Other Useful Numeric Functions

In this section I want to briefly describe the most important of the remaining numeric functions that VB has to offer. Obviously these functions will be of most use to people doing mathematical or engineering type calculations.

Sgn( ) The Sgn( ) function gives you a +1 if what is inside the parentheses is positive, -1 if negative, and a 0 if it's zero. One non-obvious use of this for integers or long integers is a For-Next loop in this form,

```
For I = A To B Step Sgn(A - B)
```

which, as long as A <> B, runs through the For-Next loop the correct number of times, regardless of whether A is greater than B or not.

Abs( ) The Abs function gives the absolute value of whatever is inside the parentheses. All this function does is remove minus signs:

Abs(-1) = 1 = Abs(1).

One common use of the absolute value function is Abs(B-A). This gives the distance between the numbers A and B. For example, suppose

A = 3 and B = 4.

Then,

Abs(A-B) = Abs(B-A) = 1

because 3 and 4 are one unit apart. As another example,

```
Abs(ASC(A$) - ASC(B$))
```

gives the "distance" between the first two characters of the strings A$ and B$.

You will often use the Abs function to set up a tolerance test in a Do loop, the framework looks like this:

```
Do Until Abs(Target - Source) < .0001

Loop
```

Sqr( ) The Sqr function returns the square root of the numeric expression inside the parentheses, which must be non-negative or a run-time error follows.

Exp( ) The Exp function gives e (e is roughly 2.7182) to the power x, where e is the base for natural logarithms, and x is the value in the parentheses. The answer is single precision if x is an integer or is itself a single-precision number; otherwise, the answer is a double-precision number.

Log( ) The Log function gives the natural logarithm of a number. To find the common log (log to base 10) use

```
Log10(x)=Log(x)/Log(10)
```

which gives the common logarithm of the value (which must be positive) inside the parentheses.

Another way to find the number of digits in a number is to use, for a number greater than 1:

```
Int(Log10(x)) + 1
```

For example, Log10(197) is between 2 and 3 because Log10(100) is 2 and Log10(1000) is 3.

As with the Exp function, the answer is single precision if *x* is an integer or is itself a single-precision number; otherwise, the answer is a double-precision number.

Trig Functions Also, for those who need them, Visual Basic has the built-in trigonometric functions Sin (sine), Cos (cosine), and Tan (tangent). The only problem is that Visual Basic expects the angle inside the parentheses following the functions to be in radian measure. To convert from degrees to radians, you need the value of π. The formula is

$$\text{radians} = \text{degrees} * \pi/180$$

TIP: The easiest way to find the value of π is to set up, early in your program, a form level (or even a global variable—see Chapter 9) PI# using the Atn (arctangent) function in the form:

Pi = 4 * Atn(1#)

This procedure works because the arctangent of 1 is $\pi/4$. You can also use the Atn function to find all the other inverse trigonometric functions.

The following table summarizes the inverse trigonometric functions, as well as some other useful functions you may want to build from the built-in ones.

Function	Result
pi = 4*Atn(1#)	Value of π in double precision
e = Exp(1#)	Value of e in double precision

Function	Result
Degrees to radians	Radians = degrees * π/180
Radians to degrees	Degrees = radians * 180/π
Sec (x)	1/Cos (x)
Csc (x)	1/Sin (x)
Cot (x)	1/Tan (x)
ArcCos (x)	Atn (x/Sqr(-x * x + 1)) + π/2
ArcSin (x)	Atn (x/Sqr(-x * x + 1))
ArcCot (x)	Atn (x) + π/2
Cosh (x)	(Exp(x) + Exp(-x))/2
Sinh (x)	(Exp(x) – Exp(-x))/2
$Log_{10}(x)$	Log(x)/Log(10)
Log_a (x)	Log(x)/Log(a)

Date and Time Functions

Visual Basic has many built-in functions you can use to read the information contained in the system clock about the time, day, and year. If you combine this with built-in functions for converting dates to numbers, financial calculations become much easier.

NOTE: All Date functions support named arguments.

The Date Function

The Date function returns a date of the form month-day-year (mm-dd-yyyy) for the current date. The month and day always use two digits; the year uses four (for example, 01-01-1999 for 1 January 1999). You can also use this function as a statement to reset the current date in the system. The least ambiguous way to do this is by assigning a string to Date in one of the following forms,

```
Date = "mm-dd-yyyy"
Date = "mm/dd/yyyy"
```

where *mm* are numerals between 01 and 12, *dd* are days between 01 and 31, and *yyyy* are years between 100 and 9999.

If you try to reset the date to an illegal date, such as 31 February, you get an "Illegal function call" message box when you run the program. You can also use a two-digit year, but this is not practical for forward-looking programs; Visual Basic assumes you mean 20th-century and not 21st-century dates when there is an ambiguity.

One point to remember: if your computer has a built-in clock calendar, then to permanently reset the clock, you may have to use the setup program that came with the computer. The changes made by Date may remain only until you reboot your computer.

You can also read the time in the system clock or temporarily (see the preceding paragraph) reset it with the Time function. The Time function returns an eight-character date of the form hh:mm:ss. To reset it, assign a string of the correct form to Time, as shown in the following table. The hours range between 00 for midnight and 23 for 11:00 P.M.

Example of Time Command	Effect
Time ="hh"	Sets the hour; minutes and seconds are set to 0
Time ="hh:mm"	Sets the hour and minutes; seconds are set to 0
Time ="hh:mm:ss"	Sets the hour, minutes, and seconds

8

Numeric Calendar Functions

To do financial calculations accurately, your programs must be able to calculate the number of days that have passed between two dates—taking leap years into account, if possible! Visual Basic makes this easy. You simply store the information in two variables of Date type, subtract them, and you're done. (Remember, you surround a date variable with #.)

Sometimes it isn't convenient to use the # notation. When it isn't, Visual Basic supplies the function DateValue(String). This function yields an expression of Date type representing the date defined by the string expression inside the parentheses. Besides accepting strings in the expected form of mm-dd-yyyy, this function can also accept the name of the month or any unambiguous abbreviation for the month. For example, all of the following give the same value to the variable PreMillennium:

```
Dim PreMillennium As Date
PreMillennium = DateValue("12-31-1999")
PreMillennium = DateValue("December 31, 1999")
PreMillennium = DateValue("Dec 31, 1999")
PreMillennium = DateValue("31 December 1999")
PreMillennium = DateValue("31-Dec-1999")
```

You cannot use this function if the date doesn't make sense. For example,

DateValue("2-30-1998")

gives a "Type mismatch" message at run time.

Of course, you will usually need to know what today's date is. For this, Visual Basic has three functions, as summarized in the following table.

Function	Description
Now	Returns the date and time as stored in the system clock
Date	Returns the current date
Time	Returns the current time

For example, suppose you want to write a program that uses these functions to calculate how many days someone has been alive. The form might look like Figure 8-3. It has two text boxes, one label, and a command button named cmdCalculate. Let's call the first text button txtBirthDate and the other txtDaysAlive. Set the Text property of both text boxes to be "", and set the Locked property of the second button to True. The code is simply:

```
Private Sub cmdCalculate_Click()
  Dim BirthDate As Date, CurrentDate As Date
  If Not IsDate(txtBirthDate.Text) Then
    MsgBox ("I don't recognize that format, please retry.")
    txtBirthDate = ""
  Else
    BirthDate = txtBirthDate
    txtDaysAlive.Text = "You have been alive " & Date - _
BirthDate & " days."
  End If

End Sub
```

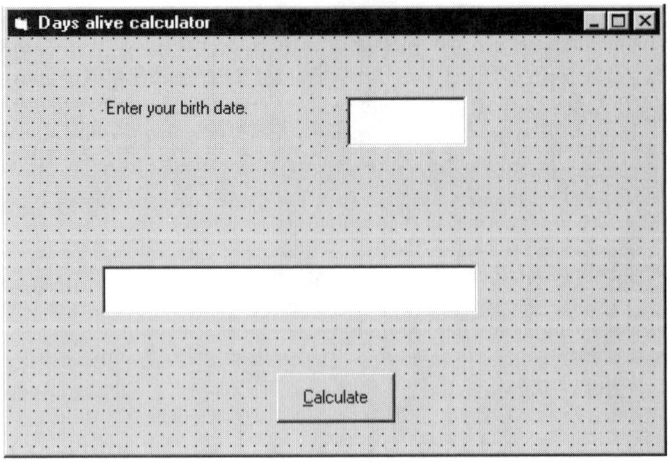

Form for days
alive program
Figure 8-3.

You will also occasionally need the DateSerial function. This returns a number that you can use for date calculations. Its syntax is

DateSerial(*Year, Month, Day*)

Year is an integer between 0 and 9999 inclusive (or an integral expression that Visual Basic can reduce to this form), *Month* is an integer (or integral expression) with a value between 1 and 12, and *Day* should be some number between 1 and 31 depending on the month. (If you go beyond these limits, Visual Basic wraps into the next month!) For example,

DateSerial(1998, 1, 35)

will give you a date in February!

You can apply the Format function to any date expression to display the information contained in the number. For example, if it is now 10:01 P.M. on January 1, 1998, the results are as follows:

Form	Display
Format(Now,"m/d-yy")	1/1/98
Format(Now,"hh:mm")	22:01
Format(Now,"hh:mm AM/PM")	10:01 PM
Format(Now,"hh:mm AM/PM mm/dd/yy")	10:01 PM 01/01/98

8

There are many other possibilities for format strings for dates. The online documentation is very useful if you need a special format.

Financial Functions

Visual Basic comes with a library of financial functions for handling standard calculations that everyone will occasionally need to do. (In fact, some of the financial example programs in Chapters 5 and 7 could have fewer lines of code and run faster if you use these functions.) Source code, however, is not supplied for these functions, which are installed in compiled form as part of the Visual Basic for Applications library.

NOTE: Since all these functions come from the Visual Basic for Applications library, they all support named arguments.

Since the terminology in the help files may be obscure to people with no accounting or economics training, this section describes the functions most often used and the terms used in the help files to describe them.

Let's start with the function that will let you do a mortgage calculation. First off, if you look in the help file for financial functions, all you will see is a list as follows:

DDB Function
FV Function
IPmt Function
IRR Function
MIRR Function
NPer Function
NPV Function
Pmt Function
PPmt Function
PV Function
Rate Function
SLN Function
SYD Function

None of these seem to have anything to do with a mortgage calculation. It turns out that the function you need is the Pmt function. In the online help it is described as follows:

Returns the payment for an annuity based on periodic, constant payments and a constant interest rate.

The keyword here (in fact the keyword for most of the financial functions) is "annuity." An *annuity* is a fancy term for a series of payments made over time. For example, when you have a mortgage, you start out with a (large) amount, make (many) payments over time, and end up with a zero balance. (There are also balloon mortgages in which the balance isn't zero.) In the retirement calculator from Chapter 7, you made periodic deposits over time and thereby ended up with a (large) amount of money at the end.

The syntax for the Pmt function is best explained as:

Pmt(*RatePerPeriod, NumPeriods, WhatYouStartWith, WhatYouEndUpWith, WhenDoYouPay*)

For example, to calculate a 30-year $100,000 mortgage at 8 percent, use

```
MortgagePayment = Pmt(.08/12, 30*12, 100000, 0, 1)
```

NOTE: In all the entries (and the result as well), moneys paid out are represented by negative numbers; moneys received are represented by positive numbers.

Here's a description of what the parameters in the Pmt function stand for:

◆ *RatePerPeriod*—Usually the interest rate is quoted per year, but you pay every month. This entry needs the interest rate per payment rate. You can ask Visual Basic to do the calculation. So if the yearly rate for the mortgage was 8 percent, the RatePerPeriod would be .08/12, and you would use this in the first position.

◆ *NumPeriods*—This is the number of periods. For example, for a 30-year mortgage, this would be 30*12. For a 20-year biweekly mortgage, this would be 20*26.

◆ *WhatYouStartWith*—In a mortgage, this would start out as the balance. If you were saving money for college, it would be what your initial balance was.

◆ *WhatYouEndUpWith*—In a mortgage, this would be zero. (In a balloon mortgage, this would be the "balloon payment.") For a savings plan, this would be the amount you wanted to end up with for retirement or college.

◆ *WhenDoYouPay*—Do you pay at the beginning of the period or at the end? Use a 0 for the end of the month and a 1 for the beginning. (For a $100,000 mortgage at 8 percent, it costs about $5 more per month to pay at the end of the month. Not that many banks allow you to do this, though.)

NOTE: In the help files, this function is described as:

Pmt(*rate, nper, pv*[, *fv*[, *type*]])

8

Although you need to use these names for the parameters if you use them as named arguments, Microsoft's notation does not stress enough that the units you use for the various entries must be the same. For example, if *rate* is calculated using months, *nper* must also be calculated using months.

Example: Rewriting the Mortgage Program Using the Pmt Function

All we have to do is change one line in the program from the section called "Example: Improving the Mortgage Calculator" in Chapter 7. It's indicated in bold below. The trick was to remember to

1. Change the sign to a negative because the Pmt function reports a negative number for amounts you have to pay

2. Use the right interest rate by dividing the yearly interest rate by 12

3. Use the right number of periods by multiplying the number of years by 12

Here's the procedure with the single change in bold:

```
Private Sub cmdCalculate_Click()
    'Calculates a mortgage table using original amounts
    'but having the interest rate move up by 1/8%
    'local variables and constants
```

```
'use the built in Pmt function this time
Dim SpaceChar As String, T$
Dim Years As Integer, Payment As Currency
Dim MonthInt As Single, Principal As Currency
Dim Percent As Single, Interest  As Single
Dim StartInterest As Single, EndInterest As Single
Dim Amount As Currency, StartAmount As Currency
Dim EndAmount As Currency

Const DAMOUNT = "###.00"
Const IRATE = "00.00%"

'Get info
Years = CInt(txtMortgageTerm.Text)
Principal = CCur(txtMortgageAmount.Text)
Percent = CInt(txtInterestRate.Text) / 100
StartInterest = Percent - 0.01             '1% change
EndInterest = Percent + 0.01
StartAmount = Principal - 25000
EndAmount = Principal + 25000
For Amount = StartAmount To EndAmount Step 5000
  For Interest = StartInterest To EndInterest Step 0.00125
    MonthInt = Interest / 12
    Payment = -Pmt(Interest / 12, Years * 12, Amount, 0, 1)
    T$ = T$ & Format$(Interest, IRATE) & Space$(20) + _
"for " & Amount & " =" & Space$(7) & Format$(Payment, DAMOUNT) & vbCrLf
  Next Interest
  txtMortgageTable.Text = T$
Next Amount
End Sub
```

Other Financial Functions

Now that you know the key terms and how one of these functions works, here are
short descriptions of the other financial functions.

FV   This is the function used, for example, for a retirement calculation, because it
gives you the future value of an annuity based on periodic payments (or withdrawals)
and a constant interest rate. The syntax in the online help is

   FV(*rate, nper, pmt*[, *pv*[, *type*]])

and you can think of this as:

   FV(*InterestRatePerPeriod, NumPeriods, PaymentPerPeriod* [, *StartAmount*[, *WhenDue*]])

Again, the first two arguments must be expressed using the same units. And, as for all
financial functions, moneys paid out will be given by negative numbers; moneys
received are given by positive numbers.

IPmt   This gives the interest paid over a given period of an annuity based on
periodic, equal payments and a constant interest rate. For example, you could use this

to check that your mortgage company's computers are reporting the correct number to the IRS for the interest you paid in a
given year.

The syntax (using Microsoft's notation) is

> IPmt(*rate, per, nper, pv, fv, due*)

where *rate* is the interest rate per period, and *per* is the period in the range 1 through the number of periods (*nper*). For example, the interest paid in the first month of the third year of a 30-year $100,000 mortgage at 8 percent is

```
IPmt(.08/12, 25, 360, 100000, 0, 1)
```

(So you would modify this code in a loop to calculate the interest over a given year.)

NPer   This function tells you how long it will take (the number of periodic deposits/withdrawals) to accumulate (disburse) an annuity. The syntax is

> NPer(*rate, pmt, pv, fv, due*)

For example, suppose you are getting 5 percent on your money and you have $100,000 in the bank. To calculate how long it would take to spend the $100,000 that you have saved if you withdrew the money at a rate of $1,000 a month, use

8

```
NPer(.05/12, -1000, 100000, 0, 1)
```

PV   This is the functional equivalent of "a bird in the hand is worth two in the bush." Getting $1,000 ten years from now is not the same as getting $1,000 now. How bad it is depends on the prevailing interest rates. What this function does is tell you how much periodic payments made over the future are worth now. (The technical term for this is *present value*.)

The syntax is

> PV(*rate, nper, pmt, fv, due*)

The *rate* is, as usual, the interest rate per period, *nper* is the total number of payments made, *pmt* is the number of payments made each period. The *fv* entry is the future value or cash balance you want after you've received (made) the final payment.

For example, if someone agrees to pay you $1,000 a month for ten years and the assumed prevailing interest rate is 6 percent, then this deal is worth

```
PV(.06/12, 120, -1000, 0, 1)
```

to you now. (This is why lotteries can advertise big prizes but pay out relatively little. A $10 million prize paid out over 20 years if the prevailing interest rate is 6 percent is worth about $6 million.)

NPV   This is the net present value function. This function is used, for example, if you start out by paying money as startup costs but then get money in succeeding years. The syntax is

   NPV(*RatePerPeriod, ArrayOf*( ))

You have to fill the array with the appropriate values in the correct order. For example, the first entry could be a negative number representing startup costs and the remaining entries a positive number representing value received. At least one entry must be positive and one entry must be negative. This function is more general than the PV function because using an array allows the amounts received or disbursed to change over time.

Rate   This function gives the interest rate per period for an annuity. You would use this to check on the interest rate you would really be paying if you actually responded to the standard advertising come-on of "Only $49.95 a month for three years will buy you this gadget." (Use the cost today for the *pv* parameter.)

The syntax is

   Rate(*nper, pmt, pv, fv, due, guess*)

The only entry you haven't seen is *guess*. The Rate function uses an iterative procedure to arrive at the true interest rate. You can usually just guess .01 and let Visual Basic do the rest. What happens is, the answer Rate is calculated by iteration. Visual Basic starts with the value of *guess* and repeats the calculation until the result is accurate to within 0.00001 percent. If, after 20 tries, it can't find a result, the function fails. If the function fails, try a different value for *guess*.

The Remaining Financial Functions

The remaining financial functions are mostly used by business. Explaining them would take us too far afield.

SLN and DDB   These functions return the straight line and double declining balance depreciation of an asset over a given period. The syntaxes are

   SLN(*Cost, SalvageValue, LifeExpectancy*)

and

   DDB(*Cost, SalvageValue, LifeExpectancy, PeriodOfCalculation*)

IRR, MIRR   These give versions of the internal rate of return for a series of payments and receipts. IRR gives the ordinary internal rate of return, and MIRR gives the modified rate in which you allow payments and receipts to have different interest rates. The syntax for the IRR function is

IRR(*ValueArray( )*, *Guess*)

As with the NPV function, the *ValueArray( )* contains the receipts and disbursements and must contain at least one negative value (a payment) and one positive value (a receipt). Also, as before, the value of Guess is your best estimate for the value returned by IRR. In most cases, start with a guess of 1 percent (.01).

The MIRR function has the following syntax:

MIRR(*ValueArray( )*, *FinanceRate*, *ReinvestRate*)

Tables with the Most Useful Functions

This chapter ends with some tables that summarize the functions I use most. You can check the online help for more details on them if they are not covered in this chapter. Table 8-1 lists the most common functions, Table 8-2 lists the most common string functions, and Table 8-3 gives you the functions for handling dates and times.

NOTE: Remember, most of the string functions have a form with a dollar sign at the end of them, for example Left$, Mid$, and so on. The difference is that the dollar form returns a string rather than a string inside a variant. For this reason, the $ variant will often run faster.

8

Function	Purpose
Abs	Finds the absolute value of a number
Atn	Finds the arctangent
Cos	Finds the cosine
Exp	Raises e (2.7182...) to the given power
Fix	Returns the integer part of a number
FV	Future value
Hex	Gives the hex equivalent
Int	Finds the greatest integer
IPmt	Interest paid over time
IRR	Internal rate of return
Log	Common logarithm
MIRR	Modified internal rate of return

Common
Functions
Table 8-1.

Function	Purpose
NPer	Time to accumulate (disburse) an annuity
NPV	Net present value
Pmt	Pay out for annuity
PPmt	Principal paid out in an annuity payment
PV	Present value
Rate	Interest rate per period for an annuity
Rnd	Calls the random number generator
Round	Rounds the number
Sgn	Returns the sign of a number
Sin	Returns the sine of the number
SLN	Straight line depreciation
Sqr	The square root function
SYD	Sum of years depreciation
Tan	The tangent of an angle in radians

Common Functions (*continued*)
Table 8-1.

Function	Description
Asc	Returns the character code corresponding to the first letter in a string
InStr	Returns the position of the first occurrence of one string within another
InStrRev	Returns the position of the last occurrence of one string within another
Join	Lets you build a larger string out of smaller strings (see Chapter 10)
LCase	Converts a string to lowercase
Left	Finds or removes a specified number of characters from the beginning of a string
Len	Gives the length of a string
LTrim	Removes spaces from the beginning of a string
Mid	Finds or removes characters from a string
Replace	Allows you to replace one or more occurrences of a string inside another

The Most Common String Functions
Table 8-2.

Function	Description
Right	Finds or removes a specified number of characters from the end of a string
RTrim	Removes spaces from the end of a string
Split	Allows you to break up a string at specified places (such as spaces). Please see Chapter 10 for more on this very useful function.
Str	Returns the string equivalent of a number (the numeral)
StrComp	Another way to do string comparisons
StrConv	Converts a string from one form to another
String	Returns a repeated string of identical characters
Trim	Trims spaces from both the beginning and end of a string
UCase	Converts a string to uppercase

The Most Common String Functions (*continued*)
Table 8-2.

Function	Description
Date	Returns the current date (from the system clock)
DateAdd	Lets you add a specified interval to a date
DateDiff	Lets you subtract a specified interval from a date
DateSerial	Returns a Date corresponding to the specified day, month, and year
DateValue	Takes a string and returns a date
Day	Tells you what day a string or number represents
Hour	Tells you what hour a string or number represents
Minute	Tells you what minute a string or number represents
Month	Tells you what month a string or number represents
Now	Returns the current time and date
Second	Tells you what second a string or number represents
Time	Tells you the current time in the system clock
TimeSerial	Returns a variable of date type for the given time
Weekday	Tells you what day of the week a date corresponds to
Year	Tells you what year a date corresponds to

Date and Time Functions
Table 8-3.

8

CHAPTER 9

Writing Your Own Functions and Procedures

I assume that by now you're quite comfortable with the basics of using Visual Basic's event procedures. While it is true that event procedures are the core of Visual Basic programming, they shouldn't be made *too* complicated. If an event procedure is much longer than one page—or even one screen length—it will probably be too long to debug easily. You should consider doing some of the work in one or more of Visual Basic's *general* procedures. Showing you how to write this kind of helper code is the purpose of this chapter.

There are actually two kinds of general procedures in Visual Basic: Function procedures and Sub procedures. *Function procedures,* or *user-defined functions,* are simply ways of going beyond the built-in Visual Basic functions that you saw in the last chapter by building your own. In particular, regardless of whether it is a function you write or one that the creators of Visual Basic supplied, you'll want to think of a function as a self-contained piece of code designed to massage data and return a value.

Sub procedures, on the other hand, are smaller "helper programs" that are used (or *called,* in the jargon) as needed. Sub procedures are thus generalizations of the event procedures you are already familiar with. Unlike functions, which normally return values, procedures simply do things. (Ideally, one thing—well.)

To sum up, regardless of whether you choose a Function procedure or a Sub procedure, the point is that Sub and Function procedures do one or more of the following:

◆ Help you break down large tasks into smaller ones

◆ Automate repeated operations

◆ Make it clearer what it is you are trying to accomplish by "naming" a piece of code.

All these features can dramatically reduce debugging time. (See Chapters 12 and 13 for more about coding techniques to reduce bugs and make the whole coding process easier to accomplish.)

NOTE: People sometimes use the term *subprogram* when they want to refer to both functions and procedures at once. Other people simply say "procedures" and leave it to you (and the context) to determine if they mean a Function procedure or a Sub procedure.

Function Procedures

Start thinking about defining your own functions when you use a complicated expression more than once in a project. For example, suppose you need a random integer between 1 and 10. You could write

```
TheChoice = Int((10 * Rnd) + 1)
```

each time you needed it, but this might eventually grow tiresome. Also, until they really think about it, it might not be clear to someone reading your code what this line does. You could simply comment the line, but "self-documenting" code is always better. Wouldn't

```
TheChoice = RandomInt1To10
```

be clearer?

Next, suppose that the same program needs a random integer between 1 and 40, between 1 and 100, and so on. The code might look like this:

```
TheChoice = Int((40* Rnd) + 1)
TheChoice = Int((100* Rnd) + 1)
```

The statements needed for these two uses are so similar to the earlier statement that it would be nice to have a way of automating the process—to have Visual Basic do some of the work! This is the role of a subprogram. In this case, since we want to return a value, we will need to create a Function procedure—a user-defined function.

As with any code, you'll write the code for your function procedures in the usual code window.

9

TIP: Remember that on top of the vertical scroll bar in the code window is the split bar. When you are writing subprograms, being able to look at two different parts of your code simultaneously is very handy. Recall that, as you drag the split bar with the mouse, the screen splits into two parts. The size of the parts depends on how far you drag the mouse and you can eliminate one of the panes by dragging the split bar to the top or bottom. The key point is that you can then use the direction keys to cycle independently through all the procedures attached to a specific form. (Press CTRL+an arrow key if you are not in full module view.)

Writing a Simple Function

In this chapter we will always be attaching functions to the current form. To do this, open the Code window by double-clicking anywhere in the form or by pressing F7. Now choose Tools|Add Procedure from the Tools menu, and the Add Procedure dialog box will pop up, as shown here:

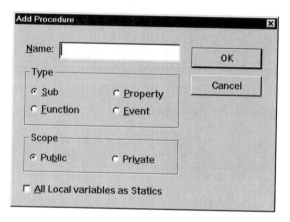

You'll learn more about this dialog box as the chapter progresses, but for now click the Function radio button (or use the ALT+F shortcut) and type a name for your function. (The example uses the name RandomRange1To because we will start our random integers at 1.) Click on OK, and a function template for the form, shown in Figure 9-1, pops up in the Code window.

Now make your code look like this. You'll need to add an X inside the parentheses but otherwise the VB supplied template gives you the first and last lines. Enter the following code:

```
Public Function RandomRange1To(X) As Integer
   Randomize
   RandomRange1To = Int(X * Rnd) + 1
End Function
```

Although this is a pretty simple function, its parts are the same as they would be in any function that you write—no matter how complicated. I want to go over them piece by piece. The first line of the function (the line containing its name) is called the *header* of the function. The keyword Public is called an *access specifier*. These specifiers are used to describe what other code can use your function. You have seen its cousin already, the more restrictive access specifier *Private*, because that specifier is the default for event procedures. You'll see more about what these two specifiers mean in Chapter 12. (And, yes, you can change the Private to Public for an event procedure. But I suggest waiting until Chapter 12 to do this when I cover the ramifications of making this change.) The X is important; it's called the (formal) parameter and I'll

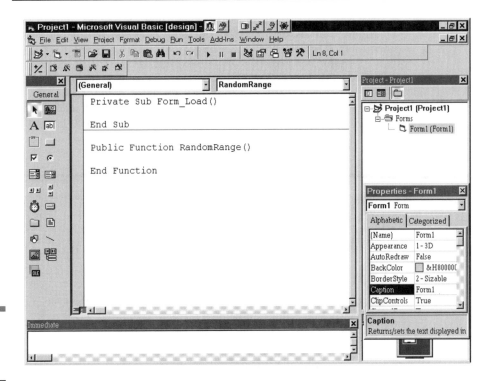

take up the whole notion of parameters in the next section. In the function templates automatically supplied by VB, you will always have to put in the parameters by hand.

When naming a function (in this case, RandomRange1To), you must follow the same rules as you would for naming variables in Visual Basic (see Chapter 5). If you prefer, you can add a type identifier at the end of the name of a function or use the As identifier. For example, you could write

```
Public Function RandomRange% ( X )
Public Function RandomRange ( X ) As Integer
```

In both cases, Visual Basic will then know that the function returns integer values.

Next comes the *body* of the function—the code that actually defines the function's power. In the body of the function, you'll always want a line that assigns a value to the function using its name. In our example the key line is

```
RandomRange1To = Int(X * Rnd) + 1
```

This assignment statement is how the function gets its value. What value it will get depends on the X that occurs both here and in the header of the function. What the X is and how it is used by Visual Basic is easy once you get the hang of it, but it can be confusing at first. Of course, the first step in understanding the X is to learn what it is called. Its imposing name is the *formal parameter* but it is easiest to think of it as a *placeholder*. (Keep in mind that you have seen parameters in various key event procedures, such as KeyUp.) To see why thinking of the formal parameter as simply being a placeholder is helpful, keep in mind that once you add this code to the current form as we just did, then to print a random integer between 1 and 10, you can write

```
Print RandomRange1To(10)
```

When Visual Basic processes a line of code like this, VB substitutes the value 10 for the placeholder X *everywhere* it appears in the body of the function. In particular, the key line inside the function becomes

```
RandomRange1To = Int(10 * Rnd) + 1
```

which you already know gives you a random integer between 1 and 10. This, in turn, is what Visual Basic will return as the value of the function. Finally, notice that when you go to use a user-defined function in your code, Visual Basic applies the same IntelliSense that it does for its own built-in functions, and it shows you what you need to feed to the function, as you can see here:

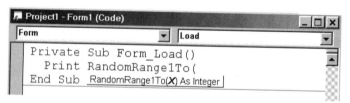

More on Parameters

Let's go back to the header of our function.

```
Public Function RandomRange1To(X) As Integer
```

Notice that in this line, the parameter is a variant because we have not used any type identifier. If we wanted to ensure that you could only send integers to the function, we could have written something like

```
Public Function RandomRange1To (X As Integer) As Integer
```

to ensure that the parameter, in addition to what the function gave back, was also always an integer.

CAUTION: Keep in mind that the type identifier and the type used for the return value determine what you can send and get out of the function. If you changed

```
Public Function RandomRange1To (X As Integer) As Integer
```

and instead wrote

```
Number% = RandomRange1To(3000000)
```

you'd get an overflow error. Similarly, the largest value that this function can return is 32,767.

Next, in our original example we replaced the parameter with a number. This is far too restrictive. For example, when you want to use (or *call*) a function you may want to replace the formal parameter (the placeholder) with an *expression*. When you do this, Visual Basic replaces all occurrences of the placeholder in the function with the value of the expression. In particular, Visual Basic does *any* necessary calculations. Therefore, if

$A = 3$ and $B = 2$

and you write

9

```
N% = RandomRange1To(A * B + 37)
```

this will have the same effect as

```
N% = RandomRange1To(43)
```

which, in turn, is the same as using code like

```
N% = Int(43 * Rnd) + 1
```

NOTE: The value you send the function is sometimes called the *actual parameter*. For more details on what happens when you send a variable to a function rather than an expression involving variables, please see the section on "Passing by Reference, Passing by Value" later in this chapter.

CAUTION: Be very careful about having a formal parameter on the left side of an assignment statement in the body of the function. As you will soon see, Visual Basic defaults to sending the memory location of the actual parameters to the function. This means that any changes you make to the parameters inside the body of the function will affect the original variables you may have used as a parameter. (See the section "Passing by Reference, Passing by Value" later in the chapter for more on this.)

Finally, the X used as a parameter (placeholder) in the definition of the function has no independent existence. If you used X as a variable somewhere earlier—even as a form or global variable—no assignment to its value ever affects the value of the function nor do any assignments you make inside the function affect even a form level variable that might have been named X elsewhere in your program.

Functions with More Than One Parameter

The function RandomRange1To works with one piece of information; that is, it's a function of one variable (or one parameter). However, you will frequently want the value of a function to depend on more than one piece of information. For example, suppose you want a range of random integers between X and Y. You can modify RandomRange1To as follows:

```
Public Function RandomRangeXToY (X As Integer, Y As Integer) As Integer
   Randomize
   RandomRangeXToY = Int((Y - X + 1) * Rnd) + X
End Function
```

This may seem a little tricky. If so, try to see what happens with numbers like X = 5 and Y = 37.

1. Multiplying the value you get from Rnd by Y - X + 1 (=33) gives a number between 0 and 32.999999.

2. Using the built-in Int function then gives you a range between 0 and 32 (= Y - X).

3. Finally, adding X gives you an integer in the desired range (5 through 37).

Next, if you want to make sure that the function can use long integer values and therefore use and return larger values, rewrite it as follows:

```
Public Function RandomRangeXToY (X As Long, Y As Long) As Long
   Randomize
   RandomRangeXToY = Int((Y - X + 1) * Rnd) + X
End Function
```

Now the placeholders can only have long integer values. In either case, as long as the parameters are defined as either type of integer, then setting

```
Number% = RandomRangeXToY (2.7, 39.2)
```

will cause 2.7 to be rounded up to 3 and 39.2 to be rounded down to 39 when Visual Basic substitutes their values into the function definition.

Example: A Postage Calculator

Just to make sure you have the concept of functions down, here is an example of a simple user-defined function. We want to write a program that lets you compute how much the postage will be for a letter. The rule is that it will cost you .32 for the first ounce and .23 for each additional ounce or fractional part. The following function calculates the cost of mailing a letter:

```
Public Function Postage(Weight As Single) As Currency
  'Calculate the cost, in cents, of mailing
  'a first-class letter of a given weight in ounces
  'the rule is .32 for the first ounce and .23 for
  'each additional ounce or fractional part

  If Int(Weight) = Weight Then
    Postage = 0.32 + (0.23 * (Weight - 1))
  Else
    Postage = 0.32 + (0.23 * (Int(Weight)))
  End If
End Function
```

Notice that we will have two alternate definitions of the function depending on which branch of the If-Then is taken. This is quite typical of a more sophisticated function definition. Now if you add a text box (name it txtWeight) and a command button (name it cmdCalculate) to a form, like the one shown here

9

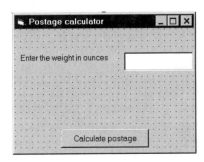

then, adding the following code to the cmdCalculate_Click procedure lets you calculate the postage:

```
Private Sub cmdCalculate_Click()
'local variables:
Dim WeightOfLetter As Single, Msg$

  WeightOfLetter = CSng(txtWeight.Text)
  Msg$ = "The cost to mail that letter is "
  Msg$ = Msg$ & Format(Postage(WeightOfLetter), "Currency")
  MsgBox Msg$
End Sub
```

Of course, this isn't a particularly robust program. To make the program more robust, we have to check the information the user placed in the text box before we send it off to the function. With the Postage function, what we need to do is check whether the weight is a positive number. The following modification of the cmdCalculate_Click procedure does this by first checking if the user entered a number, and then checking if the number is positive. (Notice how much code is needed to do even the simplest kind of validation.)

```
Private Sub cmdCalculate_Click()
'local variables:
Dim WeightOfLetter As Single, Msg$

If Not IsNumeric(txtWeight.Text) Then
  Beep
  MsgBox "Please enter a positive number for the weight"
  txtWeight = ""
  Exit Sub
End If
WeightOfLetter = CSng(txtWeight.Text)
If WeightOfLetter > 0 Then
  Msg$ = "The cost to mail that letter is "
  Msg$ = Msg$ & Format(Postage(WeightOfLetter), "Currency")
  MsgBox Msg$
 Else
  Beep
  MsgBox "A letter must have positive weight!"
  cmdText.Weight =""
End If
End Sub
```

It is possible to combine the test of being numeric and being positive into one If-Then. However, I think the above code, though a little longer, is slightly clearer than doing this in one If-Then would have been. This is because for most people, nested If-Thens tend to be harder to understand in this type of code than using the Exit Sub as I did. (That's one of the reasons why VB also has an Exit Function command to let you leave a user-defined function quickly!)

Still, the code is getting kind of long, so it is about time to think about putting the validation code in a separate function. If we want to do this, we will need a function that returns a Boolean (True/False) value. This is a more professional way of proceeding—you will often find yourself putting your validation code in a separate function.

Here's what I think is a better way of writing this program. First off, we will keep the function that calculates the postage. All we need to do is make sure we are sending it good data. Next, we add a validation function. Here's what one might look like. It is a little tricky (but typical) because it uses a nested if-then, so I'll go over it line by line after you look it over:

```
Public Function IsPositive(X As Variant) As Boolean
  If IsNumeric(X) Then
```

```
      If CSng(X) > 0 Then
         IsPositive = True
      Else
         IsPositive = False
      End If
   Else
      IsPositive = False
   End If
End Function
```

The idea is simple: we want an improved version of the built-in IsNumeric function that takes a variant. This is why the parameter for our function is a variant. Next, it should return a Boolean (True/False). The actual code does the following:

1. First, checks if the variant is a number.
2. If it is *not* a number, the outer Else clause is activated and the function gets the value "False".
3. If it *is* a number, the inner If-Then-Else starts up. This checks if the number is positive or not.

(Notice that to make this code even more bulletproof we would not only want to check that the number is positive but also that it is in the correct range for the Single type. I'll leave this extra level of safety to you.)

 TIP: Having nested If-Thens in validation code is quite common, so it is worth getting comfortable with the style. The usual way to avoid it would be to use an Exit Function statement to leave the function—see the section called "Leaving Functions Prematurely" later in this chapter for a version of the IsPositive function that uses Exit Function.

9

Finally, we can rewrite the cmdCalculate_Click code to take into account our new validation code:

```
Private Sub cmdCalculate_Click()
'local variables:
Dim WeightOfLetter As Single, Msg$

If IsPositive(txtWeight.Text) Then
   WeightOfLetter = CSng(txtWeight.Text)
   Msg$ = "The cost to mail that letter is "
   Msg$ = Msg$ & Format(Postage(WeightOfLetter), "Currency")
   MsgBox Msg$
Else
   Beep
   MsgBox "A letter must have positive weight!"
   txtWeight.Text = ""
End If
End Sub
```

Going Further with User-Defined Functions

Since the names you choose for your function have the same flexibility as the names of Visual Basic variables, choose meaningful function names; they will certainly make your program more readable, as well as easier to debug. Keep in mind that unless you give a function an explicit type identifier at the end of the name or via an As clause, the type defaults to the Variant data type (or to whatever type the active DefType statement dictates). The simplest (but still quite general) form of a function definition is

> Public Function *FunctionName* (*parameter1, parameter2, ...*)
>   *statements*
>   *FunctionName = expression*
>   *statements*
>   *FunctionName = expression*
>   *statements*
>   *etc.*
> End Function

where *parameter1, parameter2*, and so on are variables. As you have seen, these variables are referred to as the *parameters* or *arguments* of the function. The types of the parameters can be specified by type-declaration tags or with As phrases. Next, if VB ever encounters code like

> ...FunctionName (*YourExpressionForParameter1, YourExpressionForParameter2, ...*) ...

in *any* Visual Basic statement, then the value of *YourExpressionForParameter1* is assigned to all occurrences of *parameter1* inside the body of the function, the value of *YourExpressionForParameter2* is assigned to all occurrences of *parameter2* inside the body of the function, and so on. Visual Basic will do any calculations needed to get this value. The expressions you use as *YourExpressionForParameter1, YourExpressionForParameter2*, and so on can be either constants, variables, or expressions. (Remember, parameters are placeholders—they have no existence outside of this role.)

Immediately after processing a line with this kind of statement, Visual Basic sends the information to the function definition. It then executes the statements in the body of the function definition using the information contained in the parameters; the last value assigned to the *FunctionName* inside the body of the function is the one Visual Basic uses as the result of the function.

It is good to get used to the terminology that more experienced programmers like to use when working with function procedures. They would say that a Visual Basic statement using a function is *calling* the function and *passing* the various expressions to the parameters. (Sometimes people use the term "the arguments" for the function as a shorthand to describe the expressions you are passing.) The function is said to *return* its value. For instance, in the example in the previous section, the statement

```
Format(Postage(WeightOfLetter), "Currency")
```

calls the Postage function, *passing* it the argument WeightOfLetter.

The type of the value returned by the function is specified with a type-declaration tag (%, !, &, #, or $) appended to the function name, or the named used in the As clause at the end of the Function line, or by a DefType statement appearing above the Function definition.

NOTE: Unlike early versions of Visual Basic, after version 4 you can have lines in your programs that simply use

FunctionName (arg1, arg2, arg3)

without assigning the results to a variable. However, this is unusual for most Visual Basic programmers (it is C-style function calling). If you did use this form of function calling, the statements inside the function would be executed, but no value would be returned—only the side effects caused by the function would occur. Generally speaking, most Visual Basic programmers prefer to make the call to a function part of an expression or statement (most often in an assignment statement) and use the Sub procedures for when they don't need the return value.

If your user-defined function takes no arguments, you can leave off the parentheses when you assign it to a variable. For example, if you had a function

```
Public Function RandomIntegerTo10() As Integer
   Randomize
   RandomIntegerTo10 = Int(10*Rnd) + 1
End Function
```

then you can use either

```
X = RandomIntegerTo10
```

or

```
X = RandomIntegerTo10()
```

9

in your code to call the function.

Next, with one exception that you'll see shortly (see the section called "Subprograms That Have Optional Arguments"), you can only call a function when you use the same number of arguments as there are parameters in the definition of the function. Each variable that you want to send to a parameter must be of the same type (integer, long integer, and so on) as the corresponding parameter with *one exception*. The exception is exactly the one that I took advantage of in the definition of the IsPositive function: you can use *any* type of variable if the parameter is of the variant type.

What this means is that only an integer *variable* argument can be passed to an integer parameter. You could not pass it directly to a long integer parameter of a function.

This can be a bit confusing, so here is an example. To follow this example:

1. Set up a command button on an ordinary form.
2. Add the following code to the form:

```
Private Sub Command1_Click()
  Dim Foo As Integer
  Foo = 37
  Print Test(Foo)
End Sub
Public Function Test(A As Long)
  Test = A + 1
End Function
```

What this code does is try to add 1 to whatever is passed to the long integer parameter. But the Click event procedure sets up the variable Foo as being of integer type.

Okay, run this code. If you do, you will get the message box shown next:

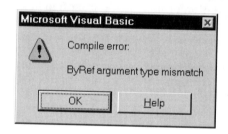

As you can see, Visual Basic refuses to pass a variable of type integer to a parameter of type long—even though in most cases an integer will work in all the places a long will. (After all, it is easy to think of the integer type as being a part of the long Integer type!)

NOTE: I certainly don't advocate using the variant type in the parameters of your functions to avoid this error message (only do that when you need the special properties of variants). Instead I suggest using the correct conversion function. For example, if you used

```
Print Test(CLng(Foo))
```

then the example above would work just fine.

Here's another example, if the function was

```
Public Function RandomRangeXToY (X As Long, Y As Long) As Long
  Randomize
  RandomRangeXToY = Int((Y - X + 1) * Rnd) + X
End Function
```

and you tried to call it with code like

```
Dim AnInteger As Integer
AnInteger = 1
Dim ALongInteger As Long, AnotherLongInteger As Long
ALongInteger = 12345678
AnotherLongInteger = RandomRangeXToY(AnInteger, AlongInteger)
```

you'll also get an error message from VB when you run this code, but change the code slightly to read

```
AnotherLongInteger = RandomRangeXToY(CLng(AnInteger), AlongInteger)
```

and it will work fine.

What makes the whole thing even more confusing is that a *number* such as 3 or 3.7 or an *expression* such 3*7+4.5 + X that would be in the right range for a long integer *can* be passed to a long integer parameter. (It will be rounded to the nearest long integer; in the second case this would be the number 4.) This chapter will have a lot more to say about the "ByRef" message a little later (it stands for "by reference"; see the section called "Passing by Reference, Passing by Value"), but for now I just hope I have successfully warned you against mismatching the types of your variables when you call a function.

NOTE: Nothing prevents a function from calling another function. You'll find yourself doing this frequently in order to increase the power of your Function procedures. Visual Basic allows you to call as many functions as you want from within a given function, but you can't nest function definitions: only one function can be defined at any one time. Functions can even call themselves. This is called recursion; the subject is so fascinating and useful that all of Chapter 21 is devoted to it.

9

Finally, at this point, please keep in mind that in all the functions that we have written so far we haven't changed the variables by having the parameter variable on the left side of an assignment statement inside the body of the function. That is, I have made *no* assignments to parameters within the body of the functions that you have seen so far. As you saw in the KeyPress event procedure, it's possible to do this. Visual Basic doesn't prevent you from assigning values to parameter variables. The problem is that doing this has definite side effects—as you saw when we made the KeyAscii parameter 0 in order to cancel a keystroke. Since the range of possible side effects is quite large and also can be quite subtle, I'll devote a whole section later in this chapter to the ramifications of doing this (see the section called "Passing by Reference, Passing by Value"). In practice, however, you should rarely have to change the value of a parameter in a Function procedure. Generally, a function should simply manipulate existing values and return a new value.

Scope of Variables Used in Function Procedures

As you already know, form-level variables are visible to all the functions attached to that form. As with event procedures, you can set up your own *local* variables inside Function procedures. The method is the same: any variable Dimmed inside the body of a Function procedure will be local to the procedure regardless of whether there is a form-level variable with the same name. (The parameters of the function are automatically local, they don't need a Dim statement.) In particular, in the following code framework

```
Public Function AnExample(Foo As Integer) As Integer
Dim Count As Integer


End Function
```

the variables Foo and Count will have no relation to any other variables named Foo and Count outside the function—no matter where they may appear.

The purpose of using local variables inside your functions is the same as the reason you usually want to use them in event procedures: to avoid inadvertent side effects. By side effect, I mean something that is done in the procedure and that affects the rest of the program. For example, if you use the Cls method in a function attached to a form, then every time you use the function, the form will clear. If you have a MsgBox statement inside the function, every time you call the function, the message box will appear. These, of course, are obvious side effects—and ones that you may very well want to happen. On the other hand, any time you change the value of a parameter or form-level variable, you will also cause side effects. Of course, it is only *unintended* side effects that are problems. There's certainly nothing wrong with *controlled* side effects. The key, though, is the word "controlled." You must know exactly when they're going to happen and what the fallout will be for the rest of the project.

Next, in addition to local variables, you can also have static variables inside your functions. Just use the same Static keyword you used in event procedures. You can even make all the variables in a Function procedure static by putting the keyword Static before the name of the function, for example:

Public Static *FunctionName* (*parameter list*)

(You can also do this by checking off the "All Local variables as Statics" box on the Insert Procedure dialog box, which puts this keyword in automatically.)

Leaving Functions Prematurely

As I briefly mentioned earlier, sometimes you are forced (or want) to exit a function prematurely; you can do this with the Exit Function statement. Here's a framework that uses the Exit Function statement:

```
Public Function BailOut (X) As Single
  If X < 0 Then
    Exit Function
```

```
   Else
      statements
   End If
End Function
```

This function bails out if a negative value is sent to it, and we therefore make no assignment to the function if it is called with a negative value. This is fine—you don't always have to give a function an explicit value. In this case, calling the function with a negative value returns a value of 0—the default value of any numeric variable.

NOTE: If you bail out of a string function before assigning it a value, it returns the null string "" (= vbNullString) as its value. Similarly, a function that returns variants would have the default value of "Empty" if you don't make an assignment in the body of the function.

I suspect that you will rarely find yourself needing the Exit Function statement, and, in fact, you probably wouldn't want to use it as it is used in the preceding example. The reason the above code is suspect for most programmers is that they think it makes for unclear code. It is clearer to validate the information you want to send to a function (possibly by using another function!) before you call the function than to exit because of a bad condition. You should only use the Exit Function statement if it makes the program clearer, or, of course, in emergencies.

As I said earlier, one example where some people would advocate using the Exit Function statement is if you want to rewrite the IsPositive function from the postage example. The idea is that you can replace the nested If-Then with a call to Exit Function. Many programmers prefer this way of writing the IsPositive function because they find it clearer:

9

```
Function IsPositive(X As Variant) As Boolean
   If Not IsNumeric(X) Then
      IsPositive = False
      Exit Function
   End if
   Dim Temp As Single
   Temp = CSng(X)
   If CSng(X) > 0 Then
      IsPositive = True
   Else
      IsPositive = False
   End If
End Function
```

I think you have to pick the way of writing code that you are most comfortable with. Just because some people religiously subscribe to the "one entry, one exit" philosophy of coding functions doesn't mean that you have to. Rigid rules are silly—you should write code in the way that is most clear to you and your colleagues!

Example: A SuperTrim Function

Let's suppose we want to write a super trim function. The function is supposed to take a string and do the following:

1. Remove all spaces at the beginning and end of the string.
2. Reduce multiple spaces inside the string to single spaces.

We can code the first step using the usual Trim function and the second using the Replace function. Here's a first attempt, but fair warning: it has a bug. (I'll show you how to detect and then fix the bug in a moment.)

```
Public Function SuperTrim(TheString As String) As String
  Dim Temp As String
  Temp = Trim(TheString)
  Temp = Replace(Temp, Chr(32) & Chr(32), Chr(32))
  SuperTrim = Temp
End Function
```

Okay, so what's the bug in the above code? The problem is that if we have a string like "a   b" with four spaces between the "a" and "b", what we end up with is the string "a b" with *two* spaces between the letters—not the one that we want. You can test for this bug by adding the following test code to a project that has the first version of the SuperTrim function:

```
Private Sub Form_Load()
  Dim Foo As String, Msg As String
  Foo = "a   b"             'three spaces between the letters
  Msg = "The length of the super trimmed version is "
  Msg = Msg & Len(SuperTrim(Foo))
  Msg = Msg & vbCrLf & "The super-trimmed string is: "
  Msg = Msg & SuperTrim(Foo)
  MsgBox Msg
  End
End Sub
```

As you will see if you run this, the length of the super-trimmed version of the string "a b" is 4 rather than 3. Thus, there are still *two* spaces between the "a" and the "b". Can you see what the solution is?

The easiest solution is to keep calling the Replace function as long as there are still double spaces in the string. This isn't hard to detect: you can find out whether you still have a double space by using the Instr function. Here's the corrected code; to make it a little clearer I first set up a variable called DoubleSpaces that consists of two spaces (Chr(32)) joined together, and I also used a helper variable named Temp.

```
Public Function SuperTrim(TheString As String) As String
  Dim Temp As String, DoubleSpaces As String
  DoubleSpaces = Chr(32) & Chr(32)
  Temp = Trim(TheString)
```

```
    Do Until InStr(Temp, DoubleSpaces) = 0
      Temp = Replace(Temp, DoubleSpaces, Chr(32))
    Loop
    SuperTrim = Temp
End Function
```

Now if you run the same test program that detected the bug, you'll see that you now get the right answer.

Example: Counting Multiple Characters

Next, let's suppose we want to write a function that counts the number of times a character appears in a string. This would be a function of two string variables, and it should return an integer. Let's call it CharCount%. Here's the code:

```
Function CharCount% (X$, Y$)
   'This function counts the number of times
   'the character Y$ is inside the string X$
   'If Y$ is not a character or Y$ does not occur in
   'X$ then this function returns zero
   'local variables: I, Count

   Dim Count As Integer, I As Integer

   Count = 0
   For I = 1 To Len(X$)
     If Mid(X$, I%, 1) = Y$ Then Count = Count + 1
   Next I
   CharCount% = Count
End Function
```

9

First, notice the extended remark section. In defining a complicated function, it's often a good idea to use comments to indicate what's supposed to happen. Explain what kind of information (parameters) the function expects to deal with, what local variables it uses, and what it is supposed to return. If the users of your code know what the function expects as parameters, they're more likely to check what they send it and keep the program from blowing up.

Of course, most of the example programs in this book have, up to this point, been sparsely commented, mostly because the surrounding text explained them. However, when you are hired to write a program, this is probably the way you would be expected to comment it. In fact, you might also explain what the local variables are doing.

Let's return to the CharCount% function. It uses two local integer variables: Count and I. As you've seen, it's good programming practice to Dim the local variables before going on to the main business of the function. Being local variables, they will have no connection with any variables that might share the same names elsewhere in the program. After all, a complicated string-handling program might have 17 different functions with 17 different variables named I or Count, and you wouldn't want their values contaminating each other. The advantages this gives over the older Def FN in interpreted BASICs can't be stressed enough.

Next, notice that the function initializes the Count variable to 0. This is done for the same reason that you would initialize a variable in the main part of a program; relying on default values is sloppy and occasionally dangerous unless you make it clear by a comment that you are doing so deliberately.

The For-Next loop runs through the string character-by-character, checking for a match and adding 1 to the value of the Count variable if it finds one. Finally, the value of the local variable Count is what this function will return. In this case, the body of the function ends with the assignment that defines the function. Using a variable such as Count to accumulate information as a function works is quite common. When you're done, you use the value of the "accumulator" to determine the value of the function in the final assignment.

Sub Procedures

Function procedures can be made to do almost anything, provided that what you want to do is get an answer—a value—out of them. As mentioned before, although functions can change properties of a form, affect the value of the variables passed as parameters, or affect form-level variables, it's not a good idea to do so unless the change is somehow related to what the function is designed to do. In any case, a function takes raw data, massages it, and then returns a single value.

Suppose, for example, you want to print a song—one with many verses but only a single chorus. The outline for the program is clear:

```
While there are verses left
    print verse
    print chorus
Loop
```

Unless you wrote a truly bizarre function, you could not easily translate this outline into Visual Basic code that uses a user-defined function. You would probably end up including many statements of the form

```
X = Chorus ()
```

even though the Chorus function would not have any real value to return. Unless you want to repeatedly type useless assignment statements, or confuse the issue by using the fact that you can throw away the return value of a function and use it solely for its side effects, you'll want to use a Sub procedure. The idea is that Sub procedures are the tool to choose if you just want to write a block of code that does something—much as an Event procedure does something.

You tell Visual Basic that you want to define a Sub procedure in much the same way you would with a Function procedure: use Tools|Add Procedure. This time, though, click the Sub option button. The structure of the simplest kind of Sub procedure—although one powerful enough to translate the outline—looks like this:

```
Public Sub Chorus( )
        ' many print statements
End Sub
```

As with the functions you write, the first line of the Sub procedure is called the *header*. Also, as with user-defined functions, headers can have access specifiers (Public in this case). Next in the header is the keyword Sub followed by the procedure's name. The name of a Sub procedure also must follow the rules for variable names. Next comes the parameter list, enclosed in parentheses, for the information the Sub procedure will use. In this case, as with the Click() event procedure, for example, the Chorus Sub procedure uses no parameters. Note that even if your procedure uses no parameters, you must have the empty parentheses in the header.

After the header are the lines that contain the statements that make up the procedure. These statements are also called the body (of the procedure). Finally, there are the keywords End Sub on their own line. These keywords, as in event procedures, are used to indicate the end of a general procedure.

NOTE: As with Function procedures, you can exit a Sub procedure prematurely. To do this you use the Exit keyword in the form of an Exit Sub statement.

If you imagine an event procedure as one of the main verses and the Sub and Function procedures as the choruses, then thinking of a program as a song with many choruses would be a good metaphor for one way of designing programs, except that it misses one key point: each time you need the procedure, it's likely to be in a different situation. The procedure must change to meet new requirements. You need a way to transfer information between the main program and the Sub procedure. You do this in the same way you did for functions: by using the parameter list. The parameter list will again be used to communicate between the main program and the procedure. When you call the Sub procedure, you use the name of the procedure, followed by the arguments (parameters), separated by commas if there are two or more:

9

>   *NameOfProcedure argument1, argument2,...*

You can also use this version:

>   Call *NameOfProcedure(Argument1, Argument2,...)*

When you use the Call keyword, you must use parentheses around the argument list; when you omit the Call keyword, you must omit the parentheses. People are about equally divided as to which form they use—many people even use both in the *same* program! In any case, since you may be working with code written by other people, you'll need to be comfortable with both forms.

CAUTION: Just as with Function Procedures, if the parameter isn't a variant, then any variables must be of the exact same type as the ones you specified for the parameters.

T IP: Remember, you can also call an event procedure directly in this way. For example, the lines:

```
Command1_Click
Me.Command1_Click
```

both call the Click event procedure for the button named Command1 on the current form. You can even give the name of the form: Form1. Command1_Click would also work for the Command1 button on the form named Form1.

Example: A Simple Program That Uses a Sub Procedure

Suppose you want to print the old song "A Hundred Bottles of Beer on the Wall" on a blank form in response to a click. As you probably recall, it begins this way:

> 100 bottles of beer on the wall,
> 100 bottles of beer,
> If one of those bottles should happen to fall,
> 99 bottles of beer on the wall.
>
> 99 bottles of beer on the wall,
> 99 bottles of beer,
> If one of those bottles should happen to fall,
> 98 bottles of beer on the wall.
>
> 98 bottles of beer on the wall,
> 98 bottles of beer,
> If one of those bottles should happen to fall,
> 97 bottles of beer on the wall.

and so on.

Here's what you might write in a Form_Click that would start the process of displaying the song. Notice the call to a Sub procedure that I called Chorus:

```
Sub Form_Click()
  Dim I As Integer

  For I = 100 To 1 Step -1
    Chorus I
  Next I
  Print "There are no more bottles of beer on the wall."
End Sub
```

Using the Call keyword, the click procedure would look like this:

```
Sub Form_Click()
  Dim I As Integer
```

```
    For I = 100 To 1 Step -1
      Call Chorus(I)
    Next I
    Print "There are no more bottles of beer on the wall."
End Sub
```

The Chorus Sub procedure looks like this:

```
Sub Chorus (X As Integer)
  Print X; " bottles of beer on the wall,"
  Print X; " bottles of beer,"
  Print "If one of those bottles should happen to fall,"
  Print (X - 1); " bottles of beer on the wall."
  Print
End Sub
```

Now suppose you click on the form. On each pass through the loop, the current value of the variable I is sent to the Chorus procedure, where it replaces the formal parameter X. (The I is also sometimes called the actual parameter, as was the case for user-defined functions.) Also, just as with user-defined functions, the names you choose for your formal parameters are irrelevant; they again serve just as placeholders. Finally, note that you do not use a type identifier at the end of a Sub procedure (because, after all, a Sub procedure does not return a value).

 NOTE: In practice, you would use a multiline text box for printing so much information on a form. If you rewrite it this way, remember that it is faster to build up the string first than to make assignments to a property repeatedly.

9

You may be thinking that this particular example seems a little forced; it's easy to rewrite the program using a For-Next loop instead of a call to a separate Chorus procedure. This is true, but writing the program using a Sub procedure changes the emphasis a little, and it's a lot closer to the outline we started with.

Also, start think big(ger)—start thinking about writing much more complicated programs. Imagine for a moment you were thinking about writing a For-Next loop that surrounds 50 lines of code. In this situation, it's easy to forget what the loop is doing, to lose the "big picture."

To avoid losing the "big picture," most programmers prefer loops to be "digestible." For example, the whole loop ideally should never be more than a single screen of code. The only way to manage this is to extract many parts of the 50-line loop and make them calls to procedures and functions, as we did in the simpler Chorus example above.

One other point worth noticing about the Chorus example is how most of the nitty-gritty details have been pushed under the rug—into the Sub procedure. This is quite common when you use procedures and functions to help your event procedures do their jobs. Using this model of programming, your event procedures will often have a fairly clean look, perhaps containing only directions and then repeated procedure and function calls. (In fact, some people would even put the directions into procedure calls and so make an event procedure simply one long sequence of procedure and function calls. This too is a matter of taste.) In any case, if you follow this model, it's unlikely that any event procedure will need to be very long.

Summary of How to Code and Use Sub Procedures

To summarize, a Sub procedure is a part of a program that performs one or more related tasks, has its own name, is written as a separate part of the program, and is accessed by using its name followed by the correct number and type of parameters separated by commas.

A Sub procedure must have the form

```
Sub SubprocedureName(parameter1, parameter2,...)
    statement(s)
End Sub
```

Next, when Visual Basic executes statements of the form

SubprocedureName parameter1, parameter2,...

or the equivalent

Call *SubprocedureName (parameter1, parameter2,...)*

then the values (actually the memory locations) of the parameters are passed to the corresponding parameters in the procedure, and the statements inside the Sub procedure are executed. (Again, these statements are collectively called the *body* of the procedure.) When the End Sub statement is reached, execution continues with the line that followed the call to the Sub procedure. Exactly as with Function procedures, you usually must use the same number of parameters when calling as there are parameters defined in the Sub procedure, and they must be of compatible types.

NOTE: If you delete a control from a form, any event procedures that you may have written for that control become general Sub procedures for that form, using the same procedure names as before. For example, suppose you have a command button with a control name of Command1 and have written a Command1_Click procedure for it. Now you delete the command button from the form. The general procedure part of your form will now have a procedure called Command1_Click. This will also happen if you change the name of the control.

Examples of Some Simple but Useful Procedures

A sophisticated program may need to beep at the user to give feedback—more beeps may indicate more feedback. Having a Sub procedure called ManyBeeps in a program is quite common:

```
Sub ManyBeeps (X As Integer)
  Dim I As Integer

  For I = 1 To X
    Beep
  Next I
End Sub
```

Since I is dimensioned inside the procedure, it is a local variable. Now you can write

```
ManyBeeps 10
```

or

```
Call ManyBeeps(10)
```

for ten beeps, and

```
ManyBeeps 100
```

or

```
Call ManyBeeps(100)
```

for overkill.

Next, Visual Basic lets you set up an event procedure that triggers itself after a set period of time has passed (the Timer event is discussed in Chapter 14). Still, you may need to write code that simply waits for a specific period of time before continuing. Rather than writing this kind of code repeatedly, why not write a procedure that wastes a fixed number of seconds. Here's a first attempt (and yes, it has a bug that I'll correct in a second):

```
Sub WasteTime(X As Single)
  Dim StartTime As Single

  StartTime = Timer
  Do Until (Timer - StartTime) > X
  Loop
End Sub
```

What's the bug? The problem is that the Timer function returns the number of seconds since midnight. This means the procedure will run into problems near midnight. (It will give a negative number and so fail the test when it really shouldn't.)

One way around this problem, as long as you don't need an interval more than one day, is to use the DateValue function. Another way is to use the Mod function and the fact that there are 86,400 (60*60*24) seconds in a day. I think this is a little easier, so here is a corrected version of the above code that uses the Mod function:

```
Do Until (Timer - StartTime + 86400) Mod 86400 > X
```

To see that this really works, assume that it is 2 seconds before midnight and that X is 3. StartTime will be 86398. Consider, for now, just the whole-number values that Timer will be taking on: 86399, 0(midnight), 1, 2, and so on. For these values, the expression involving Mod will be as follows:

```
(86399 - 86398 + 86400) Mod 86400 = 86401 Mod 86400 = 1;

(    0 - 86398 + 86400) Mod 86400 =     2 Mod 86400 = 2;

(    1 - 86398 + 86400) Mod 86400 =     3 Mod 86400 = 3;

(    2 - 86398 + 86400) Mod 86400 =     4 Mod 86400 = 4;
```

You can see from this that the expression involving Mod will equal X (which was set as 3) after 3 seconds and will exceed X after 3 seconds, thus ending the loop.

TIP: If you need to have a discernible time between beeps, place a short time interval between them with the Beep statement in the ManyBeeps procedure. You can do this by combining the ManyBeeps procedure with a call to the WasteTime procedure.

Advanced Uses of Procedures and Functions

Now that you know the basics of defining and using user-defined functions and procedures, it's time to turn to a few more advanced techniques. The first is simple, but it isn't one that occurs to even experienced VB programmers who cut their teeth on the first few versions of Visual Basic. It is based on the fact that functions or procedures you define can also use *named* arguments (as can functions from the VBA library).

If you choose to use this feature, the names you choose for the parameters of your functions and procedures become vital. For example, the header for our original CharCount% function was simply

```
Function CharCount% (X$, Y$)
```

This would be a terrible choice for the parameters of the function if I ever wanted to allow other members of my programming team (or me) to use named parameters—what's the X$, what's the Y$? Instead, it might have been better to have defined the function from the get go as:

```
Public Function CharCount(OrigString As String, CharToFind As String) As_
                         Integer

  Dim Count As Integer, I As Integer

  Count = 0
  For I = 1 To Len(OrigString)
    If Mid(OrigString, I%, 1) = CharToFind Then Count = Count + 1
  Next I
  CharCount% = Count
End Function
```

Then, you could call this function by, for example, saying:

```
Count = CharCount(OrigString:="ababa", CharToFind:="a")
```

Passing by Reference, Passing by Value

When you call a function or procedure, there are actually two ways to pass in a variable as an argument. These are called:

♦   Passing by reference

♦   Passing by value

When you pass an argument variable by *reference*, any changes to the corresponding parameter inside the procedure will change the value of the original argument when the procedure finishes. When you pass an argument by value, then the original variable retains its original value after the procedure terminates—regardless of what was done to the corresponding parameter inside the procedure. This is obviously a little confusing, so let's work through a simple example. Start up a new project and add the following Sub procedure that I'll call Triple to it. As you can see all it does is triple the value of any argument passed to it and print the result:

```
Sub Triple(Num As Integer)
  Num = 3 * Num
  Print "I am in the procedure (pass by reference)and"
  Print "the parameter variable has value " & Num
  Print
End Sub
```

Notice the assignment to the parameter Num inside the procedure via the line:

```
Num = 3 * Num
```

Now make the Form_Load read as follows:

```
Sub Form_Load()
  'local variables:
  Dim Amt As Integer
```

```
        AutoRedraw = True
        Amt = 2
        Print "I am in the Form_Load and " & _
        "the variable is now " & Amt
        Print
        Triple Amt
        Print "I called the procedure and the variable" & _
        " is now " & Amt
    End Sub
```

When the project starts running and Visual Basic executes the following lines of code, the variable named Amt is passed by *reference* to the parameter Num. What you see if you run this code is shown here:

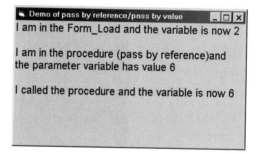

As you can see, the value of the Amt variable has been changed. Here's what happened. First off, in this case, only one memory location is involved—the place where the current value of the variable Amt is stored. In fact, the first line of code inside the Click procedure sets up a memory location to store the value of Amt (see Figure 9-2a). When we call the Sub procedure, the parameter Num becomes the procedure's name for this memory location (Figure 9-2b). When we triple the value of Num inside the procedure, the value in this memory location then becomes 6 (Figure 9-2c). After the completion of the procedure, the parameter Num is forgotten. However, its value lives on in Amt (Figure 9-2d). (Note: Naming the parameter Amt within the procedure produces the same result.)

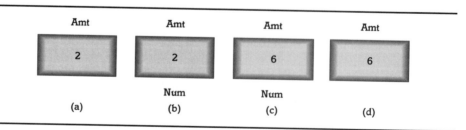

Passing a variable to a procedure by reference

Figure 9-2.

CAUTION: Argument variables are always passed by reference unless surrounded by an extra pair of parentheses.

The following statements, calling a Sub procedure named Display, will pass Variable1 by reference and Variable2 by value because of the use of parentheses:

```
Display Variable1, (Variable2)
Call Display (Variable1, (Variable2))
```

That is, the Display procedure will refer to the original copy of Variable1, but VB will create a temporary copy of Variable2 to be passed to Display, and will then abandon the copy after the routine finishes.

Now consider the previous Form_Load procedure with the key statement changed to

```
Triple (Amt)
```

so that the variable Amt is passed by value because it is surrounded by parentheses. Here's the outcome of the revised code:

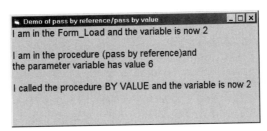

9

So what is happening here? This time two memory locations are involved. Initially, the first line of code allocates a memory location to store the value of Amt (Figure 9-3*a*) just as before. When we call the Sub procedure, VB sets aside a second *temporary* memory location for the parameter Num. This location exists only for the procedure's use and VB copies the value of Amt into this location (Figure 9-3*b*). When VB executes the line that triples the value of Num, the value of Num becomes 6 (Figure 9-3*c*). After VB finishes processing the code in the procedure, Num's temporary memory location is reclaimed (Figure 9-3*d*). Since only the value in the temporary memory location (Num) was actually tripled, the value of the original variable Amt remains the same as it was before we called the procedure. (Note: Again the outcome of the program would be the same even if the parameter in the subprogram was also named Amt. There would still be two memory locations when the procedure was called—one for the argument Amt and the other for the parameter Amt!)

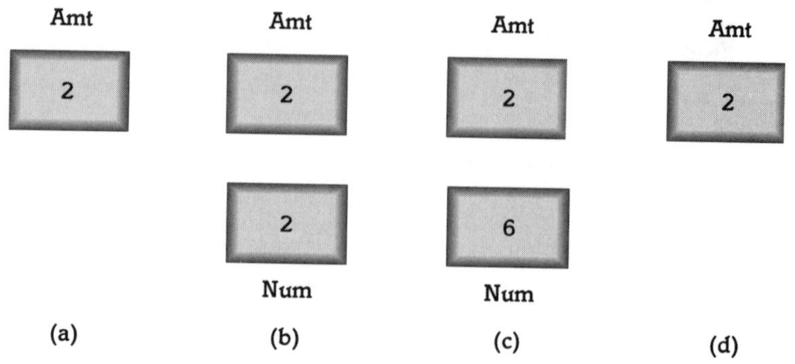

Amt	Amt	Amt	Amt
2	2	2	2

	2	6	
	Num	Num	

| (a) | (b) | (c) | (d) |

Passing a variable to a procedure by value

Figure 9-3.

When Visual Basic leaves any procedure, it releases the memory locations it had temporarily set aside for all variables that were passed by value.

Here's another example. The following Form_Click event procedure and its associated general procedure pass parameters by reference in order to validate what the user enters into an InputBox. Since we are passing them by reference the procedures can change their value. What happens is that VB changes the value of the original variable PhoneNum$ to the value that the user enters into an InputBox popped up by the code inside the procedure:

```
Sub Form_Click ()
  'local variables:
  Dim PhoneNum$

  PhoneNum$ = InputBox("Enter phone number (xxx-xxx-xxxx):")
  Validate PhoneNum$
  Print "Your phone number is "; PhoneNum$
End Sub

Sub Validate (Num$)
  Do While Len(Num$) <> 12
    MsgBox "Don't forget your area code."
    Num$ = InputBox("Enter phone number (xxx-xxx-xxxx):")
    'above was using pass by reference
  Loop
End Sub
```

As another example, suppose you want to change a phrase by stripping out all the double spaces inside it—in other words, a version of our SuperTrim function that actually changes the original string. If you want the original phrase to change, and don't want to bother using an assignment statement, as in our previous function, the easiest way is to pass by reference into a Sub procedure. For example, you can convert the function into a procedure:

```
Public Sub SuperTrim(TheString As String)
  Dim Temp As String, DoubleSpaces As String
```

```
   DoubleSpaces = Chr(32) & Chr(32)
   Temp = Trim(TheString)
   Temp = Replace(Temp, DoubleSpaces, Chr(32))
   Do Until InStr(Temp, DoubleSpaces) = 0
     Temp = Replace(Temp, DoubleSpaces, Chr(32))
   Loop
   TheString = Temp
End Sub
```

Now whenever you call the procedure via a line of code like

```
SuperTrim Phrase$
```

the original string Phrase$ changes *because the default is to pass by reference.*

As a final example, in the following code fragment and function we pass the variable Bal by *value* to the function since it is surrounded by parentheses. The outcome of the procedure is

8667.0178 is the future value of 1000

```
' Calculate future value after Yrs years with interest rate
' IntRate when Bal dollars is deposited and Dep dollars
' is added to the account at the end of each year
Dim Bal As Currency
Bal = 1000
IntRate = .05
Dep = 100
Yrs = 26
'of course in a non-example
'program you would use Format (, "Currency")!
Print NewBal((Bal), IntRate, Yrs, Dep);
Print "is the future value of"; Bal

Function NewBal (Bal, IntRate, Yrs, Dep)
  'local variables:
  Dim I As Integer

  For I = 1 To Yrs
    Bal = Bal + IntRate * Bal + Dep
  Next I
  NewBal = Bal
End Function
```

To check whether you have really understood the distinction between passing by reference and passing by value, ask yourself this question: How would removing the parentheses surrounding Bal in the previous example (i.e., going back to the default of passing by reference) affect the outcome?

Next, if you know that some of the variables sent to a procedure or function should never be passed by reference, you can specify that they will only be passed by value.

9

To do this, add the ByVal keyword before that parameter in the argument list of the function or procedure. Here's an example of the syntax:

Function *Example* (*X* As Integer, ByVal *Y* As Single)

In this example, any integer variable passed to the parameter *X* may be passed by reference (the default) or by value (when enclosed in parentheses), but any single-precision variable passed to the parameter *Y* will *always* be passed by value, whether or not it is enclosed in parentheses.

Finally, since procedures and functions can change the values of the variables used as actual parameters, any time you call a procedure attached to a form, you can think of this as temporarily making a new group of variables that have non-local scope. How do you decide whether to make a variable a form-level variable or send it as a parameter to a procedure by passing by reference?

Most programmers follow the convention that form-level variables are for information that should be available to the whole form (for example, the value of π), and therefore you should rarely change the value of these variables inside a procedure. Procedures ideally should only change the values of the variables passed as parameters. The reason for this convention stems from the methods used to debug procedures. For more on this, see Chapter 15.

Subprograms That Have Optional Arguments

Visual Basic permits you to have optional arguments in the functions and procedures you define yourself, just as it does in some of its functions. Optional arguments can be of any type, but they must be the last arguments in a function or procedure. For example, you might have a Sub procedure that looks like this:

```
Sub ProcessAddress(Name As String, Address As String, _
City As String, State As String, ZipCode As String, _
Optional ZipPlus4 As String)
```

In this case, the last argument (for a zip-plus-four code) is optional.

You can have as many optional arguments as you want—you can even provide a default value for any optional argument that isn't there by using the following syntax:

```
Sub ProcessAddress(Name As String, Address As String, _
City As String, State As String, ZipCode As String, _
Optional ZipPlus4 As String = "0000"
```

In this example, the value "0000" will be used when you don't send a zip-plus-four code to the procedure.

Next, although it will only work with optional parameters that are variants, you can use the IsMissing Function to determine if a variant parameter is missing. The syntax is simply:

IsMissing(*argname*)

The required parameter I am calling *argname* must contain the name of an optional variant procedure argument. For example,

```
Sub ProcessName(FirstName as String, LastName As String, _
MiddleInitial As Variant)
  If IsMissing(MiddleInitial) then
    MsgBox "We really need your_middle initial!"
  End If
End Sub
```

Notice that if you give a default value to a non-variant optional parameter using the syntax you saw earlier, then you can often test for this default value instead of using a variant parameter and using IsMissing. For example:

```
Sub ProcessName(FirstName as String, LastName As String, _
MiddleInitial As String = vbNullString)
  If MiddleInitial = vbNullString then MsgBox "We really need your middle_
initial!"
End Sub
```

Finally, you can also have procedures and functions that accept an arbitrary number of arguments. See the next chapter for more on these.

T IP: Functions and procedures that use the Optional keyword or that accept an arbitrary number of arguments will work more slowly than those with a fixed number of arguments of specific types. Save these kinds of procedures and functions for when you really need them.

9

Using the Object Browser to Navigate Among Your Subprograms

As your programs become more complicated, navigating among the procedures and functions that you have written for it will become more complicated as well. One of the easiest ways to navigate through the code in your project is with the Object Browser. Simply follow these steps:

1. Bring up the Object Browser (remember F2 is the shortcut).
2. Choose your project by name from the Libraries/Projects list box. (It will almost certainly be Project1 unless you have read a little bit ahead or have carefully read Chapter 2. The name of your project is unfortunately not necessarily the filename you used to save the project!)
3. Up to now all our projects have a single form and all the code is attached to that form. In this case, the name of the form will be the same as the value of the form's name property and when you click on it, the Members (second) column of the Object Browser will show the procedures attached to that form (including

the event procedures). Double-click on the name of the subprogram whose code you want to work with.

Figure 9-4 shows the Object Browser for a sample project that has three functions and three Sub procedures with the obvious names (FirstFunction, FirstSub, and so on). The project also has a command button with a Click procedure on it. Notice in Figure 9-4 that these items are in bold. This is how the Object Browser shows you that code exists for that item. (Subprograms, including event procedures, also have an icon next to them. Just what it represents has always escaped me—it seems to be a kind of green eraser.)

Next, remember that the easiest way to hide the Object Browser is to right-click inside of it and then choose Hide from its context menu.

If you want to take full advantage of the Object Browser as a way to document your code, you should supply a description of your procedures that can show up in the Object Browser—just as the builders of Visual Basic did for the built-in procedures and constants. Your descriptions will also show up in the bottom pane of the object browser as you can see in Figure 9-5 for the SuperTrim test project.

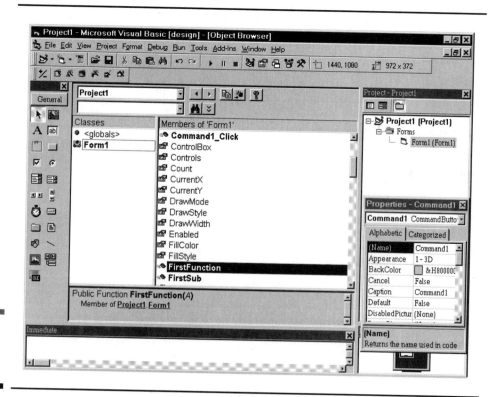

Object Browser for a sample project

Figure 9-4.

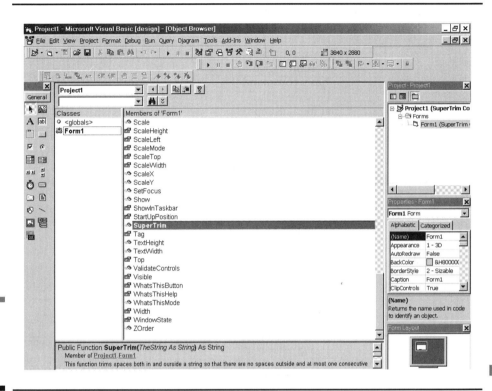

The Object
Browser for the
SuperTrim test
project
Figure 9-5.

9

To add these descriptions, you can work from the Code Window or the Object
Browser itself. To work from the Object Browser, you again use its context menu. This
time, follow these steps:

1. Highlight the function or procedure you want to document.
2. Right click and choose Properties from the Context menu that pops up.
3. In the Procedure Attributes dialog box shown here, enter the description you
    want in the Description text box.

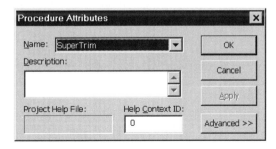

To work from the Code Window:

1. Make sure the cursor is inside the code for the procedure.
2. Choose Tools|Procedure Attributes.
3. The same dialog box that you just saw will now pop up, and you can fill it out just as before.

Finally, you may want to name your project something other than the default, Project1, so that you will see a more descriptive name in the Object Browser. To do this:

1. Choose Project|Properties.
2. Enter the name you want in the Project Name text box in the dialog box shown in Figure 9-6. (You can also get to this dialog box by right-clicking in the top line of the Project Explorer and then choosing Project1 Properties.)

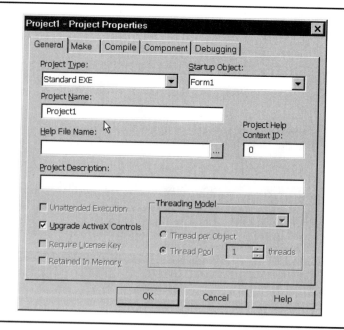

The Project Properties dialog box

Figure 9-6.

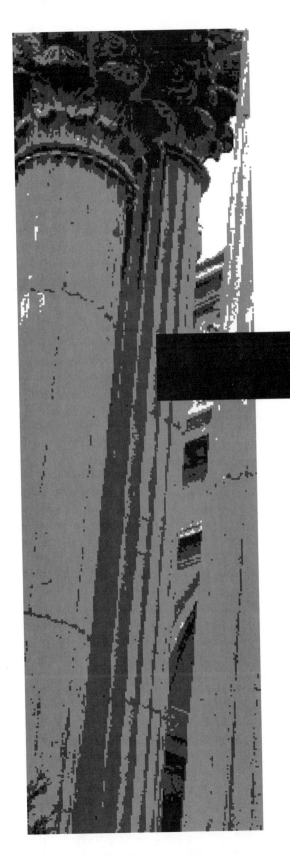

CHAPTER 10

Organizing Information Via Code

The purpose of this and the next chapter is to show you the most important of the ways that Visual Basic has to organize information. In this chapter I concentrate on how you can organize information using code. In the next chapter I'll show you the controls (such as list boxes and grids) that you would use to organize information displayed on the user's screen.

The fundamental structure for organizing information in Visual Basic is called a *variable array,* or simply an *array* for short. You can store many items in an array and get at them easily. To distinguish among the items stored in an array, you use a special kind of parameter called an *index*. Think of arrays as the computer equivalent of a list or a table.

Once you have the basics of using arrays under your belt, I'll show you the new (and really nifty) string handling functions that were added to VB6. These new string functions depend on arrays in a crucial way. For example, they allow you to split apart or join together text with almost no code. (This reduces considerably the amount of work you now need to do compared to what you had to do in previous versions of Visual Basic.)

Of course, once you start building big lists, you'll need to have fast and effective ways to search and sort the contents. This chapter covers some of the many methods known for searching and sorting. (Chapter 21 covers some more sophisticated methods.)

Finally, you'll see how to create *Enums* and *records* (user-defined types). Enums make it easier to use related sets of information; they are analogous to what is going on with properties like BorderStyle that have only a fixed number of possibilities. Records, on the other hand, let you create variables that combine variables of many types into one organized structure.

Lists: One-Dimensional Arrays

Suppose you need data for a 12-month period. You could try to write something like this:

```
'not real code
For I = 1 to 12
  MonthI = InputBox(Data for MonthI)
Next I
```

If this kind of loop were possible, then you would be all set. The information the user entered would easily be available in the various MonthI variables. Unfortunately, this is not quite correct code—it won't even compile. In Visual Basic, MonthI is a perfectly good variable name—for a single variable. Visual Basic cannot separate the I from the Month in order to make the 12 variables that you want in this example code.

The idea of a one-dimensional array (list) is to give you a systematic way to name groups of related variables that are part of a list. To Visual Basic, a one-dimensional array is just a collection of variables, each one of which is identified by two things:

◆ The name of the array

◆ The position of the item on the list

For example, you've already seen, in Chapter 7, the Fonts list that Visual Basic uses to store font names and the fonts were stored in Fonts(0), Fonts(1), and so on.

As another example, suppose you are writing a program that lets a user enter an "errand list" at the beginning of each day. You would probably choose to store the information in a one-dimensional array. The third errand might be stored as Errand$(3). The name of this list is Errand$. Notice the dollar sign ($) that indicates that the variables on this one-dimensional array will hold strings.

The number in the parentheses is usually called a subscript, a pointer, or most commonly, an *index*. The term *subscript* actually comes from mathematics, where the item that Visual Basic would call M(5) is more likely to be written M_5. The term *pointer* is sometimes used because the 5 "points" to the position holding the information. To Visual Basic, M5 is the name of a single variable, but M(5) is the name of an element on a one-dimensional array named M. In fact, it turns out to be the *sixth* element on the one-dimensional array called M. (As you saw with the Fonts list, one-dimensional arrays in Visual Basic default to having a zeroth entry, so M(5) is actually the sixth element in the one-dimensional array M(0) … M(5).) Thus, variables in a one-dimensional array share the same name but have a different index.

CAUTION: M really is the name of the one-dimensional array. For example, once you set up an array called M, you can't have an individual variable called M anymore.

Fixed Versus Dynamic Arrays

10

Arrays can't be open-ended in Visual Basic. Although the limits are quite large—they depend pretty much on the amount of memory you have—you must tell Visual Basic how much memory to set aside for the array before you use it.

There are two kinds of arrays in Visual Basic: *fixed arrays*, where the memory allocation stays the same for the whole time the program runs, and *dynamic arrays*, where you can change size on the fly while the program is running. The advantage of a fixed array is that since memory is set aside at the beginning of the program, you run a much smaller risk of running out of memory while the program is running. The advantage of dynamic arrays is the flexibility they give. You can change their sizes in response to what the program encounters, and in VB6, as you will soon see, you are now actually allowed to have them on the left side of an assignment statement.

NOTE: List boxes give you another way to store one-dimensional (list type) information (see the next chapter). In some situations, using a list box can be a better way to store data than a one-dimensional array.

You can make both fixed and dynamic arrays visible to the whole application, to a specific form or module, or only within a function or procedure. (See Chapter 12 for more on modules and multiform applications.) In this chapter we will stay with arrays attached to a form, so the only possible scopes will be arrays visible to the whole form and arrays visible to a single function or procedure.

To set up a fixed one-dimensional array visible throughout the whole form, place a statement such as

```
Private Errand$(13)
```

or

```
Private Errand(13) As String
```

in the Declarations section of the form. This line of code sets up a one-dimensional will be array for strings that has 14 "pigeon holes" named Errand(0) through Errand(13) that will be visible to every function or procedure on that form. The items would be stored in the Errand(0) through Errand(13) pigeon holes. (Remember, all one-dimensional arrays in Visual Basic default to having an entry in the zeroth position.)

To set up a dynamic one-dimensional array that will be visible to all functions or procedures in the form, place a statement such as

```
Private Errand() As String
```

in the Declarations section of the form. Notice the empty parentheses; this is what distinguishes a dynamic array from a fixed array. (One reason that using empty parentheses for a dynamic array is such a good notation is that it makes clear that the whole point of a dynamic array is to let the situation determine the size and not be rigid about it.)

How Do You Allocate Space for a Dynamic Array?

Once you have created a form-level dynamic array, you use the ReDim statement inside a function or procedure to allocate the space. For example, the following fragment of a Sub procedure asks the user for the number of items and then sets that many spaces aside:

```
Private Errand() As String 'in declaration section

Private Sub NameOfProcedure()
  Dim Number As Integer
  Number = CInt(Input Box("How many items?"))
  ReDim Errand(Number) As String
  'code to manipulate the entries in the
  'Errand array is now ok
End Sub
```

CAUTION: Each time Visual Basic processes a ReDim statement that sizes a dynamic array, the old information in the array is lost.

The advantage is clear: you can ask or calculate how much space you need before issuing the ReDim command. In the preceding example, the value of the variable Number can obviously change depending on the circumstances.

When you dynamically dimension an array, Visual Basic sets aside space at the time it processes the ReDim statement. If the program's memory requirements are very large, it's possible that VB won't have enough room for the array. If this happens, you'll get the dreaded "out of memory" error. Given Windows' memory-management skills, this is a much more rarely encountered error than you might think. I have never encountered one in a program that wasn't deliberately designed to test the limits of VB's array-handling capabilities.

Preserving Information in a Dynamic Array When Resizing

You will often need a way to increase the size of a form-level dynamic array inside a function or procedure without losing the information that is already in it. You can do this with a variation on the ReDim command that you just saw called ReDim Preserve. For example, suppose the maximum index for the form-level one-dimensional array named Errand is currently 10; then you can put the statement

```
ReDim Preserve Errand(11) As String
```

in a function or procedure to increase the number of entries in the array Errand( ) to 11 without losing the first 10 items. Similarly, the statement

```
ReDim Preserve Errand(9) As String
```

drops off the last entry in the Errand one-dimensional array but preserves all the others.

Local Arrays

As with ordinary variables, you will want to mix and match form-level and local arrays in your programs. Just as with local variables, you use a local array when you want to keep the information hidden in a single function or procedure and thereby avoid side effects.

To set up a local fixed array, simply use the Dim statement inside the function or procedure with the size. For example:

```
Private Sub ProcedureName()
  'a 14 element local fixed array named Errand
  Dim Errand(13) As String
  has Errand(0)...Errand(13)entries
  .
  .
  .
End Sub
```

10

To set up a local dynamic array, use the appropriate ReDim statement in the function or procedure without first declaring the array in the Declarations section of the form. As with a local fixed array, no other function or procedure can see the information stored in a local array. In particular, VB allocates space for that array *only* while the function or procedure is active and reclaims the space as soon as the function or procedure ends. Here's an example using a procedure.

```
Private Sub ProcedureName()
Making a dynamic local array _
Dim DynamicLocalArray() as String, Temp As Integer
  Temp = CInt(InputBox ("How many items?"))
  ReDim DynamicLocalArray(Temp) As String
  .
  .
  .
End Sub
```

NOTE: A shorthand that some VB programmers like for dynamic local arrays is to simply use the ReDim statement without first using the Dim statement for declaring the array. In this style of coding the example above would take the form:

```
Private Sub ProcedureName()
  Dim Temp As Integer
  Temp = CInt(InputBox ("How many items?"))
  'now set up the local array
  ReDim DynamicLocalArray(Temp) As String
  .
  .
  .
End Sub
```

Static Arrays

As with ordinary static variables, it is occasionally useful to have an array whose contents remain the same no matter how often the function or procedure is used. By analogy with static variables, this kind of array is usually called a *static* array. To set up a static array inside a function or procedure, you use the Static keyword:

```
Private Function FunctionName() As String

  Static Errand(13) As String
  .
  .
End Sub
```

As with static variables, the information you store in a static array remains intact. (Of course, the information in a form or global array will also remain intact until you redimension it, but form-level arrays, like form-level variables, need to be used with care.)

NOTE: You cannot use a variable inside the parentheses when you do static dimensioning. You must allocate a fixed amount of space once and for all for all your static arrays.

Some Ways of Working with One-Dimensional Arrays

Values inside one-dimensional arrays are most often assigned by using a For-Next loop or, since you often want to allow someone to stop before entering all the data, by using a Do loop with a test as in the following fragment, which assumes the user wants to enter at most 30 items (stored in boxes labeled Errand(0) through Errand(29)):

```
Static Errand(29) as String
Index = 0

Do
  M$ = "You've entered " & Str$(Index)& " entries so far."
  M$ = M$ & "Enter the next errand -- ZZZ when done"
  NextErrand$ =InputBox(M$)
  If NextErrand$ <> "ZZZ" Then
    Errand(Index) = NextErrand$
    Index = Index + 1
  End If
Loop Until Index = 30 Or NextErrand$ = "ZZZ"
NumberOfItems = Index
```

Notice that a temporary variable, NextErrand$, is set up to hold the information before it is added to the one-dimensional array. Once you know the entry is acceptable, we fill in the entry and move the index up by one. Do you see why the order is important? Notice also that this If-Then is completely skipped when "**ZZZ**" is entered, so it is not stored in the array. Enter **ZZZ**, and you move immediately to the loop test and leave the loop. The variable NumberOfItems keeps track of the number of items on the one-dimensional array. In a program that will manipulate this one-dimensional array in many ways, this variable is a good candidate for a global or form-level variable.

However, there are other ways to pass the information around than by using a form-level variable like NumberOfItems. For this, recall that in Visual Basic all one-dimensional arrays default to having a zeroth entry. In the example, if we write

```
Static Errand(30) As String
```

then Visual Basic actually sets aside 31 slots, the slots now being numbered Errand(0) to Errand(30). Many programmers would use the Errand(0) or Errand(30) slot for things like the number of significant items in the array. What you might want to do (rather than set up a new variable) is use code like

```
Errand(0) = Str$(Index)
```

10

or

```
Errand(30) = Str$(Index)
```

when you are done with the loop. Now, to find the number of items (if you want to set up a For-Next loop, for example), you can convert this entry back to a number by using the CInt command.

Another, perhaps even more popular, alternative is to keep a flag (like the "ZZZ") right after the last usable item in a one-dimensional array. This lets you use an indeterminate loop to manipulate the array (test for the flag). To do this, modify the previous fragment as follows:

```
' A simple one-dimensional array demo revisited and revised

Static Errand(30) As String
Index = 0
Do
  M$ = "You've entered "& Str$(Index)& " entries so far."
  M$ = M$ & "Enter the next errand -- ZZZ when done"
  NextErrand$ =InputBox$(M$)
  If NextErrand$ = "ZZZ" Then
    Errand$(Index) = "ZZZ"
  Else
    Errand$(Index) = NextErrand$
    Index = Index + 1
  End If
Loop Until Index = 30 Or Errand$(Index) = "ZZZ"
```

Notice that here, the If-Then-Else deals with the two possibilities—a real entry or the flag. Notice as well that the last entry could hold the flag. Of the two methods, the idea of keeping the number of items currently used in the zeroth or last entry (when possible) may be the most appealing, but this is clearly a matter of taste. You may find it comforting to always know how many entries are in a one-dimensional array. It makes debugging easier and, like most programmers, you may find For-Next loops easier to use than Do loops.

Some people may argue that this example is not really in keeping with the Visual Basic spirit (because I am using so many input boxes). Still, input boxes have their place, and this is arguably one of them. The other way you might deal with the user entering information is to have a command button to add items and another one to click on when the user is done. In this case you won't use a flag to end the process but rather to keep track of the number of items.

Example: Allowing a Form-Level List to Grow and Grow and Grow

Okay, so what do you do if you want to allow the user to keep on entering items, and you don't want to set a limit beforehand for the maximum number of items? The trick is to use ReDim Preserve to increase the size of the array by one on each pass through the loop.

Let's even make it more sophisticated: we will allow the user to repeat the process of adding items by simply clicking on a command button to start the process over again, and we won't bother storing the number of items in a form-level variable. To make this work, of course, we will need to make heavy use of the neat ReDim Preserve statement in the Click event procedure.

To see this example at work, simply add a command button to a blank form on a new project, and enter the following code:

```
Private Errand() As String 'form level
Private Sub Command1_Click()
  Dim M$
  Static Index As Integer
  Do
    M$ = "You've entered " & Str$(Index) & " entries so far."
    M$ = M$ & "Enter the next errand -- ZZZ when done"
    NextErrand$ = InputBox(M$)
    If NextErrand$ <> "ZZZ" Then
      ReDim Preserve Errand(Index)
      Errand(Index) = NextErrand$
      Index = Index + 1
    End If
  Loop Until NextErrand$ = "ZZZ"
End Sub
```

Since this kind of code will occur again and again, lets go over the key points. First off, the line

```
Private Errand() As String
```

is outside the procedure. This makes it a form-level dynamic array so that we will have access to it each time we enter the click procedure. Next, we use a static variable to keep track of the number of items entered. Since the Index variable is static, we won't lose the information. The key lines

```
ReDim Preserve Errand(Index)
Errand(Index) = NextErrand$
Index = Index + 1
```

allow us to keep on increasing the information stored without losing what was put there previously.

The Erase Statement

As your programs grow longer, the possibility that you'll run out of space increases, although, given Visual Basic's rather large limits and Windows' memory management, it's never very likely. Visual Basic allows you to reclaim the space used by a dynamically dimensioned array (that is, with ReDim or ReDim Preserve). You do this with the Erase command. For example, if the array Errand were dynamically dimensioned,

```
Erase Errand
```

would erase the Errand array and free up the space it occupied.

If an array were not dimensioned dynamically (that is, were not dimensioned using the ReDim or ReDim Preserve statement inside a procedure), the Erase command would simply reset all the entries back to zero for numeric one-dimensional arrays, to the null string for string one-dimensional arrays, and to null for variant one-dimensional arrays. Using the Erase command on a fixed or static one-dimensional array gives a fast method to "zero out" the entries. (It sets them to the null string for string arrays.)

One-Dimensional Arrays with Index Ranges

Some people never use the zeroth entry of a one-dimensional array; they just find it confusing. However, just ignoring those entries wastes space. For this reason, Visual Basic has a command that eliminates the zeroth entry in all one-dimensional arrays dimensioned in a module or form (this also keeps compatibility with older BASICs). It is the Option Base 1 statement. This statement is used in the Declarations section of a form or module, and it affects all one-dimensional arrays in the module. All new one-dimensional arrays dimensioned in that form or module will begin with item 1. After Option Base 1, Dim Errand$(30) sets aside 30 spots rather than 31.

In all honesty, the Option Base 1 statement (though you will often see it in code that you have to maintain) is a bit of an anachronism. I don't recommend using it. The reason is that, as usual, Visual Basic goes beyond what earlier versions of the BASIC language had to offer. Here's an example of what I mean. First, suppose you want to write the input routine for a bar graph program for sales in the years 1980 through 1997. You could write something like this:

```
Dim Sales$, I As Integers
Static SalesInYear(17) As Single
For I = 0 To 17
  Sales$=InputBox("Enter the sales in year" + Str$(1980 + I))
  SalesInYear(I) = CCur(Sales$)
Next I
```

However, this program requires 18 additions (one for each pass through the loop) and is more complicated to code. This situation, where you want to go from the beginning of a range of indexes to the end of the range is so common that Visual Basic enhanced the original BASIC language by allowing subscript ranges. Instead of writing

```
Dim SalesInYear(17)
```

you can now write

```
Dim SalesInYear(1980 To 1997)
```

and now the array will have 18 boxes labeled SalesInYear(1980), SalesInYear(1981), ... SalesInYear(1997).

One nice point of using an index range is that you can rewrite the preceding fragment as

```
Static SalesInYear(1980 To 1997) As Single
Dim I As Integer, Sales$

For I = 1980 To 1997
  Sales$=InputBox("Enter the sales in year"+ Str$(I))
  SalesInYear(I) = VCCur(Sales$)
Next I
```

Besides being much cleaner, this new fragment runs more quickly since you don't have to do any additions. In a large program with one-dimensional arrays containing thousands of entries, the savings can be substantial.

In general, the keyword To marks the range to be used for the indexes. Put the smaller number first (as I did when I went from 1980 to 1997). You can use both positive and negative long integers for the range. But memory constraints would almost certainly intervene before you could go beyond a few million entries. Thus, while in theory, a statement like

```
Dim RidiculousArray(-2147483648 To 2147483647) 'long integer range
```

would work in Visual Basic, you would get an Out Of Memory error if you tried it.

NOTE: You can use all the other keywords for arrays, such as Dim, ReDim, and ReDim Preserve, in order to have both fixed and dynamic arrays that use index ranges.

10

Finally, you can always find out the lower index or upper index in an array by using the commands LBound and UBound. LBound gives the lowest possible index and UBound the highest in a list. For example:

```
Dim foo(3 To 37)
Print "Lower bound of foo is " & LBound(foo)
Print "Upper bound of foo is " & UBound(foo)
```

gives

```
Lower bound of foo is 3
Upper bound of foo is 37
```

Iterating Through Array Entries

Visual Basic allows you two ways to construct a loop that iterates through all the elements in an array. The fastest is to use the LBound and UBound functions in a loop:

```
Dim I As Integer
For I = LBound(AnArray) To UBound(AnArray)
' do what you want with AnArray(I)
Next
```

Unfortunately VB allows you another way to iterate through an array, and in code that you may be asked to maintain you may run across it. You will sometimes see people use a construct called a "For Each" to walk through the items in an array. The format for a For-Each that works through the items in an array looks like this:

```
Dim Item As Variant
For Each Item In AnArray
  ' do what you want with the item
Next
```

Note that the Item variable you use to iterate through the array in a For-Each *must be a variant*. This form, though it looks cleaner and obviously avoids the LBound and UBound functions, is actually *much* slower than the usual loop using LBound and UBound. Because using For-Each for an array is so much slower than using a For-Next, I know of no examples where you would want to use a For-Each. I rarely suggest changing code that works, but changing a For-Each for an array to a For-Next loop is one change that may pay in code that you are maintaining.

NOTE: The For-Each construct should be reserved for Collections. See Chapter 13 for more on collections.

Start up a new project and add the following code to it and you will see what I mean! (You should find that a For-Each is about four to ten times slower than a For-Next loop.)

```
Private Sub Form_Load()
  Dim TestArray(1 To 5000000)
  Dim StartTime As Single, EndTime As Single
  Dim I As Long, Message As String
  Dim ForNextTime As Single
  Dim ForEachTime As Single
    StartTime = Timer
    For I = LBound(TestArray) To UBound(TestArray)
      'do nothing
    Next I
```

```
   EndTime = Timer
   ForNextTime = EndTime - StartTime
   Message = "Using a For-Next loop took "
   Message = Message & ForNextTime & " seconds"
   MsgBox Message
 Dim Item As Variant
   StartTime = Timer
   For Each Item In TestArray
     'do nothing
   Next
   EndTime = Timer
   ForEachTime = EndTime - StartTime
   Message = "Using a For-Each loop took "
   Message = Message & ForEachTime & " seconds"
   MsgBox Message
   MsgBox "For-Each was " & (ForEachTime / ForNextTime) & _
   " times slower"
 End
End Sub
```

Assigning Arrays

One of the more useful features added to VB6 is the ability to make array assignments.
Suppose you have a dynamic array called MyErrands and another array called
YourErrands that hold the same type of information. (For example, both are string
arrays.) Then the line

```
MyErrands = YourErrands
```

will automatically change the size of the dynamic array named MyErrands to be the
size of the array YourErrands and copy all the information from YourErrands into the
corresponding slots in the MyErrands array. For example, in this code

```
ReDim M(1 To 10) As String
Dim foo(3 To 37) As String
Print "Lower bound of M is " & LBound(M)
Print "Upper bound of M is " & UBound(M)
Print "Assigning the foo array to the M array"
M = foo
Print "Lower bound of M is now " & LBound(M)
Print "Upper bound of M is now " & UBound(M)
```

you would see

```
Lower bound of M is 1
Upper bound of M is 10
Assigning the foo array to the M array
Lower bound of M is now 3
Upper bound of M is now 37
```

10

The Array Function

Occasionally you will want to store an array in a variant. If you store an array in a variant, use the ordinary index to get at it.

It is a little less than elegant to store arrays in variants, but this technique does get around the limitation that only allows dynamic arrays on the left side of an assignment statement. For example, this technique gives you a quick way to swap the contents of two nondynamic arrays, as shown here:

```
Dim I As Long
Dim A(1 To 20000) As Long
Dim B(1 To 20000) As Long
For I = 1 To 20000
  A(I) = I
  B(I) = 2 * I
Next I
Dim Array1 As Variant, Array2 As Variant, Temp As Variant
Array1 = A()
Array2 = B()
Temp = Array1
Array1 = Array2
Array2 = Temp
Print "The third entry in Array1 is now" & Array1(3)
```

would produce the result

```
The third entry in Array1 is now 6
```

Note that when this code finishes processing, the variants Array1 and Array2 contain the original array that was in the other variable. Also, since these were not dynamic arrays there's no way to reclaim the memory; the erase statement would only zero the arrays out. Thus, you now have *four* objects taking up memory instead of two, so this technique can be a bit memory hungry (needing about an extra 40,000 bytes, in this case). On the other hand, if you need to swap two non-dynamic arrays, this is a whole lot faster than copying the 20,000 entries one by one!

Finally, occasionally you need to create an array in a variant directly. For this you use the Array function, whose syntax is

Array(*arglist*)

where the *arglist* argument consists of a list of items separated by commas. For example:

```
Dim A As Variant
A = Array(1,2,3,4,5)
```

Arrays with More Than One Dimension

You can also have arrays with more than one dimension; they're usually called *multidimensional arrays*. Just as lists of data lead to a single subscript (one-dimensional arrays), tables of data lead to double subscripts (two-dimensional arrays). For example, suppose you want to store a multiplication table in memory—as a table. You could do this with the following code:

```
Static MultTable(1 To 12, 1 To 12) As Integer
Dim I As Integer, J As Integer

For I = 1 To 12
  For J = 1 To 12
    MultTable(I, J) = I*J
  Next J
Next I
```

To compute the number of items in a multidimensional array, multiply the number of entries. The dimension statement for the two-dimensional array that I used here sets aside 144 elements.

The convention is to refer to the first entry as giving the number of rows and the second as giving the number of columns. Following this convention, you would describe the fragment for the multiplication table above as filling an entire row, column by column, before moving to the next row.

Visual Basic allows you up to 60 dimensions with the Dim statement and 8 with the ReDim statement. A statement like

```
Dim LargeArray%(2,2,2,2,2,2,2,2)
```

would set aside either $2^8 = 256$ or $3^8 = 6,561$ entries (depending on whether an Option Base 1 statement has been processed). But you almost never see more than four dimensions in a program, and even a three-dimensional array is uncommon. You can use index ranges in multidimensional arrays as well. For example, the following would give you a sales table for the months in the years 1990 to 1997:

```
Dim SalesTable(1 To 12, 1990 To 1997)
```

Finally, note that you can use ReDim for multidimensional arrays in exactly the same way as with one-dimensional arrays. For example:

```
ReDim LargeArray%(2,2,2,2,2,2,2,2)
```

Since you can have index ranges in multidimensional arrays, you obviously need versions of LBound and UBound. The commands

LBound(*NameOfArray*, *I*)
UBound(*NameOfArray*, *I*)

10

give the lower and upper bounds for the I'th dimension of the array. (For a one-dimensional array the I is optional, as you have already seen.) Therefore,

```
Dim Test%(1 To 5,6 To 10,7 To 12)
Print LBound(Test%, 2)
```

gives a 6 and

```
Print UBound(Test%, 3)
```

gives a 12.

Using Lists and Arrays with Functions and Procedures

Visual Basic has an extraordinary facility for using lists and arrays in procedures and functions. Unlike many languages, it's easy to send any size list or array to a procedure. Arrays are *always* passed by reference. This means any changes you make to the array or to the entries in the array will persist after VB leaves the function or procedure.

Of course, having arrays passed by reference means that you don't need to use form-level arrays unless you want the array to be visible everywhere. To send an array parameter to a procedure or function, just use the name of the array followed by opening and closing parentheses in the list of parameters.

For example, assume that List# is a one-dimensional array of double-precision variables, Array$ is a two-dimensional string array, and BigArray% is a three-dimensional array of integers. Then,

```
Private Sub Example(List#(), Array$(), BigArray%(), X%)
```

would allow this Example procedure to use (and change) a list of double-precision variables, an array of strings, a three-dimensional array of integers, and a final integer variable. Note that, just as with variables, list and array parameters are placeholders; they have no independent existence. To call the procedure, you might have a fragment like this:

```
Dim PopChange#(50), CityState$(3,10), TotalPop%(2,2,2)
```

Now,

```
Example PopChange#(), CityState$(), TotalPop%(), X1#
```

would call the Example procedure by sending it the current location (passed by reference) of the three arrays and the integer variable. And just as before, since the compiler knows where the variable, list, or array is located, it can change the contents.

Suppose you want to write a function procedure that would take a list of numbers and return the maximum entry. Since you may want to do this for many different lists, you decide to write a procedure that follows this outline:

Function FindMaximum(List( ))
 Start at the top of the list
 If an entry is bigger than the current Max "swap it"
 Until you finish the list
 Set the value of the function to the final "Max"

This kind of outline obviously calls for a For-Next loop. But the problem with translating this outline to a program is, how do you know where the list starts or ends? You could arrange for every list to have a flag at the end, but then you would have trouble combining this with Visual Basic's Range feature. Or you could use the trick of reserving one entry in the list for the number of items in the list, but it is obviously much easier to simply use the LBound and UBound functions. For example, you can easily translate the preceding outline to the following:

```
Function FindMax(A() As Single) As Single
  ' local variables Start, Finish, I, Max
  Dim Start As Integer, Finish As Integer, I As Integer
  Dim Max As Single
  Start = LBound(A)
  Finish = UBound(A)
  Max = A(Start)
  For I = Start  To Finish
    If A(I) > Max Then Max = A(I)
  Next I
  FindMax = Max
End Function
```

10

When this procedure is finished, the value of this function would be the largest entry in the list of single-precision variables.

Here's another example. Suppose you want to write a general procedure to copy one two-dimensional fixed string array to another. The LBound and UBound commands allow you to copy lists or arrays with different ranges, provided the total number of rows and columns is the same. (Subtract the LBound from the UBound for each dimension, and see if they match.)

It's hard to stress enough the flexibility that Visual Basic's method for handling lists and arrays within procedures gives, especially when combined with the LBound and UBound commands. For example, you may have learned about matrices in math or engineering courses. It is close to impossible to write a general matrix package in standard Pascal, yet it's almost trivial in Visual Basic.

One last point: using LBound and UBound is not a cure-all. If part of the list or array hasn't yet been filled, these commands may not help. Therefore, although using a flag or adding the number of items on a list as the zeroth item on the list was a more common programming trick for earlier BASICs (that didn't have UBound and LBound), it is still sometimes useful in Visual Basic.

NOTE: VB6 now allows you to return an array as the value of a function.

The ParamArray Keyword: Procedures with a Variable Number of Arguments

It is sometimes convenient to have a function or procedure where the number of arguments is arbitrary. This is done using the keyword ParamArray, followed by an array of variants. For example, the following function computes an average of the numbers that are sent to it and returns the answer as a single:

```
Function Average(ParamArray Numbers()) As Single
Dim Count as Integer, I as Integer
Dim Sum As Single
Count = UBound(Numbers) - LBound(Numbers)  + 1
For I = LBound(Numbers) To UBound(Numbers)
  Sum = Sum + Numbers(I)
Next I
Average = Sum/Count
End Function
```

You can then call this function in code like the following:

```
YourAverage =  Average(90, 100, 95, 80, 100).
```

The New Array-Based String Handling Functions

The first of the new array-based String functions added to VB6 is the Join function. This takes an array of strings and makes a new string out of all the entries. This saves you the work of coding a For-Next loop to join together the individual strings—and it even works faster. Here's an example of the Join function. Let's suppose I have previously stored a list of names in an array, as shown in the following code:

```
Dim MyNieces(1 To 6)
MyNieces(1) = "Shara"
```

```
MyNieces(2) = "Rebecca "
MyNieces(3) = "Alysa"
MyNieces(4) = "Deborah"
MyNieces(5) = "Emma"
MyNieces(6) = "Julia"
```

Now I can simply write one line of code to display all their names in a message box, as shown here:

```
MsgBox Join(MyNieces) & " are the joy of my life."
```

The Join function is convenient but not really essential; the equivalent For-Next loop is pretty trivial to write. The next two functions, though, are a real pain to write.

The Split Function

Suppose you have somebody's full name, and you want to split it up into the three names: first, middle, and last. For example, "William Jefferson Clinton."

This is an extraordinarily common task in programming, and VB now has a function that does the work for you. (In previous versions of VB you had to write this "parsing" code yourself.) The Split function can take this string and return an array of three strings:

◆ First array entry = "William"

◆ Second array entry = "Jefferson"

◆ Third array entry = "Clinton"

Here's some sample code you can add to a new project to do this, and also to display the results in successive message boxes (note the use of the UBound function):

10

```
Private Sub Form_Load()
  Dim TestString As String
  Dim A() As String
  Dim I As Integer

  TestString = "William Jefferson Clinton"
  A = Split(TestString)

  For I = LBound(A) To UBound(A)
    MsgBox A(I)
  Next
  End
End Sub
```

This kind of code shows off the simplest form of the Split function, which involves breaking down a string into the parts that are separated by individual spaces. However, it doesn't work very well if the user has inadvertently added multiple spaces. For example, if you change the code to read as follows, it will display a bunch of "empty" message boxes because of the extra spaces:

```
Private Sub Form_Load()
  Dim FileName As String
  Dim TestString As String
  Dim A() As String
  Dim I As Integer

  TestString = "William     Jefferson     Clinton"
  A = Split(TestString)

  For I = LBound(A) To UBound(A)
    MsgBox A(I)
  Next
  End
End Sub
```

The easiest solution to the problem of multiple spaces is to simply use the Replace function to remove extra spaces. As you saw earlier, you can do this by using the SuperTrim function from Chapter 9, *before* using the Split function. Try the following code in a new project:

```
Private Sub Form_Load()
  Dim TestString As String
  Dim A() As String
  Dim I As Integer

  TestString = "William     Jefferson     Clinton"
  A = Split(SuperTrim(TestString))

  For I = LBound(A) To UBound(A)
    MsgBox A(I)
  Next
  End
End Sub

Public Function SuperTrim(TheString As String) As String
  Dim Temp As String, DoubleSpaces As String
  DoubleSpaces = Chr(32) & Chr(32)
  Temp = Trim(TheString)
  Temp = Replace(Temp, DoubleSpaces, Chr(32))
  Do Until InStr(Temp, DoubleSpaces) = 0
    Temp = Replace(Temp, DoubleSpaces, Chr(32))
  Loop
  SuperTrim = Temp
End Function
```

As you will see if you run this code, since the SuperTrim function allows us to replace multiple spaces by a single space, we will now be feeding good data to the Split function and the result is what we want.

The Full Power of the Split Function

Although the Split function defaults to splitting a string at its spaces, you can do more when you use some of its optional parameters. For example, you can tell the Split function that backslashes mark the breaks. (Whatever character you specify is called the *delimiter*.) This lets you easily analyze the full path of a filename. The following sample code shows you how to split a filename into its separate path components:

```
Private Sub Form_Load()
   FileName = "C:\windows\Temp"
   Dim A() As String
   A = Split(FileName, "\")
   For I = LBound(A) To UBound(A)
      MsgBox A(I)
   Next
   End
End Sub
```

The full syntax for the Split function looks like this:

Split(*expression*[, *delimiter*[, *count*[, *compare*]]])

The *delimiter* parameter is the string that marks the breaks. (It doesn't have to be a single character, by the way; you could split on a "\\" string, for example.) If you omit it, as I said before, VB simply assumes that you want the string split at the space characters. The optional *count* parameter tells VB how many substrings you want in the array. Omitting it (or using a -1) tells VB to return all the substrings. The *compare* parameter works as usual; it determines whether VB should be case sensitive if the delimiter is a letter. You can use either vbCompareText for a case-insensitive comparison or vbCompareBinary (the default) for a case-sensitive comparison.

10

 NOTE: You might see the individual substrings that result from using the Split function referred to as *tokens*.

What to Do About Multiple Delimiters?

Even the full power of the Split function is not a panacea. Suppose the string was:

"Clinton, William Jefferson"

Then even the SuperTrim function won't help you. The solution is either to write your own version of the Split function that allows multiple delimiters or simply to use the

Replace function to replace things like a comma by a single delimiter (say a space). Probably the easiest way to do this is to write a function that mimics the SuperTrim function but allows you to use the ParamArray keyword to allow for a varying number of delimiters. Here's a version of that function:

```
Public Function ReplaceDelimiters(TheString As String, ParamArray _
Delim()) As String
  Dim Delimiter As Variant, Temp As String, DoubleDelim As String
  Temp = TheString
  For Each Delimiter In Delim
     DoubleDelim = Delimiter & Delimiter
     Do Until InStr(Temp, DoubleDelim) = 0
       Temp = Replace(Temp, DoubleDelim, Delimiter)
     Loop
     Temp = Replace(Temp, Delimiter, Chr(32))
  Next
  ReplaceDelimiters = Temp
End Function
```

Notice how we even allow for multiple consecutive delimiters, as in the string: " Clinton, William Jefferson!!". For a string like this, you would call the ReplaceDelimiters function like this:

```
TestString = ReplaceDelimiters(TestString, ",", "!")
```

Here's a program that you can use to test that this function works as promised:

```
Private Sub Form_Load()
  Dim TestString As String
  Dim A() As String
  Dim I As Integer

  TestString = "   Clinton,,, William Jefferson!!"
  TestString = ReplaceDelimiters(TestString, ",", "!")
  A = Split(SuperTrim(TestString))
  For I = LBound(A) To UBound(A)
    MsgBox A(I)
  Next
  End
End Sub

Public Function SuperTrim(TheString As String) As String
  Dim Temp As String, DoubleSpaces As String
  DoubleSpaces = Chr(32) & Chr(32)
  Temp = Trim(TheString)
  Temp = Replace(Temp, DoubleSpaces, Chr(32))
  Do Until InStr(Temp, DoubleSpaces) = 0
    Temp = Replace(Temp, DoubleSpaces, Chr(32))
  Loop
  SuperTrim = Temp
End Function
```

```
Public Function ReplaceDelimiters(TheString As String, ParamArray Delim()) As
String
  Dim Delimiter As Variant, Temp As String, DoubleDelim As String
  Temp = TheString
  For Each Delimiter In Delim
    DoubleDelim = Delimiter & Delimiter
    Do Until InStr(Temp, DoubleDelim) = 0
      Temp = Replace(Temp, DoubleDelim, Delimiter)
    Loop
    Temp = Replace(Temp, Delimiter, Chr(32))
  Next
  ReplaceDelimiters = Temp
End Function
```

Example: Parsing Text

Suppose you want to examine the contents of a text box and print out the words
one-by-one in a second text box, in response to each click on a command button. The
screen might look like the one in Figure 10-1. You want each click to print the next
word. This is an almost trivial application of the techniques you have seen already.

Supposing the command button is called cmdFindWords. Then the key will be to put
calls to the ReplaceDelimiters and SuperTrim functions in the Click event procedure.
Here's how the whole program might go.

```
Sub cmdFindWords_Click()
  Dim Temp As String, Tokens() As String

  Static CurrentIndex As Integer
  txtString.Locked = True
  Temp = ReplaceDelimiters(txtString.Text, ".",",", "!",":",";","?")
  Temp = SuperTrim(Temp)
  If Len(Temp) = 0 Then
    MsgBox "Please enter some text!"
    txtString.Locked = False
    txtString.Text = vbNullString
    txtString.SetFocus
    Exit Sub
  End If
  Tokens = Split(Temp)
  txtNextWord.Text = "Word #" & (CurrentIndex + 1) _
  & " = " & Tokens(CurrentIndex)
  CurrentIndex = CurrentIndex + 1
  Dim YesNo As Integer
  If CurrentIndex > UBound(Tokens) Then
    YesNo = MsgBox("Done! -- Click on Yes to enter more text, no to end",
vbYesNo)
    If YesNo = vbYes Then
      CurrentIndex = 0
      txtNextWord.Text = vbNullString
      txtString.Text = vbNullString
```

10

```
        txtString.Locked = False
        txtString.SetFocus
    Else
        End
    End If
  End If
End If
End Sub


Public Function SuperTrim(TheString As String) As String
  Dim Temp As String, DoubleSpaces As String
  DoubleSpaces = Chr(32) & Chr(32)
  Temp = Trim(TheString)
  Temp = Replace(Temp, DoubleSpaces, Chr(32))
  Do Until InStr(Temp, DoubleSpaces) = 0
    Temp = Replace(Temp, DoubleSpaces, Chr(32))
  Loop
  SuperTrim = Temp
End Function


Public Function ReplaceDelimiters(TheString As String, ParamArray Delim()) As
String
Dim Delimiter As Variant, Temp As String, DoubleDelim As String
  Temp = TheString
  For Each Delimiter In Delim
     DoubleDelim = Delimiter & Delimiter
     Do Until InStr(Temp, DoubleDelim) = 0
       Temp = Replace(Temp, DoubleDelim, Delimiter)
     Loop
     Temp = Replace(Temp, Delimiter, Chr(32))
  Next
  ReplaceDelimiters = Temp
End Function
```

Example: A Pig Latin Generator

This section shows you how to write a "Pig Latin converter." It will demonstrate many of the techniques you've learned so far. For those who aren't familiar with it, Pig Latin is a well-known variant on English that children often use: Ancay ouyay understandway isthay? Although Pig Latin itself is perhaps somewhat frivolous, the techniques of analyzing and then modifying strings obtained through parsing are ones that you will use frequently.

The rules for converting English to Pig Latin are simple:

◆   All one-letter words stay the same.

◆   Words beginning with vowels get the suffix "way."

◆   Words beginning with a string of consonants have the consonants shifted to the end and the suffix "ay" added.

◆   Any *q* moved because of the preceding rule carries its *u* along with it.

◆   *Y* is a consonant.

◆   There are no more rules.

Here is an outline for a Pig Latin converter in its simplest form:

```
While there are still words
    "Pig Latinize" the next word
```

To "Pig Latinize" a word, we have to follow the rules just given. You will need two text boxes (txtSource and txtTranslation) and a command button (cmdTranslate) to start the process.

As mentioned earlier, the first step is simply to change the "Find Words" program from the previous section to one that, instead of printing the next word, prints the converted form by feeding the result to a "Latinize" function.

The Latinize function starts out by dealing with the special case of one-letter words and follows the first rule: it does nothing to them. Then, the first case in the Select Case deals with vowels: words with a leading vowel add "way." The next case makes sure numbers and other special characters are not transformed. The Else case calls the most complicated function—the one that shifts consonants to the end.

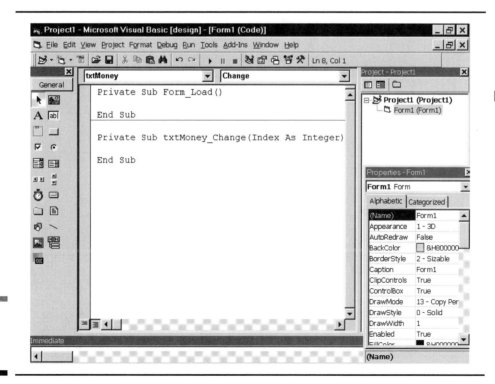

Form for
Find Words
program
Figure 10-1.

10

The ShiftCons$ function works by using a flag to detect when, moving letter-by-letter, Visual Basic finally hits a vowel. By adding 2 to the count, you carry the *u* along with the *q* for this special case. The trick is that by starting with the count equal to 1 and incrementing the count every time a consonant shows up, Left(A$, Count - 1) must, when the loop ends, contain the leading consonants.

Finally, this program replaces all punctuation in the original text with spaces. It would be possible but tricky to change the program so that the converted phrase retains the original punctuation.

This program is a good demonstration of how longer programs can be built from "building blocks." You'll see more about this in Chapter 12 under the section "Some General Words on Program Design."

Here's the full source code for the Pig Latin program:

```
Option Explicit

Private Sub cmdTranslate_Click()

  Dim Phrase$, Tokens() As String
  Dim PigWord$, I As Integer, T$, Temp As String

  Phrase$ = txtSource.Text
  Temp = ReplaceDelimiters(Phrase$, ".", ",", "!", ":", ";", "?")
  Temp = SuperTrim(Temp)
  If Len(Temp) = 0 Then
    MsgBox "Please enter some text!"
    txtSource.Text = vbNullString
    txtSource.SetFocus
    Exit Sub
  End If
  Tokens = Split(Temp)
  For I = 0 To UBound(Tokens)
      PigWord$ = Latinize$(Tokens(I))
      T$ = T$ + PigWord$ + Space$(1)
  Next I
  txtTranslation.Text = T$
  Dim YesNo As Integer
  YesNo = MsgBox("Done! -- Click on Yes to enter more text, no to end", _
    vbYesNo)
  If YesNo = vbYes Then
    txtSource.Text = vbNullString
    txtTranslation = vbNullString
    txtSource.SetFocus
  Else
    End
  End If
End Sub

Public Function Latinize$(A$)
  Dim FirstChar$
  If Len(A$) = 1 Then
```

```
      Latinize$ = A$
  Else
     FirstChar$ = UCase$(Left(A$, 1))

     Select Case FirstChar$
       Case "A", "E", "I", "O", "U"
         Latinize$ = A$ + "way"
       Case Is < "A"
         Latinize$ = A$
       Case Is > "Z"
         Latinize$ = A$
       Case Else
         Latinize$ = ShiftCons$(A$) + "ay"
     End Select
  End If
End Function

Public Function ShiftCons$(A$)
  ' local variables
  Dim Count As Integer, Done As Integer
  Dim NextChar As String

  Count = 1
  Done = False
  Do
    NextChar = UCase$(Mid(A$, Count, 1))
    Select Case NextChar
      Case "A", "E", "I", "O", "U"
        Done = True
      Case "Q"
        Count = Count + 2
      Case Else
        Count = Count + 1
    End Select
  Loop Until Done Or Count > Len(A$)
  ShiftCons$ = Mid(A$, Count) + Left(A$, Count - 1)
End Function

Public Function SuperTrim(TheString As String) As String
  Dim Temp As String, DoubleSpaces As String
  DoubleSpaces = Chr(32) & Chr(32)
  Temp = Trim(TheString)
  Temp = Replace(Temp, DoubleSpaces, Chr(32))
  Do Until InStr(Temp, DoubleSpaces) = 0
    Temp = Replace(Temp, DoubleSpaces, Chr(32))
  Loop
  SuperTrim = Temp
End Function


Public Function ReplaceDelimiters(TheString As String, _
ParamArray Delim()) As String
  Dim Delimiter As Variant, Temp As String, DoubleDelim As String
```

10

```
   Temp = TheString
   For Each Delimiter In Delim
     DoubleDelim = Delimiter & Delimiter
     Do Until InStr(Temp, DoubleDelim) = 0
       Temp = Replace(Temp, DoubleDelim, Delimiter)
     Loop
     Temp = Replace(Temp, Delimiter, Chr(32))
   Next
   ReplaceDelimiters = Temp
End Function
```

The Filter Function

The Filter Function takes an array of strings and returns a new array by including only those entries that satisfy the filter or only those that do not. Obviously, you will most often apply the Filter function to an array that you got from using the Split function. For example, suppose that an array named NamesOfNewsgroups contains the names of Internet newsgroups. As you may know, Internet newsgroup names include dots—for example, rec.art.dance or comp.lang.basic.visual. The first part of the name (up to the first dot) defines the *hierarchy*. You want to filter out all the newsgroups in the *alt* hierarchy because this is the hierarchy containing newsgroups with messages you don't want your children to see. Here's all the code that you need:

```
FilteredNewsgroups = Filter(NamesOfNewsgroups, "alt.", False)
```

Now the FilteredNewsgroups array contains exactly what you want.

In that example, the new array *eliminated* entries that contained the search string. This was controlled by the third parameter. If you change this parameter to True, you include the entries that contain the search string:

```
CompNewsgroups = Filter(NewsgroupNames, "comp.", True)
```

The full syntax for the Filter function looks like this:

```
Filter(inputStrings, value[, include[, compare]])
```

The default for the Include parameter is True, and the Compare parameter works as before.

Sorting and Searching

Sorting and searching through lists of names is one of the most common tasks people use computers for. The next part of this chapter takes you through the basic techniques. (See Chapter 21 for a few more sophisticated techniques.) Let's start with the techniques needed for searching through a list.

Searching

Suppose a long list of names is stored in the computer's memory, and you want to find out whether a certain name is on the list. You can do this easily: just write a program to compare the name you want with all the names on the list. Visual Basic generates code quickly, so this method is effective for short lists.

However, if the list has 5,000 names, all in alphabetical order, this method would be a waste of time. If you are looking in a telephone book for a name beginning with K, you don't start at page 1; you open the book roughly in the middle and proceed from there. When the information in the list you're searching is already ordered, you can speed things up by using an extension of this method: the program looks at the middle of the list, ignores the half of the list that the information isn't in, and repeats until it finds the information. Each time it repeats, the program will look at a list that is only half the size of the previous list. This procedure speeds up a search almost beyond belief. Here's an outline for a program that searches through a list of names that is already in alphabetical order:

1. Divide the list in half.
2. Determine whether you have gone too far. (Does the entry at the halfway mark come before or after the name you're looking for?)
3. If you have gone too far, look at the first half of the list; otherwise, look at the second half.
4. Go back to step 1 as long as there are names left to look at.

Suppose your list has 5,000 names. After completing step 4, you will go back to step 1 with a list of 2,500 names. Complete step 4 again and you will have only 1,250 names, then only 625, and so on. By the 12th time, you will have only 2 names to search. This type of search is called a *binary search*.

10

An extraordinary feature of the binary search is that it works almost as quickly for large lists as for small. For example, suppose you are searching through the New York City telephone directory, with roughly 10,000,000 entries, to find a name. Just by following this outline (and not doing any estimating of where the letters are), you would find the name, if it is in the directory, in no more than 25 applications of step 4.

The procedure is a bit tricky, so it's worth spending time on. What follows is a first attempt to follow the outline. (It has a subtle bug; try to find it before you go any further.)

```
Private Sub BinarySearch (X$(), Target$)
    ' LOCAL variables are Low, High, Middle
    ' A global variable called TargetPosition
    Dim Low As Integer, High As Integer, Middle As Integer
    TargetPosition = 0
    Low = LBound(X$)
    High = UBound(X$)
```

```
  Do
    Middle = (Low + High) \ 2 'integer division since using integers
    Select Case X$(Middle)
      Case Is = Target$
        TargetPosition = Middle
      Case Is > Target$
        High = Middle - 1
      Case Is < Target$
        Low = Middle + 1
    End Select
  Loop Until TargetPosition <> 0
  Print TargetPosition
End Sub
```

Setting the variable TargetPosition to zero initializes the global variable at the beginning of the list. At the end of the procedure, this variable will contain the position of the target. (You also could set up another parameter for this information, and an even better idea would be to turn the whole procedure into a function whose value is the location of the target.)

Notice that this procedure uses the UBound/LBound method of finding the limits. The method described earlier for storing the number of entries in the list as the zeroth entry is not needed here because this procedure assumes that the entire list is ordered.

The Do loop does the work. First it finds the middle of the list by using the integer division operator. (List indexes are always integers.) There are three possibilities in the search, so I chose to use the Select Case command. (You can also use If-Then-ElseIf, of course, but see the next version of this routine, for another option.) If the entry in the middle position is too large, you know that you should look at the first half of the list. Your target can't be the middle entry (you eliminated that in the first case), so you can move the "High" index down to the entry before the middle. (The opposite situation holds in the next case.)

Now comes the problem in this preliminary version of a binary search routine: the loop stops only if TargetPosition has a nonzero value—in other words, if the function finds the target. But suppose the target isn't in the list? The loop never stops; the program is stuck in an infinite loop.

How can you fix this procedure so it stops when there are no more entries left to check? Consider the following example. Suppose you are down to a list that consists of two names, say, in the 42nd and 43rd positions, and the 42nd entry is too small and the 43rd entry too large. What happens? The first time you're in this situation, the value of Middle is set to $(42+43)\backslash2 = 42$. Since the value in the 42nd position is too small, the value of Low is set to one more than Middle—that is, to 43. The value of Low and High are now the same. What happens next? Both Low and High are the same, and the value of Middle is also the same. Now the entry in the Middle position is too large, so the value of High shrinks by one, to 42—less than the value of Low. This gives you one way to end the loop. Change it to read

```
Loop Until (TargetPosition <> 0) Or (High < Low)
```

There's another way to write this loop that some people find easier to understand. This method is based on the assumption that something special happens in small lists when the difference between the High and Low indexes is 1. Arrange to leave the loop when the list has size 1 and add a few lines to take care of this special case:

```
If (High - Low) <= 1 Then
   If A$(High) = Target$ Then TargetPosition = High
Else
   If A$(Low) = Target$ Then TargetPosition = Low
End If
```

Notice that both these possibilities take care of the case when the list has only one entry, or even no entries. Remember: it's the boundary cases that often cause the most subtle bugs in a program!

The StrComp Function

The situation in which you need to know whether some string is less than, equal to, or greater than another is so common that Visual Basic has a special function for this: the StrComp function. (It works a little faster than the three tests.) Its syntax is

StrComp(*string1*, *string2*[, *compare*])

(StrComp supports named arguments, by the way.)

The optional *compare* argument specifies whether the comparison is case-sensitive or not. Use a 0 (the default) for a case-sensitive comparison and 1 for one that is not case-sensitive. The point of StrComp is the return values, which are described in the following table:

The Comparison Gives	StrComp Returns
string1 is less than *string2*	−1
string1 is equal to *string2*	0
string1 is greater than *string2*	1
string1 or *string2* is Null	Null

10

Using StrComp, you can rewrite the comparison part of the binary search routine as

```
Select Case StrComp(X$(Middle), Target)
   Case 0
     TargetPosition = Middle
   Case 1
     High = Middle - 1
   Case -1
     Low = Middle + 1
End Select
```

How Do You Test a Binary Search Routine?

On the subject of bugs, how would you write a test module for a binary search module in order to determine what was wrong with the preliminary program given earlier? You need a long, ordered list. One way to test the program is to use a list that consists of all possible two-letter strings:

AA, AB, AC, ... BA, BB, ... ZZ

There are 26 * 26 = 676 two-letter combinations. (Using three-letter combinations allows a list of $26^3 = 17,576$ entries.)

To create this list, you can use this code fragment:

```
Dim A$(1 To 676)
Dim Index As Integer, I As Integer, J As Integer
Index = 1
For I = 65 To 90
  For J = 65 To 90
    A$(Index) = Chr$(I) + Chr$(J)
    Index = Index + 1
  Next J
Next I
```

Now you can test the binary search module by trying various possibilities, such as searching for a two-letter string that is on the list and another two-letter string that is not on the list, or searching for the first entry and the last.

Sorting

Programmers prefer ordered lists, just as people prefer alphabetized lists, because techniques such as binary searching work so quickly. Sorting data is one of the most common jobs a computer is asked to do. Unfortunately, sorting is also one of the most time-consuming tasks for a computer. Because of this, computer scientists have developed hundreds of different ways to sort lists, and it's impossible to say which is best in all possible circumstances. This section discusses four methods. The first two are useful for short lists. The third is often the method of choice, even for lists having thousands of entries. The last sort method is called the *bubble sort* and seems to be the sort most commonly given in elementary books. Unfortunately, it has few, if any, redeeming features, and you may find it better not to use it even if you are adapting code already written. It is usually better to switch to one of the other three sort procedures given here. Chapter 16 discusses three more sorting methods. Two of those three are usually better than even the fastest sort presented in this section, but unfortunately they are much more difficult to program.

When you sit down to write a program, it's always a good idea to ask yourself if there's anything you do in real life that's analogous to what you want the computer to do. For sorting lists, what often comes to mind is ordering playing-card hands. There seem to be two types of people: those who pick up all the cards at once and sort their hands by first finding the smallest card, then the next smallest, and so on; and those who pick up one card at a time, scan what they have already sorted, and then immediately place the new card in the correct place. (For what it's worth, computer scientists have proved that these two methods take roughly the same amount of time, with the second method usually being a tiny bit faster.) Each of the methods for ordering playing cards translates into a way to sort lists, and each is taken up in turn.

Ripple Sort
The sorting method analogous to the first way of sorting cards just described is usually called a *ripple sort*. Here's an outline for it:

1. Start with the first entry.
2. Look at the remaining entries one by one. Whenever you find a smaller entry, swap it with the first entry, so that the first entry always holds the candidate for the smallest entry.
3. Now shrink how you *look* at the list by starting with the second entry and look at the remaining entries (3, 4, and so on).
4. Continue step 3 until all items are worked through.

Notice that if, say, the list has 50 entries, you only have to do the fourth step of this outline 48 times. This is because by the time this procedure works its way to the last entry, enough switching has happened that it has to be the largest entry. Here's the procedure. (Like many of the sorts in this chapter, it assumes you've written a SWAP general procedure to interchange the values of two variables, filling in the gap left by the designers of Visual Basic.)

```
Private Sub RippleSort (A$())
  'Local variables NumOfEntries%, NumOfTimes%, I%, J%
  Dim NumOfEntries%, NumOfTimes%, I%, J%

  NumOfEntries% = UBound(A$)
  NumOfTimes% = NumOfEntries% - 1
  For I% = LBound(A$) To NumOfTimes%
    For J% = I% + 1 To NumOfEntries%
      'need to write the SWAP routine!!
      If A$(J%) < A$(I%) Then SWAP A$(J%), A$(I%)
    Next J%
  Next I%
End Sub
```

10

This procedure assumes the list starts from 1 and that you have written a SWAP routine like the following:

```
Sub SWAP(X As String, Y As String)
Dim Temp As String
  Temp = X
  X = Y
  Y = Temp
End Sub
```

An even more elegant idea is to make this procedure depend on two more parameters, say Low and High, and use these to establish the bounds on the loops. (That way you can sort all or part of the list.)

First Steps for Testing Sorts

How do you write a module to test a sort? Well, you need a way of creating random lists of strings. Here's one way we create a list of 1000 four-letter "words" by adding the following lines to a Form_Click procedure:

```
Dim B$(1000)
Dim I As Integer, RndInt1 As Integer, RndInt2 As Integer

Randomize
For I = 1 To 1000
   RndInt1 = Int(26*Rnd(1)): RndInt2 = Int(26*Rnd(1))
   B$(I) = Chr$(RndInt1 + 65) + Chr$ (RndInt2 + 65)

   RndInt1 = Int(26*Rnd(1)): RndInt2 = Int(26*Rnd(1))
   B$(I) = B$(I) & Chr$(RndInt1 + 65) + Chr$ (RndInt2 + 65)

Next I
```

At this point, of course, you have only one sort to test, although this method can be used to test any sort. In any case, to test ripple sort use the following:

```
RippleSort B$()
```

Now print out the list to make sure it's been sorted, you might want to consider adding a text box whose multiline property is set to True and then using code like this:

```
Dim Temp As String
For I = 1 To 100
   Temp = B$(I) & "    ";
Next I
Text1.Text = Temp
```

Insertion Sort

The second sorting method, usually called *insertion sort*, is no harder to program. In this sort, at every stage you'll have an already sorted, smaller list. Look through the list, from the first entry to what is currently the last, until you find something smaller than the new entry. Unfortunately, unlike the case of playing cards, you have to move all the entries down by one to make room for the new entry. This leads to a *tweak* (computer jargon meaning "a small change that improves performance"). The new version is even easier to program. Instead of moving forward from the start of the list, move backward from the end of the list. Now, each time the comparison fails, move the old entry down by one. If you do this, you'll be moving a "hole" along as you move through the list. When the comparison finally fails, you drop the new entry into the hole. Here's that procedure:

```
Private Sub InsertionSort (A$())
   'LOCAL Variables are NumOfEntries%, I%, J%, Temp$
   Dim NumOfEntries%, I%, J%, Temp$

  NumOfEntries% = UBound(A$)
  For I% = 2 To NumOfEntries%
    Temp$ = A$(I%)
    For J% = I% - 1 To 1 Step -1
      If Temp$ >= A$(J%) Then Exit For
      A$(J% + 1) = A$(J%)
    Next J%
    A$(J% + 1) = Temp$
  Next I%
End Sub
```

As with the ripple sort, you might want to make this procedure depend on a Low and High parameter. Notice, however, that starting the For-Next loop at 2 takes care of the special case of the list having one entry. The loop moves entries forward until conditions are ripe for the Exit For statement. This occurs when you have located the position of the hole—in preparation for the statement A$(J%+1) = Temp$, which fills the hole.

Since these methods follow the playing-card analogy closely, they are not hard to program. Both sorts work essentially equally fast. Moreover, for small lists, they are reasonably fast. Sorting 1,000 strings on using the ripple sort takes about .5 seconds on my 333 MHz Pentium II. Unfortunately, sorting 2,000 entries takes about 2 seconds, 4,000 entries takes about 8 seconds, sorting 8,000 entries takes about 32 seconds. As you might guess from this data, both these types of sorts have the unfortunate property that doubling the list quadruples the time. Sorting a list of 128,000 names (by no means a very large list) would take over an hour—even on a 333 MHz Pentium II, so you can see that these are not the methods to use for lists much longer than 500 or so entries. You need to turn to a faster method. (Now you can see why the binary search is so nice—doubling the length of the list adds only one step.)

The next section shows you one of the very fastest all-purpose sorts.

Shell Sort
The faster sort discussed in this section, the *Shell sort*, was discovered by Donald Shell around 30 years ago. (Two other fast sorts are discussed in Chapter 21.)

Shell sort is unusual because while the procedure is simple—and short—understanding what makes it work is not. This is partially because there is nothing that you do in real life that's analogous to Shell sort and partially because it's a really neat idea. Another problem is that even after you understand why it works, it's unclear why it's so much faster than the previous two methods.

To understand Shell sort, you should ask yourself what are the advantages and disadvantages of the two previous sorting methods. One obvious disadvantage of ripple sort is that most of the time, the comparisons in the various loops are wasted. The disadvantage of insertion sort is that most of the time it moves objects inefficiently. Even when the list is mostly sorted, you still have to move the entries

10

one-by-one to make the hole. The big advantage of ripple sort is that it moves objects efficiently. Once the smallest object gets to the top, it stays there.

In a sense, then, insertion and ripple sorts are opposites. Donald Shell decided to improve insertion sort by moving the data long distances, as is done in ripple sort. Consider the following list of numbers to sort:

57, 3, 12, 9, 1, 7, 8, 2, 5, 4, 97, 6

Suppose, instead of comparing the first entry with the second, you compare it with the seventh, and instead of comparing the second with the third, you compare it with the eighth. In short, cut up the list into six different lists. Now do an insertion sort on these six small lists. After this, you have six lists, each of which is sorted, while the whole list is probably still not sorted. Merge the smaller lists and break up the result into three new lists (compare the first entry with the fourth, seventh, and so on, and the second with the fifth, eighth, and so on). Do an insertion sort on these three smaller lists and merge again. Now the resulting list is very close to being sorted. A final sort finishes the process. (Insertion sort is efficient when it doesn't have much work to do.)

If the numbers are already stored in a list, you never have to break up the list into smaller lists. Instead, you shift your point of view by concentrating on the different sublists. Also, because on the earlier passes the entries moved fairly long distances, when you're down to the final step, not many more moves are needed. Here's a version of Shell sort that assumes the array index starts at 1:

```
Public Sub ShellSort (A$())
  'LOCAL variables are NumOfEntries%, Increm%, J%, Temp$
  Dim NumOfEntries%, Increm%, J%, Temp$
  NumOfEntries% = UBound(A$)
  Increm% = NumOfEntries% \ 2
  Do Until Increm% 1
    For I% = Increm% + 1 To NumOfEntries%
      Temp$ = A$(I%)
      For J% = I% - Increm% To 1 Step -Increm%
        If Temp$ >= A$(J%) Then Exit For
        A$(J% + Increm%) = A$(J%)
      Next J%
      A$(J% + Increm%) = Temp$
    Next I%
    Increm% = Increm% \ 2
  Loop
End Sub
```

The Do loop gives you the way of dividing the lists into smaller lists. Inside the Do loop, the inner For-Next loop does an insertion sort on the smaller lists. Since each entry on the smaller list differs from the next by the number given in the variable Increm%, the Step command gives you a way of working with the smaller lists.

TIP: To modify the previous Shell sort to work with any kind of array, replace the NumOfEntries% with UBound – LBound + 1 and the other various occurrences of "1" in the For-Next loops in the example code with a reference to the LBound of the array.

What's amazing about Shell sort is that it's so much faster than the ripple or insertion sort—which is why I allowed long integers for the size, although, surprisingly enough, nobody yet knows how much faster it will be in general. (A way to get a first-rate Ph.D. would be to fully analyze Shell sort.) In any case, sorting a list of 128,000 names will take around 18 seconds using Shell sort on my Pentium 333—which is a far cry from an hour!

The speed of Shell sort depends somewhat on the numbers you use to split the list into smaller ones. These are usually called the increments (the 6, 3, and 1 used in the preceding example), and they should be chosen with care. (Because the increments get smaller on each pass, Shell sort is sometimes known as a "diminishing increment" sort.) The numbers used in the example (half the current size of the list) are Shell's original choice. Today we know you can obtain slightly better results with other increments. One of the simpler choices that gives slightly better results is

... 3280, 1093, 364, 121, 40, 13, 4, 1

where each number is arrived at by multiplying the next smaller number by 3 and adding 1. (You start with the largest increment that's smaller than the size of your list, so a list with 5,000 entries would start with an increment of 3,280.) In any case, no one yet knows the best choice of increments. Try other sequences and see if you get better results.

NOTE: In Chapter 21, I'll show you sorts that are significantly faster than even Shell sort.

10

How do you write a realistic test module for a fast sorting routine? First, you want to create a long list of random strings. This is not very difficult to do, but it can sometimes take longer than the sort. For a list of random four-letter strings for Shell sort, I used

```
Dim I As Long, RndInt1 As Integer, RndInt2 As Integer

Randomize
For I = 1 To 128000
  RndInt1 = Int(26 * Rnd(1)): RndInt2 = Int(26 * Rnd(1))
  B$(I) = Chr$(RndInt1 + 65) & Chr$(RndInt2 + 65)
  RndInt1 = Int(26 * Rnd(1)): RndInt2 = Int(26 * Rnd(1))
  B$(I) = B$(I) & Chr$(RndInt1 + 65) & Chr$(RndInt2 + 65)

Next I
```

and then I called Shell sort. (I wouldn't recommend trying to sort a list of 128,000 names with insertion or ripple sort.) Finally, add a routine to print out (or put into a multiline text box) the beginning and end of the transformed list. If the results are ordered, then you can be satisfied. Once you are, you might want to add a routine to time the various sorts. (If you devise your own sort or want to test these, you might want to test the sorts on the two "boundary cases" also. For a sorting routine, this is usually thought as being when the list is either already ordered or completely in reverse order.)

NOTE: Remember, there are projects showing off the most interesting code (including the sort code) at http://www.osborne.com.

A Common But Bad Sort: Bubble Sort

Finally, you should be aware of (or may already be using) bubble sort. The idea of bubble sort is the easiest of all: you constantly compare an entry with the one below it. This way, the smallest one "bubbles" to the top. The code for this is almost trivial:

```
Private Sub BubbleSort(A$())
  'assume slist starts with 1
  N = UBound(A$)
  For I = 2 To N
    For J = N To I Step -1
      If A$(J-1) > A$(J) Then
        ' need to SWAP A$(J-1), A$(J)
        Temp$ = A$(J-1)
        A$(J-1) = A$(J)
        A$(J) = Temp$
      End If
    Next J
  Next I
End Sub
```

The problem is that bubble sort is almost always the slowest sort of all. Since it has few, if any, redeeming virtues, it should be replaced, at the very least, with an insertion or ripple sort (which are just as easy to program) for small lists, and with one of the faster sorts, such as Shell sort, for longer lists. (The only place to use it is if the list to be sorted is already essentially sorted!)

Records (User-Defined Types)

Suppose you want to have a three-dimensional array for 100 employees in a company. The first column is to be for names, the second for salaries, and the third for social security numbers. This common situation can't be programmed in a multidimensional array except by using the variant data type. Some people would call using the variant data type in this situation a *kludge*. The problem is that variants use more memory and are slower than other data types. For both speed and memory reasons, you might prefer to set up three parallel lists—one for the names, the second for salaries, and the third for social security numbers (they're strings so they can include the dashes), as shown here:

```
Dim Names$(100), Salary!(100), SocSec$(100)
```

Having done this, you now would use the same pointer (that is, the row number) to extract information from the three lists.

The way around this extra work is to use a new structure called a *record*. Records are not part of traditional BASICs, although they are common in programming languages such as C and Pascal. Essentially, a record is a type of "mixed" variable that you create as needed. It usually mixes different kinds of numbers and strings. Visual Basic makes it easy to avoid maintaining parallel structures or using arrays of variants.

Here's the first step: in the Declarations section of a code module, enter

```
Type  VitalInfo
    Name as String
    Salary as Long
    SocSec as String
End Type
```

This defines the type. From this point on in the program, it's just as good a variable type as single precision, double precision, or variants.

Now, to make (set up) a single variable of "type" VitalInfo, write either

```
Private YourName as VitalInfo
```

or

```
Public HisName As VitalInfo
```

in the Declarations section of any form or module (see Chapter 12 for modules). (YourName would then be private to the form or module, and HisName would be global to the project.) You can also write

```
Static MyName As VitalInfo
```

inside a procedure. You can also set up global variables of this type using the Global statement. Each of these statements sets up a single "mixed" variable. The jargon is to say, "YourName is a record variable of type VitalInfo."

10

Now you use a dot (period) to isolate the parts of this record:

```
YourName.Name = "Howard"
YourName.Salary = 100000
YourName.SocSec = "036-78-9987"
```

T IP: Many of the Windows API functions require being passed a record of a specific form. The API viewer gives you the structure needed. See Chapter 12 for more on the Windows API.

You can make up an array of records. For example,

```
Dim CompanyRecord(1 To 75) as VitalInfo
```

sets up a list capable of holding 75 of these records.

Now imagine you want to design a form to allow a user to input the data needed to fill the 75 records. Set up a form-level array called CompanyRecord to hold the 75 records. Next, the form used for this input operation requires three labels to identify the text boxes, three text boxes (control names of Names, Salary, and SSNum), and a command button. If you give the command button the control name (value of Name property) AddButton and add to the Form the form name of DataForm, you can use the following code to add up to 75 records.

```
Private Sub AddEmpData_Click ()
  Static Count As Integer
  Count = Count + 1
  If Count > 75 Then
    MsgBox("Too Many records")
    Exit Sub
  End If
  DataForm.Caption = "Adding data for entry " + Str$(Count)
  CompanyRecord(Count).Name = Names.Text
  CompanyRecord(Count).Salary = Val(Salary.Text)
  CompanyRecord(Count).SocSec = SSNum.Text
End Sub
```

Note that the caption on the form changes to reflect the number entered. Making Count a static variable and adding 1 before checking ensures that at most 75 entries are allowed. Also, note the periods for each component, or element, of the record.

You can even have a component of a record be a record itself. For example, you could make up a RecordOfSalary type to keep track of monthly earnings along with the previous year's salary:

```
Type RecordOfSalary
   SalInJan As Integer
   SalInFeb As Integer
   SalInMar As Integer
   SalInApr As Integer
   SalInMay As Integer
   SalInJun As Integer
   SalInJul As Integer
   SalInAug As Integer
   SalInSep As Integer
   SalInOct As Integer
   SalInNov As Integer
   SalInDec As Integer
   SalInPrevYear As Long
End Type
```

Now you can set up a record of records:

```
Type ExpandedVitalInfo
   Name As String
   Salary As RecordOfSalary
   SocSec As String * 11
End Type
```

Of course, filling out all the information needed for a single record is now that much harder. Filling in the record RecordOfSalary for a single employee requires at least 13 lines of code, so filling in a record of type ExpandedVitalInfo requires at least 15. It also gets a little messy to refer to the information in ExpandedVitalInfo. You thread your way down by using more periods. After using

```
Dim GaryStats As ExpandedVitalInfo
```

10

to set up a variable of this new type, use a statement like

```
Print GaryStats.Salary.SalInPrevYear
```

to display the information on the previous year's salary.

You can have records as one of the parameters in functions or subprograms. For example, you might write a general procedure to analyze salary data. The first line in the procedure would look like this:

```
Private Sub AnalyzeSalary (X As ExpandedVitalInfo)
```

This procedure allows (and in fact requires) that only variables of type ExpandedVitalInfo be passed to it. Now you can call it at any time by using a line of code like this:

```
AnalyzeSalary(BillStats)
```

This would analyze Bill's salary information. You also can pass individual components of a record whenever they match the type of the parameter.

NOTE: You can also use arrays in user-defined records. For example:

```
Type RecordOfSalary
  Salaries(1 To 12) As Integer
  SalInPrevYear As Long
End Type
```

You can then use a loop plus one individual statement to fill a record rather than using 13 statements.

The With Statement

By now, navigating through multiple periods in a record has gotten tiring. You will be happy to know that Visual Basic offers a shortcut. You can use the With statement as a convenient method for quickly getting at the parts of a record. For example,

```
With YourName
  .Name = "Howard"
  .Salary = 100000
  .SocSec = "036-78-9987"
End With
```

lets you avoid some typing. You can even nest With statements if one of the components of a record is itself a record:

```
Dim MyStats As ExpandedVitalInfo
With MyStats
 .Name = "Gary Cornell"
  With .Salary    'notice the period is still needed
    .SalInJan = 1000
    .SalInFeb = 2000
    .
    .
    .
  End With
End With
```

You can also use the With statement with properties of objects. For example:

```
With txtBox
  .Height = 2000
  .Width = 2000
  .Text = "This is a text box"
End With
```

And you can nest Withs when dealing with objects or records, if appropriate:

```
With txtBox
  .Height = 2000
  .Width = 2000
  .Text = "This is a text box"
  With .Font
    .Bold = True
    .Size = 18
  End With
End With
```

Note the use of .Font in the inner With. Remember, Font is itself an object—we need the period here.

Enums

Wouldn't it be nice to be able to write

```
Appointment = Weekday(Now)
```

and then have code like this,

```
If Appointment < Wednesday Then ...
```

where the word *Wednesday* really referred to Wednesday? One of the neatest new features of Visual Basic lets you do this. The feature is called *enumerated constants* or *Enums*. You place the definition of the Enum in the declaration section of the form or module. For example:

```
Enum DaysOfTheWeek
  Sunday = 1
  Monday
  Tuesday
  Wednesday
  Thursday
  Friday
  Saturday
End Enum
```

10

Once you do this, Visual Basic automatically assigns successive integers to the days of the week. (Monday = 2, Tuesday = 3, and so on.) You can then use these integers in code, as in the following:

```
If Weekday(Now) = Friday Then MsgBox("TGIF!")
```

After they have been defined, Enums can be used as the parameters for functions and procedures, so they can make code much clearer:

```
Function SalaryMultiplier(X As DaysOfTheWeek) as Single
  Select Case X
    Case Saturday, Sunday
      SalaryMultiplier = 1.5
    Case Else
      SalaryMultiplier = 1.0
  End Select
End Function
```

In the preceding DaysOfTheWeek Enum, the values would increase by 1 starting at 1. By the way, the IntelliSense feature recognizes the Enums that you add, as you can see in Figure 10-2.

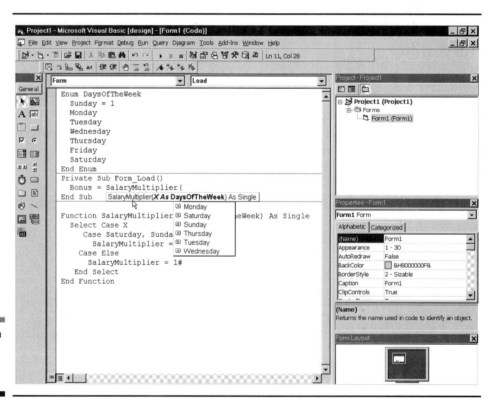

IntelliSense with user-defined Enums

Figure 10-2.

Finally, you can also use Enums to create constants that do not follow any order,

```
Enum BonusLevel
   NoBonus = 0
   StandardBonus = 5
   SpecialBonus = 10
   BossesBonus = 100
End Enum
```

and use code like this,

```
Dim YourBonus As BonusLevel
YourBonus = SpecialBonus
```

to give the YourBonus variable the value 10. (If you leave off the initial value, the Enum starts at 0. If you leave off the succeeding values, they automatically increase by 1 for each enumerated constant.)

10

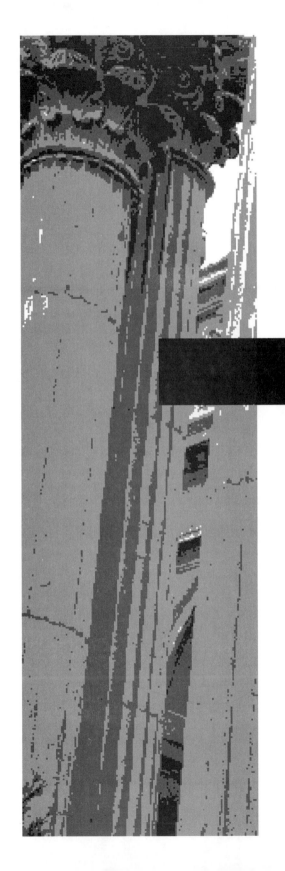

CHAPTER 11

Organizing Information via Controls

The last chapter showed you how you can use arrays and code to organize information. This chapter shows you how to use various Visual Basic objects, such as list boxes and grids, in order to do the same. Note that these controls work best when combined with arrays. And, in fact, many of the techniques you'll need for manipulating them are similar to the techniques you have just seen for manipulating arrays. This is because many of the properties of these controls are, for all practical purposes, arrays. For example, a list box has a List property which works just like an array: if List1 is the name of a list box, then List1.List(0) is the first item in the list box, List1.List(1) is the second, and so on. Similarly, the contents of a grid control can best be thought of as being stored in a structure analogous to a two dimensional array.

Before we get to these controls, however, I want to introduce you to *control arrays*. The controls in a control array share common properties but, just like an array, use an *index* to distinguish among them. This index parameter identifies the specific control and gives you the flexibility you will need to organize information at run time. Control arrays also were the traditional method of adding new controls to a form at run time and are still very useful for this task. (VB6 has a nifty new way to add controls at run time that I'll explain in Chapter 13.)

Control Arrays

As you may have observed, anytime you use the same control name (that is, the same string as the value of the Name property) more than once while designing a Visual Basic application or use CTRL+C, CTRL+V to copy an existing control from one place on the form to another (when you copy a control, it always appears in the top left-hand corner), Visual Basic asks you whether you really want to create a control array by popping up the message box you can see in Figure 11-1. Clicking the Yes button (or pressing ENTER) tells Visual Basic that you do want to make a control array.

So, what's a control array and why would you want to create one? Well, as I said in the introduction to this chapter, they are a bunch of related controls that you distinguish with an index—just as you distinguish the elements of an array by its index. When Visual Basic creates a control array, it gives the first control an Index property of zero, the second control an Index property of 1, and so on.

NOTE: By analogy with the case of arrays, each control in a control array is called an *element* of the control array.

Like most properties of Visual Basic objects, you can change the Index property at design time using the Properties window. In fact, if you assign any number to the Index property of a control at design time, Visual Basic automatically creates a control array for you. This lets you create a control array without having to use two controls at design time. In theory, you can have up to 255 elements in a control array, but that would be very unusual, as it would waste too many Windows resources.

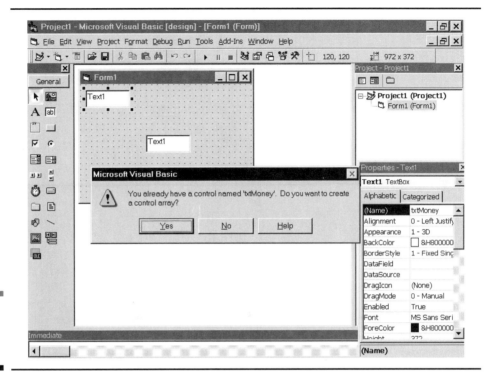

Message box to
create a control
array
Figure 11-1.

Working with a Control Array

NOTE: To follow along with the discussion in this section you might want to
create a control array of two text boxes with a control name of txtMoney. You can do
this by, for example, adding two controls to the form and changing the control name
of both of them to be txtMoney and answering Yes to the dialog box that pops up.

Suppose you want to work with the Change procedure for one of the two elements of
the txtMoney text box control array. When you move to the Code window, by
double-clicking one of these text boxes from the control array, you'll see something
like the screen in Figure 11-2. Notice that the Change event procedure template looks
a little different from anything you've seen before. Instead of having no parameters, as
the Change procedure ordinarily does, this event procedure now uses a new
parameter, Index As Integer.

As with arrays, the index parameter is the key to the smooth functioning of control
arrays. For example, add the following code to the event procedure template shown in
Figure 11-2.

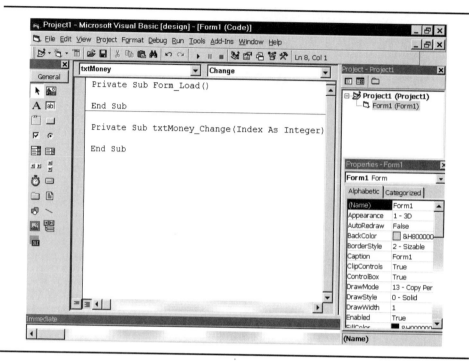

Event procedure
template with an
index parameter
Figure 11-2.

```
Private Sub txtMoney_Change (Index As Integer)
  If Index = 0 Then
    MsgBox "You typed in the text box with index 0."
  Else
    MsgBox "You typed in the text box with index 1."
  End If
End Sub
```

Now, when you type in one of the text boxes:

1. Visual Basic calls this event procedure.
2. VB passes the index parameter of the control you typed in to the procedure.

In this way, the event procedure (and you!) can use the index to determine what to do. When you type in the text box with the Index property of zero, Visual Basic activates the If clause inside this event procedure and so displays text telling you which box you typed in. Otherwise, Visual Basic processes the Else clause. The If-Then-Else, combined with the index parameter, lets the event procedure determine where you typed.

What Visual Basic did for the Change event is an example of a general phenomenon: *any* event procedure that would work for a single control can be used for a control array of controls of that type. Visual Basic simply adds an index as the first parameter to the parameter list for the given event procedure in the Code window. For example, the KeyPress event procedure for the control array of txtMoney text boxes now starts out as

```
Private Sub txtMoney_KeyPress(Index As Integer, KeyAscii As Integer)
```

instead of

```
Private Sub txtMoney_KeyPress(KeyAscii As Integer)
```

as it would for an ordinary text box.

Adding and Removing Controls in a Control Array

If you inadvertently add a control to a control array at design time, you can remove it by changing the control name or deleting the control at design time. However, once you tell Visual Basic to create a control array, you must change all the names of all the controls in the control array before Visual Basic will let you eliminate the Index property. (You can, of course, simply delete all the controls in the array in order to eliminate the control array.)

The Load Statement

The nifty part is that once you've created a control array at design time, you can add controls while the application is running. To do this, you use a method called Load that you haven't seen yet. The syntax for using Load is pretty simple; for our txtMoney control array it would be

```
Load txtMoney(I)
```

where I will be the index of the element.

There is actually one "gotcha" when adding controls to a control array at run time that you need to be aware of. To see this gotcha at work, start up a new project and add the following code to the Form_Load event procedure for the startup form:

11

```
Private Sub Form_Load()
  Dim I As Integer

  For I = 2 To 5
    Load txtMoney(I)
    txtMoney(I).Text = "Text box #" + Str$(I)
  Next I
End Sub
```

If you run this program, you won't see any of your new controls! The gotcha is that whenever Visual Basic loads a new element of a control array, the object is invisible—the Visible property of the new control is set to *False*. You'll need to change this to true. But even if you do, there is *another* problem you'll need to cure: *all* other properties (except the Tab Index and Control Array Index) of your new control are copied from the object that has the lowest index in the array. In particular, even if you modify the preceding Form_Load procedure to read

```
Private Sub Form_Load()
   For I = 2 To 5
      Load txtMoney(I)
      txtMoney(I).Text = "Text Box #" + Str$(I)
      txtMoney(I).Visible = True
   Next I
End Sub
```

you will only see the text box with index number 5 (which is the *sixth* box since indices for control array elements start out at 0). This is because the Left and Top properties start out the same for all four of the newly created controls. In our situation they are the same as txtMoney(0).Left and txtMoney(0).Top. Since these properties determine where you see the control, this means that newly created controls in a control array default to being stacked one on top of the other! Because of this, you'll often find yourself applying the Move method to controls in a control array after you tell Visual Basic to load them. For example, suppose you want to place all the text boxes (both the original ones and the newly loaded ones) running down the left-hand side of a form as in Figure 11-3. You could use code like this in the Form_Load:

```
Private Sub Form_Load()
   Dim I As Integer
   Const SPACING = 10
   txtMoney(0).Move 0, 0
   txtMoney(0).Text = "Text Box in control array #0"
   txtMoney(0).Width = TextWidth("  Text Box in control array #0  ")
   txtMoney(1).Move 0, txtMoney(0).Top + txtMoney(0).Height + SPACING
   txtMoney(1).Text = "Text Box in control array #1"
   txtMoney(1).Width = TextWidth("  Text Box in control array #1  ")
   For I = 2 To 5
      Load txtMoney(I)
      txtMoney(I).Text = "Text Box in control array #" + Str$(I)
      txtMoney(I).Move 0, txtMoney(I - 1).Top + txtMoney(I - 1).Height_
         + SPACING
      txtMoney(I).Visible = True
   Next I
End Sub
```

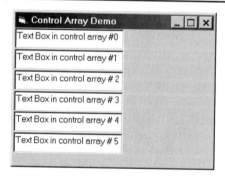

Demonstration
of control arrays
Figure 11-3.

The key line

```
txtMoney(I).Move 0, txtMoney(I - 1).Top + txtMoney(I - 1).Height + SPACING
```

uses the position and height of the previous control (plus a little spacing set by the constant) to determine the position of the new control. Notice how on each pass through the loop, the location for the top of the newly loaded text box moves down depending on the location of the previous control in the control array. (We have made the width of the text boxes reflect the size of the string inside of them.)

 T IP: Using the position of the previous element in a control array to reposition the next one is a standard technique for making a professional quality user interface.

The Unload Statement

You use the Unload statement to remove any element of a control array that you added at run time via the Load command. You cannot use the Unload statement to remove original elements of a control array that were created at design time. For example, if you add the Click procedure,

```
Private Sub Form_Click()
  Static I As Integer

  If I < 4 Then
    Unload txtMoney(I+2)
    I = I + 1
  Else
    Exit Sub
  End If
End Sub
```

each click on an empty place in the form removes the next control in the control array. However, this routine will not remove the initial two elements in the control array because of the line

```
If I < 4 Then ...
```

This extra precaution is necessary because you can only load or unload an element of a control array once. If you try to load or unload a control array element twice in succession, Visual Basic gives a run-time error.

 T IP: If you need to change the container control for an element of a control array that you added at run time, just reset the value of the Container property.

11

Example: Creating a Square Array of Labels via Control Arrays

The ability to position the elements of a control array precisely is important. In fact, as mentioned earlier, new elements of a control array start out being located at exactly the same place their parent was. You saw the first inklings of how to precisely position controls when we "stacked" the text boxes in the previous example. This next example requires positioning and sizing a group of labels so they fit into a perfect square that fills up, as best it can, a maximized form. Moreover, the labels themselves should be square with a size in twips determined by a variable called LabelSize that can be set in the program.

We will then use this code, in the section "Making a Magic Square," to build a program that creates magic squares. (A magic square is one in which the sum of all the rows, columns, and diagonals add up to the same number.) That program also requires an odd number of rows and columns. (Making magic squares is only simple for an odd number of rows and columns.) Figure 11-4 shows an example of a magic square created by the program from that section.

NOTE: I am showing you this program as an example of how to precisely position controls that are in a control array. This is an important technique that you will use a lot when working with Visual Basic. However, for displaying information in a table (like a magic square), it is usually much more efficient to use the flex grid control than to use a control array. (See the section "The Flex Grid Control" later in this chapter, which gives another version of the magic square program. Compare the speed of the two, for example!)

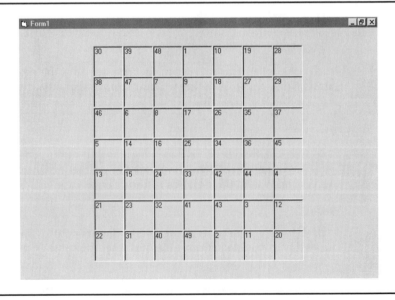

A 7 X 7 magic
square
Figure 11-4.

Here's a basic outline of the steps needed to put a square array of labels on a maximized form for the magic square program:

1. Add a label to the form and set the Border property of the label to 1 (fixed single). Set its Index property to be 0 to make it the first element of a control array. (In what follows, we suppose its Name property is set to lblBox.)

2. Maximize the form and find its usable height and width using the ScaleHeight and ScaleWidth properties.

3. Ask how large (number of rows and columns) the square should be. This translates into the number of labels we will add to the control array. This program prohibits you from having more than 15 rows and columns.

4. Calculate the maximum size for each label. The program loads the labels.

5. Then the program arranges the labels in a square on the form by moving them to the correct places.

Where should the labels be moved? Since ScaleWidth/2 is the center of a horizontal line down the form and ScaleHeight/2 is the center of a vertical line down the form, for the horizontal location of the first label, we need to start at

ScaleWidth/2 - (n/2) * LabelSize

where n is the number of controls in a row. We can use

ScaleHeight/2 - (n/2) * LabelSize

for the vertical positioning.

The program is a bit more elaborate than the simple outline would suggest, in order to allow for more informative messages if users enter unusable data. The extra things the code includes will be discussed as the code is presented.

First, you'll need some form-level variables and, of course, the Option Explicit command. For these, enter

```
Option Explicit
Private fNumberOfDim As Integer, fSize As Integer, fLabelSize As Integer
```

Here's the Form_Load procedure:

```
Private Sub Form_Load()
  Show
  WindowState = 2                              'maximal
  '    Call the GetDimensions procedure
  GetDimensions
  MsgBox "Please click on the form in order to see the control array."
End Sub
```

Here's the GetDimensions procedure that asks for the size of the box and insists that the size fit the form:

11

```
Sub GetDimensions()
'Local variables
  Dim I As Integer, BoxSize As Single
  Dim X As String, L As String
  Dim LabelSizeMessage As String

  'Get number of rows/columns
  X = InputBox("Number of dimensions?")
  fNumberOfDim = Val(X)
  'Call a function to check the number of dimensions.
  'This will return a message that we use for the loop.
  LabelSizeMessage = CheckDimensionNumber(fNumberOfDim)
  Do Until LabelSizeMessage = "OK"
    X = InputBox(LabelSizeMessage & "Reenter the number of dimensions.")
    fNumberOfDim = CInt(X)
    LabelSizeMessage = CheckDimensionNumber(fNumberOfDim)
  Loop

  'Call a similar function to check the size of the labels.
  L = InputBox("fSize of Labels?")
  fLabelSize = CInt(L)
  LabelSizeMessage = fLabelSizeOk(fLabelSize)
  Do Until LabelSizeMessage = "OK"
    L = InputBox(LabelSizeMessage & " Please reenter label size")
    fLabelSize = CInt(L)
    LabelSizeMessage = fLabelSizeOk(fLabelSize)
  Loop

End Sub
```

Notice that the GetDimensions procedure uses two string functions that return messages that depend on whether the data entered will work.

Here is the code for these functions. Notice that both these functions return strings that tell the program whether the data was usable or not. The CheckDimensionNumber function is the easiest. It just checks whether the number entered is odd (remember, you will need this for your magic square program) and whether it's less than 16.

```
Function CheckDimensionNumber(X As Integer) As String
  If X Mod 2 <> 1 Then
    CheckDimensionNumber = "Number of rows/columns must be odd. "
  ElseIf X > 15 Then
    CheckDimensionNumber = "Number of rows/columns must be < 16. "
  Else
    CheckDimensionNumber = "OK"
  End If
End Function
```

The fLabelSizeOk routine is a bit more complicated, as you want to be sure that you have enough room on the labels for the numerals. It looks like this:

```
Function fLabelSizeOk(X As Integer) As String
  Dim SpacedUsed As Integer, MaximumWidth As Integer
  MaximumWidth = fNumberOfDim*fNumberOfDim
  'MaximumWidth is the width of the largest number that we use
  MaximumWidth = TextWidth(Trim(Str$(MaximumWidth)))
  SpacedUsed = X * fNumberOfDim
  If SpacedUsed > ScaleHeight Or SpacedUsed > ScaleWidth Then
    fLabelSizeOk = "Labels too large. "
  ElseIf X < MaximumWidth Or X < TextHeight("1") Then
    fLabelSizeOk = "Labels too small. "
  Else
    fLabelSizeOk = "OK"
  End If
End Function
```

Here's the Form_Click procedure that actually does the work. It calls a procedure for making the boxes and then one for locating them.

```
Private Sub Form_Click()
  Static BoxesMade As Integer
  Cls
  If Not (BoxesMade) Then
    MakeBoxes fLabelSize
    BoxesMade = True
  End If
  LocateBoxes fLabelSize, fNumberOfDim
End Sub
```

Here's the procedure that makes the boxes:

```
Private Sub MakeBoxes(HowBig)
  Dim I As Integer

  lblBox(0).Visible = 0    'temp hide original label
  lblBox(0).Height = HowBig
  lblBox(0).Width = HowBig
  fSize = fNumberOfDim * fNumberOfDim
  For I = 1 To fSize - 1    'already have one label lblBox(0)
    Load lblBox(I)
    lblBox(I).Height = HowBig
    lblBox(I).Width = HowBig
  Next I
End Sub
```

11

Finally, the procedure that locates the labels is shown next. Inside the procedure, the For-Next loop does all the work. By setting the starting width and height as indicated, you can use integer division to find the row. For example, when I is between 0 and fNumberOfDim, then Row = 0; and when I is between fNumberOfDim and one less than twice the number of dimensions, then Row = 1. Columns are given by the remainder. The line

```
lblBox(I).Caption = Trim(Str$(I+1))
```

was put in to display the ordering of the boxes.

```
Private Sub LocateBoxes(HowBig As Integer, Number As Integer)

  Dim I As Integer, Row As Integer
  Dim Column As Integer
  Dim StartWidth As Integer, StartHeight As Integer
  Dim CurrentHeight As Integer, CurrentWidth As Integer

  StartHeight = ScaleHeight / 2 - ((Number / 2) * HowBig)
  StartWidth = ScaleWidth / 2 - ((Number / 2) * HowBig)
  For I = 0 To fSize - 1
    Row = I \ Number
    Column = I Mod Number
    CurrentHeight = StartHeight + (Row * HowBig)
    CurrentWidth = StartWidth + (Column * HowBig)
    lblBox(I).Move CurrentWidth, CurrentHeight
    lblBox(I).Caption = Trim(Str$(I + 1))
    lblBox(I).Visible = True
  Next I
End Sub
```

Of course, you need a way to end the program, so:

```
Private Sub Form_QueryUnload(Cancel As Integer, UnloadMode As Integer)
  Unload Me
  End
End Sub
```

One nice point about the procedures in this program is that you can easily adapt them to many situations. For example, minor changes to the Locate procedure allow you to use it whenever you'll need to load and position multiple controls on a form.

Making a Magic Square

Now that we have the form filled with an array of controls, we want to write the code that fills in the labels with the numbers that will make it into a magic square. As mentioned earlier, a magic square is one in which all the rows, columns, and long diagonals add up to the same number. This will be a good example of how you translate rules for working with array elements into code—and besides, these squares were once thought to have magical properties and bring you good luck, if printed out and hung on a wall!

Many people have devised rules for constructing magic squares. The one used in this section is called Loubre's rule and works only for odd-order magic squares—those with an odd number of rows and columns. Here's the method:

1. Place a 1 in the center of the first row.

2. The numbers now go into the square in order, by moving up on the diagonal to the right.

   Of course, you're immediately met with the problem of where to put the 2. If you've placed a 1 in the top row, going up takes you out of the square.

3. If you go off the top, wrap around to the corresponding place in the bottom row. On the other hand, going to the right eventually drops you off the side.

4. If you go off to the right end, wrap around to the left column.

5. Finally, if a square is already filled, or the upper right corner is reached, move down one row and continue applying these rules.

Here's a 5 × 5 magic square constructed with this rule.

```
17  24   1   8  15
23   5   7  14  16
 4   6  13  20  22
10  12  19  21   3
11  18  25   2   9
```

Suppose you store the numbers that will appear in the magic square in an array called Magic(,), where the first index is the row number and the second the column number. You can use all the procedures in the original program except that you need a form-level array, Magic, of integers, and:

◆ The Form_Click program will also call the program that fills the Magic array.

◆ The line that placed a number in the labels now uses the numbers stored in the Magic array.

Here are the form-level declarations for the magic square program:

```
Option Explicit
Dim fNumberOfDim As Integer, fSize As Integer
Dim fLabelSize As Integer, Magic() As Integer
```

Here's the modified Form_Load:

```
Private Sub Form_Load()
'Local variables
  Dim I As Integer, BoxSize As Single
  Dim X As String, L As String
  Dim LabelSizeMessage As String

  Show
  WindowState = 2                              'maximal

  'get number of rows/columns
  X = InputBox("Number of dimensions?")
  fNumberOfDim = Val(X)
  LabelSizeMessage = CheckDimensionNumber(fNumberOfDim)
  Do Until LabelSizeMessage = "OK"
     X = InputBox(LabelSizeMessage & "Reenter the number of dimensions.")
     fNumberOfDim = Val(X)
     LabelSizeMessage = CheckDimensionNumber(fNumberOfDim)
```

11

```
   Loop
   ' get size
   L = InputBox("fSize of Labels?")
   fLabelSize = Val(L)
   LabelSizeMessage = fLabelSizeOk(fLabelSize)
   Do Until LabelSizeMessage = "OK"
     L = InputBox(LabelSizeMessage & " Please reenter label size")
     fLabelSize = Val(L)
     LabelSizeMessage = fLabelSizeOk(fLabelSize)
   Loop

   Me.Print "Please click on the form in order to see the magic square."
End Sub
```

The functions

```
Function CheckDimensionNumber(X As Integer) As String
```

and

```
Function fLabelSizeOk(X As Integer) As String
```

are identical to the ones in the previous program, as is the Procedure to make the labels:

```
Private Sub MakeBoxes(HowBig)
```

The only change in the Locate procedure is to change the caption of the labels to reflect the value of the Magic array:

```
Private Sub LocateBoxes(HowBig As Integer, Number As Integer)

   Dim I As Integer, Row As Integer
   Dim Column As Integer
   Dim StartWidth As Integer, StartHeight As Integer
   Dim CurrentHeight As Integer, CurrentWidth As Integer

   StartHeight = ScaleHeight / 2 - ((Number / 2) * HowBig)
   StartWidth = ScaleWidth / 2 - ((Number / 2) * HowBig)
   For I = 0 To fSize - 1
     Row = I \ Number
     Column = I Mod Number
     CurrentHeight = StartHeight + (Row * HowBig)
     CurrentWidth = StartWidth + (Column * HowBig)
     lblBox(I).Move CurrentWidth, CurrentHeight
'the next line is the changed line
     lblBox(I).Caption = Trim(Str$(Magic(Row + 1, Column + 1)))
     lblBox(I).Visible = True
   Next I
End Sub
```

The Form_Click program now looks like this:

```
Private Sub Form_Click()
  Static BoxesMade As Integer
  Cls
  If Not (BoxesMade) Then
    MakeBoxes fLabelSize
    BoxesMade = True
  End If
  MakeMagic ' calls the MakeMagic routine
  LocateBoxes fLabelSize, fNumberOfDim
End Sub
```

Finally, the key MakeMagic routine that implements Loubre's rule looks like this:

```
Private Sub MakeMagic()
  'local variables
  Dim I As Integer, RowNumber As Integer, ColNumber As Integer
  Dim NewRow As Integer, NewCol As Integer
  ReDim Magic(1 To fNumberOfDim, 1 To fNumberOfDim)

  RowNumber = 1
  ColNumber = (fNumberOfDim \ 2) + 1
  Magic(RowNumber, ColNumber) = 1
  For I = 2 To fSize
    If RowNumber = 1 And ColNumber = fNumberOfDim Then
    ' at right hand corner
      NewRow = 2
      NewCol = ColNumber
    Else
      'move up one row and to the right
      NewRow = RowNumber - 1
      NewCol = ColNumber + 1
      'next line means we have gone off the top
      If NewRow < 1 Then NewRow = NewRow + fNumberOfDim

      'next line means we have gone off the right
      If NewCol > fNumberOfDim Then NewCol = NewCol - fNumberOfDim

    End If
  ' find empty slot by going down row by row
    Do Until Magic(NewRow, NewCol) = 0
      NewRow = RowNumber + 1
      NewCol = ColNumber
    Loop
    RowNumber = NewRow
    ColNumber = NewCol
    Magic(RowNumber, ColNumber) = I
  Next I
End Sub
```

11

Notice that the If clause inside the For-Next loop corresponds to the special case of the upper right corner. The two If statements inside the Else clause correspond to the first rule, "up and to the right." Of course, this row may be out of the bounds of the square, and the If-Thens take care of this.

The Do loop stops when you get to an unoccupied square. One of the nice properties of Loubre's method of constructing magic squares is that you know this will always work.

List and Combo Boxes

Use list boxes when you have a fixed list of choices. For example, suppose you are designing an application to provide information about the presidents of the United States. The form might look like the one in Figure 11-5. Note that (as in this figure) Visual Basic automatically adds vertical scroll bars whenever the list box is too small for all the items it contains.

On the other hand, you might want this application to let the user select a president by number rather than by scrolling through the list. To allow users to input data as well as make choices from a list, use a combo box, as shown in Figure 11-6. Notice that this form has a label near the combo box to identify what the user should type into the input area of the combo box.

There are actually two types of combo boxes, and which one you get depends on the value of the Style property.

◆ If the value of the Style property is set to the default value of 0, you get a combo box with an arrow. If the user clicks the arrow, he or she will see the drop-down list of choices given in the box.

◆ If the value of the Style property of a combo box is 1, the user sees the combo box with the list already dropped down.

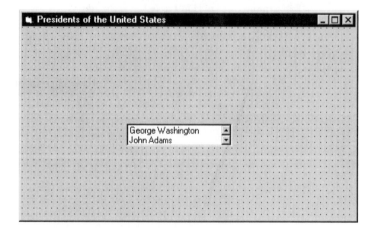

List box with presidents' names

Figure 11-5.

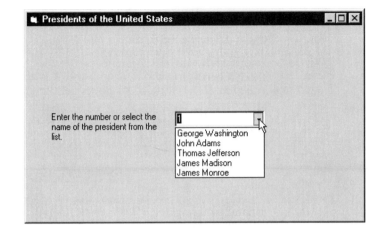

Combo box with
label for
presidents'
names
Figure 11-6.

Here are examples of these two types of combo boxes:

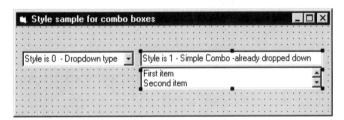

Notice that, in both cases, the user still has a text area to enter information. There is one other possible choice:

11

◆ If the value of the Style property of a combo box is 2, you will see a pull-down list box (as in the following).

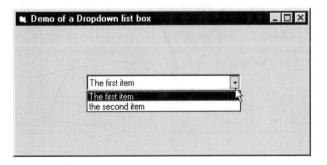

Thus, although you draw a pull-down list box by using the Combo Box icon, once you set the Style property to 2 (either via code or at design time), the text area disappears and what appears on the screen looks like a different version of a list box. On the other hand, the events that this "pull-down list box" will respond to are those of a combo box and not those of a list box.

There are also two kinds of list boxes, and working with the Style property lets you determine if the box shows little check boxes next to the items as you can see here:

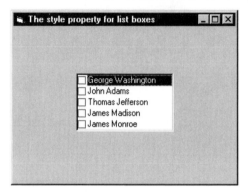

You can even change this property at run time using one of the built-in constants vbListBoxStandard or vbListBoxCheckBox.

Sorting Lists and Combo Boxes

As you saw in the last chapter, sorting items in an array requires a non-trivial amount of code. However, items in a list or combo box can be sorted in ASCII order by simply setting the Sorted property to be True. (Many VB programmers use an invisible list box to sort the items. This is fine as long as the list isn't too large—if it is, you are usually better off "rolling your own" sort code.)

If you set the Sorted property to True, Visual Basic will order the items in ANSII order. Otherwise, the order of the items depends on the order in which you placed them in the list box. You can set the Sorted property to True at design or run time, as well as switch it back and forth via code as necessary.

Manipulating the Items on a List or Combo Box

You usually add or remove items from a list or combo box while the project is running. (Visual Basic also allows you to populate list and combo boxes at design time. See the next section.) Use the AddItem method to add an item to a list or combo box. The syntax for this method is

    ListName.AddItem *Item* [, *Index*]

ListName is the control name of the list or combo box, and *Item* is a string or string expression. If the Sorted property is True for the list or combo box, then *Item* goes where ANSII order places it. If the Sorted property is False, Visual Basic places *Item* either at the position determined by the *Index* parameter or at the end of the list when you do not specify the index. The *Index* parameter must be an integer or integral expression. An *Index* value of 0 (not 1) means you are at the beginning of the list. The

Index option has no effect on where the item is added to the list if the Sorted property of the list box is set to True.

If you don't add the initial items to a list or combo box at design time, then the most common place to do so is in the Form_Load or Form_Initialize procedure. For example, if the list or combo box had the control name of lstPresidents, the code to build the list might start like this:

```
Private Sub Form_Load()
  lstPresidents.AddItem "George Washington"
  lstPresidents.AddItem "John Adams"
  lstPresidents.AddItem "Thomas Jefferson"
  lstPresidents.AddItem "James Madison"
...
End Sub
```

GW-BASIC and QuickBASIC users should note that there is no direct analogue of the READ/DATA combination to build information into your program. Of course, you can store the information that will go on the list in a file (see Chapter 18) or in a collection (Chapter 13).

You can also remove an item from a list while the program is running. The syntax for the RemoveItem method is

   ListName.RemoveItem *Index*

where, as before, *ListName* is the control name for the list or combo box and *Index* is the position where the item was located.

In addition to removing individual items on a list, you can use the Clear method to remove all the items on the list. The syntax is

   ListName.Clear

Other Common List and Combo Box Properties
Many of the properties of list and combo boxes determine how the information will appear. These properties work the same in list and combo boxes as they do in other controls. For example, the Font properties determine which font is used to display the items in the list or combo box; the BackColor and ForeColor properties control what colors are used for the background and foreground, respectively. Similarly, properties such as Height, Left, Top, and Width control the shape and location of the list or combo box.

The properties special to list and combo boxes let you get at the information in the box or the item the user has moved to within the box. They also allow you to have multiple columns in a list box. For example, when a user moves the focus to a list or combo box, he or she can select an item by using the ordinary Windows conventions—the arrow keys, PAGE UP, PAGE DOWN, the END key, and so on. In fact, once the user moves the focus to the list or combo box, he or she can also use the Windows shortcut of pressing a letter key to move to the first item in the list beginning with that letter. The item the user selects is always highlighted. All these details are handled automatically by Visual Basic.

Here are descriptions of the six list and combo box properties you'll be working with most frequently for these controls.

List   This is a property of both list and combo boxes, and it is for all practical purposes like a zero-based string array that contains all the items on the list.

```
lstTheBox(0)    'first item
lstTheBox(1)    'the SECOND item
lstTheBox(2)    'third item
```

Ever since Visual Basic 5, the List property has also been available to you at design time (that it wasn't was very annoying in early versions of VB!). This gives you another way to initialize the items in the list or combo box instead of doing it at run time. When you choose the List property in the Properties Window, VB opens up a list box where you can type the items. You'll need to place each item on a separate line, and this must be done by pressing CTRL+ENTER and *not* the ENTER key between items. (Pressing ENTER just closes the box where you are entering data—I can't tell you how many times I have done this inadvertently by hitting ENTER instead of using the CTRL+ENTER combination.)

ListCount   This is a property of both list and combo boxes, and it gives you the number of items on the list. Since the Index property starts at 0, in order to analyze the contents of the list using a For-Next loop, write the limits of the loop as

```
For I% = 0 To lstBoxName.ListCount-1
```

For example, the following loop lets you remove a specific item from a list box that I called "TheItemToGo".

```
Dim I%
For I% = 0 To lstBoxName.ListCount-1
  If lstTheBox.List(I%) = "TheItemToGo" Then
    lstTheBox.RemoveItem I%
    Exit For
  End If
Next I%
```

NOTE: Searching for an item can be done in a similar way, and it works well when there is a small number of items in the list box. However, there is a way to use Windows API calls to search through the items in a list box that is amazingly quick, pretty much regardless of how many items are in the list box. I'll show you that method in the next chapter.

ListIndex   This is a property of both list and combo boxes. The value of the ListIndex property gives the index number of the highlighted item, which is where the user has stopped in the list. If no item was selected, the value of this property is -1. For example, suppose you've stored information about the presidents in a string array named PresidentInfo$, which is dimensioned as being from 1 to 42, and you need to get at the item in this array containing information about the president that the user has selected from the lstPresidents list box. That is, your array of presidential information comes from lines like:

```
ReDim Presidents$(1 To 42)
Presidents$(1) = "George Washington"
Presidents$(2) = "John Adams"
Presidents$(3) = "Thomas Jefferson"
Presidents$(4) = "James Madison"
```

A statement such as

```
If ListIndex = -1 Then
  MsgBox "No president selected!"
Else
  Info$ = Presidents$(lstPresidents.ListIndex + 1)
End If
```

sets the value of the Info$ string variable to the value you'll need. Note that we need to shift the index given by the ListIndex property by 1 to take into account that the Presidents$ array goes from 1 to 42. If you've put the information about George Washington in the zero slot by starting the array from 0, you won't need to add 1 to the value of lstPresidents.ListIndex to get at this information.

Text   This is a property of both list and combo boxes, and it gives the currently selected item stored as a string. This, of course, changes as the user moves through the list box. If you need the numeric equivalent of this string, just apply the correct conversion function (CInt, CSng, etc.). Notice that if lstBoxName is the name of the list box, then the value of the lstBoxName.Text property for a list or combo box is the same as that of lstBoxName.List(ListIndex) as long as only one item was selected.

11

Columns and MultiSelect   The Columns property controls the number of columns in a list box. If the value is 0 (the default), you get a normal single-column list box with vertical scrolling. If the value is 1, you get a single-column list box with horizontal scrolling. If the value is greater than 1, you allow (but do not require) multiple columns.

T ....
  IP: Multiple columns show up only when the items don't fit into the list box. To force multiple columns, reduce the height of the list box accordingly.

The MultiSelect property controls whether the user can select more than one item from the list. (Of course, you may have to parse the resulting string assigned to the Text property to determine the individual items selected.) There are three possible values for this property:

Type of Selection	Value	How It Works
No multiselection allowed	0	
Simple multiselection	1	Use ordinary Windows techniques and mouse dragging (SHIFT+arrow keys, CTRL+RIGHT ARROW, and so on) to select more items.
Extended multiselection	2	SHIFT+mouse click extends the selection to include all list items between the current selection and the location of the click. Pressing and clicking the mouse selects or deselects an item in the list.

List Box Events

List boxes respond to 12 events. The KeyUp, KeyDown, and KeyPress events work exactly as before. The mouse events are covered in Chapter 17. List boxes can also tell you whether they've received or lost the focus.

However, the two most important events for list boxes are the Click and Double-click events. An important Windows convention is that clicking on an item selects the item but does not choose the item. This is reserved for double-clicking on the item. In general, therefore, you do not write code for the Click event procedure for a list box but only for the Double-click event procedure.

Another reason not to write code for the Click event procedure unnecessarily is that each time the user moves through the list, Visual Basic generates the Click event. Landing on an item in a list box by using the keyboard is the functional equivalent of clicking on the item. (There is no keyboard equivalent for double-clicking, although you can write your own for a specific list box by using the key events.)

 T IP: You might have the Click event update a status bar (see the next chapter) that gives information about the item.

Combo Box Events

Combo boxes respond to many of the same events as list boxes. You can analyze which keys were pressed or whether the box has received or lost the focus.

The first event that is different is the Change event. The Change event occurs only for pull-down combo boxes and simple combo boxes (Style = 0 or 1). Visual Basic does not generate this event if you are using a pull-down list box (Style = 2). Visual Basic generates this event whenever the user enters data in the text area of the combo box or when you change the Text property of the combo box from code.

As an example of where you might use this, suppose you've set up the list of presidents using a simple combo box (Style = 0, control Name = cboPresidents). Again, let's assume the information you want to display about each president is stored in the string array PresidentsInfo$. As the directions on the screen in Figure 11-6 indicate, you want to allow the user the possibility of entering the number of the president instead of scrolling through the list. Now, suppose someone types a number in the text box. Then you *might* first try to use the following Change event procedure for the Combo to give the user the information he or she is looking for:

```
Private Sub cboPresidents_Change()
  Dim PresidentNumber%
  If IsNumeric(cboPresidents.Text) Then
    PresidentNumber% = CInt(cboPresidents.Text)
    If PresidentNumber% < 1 Or PresidentNumber% > 42 Then
      MsgBox("Only 42 presidents with Clinton's re-election!")
    Else
      MsgBox(Presidents$(PresidentNumber% + 1))
    End If
  End If
End Sub
```

The trouble with this is that the Change event procedure is *too* responsive for this particular task. Visual Basic calls this event procedure every time the user types a character in the text area of the combo box. This means that for all but the first nine presidents, the procedure is called twice. (For example, if the user entered 16, he or she would see information about both Washington and Lincoln!) Also, if the user drops down the list and clicks, text rather than a number fills the text box. A better way to analyze the information is to put this code inside the KeyPress event procedure, but check for the user's pressing ENTER. You can do this with the following code:

```
Private Sub cboPresidents_KeyPress(KeyAscii As Integer)
  If KeyAscii = vbKeyReturn Then     'or 13 - the Enter key
    If IsNumeric(cboPresidents.Text) Then
      PresidentNumber% = CInt(cboPresidents.Text)
      If PresidentNumber% < 1 Or PresidentNumber% > 42 Then
        MsgBox("Only 42 presidents with Clinton's re-election!")
    Else
      MsgBox(Presidents$(PresidentNumber% + 1))
    End If
  End If
End Sub
```

11

Since simple combo boxes (Style = 1) recognize the Double-click event, another possibility is to put this kind of code in the Double-click event procedure. However, since there is no keyboard equivalent for double-clicking, you still might want to write a KeyPress event procedure to add keyboard equivalents for the user.

Visual Basic calls the DropDown event procedure right after the user clicks the arrow to drop the list box down or presses ALT+DOWN ARROW when the combo box has the focus—before the list drops down. For this reason, this event procedure is mostly used to update a combo box before the list appears. Since you can have a pull-down list only when the Style property is 0 or 2, this event is not invoked for simple combo boxes (Style = 1).

Associating Numbers with Items in List or Combo Boxes

Needing to associate integers with items in a list or combo box is so common that a simple method of doing this was added way back in Visual Basic 2. Of course, you could create an array to store this information and keep track of this array yourself, but you no longer need to do that—at least as long as all you need is a (long) integer associated with the item. For example, since we already have the Presidents' names in the Presidents combo box, we might want to associate their numbers with them when we build the combo box.

Whenever you create a list or combo box, Visual Basic automatically creates a long integer array called the ItemData array. This array is another property of the box, like the List array that you saw previously. And, like any property of a Visual Basic control, you can examine it or modify it.

If you want to add the numeric data to an entry in this ItemData array, you need to know the array index of the item. This is taken care of by the NewIndex property of the box. This property gives you the index of the last item added to the box. (If the Sorted property is True, this is particularly useful information, since you have no idea where this item will end up.)

At this point you need to write the code to update the ItemData array. The code will always look something like this.

```
cboPresidents.AddItem "William Jefferson Clinton"
cboPresidents.ItemData(cboPresidents.NewIndex) = 42
```

Example: Making a Dual List Box "Pick List" Form

One of the most common user interface features can be seen in Figure 11-7. We want to allow the user to move choices back and forth between the two columns. This turns out to be slightly more difficult to code than one would think. The problem is that once you remove an item from a box, the previous ListIndex property is no longer valid, so naively using a For-Next loop can run into problems. To follow along with this example, you might want to build a form like the one in Figure 11-7. Set the MultiSelect property to be 2 (Extended) and the Sorted property to be True. Name the two list boxes lstPossibleToppings and lstChosenToppings.

First off, we need two form-level variables that will keep track of the number of items on the list.

```
Private mItemsInPossibleList As Integer
Private mItemsInChosenList As Integer
```

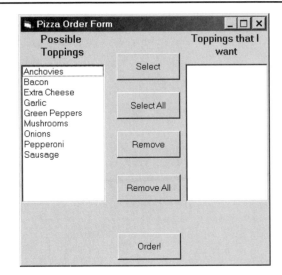

A Dual List Box
"Pick List" form
Figure 11-7.

The Form_Load then initializes these form-level variables to the correct values:

```
Private Sub Form_Load()
  Show
  mItemsInPossibleList = lstPossibleToppings.ListCount
  mItemsInChosenList = 0
End Sub
```

Suppose the user has selected a bunch of items and then clicks on the Select button. What we need to do is walk through the list and look for the items that the user has selected. Since we are allowing multiselection, this is a bit more complicated than it would be if we were not allowing this. The easiest way to do this is to remove the items one at a time and then start walking through the list from the first item after each item was removed. Every time we find an item, we adjust the current values of mItemsInPossibleList and mItemsInChosenList to reflect the current values and then start the search from the top again. Here's the code:

11

```
Private Sub cmdSelect_Click()
  Dim I As Integer
  Do Until I >= mItemsInPossibleList
    If lstPossibleToppings.Selected(I) Then
      lstChosenToppings.AddItem lstPossibleToppings.List(I)
      lstPossibleToppings.RemoveItem I
      mItemsInPossibleList = mItemsInPossibleList - 1
      mItemsInChosenList = mItemsInChosenList + 1
      I = 0
    Else
      I = I + 1
```

```
      End If
   Loop
End Sub
```

The code for the Remove button is essentially the same: just reverse the roles of the two list boxes.

```
Private Sub cmdRemove_Click()
   Dim I As Integer
   Do Until I >= mItemsInChosenList
      If lstChosenToppings.Selected(I) Then
         lstPossibleToppings.AddItem lstChosenToppings.List(I)
         lstChosenToppings.RemoveItem I
         mItemsInChosenList = mItemsInChosenList - 1
         mItemsInPossibleList = mItemsInPossibleList + 1
         I = 0
      Else
         I = I + 1
      End If
   Loop
End Sub
```

NOTE: If you wanted to avoid having to waste time constantly walking through the list, you could store the items in a two-dimensional array and keep track of which item was where using the second column.

The code for the Select/Remove All buttons works identically. Here the trick is to remember to clear the items you are removing from one list box after you are done moving the items to the other list box.

```
Private Sub cmdSelectAll_Click()
   Dim I As Integer
   For I = 0 To mItemsInPossibleList - 1
      lstChosenToppings.AddItem lstPossibleToppings.List(I)
      mItemsInChosenList = mItemsInChosenList + 1
   Next
   lstPossibleToppings.Clear
   mItemsInPossibleList = 0
End Sub

Private Sub cmdRemoveAll_Click()
   Dim I As Integer
   For I = 0 To mItemsInChosenList - 1
      lstPossibleToppings.AddItem lstChosenToppings.List(I)
      mItemsInPossibleList = mItemsInPossibleList + 1
   Next
   lstChosenToppings.Clear
   mItemsInChosenList = 0
End Sub
```

Finally, we want to allow the user to simply double click on an item to move it from one box to the other. This code must be in the DblClick event for the list box, and it needs to use the fact that the ItemChosen property gives you the index of the item currently selected. Otherwise the code shown here would simply adjust the values of the form-level variables that let us keep track of the number of items in each box.

```
Private Sub lstPossibleToppings_DblClick()
  Dim ItemChosen As Integer
  ItemChosen = lstPossibleToppings.ListIndex
  lstChosenToppings.AddItem lstPossibleToppings.List(ItemChosen)
  lstPossibleToppings.RemoveItem ItemChosen
  mItemsInPossibleList = mItemsInPossibleList - 1
  mItemsInChosenList = mItemsInChosenList + 1
End Sub

Private Sub lstChosenToppings_DblClick()
  Dim ItemChosen As Integer
  ItemChosen = lstChosenToppings.ListIndex
  lstPossibleToppings.AddItem lstChosenToppings.List(ItemChosen)
  lstChosenToppings.RemoveItem ItemChosen
  mItemsInPossibleList = mItemsInPossibleList + 1
  mItemsInChosenList = mItemsInChosenList - 1
End Sub
```

Example: Adding What the User Enters to the Data in a Combo Box

When you add one of the usual combo boxes to a form (one whose Style property is 0 or 1), you are doing it because you presumably want the user to have the capability to choose items not already in the box. Suppose you want to carry this idea further and add the item to the box either:

◆   When the user moves the focus away from the combo box or

◆   When the user presses ENTER

You will probably also want to check that the item isn't already in the box. Here's a sample of what the code in the LostFocus event might look like if the combo box is named cboBox:

11

```
Private Sub cboBox_LostFocus()
  Dim NewItem As String
  Dim I As Integer
  With cboBox
    NewItem = cboBox.Text
    For I = 0 To .ListCount -1
      If .List(I) = NewItem Then
        Exit Sub
      End If
    Next I
    .AddItem NewItem
  End With
End Sub
```

Notice the systematic use of the dot notation inside the With statement to simplify typing. The idea is simple—if we find the item, we exit the Sub, otherwise we know we have to add it.

Finally, to have the same kind of effect if the user presses ENTER, simply put similar code in the KeyPress event and then check if the KeyAscii key code is vbKeyReturn:

```
Private Sub cboBox_KeyPress(KeyAscii As Integer)
  Dim NewItem As String
  Dim I As Integer
  If KeyAscii = vbKeyReturn Then
    With cboBox
      NewItem = cboBox.Text
      For I = 0 To .ListCount -1
        If .List(I) = NewItem Then
          Exit Sub
        End If
      Next I
      .AddItem NewItem
    End With
  End If
End Sub
```

The Flex Grid Control

In this section I want to introduce you to the flex grid control supplied with most versions of Visual Basic. It is far more powerful than the grid control that came with early versions of Visual Basic. Of course, since the flex grid control has more than 80 properties, 20 events, and 10 methods, this section can only be an introduction!

The flex grid control lets you build spreadsheet-like features into your projects or display tabular information neatly and efficiently. For example, as you will see later in this chapter, you can use a flex grid control to display larger magic squares than the control array of labels allowed you to do earlier. Moreover, the flex grid version works faster and uses fewer Windows resources than a control array.

As the screen in Figure 11-8 shows, this control displays a rectangular grid of rows and columns at design time. How many rows and columns you see at design time depends both on the number of rows and columns you have set *and* the current size of the grid. (For example, in Figure 11-8 there is not enough room to see all of the eight rows and all of the five columns.)

NOTE: If the flex grid control (pointed to in Figure 11-8) is not part of your toolbox, choose Project|Components and check off Microsoft Flex Grid Control 6.0 in the dialog box.

Each grid member (intersection of a row and column) is usually called a *cell*. Cells can hold text, bitmaps, or icons, and you can even have some cells holding text and

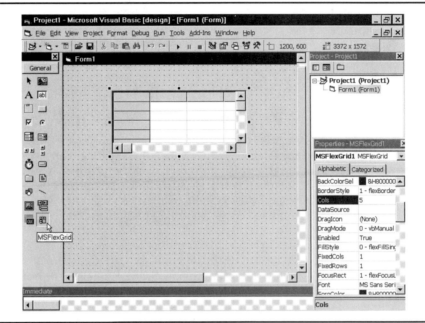

Sample flex grid
control with
eight rows and
five columns

Figure 11-8.

others holding graphics. Numbers must be translated back and forth using the right
conversion (CInt, CDbl and so on) and Str($) functions or the Variant data type must
be used—as you would do with text boxes. You can specify the contents, as well as the
width and height of a row or column, and you can use code to control each cell
individually while your project is running. For example, the value of the Text
property lets you read or change whatever text is in the current cell. The grid control
even includes a built-in word-wrap feature that you can activate via code or the
Properties window so users can enter text more easily.

NOTE: You must program in the ability for cells to actually accept text—it's a
little tricky so I'll show you how in the section called "Adding the Ability to Enter Text
in a MSFlexGrid Cell" later in this chapter.

11

Users can move from cell to cell by using the arrow keys or the mouse; Visual Basic
handles such movement automatically. As the user of your control moves around the
grid, Visual Basic keeps track of what the current cell is as the values of the Row and
Col properties.

Users can work with contiguous groups of cells in the grid, usually called *regions*, by
clicking a cell and dragging the mouse or by pressing SHIFT plus an arrow key to select
the region. Once a region is selected, code can be used to analyze or change the
contents.

NOTE: If you give someone an application that uses the grid control, you must install MSFlxGrd.ocx in their \Windows\System directory or in some other place that Windows knows about. The Setup and Deployment Wizard (see Chapter 10) can do this automatically.

General Properties of the Flex Grid Control

Many properties of the flex grid control are the same as those for the controls that you're already familiar with. For example, the Height and Width properties tell you how large the grid will appear; the Enabled property determines whether the grid will notice keystrokes or mouse activity. Similarly, if you set the ScrollBar property to a nonzero value (1 for Horizontal, 2 for Vertical, 3 for both), Visual Basic automatically adds the appropriate scroll bars when there is information on the grid that cannot be seen.

NOTE: It is important to refer to the online help as needed. Certain properties of the flex grid that you would think apply to the current cell, don't. The most obvious example of this is the Picture property, which returns a bitmap image of the flex grid and does not assign a picture to a cell. (Use the CellPicture property for this.)

Before we go over the most interesting properties that are special to the flex grid, be aware that there are a slew of properties like the CellPicture property I just mentioned. Some other examples of these are CellFontBold, CellFontItalic, CellBackColor, and CellForeColor. As you might expect from the names, these properties affect the text or color of the current cell.

The remainder of this section takes you through the most important properties that are special to grids.

TIP: The flex grid control comes with a custom property page, as shown in Figure 11-9. (Click on Custom in the Properties window to see this dialog box.) Once you are comfortable with the various properties of the flex grid control, you can use this dialog box to quickly set the values of the properties you need to change.

Cols, Rows These properties determine the number of rows and columns in the grid. The default values for each of these properties is 2, but you can reset them in code or via the Properties window, as needed. They must be integers, and the syntax is

GridName.Cols = *NumOfCols%*
GridName.Rows = *NumOfRows%*

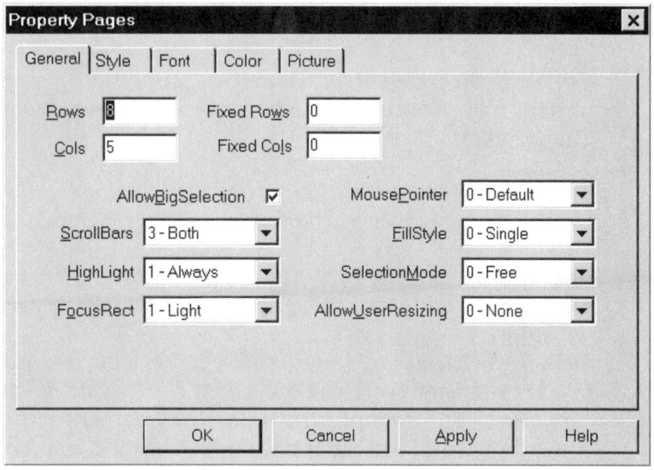

Property Pages

General | Style | Font | Color | Picture

Rows: 8   Fixed Rows: 0
Cols: 5   Fixed Cols: 0

AllowBigSelection ☑   MousePointer: 0 - Default

ScrollBars: 3 - Both   FillStyle: 0 - Single

HighLight: 1 - Always   SelectionMode: 0 - Free

FocusRect: 1 - Light   AllowUserResizing: 0 - None

OK   Cancel   Apply   Help

Custom property
page for the flex
grid control
Figure 11-9.

You can also add an optional form name. For example:

```
frmDisplay.Cols = 10
```

Col, Row   These properties (which shouldn't be confused with Cols and Rows!) set
or return the row and column for the currently selected cell inside the grid. These
properties are only available at run time. As the user moves around the grid, the
values of these properties change. You then use their values to determine where inside
the grid the user is. By adjusting their values via code, you can specify the current cell
directly. Since both Col and Row start out at zero, the top left corner cell has Col
value 0 and Row value 0.

ColPosition, RowPosition   These occasionally useful properties let you move whole
rows and columns around in your grid. The syntax is

> *GridName*.ColPosition(*number*) [= *value*]
> *GridName*.RowPosition(*number*) [= *value*]

For example, the following code is guaranteed to drive users of your grid crazy since
every time they click in a cell, the column containing that cell moves to a random
location within the grid:

```
Sub MSFlexGrid1_Click ()
  MSFlexGrid1.ColPosition(MSFlexGrid.MouseRow) = Int(Rnd*Rows)
End Sub
```

11

(As you might expect, the MouseRow property tells you in what row the mouse pointer is currently located. MouseCol does the same thing for the column.)

ColWidth, RowHeight   These two properties specify the width of a specific column or height of a specific row. They can only be set via code. Both are measured in twips. The syntax is

> *GridName*.ColWidth(*ColNumber%*) = *Width%*
> *GridName*.RowHeight(*RowNumber%*) = *Height%*

(If text has been automatically word wrapped, adjust ColWidth or RowHeight to display the text by checking its TextWidth and TextHeight properties.)

Text, TextMatrix   As mentioned earlier, the Text property sets or returns the text inside the current cell (the one given by the *current* values of the Col and Row properties). For example, the following fragment sets up a grid (the control name is the default—MSFlexGrid1) with four rows and four columns. Then we make the cell in the bottom right corner the current cell. We add some text to that cell and then display it on the form.

```
MSFlexGrid1.Cols = 4 'have four rows
MSFlexGrid1.Rows = 4  'have four columns
MSFlexGrid1.Col = 3
MSFlexGrid1.Row = 3
MSFlexGrid1.Text = "This would go in the bottom right corner"
MsgBox MSFlexGrid1.Text & "is in cell 3, 3"
MSFlexGrid1.Col = 0
MSFlexGrid1.Row = 0
MsgBox MSFlexGrid1.Text & "is in cell 0, 0"
```

NOTE: Because rows and columns in grids are numbered from 0, the bottom right corner of a 4 × 4 grid has col (and row) index 3.

Next, the TextMatrix property, which has the following syntax,

> TextMatrix(*rowindex, colindex*) = [*string*]

lets you set or retrieve the text in an arbitrary cell *without* needing to change the Row and Col properties.

CellLeft, CellWidth, CellTop, and CellHeight   As the name suggests, these properties give you the size and location of a cell relative to its container. We will use these extensively in the section on adding an editing capability to our grid.

ColAlignment   There are three possible settings for data inside a column. You can left-justify (value = 0), right-justify (value = 1), or center the text (value = 2). The syntax is

GridName.ColAlignment(*Index%*) = *Setting%*

TIP: You can also use the ten possible values for the CellAlignment and PictureAlignment properties to control the alignment of information in a specific cell.

FixedCols, FixedRows, and FixedAlignment   Often when you are working with a grid, you will want to use certain cells to display information at all times. For example, regardless of how the user scrolls through a spreadsheet, you may want to display the column headings. Fixed rows and columns are always displayed in gray and must be at the top and left sides of the grid. The default is that there is one fixed row and one fixed column. The FixedAlignment property works exactly like the ColAlignment property but applies only to fixed columns. The syntax for these three properties is

GridName.FixedCols = *NumberOfFixedCols%*
GridName.FixedRows = *NumberOfFixedRows%*
GridName.FixedAlignment = *SettingNumber%*

As before, the setting for the alignment property has the possible values 0, 1, and 2, and you can add an optional form name, of course.

GridLines, ScrollBars   These two properties control whether grid lines (these make it easier to see cell boundaries) and scroll bars appear. The default is to show grid lines and to have both horizontal and vertical scroll bars.

LeftCol, TopRow   These two properties control which are the leftmost column and highest row displayed from a grid. You use these properties when the entire grid is too large to fit on the form. These properties can only be set in code, and the syntax for both of these properties is similar:

GridName.LeftCol = *LeftmostCol%*
GridName.TopRow = *HighestRow%*

Properties of Selected Cells Inside Grids

Although grids are often used passively to display data (or pictures), it is even more common to make them responsive to users. Users can select cells or regions and change their contents. This section takes you through the properties that let you work with regions selected by the user.

11

ColSel, RowSel These properties work with the Row and Col properties to determine the size of the current selection. Like Row and Col, they start at 0. If all four of these values are the same, the user has selected a single cell.

For example, the following code selects columns 0 through 4 and rows 0 through 3 (five columns and four rows).

```
MSFlexGrid1.Row = 0: MSFlexGrid1.Col = 0
MSFlexGrid1.ColSel = 4: MSFlexGrid1.RowSel = 3
```

You must first set the Row and Col properties and then set the ColSel and RowSel properties in order to define a region in your grid.

Clip The Clip property is among the most important when dealing with selected regions. This property sets or returns the contents of the selected region. The syntax is

   GridName.Clip = *String*$

The string expression on the right-hand side contains the entire contents of the selected region. The contents of each cell on the same row are separated from the adjacent cell by the tab character (ASCII 9 = vbKeyTab), and each row is separated from the next by the carriage return character (ASCII 13 = vbKeyReturn). For example, if you start up a new project and add an MSFlexGrid first to the toolbox and then to the form, the following code fills up the first three columns and two rows with the string equivalents of the numbers 1 through 6.

```
Private Sub Form_Load()
  Dim S$
  MSFlexGrid1.Rows = 3
  MSFlexGrid1.Cols = 3
  MSFlexGrid1.Row = 0: MSFlexGrid1.Col = 0
  MSFlexGrid1.ColSel = 2: MSFlexGrid1.RowSel = 1
  S$ = Str$(1) + vbTab + Str$(2) + vbTab + Str$(4)
  S$ = S$ + vbCr + Str$(4) + vbTab + Str$(5) + vbTab + Str$(6)
  MSFlexGrid1.Clip = S$
End Sub
```

FillStyle Sometimes you want what the user enters into one cell of the selected region to fill up the entire region. You can control this by changing the FillStyle property from its default value of 0 (flexFillSingle) to the value 1 (flexFillRepeat). In addition, when FillStyle is 1, any image assigned with the Picture property automatically fills all cells in the selected region.

HighLight This has three values. The value 0 (flexHighlightNever) means that the user can't tell when a cell is selected. The other two values 1 (= flexHighlightAlways) and 2 (flexHighlightWithFocus) give the user a visual clue. (The difference between the two is whether the control stays highlighted after it loses the focus.)

AllowBigSelection This True/False property determines whether clicking on a column or row header selects the entire row or column.

AllowUserResizing This determines whether the user can resize a row or column at run time using the mouse. The possible values are described in the following table.

Constant	Value	Description
flexResizeNone	0	(Default) The user can't resize rows or columns.
flexResizeColumns	1	The user can resize columns.
flexResizeRows	2	The user can resize rows.
flexResizeBoth	3	The user can resize both rows and columns.

Sorting a Grid

One of the most powerful features of the flex grid is its ability to sort rows according to the columns you select. If you change the Sort property at design time, the grid starts out sorted. If you change it at run time, Visual Basic sorts the (selected) rows of the grid immediately after it processes the statement. The syntax for the Sort property takes the form,

FlexGridName.Sort = *Value*

where the possible values are described in the following table.

Constant	Value	Description
flexSortNone	0	None
flexSortGenericAscending	1	Sort in ascending order
flexSortGenericDescending	2	Sort in descending order
flexSortNumericAscending	3	Ascending but converts strings to numbers
flexSortNumericDescending	4	Descending but converts strings to numbers
flexSortStringNoCaseAscending	5	Ascending but case-insensitive
flexSortStringNoCaseDescending	6	Descending but case-insensitive
flexSortStringAscending	7	Ascending but case-sensitive
flexSortStringDescending	8	Descending but case-sensitive
Custom	9	Uses the Compare event (described in the next section) to compare rows

11

Note that if you set the Sort property to a nonzero value, it will sort entire rows regardless of whether only a few columns are selected. If you have set the Row and RowSel properties to be equal, you will sort all nonfixed rows. The custom version allows you to control the sort by using a special event of the flex grid called the Compare event, described in the next section.

Finally, the rows are sorted depending on the columns you have selected, going from left to right. For example, if Col = 2 and ColSel = 1, the sort would be done using Column 2 for the keys. (You can even sort on invisible rows.)

Events and Methods for Grid Controls

Grids respond to many of the standard events; for example, you can use the Click event to determine whether (and where) the user has clicked inside the grid and the KeyPress event to send what a user is typing inside the grid directly to the currently selected cell. Using the KeyPress event to accumulate keystrokes with a static variable and then testing for the ENTER key is a common way to allow direct entry of data into the grid. All you need to do after the ENTER key is pressed is assign the data accumulated by the static variable to the Text property of the grid. However, since the code to activate a grid control must constantly monitor when the selected region changes, Visual Basic provides you with two events unique to grids that you might want to consider allowing along with (or instead of) the ENTER key.

EnterCell, LeaveCell   EnterCell is triggered when the user clicks inside a cell that is different from the one currently selected. LeaveCell is triggered right before the active cell changes to a new one (and thus right before EnterCell is triggered).

RowColChange   This event is also triggered when the current cell changes. It occurs after LeaveCell and EnterCell. If you make the variable used in the KeyPress event procedure a form-level variable instead of a static variable, you can use an assignment to the Text property of the grid in this event procedure to make the changes.

SelChange   This event is activated when the selected region changes—either because the user has moved around in the grid or the code has directly changed one of the properties given in the previous section.

Compare Event   As I mentioned before, this event lets you order the columns any way you want. The idea is that when you set the Sort property to 9, Visual Basic will automatically trigger this event. The syntax for this event procedure looks like this:

Private Sub *object*_Compare(*row1* As Integer, *row2* As Integer, *cmp* As Integer)

You change the value of the *cmp* parameter in order to tell Visual Basic which row to consider as being less than the other row. The idea is that you can say that one row is less than another even if the usually alphabetical order wouldn't make it so. The three possible ways to change the *cmp* parameter are described in the following table.

cmp Setting	Description
–1	If row1 should appear before row2 when you tell VB to sort the grid
0	If both rows are equal or the order in which they appear is irrelevant
1	If row1 should appear after row2 when you tell VB to sort the grid

Methods for Resizing a Grid

There are also methods that let you insert or delete rows from a grid. The syntax to add a row is

GridName.AddItem *Item$* [,*Index%*]

The optional *index* parameter allows you to add the row at a specific location.

The string given by *Item$* is placed in the first column of the new row; you separate successive items in the same row by tab characters (vbTab). For example, the following code

```
Dim TheItem As String
For I = Asc("A") To Asc("Z")
  TheItem = Chr$(I) & vbTab & I
  MSFlexGrid1.AddItem TheItem
Next I
```

adds 26 two column rows to those *already* in the grid. The first column has the letters A through Z, the second has their ASCII codes.

If you wanted to start the grid from scratch, you would rewrite the above code as:

```
Dim TheItem As String
MSFlexGrid1.Rows = 0
For I = Asc("A") To Asc("Z")
  TheItem = Chr$(I) & vbTab & I
  MSFlexGrid1.AddItem TheItem
Next I
```

11

Because we set the Rows property to zero before starting, the finished grid will have only 26 rows in total.

RemoveItem, on the other hand, removes a row from a grid. Its syntax is

GridName.RemoveItem *Index%*

For example, to remove the first row of a grid, you might use

```
MSFlexGrid1.RemoveItem 0
```

(because the first index starts out at zero).

Adding the Ability to Enter Text in a MSFlexGrid Cell

Unfortunately, the MSFlexGrid, as useful as it is, doesn't have the ability to let the user type into a cell automatically. You have two choices in order to add this ability. The first is simply to monitor the various KeyEvents and then assign the string (say, when the user presses the ENTER key) to the Text property. This may seem like the simplest solution, but it really doesn't provide what users really want.

What they *really* want is the ability to do all the usual Windows editing tricks, such as cut and paste and undo (CTRL+Z). The way professionals deal with this request is to use a floating text box that "hovers" over the current cell. To make the text box seem to be even more like a cell, you should set the Appearance property of that text box to be = 0 (flat), and the BorderStyle property to be 0 (none). The result is that the user thinks he or she is entering the data directly into the grid, but what they are really doing is entering the data in a text box. When they press ENTER or an UP or DOWN ARROW key or move the focus within the grid by clicking on a new cell, you simply copy the information from the text box to the old cell and no one is the wiser. The only tricky thing is to position the text box just right so that the user doesn't realize he or she is not entering data in the cell.

To follow along, you might want to start up a new project, add the MSFlexGrid control to your toolbox, and then add one to a form. Make sure it has neither fixed rows nor fixed columns. Also add a Text box whose Text property is set to be empty (so that it is blank), and as I mentioned a moment ago, set the Appearance property to be = 0 (flat), and the BorderStyle to be 0 (none).

In the code that follows we'll simply assume that whenever the user starts typing, he or she wants to edit the contents of the cell. (One can get quite elaborate in how much editing one wants to allow: for example, at the cost of making it significantly longer, you could modify this code to allow for a double click ("Excel" style) editing.)

First off, you might want to enter the following Form_Load to start things off. This initializes the Text box so that it is invisible and there is nothing in it. The line

```
Set Text1.Font = MSFlexGrid1.Font
```

uses a command you'll see in Chapter 13; for now just accept that this makes all the font properties of the text box be the same as the font properties of the grid control. The real work is done by a call to a routine I called PositionTextBox that I'll show you in a second.

```
Private Sub Form_Load()
  Text1.Visible = False
  Set Text1.Font = MSFlexGrid1.Font
  MSFlexGrid1.Cols = 5
  MSFlexGrid1.Rows = 10
  Show
  MSFlexGrid1.Col = 0
  MSFlexGrid1.Row = 0
  PositionTextBox
End Sub
```

The PositionTextBox routine uses the current values of the CellLeft, CellWidth, CellTop, and CellHeight properties in order to make the text box sit perfectly inside a cell. Then we make the text box visible and set the focus there.

```
Private Sub PositionTextBox()
    Text1.Left = MSFlexGrid1.CellLeft + MSFlexGrid1.Left
    Text1.Top = MSFlexGrid1.CellTop + MSFlexGrid1.Top
    Text1.Width = MSFlexGrid1.CellWidth
    Text1.Height = MSFlexGrid1.CellHeight
    Text1.Visible = True
    Text1.SetFocus
End Sub
```

Next, although there isn't much code in it, comes one of the keys. In the EnterCell event procedure of the grid—which is triggered whenever the current cell changes—we:

1. Set the text box's contents to what was in the cell
2. Position the text box correctly

Here's the code:

```
Private Sub MSFlexGrid1_EnterCell()
    Text1.Text = MSFlexGrid1.Text
    PositionTextBox
End Sub
```

Next, to allow for cut and pasting and to make sure the text box and the cell stay in synch, we update the cell's content in the Change event of the text box:

```
Private Sub Text1_Change()
    MSFlexGrid1.Text = Text1.Text
End Sub
```

11

Finally, to allow for the user to press ENTER or the UP/DOWN ARROW keys to move out of the cell, we will work with both the KeyDown and KeyPress events of the text box. In all cases the ideas are the same: the code simply moves the current cell down, up, or to the side depending on whether the user pressed the DOWN or UP ARROW or the ENTER key. (I use the Mod function to "wrap" around when we get to an edge.)

```
Private Sub Text1_KeyDown(KeyCode As Integer, Shift As Integer)
    If KeyCode = vbKeyDown Then
        MSFlexGrid1.Row = MSFlexGrid1.Row + 1 Mod MSFlexGrid1.Rows
    End If
    If KeyCode = vbKeyUp Then
        MSFlexGrid1.Row = MSFlexGrid1.Row - 1 Mod MSFlexGrid1.Rows
    End If
End Sub
```

```
Private Sub Text1_KeyPress(KeyAscii As Integer)
  If KeyAscii = vbKeyReturn Then
    MSFlexGrid1.Col = MSFlexGrid1.Col + 1 Mod MSFlexGrid1.Cols
  End If
End Sub
```

Magic Squares Using a Grid Control

You can easily modify the magic square program to use a grid rather than a control array. However, let's change the program so that the user can scroll through the grid. This will allow extraordinarily large magic squares. First of all, you will need a form with a grid control that has both vertical and horizontal scroll bars enabled. Let's leave it at the default name of MSFlexGrid1. Once you do this, here is the code that gives this version of the magic square program. To begin with, you need fewer form-level variables:

```
Dim fNumberOfDim As Integer
Dim CellfSize As Integer, Magic() As Integer
```

Next, the Form_Load is much simpler, as you don't have to check the size (because the user can now scroll through the grid).

```
Private Sub Form_Load()
'Local variables
  Dim I As Integer
  Dim X As String

  Show
  WindowState = 2                          'maximal

  'get number of rows/columns
  X = InputBox("Number of rows/columns?")
  fNumberOfDim = Val(X)
  Do Until fNumberOfDim Mod 2 = 1
    X = InputBox("The number of rows/columns must be odd.")
    fNumberOfDim = Val(X)
  Loop
  ' the next two lines calculate how wide a cell should be, based on
  ' the largest number that is going into it
  'this line finds the number of digits
  CellfSize = Len(Trim(Str$(fNumberOfDim * fNumberOfDim)))
  'this one multiplies it by the width of a digit
  CellfSize = CellfSize * (TextWidth("1"))
  Me.Print "Please click on the form in order to see the magic square."
End Sub
```

This routine makes the grid the correct size. To make the scroll bars easier to see, make the grid 90 percent of the size of the form. It also makes each row and column the correct height and width (as measured by the HowBig parameter).

```
Private Sub MakeGrid(HowBig)
  Dim I As Integer

  MSFlexGrid1.Cols = fNumberOfDim
  MSFlexGrid1.Rows = fNumberOfDim
  MSFlexGrid1.Height = 0.9 * ScaleHeight
  MSFlexGrid1.Width = 0.9 * ScaleWidth
  MSFlexGrid1.Move ScaleWidth / 2 - (MSFlexGrid1.Width / 2), _
  ScaleHeight / 2 - (MSFlexGrid1.Height / 2)
  For I = 1 To MSFlexGrid1.Cols
    MSFlexGrid1.ColWidth(I - 1) = HowBig
    MSFlexGrid1.RowHeight(I - 1) = HowBig
  Next I
End Sub
```

As before, Form_Click calls the procedure that builds the array for the magic square. In this case you also fill the cells in the grid using the array and then make the grid visible.

```
Private Sub Form_Click()
Dim I As Integer, J As Integer
  Cls
  MakeGrid CellfSize
  MakeMagic
  MousePointer = 11
  For I = 1 To fNumberOfDim
    For J = 1 To fNumberOfDim
      MSFlexGrid1.Col = J - 1
      MSFlexGrid1.Row = I - 1
      MSFlexGrid1.ColAlignment(J - 1) = 2 'centered
      MSFlexGrid1.Text = Str$(Magic(I, J))
    Next J
  Next I
  MSFlexGrid1.Visible = True
  MousePointer = 0
End Sub
```

The MakeMagic routine is the same as before, as is the QueryUnload event.

11

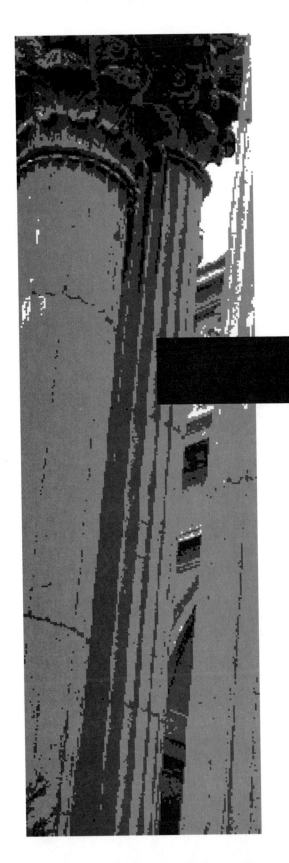

CHAPTER 12

Building Larger Projects

While it is quite amazing how much one can do with Visual Basic with the code attached to a single form, to take full advantage of VB you'll need to start using multiple forms and having the code on all the forms in your project interact. The first part of this chapter shows you how to add multiple forms to a project. Next, you'll want to start writing code that doesn't belong to any particular form but can easily work with all the forms in your project. This kind of code is often thought of as a *library* and you'll also want to know the techniques for starting to build libraries, so this chapter explains how to add modules for code alone. Such code allows you to build global variables and global procedures into a project.

Occasionally you will need to use a function internal to Windows that is not part of Visual Basic itself; you'll learn the basic techniques for using these "Windows API functions" in this chapter as well. Then it's on to error trapping. Up to this point we have been living in the never-never land of programming. We have assumed that nothing ever goes wrong with a program: that printers are always available and files always exist. Error trapping is needed when you move to the real world. Learning these techniques is necessary if you want your program to be able to respond to errors (both internally and externally generated) without just rolling over and dying.

The chapter ends by spending a bit more time on the anatomy of a project and some general words on styles for making writing maintainable programs easier.

Projects with Multiple Forms

As your applications grow more complicated, you won't want to restrict yourself to applications that are contained in only a single form. Multiple forms will add flexibility and power to your applications. This is over and above solving the problems you've already seen, with controls blocking out text that you've printed to a form as opposed to placing the text in a multiline text box or rich text box.

To add more forms to an application you're designing, open the Project menu and choose Add Form. (You can also use the Add Form tool.) Regardless of which method you choose, you'll see the Add form dialog box, an example of which is shown in Figure 12-1. (Different editions of Visual Basic may have fewer or more items in this dialog box.)

As you can see in Figure 12-1, Visual Basic supplies you with quite a few prebuilt forms that you can add to your project without doing any work. You can scroll through this dialog box in order to see the other possibilities. For example, Figure 12-2 shows you the basic form for a "Splash Screen"—the name given to a form on which you can put things like your company logo or copyright screen. (You won't see it as one of the options in Figure 12-2—it is towards the bottom of this dialog box.) If you add this form to your project, you can adjust the picture and caption of the labels to match your company. (See the Section on "Sub Main" later in this chapter for more on how to build Splash Screens into your programs.)

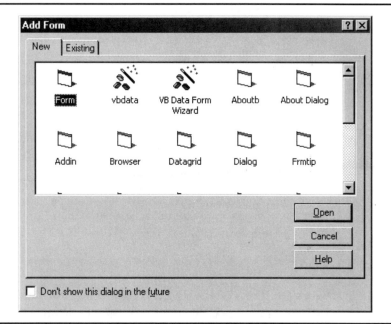

The Add Form
dialog box
Figure 12-1.

TIP: As you saw in Chapter 4, every form is stored in an .frm file that lists the controls and properties. If you store an .frm file in the \Template\Forms directory, below where Visual Basic is stored, that form will automatically get added to the Add Form dialog box for automatic reuse.

A sample splash
screen form
supplied by
Visual Basic
Figure 12-2.

12

For example, my \Template\Forms directory has files named

```
\Template\Forms\Aboutb.frm
\Template\Forms\Addin.frm
\Template\Forms\Browser.frm
\Template\Forms\Datagrid.frm
```

and so on.

NOTE: If you look in the \Forms directory (or have looked closely at a form you have created that has a picture attached to it), you'll often see a matching file with an .frx extension. For example: \Template\Forms\Aboutb.frx, These .frx files aren't always necessary; they are needed when there are pictures attached to the form or to one of the controls on the form. You'll need to make sure the associated .frx file is in the \Forms directory as well as its parent .frm file if you want to use your form as a template.

Navigating Among Forms: The Project Explorer

The Project Explorer window lists by name all the forms. The actual files of course have the .frm extension. If the forms aren't visible, expand the tree by clicking on the plus sign next to the Forms folder. Visual Basic stores each form as a separate .frm file and uses the .vbp (project) file to keep track of where they are stored, along with any .frx file that is needed for the images attached to a form. The following illustration shows unexpanded and expanded views of the Project Explorer window with an application that has three forms:

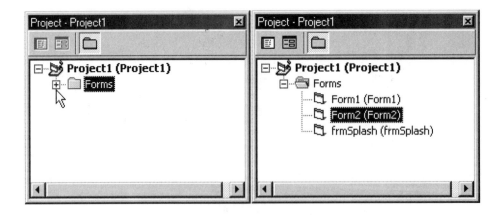

TIP: The easiest way to bring a form to the foreground so you can work with it is to open the Project window and double-click the form's name, or select the form by name in the Project Explorer and choose View Object from the right-click menu in the Project Explorer.

Note that you can see how all the forms in your project will appear relative to the users screen in the Form Layout window. And, although it is not as precise as setting the Left and Top properties, you can drag forms around in this window in order to position them for how they will appear on the user's screen.

TIP: If you are running at a higher resolution, the Form Layout window shows you how the form will appear at a lower resolution. The lower the resolution, the larger the form will appear. (See Chapter 14 for more on how to make your programs behave well regardless of the resolution of an individual user's screen.)

The Name Property for Forms

Although you never use the Name of the form when writing event code attached to the form, forms, like controls, do have a Name property that you can use to refer to properties of the form. The default value for the Name of a form starts at Form1 for the first form, Form2 for the second form, and so on.

Form names are never needed when using code attached to the current form. Most people use the reserved keyword Me or simply leave it out. However, using the default value for the form's name means you have to refer to its properties when you access it from another form with code like this:

```
Form3.Height = Screen.Height/2    'cut the default height in 2
```

If Form3 is your "Help Form," for example, the code will be a lot easier to read if you set the form name to HelpForm or frmHelp (following the standard Microsoft naming convention for forms) and write

```
HelpForm.Height = Screen.Height/2 'set HelpForm height to
                                  'half normal
```

or

```
frmHelp.Height = Screen.Height/2  'set HelpForm height to
                                  'half normal
```

12

Thus, setting the Name property of the form to something meaningful via the Properties window makes it both clearer and easier to refer to the properties or apply a method to the form from code attached to a *different* form. And, as always, the clearer your code, the easier it will be to debug.

On the other hand, regardless of how you name a form, the Click event procedure template attached to the form itself will always look like this in the Code window attached to that form:

```
Private Sub Form_Click ()

End Sub
```

In particular, even if you named the form frmHelp, code like this will have *nothing* to do with the Click event of the form.

```
Sub frmHelp_Click()

End Sub
```

It would simply be a strange procedure named frmHelp_Click!

How to Handle Multiple Forms at Run Time

Visual Basic displays at most one form when an application starts running. This is called the *startup form*. Any other forms in your application must be explicitly loaded and displayed via code. The startup form defaults to being the first form that appears when you begin a new project. If you want to change this default, select Project|Project Properties and then click on the General tab if it isn't showing. This gives you the dialog box shown in Figure 12-3. All you need to do is select the new startup form (by name) from the Startup Object drop-down list box that is shown in Figure 12-3.

Methods for Forms

Since Visual Basic only shows the startup form by default, you'll need to write code in order to display any other form you've added to your projects. There are four methods for working with forms, two of which you have already seen for working with control arrays. You will be using these methods constantly when you work with multiple form applications.

Show   As its name suggests, the Show method shows the form on the screen and will also move the current form to the top of the desktop if it was covered by another form. To make this possible, when you use the Show method, Visual Basic first checks that the form is loaded into memory. If it isn't, then it loads the form first. The basic syntax for the Show method is

   FormName.Show

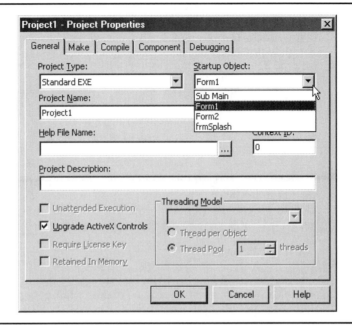

Selecting the
startup form
Figure 12-3.

In this case, including the *FormName* is a very good idea, as otherwise you will simply (and probably unintentionally) move the current form to the top.

T IP: Remember, Show can also be used in the Form_Load event of any form prior to using a Print statement on the form to let the user see the information. If you forget the Show keyword and haven't set the Auto Redraw property to True, nothing will happen!

Load The Load keyword places the form into memory but does *not* display it. Visual Basic also loads the form into memory whenever you refer to its properties or controls in code. (This is usually called *implicit* form loading.) Because of this, the main reason to load a form prior to showing it or referring to its properties via code is to speed up response time. The trade-off is that you use up more memory, since VB has to set aside enough memory for the form. Its syntax is

    Load FormName

When Visual Basic loads a form, it sets all the properties of the form to the ones you initially set at design time and invokes the Form_Initialize and then the Form_Load event procedures.

12

Hide   The Hide keyword removes the form from the screen but doesn't unload it from memory. The controls are not available to the user, but you can still refer to them in code. The values of the form-level variables do not disappear. As with loading a form, hiding a form improves response time if you will need the form again, but at the expense of continued use of memory to hold the form's bits. The syntax is

> *FormName*.Hide

For example, to hide the current form, you can always use the Me keyword:

```
Me.Hide
```

Unload   The Unload keyword removes the form from memory. (It has the same effect as someone clicking the exit button or double-clicking the control box icon on the left of the title bar.) All information contained in its form-level variables is lost. The syntax for this command is

> Unload *FormName*

Note that when you cycle a form by loading, unloading, and then loading it again, you will always trigger the Form_Load event, but only the first call to the Load method triggers the Initialize event.

TIP: When Visual Basic starts the process of unloading a form, it generates the QueryUnload event. This event procedure is a good place to put code that you want to be activated at the end of the useful life of the form; for example, when the user chooses Close from the control box or presses the ALT+F4 combination. For more on this event, see the next two sections in this chapter.

An Example Using Multiple Forms

For a simple example of an application with multiple forms, let's create a project with two forms and add a command button to each form. The command button on the first form will move the second form to the left and bring it to the forefront. The command button on the second form will bring the first form back to the top without moving it from its original place. You will also prevent the second form from closing down and have the application end only when the first form is closed. For illustration purposes, the default names for all the objects will be left unchanged.

First off, let's begin with a way to close the project. This is simply two Unload statements in the QueryUnload event for the main form.

NOTE: Visual Basic ends a normal program when there are no more loaded forms, so while some people might add an End statement here, it really doesn't do anything.

```
Private Sub Form_QueryUnload(Cancel As Integer, UnloadMode As Integer)
  Unload Form2
  Unload Me
  'an End statement isn't needed but here does no harm
End Sub
```

The command button for the first form needs the following code:

```
Private Sub Command1_Click ()
  ' Moves the second form around and displays it
  Form2.Show
  Form2.Left = Form2.Left - 75
End Sub
```

Because the control's name is deliberately not set to be more meaningful, the event procedure for the command button on the *second* form starts off just like the first:

```
Private Sub Command1_Click ()
  ' Show original form
  Form1.Show
End Sub
```

I left the control names unchanged here to make the point that this is sloppy programming. Although Visual Basic will know which Command1_Click procedure belongs where, in a more sophisticated program, this sloppiness would be an obvious breeding ground for confusion and bugs. Even if the form names seem clear enough as you create the program, it is better to use control names such as Form2Shift (or, if I used Microsoft's convention, it would be called cmdfrm2Shift—now you see why I don't like the prefix notation so much!) for the first command button and Form1ToTop for the second (cmdForm2Shift). You will probably also want to set the caption properties to explain what actions the buttons perform.

Finally, since I don't want someone to be able to close the second form, I'll use the following QueryUnload event procedure attached to the second form:

```
Private Sub Form_QueryUnload(Cancel As Integer, UnloadMode As Integer)
  Cancel = True
End Sub
```

12

Applications that Look Like They Are Over—but Aren't

One of the most common problems when dealing with a multiple form application is when users close a form by accident—but no other form is visible since the other forms were hidden or minimized. At this point they would have to know enough to use the Windows Task Manager to kill the project. Since naive users are unlikely to know this, you need to be aware of the possibility so you can deal with it.

The easiest way to deal with this all too common problem is to write code in the QueryUnload event that either:

◆ Prevents the user from closing down the form (as I did above, for the second form), or

◆ Ends the project if that form is closed

Both of these depend on the QueryUnload event being triggered before the form is purged from memory. As you saw in the previous example, to prevent someone from closing down a form, you just need to set the Cancel argument in the QueryUnload event to True. To allow the user to end the program when he or she closes a specific form, you'll need to place code in that form's Query_Unload event that unloads all the remaining forms. You can even follow this code by an End statement.

To make this possible, you need to have a way to get at all the loaded forms in a project. Visual Basic does this through the *Forms collection*. Like the Printers collection you saw in Chapter 6, you can access this with either a For-Next or (better) the For-Each construct. You'll want to make a variable of "Form" type as well. (See the next chapter for more on these object variables.)

```
'useful code to attach to any form whose closing
'you want to end the WHOLE program
Private Sub Form_QueryUnload(Cancel As Integer, UnloadMode As Integer)
  Dim AForm As Form
  For Each AForm in Forms
    Unload AForm
  Next
  End
End Sub
```

The Activate/Deactivate Events

When you start working with projects that involve multiple forms, you may want to take advantage of the Activate/Deactivate events. Visual Basic invokes the Activate event for a form whenever a form becomes the active window *within the current Visual Basic project* (and not when the user moves back from another Windows application to the form). In general, Visual Basic will call the Activate event when:

◆ A form becomes active within the current Visual Basic application

◆ The user clicks on the form

◆ You use the Show or SetFocus method in code

The Activate event occurs before the GotFocus event. Note that Visual Basic will call the Activate event only when a form is visible. This means that if you load the form using the Load method, Visual Basic won't call the Activate event until the form becomes visible (for example, by using the Show event or setting the form's Visible property to True).

Visual Basic invokes the Deactivate event when the form stops being the active window *within the current Visual Basic program*; it doesn't call it when you unload a form (use the Unload or QueryUnload events for this) or when the user moves to another running application. Visual Basic also calls the LostFocus event before the Deactivate event.

Keeping the Focus in a Form (Modality)

Message boxes require that users close them before they can go back to working with the application. (Users can still switch to a completely different application within the Windows environment when a message box is displayed.) This "in your face" property is often useful for a form, as well. For example, you may want to make sure a user has digested the information contained in a form before he or she shifts the focus to another form in the application. This property is called *modality* in the Microsoft Windows documentation. You make a form modal by adding an option to the Show method that displays the form. If you have a line of code in a procedure that reads

```
FormName.Show vbModal  '=1
```

then Visual Basic displays the form modally. No user input to any other form in the application will be accepted until the code that hides or unloads the modal form is processed. In particular, once a form is shown using the vbModal setting, a user cannot move the focus to any other form in the application until the modal form is hidden or unloaded.

NOTE: Although other forms in your application are disabled when you display a modal form, other applications aren't.

In particular, neither mouse clicks nor keypresses will register in any other form. Usually you will have a default command or cancel button on a modal form to unload it.

TIP: A dialog box is usually a modal form with a fixed double border.

Forms default to be nonmodal, but you can also use the following code to force them to be nonmodal:

12

```
FormName.Show vbModeLess  '=0
```

Code Modules: Global Procedures and Global Variables

When you start building larger projects with Visual Basic, you will probably want to reuse code as much as possible. For this reason you will often want to store your procedures and functions in separate modules rather than leaving them attached to a form. The next section explains the techniques needed for doing this.

A Standard (code) module is where you put code that you want to be accessible to all code in a project. Standard modules have no visual components. They are also useful for reusing code. (Just save the code in a Standard module and then add it to another project.) You add a new Standard module by choosing Project|Add Module; you add an existing one to your project by choosing Project|Add File. By convention, Standard modules have a .bas extension.

The Sub and Function procedures in code modules default so that they are available to the *whole* project. The buzzword is that they have *global* scope. This is because your placement of a procedure or of a declaration of a variable or constant determines which parts of the project can use it. To summarize:

If you attach a procedure to a form, the procedure will default to being usable only by procedures attached to the form. If you put the procedure in a code module, the procedure will default to being available to the whole project.

Still, don't rely on defaults. Just as Visual Basic automatically puts the keyword Private in front of any event procedures attached to a form, you should use the keyword Private for any Sub and Function procedures that are attached to a form. The opposite of Private, of course, is Public, and any code attached to a form that is marked Public can be used by simply prefixing it with the form's name.

For example, start up a new project with two forms and two command buttons. Name the button on Form1 cmdOnForm1 and name the button on Form2 cmdOnForm2. Change the Private keyword to the Public keyword in the cmdOnForm2_Click event procedure. Finally, add code to this event procedure so that it looks like the following:

```
Public cmdOnForm2_Click()
  MsgBox "This is the code in the now public click event attached to Form2"
End Sub
```

Make the code in the cmdOnForm1 button read:

```
Private cmdOnForm1_Click()
  Form2.Show
  Form2.cmdOnForm2_Click
End Sub
```

If you run this and click on the button on Form1, you'll see the message box, proving that we accessed the event procedure on Form2. If you went back and changed the Public keyword back to Private keyword in the event procedure on Form2, you wouldn't.

Public Variables
Similarly, to make a variable attached to a form into a global variable visible to every part of a project, use a statement of the form

Public *VariableName* As *VariableType*

Then somebody can see that variable by using *FormName.NameOfVariable.*

NOTE: Public variables attached to a form essentially become Read/Write properties of the form (hence the use of the dot notation).It is often better to add properties using the techniques you'll see in the next chapter rather than making them available via a Public variable.

Where it gets interesting is that if you use the Public identifier on variables or procedures attached to a *code* module, you don't need to use the name of the code module. For example, if you added the following line to the Declarations section of any code module named MyCode.bas,

```
Public gInterestRate As Single
```

then every bit of code in your project can see (and change) the variable named gInterestRate simply by using the name gInterestRate—you wouldn't have to say MyCode.gInterestRate like you would for public variables attached to a form.

TIP: Since global variables are breeding grounds for bugs, a very good convention is to identify global variables by prefixing them with a lower case "g", as I did here.

NOTE: When maintaining code, you may see the older "Global" keyword instead of Public; it has the same effect. Microsoft discourages you from using this keyword because they may stop supporting it in future versions of Visual Basic.

12

Once you create a code module, saving it to disk is easy. When you are working with the module, open the File menu and choose Save Module As. (You can also right-click and use the context menu in the Project Explorer.) You'll be presented with a dialog box. Enter the path name under which you want the module saved and press ENTER. Visual Basic will do the work.

Finally, you can have as many code modules as you want in a project. To open a specific code module window for any code module in the current project, double-click on the name of the module in the Project Explorer, or use the Object Browser.

TIP: Professional VB programmers suggest using one code module that has only the global constants and global variables, with no code. This makes it easier to isolate bugs caused by inappropriate use of global variables and global constants.

Fine Points About the Scope of Procedures

Code modules can also have module-level variables that are visible only to the code attached to that module. To make a variable a global variable requires the Public (or Global) keyword or leaving off the Public (Global) access modifier. (These keywords are called *access modifiers*, because they control what code can see (access) the code so identified.) If you use the ordinary Private (Dim) declaration syntax that you have been using for code attached to a form in the Declarations section of a code module, then the variable is visible only to the procedures attached to that code module. Similarly, if you use the Private (Dim) statement inside a procedure attached to a code module, that variable is *local* to the procedure. Figure 12-4 shows you the scope for variables within a Visual Basic project.

When you use a Sub or Function procedure inside another procedure, Visual Basic follows these steps to determine where to look for it:

1. Visual Basic first looks at procedures attached to the current form or module.
2. If the procedure is not found in the current form or module, Visual Basic looks at all code modules attached to the project.

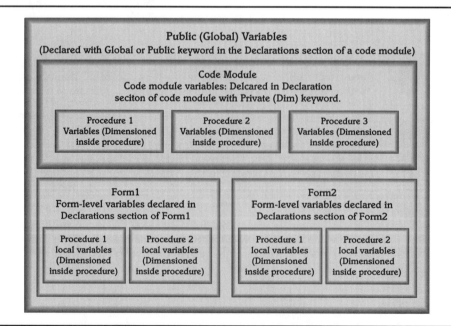

Scope of variables in a Visual Basic project

Figure 12-4.

The second of these options explains why the name of a global procedure must be unique throughout all code modules. On the other hand, you certainly can have the same procedure name attached to two different forms; otherwise, forms could not have their own Form_Load procedures.

Adding or Removing Existing Code Modules

Just as you can add a form module to your project, you can add text or complete Standard (code) modules that are stored on a disk. This lets you share code between projects (and often means you won't have to reinvent the wheel). On the other hand, code from one module may conflict with code from another module, especially if you are incorporating other people's code. (For example, names of public procedures in Standard modules must be unique, regardless of how many modules you have.)

To add an existing code module, open the Project menu and choose the Add Module option. Choose the Existing tab on the dialog box that opens; this gives you a standard File Open dialog box asking for the name of the file. Remember, the convention is that code modules have a .bas extension and form modules use .frm. To add code from another file to an existing module, choose Insert|File and then work with the dialog box that pops up. (The file will be inserted at the current cursor location.)

Occasionally, you will need to remove a code or form module from a project. Follow these steps:

1. Open the Project Explorer window by clicking on any part that's visible or by choosing View|Project Explorer.
2. Select the code module or form module you want to remove.
3. Either choose Remove from the right-click menu, or choose the Remove item from the Project menu.

The DoEvents Function and Sub Main

Usually you want Windows (and Visual Basic) to monitor the environment constantly for events to respond to, and most of the time this will happen automatically as the Windows operating system gives each program a "slice" of time to work before giving the next program a chance.

12

NOTE: The buzzword for this process is "preemptive multitasking via time slicing," which is why Windows can give the impression of running many programs simultaneously—it is switching between all the active programs so rapidly that, to the user, it looks like it is doing many things at once. Windows 3.1 programs don't usually allow time slicing—which is why they occasionally won't run smoothly on Windows 95/98 or NT.

On the other hand, you can foul up your own program by preventing Windows from sending information about events that happened to the running program. To see this at work, start up a new project and add the following code to the Form_Load:

```
Private Sub Form_Load()
  Show
  Do ' an infinite loop
    ' nothing being done
  Loop
End Sub
```

If you run this program, you'll see that clicking on the Exit button doesn't end the program—it doesn't even close the form! The problem is that we have written what programmers call a *tight loop*—there's no time left for Windows to report to the program: "Hey somebody clicked on the Close button of the form."

The solution is to add a command that tells VB to "listen" to any events. This command is called, naturally enough, DoEvents. More precisely, Windows maintains a list of pending events in what is called an *Event Queue*. The DoEvents statement passes control to Windows, and VB gets control back only after the operating system has finished processing the events in its queue. Thus, if you changed the above code to read

```
Private Sub Form_Load()
  Show
  Do ' an infinite loop
    DoEvents  'hey, what is happening?
  Loop
End Sub
```

the form will close normally when you click on the Exit button. However, the application will still not be over, as you can see by looking at the title bar. Tight loops are tricky—even DoEvents is not a cure-all!

The final trick you need for this kind of code is to keep in mind that since the form is now closed, you can simply put an End statement in the Query_Unload event of that form in order to end this program naturally.

 TIP: If your programs don't end normally even after putting a DoEvents statement inside your tight loops, consider putting the End statement after the code that unloads all forms in the Query_Unload event that you saw earlier in this chapter (in the section "Applications that Look Like They Are Over—but Aren't").

Another common use of the DoEvents function is to put it inside a procedure that is making a time-consuming numeric computation. Set up a timing loop so that Visual Basic periodically processes a DoEvents function to check what events may have taken place while it was calculating. The little extra time that Visual Basic uses to manage the timing loop inside the function is well worth it.

C AUTION: Do not use the DoEvents function inside an event procedure if it is possible to reenter the same event procedure again. For example, a Click event procedure may be called again by the user's clicking the mouse. If you forget about this possibility, your program may be caught in an infinite regression.

Sub Main

DoEvents can actually be used as a function—in this case it returns the number of *loaded* forms. This ability is most commonly used when you choose to start a program from a code module rather than from a startup form. Of course, since there is no startup form, you have to manage the code for loading all the forms yourself. This is done inside a special Sub procedure called Main that may be attached to any code module. You can have only one Sub Main procedure in any project. For example, if you use the Application wizard to add a splash screen to a project, you'll see code that starts like this in the Sub Main:

```
Sub Main()
  frmSplash.Show
  frmSplash.Refresh
  frmMainForm.Show
  'more code supplied by the Wizard deleted
End Sub
```

To use a Sub Main, though, you not only have to add the code, you have to make the code module containing the Sub Main procedure be the startup module. To do this, choose Project|Project Properties and then choose the General page. On this page, drop down the Startup Object list box and choose Sub Main instead of a form. Once you've set Sub Main as the startup object, Visual Basic does not load any forms automatically. You will have to write the code for this yourself using the Load and Show keywords, as you saw in the code earlier in this chapter.

Sub Main and DoEvents

You can use DoEvents as a function. In this case it returns the number of loaded forms. The framework for this takes the following form:

12

```
Sub Main()
  frmSplash.Show
  frmSplash.Refresh
  Do While DoEvents()
    frmMainForm.Show
    'more code
  Loop
  End
End Sub
```

In this case you are guaranteed that the End statement will only be reached when there are no more loaded forms. This is because the line

```
Do While DoEvents()
```

means "Do while the number of loaded forms is at least 1."

Idle Time

There can be a lot of idle time in your application that you can use to do, for example, time-consuming numeric calculations or sorts. However, you don't want a Visual Basic application to stop responding to events completely. A loop that is processed only when no events are occurring is called an *idle loop*. Idle loops are written inside Sub Main. The format looks like this:

```
Sub Main ()
  Load StartUpForm
  Do While DoEvents()
    'Code to load forms goes here
    'Code you want to be processed during idle time
  Loop
End Sub
```

Again, this kind of code will continue to execute as long as there are any loaded forms. Here's a simple example of an idle loop at work. Start a new project and add a code module. Next, add a global variable named gCounter as a long integer by adding this statement to the code module:

```
Public gCounter As Long
```

Next, add this code to the code module:

```
Sub Main ()

  Form1.Show
  Do While DoEvents()
    gCounter = gCounter + 1
  Loop
End Sub
```

Finally, make Sub Main the startup module in the Project|Properties dialog box and add a Form_Click procedure to the first form that says

```
Private Sub Form_Click()
  Me.Cls
  Print "The counter is " & gCounter
End Sub
```

When you run this program, you'll notice that the number gets larger each time you click on the form. The reason is that during the idle time (when you are not clicking),

Visual Basic moves to the Main procedure and keeps adding 1 to the count. Since gCounter is a global variable, Visual Basic preserves the value for each call.

Accessing Windows Functions

You have already seen that when you create a stand-alone Visual Basic program, you must include the Visual Basic .dll file in order to actually run it. A dynamic link library like this one contains specialized functions that a Windows program can call on as needed. Windows itself can be thought of as an interlocking set of DLLs containing hundreds of specialized functions. These are called Application Programming Interface (API) functions. Most of the time, Visual Basic is rich enough in functionality that you don't need to bother with API functions. But some tasks, such as learning whether users have swapped their mouse buttons or putting a window always on top, or checking or setting the state of the keyboard, must be done with an API function. You can even use an API function to reboot a user's computer and start a program when Windows reboots.

NOTE: This book covers only the barest basics of using the API. Completely covering the Windows API would require another book roughly twice(!) this size. The reference work you'll want to own is Daniel Appleman's *Visual Basic Programmer's Guide to the Windows 32 Bit API* (Emeryville, CA: Ziff-Davis Press, 1998) although, as I said, it is twice the size of this book and weighs in at roughly 5 lbs. For a tutorial, he will have a new book called *Dan Appleman's API Puzzle Guide and Tutorial* that should be more accessible. This will be out in late 1998 from APress (http://www.apress.com).

CAUTION: If you use API functions at all carelessly, your system is likely to crash. Since you may have to reboot frequently when experimenting with API functions, I suggest setting the "Save before run" option by going to the Tools|Options|Environment page and checking off this box.

Using an API statement requires a special type of declaration that is much more complicated than the ones used for variables; these are called Declare statements. As a first example of using an API call, consider the plight of left-handed users of Windows. They might like to swap the left and right mouse buttons via the Windows control panel. If you wanted to make your programs truly user friendly, you would want to take this into account. (Visual Basic automatically adjusts the left and right buttons for all its mouse events when somebody does this, so there is less work involved than you think!) Before you can do this, you need to find out if the buttons have been swapped. The only way to do this is by using a Windows API function called GetSystemMetrics. To use this function, add the following Declare statement to the general section of a Code module.

12

```
Declare Function GetSystemMetrics Lib "user32" Alias _
"GetSystemMetrics" (ByVal nIndex As Long) As Long
```

As the Declare statement indicates, you send this function a long integer value that tells the function what information you want reported back. This function returns a long integer that you can analyze. For example, here's how to use this API function to find out if the mouse buttons have been swapped: First you need a constant for the GetSystemMetrics function parameter that tells it you want to know the status of the mouse buttons. The constant must have the value 23 and is usually called SM_SWAPBUTTON. Here's some code that will detect a mouse swap:

```
Sub Form_Load
  Const SM_SWAPBUTTON = 23
  If GetSystemMetrics(SM_SWAPBUTTON) Then
    MsgBox "Mouse buttons switched. I'm a lefty too."
  End If
End Sub
```

NOTE: Most API functions expect the parameters used to be passed by value. As the preceding example indicates, you specify this in the Declare statement that specifies which API function you will be using.

There are two possibilities for the general form of the Declare statement. For a Sub program in a DLL (one that doesn't return a value), use

[*Public* | *Private*] Declare Sub *name* Lib "*libname*" [Alias _
"*aliasname*"][([*arglist*])]

For a function (something that returns a value), use

[*Public* | *Private*] Declare Function *name* Lib "*libname*" [Alias _
"*aliasname*"] [([*arglist*])][As *type*]

Most of the elements in a Declare statement should be familiar to you (Public, Private, and so on). For the new ones, the Lib keyword is just bookkeeping—it tells Visual Basic that a DLL is being called. The *libname* argument is the name of the DLL that contains the procedure you will be calling. The Alias keyword is used when the procedure has another name in the DLL but you don't (or can't) use it.

For example, to go beyond the built-in beep command, you can use the Windows API version of Beep. The API version allows you to set the frequency and duration. Since Beep is a reserved word in Visual Basic, you probably want to use an alias here (the example uses APIBeep). The Declare statement for the Windows API version of the Beep function looks like this:

```
Declare Function APIBeep Lib "kernel32" Alias "Beep" (ByVal _
dwFreq As Long, ByVal dwDuration As Long) As Long
```

As you might expect, the dwFreq parameter gives the frequency of the beep, and the dwDuration parameter gives the duration in milliseconds.

It is extremely important that the Declare statement for an API function be exactly as Windows expects. Leaving off a ByVal keyword will almost certainly lock your system. One nice feature of the Professional and Enterprise editions of Visual Basic is that both come with a file with all the Declare statements and values of the constants needed for the Windows API functions—and an API Text Viewer program for dealing with this file. You can get to the API Viewer (shown in Figure 12-5) from the Visual Basic (or Visual Studio Tools) project group on the Start menu, or directly from the Winapi subdirectory of the VB directory (or the common directory if you are using a Visual Studio Intallation), or by using Add-In Manager. You can use the API Viewer to copy and paste the necessary information about an API function directly in your program.

To use the API Viewer, follow these steps:

1. Open the File menu in the API Viewer and choose the file you want to look at. Figure 12-6 shows what you will see if you load Win32api.txt.

NOTE: The first time you ask to load Win32api.txt the API Viewer asks if you want to convert the text file into a database. This speeds things up, so I would suggest doing it if you have enough hard disk space.

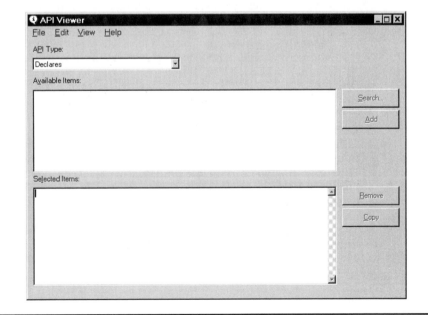

API Viewer main
screen
Figure 12-5.

12

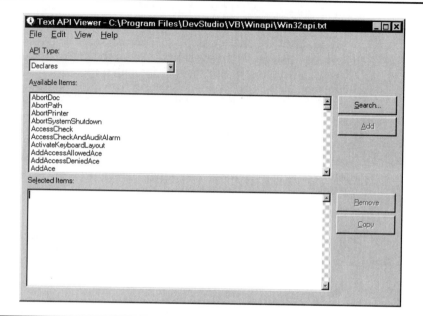

API Viewer for
Win32api.txt
Figure 12-6.

2. After the text file loads, choose what part of the API you need to look at (Declares, Constants, and so on) from the API Type list box.

3. Choose the item you want by scrolling through the Available Items list box.

4. Click on the Copy button to place the item in the clipboard.

5. Move the insertion point inside your Code window where you want the item to appear, and choose Edit|Paste (or CTRL+V) to copy the item from the clipboard.

For any serious use of API functions, having the necessary documentation about what the API call does is essential!

Example: A Searchable List Box

Although we can't cover a whole lot of the API in an introductory book like this one, there is one use of it that is so striking and so useful, I can't resist showing it to you. The trick is that you can use the SendMessage API to quickly search a list or combo box. Even if the list box has thousands of items, the search will be done almost instantly! Here's what you need to do.

1. Add the following Declare and constant to a code module:

```
Declare Function SendMessage Lib "user32" _
    Alias "SendMessageA" _
        (ByVal hwnd As Long, _
         ByVal wMsg As Long, _
```

```
      ByVal wParam As Long, _
      ByVal lParam As Any) As Long

   Public Const LB_FINDSTRING = &H18F
```

2. Now add a list box named lstBoxToSearch to a form, along with a text box called txtSearch.

3. Add the following code to the form; it fills a list box with the strings "1", "2" ..., "20000", and the string "Wow!" at the end.

```
Private Sub Form_Load()
   Dim I As Integers
   For I = 1 to 20000
      lstBoxToSearch.AddItem Str(I)
   Next I
   lstBoxToSearch.AdddItem "Wow!"
End Sub
```

4. Now add the following Change event procedure:

```
Private Sub txtSearch_Change()
   Dim Temp As String
   Dim TheHandle As Long
   Dim Position As Long
   Temp = txtSearch.Text
   TheListBoxHandle = lstBoxToSearch.hwnd
   If Len(Temp) = 0 Then
      lstBoxToSearch.ListIndex = 0
   Else
   'find the right entry or first entry if nothing found
      Position = SendMessage(TheListBoxHandle, _
        LB_FINDSTRING, -1, TempString)
      If Position = -1 Then
        lstBoxToSearch.ListIndex = 0
      Else
        lstBoxToSearch.ListIndex = Position
      End If
   End If
End Sub
```

Now run the program and type a W into the text box. Pretty amazing response considering there are 20,000 entries ahead of it. (Imagine how long it would take to search through 20,000 items in a For-Next loop.)

12

NOTE: The SendMessage API I used here is probably the most powerful API call. For example, most events in VB are triggered in response to Windows sending out a message to the control, and most controls can be sent various kinds of messages, just as I used here to tell the box to "search itself." I'd estimate that around 200 pages (!) of Appleman's reference book are devoted to various uses of SendMessage.

Error Trapping

Regardless of how carefully you debug your own program, it's impossible to anticipate all the crazy things a user may do. If you want your program to "degrade gracefully" and not just roll over, you'll want to prevent fatal errors. The command that activates (enables) error trapping within a given procedure is

```
On Error GoTo...
```

where the three dots stand for the label (line number) that defines the error trap. The labeled code must be in the current procedure. You cannot jump out of a procedure using an On Error GoTo command. On the other hand, the code for the error trap will often use other Sub or Function procedures to process the error information.

A label for an error trap is exactly like the one for the GoTo from Chapter 7. It is any identifier ending with a colon that satisfies the rules for variables. The label identifies the island of code starting on the next line, as shown here:

```
ErrorTrap:
  ' error code goes here
```

Since you don't want Visual Basic to inadvertently "fall" into the error-trapping code, it is a good idea to have an Exit (Sub or Function) statement on the line immediately preceding the label for the error trap.

The On Error GoTo command can occur anywhere in an event, Sub, or Function procedure. Usually, the error-trapping code is inside that procedure. The only exception to this is when one procedure has been called by another. In this case, Visual Basic will look to see if an error trap was enabled in the earlier procedure if one does not exist in the second procedure.

Once you start error trapping with the On Error GoTo command, a run-time error will no longer bomb the program. (Operating system errors cannot be helped, of course; Windows 98 is supposed to have fewer of them than Windows 95 or 3.X had.) In any case, the On Error GoTo command should transfer control to a piece of code that identifies the problem and, if possible, fix it.

If the error can be corrected, the Resume statement takes you back to the statement that caused the error in the first place. However, you can't correct an error if you don't know why it happened. You identify the problem by means of either the Err function or the Err object. This gives you an integer that you can assign to a variable. For example, if you write

```
ErrorNumber = Err.Number
```

the value of the variable ErrorNumber is the error number.

Visual Basic can identify more than 80 run-time errors. (Search for "trappable errors" in the online help.) Here are a few examples:

Error Code	Explanation
57	Device I/O error (for example, trying to print when the printer is offline)
68	Device unavailable (the device may not exist or is currently unavailable)
482	A general printer Error. Visual Basic reports the error whenever the printer driver returns an error code.
483	The Printer driver does not support the property.

The way you use this information is simple. Suppose an event procedure will be using the printer. Somewhere in the procedure, before the error can occur, place a statement such as this:

```
On Error GoTo PrinterCheck
```

Now, before the End Sub, add code that looks like this:

```
Exit Sub
PrinterCheck:
  ErrorNumber = Err.Number
  Beep
  Select Case ErrorNumber
    Case  57
      MsgBox "Your printer may be offline."
    Case 68
      MsgBox "Is there a printer available?"
   Case 482, 483
      M$ = "Please tell the operator (= program author?) that"
      M$ = M$ & vbCrLf '=  Chr$(10) + Chr$(13) New Line
      M$ = M$ & "a general printer error with "&  ErrorNumber _
& " occurred."
      MsgBox M$
      End
    Case Else
      M$ = "Please tell the operator (= program author?) that"
      M$ = M$ & vbCrLf '=  Chr$(10) + Chr$(13) New Line
      M$ = M$ & "error number " & ErrorNumber & " occurred."
      MsgBox M$
      End
  End Select
```

12

```
M$ = "If the error has been corrected click on OK."
M$ = M$ & vbCrLf
M$ = M$ & "Otherwise click on Cancel."
Continue = MsgBox(M$, vbOKCancel)
If Continue = vbOK Then Resume Else End
```

The idea of this error trap is simple, and the Select Case statement is ideal. Each case tries to give some indication of where the problem is and, if possible, how to correct it. If you reach the Case Else, the error number has to be reported. In any case, the final block gives you the option of continuing or not by using a message box with two buttons. You might want to get into the habit of writing a general procedure that analyzes the error code. The error trap inside a procedure just sends control to the general procedure. If you do this, you can reuse the general procedure in many different projects.

Error trapping isn't a cure-all. For example, very little can be done about a hard disk crash or running out of paper.

More on the Resume Statement

A variant on the Resume statement lets you bypass the statement that may have caused the problem. If you use

```
Resume Next
```

Visual Basic begins processing at the statement following the one that caused the error. You can even use

```
OnError Resume Next
```

to automatically bypass any code that causes an error. (Not to be done casually, but as you will see in the chapter on writing your own controls, this kind of error trapping is sometimes necessary.)

You can also resume execution at any line of code that has been previously identified with a label. For this, use

Resume *Label*

It is unusual to have labels in Visual Basic except in connection with error trapping. For compatibility with older BASICs, Visual Basic does let you use the unconditional GoTo (see Chapter 7), but there is rarely any reason to use it.

Both the Resume and Resume Next statements behave differently if Visual Basic has to move backward to find the error trap in a calling procedure. Recall that this happens when one procedure is invoked by a previous procedure and the current procedure doesn't have an error trap. For both Resume and Resume Next, the statement executed by Visual Basic will not be in the procedure where the error occurred. For the Resume statement, Visual Basic will call the original procedure again. For the Resume Next command, Visual Basic will execute the statement after the call to the original procedure. You will never get back to the original procedure.

Suppose the chain of procedural calls goes back even farther: Procedure1 calls Procedure2, which calls Function3. Now an error occurs in Function3, but the only error handler is in Procedure1. If there is a Resume statement in the error handler in Procedure1, Visual Basic actually goes to the statement that called Procedure2. Because this is unwieldy and so prone to problems, it is probably better to rely only on error handlers that occur in the specific procedure. If one procedure calls another, turn off the error handler in the calling routine.

The Erl (Error Line) Function

There's one other error-handling function: Erl (Error Line). If you get really desperate and need to find the line that caused the error, and Visual Basic isn't stopping the program at that line, you can do the following:

1. Add line numbers before every statement in the procedure.
2. Add a Debug.Print Erl statement inside the error trap.

When developing a program, you may want to test how your error handler works. Visual Basic includes the statement

```
Error(ErrorcodeNumber)
```

which, when processed, makes Visual Basic behave as if the error described by the given error number had actually occurred. This makes it easier to develop the trap.

Disabling Error Trapping

If you are confident that you will no longer need an error trap, you can disable error trapping with the statement

```
On Error GoTo 0
```

(although, strictly speaking, the 0 is not needed). Similarly, you can change which error trap is in effect by using another On Error GoTo statement. Be sure to have an Exit command between the error traps. Visual Basic uses the last processed On Error GoTo statement to decide where to go.

12

More on the Err Object

To allow for more centralized error handling when necessary, Visual Basic provides the special Err object, which can be analyzed when an error occurs. You have already seen how the Number property of the Err object (Err.Number) gives you the error number. Err.Description gives a (hopefully) understandable description of the error. Finally, Err.Source gives you the source of the error if you are accessing another Windows application through OLE (see Chapter 20 for more on this topic).

NOTE: Microsoft recommends that, except for legacy code, you switch to using the properties and methods of the Err object instead of using the various error functions. Most code that you will maintain, however, uses the various error functions I have just showed you.

All the Err object's properties are reset to 0 or zero-length strings ("") after Visual Basic processes either a Resume or a new On Error statement. The properties of the Err object are also reset after you leave the function or procedure. You can also use

```
Err.Clear
```

to reset the Err object's properties.

NOTE: Setting up a centralized error handler is very useful. However, you must pass that procedure the current values of the various Err object's properties. If you call the Err object from a new procedure, all its values will have been reset.

If you want to generate an error for testing purposes, use the Raise method of the Err object. Its syntax is

Err.Raise(*Number*)

TIP: You can use the Raise method to define your own custom errors.

Some General Words on Program Design

The usual improved methods for writing programs—often called modular, top-down, structured program design—were developed in the 1970s and 1980s from rules of thumb that programmers learned through experience in using conventional programming languages. An event-driven language such as Visual Basic requires some obvious shifts. For one thing, there is no "top" of the program. Also, the new object-oriented features of Visual Basic (see Chapter 13) shift things even more.

Nonetheless, when you have something hard to do, you first divide it into several smaller jobs. Moreover, with most jobs, the subtasks (the smaller jobs) have a natural order in which they should be done. (You dig a hole for the foundation before you bring in the cement truck.) Write programs from the general to the particular. Stub out the code that you'll later implement more fully. After you design the interface for your Visual Basic project, start by looking at the big picture (what are the event procedures supposed to do?), and then, in stages, break that down. This lets you keep track of the forest even when there are lots of trees.

Your first outline should list the event procedures and the jobs they have to do. Keep refining your outline by adding helper Sub and Function procedures for the jobs the event procedures are supposed to do until the pieces to be coded for all the procedures are well within your limits. Stop massaging the problem (breaking down the jobs) when you can shut your eyes and visualize the code for the procedure to accomplish the task you set out for it. Sometimes this "step-wise refinement" is described as "relentless massage." Since programmers often say "massage a problem" when they mean "chew it over and analyze it," the metaphor is striking—and useful.

Even if you can see how to program two completely separate jobs in one Sub or Function procedure, it's usually better not to do so. Sticking to one job per procedure makes it easier both to debug the procedure and to optimize the code in it.

Often, professional programmers are hired to modify programs written by other people. Imagine trying to modify a big program that wasn't written cleanly—if, for example, no distinction was made between local and global variables (all variables were global) and no attempt was made to write the program in digestible pieces with clear lines of communication between the pieces.

What happens? Because all variables are global, making a little change in a small module could foul up the whole program. Because the pieces of the program aren't digestible and the way they communicate is unclear, you can't be sure how they relate. Anything you do, even to one line of code, may introduce side effects— possibly disastrous ones.

This kind of disaster was common until the late 1960s or early 1970s. Companies first spent millions of dollars having programs modified; then they spent more money trying to anticipate the potential side effects the changes they just paid for might cause. Finally, they hoped that more time (and more money) would fix the side effects. No matter where they stopped, they never could be certain that the programs were free of bugs. Top-down design, when combined with programming languages that allow local and global variables, can stop side effects completely; programs still have bugs, but these bugs don't cause epidemics. If you fix a small module in a giant but well-designed program, then you know how the changes affect everything; it is clear how the parts of the program communicate with each other. Only global form-level variables and parameters need to be checked.

12

Ultimately, you will develop your own style for writing Visual Basic programs, and what works for one person may not work for another. Still, just as artists benefit from knowing what techniques have worked in the past, programmers can learn from what programmers have done before them.

The first rule is still: Think first—code later. You have some idea of what needs to be done, so you design the interface and start writing code. When your first attempt doesn't work, you keep modifying your project until it does (or seems to) work. This is usually referred to (sometimes with pride, sometimes with disdain) as "hacking away at the keyboard."

Of course, almost everyone will occasionally write programs with little or no preparation (you may need a ten-line program to print out a label or something); that's one of the virtues of any BASIC, and Visual Basic is no exception. Where do you draw the line? How long must a program be before it can benefit from some paper and pencil? The answer is to know your own limits. You may find it hard to write a program longer than one screen or with more than one event procedure without some sort of outline. If you try to do it without an outline, it might end up taking longer than if you had written an outline first.

Outlines don't have to be complicated. The complete outline for the pig Latin program is as follows:

```
Two text boxes and a command button
text1 for text
text2 for translation
Command button starts process
While there are still words
    latinize the next word
To latinize a word
    one-letter words stay the same
    beginning vowels -> add way
    beginning consonants (y, qu = conson) -> ROTATE and add ay
ROTATE
    find conson
    move it to end
```

This may be a little hard for other people to use, but that's not the point of an outline. Your outlines are for you. In particular, outlines should help you fix the concepts that you'll use in the program. You may find it a good rule that when each line in your outline corresponds to ten or fewer lines of code, you've done enough outlining and should start writing. (Of course, only practice will let you see at a glance how long the coded version is likely to be.)

Some people like to expand their outlines to pseudocode. This is especially common if you are developing a program with or for someone else. Pseudocode is an ill-defined cross between a programming language and English. While everyone seems to have his or her own idea of what pseudocode should look like, most programmers do agree that a pseudocode description (unlike an outline) should be sufficiently clear and detailed that any competent programmer can translate it into a running program.

Here's a pseudocode version of part of the preceding outline:

```
Function(latinize NEXT WORD)
  IF Length(NEXT WORD) = 1 THEN do nothing
  IF FirstLetter(NEXT WORD) = a,e,i,o,u THEN
    latinize(NEXT WORD)  = NEXT WORD + WAY
  ELSE
    Find(leading consonants of NEXT WORD)   ' (qu a consonant)
  latinize(NEXT WORD) = NEXT WORD - leading consonants + ay
```

The point is that, although a phrase such as

latinize(NEXT WORD) = NEXT WORD - leading consonants + ay

doesn't seem on the surface to be very close to Visual Basic code, it is perfectly understandable for an experienced programmer.

NOTE: Probably the key technique for making code less prone to bugs is to make sure that the information being passed is exactly what you want—and no unwanted side effects happen. Object-oriented programming techniques (see Chapter 13) make this even easier—although they do require a different type of analysis than the one I just outlined.

CHAPTER 13

VB Objects and an Introduction to Object-Oriented Programming

At this point, you are probably pretty comfortable with the basic techniques for manipulating Visual Basic's built-in objects. To go further with Visual Basic, you will need to know more than just how to manipulate objects by setting properties and applying methods—and this chapter will teach you how. This chapter will show you the most powerful techniques available for working with VB's objects, including VB6's new method for adding controls at run time. (This new method goes way beyond what you can do with the control arrays that you saw in Chapter 11.)

In all honesty, while this chapter will certainly teach you the most powerful ways of manipulating Visual Basic's built-in objects, the real point is to get you started on creating your own objects. You can't move to the next level of VB mastery until you can build *reusable* objects for use not only by yourself but also by other programmers. Visual Basic 6 goes a lot further than earlier versions of Visual Basic in giving you access to the power, and thus the advantages, of *object-oriented programming (OOP)*.

Object-oriented programming is the dominant programming paradigm these days, having replaced the *structured* programming techniques that were developed in the early 1970s. If you haven't formally worked with OOP before, you are probably wondering what all the hoopla is about. This chapter will also try to explain what the hoopla is about. Since there's a fair amount of terminology needed to make sense of OOP, the chapter also has a discussion of the needed concepts and definitions.

NOTE: Actually, VB always was an *object-based* language, and such languages are close cousins to full OOP languages. As you'll soon see, VB programmers have been benefiting from the advantages of OOP since VB1.0 (this is the VB equivalent of the writer's discovery, "I've been speaking prose all my life!").

The Object Browser

You've seen how to use the Object Browser (shown in Figure 13-1) to look at the built-in constants in Visual Basic and to navigate among the procedures you have written. The Object Browser can do far more. In particular, it gives you complete access to the classes and objects, and their methods and properties, all of which you can use in your Visual Basic projects. It lets you see the values of constants—or even if there are any constants. You can search through all the methods and properties of all the parts of Visual Basic with a single click of a button.

The idea is that the objects that are usable in Visual Basic are collected into *object* (or *type*) *libraries*, for example, Visual Basic's object library, the Visual Basic for Applications' object library, Excel's object library, and so on. An object library contains the information that Visual Basic needs to build instances of its objects, as well as information on the methods and properties of the object in the library. The Object Browser is your porthole into the object libraries used in your project. To bring up the Object Browser, shown in Figure 13-1, either:

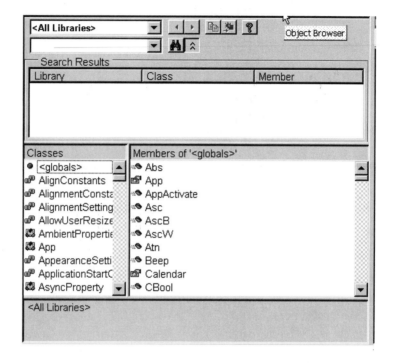

The Object
Browser
Figure 13-1.

◆   Choose View|Object Browser

◆   Press F2

◆   Use the toolbar shortcut

To hide the Object Browser, right-click anywhere inside the Object Browser and choose Hide from the context menu that pops up.

Since the Object Browser is so potentially useful to you when working with VB objects, I want to go over its main parts in detail. Table 13-1 describes the toolbar in the Object Browser.

Finally, before I can go further with the Object Browser, I need to recall one buzzword: *member*. Recall that this means a constant, property, or method in an object.

Libraries/Projects Drop-Down List Box

The list box at the top of the Object Browser displays the libraries available to your project, and as you have seen earlier, it also lists the modules in your project. In general, you can select from available object libraries, including the ones in the current Visual Basic project. Once you choose a library, other parts of the Object

13

Tool	Name	Description
◄	Go Back	Keeps track of where you last were inside the Browser and returns there.
►	Go Forward	Keeps track of where you just were in the Browser (before you clicked Go Back) and returns there.
(copy icon)	Copy to Clipboard	Copies the currently displayed information (constant, method signature, and so on) into the clipboard. You then use Paste from the Edit menu to place the information in your code at the current insertion point.
(definition icon)	View Definition	If the member is defined by code inside your current project, clicking this button sends you to the code. (Same as double-clicking on the name of the element in the Members column.)
?	Help	Gives online help for the item currently selected.
(binoculars icon)	Search	Lets you search through whatever libraries are indicated in the Libraries/Projects list for the text you entered in the Search text box. The results of a successful search are displayed in the Search Results pane.
˄˄	Show/Hide Search Result	Opens or hides the Search Results pane.

Tools in
the Object
Browser
Table 13-1.

Browser let you look at the classes, modules, procedures, methods, and properties of that library. Here's a picture of the standard libraries you will see if you drop this box down:

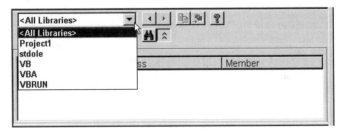

For example, if you add an MSFlexGrid to your project, you'll see MSFlexGridLib listed in this drop-down list box.

Search Text Box

The Search text box, just below the Libraries/Projects list box, contains the string you want to search for. The libraries that the Browser searches through are determined by the current setting in the Libraries/Projects drop-down list box.

Classes Pane

All the classes in the currently selected library are displayed in the Classes pane. As you have already seen in Chapter 9, if you select your own Visual Basic project in the Libraries/Projects list box, this pane displays modules from your project, including any classes you defined in the current project. You also have already used this box to get at the library of built-in constants in both Visual Basic and Visual Basic for Applications. When you select another object library in the Libraries/Projects list box, the Classes pane displays the classes available in that library.

Members Pane

You also saw in Chapter 9 how to use the Members dialog box to get at the procedures and functions in your project. Once you select an object library in the Libraries/Projects list box, the Object Browser gives you a list of the methods and properties for the class that you have selected in the Classes pane.

Details Pane

The bottom pane in the browser gives a short definition of the object. For example, if you select a constant in the Members pane, the Details pane gives you its value; if you select a function or procedure, it gives you its signature.

Manipulating Objects Built into Visual Basic   13

The key to working with objects in Visual Basic is using variables of the special *object* type. For example, when you use the Me keyword to refer to the current object, you are using an object variable. In general, you give the scope of an object variable with the same Dim, Private, Public, Static (and so on) keywords that you've already seen. Thus, you can have local, form-level, or public (global) object variables. The convention is to use the same prefix for the name of an object variable as you would use for the Name property of a control or form. Here are some examples:

```
Dim frmVariable As Form
Dim txtInfoBox As TextBox
Public gcmdAButton As CommandButton 'global in a code module
Private scrMyBar As ScrollBar
Dim objTheLabel As Object
```

In general, the name used after the "As" keyword for an object variable of a given control type is the name given in the Properties window for that control. (You can also look in the Help system.)

You can define arrays of object variables in the same way you define an ordinary array:

```
Dim LotsOfTextBoxes(1 To 100) As TextBox
```

These kind of arrays are very different than the control arrays you saw in Chapter 11. Those were controls related by an index parameter. An array of control objects like the ones in the code above is simply an ordinary array that happens to be filled with object variables of control type—they are not even as general as an array of variants.

When you want to make an object variable refer to a specific object of that type in your project, use the Set keyword. For example, if your project has a form named Form1 and a command button named Command1, your code would look like this:

```
Set frmAForm = Form1
Set cmdAButton = Command1
```

T IP: The Set command can also be used to simplify lengthy control references.

Here's an example:

```
Set Foo = frmHelp.txtHelp
```

Now you can write

```
Foo.BackColor
```

instead of

```
frmhelp.txtHelp.BackColor
```

C<small>AUTION:</small> It is important to remember that the Set command does not make a copy of the object as a variable assignment would. Instead, the Set command points the object variable to the other object.

In particular, you cannot use an assignment statement to make an object variable equal to, say, a text box. Suppose you have a text box named Text1. Trying to use code like the following will give you an error message:

```
Dim txtFoo As TextBox
txtFoo = Text1
```

A Pitfall to be Wary of When Using Set

That all the Set keyword does is *point* your variable to an object can occasionally lead to problems. For example, if you change a property of an object variable that is Set to another object, the property of the original object changes as well (much like passing by reference in procedures does). Here's an example of what I mean. Start up a new project and add a text box to it. Add the following Form_Load():

```
Private Sub Form_Load()
  Set Text1.Font = Me.Font
  Me.Font.Size = 18
End Sub
```

If you run this program, you'll see that the text in the text box will also be shifted to 18 point! This is because the line

```
Set Text1.Font = Me.Font
```

made the Font objects in both the Form and the TextBox refer to the same thing. Thus, any change to the font size of the form would impact the font size of the text box.

The Is Keyword

Since it is important to know when two object variables point to the same object, VB supplies the Is keyword for this test. A line like

```
If AnObjectVariable Is AnotherObjectVariable Then
```

lets you test whether they refer to the same object. (It is a wise precaution to find out whether changing the properties of one variable will also change the properties of the other!)

13

The Nothing Keyword

Once you use the Set keyword to assign an object to an object variable, you need to release the memory used for the object. You do this by setting the object variable to the keyword Nothing. For example,

```
Dim AFont As Font
   ' code to manipulate the new instance of the Font would go here
   '
   '
Set AFont = Nothing
```

NOTE: Since object variables merely point to the object, it is possible for several object variables to refer to the same object. When several object variables refer to the same object, you must set all of them to Nothing in order to release the memory and system resources associated with the object.

Memory may be released automatically: this happens, for example, after the last object variable referring to the object goes out of scope. However, relying on this is sloppy. For example, if you set a local object variable inside a procedure, set it to Nothing before the Sub is exited; don't rely on Visual Basic to clean up after you!

NOTE: An uninitialized object variable can be thought of as having a current value of Nothing.

The New Keyword with Forms

The New keyword is the most common method of creating VB objects at run time. For example, one case in which you can create a new instance of a Visual Basic object at run time is when you use an existing form as the class and make multiple instances (copies) of it. The most common syntax for using New is a little different than what you have seen before. Assume you have a form named Form1 in your project already. Then the statement

```
Dim frmAForm As New Form1
```

creates a new instance of Form1. The line

```
Private frmAForm As New Form1
```

in the declaration section of a form would create a copy of Form1, visible to all the code in the form. This new instance has the same properties as the original Form1 at the time the code was executed and the new instance created. Moreover, a duplicate of the code in the original will be attached to the same procedures in the new instance. All the event procedures, for example, will work the same way.

Use the New keyword only when you want Visual Basic to create a new instance of the original object. For example,

```
Dim frmAForm As New Form1
Dim frmBForm As New Form1
frmAForm.Show
frmBForm.Show
frmAForm.Move Left - 199, Top + 100
frmBForm.Move Left - 399, Top + 200
```

shows two copies of the original Form1. The locations are determined by the value of the Left and Top properties of the original Form1. (We needed to change them to prevent them from stacking one on another, because instances inherit all the properties of the parent.)

NOTE: It would be logical if you could also use the New keyword to create controls at run time; unfortunately, that isn't the way it works. In addition to the control arrays that you saw in Chapter 11, Visual Basic 6 uses another method that is equally elegant; you'll see that a little later in this chapter (see the section called "The Controls Collection").

Regardless of the nifty new method for adding controls at run time, only forms in Visual Basic 6 are classes (templates for new objects)—controls on a form are not. This means that a statement such as

```
Dim Foo As New Text1
```

gives an error message when you try to compile it.

Finally, you will also use the New keyword with objects you create yourself. (See the sections "Collections" and "Creating a New Class Module" later in the chapter for more examples of using the New keyword.)

An Example of Using New (and a Warning)

13

Although the ability to use an existing form as a template to make copies of it at run time is very useful, there are some pitfalls to be wary of. To see both how to use the New keyword and what can go wrong:

1. Start up a new project and add a code module (we need a true global variable).
2. In the code module, add a global variable via the line:

   ```
   Public gFormCounter As Integer
   ```

3. Add the following code to the Form_Load:

```
Private Sub Form_Load()
  Me.Show
  Me.Caption = "This is the " & _
  gFormCounter & "'th copy of Form1 created so far."
  MsgBox "Please click inside of me to see a new form."
  gFormCounter = gFormCounter + 1
End Sub
```

4. Add the following code to the Form_Click:

```
Private Sub Form_Click()
  Unload Me
  Dim ACopyOfForm1 As New Form1
  ACopyOfForm1.Show
End Sub
```

If you run this program, you'll see that after each click on the form, the previous form vanishes and you will see a new form with a caption indicating which form it is. There are a lot of tricky things going on under the hood of this simple program that you need to understand, so I want to spend a bit of time on them.

First off, notice the use of the Me keyword in the Form_Load. Copies of Form1 will get the same code as the original, including the Form_Load, which will be executed immediately after they are created. This feature, when combined with the line

```
Me.Caption = "This is the " & _
  gFormCounter & "'th copy of Form1 created so far."
```

allows us to change the caption of the *current* form. We then update the counter. The MsgBox statement in the Form_Load procedure also will be displayed for each instance (copy) of Form1.

The Click procedure unloads the current form and then creates and shows a new copy of Form1 via the lines

```
Dim ACopyOfForm1 As New Form1
ACopyOfForm1.Show
```

Because creating the copy makes *its* Form_Load run, the caption of the form gets updated appropriately.

Okay, now for the subtleties. The first is: Why did I put the creation of the new form instance in the Click event rather than in the Form_Load? Move it and see what happens! If you do this, you'll quickly get an "Out of Memory Error." The reason is that moving the creation process into the Form_Load puts it on "automatic pilot." The Form_Load of the original form creates a copy whose Form_Load creates another copy and so on until you run out of memory. Ergo: *Never create new copies of a Form in its Form_Load.*

The next subtlety is: Why did I put the code to create the Caption in the Form_Load, rather than in the Form_Click? Try to move it and see what happens. If you do, you'll see that it doesn't update itself correctly. This is because only after you click in the form does the updating occur—you have a built in "off by one" error.

The final subtlety is: Why did I unload the current form with the line Unload Me in the Form_Click? To see why this is important, replace this line by a simple Me.Hide. If you do, you have one of those applications that seems to be over, but really isn't. There will be lots of hidden forms around when you click on the exit button of the current form.

General Object Variables

There are a few general types of object variables for use when you need to refer to objects of many different types. For example,

```
Dim ctlFoo As Control
```

gives you a way to refer to any control. Similarly,

```
Dim objGeneral As Object
```

lets you set the variable named objGeneral to *any* Visual Basic object.

Although you can use a variable of Object or variant type to refer to any Visual Basic object, generally speaking, don't do it. Your code will run a lot faster and be less bug prone if you always follow the following rule:

> *Always use the most specific type of object variable you can.*

For example, code with this statement

```
Dim txtFoo As TextBox
Set txtFoo = Text1
```

will always run faster than

```
Dim ctlFoo As Control
Set ctlFoo = Text1
```

which, in turn, will always run faster than

```
Dim objFoo As Object
Set objFoo = Text1
```

And this will run the slowest of all:

```
Dim varFoo As Variant
Set varFoo = Text1
```

13

Manipulating Object Variables via Procedures

You have already seen how to manipulate individual objects by setting their properties or applying one of their methods to them. Suppose, however, you want to write a general procedure to manipulate properties of forms or controls, or the forms and controls themselves—you simply don't yet have the techniques needed for this. This section explains them.

First off, *properties* of forms and controls can only be passed by value. For example, consider the following simple Sub procedure. If you call it using the following code,

```
Call ChangeText(Form1.Caption, Y$)
```

then the current value of Y$ is the caption for Form1.

T IP: You can set the Tag property of the form or control to contain information otherwise not available at run time. Then, you can write a general procedure using this technique to analyze the Control.Tag property and retrieve information about the control that would otherwise not be available at run time.

On the other hand, you will often want to affect the properties of a form or control by using a general procedure. For this, you have to pass the form or control as a parameter by reference. To do this, declare the argument to the procedure to be one of the object types. (You could use variants too, of course, but this should be avoided unless absolutely necessary because it is slower and also leads to code that is harder to debug.) For example, the following code makes a form visible if it is invisible:

```
Sub MakeVisible (frmX As Form)
  If frmX.Visible = False Then
    frmX.Visible  = True
  End If
End Sub
```

Notice that the parameter is declared to be an object variable of Form type and will be passed by reference (the default behavior for procedures). Otherwise, the code is pretty straightforward. Since frmX is being passed by reference, Visual Basic knows where in memory the form object is located. Since it knows this location, it can change the properties of the object. You access properties of an object variable inside a procedure using the dot notation you have become familiar with. In this case, the code is straightforward: if the form isn't visible (so frmX.Visible = False), the procedure makes it visible.

T IP: This kind of procedure would usually be in a code module, since you will want to use it for many different forms.

As another example, if you often find yourself writing code to center a form on the screen, why not use the following general procedure:

```
Public Sub CenterForm(frmX As Form)
  frmX.Move (Screen.Width - frmX.Width)/2, _
(Screen.Height - frmX.Height)/2
End Sub
```

Then, whenever you are in a procedure attached to a specific form, you can simply write

```
CenterForm Me
```

to center the form on the screen.

Similarly, you can have a Sub or Function procedure that affects a property of a control. For example, a first approximation to a general procedure to change the caption on a control might look like this:

```
Sub ChangeCaption (ctlX As Control, Y As String)
  ctlX.Caption = Y
End Sub
```

Notice that this procedure uses the general Control type. However, suppose you tried to use this procedure in the following line,

```
Call ChangeCaption(Text1, "New text")
```

or equivalently

```
ChangeCaption Text1, "New text"
```

where Text1 was the name of a text box. Then Visual Basic would give you a run-time error because text boxes do not have a Caption property. The next section explains how to overcome this problem.

Run-Time Type Information

Run-time type information is a fancy buzzword for inquiring into what type of object is stored inside an object variable. Knowing this is one solution to the problem of asking if the control passed to a procedure has a Caption property.

13

There are two methods to get run-time type information. The first is to use a slightly different version of the standard If-Then-Else loop to determine what type of control is being manipulated. This control structure takes the following form,

> If TypeOf *Control* Is *ControlType* Then
> .
> .
> .

```
Else
    .
    .
    .
End If
```

where the *ControlType* parameter is the same one used in declaring an object variable (Form, Label, TextBox, and so on).

For example, if all you wanted to do was work with both text boxes, and all the other controls you wanted to change *did* have Caption properties, you could use

```
Sub ChangeCaptionOrText (ctlX As Control, Y As String)
  If TypeOf ctlX Is TextBox Then
    ctlX.Text = Y
  Else
    ctlX.Caption = Y
  End If
End Sub
```

You will often find yourself using an empty If clause in this type of control structure. For example, if you wanted to play it safer:

```
Sub ChangeCaption (ctlX As Control, Y As String)
  If TypeOf ctlX Is TextBox Then
    '  Do Nothing
  Else
    ctlX.Caption = Y
  End If
End Sub
```

Since there is also no version of the Select Case for controls, you may need the If-Then-ElseIf version of this control structure:

```
If TypeOf ctlX Is...Then
  .
  .
  .
ElseIf TypeOf ctlX Is...Then
  .
  .
  .
ElseIf TypeOf ctlX Is...Then
  .
  .
  .
Else
  .
  .
  .
End If
```

TIP: You can also usually use the On Error Resume Next statement to eliminate the numerous tests in code like this (see Chapter 12).

The TypeName Function and Object Variables

You don't have to use the TypeOf operator to determine what object you are dealing with. You can use the TypeName function to determine the type of an object as well as the type of any variable. For example, start up a new project and add a command button to it. Run the following code:

```
Private Sub Command1_Click()
  Dim AButton As Object
  Set AButton = Command1
  MsgBox "You clicked on me. I am a " & TypeName(AButton)
End Sub
```

As you can see, the TypeName function tells you what kind of control you have stored in an object variable. Be sure to do the Set before the test. If you try

```
Private Sub Command1_Click()
  Dim AButton As CommandButton
  MsgBox "You clicked on me. I am a " & TypeName(AButton)
End Sub
```

you'll see the string Nothing and not the string CommandButton. In general, the TypeName function returns the string equivalent of what you use in the If TypeOf structure.

TIP: Since the TypeName function returns an ordinary string, you can use its results in every VB control structure. For example:

```
ObjectType = TypeName(AnObject)
Select Case ObjectType
  Case "TextBox"
    'now know it is a text box
  Case "CommandButton"
    'do what you want, assuming it's a Command button
'and so on
```

13

Collections

A Collection is a special type of object whose parts can be referred to individually as needed, *and* you still can refer to the object as a whole when needed. Think of collections as being smart arrays that can grow and shrink themselves automatically on demand. You have already seen the Printers collection in Chapter 6 and the Forms collection in Chapter 12. Visual Basic also has a built-in collection that gives you information about all the loaded controls on a specific form: it's called, naturally enough, Controls. Just as with the Printers collection and the Forms collection, the Count property of the Controls collection tells you how many controls are loaded on a specific form.

The Controls Collection

You can access individual controls by writing, for example, Controls(0), Controls(1), and so on. Unfortunately, although the count starts at 0, Controls(0) is not necessarily the first control you added to the form. The order of the Controls collection is unpredictable, like the order of the forms. For example, the following code prints the names of all the *loaded* controls in the current form in the Debug window.

```
Dim I As Integer
For I = 0 To Controls.Count - 1
  Debug.Print Controls(I).Name
Next I
```

(Since the Count property starts at 0, we go to one less than Controls.Count.) Although the preceding code works fine, most programmers would use the For-Each structure for iterating through a collection. They feel the For-Each structure makes the code a bit clearer when you need to iterate through all the elements in a collection, and it is also *much, much faster*. A framework for using the For-Each structure takes the following form,

```
For Each Element In TheCollection
  'do something
Next
```

as shown in the following rewritten version of the program to print the captions of all the loaded forms in a project:

```
Dim ctrlAControl As Control
For Each ctrAControol In Controls
  Debug.Print ctrlAControl.Name
Next
```

You get a reference to this collection with lines like

```
Me.Controls
```

and so you can use the Set command in the folllowing form:

```
Dim TheControls 'can use a variant to hold this
Set TheControls = Me.Controls.
```

NOTE: Dim TheControls As Collection won't work. The collection type turns out to not be useable for the most built-in collections but is reserved for collections you build yourself. (See later in this chapter.)

Adding Controls at Run Time

One of the most exciting features of VB6 is the ability to add new controls at run time to the Controls collection of a form via a method called, naturally enough, Add. These controls then become as much a part of that form as if you had added them at design time. The syntax for using this new feature of VB6 takes a bit of getting used to!

Set *CtrlObjectName* = *FormName*.Controls.Add ("*ProgID*", "*key*" [, *ContainerName*])

If you leave the parameter for the *ContainerName* off, the new control gets attached to the form. The *CtrlObjectName* is an object variable that you have previously declared to be of a compatible type. The parameter that is the most tricky is the *ProgID*. This stands for programmatic ID, and you can think of it as a string that helps Windows identify the OCX file. However, it isn't the actual file name. (Exactly what it is is not worth getting into for most VB programmers—it is part of Microsoft's COM/OLE machinery.) The rule for what the ProgID is for intrinsic VB controls—the ones you don't have to add via a check box on Tools|Components—is simple. The ProgID for intrinsic controls is a string of the form

VB.*ControlType*

The Key parameter is simply a string you can use to pull out the control from the controls collection—it is not the name of the control.

Here are some examples of using the Add method with the intrinsic controls:

```
Dim ALabel As Label
Set ALabel = Form1.Controls.Add("VB.Label", "AReallyNewLabel")
Dim ATextBox As TextBox
Set ATextBox = Form1.Controls.Add("VB.TextBox", "AReallyNewTextBox")
```

13

Once VB processes this code, you'll have a label and a control that you can get at by using the ALabel and the ATextBox object variables. These new controls need to have their properties set to reasonable values before you can use them. (For example, the Visible property of all newly added controls is at the default value of 0 = false!)

To actually see the Add method in action, start up a new project and run the following Form_Load. Notice how we need to set all the relevant properties for the new controls. Also notice how I could use the properties of the new label in setting the properties of the new text box. (The results are shown in Figure 13-2.)

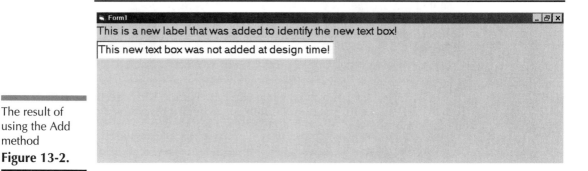

The result of
using the Add
method
Figure 13-2.

```
Private Sub Form_Load()
  WindowState = 2
  Me.Font.Size = 14
  Dim ALabel As Label
  Set ALabel = Form1.Controls.Add("VB.Label", "AReallyNewLabel")
  Dim ATextBox As TextBox
  Set ATextBox = Form1.Controls.Add("VB.TextBox", "AReallyNewTextBox")

  With ALabel
    .Visible = True
    .Height = 300
    .Left = 0
    .Top = 0
    .AutoSize = True
    .Caption = "This is a new label that was added to identify the new text box!"
  End With

  With ATextBox
    .Visible = True
    .Width = TextWidth(" This new text box was not added at design time! ")
    .Height = 300
    .Left = 0
    .Top = ALabel.Height + 100
    .Text = "This new text box was not added at design time!"
  End With
  Show
End Sub
```

For controls that you add with the Tools|Components dialog box, the rules for the ProgID are a lot more complicated. Most of the time the rule is that the ProgID begins with the name of the library you'd see in the Object Browser if you added the control at design time, followed by a dot, followed by the name that shows up in the Properties Window. For example, if you want to add an MSFlexGrid control, you could first load one into VB on a blank project. If you do, you'll see that what shows up in the drop-down list box in the Object Browser is "MSFlexGridLib". What shows up in the Properties window is "MSFlexGrid". Therefore, a good guess for how to use the ADD method is:

```
Dim MyGridfoo As MSFlexGrid
Set MyGrid = Form1.Controls.Add("MSFlexGridLib.MSFlexGrid", "ANewGrid")
```

Unfortunately, things get strange for some controls. If you follow the procedure outlined for a RichTextBox, you would get "RichTextBoxLib.RichTextBox", but if you run code like the following:

```
Private Sub Form_Load()
  Dim ARichTextBox As RichTextBox
  Set ARichTextBox = Form1.Controls.Add("RichTextBoxLib.RichTextBox", _
"ANewBox")
  ARichTextBox.Visible = True
  ARichTextBox.Width = 2000
  ARichTextBox.Height = 2000
End Sub
```

you'll see this:

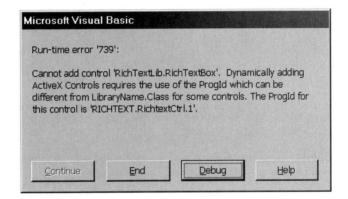

Luckily this message box tells you the correct ProgID!

NOTE: It is possible but very unusual to add controls that can also respond to events at run time. Most of the time you simply use properties to get them to behave the way you want. For more details on this unusual situation, please see the online help.

13

Example: Using the Controls Collection with Set
The Set statement is also useful when working with collections of objects. For example, suppose you need to know if there is a disabled control on your form, so you can enable it. The following code finds one and assigns it to an object variable named NotEnabledControl:

```
Dim AControl As Control
Dim ToBeEnabledControl As Control
```

```
For Each AControl in Me.Controls
   If Not(AControl.Enabled) Then
      Set ToBeEnabledControl = AControl
      Exit For
   End If
Next
```

This code moves through all the controls on a form until it finds one that is not enabled, and then it sets the AControl object variable to it. At this point you can say

```
ToBeEnabled.Enabled = True
```

and the control will now be enabled.

Building Your Own Collections

Since collections are so powerful, it is often useful to build your own. The items in a collection (usually called its *members* or *elements)* can be of any type, and you can mix types in a collection if necessary. (Such heterogeneous collections are obviously more bug prone and require more code to work with than collections that contain objects of only one type—since you need to check the type of each element before you work with it.).

NOTE: Although collections are more powerful and easier to use than arrays, they will run slower (roughly twice as slow) and often require more code to maintain.

Since a collection is an object, you must create it as an instance of a built-in class in Visual Basic. The class you need is named, naturally enough, the Collection class. For example, the line

```
Dim collX As New Collection
```

creates a new collection named collX as an instance of the Collection class.

NOTE: Certain editions of Visual Basic come with a Class Builder add-in that lets you build collections in your code more easily. You might want to check Tools|Add-Ins to see if your edition of Visual Basic has this nifty tool as part of its arsenal. The help file explains how to use this tool.

Just as with the Forms, Controls, or Printers collection, the Count property of each collection you create tells you the number of items in the collection. (Collections start out with no elements, so Count is 0.) Each element in a collection can be referred to by its index—just as you saw in the Forms and Controls collections. This means that the following code gives you one way of dealing with all the elements in a collection that you build:

```
For I = 1 To NameOfCollection.Count-1
  'work with NameOfCollection(I)
Next I
```

However, it is always faster (and certainly clearer) to use the For Each structure.

Of course, you still don't know how to add or remove elements from a collection. But before moving on to the important Add and Remove methods that do this, you need to learn about one other method for working with a collection.

The Item Method

The Item method is the default method for a collection; it is how you refer to (or return) a specific element of a collection. Its syntax is

NameOfCollectionObject.Item(*index*)

The *index* parameter specifies the position of a member of the collection or a key you can use to quickly pull out the element from the collection (see below for more on the nifty "Keyed Acesss" feature of collections). If you want to specify an item by its position in the collection, you can use any long integer here (you can have *lots* of elements in a collection). Visual Basic then goes to the item with that number in the collection. For example,

```
MyCollection.Item(1)
```

is the first item in the collection.

CAUTION: Collections you create start with an index of 1 and go up to the count of the collection. The built-in collections (Forms, Controls, and Printers) start at 0 and go up to Count -1 (which explains why you can't use a collection object variable in referring to built-in collections).

13

However, Visual Basic lets you use a key to access the elements in a collection. This key is set up at the time you add the element to the collection (see the Add method below). Using a key rather than an index is often more effective: you can easily associate a useful mnemonic as the key as you will see in the next section.

NOTE: The Item method is the default method for a collection, so

```
Print Forms(1).Caption
```

is actually the same as

```
Print Forms.Item(1).Caption
```

and is one of the few cases where even experienced VB programmers use the default property.

The Add Method

Once you create the collection by using the New keyword, you use the same Add method that you saw for the Controls collection to add items to it.

```
Dim Versions As New Collection
Dim Foo As String
Foo = "Visual Basic 4.0"
Versions.Add(Foo)
Foo = "Visual Basic 5.0"
Versions.Add(Foo)
Foo = "Visual Basic 6.0"
Versions.Add(Foo)
```

In general, the Add method has the following syntax (it supports named arguments, by the way):

CollectionObject.Add *item* [, *key* As string] [, *before* As Long] [, *after* As Long]

Here are short descriptions of the parts of the Add method:

◆   *CollectionObject* is any object or object variable that refers to a collection.

◆   The *item* parameter is required. Unlike arrays, the information can be of any type and you can mix types in a collection.

◆   The *key* parameter is optional. It must be a string expression, and within the collection it must be unique or you'll get a run-time error. For example:

```
Dim Presidents As New Collection
Dim Foo As Variant
Foo = "George Washington"
Presidents.Add Foo, "Didn't lie"
```

```
Foo = "John Adams"
Presidents.Add item:= Foo, key:= "Proper Bostonian"
```

Now you can access George by:

```
Presidents.Item("Didn't lie")
```

But remember that the match to the string in the key must be perfect. For example, this doesn't work:

```
Presidents.Item("Didn't  lie")   'used an extra space
```

NOTE: Although case doesn't seem to matter for the key, to play it safe, I would respect case since the case insensitivity of the key for a collection isn't documented.

◆   The optional *before* and *after* parameters are usually numeric expressions that evaluate to a (long) integer. The new member is placed right before (or right after) the member identified by the *before* (or *after*) argument. If you use a string expression, it must correspond to one of the keys that was used to add elements to the collection. You can specify before or after positions but not both.

The Remove Method
When you need to remove items from a collection, you use the Remove method. It too supports named arguments, and its syntax is

> *CollectionObject*.Remove *index*

Here, as you might expect, the *index* parameter is used to specify the element you want removed. If *index* is a numeric expression, it must be a number between 1 and the collection's Count property. If it's a string expression, it must exactly match a key to an element in the collection.

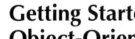

Getting Started with Object-Oriented Programming

Let's start with a question that, on the surface, seems to have nothing to do with programming: How did Gateway 2000 become a billion-dollar company faster than any other company in American history? Most people would probably say they made good computers and sold them at rock-bottom prices. But go further—how did they do *that*? Well, a big part of the answer is that they farmed out a lot of the work. They bought components from reputable vendors and then assembled them. They didn't invest any money in designing and building power supplies, disk drives, motherboards, and so on. This made it possible for them to have a good product at a low price.

13

Ask yourself for a second how this could work. The obvious (and to a large extent, correct) answer is that what they were buying was "prepackaged functionality." For example, when Gateway bought a power supply, they were buying something with certain properties (size, shape, and so on) and a certain functionality (smooth power output, amount of power available, and so on).

Object-oriented programming (OOP) springs from the same idea. Your programs will now be made up of objects with certain properties and functionality. You will depend on the objects not interacting in undocumented ways with other objects or with the rest of the code in your project. Whether you build the object or buy it might depend on the state of your wallet or how much time you have free. In either case, as long as the objects satisfy your specifications, you won't much care how the functionality is implemented. In OOP, the way people put it is that what you care about is what the objects *expose*.

NOTE: One of the funny things about the whole hoopla about productivity improvements coming from object-oriented techniques is that Visual Basic programmers are probably the first to benefit from them. After all, Visual Basic is the most productive tool for programmers partially because you don't need to care how command buttons are implemented in Visual Basic as long as they do what *you* want. And, as you certainly know by now, on the whole, Visual Basic's objects do what you would expect them to!

Why can this simple idea lead to amazing productivity improvements? I am tempted to say, well, just look at how productive VB programmers are. But the next step is to imagine that you are part of a team of programmers working on objects that the other teams can use—just as you will be using the objects they produce. Now, just as Gateway doesn't care about the internals of a power supply as long as it does what they want, your team doesn't need to care how the objects you will be using are implemented—as long as they do what you want. The key point is that, *as much as possible*, you should have the other objects and parts of your program communicate via messages that tell them what to do. They never muck around in the "innards" of the object. For example, think of the power supply as sending out current in response to a message from the modem saying, "I'm turning myself on." OOP jargon describes this by saying that what you do in object-oriented programming is *have client objects send messages to server objects*. (Which object is the client and which is the server can switch depending on the message being sent.) By designing your objects to handle all appropriate messages and to manipulate their data internally, you maximize reusability and minimize debugging time. (By now you have seen pretty clear evidence that Visual Basic's built-in objects fit this model well. They are extremely rich in functionality.)

TIP: As you move further along in your VB mastery, you'll start thinking about building more and more and more objects. Don't go overboard; don't fall victim to the "not invented here" syndrome. Generally speaking, it is rarely worth reinventing the wheel. If it takes you 40 hours to build a component in Visual Basic and you can buy it for $200, you really should ask: is it worth it? Commercial vendors usually produce quality products that are worth the (usually) small cost. I have always used commercial products in my applications and have been generally happy with the results.

On the other hand, if you are constantly using a text box that accepts only numbers, why not use the control-creation power built into VB6 to make a "NumericTextBox" once and for all? As you will see in Chapter 23, it will take a lot less than an hour to do this!

NOTE: On the surface, Visual Basic misses implementing one of the key features of OOP here. Ideally, if you do have to write your own objects, another tenet of traditional OOP languages can make this easier as well: objects can be built based on other objects. When you do this in a classic OOP language like C++ or Java, the new object starts out by inheriting all the properties and functions of its parent—you can pick and choose whether you want to keep or modify any property or function of the parent. Visual Basic 6 doesn't allow this, but it does replace it with another notion called an *interface* that you will see shortly.

Vocabulary of OOP

Traditional structured programming consists of manipulating data. (This is one reason computer programming used to be called data processing.) You manipulate the data in specific ways that are theoretically sure to terminate. (These are usually called *algorithms*.) Computer scientists talk about *data structures* when they want to single out the arrangements used in your program for the data. All of this explains, in part, why Niklaus Wirth, a Swiss professor and computer scientist (who designed Pascal among other achievements) called his famous book on programming *Algorithms + Data Structures = Programs* (Prentice Hall, 1976). Notice that in Wirth's title the algorithms come first and the data structures come after. This mimics the way programmers worked at that time. First, you decided how to manipulate the data, then you decided what structure to impose on the data in order to make the manipulations easier. OOP puts both algorithms and data structures on the same level. With OOP you work with packages consisting of both data and the functions that manipulate them.

13

TIP: Many people like to think of an object as simply a user-defined type that includes not only data but functions. If this is helpful to you, there is no reason not to use this model.

The rest of this section explains the basic terminology of OOP. There's a fair amount of it, but it is worth learning for two reasons. The first is that you will need some of this terminology to understand the discussions in this chapter; the second is that knowing this terminology is useful if you move on to other OOP languages, such as C++ or Java.

Classes

A *class* is usually described as the template or blueprint from which an object is actually made. The standard way of thinking about classes is to think of them as the cookie cutter and the object as the cookie. The "dough," in the form of memory, will sometimes need to be allocated as well. Visual Basic is pretty good about hiding this "dough preparation" step from you. You almost never have to worry about specifying memory for an object. (However, you do have to be a little careful about releasing the memory you used when a VB program ends.)

When you create an object from a class, you are said to have created an instance of the class. The instances of your class are the actual objects. All the tools on the toolbox are classes, and when you add a text box to a form you have made an instance of the text box class. Also, as you already saw: an individual form in your application is a class that you can use to create new forms that will be modeled on it. (See the section "The New Keyword with Forms".)

NOTE: As you will see in Chapter 23, it is possible to create new controls with Visual Basic 6. It is worth keeping in mind that what you are doing then is creating a new control class of a specific type.

Finally, the *members* of a class are the properties, constants, and methods that belong to the class. The public members of your class define its functionality.

Encapsulation

Encapsulation (sometimes called *data hiding*) is another key concept in working with objects. Formally, encapsulation is nothing more than combining the data and behavior in one package and hiding the implementation of the data. Nobody should care whether you store dates as date variables or as date serial numbers, for example.

NOTE: The data in an object is usually called its *instance* variables or fields, and the functions and procedures are its methods or properties.

A key rule in making encapsulation work is that programs should *never* access the instance variables (fields) in an object directly; programs should interact with this data only through an object's methods and properties. (Properties and methods for Visual Basic objects are designed so as to give you a way to interact with the instance variables without violating encapsulation.) Encapsulation is the way to give an object its "black box" behavior, which is the key to reuse and debugging efficiency.

NOTE: Visual Basic fully supports encapsulation.

Inheritance

The ability to make classes that are based on (descend from) other classes is called *inheritance*. The main purpose of inheritance is to make it easier to build code for specialized tasks by:

◆ Letting you reuse code that won't change automatically.

This is because in an inheritance-based OOP language the instance variables and methods of the descendent classes (sometimes called the *subclasses*) start out being the same as in the parent class; you only have to code the changes.

NOTE: Visual Basic does not support inheritance and so you have to do a bit more typing than in other OOP languages. Luckily, to a great extent the VB IDE and the Wizards supplied with VB will do an equally good job of saving you from needless typing.

13

Inheritance has another purpose; it:

◆ Makes it easier to send a single message out and rely on the object itself to know how to deal with it.

(We will discuss the second feature (called *polymorphism*) in the next section.)

Interfaces and Polymorphism

While Visual Basic 6 doesn't have inheritance, it does have something that will accomplish the main point—which is making it easier to build code that adapts itself to working with different objects. The idea that the designers of Visual Basic decided to use came from the mechanism used in Windows to implement controls and other OLE objects. This idea is usually called an *interface*, and the purpose of interfaces is to implement a programming idea that is usually called *polymorphism*. Polymorphism, which comes from the Greek words meaning "many faces," has many aspects, but the key one is this: When you write the code that sends an object a message, you don't need to know what class an object belongs to. All you need to know is the name of the message and its parameters. The combination of the name and parameters of a method is usually called its *signature*.

Polymorphism is sometimes described as "objects know how to do their own work." What this means is best explained by a simple example: Suppose you are writing an object-based e-mail system. The idea is that whether you have an E-Mail message object, or a VoiceMail message object, when you send the object a "play" message, the object will know how to respond.

Polymorphism is helpful when creating new objects from old ones because it makes a programmer's job simpler. When you define a new object that is related to an existing object, you do not want to rebuild some previously existing code in order to take into account that a new object exists. Imagine the alternative, some giant Case statement somewhere that just grows and grows in your code:

```
Case E-mailMessage
  'do this
Case VoiceMailMessage
  'do that
Case Post-ItMessage
  'etc., etc.
```

Polymorphism often depends on what is called *late binding*. This means the compiler doesn't generate the code to call a method at compile time. Instead, every time you use a method with an object, the compiler generates code that lets it calculate which method to call by using pointer information built into the object that called it. Methods that allow late binding are called *virtual methods* because they do not exist in the .exe file but are only potentially there. What Visual Basic does is use the notion of *interface* to allow this key part of polymorphism.

So what's an interface? It is nothing more than a contract between the class and the user of the class that says: "I have a method with this signature; if you call me and pass me the name and the parameters indicated in the method's signature, I will use my version of the method and you won't have to worry."

One big advantage to interfaces is that they make using your Visual Basic objects extremely efficient; you can often avoid late binding if you use them. Since late binding is much slower than doing it at compile time (early binding), this can be a big win. The idea is that if you call a method to change a property of a control, for example, Visual Basic can find out at compile time what code to call in your object. This works at compile time roughly as follows:

1. Visual Basic looks to see if your object says it supports the method in one of its interfaces. (*Implements* is the technical term for "supporting" an interface.)
2. If your object does expose this method in one of its interfaces, then at compile time Visual Basic looks in the code for the object and generates code that says "Go to this method."

Now compare this to what happens if you don't give your objects an interface that says the object will support the method with that signature:

1. Since you haven't promised you will support the method, at compile time Visual Basic is smart enough not to go looking for what may or may not be there yet.
2. At compile time, Visual Basic generates a lot more code. This code allows Visual Basic to politely ask the object at run time if it supports the method with the signature you specified and would it mind running the method if it does? (This is the essence of late binding.)

This kind of code has two features that make it slower:

◆ It needs error trapping, in case you were wrong.

◆ In any case, since you don't know the location of the method inside the object, you have to rely on the object to send you the information at run time.

Finally, another advantage of the interface approach is that objects that support interfaces can make multiple contracts—support multiple interfaces—without the complexity of managing multiple inheritance chains (one of the real pains in C++).

Object-Oriented Design

There are dozens of books on the topic of object-oriented design. The idea, however, is simple. When designing an object-oriented program, you follow three basic steps:

1. Find the classes.
2. Then find their methods.
3. Then find the relationships between the classes.

So the question is, how do you do this? A good rule of thumb is that the classes in your program correspond to the nouns, and the methods correspond to the verbs. For example, in an object-oriented approach to designing a "Rolodex" program, some of the nouns (classes) would be:

13

◆ An individual card

◆ The collection of all the cards

◆ The index of all the cards

Some of the verbs (methods) might be EnterDataInCard, EnterCardInCollectionOfCards, UpdateIndex, DeleteCard, SortIndex, FindCard, and so on. For example, after you finish the data entry for a specific card, the data entry method of the card class could call the UpdateIndex method of the Card Collection class.

Creating an Object in Visual Basic

You can build objects in three ways in Visual Basic. One is by adding custom properties to an existing form and then using that form as a class (template) for new instances of the form. Each new instance of the form will have the new properties. You have already seen this feature at the beginning of the chapter.

The second way is by using a special type of module called a *class module*. Class modules have the advantage that they can be compiled separately (see Chapter 20) and used by other Windows applications—even other VB programs. You can think of a Class Module as a control without a visual interface. The third alternative is, of course, to create a custom control (see Chapter 23).

In all three cases you start with the same ideas for adding properties to these classes (templates). First off, what are the most basic things you will want to be able to do with a new property?

◆   You want to get its current value.

◆   You want to assign a new value to it.

For the first situation, you use a special type of procedure called a *Property Get* procedure. For the second, you use a *Property Let* procedure. (The way I remember the terminology is that a Let statement is the way you made assignments in early versions of BASIC—you can even still use them in Visual Basic!)

NOTE: If the value you are assigning is itself an object, you use a *Property Set* rather than a Property Let.

For example, suppose you want to add a custom property to a form that will tell you whether a form named frmNeedsToBeCentered is centered, and also to center it if you set the property to True. Here's what you need to do.

Set up a Private variable in the declarations section of the form. (It's a Private variable to enforce encapsulation.)

```
Private IsCentered As Boolean
```

Then add the following procedures to the form:

```
Public Property Let Center(X As Boolean)
  IsCentered = X 'used for the current state of the property
  If X then
    Me.Move (Screen.Width - Me.Width)/2, _
Screen.Height - Me.Height)/2
  End If
End Sub
```

The first line of code uses the Private variable to store the current value of the property. Now you can use a line of code like

```
Me.Center = True
```

to center the form (or any instance of it). From another form or code module, you can use a line of code like this:

```
frmNeedsToBeCentered.Center = True
```

Of course, it might also be useful to know whether a form is centered. For this you need to use a Property Get procedure that returns a Boolean:

```
Public Property Get Center() As Boolean
  Center = IsCentered
End Sub
```

This picks up the current value of the IsCentered Private variable that you are using to hold the information about the current value of the property. (Notice that Property Get procedures are a bit like Function procedures: you assign a value to them within the body of the procedure.)

NOTE: You may be wondering, why all this bother? You can certainly use a Public variable to determine whether a form is centered or not. The point is that the designers of Visual Basic 6 are trying to give objects as much "black box" behavior as they can. Using a Public variable to determine whether a form is centered would partially defeat this. At the risk of sounding repetitive: never use public variables for properties.

13

In any case, you can use code like this:

```
If Not(frmNeedsToBeCentered.Center) Then MsgBox _
("Why did you move the form?")
```

Finally, you'll need to have some code in the Form_Resize event to check if the user actually centered the form by hand. One possibility is code like this:

```
Sub Form_Resize()
  If Me.Left = (Screen.Width - Me.Width)/2 And Me.Height = _
Screen.Height - Me.Height)/2 Then
    IsCentered = True
  End If
End Sub
```

General Property Procedures

Did you notice how the Property Let and Property Get procedures in the example worked in tandem? The value returned by the Property Get procedure is of the same type as the one used in the assignment for Property Let. Also, in general, the number of arguments for a Property Get is also one less than that of the corresponding Property Let (the last argument being the one that will be changed). A Property Get procedure that you write without a corresponding Property Let procedure gives you a read-only property—since you provide no way to change it.

The usual syntax for a Property Let procedure template looks like this:

> [Public | Private][Static] Property Let *name* [(*arglist*)]
>   [*statements*]
>   [*name* = *expression*]
>   [Exit Property] ' if need be
> End Property

◆ Use Public to make the Property Let procedure accessible to every procedure in every module.

◆ Use Private to make the Property Let procedure accessible only to other procedures in the module where it is declared.

The other keywords work as they would in any procedure. Use the Static keyword if you need the Property Let procedure's local variables preserved between uses. The Exit Property keywords give you a way to immediately exit from a Property Let procedure, and so on. The name of the Property Let procedure must follow standard variable-naming conventions, except that the name can, and most often will, be the same as a Property Get or Property Set procedure in the same module.

The usual syntax for a Property Get procedure template looks like this:

> [Public | Private][Static] Property Get *name* [(*arglist*)][As *type*]
>   [*statements*]
>   [*name* = *expression*]
>   [Exit Property] ' if need be
> End Property

NOTE: The name and type of each argument in a Property Get procedure must be the same as the corresponding arguments in the corresponding Property Let procedure—if it exists. The type of the value returned by a Property Get procedure must be the same data type as the last argument in the corresponding Property Let procedure, if it exists.

The last type of Property procedure is the Property Set statement. Use this when you need to set a reference to an object instead of just setting a value (for example, when you want to set a Font as the value of a property). Here is the usual syntax:

```
[Public | Private][Static] Property Set name [(arglist)]
    [statements]
    [Exit Property]
    [statements]
End Property
```

TIP: If you choose Tools|Add Procedure and choose "Property" type, Visual Basic automatically gives you the following templates:

```
Public Property Get ExampleProperty( ) As Variant
End Property
Public Property Let ExampleProperty(ByVal vNewValue As Variant)
End Property
```

Now all you have to do is change the signatures to reflect what you want.

Building Your Own Classes

Although you can add custom properties to a form and then use them as templates for new objects, the most common way to build a new class (template) for new objects in Visual Basic is to use a class module. A class module object contains the code for the custom properties (in the Property procedures you write) and methods that objects defined from it will have.

You can then create new instances of the class from any other module or form in your project. (You can even compile class modules for use by other applications as in-process OLE servers—see Chapter 20 for more on this important concept.) A class module cannot have a visible interface of its own. Each class module you create gives you, naturally enough, a single class (template) for building new instances of that class. However, you can have as many class modules in a project as you like (subject only to operating system constraints).

As you might expect, once you have a class module, you use the New keyword to create new instances of it. For example, if FirstClass is the name of a class module in your project, you would create an instance as follows:

```
Dim AnInstance As New FirstClass
```

13

You use Property procedures to define the properties of your class and use Public Sub and Public Function procedures for its methods.

Creating a New Class Module

You create a new class module at design time by choosing Project|Add Class Module. Each class module can respond to only two events: Initialize and Terminate. They are triggered when someone creates an instance of your class or terminates it. (Note that the Terminate event for a class module is triggered when the class created via the New keyword is set to Nothing. *It does not occur if the application stops because of the End statement.*) As you might expect, the Name property determines the name of the class.

NOTE: Since you cannot give parameters to the Initialize event, the custom is to have a Create event that the Initialize event calls when you need to send parameters to define your class's initial state.

Example: A Deck of Cards Class Module

Start by imagining you want to provide a toolkit for the designers of computer-generated card games. You obviously need an object that takes the place of a deck of cards. Since class modules in Visual Basic can't be visual, you only need to be concerned about the data and methods this deck-of-cards object must support.

Let's call this class module CardDecks. This object needs to expose individual cards and have methods for shuffling the deck and dealing the cards. (You will use the Initialize event to build up the deck of cards.)

The code for creating this nonvisual object might look like what follows. First off, start with the Private variables used for the data:

```
Private Deck(0 To 51) As Integer
Private TheCard As String
Private Position As Integer
```

The Deck array will be used to hold the integers that are the internal representation of the cards. The Private TheCard variable will be used for the Property procedures to encapsulate the card. (This will make it easy to change the names of the cards for a different country, for example.)

The Initialize procedure simply fills the array with 52 consecutive integers:

```
Private Sub Class_Initialize()
  Dim I As Integer
  For I = 0 To 51
    Deck(I) = I
  Next I
End Sub
```

Now it's on to the methods. First off, there's got to be a Shuffle method for shuffling the deck. It might look like this:

```
Public Sub Shuffle()
  Dim X As Integer, I As Integer
  Dim Temp As Integer, Place As Integer
  Randomize
  For I = 0 To 5199 '10 times through the deck should be enough
    Place = I Mod 52
    X = Int(52 * Rnd)
    Temp = Deck(Place)
    Deck(Place) = Deck(X)
    Deck(X) = Temp
  Next I
End Sub
```

You can easily add an argument to this procedure to control how many "shuffles" are made. If you do, then the method this procedure generates would have an argument:

```
Foo.Shuffle 10
```

Next, create the read-only property that tells you the current card. It simply looks up the current value of the Private TheCard variable:

```
Public Property Get CurrentCard() As String
  TheCard = CalculateCard(Deck(Position))
  CurrentCard = TheCard
End Property
```

(It is read-only because there is no associated Property Let procedure to change the current card.)

The method that deals the card will need to call a private procedure that converts the integer in the Deck array to a card. Assuming that function is called CalculateCard, the DealCard method might look like this:

```
Public Function DealCard() As String
  If Position > 51 Then Err.Raise Number :=vbObjectError + _
32144, Description := "Only 52 cards in deck!"
  TheCard = CalculateCard(Deck(Position))
  DealCard = TheCard
  Position = Position + 1
End Function
```

Finally, here's the Private procedure for converting a number in the card array to a string describing the card:

```
Private Function CalculateCard(X As Integer) As String
  Dim Suit As Integer, CardValue As Integer
  Suit = X \ 13
  Select Case Suit
```

13

```
    Case 0
      TheCard = "Clubs"
    Case 1
      TheCard = "Diamonds"
    Case 2
      TheCard = "Hearts"
    Case 3
      TheCard = "Spades"
  End Select

  CardValue = X Mod 13
  Select Case CardValue
    Case 0
      TheCard = "Ace of " + TheCard
    Case 1 To 9
      TheCard = Str$(CardValue + 1) + " of " + TheCard
    Case 10
      TheCard = "Jack of " + TheCard
    Case 11
      TheCard = "Queen of " + TheCard
    Case 12
      TheCard = "King of " + TheCard
  End Select
  CalculateCard = TheCard
End Function
```

Now all you have to do to use this class module is have a line such as

```
Dim MyDeck As New CardDeck
```

before you start working with it. For example, you could test it with the following code:

```
Private Sub Form_Load()
  Dim MyDeck As New CardDeck, I As Integer
  MyDeck.Shuffle
  For I = 1 To 20
    MyDeck.DealCard
    MsgBox MyDeck.CurrentCard
  Next I
End Sub
```

Improving the Deck of Cards Example
Actually, the previous example, though it works fine, can be significantly improved. Many object-oriented programmers would say (and I agree) that the previous design of the CardDeck class was not ideal. Why? Well, because the CardDeck class is too big, it has too many *responsibilities*. Just like you don't want your procedures to be too big, you don't want your classes to try to do too much.

A better design would be to make each card itself an object. Each individual card would then have a method that gives its value. (I'll call this version of the Class Module "DeckOfCards" so that it is easier for you to distinguish them if you want to download the code from Osborne's web site: http://www.osborne.com.)

Here's how the code for this version of a DeckOfCards class would go. First off, we have the class for individual cards. Notice that we give this a Create routine in order to give a card a specific value. The CalculateCard routine is the same, and we have a read-only property that returns a string for the card value. All this is much like before:

```
Private CardIndex As Integer
'Need a way to create a card with a specific value

Public Sub Create(Index As Integer)
  If Index > 51 Or Index < 0 Then
    Err.Raise Number :=vbObjectError + 32144, _
Description :=  "Only 52 cards in deck!"
    Exit Sub
  End If
  CardIndex = Index
End Sub

Private Function CalculateCard(X As Integer) As String
  Dim Suit As Integer, CardValue As Integer
  Dim TheCard As String
  Suit = X \ 13
  Select Case Suit
    Case 0
      TheCard = "Clubs"
    Case 1
      TheCard = "Diamonds"
    Case 2
      TheCard = "Hearts"
    Case 3
      TheCard = "Spades"
  End Select

  CardValue = X Mod 13
  Select Case CardValue
    Case 0
     TheCard = "Ace of " + TheCard
    Case 1 To 9
     TheCard = Str$(CardValue + 1) + " of " + TheCard
    Case 10
     TheCard = "Jack of " + TheCard
    Case 11
     TheCard = "Queen of " + TheCard
    Case 12
     TheCard = "King of " + TheCard
  End Select
  CalculateCard = TheCard
End Function

'ReadOnly property
Public Property Get CardValue() As String
  CardValue = CalculateCard(CardIndex)
End Property
```

13

Next, we have the new DeckOfCards class module. Notice how it is a little simpler, but we need to use the Set keyword because each card is now an object:

```
Private ACard As Card
Private DeckOfCards(0 To 51) As Card

'create the deck of cards
Private Sub Class_Initialize()
  Dim I As Integer
  For I = 0 To 51
    Set ACard = New Card
    ACard.Create I 'create the card with the right value
    Set DeckOfCards(I) = ACard
  Next I
End Sub

Public Sub Shuffle()
  Dim X As Integer, I As Integer
  Dim Temp As Card, Place As Integer
  Randomize
  For I = 0 To 5199 '10 times through the deck should be enough
    Place = I Mod 52
    X = Int(52 * Rnd)
    Set Temp = DeckOfCards(Place)
    Set DeckOfCards(Place) = DeckOfCards(X)
    Set DeckOfCards(X) = Temp
  Next I
End Sub


Public Property Get CardValue(Position As Integer) As String
  CardValue = DeckOfCards(Position).CardValue
End Property
```

Finally, here's a somewhat slicker test routine you can use:

```
Private Sub Form_Load()
  Dim MyDeck As New DeckOfCards, I As Integer
  Dim YourHand As String, MyHand as String
  MyDeck.Shuffle
  For I = 1 To 5
    YourHand = YourHand & MyDeck.CardValue(I) & "  "
  Next I
  MsgBox "Your hand is: " & YourHand
  For I = 6 To 10
    MyHand = MyHand & MyDeck.CardValue(I) & "  "
  Next I
  MsgBox "My hand is: " & MyHand
  End
End Sub
```

CHAPTER 14

Finishing the Interface

To this point, we've looked at a fairly limited subset of the controls that are available and concentrated on learning the underlying Visual Basic programming language. Since you have now seen most of VB's programming language constructs, it is time to return to interface development. While it is impossible to cover completely all the controls supplied with Visual Basic, let alone the thousands of controls available commercially, this chapter will survey most of the remaining standard controls that you'll find on the toolbox or will be most likely to add via the Project|Components dialog box. Luckily, once you get a feel for how controls work, using the supplied help file makes it simple to master new controls.

For example, the controls covered in this chapter let you add check boxes and option (radio) buttons. In addition, you'll learn how to use timers so that parts of your program will spring to life at specified time intervals. You'll also see another method for creating multiple controls on a form at design time. Then we'll look at using the common dialog control; this control lets you add the dialog boxes users expect to see in your projects, as well as some of the other common controls, such as toolbars and status bars. Menus are covered in the second half of this chapter. Think of menu items as specialized controls that you add to your forms. Menu items respond only to the Click event, and unlike all the other controls in Visual Basic, menus are not added to forms by using the toolbox. Instead, you use the Menu Editor window, which is available from the Window menu on the main menu bar or via the Menu Editor tool on the toolbar.

This chapter ends with a short general discussion of interface design. In particular, you will learn techniques for keeping the controls on a form in proportion, regardless of size or display changes.

How Visual Basic Displays Work: ZOrder

Before you start using lots of complicated controls, you need to step back for a moment and understand how Visual Basic displays information on a form. The idea is that when Visual Basic paints the parts of a form, it does so in three layers. The back (bottom) layer is where you draw information directly on the form using the graphical methods that you will see in Chapter 16. The middle layer contains the graphical controls (lines, shapes, picture boxes, and the image control). The top layer contains the nongraphical controls, such as command buttons, list boxes, check boxes, and option buttons.

As you have seen already, certain controls, such as labels, have a FontTransparent property that lets information from the layers below show through. Within each layer you can control the order in which controls appear. For example, if you overlap two command buttons, you can specify which one appears on top. You can do this in two ways. At design time you can use the Bring To Front option and Send To Back option from the Edit menu to specify the initial ordering of what's on top. To change the ordering dynamically, while the program is running, you need the ZOrder method. Its syntax is:

[*object.*]ZOrder [*position*]

The *position* parameter can be 0 or 1. If it is 0 or omitted, the *object* named moves to the front. If it is 1, the *object* moves to the back. If you omit the *object* name, the current form moves to the top.

The Toolbox Revisited

In Chapter 4 you saw the basic controls for a Visual Basic project: command buttons, image controls, text boxes, and labels; Chapters 6 and 11 added a few more. Figure 14-1 shows you the controls from the standard toolbox that we'll cover in this chapter. First, though, here are brief descriptions of each of these controls. See the appropriate sections following this one for more on the individual controls.

◆ The frame control icon looks like a box with a bit of text (xyz) at the top. This control is mainly used to group other Visual Basic controls. As you'll soon see, frames give you a way to visually separate parts of a form from other parts.

◆ The icon for check boxes gives a good feel for what the control will look like on your form: a box with a check mark in it. When your project is running, check boxes are toggled on and off via mouse clicks or by using the TAB key to move the focus to the control and then pressing the SPACEBAR.

◆ The option buttons icon looks like an old-fashioned radio button—hence the other popular name for this control. Unlike check boxes, option buttons work in groups. When the user chooses one button in the group, all the others are turned off. Option buttons are also toggled on and off via mouse clicks or the TAB and SPACEBAR combination.

◆ The controls for vertical and horizontal scroll bars can give you another way of getting user input. Another possibility is to use them to display how close you are to the beginning or end of a time-consuming process. (You can also use a ProgressBar control supplied with most editions of Visual Basic; progress bars are also covered later in this chapter.)

◆ The timers icon looks like an old-fashioned alarm clock. This reminds you that this control will wake up at specified time intervals. Unlike all other controls in the standard edition of Visual Basic, timers are always invisible to the user. You can see them only during the design phase of your project.

◆ The dialog boxes icon lets you add common dialog boxes, which you've seen in previous chapters, to your Visual Basic application. Whether they are used for opening or closing a file, choosing a font, printing a page, or changing the color of a Windows object, these are the standard dialog boxes that users expect to see.

14

Frames

You rarely write event procedures for frames. In fact, currently there are only seven events to which frames can respond. (Besides the usual Click and Double-click events, there are the mouse events that tell you whether a control was dragged over or dropped onto the frame. See Chapter 17 for these events.) You usually use frames

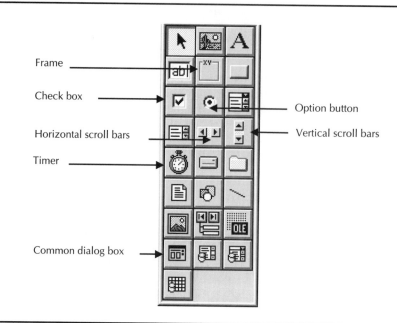

Frame

Check box

Horizontal scroll bars

Timer

Option button

Vertical scroll bars

Common dialog box

Additional
controls for
a Visual
Basic project
Figure 14-1.

passively to group images or controls. For example, a frame with image controls is one of the standard ways of creating a toolbar in some versions of Visual Basic. (See later in this chapter for the more direct way using the Toolbar control.) The screen in Figure 14-2 is an example of a form with multiple frames used to divide the form functionally.

There are 31 properties for frames, and all of them are common to the controls you are already familiar with. For example, the font properties control how the caption appears, MousePointer controls how the mouse pointer appears, and so on. The only properties you haven't seen for frames are the ones for mouse activities; they're covered in Chapter 17.

Finally, the important point to keep in mind when using a frame is that you usually will draw the frame before the controls. Only after the frame is on the form should you attach controls by placing them inside the frame. You'll need to do this by:

1. Clicking on the tool in the toolbox
2. Moving to the frame
3. Dragging the mouse *within the frame* to create the control.

In this way, Visual Basic knows the controls are attached to the frame. If you don't make it clear that the controls are attached to the frame, Visual Basic will not let the control respond to events that the frame can respond to, nor will VB move the control when you move its containing frame. In particular, do *not* use the

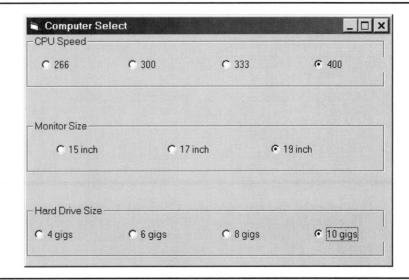

Form with
frames
Figure 14-2.

Double-click method for creating a control when you want to attach a control to a frame. The Double-click method places the control in the center of the screen, but even if the frame is there, Visual Basic will not attach the control to the frame.

IP: You can attach a control directly to a frame or picture box at design time by cutting the control out of the form, selecting the frame, and then pasting the control into the frame. You can also do this at run time by setting the Container property of that control to the name of the frame.

Option (Radio) Buttons

Option buttons always work together. When the user chooses one button, all the other buttons in the group are turned off. For this reason, any application that uses more than one group of option buttons on a form must use a frame to separate the groups. (See the "Frames" section earlier in this chapter.) You add option (radio) buttons to a form when you want the user to choose one option from a finite list of possibilities. For example, the screen in Figure 14-3 shows how a form for a database might look.

The Value property of the option button tells you whether a button was selected by the user. If the Value property is True, the user selected that button; otherwise, its Value property is False.

14

If you give the option buttons in Figure 14-3 control names of optMr, optMs, optMrs, and optOther, you could use code like the following to pick up the information:

```
If optMr.Value Then
  Title$= "Mr."
ElseIf optMs.Value Then
  Title$= "Ms."
ElseIf optMrs.Value Then
  Title$= "Mrs."
Else
  Title$=InputBox("Please enter the title you want us to
use.")
End If
```

This code works because of the Boolean (True/False) nature of the Value property. For example, the clause optMs.Value will be True only when the user has chosen the optMs option button.

Option buttons respond to the Click and Double-click events as well as to the key events. They can also detect whether a button has received or lost the focus. Visual Basic generates the Click event when the user selects the button by clicking with the mouse or moving via the TAB key and pressing SPACEBAR. If you reset the Value

---

IN DEPTH

The Sticky Click Method for Creating Controls

Visual Basic has another way to create controls on a form—other than the click and drag method. It is especially useful when working with frames (or picture boxes used as containers). This method is a cross between the Double-click and the drag-and-drop methods you've seen already. Using the *sticky click method*, you can create multiple copies of the same control but position and size them as you see fit. (Recall that the Double-click method always gives you similarly sized controls, stacked one on another, in the center of the form.) To create controls using the sticky click method, follow these steps:

1. Move to the toolbox and press CTRL while clicking the left mouse button. The control in the toolbox is highlighted.

2. Move to the form or frame and click the left mouse button. The top left corner of the new control is "stuck" at this location.

3. Hold the left mouse button down and drag until you are happy with the size of the control.

4. Release the mouse button and repeat steps 2 and 3 until you have finished placing all the controls of that type on the form or in the frame.

To change to another way of working with the toolbox, go back to the toolbox and click the pointer, or any control other than the one you were working with.

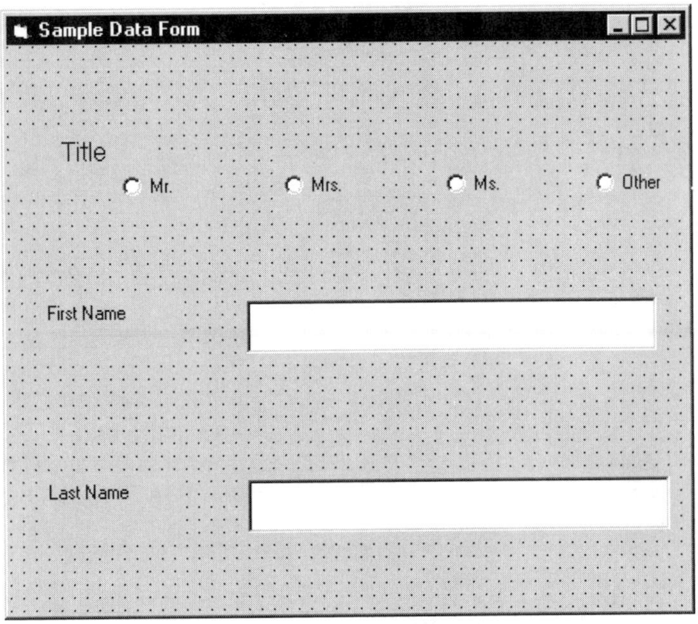

Form for
possible
database
Figure 14-3.

property of the option button to True inside code, then you also generate the Click
event. This is occasionally useful for demonstration programs. You can also turn on
one of the buttons at design time by setting its Value property to True via the
Properties window.

The 31 properties for option buttons are a subset of those for command buttons. For
example, you can set the Caption property to change how Visual Basic displays the
caption. You can also temporarily disable the button by setting the Enabled property
to False at design or run time, as you see fit.

The Bill Gates Wealth Calculator

I can't resist showing you what I like to call my "Bill Gates Wealth Calculator," which I
have people program every time I teach Visual Basic. It is sometimes hard to realize
just how rich Bill Gates is and how much a small change in the value of Microsoft
stock affects his wealth. As you can see in Figure 14-4, even a 1 percent increase in
Microsoft stock price from the value initially entered has rather amazing results—even
on a second by second basis!

14

There's really nothing tricky in the following code. I simply use publicly available
information on how many shares of Microsoft stock Bill owns as of this writing
(564,639,960 as I write this) as a constant:

```
Const BillsShares = 564639960
```

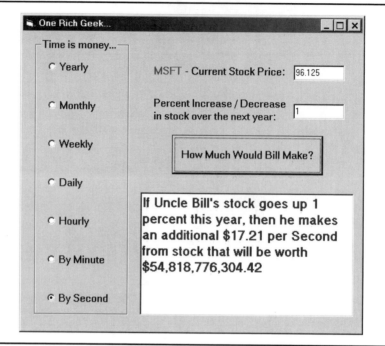

The Bill Gates
Wealth
Calculator
Figure 14-4.

Then in the cmdCalculate procedure:

1. I check via a simple user-defined function using the built-in IsNumeric function whether or not the text boxes contain numbers.
2. If they do I make the appropriate calculation, if not I pop up a message box and reset the focus and the values.
3. I assume Microsoft's stock doesn't ever go down.

Here's the rest of the code:

```
Private Sub cmdCalculate_Click()
Dim BillsMoney As Currency, TheAmount As Currency, ThePeriod As String
  Dim ThePercentIncrease As Single, BillsIncrease As Currency
  If EntriesOk Then
    ThePercentIncrease = CSng(txtPercentage.Text) / 100
    BillsMoney = CCur(txtStockPrice.Text) * BillsShares
    BillsIncrease = ((1 + ThePercentIncrease) * BillsMoney) - BillsMoney
  Else
    MsgBox "Please check that you have entered numbers in the two text boxes"
    txtStockPrice.Text = vbNullString
    txtPercentage.Text= vbNullString
    txtStockPrice.SetFocus
    Exit Sub
  End If
  If optYear Then
```

```
      TheAmount = BillsIncrease
      ThePeriod = "Year"
   End If
   If optMonth Then
      TheAmount = BillsIncrease / 12
      ThePeriod = "Month"
   End If
   If optWeek Then
      TheAmount = BillsIncrease / 52
      ThePeriod = "Week"
   End If
   If optDay Then
      TheAmount = BillsIncrease / 365
      ThePeriod = "Day"
   End If
   If optHour Then
      TheAmount = BillsIncrease / (365 * 24)
      ThePeriod = "Hour"
   End If
   If optMinute Then
      TheAmount = BillsIncrease / (365& * 24 * 60)
      ThePeriod = "Minute"
   End If
   If optSecond Then
      TheAmount = BillsIncrease / (365& * 24 * 60 * 60)
      ThePeriod = "Second"
   End If
   txtResult.Text = "If Uncle Bill's stock goes up " _
      & txtPercentage.Text & " percent this year, then " & _
      "he makes an additional " & _
      Format(TheAmount, "Currency") & " per " & ThePeriod _
      & " from stock that will be worth " & _
      Format(BillsMoney * (1 + ThePercentIncrease), "Currency")
End Sub
Function EntriesOk() As Boolean
   EntriesOk = IsNumeric(txtStockPrice.Text) _
   And IsNumeric(txtPercentage.Text)
End Function
```

Check Boxes

Check boxes differ from option buttons in that, regardless of how many check boxes you place on a form, they can all be turned on and off independently. For this reason, placing check boxes in a frame is necessary only when you think it polishes the appearance of your form.

However, like option buttons, whether a check box is on or off is also determined by its Value property. If the user has selected a check box, the Value property switches to True. It stays True until the user deselects that box. (This is unlike the situation with option buttons, where selecting one of the buttons sets the value of all the others to False.) If you want a check box to be on when the project starts up, either set the Value property of the box to True at design time or set it to True in the Form_Load or Form_Initialize procedure.

14

As an example of where you might want to use check boxes, consider the following form:

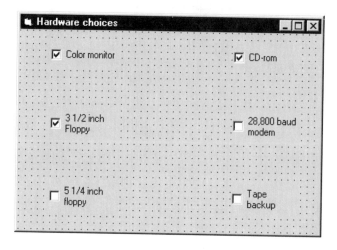

Notice that several of the check boxes are already on by default. (After all, most people want color monitors for their computers.) On the other hand, the user can choose no monitor by deselecting the check box.

You can combine check boxes and radio buttons. A good example of this is the Print dialog box on the File menu:

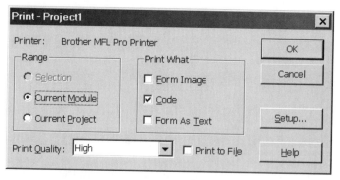

As with option buttons, check boxes will respond to the Click and Double-click events as well as to the key events. They will also detect whether a button has received or lost the focus. As with option buttons, Visual Basic generates the Click event when the user selects the button by clicking with the mouse or moving the focus via the TAB key and pressing SPACEBAR. If you reset the Value property of the button to True inside code, you also generate the Click event.

Scroll Bars

Scroll bars are used to receive input or display output when you don't care about an exact value but you do care whether the change is small or large. A good example of using scroll bars to accept input may be found in the Custom Color dialog box available from the color palette. As you saw in Chapter 3, this dialog box lets you adjust the amount of red, green, or blue for the custom color by moving the scroll bars. Although you can use the Color common dialog box to get this information (see the section "The Color Choice Box," later in this chapter), you may occasionally want to let users adjust the color of a form or picture box by using scroll bars. The upcoming example shows you how to code this.

Vertical scroll bars and horizontal scroll bars work the same way. Scroll bars span a range of values; the scroll box shows where the value is, relative to the two extremes. Scroll bars work with 9 events and 26 properties. The event that is the key to using scroll bars is the Change event. This is activated whenever the user manipulates the scroll bar.

Scroll Bar Properties

Only 5 of the 26 properties are special to scroll bars. What follows is a short description of those properties.

Min   An integer that defines the smallest value for a scroll bar. For red, green, or blue color codes, which range from 0 to 255, the Min property would be set to zero for a project that sets colors via scroll bars. Since Min takes integer values, the possible settings are from -32,768 to 32,767.

Max   An integer that defines the largest value for a scroll bar. For the primary color codes, the Max property would be set to 255 for a project that sets the colors via a scroll bar. Since Max takes integer values, the possible settings are from -32,768 to 32,767. You can set the Max value to be less than the Min value. This causes the maximum value of the scroll bar to be reached at the left or top of the scroll bar, depending on whether it's a horizontal or vertical scroll bar. Both Max and Min are usually set at design time, but you can change them with code while a project is running.

Value   Tells you where the scroll bar is. It is always an integer. The range is determined by the Min property and the Max property. The Value property can be as small as the Min value or as large as the Max value.

SmallChange   The setting for SmallChange determines how Visual Basic changes the Value property of the scroll bar in response to a user's clicking one of the scroll arrows. If the user clicks the up scroll arrow, the Value property of the scroll bar increases by the amount of SmallChange until the Value property reaches the value of the Max property. If the user clicks the down scroll arrow, Visual Basic decreases the Value property similarly. The default value of SmallChange is 1, and it can be set to

14

any integer between 1 and 32,767. As with Min and Max, this property is usually set at design time but can be changed in code as well.

LargeChange　　The setting for LargeChange determines how Visual Basic changes the Value property of the scroll bar in response to a user's clicking between the scroll box and the scroll arrow. The default LargeChange value is also 1 but is usually set to a multiple of the SmallChange value. It too is an integer between 1 and 32,767. As with Min, Max, and SmallChange, this property is usually set at design time but can also be changed at run time.

Example: Adjusting Color Codes via Scroll Bars

Suppose you want to begin an application by letting the user adjust the background and foreground colors. The initial form might look like the one in Figure 14-5. Notice that this application has three vertical scroll bars, a picture box, and two radio buttons.

Here is a table describing the important properties of the controls that make up this application:

Control Name	Property	Setting
vsbRedBar	Min	0
	Max	255
	SmallChange	5
	LargeChange	25
vsbGreenBar	Min	0
	Max	255
	SmallChange	5
	LargeChange	25
vsbBlueBar	Min	0
	Max	255
	SmallChange	5
	LargeChange	25
cmdBkColor	Caption	BackColor
cmdFrColor	Caption	ForeColor

Leave the picture box with the default name of Picture1. Here's an example of the first step in the code you would use for this project:

```
Sub vsbRedBar_Change()
  If cmdBkColor.Value Then
    Picture1.BackColor = RGB(vsbRedBar.Value,vsbGreenBar.Value, _
```

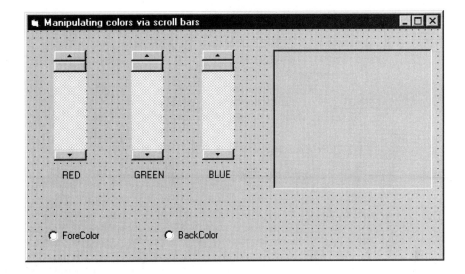

Form to adjust
color using
scroll bars
Figure 14-5.

```
vsbBlueBar.Value)
  ElseIf cmdFrColor.Value Then
    Picture1.ForeColor = RGB(vsbRedBar.Value,vsbGreenBar.Value, _
vsbBlueBar.Value)
    Picture1.Cls
    Picture1.Print "This is displayed in the current
foreground color."
  End If
End Sub
```

The other Change procedures would work the same way, which should immediately make you think that this is a perfect situation for using a general procedure attached to the form that does it once and for all. Here's the code for the more sophisticated version of this procedure:

```
Sub vsbRedBar_Change()
  ColorChange
End Sub

Sub ColorChange()
  If cmdBkColor.Value Then
    Picture1.BackColor = RGB(vsbRedBar.Value,vsbGreenBar.Value, _
vsbBlueBar.Value)
  ElseIf cmdFrColor.Value Then
    Picture1.ForeColor = RGB(vsbRedBar.Value,vsbGreenBar.Value, _
vsbBlueBar.Value)
    Picture1.Cls
    Picture1.Print "This is displayed in the current
foreground color."
```

14

```
    End If
End Sub
```

Notice that to show the ForeColor change requires displaying some text inside the picture box. Finally, notice that in an actual application, you would probably add a command button called Finished, perhaps, and have a click on that button hide this form, saving the BackColor and ForeColor information as the values of global variables to use for the other forms in your project. You might also combine all this code into a single general procedure that uses a color as the parameter.

Timers

Use a timer control whenever you want something to happen periodically. You might want to have a program that wakes up twice a day and checks stock prices. On a more prosaic level, if you want to display a "clock" on a form, you might want to update the clock's display every minute or even every second. Timers are not visible to the user; the icon appears only at design time. (Of course the effect of the timer will typically be visible to the user—but this depends on the code that you write!) Since users can't see the Timer control, where you place or how you size the timer control at design time is not important. (You can use one of the icons supplied with VB if you want to indicate to a user that a timer is ticking—also, having the appropriate audio file playing in the background would be even more professional!)

CAUTION: Although timers are an important tool for Visual Basic programmers, they shouldn't be overused; having too many timers waking up and doing things automatically will make your programs seem unresponsive to the user and goes against the spirit of VB.

The screen in Figure 14-6 shows an example of a form at design time with a label and a timer control that you can use to develop a simple clock (see "The Timer Event and Some Sample Uses").

Timer Properties
Besides the control name of the timer (the defaults are Timer1, Timer2, and so on), there are two important properties of timer controls: Enabled and Interval.

Enabled A Boolean (True/False) property that determines whether the timer should start ticking or not. If you set this to True at design time, the clock starts ticking when the form loads. Note that "ticking" is meant metaphorically; there's no noise unless you program one. Also, because timer controls are invisible to the user, he or she may well be unaware that a timer has been enabled. For this reason, you may want to notify the user that a timer is working, by means of a message box or picture box with a clock icon.

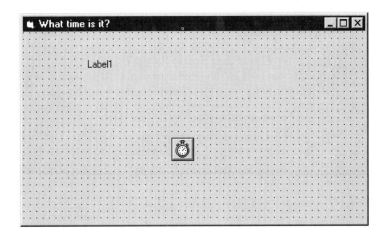

Form for a
simple clock
Figure 14-6.

If you set the Enabled property to False at design time, the timer control starts working only when you switch this property to True in code. Similarly, you can disable a timer in code by setting its Enabled property to False.

Interval Determines how much time Visual Basic waits before calling the Timer event procedure (see the next section). The interval is measured in milliseconds, and the theoretical limits are between 1 millisecond and 65,535 milliseconds (a little more than one minute and five seconds). The reason these are only theoretical limits is that the underlying hardware reports the passage of only 18 clock ticks per second. Since this is a little less than 56 milliseconds per clock tick, you can't really use an Interval property of any less than 56, and intervals that don't differ by at least this amount may give the same results.

The smaller you set the Interval property, the more CPU time is spent waking up the Timer event procedure. Set the Interval property too small and your system performance may slow to a crawl.

NOTE: An Interval property of zero disables the timer.

Finally, since the CPU may be doing something else when the interval time elapses, there is no guarantee that Visual Basic will call the Timer event procedure exactly when you want it. (Visual Basic will know when the interval has elapsed; either it or the underlying operating system just may need to finish what it is doing before

14

activating the Timer event.) If the interval has elapsed, Visual Basic will call the Timer event procedure as soon as it is free to do so. The next section explains how to deal with this problem.

The Timer Event and Some Sample Uses

Suppose you want to develop a project with a clock that will update itself every second, using the form shown in Figure 14-6. To design the form, follow these steps:

1. Add a label and a timer to a blank form.

2. Set the AutoSize property of the label to True and the Font.Size to 18. Set the Interval property of the timer control to 1000 (1000 milliseconds = 1 second).

3. Now write the following code in the Timer event procedure for the Timer1 control:

```
Sub Timer1_Timer()
   Label1.Caption = "The time is " + Format(Now,"Long Time")
End Sub
```

Visual Basic will call this event procedure and update the clock's time roughly every second because the Interval property is 1000. (See Chapter 6 for the Format function.) It would be easy enough to add an option button to let the user switch to an AM/PM display if he or she wanted.

Here is another example. One of the problems with computer screens is that they may be left on too long. This can (especially with older or cheaper monitors) cause an image to be burned into the screen, its ghostly presence interfering with efficient use of the monitor forever after. Screen-saving programs work by constantly drawing a different image in a different color, preventing burn-in. It is trivial to use a timer control to write a screen-saving program. While commercial programs provide beautiful images, the following project gives you a randomly colored, randomly placed "Press any key to end" message.

For this, start up a new project and add a timer control to the form. Next, make the BackColor property of the form be black. You can do this either by using the color palette or by directly setting the BackColor property color code to the color code for black (&H0&). Finally, since you want to have this form take over the whole screen, set the Border property of the form to None (0) and the WindowState property to Maximal (2).

Here's the code for the Timer1_Timer event procedure:

```
Sub Timer1_Timer()
  Dim X As Integer
  Cls
  X = DoEvents()
  CurrentX = Rnd*ScaleWidth
  CurrentY = Rnd*ScaleHeight
  ForeColor = QBColor(16*Rnd)
  Print "Press any key to end!"
End Sub
```

This program first clears the screen. Next, it calculates a random location on the screen and sets the ForeColor, randomly using the QBColor function. (See Chapter 16 for more on this function.) Of course, since you are taking a percentage of the screen height and width, this may occasionally not give the program enough room to display the full message. If this bothers you, you can easily add code using the TextHeight and TextWidth methods to make sure the text is always completely on the screen.

Now, having the program end when the user presses a key requires only a simple KeyDown event procedure to unload the form and the QueryUnload event to end.

```
Sub Form_KeyDown(KeyCode As Integer, Shift As Integer)
   Unload Me
End Sub

Private Sub Form_QueryUnload(Cancel As Integer, UnloadMode As Integer)
   End
End Sub
```

The KeyDown event is triggered whenever the user presses any key, thus ending the application.

To make this into a practical screen-saving program, you have to choose a value for the Interval property. A relatively large value such as 1000 (one second) or even 2000 (two seconds) for the Interval property seems to work best.

Next, suppose you want to have a Timer event procedure do something even less frequently than the maximum setting for the Interval property—much more slowly than once a minute. The trick is to add a static variable to the Timer event procedure. For example, suppose you want to have a Timer event procedure wake up only once an hour. Set the Interval property to 60,000 (one minute) and use the following code:

```
Sub Timer1_Timer()
   Static TimerTimes As Integer
   TimerTimes = TimerTimes + 1
   If TimerTimes = 60 Then
     TimerTimes = 0              'reset counter
     'Here's where the once an hour code would go
   Else
     Exit Sub
   End If
End Sub
```

The If clause is activated only when the counter TimerTimes reaches 60. But this happens only when the Timer event procedure has been called 60 times, because TimerTimes is a static variable. Now, put whatever code you want inside the If clause. That code will be processed only once an hour (because you reset TimerTimes back to 0).

14

Finally, to take into account the possibility that Visual Basic was doing something else exactly when the timer elapsed, you can add code inside the Timer event procedure to check the system clock if you feel this is necessary. (See Chapter 8 for the functions that check the clock.)

Common Dialog Boxes

While working with Windows and Visual Basic you've become accustomed to seeing one of the five standard "common" dialog boxes for opening or saving a file, printing, choosing fonts, or setting colors. Common dialog boxes are easy to use in principle, but they are somewhat less easy to use in practice. This is because they may require a fair amount of initializing to get them to look exactly the way you want. The online help is essential for working with common dialog boxes. This section can only give you a feeling for how to use them.

NOTE: The common dialog boxes take no actions; they accept information only. You will always need to write the code that gets Visual Basic to read off the information that is entered and then write the code that takes the appropriate actions when the user clicks OK.

The common dialog box control will probably need to be added to your toolbox (look for Microsoft CommonDialog Control 6.0 in the Project|Components dialog box). To use a common dialog box, you will need to place a common dialog control on the form. Here's a picture of this control:

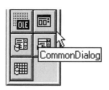

You determine which common dialog control pops up by applying one of the following methods to the common dialog control:

Method	Dialog Box
ShowSave	Shows a File Save dialog box
ShowOpen	Shows a File Open dialog box
ShowColor	Shows the color choice dialog box

Method	Dialog Box
ShowPrint	Shows the Print dialog box
ShowFont	Brings up the font choice dialog box

(You can also bring up the Windows help engine via a common dialog control. This is done with the ShowHelp method and is discussed at the end of this chapter.)

A Simple File Viewer Example

As an example of using a common dialog box, let's build a simple bitmap viewer. For this, start up a new project by selecting File|New Project. Make sure that you have added the Common Dialog control in the Project|Components dialog box. Add an image control for displaying graphics, and a command button. Use the default name of Image1 but set the command button to be named cmdShowBitmap. You will also want to set the caption of the command button to be "Show Bitmap". Finally, add a common dialog control. Your screen will look like Figure 14-7.

You now need to set the Filter properties of the common dialog control so that only files with the .bmp extension, which indicates a bitmap file, will be shown. Set the Filter property of the common dialog control to Bitmaps|*.bmp. Next, enter the text **Choose bitmap** as the value of the DialogTitle property. (This property controls the title bar of the dialog box.) Since you want to show an Open File dialog box, you use the ShowOpen method, which tells Visual Basic to display the File Open common dialog box. Here's all the code you need to get the most primitive form of the bitmap viewer working:

```
Private cmdShowBitmap_Click()
  CommonDialog1.ShowOpen
  Image1.Picture = LoadPicture(CommonDialog1.FileName)
End Sub
```

That's it. If you run this project, you'll be presented with an ordinary Windows dialog box (with the caption "Choose Bitmap") that will be restricted to displaying only files with the .bmp extension. You can navigate among the directories on your drives by clicking and double-clicking as is usual with any common dialog box in Windows. Find a bitmap, click on OK, and Visual Basic will display the bitmap on the form.

TIP: You'll find a large number of bitmaps in the directories under \Graphics \Bitmaps, within the directory containing VB or the common subdirectory of Visual Studio.

14

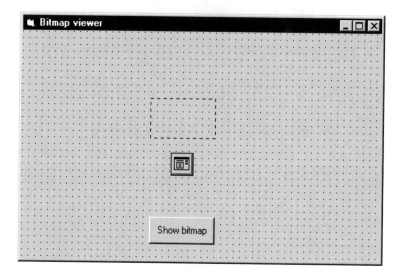

Of course, this is by no means a bulletproof application: if the user selects a
non-image file, the application will crash. Also, if the user selects the Cancel button,
one cannot be sure of what might happen! (The next section explains how to deal
with these problems.)

Working with Common Dialog Boxes

As you saw in the preceding example, before you pop up a dialog box, you need to
initialize the various properties that determine how the common dialog box looks. As
with any Visual Basic object, this can be done at run time or design time.

The first problem you encounter when using a common dialog property in real life is
distinguishing between the user clicking the OK button (in which case you want to
use the information) and clicking the Cancel button (in which case you don't want to
do anything). All the common dialog boxes can generate an error if the user clicks the
Cancel button. Whether they *will* generate the error depends on the current value of
the CancelError property. If you want to trap a user clicking the Cancel button, either
set this property to True at design time or use code like:

> *[FormName]*.*CommonDialogControlName*.CancelError = True

The default is False, so that no error is reported when the Cancel button is clicked.
However, it is hard to imagine a use of the common dialog control that would not
require trapping this error!

The reason why setting the CancelError property to True and then trapping this error
is important is that whether the user clicks OK or Cancel, certain property values of
the common dialog control may have been changed. For example, a user may have

entered a new filename, changed his or her mind, and clicked the Cancel button. However, the FileName property of the common dialog box would still have changed. Since you only want to use the information when the OK button is clicked, you must have a way to know whether the Cancel button was used to close the dialog box. This is done with an error trap. For example, here's a modification of the image viewer that uses an error trap to detect whether the Cancel button was pressed—in which case you do nothing.

```
Private cmDShowBitmap_Click()
  Dim TheFile As String
  CommonDialog1.CancelError = True
  On Error GoTo DoNothing
 CommonDialog1.ShowOpen
  TheFile = CommonDialog1.FileName
  If Right(TheFile, 3) = "bmp" Then
  Image1.Picture = LoadPicture(CommonDialog1.FileName)
  End If
   Exit Sub
DoNothing:
  If Err.Number= cdlCANCEL Then
    'do nothing, Cancel button clicked
  Else
    MsgBox Err.Description 'you have a real error to handle
  End If
End Sub
```

More on the File Open and File Save Dialog Boxes

Just as the ShowOpen method is used to show an Open dialog box, the ShowSave method is used to display the File Save dialog boxes. Other than that, the properties are essentially the same for both these dialog boxes. For example, you use the CancelError property the same way for both dialog boxes. Similarly, the DialogTitle property lets you set the text for the title bar. Note that you do not need to use Open and Save as the titles of these boxes if you are using them in other contexts.

Here is a table with descriptions of the most important properties used for these dialog boxes:

Property	What It Does
DefaultExt	Sets the default extension for files shown in the box.
FileName	Gives the name and full path of the file selected.
FileTitle	Gives the filename *without* the path.
Filter	Affects the Type box in the dialog box. You saw an example of this earlier when the example bitmap viewer used a Filter property of Bitmaps|*.bmp. You can have multiple filters by separating them with a pipe symbol (| = CHR$(124) found usually above the backslash on your keyboard). In general, the format is the description string, the pipe symbol, the filter, another pipe symbol, and so on.

14

Property	What It Does
FilterIndex	This is used when you set up many filters using the Filter property.
Flags	This property is used to set various possible options on how the box will look or behave (explained in the next section).
InitDir	Specifies the initial directory.
MaxFileSize	Sets the maximum size of the filename, including all the path info.

More on the Flags Property of the File Dialog Boxes

The Flags property is very important in determining the final look and feel of the box. For example, a line of code like

```
CommonDialog1.Flags = cdlOFNAllowMultiselect
```

allows the File name list box to use multiple selections. You can combine more than one flag by adding them together. You read back their current values using bit-masking techniques with the And operator. The following summarizes the most important of the possible flags for the File dialog boxes.

NOTE: You must set the values of the Flags property before you display the dialog box.

cdlOFNAllowMultiselect This flag (as you just saw) allows multiselection using the standard Windows techniques of holding down the SHIFT key and using the UP ARROW and DOWN ARROW keys to select the desired files.

NOTE: If you allow multiselection, the value of the FileName property is a string containing the names of all selected files. Each filename is separated from the next by spaces, so you can use the standard techniques you have already seen for parsing text to identify them.

cdlOFNCreatePrompt Suppose you are generally going to be working with existing files. This flag lets you give users a warning that they are using a new filename. When you set the Flags property to this constant, Visual Basic pops up a message box that asks the user if he or she wants to create the file when it doesn't already exist, as shown next:

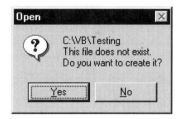

Setting this flag automatically sets the cdlOFNPathMustExist and cdlOFNFileMustExist flags.

cdlOFNExtensionDifferent   After the user clicks on OK, you can analyze the current value of the Flags property to see if it contains this constant (use the And operator). You may need to do this because you will often need to know if the user is using a nonstandard extension on a file. If you set the Flags property to this value at design time, Visual Basic will let you determine after the user closes the dialog box whether the user has specified a filename with an extension different from the one specified in the DefaultExt property. After the dialog box is closed, you could use code that begins like this:

```
If (CommonDialog1.Flags And cdlOFNExtensionDifferent) = _
cdlOFNExtensionDifferent Then 'has a different extension
```

Note that this flag isn't set if the DefaultExt property is Null, if the extensions match, or if the file has no extension.

cdlOFNFileMustExist   If you set this flag, a message box pops up if the user tries to enter a file that doesn't already exist. This flag automatically sets the cdlOFNPathMustExist flag as well.

cdlOFNHideReadOnly, cdlOFNReadOnly   The first flag hides the Read Only check box. The second flag sets the Read Only check box to be checked when the dialog box first appears. (You can also check whether the return value of the Flags property contains this value by bit masking. This lets you check the state of the Read Only check box when the user closes the dialog box.)

cdlOFNNoChangeDir   If you don't want the user to be able to change the directory from its initial setting, set this flag.

cdlOFNNoValidate   This allows the common dialog box to use invalid characters in the returned filename. (This is useful if you are not actually using the name entered as the filename but only as an identifier.)

14

cdlOFNOverwritePrompt   If you use ShowSave and the file already exists, Visual Basic will pop up a message box asking the user to confirm that he or she wants to overwrite the file.

cdlOFNPathMustExist   If you set this flag, the user can't enter an invalid path without generating a warning message box.

cdlOFNShareAware   If this flag is set, Windows will ignore sharing violation errors.

cdlOFNHelpButton   This flag makes the dialog box display a Help button.

cdlOFNLongNames   This flag controls whether you can use long filenames or are restricted to the older Windows 3.1 "8+3" rules.

The Color Choice Box

To show the Color dialog box, you use the ShowColor method of the common dialog control. The Flags property also controls how this box appears, and the symbolic constants for this box also begin with "cdl".
For example, if

```
CommonDialog1.Flags = cdlCCFullOpen
```

then the entire Color dialog box is displayed. If, on the other hand,

```
CommonDialog1.Flags = cdlCCPreventFullOpen
```

then you will disable the Define Custom Colors section of the dialog box. (The other constants are cdlCCRGBInit, which lets you set the initial color value, and cdlCCHelpButton, which determines whether you see a Help button or not.)

As always, you need to check whether the user clicked the Cancel button before using the value of, for example, CMDialog1.Color to get the color. (This is a long integer for the color, selected using the &HRRGGBB& code you have seen before.)

The Font Choice Box

You pop up this dialog box by using the ShowFont method of the common dialog control. However, before showing the remaining properties for this box, you'll need to know something about how the Flags property works here. Since you might want to have the font choice box reflect printer fonts only, screen fonts only, or both at once, Visual Basic requires you to set the Flags parameter correctly before it will display the Font dialog box. The symbolic constants used are cdlCFPrinterFonts, cdlCFScreenFonts, and cdlCFBoth. If you don't set the Flags property of the common dialog control to one of these three values and still try to show the Font box, the program generates an error and dies.

There are 15 different Flags property values for the font dialog box. As always, you combine them using the Or operator. Here is a table with descriptions of the remaining values for the Flags property.

Flag	What It Does
cdlCFHelpButton	Determines whether the dialog box displays a Help button.
cdlCFEffects	Determines whether you want to allow strikeout, underline, and color effects.
cdlCFApply	Determines whether the dialog box enables the Apply button.
cdlCFANSIOnly	Determines whether the dialog box displays only the fonts that include the Windows character set.
cdlCFNoVectorFonts	Determines whether the dialog box should not display vector-based fonts.
cdlCFNoSimulations	Determines whether the dialog box will not allow graphic device interface (GDI) font simulations.
cdlCFLimitSize	Determines whether the dialog box should show only font sizes between those specified by the Max and Min properties (see the next table).
cdlCFFixedPitchOnly	Determines whether the dialog box should display only fixed-pitch fonts.
cdlCFWYSIWYG	Determines whether the dialog box should show only fonts common to both the screen and printer.
cdlCFForceFontExist	Determines whether a message box pops up if a user selects a font or style that doesn't exist.
cdlCFScalableOnly	Determines whether the dialog box will allow the user to only select scalable fonts, such as TrueType fonts.
cdlCFTTOnly	Specifies that the dialog box should allow the user to select only TrueType fonts.
cdlCFNoFaceSel	This is returned if no font name is selected.
cdlCFNoStyleSel	This is returned if no font style is selected.
cdlCFNoSizeSel	This is returned if no font size is selected.

(As usual, you can determine which flag was returned using bit masking with the And operator.)

14

Here is a table with descriptions of the most important properties of the Font dialog box:

Property	Use
Color	Only used for color printers.
FontBold, FontItalic, FontStrikeThru, FontUnderline	True/False properties. If the cdlCFEffects flag is set, you can allow the user to choose these properties.
FontName	Sets or returns the font name.
FontSize	Sets or returns the font size.
Max, Min	These affect the point sizes shown in the size box. You need to have the cdlCFLimitSize flag set before you can use these properties.

You read back the value of the various font properties to see what the user wants. For example, the value of CommonDialog1.FontName is the name of the font the user chose. Then you can have Visual Basic process the code to have the new value go into effect.

The Printer Dialog Box

As before, the Flags property controls how the box appears. For example, if the flag parameter is cdlPDAllPages, then the All option button in the Print Range frame is set. Again, this means you will need bit-masking techniques to determine what the user did with the box. Use code like this:

```
If (CMDialog1.Flags And cdlPDAllPages) = cdlPDAllPages Then
   'all pages button checked
```

Here is a table with the flags for this dialog box:

Flag	What It Does
cdlPDAllPages	Returns the value or sets the All Pages option button.
cdlPDCollate	Returns the value or sets the Collate check box.
cdlPDDisablePrintToFile	Disables the Print to File check box.
cdlPDHidePrintToFile	Hides the Print to File check box.
cdlPDNoPageNums	Returns the value or sets the Pages option button.
cdlPDNoSelection	Disables the Selection option button.

Flag	What It Does
cdlPDNoWarning	Prevents Visual Basic from issuing a warning message when there is no default printer.
cdlPDPageNums	Returns the value or sets the Pages option button.
cdlPDPrintSetup	Displays the Print Setup dialog box rather than the Print dialog box.
cdlPDPrintToFile	Returns the value or sets the Print to File check box.
cdlPDReturnDC	Returns a device context for the printer selection from the hDC property of the dialog box.
cdlPDReturnDefault	Returns the default printer name.
cdlPDReturnIC	Returns an information context for the printer selection value from the hDC property of the dialog box.
cdlPDSelection	Returns the value or sets the Selection option button.
cdlPDHelpButton	Determines whether the dialog box displays the Help button.
cdlPDUseDevModeCopies	Sets support for multiple copies. (This, of course, depends on whether or not the printer supports multiple copies.)

The following table contains descriptions of the remaining properties you are likely to use for the Printer dialog boxes:

Property	Use
Copies	Sets or returns the number of copies the user wants.
FromPage, ToPage	Specifies what pages are wanted.
hDC	This is the device context number. It is used for API function calls.
Max, Min	Specifies the maximum and minimum pages the user can put in the Print Range frame.
PrinterDefault	Set this to True and the user can click the Setup button to change the WIN.INI file.

14

The Microsoft Windows Common Controls 6.0

You can add the eight basic Windows 95 common controls to your toolbar in one fell swoop by choosing Microsoft Windows Common Controls 6.0 from the Project|Components dialog box. This section gives you brief descriptions of these controls.

TIP: If you add the controls and can't see all of them in your toolbox, try widening the toolbox. Also, all these controls will have a (Custom) item in the Properties window. Clicking on this gives you a quick way to work with the most common properties of these controls.

NOTE: Some versions of VB come with two extra sets of "common controls." The first set includes a neat Animation and Calendar (Date Picker) control. The second set includes the "coolbar" control for making Internet Explorer type interfaces. If you have these controls, check out the online help for more details.

ImageList Control

The ImageList control gives you another way to store a group of images in a single place. You can then use these images in other parts of your application (for example, as the images used in a toolbar). The key to working with an ImageList control is knowing about ListImage objects (and the ListImages collection), which specify the images stored in the control. (You can think of an ImageList control as a container for a ListImages collection.) The easiest way to work with an ImageList control is via its (Custom) property, which pops up the Property Pages dialog box that looks like this:

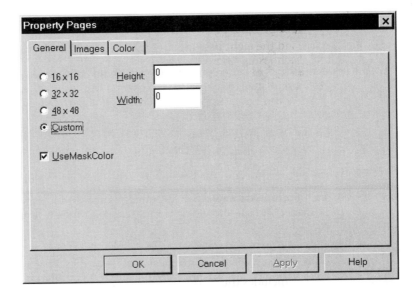

The Images tab on this dialog box (shown next) gives you a convenient way to add images at design time.

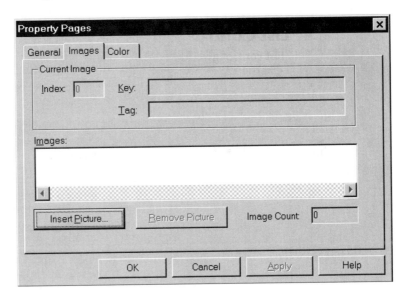

(At run time, you can add images to the ListImages collection using the Add method.)

As long as all the images are the same size, the ImageList control can store both bitmaps and icons at the same time. As with all collections (see Chapter 13), you can refer to the items (images) stored in the ListImages collection either by an index or a key. For example, suppose you have assigned an image to ImageList1.ListImages(1), then,

```
Set Picture1.Picture = ImageList1.ListImages(1).Picture ' Set Picture
```

fills the picture box with the first image. (The ListImages collection starts at 1.)

You are not limited to any particular image size, but the total number of images that can be loaded is limited by the amount of available memory.

TIP: The ListImage control need not be used as a passive storage container. The Overlay method creates a composite image from two images.

ListView Control

The ListView control lets you display items in various ways—essentially the ways you see when working with the Windows desktop. You can use this control to arrange items into columns (with or without column headings). The items can be accompanied by both icons and text. The value of the View property, as described in the following table, determines what the user sees.

Constant	Value	Description
lvwIcon	0	(Default) Each ListItem object is represented by a full-sized icon and a label.
lvwSmallIcon	1	Each ListItem object is represented by a small icon and a label that appears to the right of the icon. The different items are arranged horizontally.
lvwList	2	Each ListItem object is also represented by a small icon and a text label that appears to the right of the icon. The ListItem objects are vertical on different lines, and the text information is organized into columns.

Constant	Value	Description
lvwReport	3	Each ListItem object is displayed with a small icon and a label. The icons and labels appear in columns. (Additional columns are used to display additional text.)

The items displayed in the ListView control are called, naturally enough, ListItem objects. A ListItem object has its own properties that describe the item, the most important of which are shown in the following table.

Property	Description
Icons	Returns or sets the index or key for the icon associated with the ListItem object.
Selected	Tells you whether the ListItem was selected (or selects it).
SmallIcons	Returns or sets the index or key for the small icon associated with the ListItem object.
SubItems	Returns or sets the string representing the data for the subitem associated with a specific ListItem.
Text	As you might expect, this is the text the user sees.

Finally, you can choose to display column headings in the ListView control by setting the value of the True/False HideColumnHeaders property. The actual heading is stored in the ColumnHeader object, and all the column headers are stored in the ColumnHeaders collection.

TIP: To conserve system resources, you can bind an ImageList control to a ListView control. To do this, set the Icons and SmallIcons properties of the ListView control to the ImageList control(s). You can also specify the associated ImageList control at design time, using the (Custom) property dialog box.

ProgressBar Control

The ProgressBar control is similar to using a vertical bar in the gauge control. It fills in a bar with rectangular chunks. The key properties are described next.

Use the Align property to position the control where you want it. The possible values are described in the following table.

14

Setting	Description
0	(Default) Size and location are arbitrary.
1	Bar is at the top of the form, and it is as wide as the form.
2	Bar is at the bottom of the form, and it is as wide as the form.
3	Bar is left-aligned at the edge of the form, and it is as tall as the form.
4	Bar is right-aligned at the edge of the form, and it is as tall as the form.

Much like a scroll bar, you specify the Min and Max properties to give the range of values the progress bar will show. The Value property specifies the current position within that range.

TIP: To display more chunks, decrease the control's height or increase its width.

For example, suppose you want to give people a feeling of time passing in some way. Add a timer control, a label, and a progress bar, as shown here:

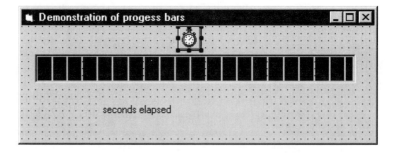

Now set the Min property of the progress bar to 0 and the Max property to 60. Set the Interval property of the Timer control to 1000 (one second). The following code will show you how the progress bar updates itself (compared to the seconds actually elapsed).

```
Private Sub Timer1_Timer()
  Static Progress As Integer
  Progress = (Progress + 1) Mod 60
  Label1.Caption = Str$(Progress) & " seconds elapsed."
  ProgressBar1.Value = Progress
End Sub
```

Slider Control

The Slider control works similarly to a scroll bar. It is a little box with optional tick marks that contains a slider, as shown here:

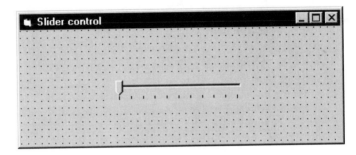

The user can move the slider by dragging it, clicking the mouse to either side of the slider, or using the keyboard. Just as for scroll bars, the key properties are Max, Min, and Value, which determine the largest, smallest, and current values for the slider. The key event is the Scroll event, which is triggered when the user moves the slider on a Slider control, either by clicking on the control or using the keyboard.

StatusBar Control

The StatusBar control gives you a window (usually at the bottom of a form) that you can use to display the status of the application. (For example, word processors such as Microsoft Word use a status bar to tell you where you are on a page, whether you are in insert mode or overstrike mode, and so on.) The Align property governs where the status bar appears. It has the same values as the Align property for a progress bar.

Each status bar can be divided into (at most) 16 panels. At design time you can add the individual panels by using the Panels page of the custom property dialog box, as shown here:

14

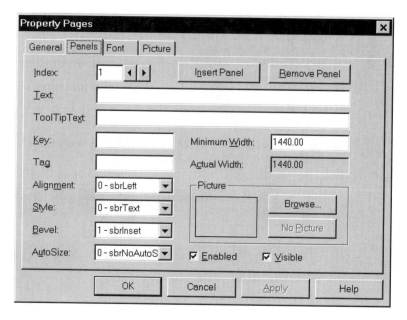

You can add both text and a picture to the panel by working with this dialog box. At run time you will usually use the Add method by first declaring a variable of Panel type and then using the Add method with a syntax that looks like this,

Set *PanelObject* = *NameOfStatusBar*.Panels.Add([*index*], [*key*], [*text*], [*style*], [*picture*])

where all the parameters are optional. (Since this method does not support named arguments, you need commas for the items you leave out.) The *index* parameter specifies the index where the panel will be added. If you leave it out, the item goes after all the existing panels. (Since you can have at most 16 panels, the index must be between 1 and 16.) The *key* parameter (as in any collection) gives you another way to refer to the items. The *text* parameter is the text for the panel. The *style* property lets you specify how the information appears in the status bar. The values for this parameter are shown in the following table.

Constant	Description
sbrText	(Default) Text and/or a bitmap. Set text with the Text property; set the picture with the LoadPicture method.
sbrCaps	Caps lock. Displays the letters CAPS in bold when CAPS LOCK is enabled; otherwise they are dimmed.
sbrNum	Number lock. Displays the letters NUM in bold when the NUM LOCK key is enabled; otherwise they are dimmed.
sbrIns	Displays the letters INS in bold when the INS key is enabled; otherwise they are dimmed.

Constant	Description
sbrScrl	Displays the letters SCRL in bold when SCROLL LOCK is enabled; otherwise they are dimmed.
sbrTime	Displays the current time in the current system format.
sbrDate	Displays the current date in the current system format.

Finally, the optional *picture* parameter specifies the bitmap. For example,

```
Private Sub Form_Load()
  Dim MyPanel As Panel

  StatusBar1.Panels(1).Text = "Default panel exists already"
  Set MyPanel = StatusBar1.Panels.Add(, , , sbrTime)
  Set MyPanel = StatusBar1.Panels.Add(, ,"Panel demo")
  Set MyPanel = StatusBar1.Panels.Add(, , , LoadPicture _
("C:\VB\ICONS\TRAFFIC\TRFFC01.ICO"))    ' may change depending on your machine
End Sub
```

would give you a status bar like this:

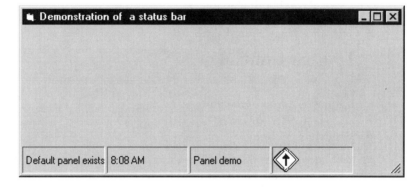

Notice that you need to use an object variable because you want to create the panel as well as refer to its properties. You could have replaced this with two lines of code, by adding the panel first. For example:

```
MyPanel = StatusBar1.Panels.Add
MyPanel = StatusBar1.Panels(2).Text = "Panel demo" 'remember they
'start at 0 so this is the THIRD panel'
```

The next useful property of the Panel object associated with a status bar is the AutoSize property, which has three possibilities, as described in the following table.

14

Constant	Description
sbrNoAutoSize	(Default) No automatic resizing occurs.
sbrSpring	When the parent form resizes and extra space is available, the panel resizes by dividing the available space and growing or shrinking accordingly. (The panel's width is always at least the current value of the status bar's MinWidth property.)
sbrContents	The panel resizes to fit its contents if space is available.

NOTE: Occasionally you will want a status bar to have only one item. (For example, many programs use this type of status bar to explain a menu item but return to displaying more general status information when the menu bar is closed.) To do this, set the Style property to Simple (sbrSimple is the constant to use at run time). Then, use the SimpleText property for the actual text.

TabStrip Control

A TabStrip control provides another way to give a form the look of a tabbed dialog box. However, since it is not a container, it is not as flexible as the tabbed dialog box that you have already seen, so I won't cover it here.

Toolbar Control

The Toolbar control makes it easy to build toolbars into your Windows 95 projects. Features like ToolTips come essentially for free (see the section on ToolTips coming up shortly). First off, the Align property that you have already seen controls where the toolbar appears. Normally, toolbars appear on the top, so the Align property defaults to 1 (Top).

Next, if you want images to appear in your toolbar, you must first store them in an ImageList control (either at design time or run time). *If you intend to set the images at design time, the associated ImageList control must be on the same form as the toolbar control.* After the images are stored in an ImageList control, you set the ImageList property of the Toolbar control to be the name of the ImageList control. For example, add a Toolbar control and an ImageList control to a blank form at design time using the default names. If you look at the General page of the toolbar's Property Pages dialog box, you can see that the ImageList drop-down list box will show the ImageList1 control.

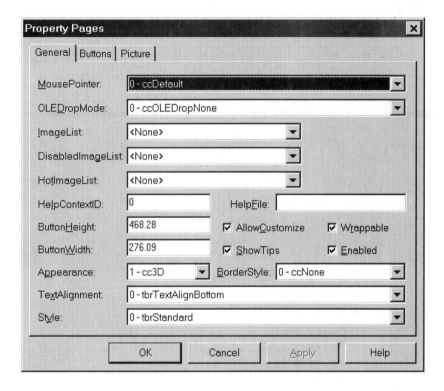

Once you have associated the ImageList control, the next (Buttons) page of this dialog box lets you associate the images stored in the ImageList control with the buttons. You do that by setting the Image text box on this page to the number of the image in the ImageList control. In the example shown here, the second button is associated with the first image (0) stored in the ImageList control.

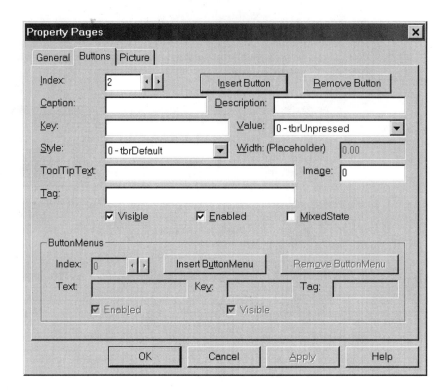

TIP: If you run the Application Wizard, you can see a good example of how the Toolbar and ImageList controls interact in a complete application. The wizard uses these controls to build up the toolbar from the tools you selected.

NOTE: The Professional and Enterprise editions of VB come with a "coolbar" control in "The Windows Common Controls 3" that lets you create toolbars similar to the one in Internet Explorer 4.0. See the online help for more on the coolbar.

Example: Working with the Toolbar at Run Time
The Toolbar control holds a collection of button objects. At run time you must use the Add and Remove methods to add the buttons. As you might expect, each

button has a ButtonClick event that lets you take actions depending on which button is clicked.

The usual way to use the Add method is to declare an object variable to be of Button type. Then the syntax for using the Add method looks like this,

Set *ButtonObject* = *NameOfToolbar*.Buttons.Add([*index*], [*key*], [*caption*], [*style*], [*image*])

where all the parameters are optional. (Since this method does not support named arguments, you will need commas for the items you leave out.) The *index* parameter specifies the index where the button will be added. If you leave it out, the button goes at the end. The *key* parameter (as in any collection) gives you another way to refer to the buttons. The *caption* parameter is the text that will appear beneath the Button object. The *style* property lets you specify how the button appears. The values for this parameter are shown in the following table.

Constant	Description
tbrDefault	(Default) The button is a regular push button.
tbrCheck	The button is a check button.
tbrButtonGroup	The button is part of a button group. This means that the button remains pressed until another button in the group is pressed. Only one button in a group can be pressed at any one time.
tbrSeparator	The button is simply a separator. (It will have a fixed width of eight pixels.)
tbrPlaceholder	The button is a variable width separator.

Finally, the *image* parameter is the index or key that describes which image you want from the previously associated ImageList control.

As with Panel objects, you can first add the button and then describe its properties. For example, if you have added only one button at design time with a caption of "First button" then,

```
Toolbar1.Buttons.Add
Toolbar1.Buttons(2).Caption = "Second button"
Toolbar1.Buttons.Add
Toolbar1.Buttons(3).Caption = "Third button"
```

gives you a toolbar that looks like this:

14

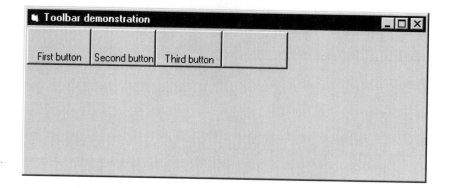

NOTE: Unless you set the AllowCustomize property to False, Visual Basic will pop up the Customize Toolbar dialog box when the user double-clicks on a toolbar at run time, which allows the user to hide, display, or rearrange the toolbar buttons. See the online help for more on run-time customization of toolbars.

ToolTips

Providing ToolTips, the little labels that appear below a tool whenever the mouse moves over the tool and remains there for about one second, can be done automatically. To display ToolTips for a Toolbar control, you must:

1. Set the ShowTips property to True.
2. Set the ToolTipText property of each button object to the text you want as your ToolTip.

TreeView Control

The TreeView control, as its name suggests, lets you build an outline similar to the one used in Windows Explorer. The individual objects are usually called nodes, and the TreeView control has a Nodes collection that holds information about the nodes in the control. The highest node is given by the Root property. For more on the TreeView control, consult the online help.

Microsoft Comm Control 6.0

The communications control makes it easy for you to design a communi- cations package that works over ordinary phone lines (not the Internet!). You can customize it for your needs by setting some of its many properties. (In VB6 it is limited to 256,000 baud—more than enough for most applications.) The various properties of this control let you set the communications port and the settings needed, such as baud rate, number of data bits, and parity. As you would expect, an event-driven language is ideal for dealing with communications. You can program the communications custom control so that it wakes up only when your hardware detects activity at a communications port, for example.

NOTE: For communicating via the Internet using the Microsoft WebBrowser Control 6.0, please see Chapter 24.

The following table summarizes the key properties of the communications control.

Property	Description
CommEvent	This is the key property for the communications control. The various values of this property correspond to either events or errors in the communications port. For example, if the value of this property is the constant comEvEOF (= 7), then the traditional end-of-file character (ASCII character 26) was received in the buffer.
CommPort	Sets and returns the communications port; use a 1 for COM1, 2 for COM2, and so on.
Settings	Sets and returns the baud rate, parity, data bits, and stop bits. Can be set at design or run time.
PortOpen	Opens and closes a communications port.
Input	Removes characters from the receive buffer.
Output	Writes a string of characters to the transmit buffer.

The only event for the communications control is the OnComm event. This is triggered whenever the value of the CommEvent property changes. Thus, by analyzing the current value of the CommEvent property in the OnComm event, you can have your code take the actions you want.

Like many custom controls, the communications control gives you a dialog box to set many of its properties more easily. Simply go to the Properties window and click on the (Custom) property. If you click on this property, you get a dialog box that lets you set the special properties of the custom control. Here's a picture of this dialog box for the communications control:

14

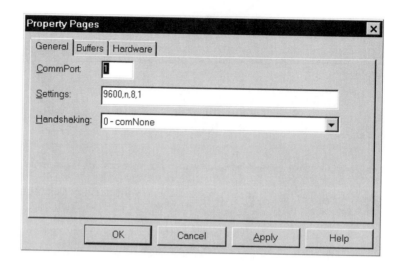

Example: Using the Communications Control

As a simple example of using the communications control, suppose you want to check what is coming into one of the COM ports after a button click. (COM1 is used in this example.)

```
Private Sub cmdGetData_Click ()
  Dim Foo As Integer, TheData As String
  MsComm1.CommPort = 1  ' COM1
  '28800 baud, no parity, 8 data, and 1 stop bit.
  MsComm1.Settings = "28800,N,8,1"
  MsComm1.InputLen = 0  ' Clear the comm buffer
  MsComm1.PortOpen = True
  'Send the usual wake up signal to the modem.
  MsComm1.Output = "AT" + Chr$(13)
  Do
    Foo = DoEvents()
    MsComm1.InputLen = 0  'clear buffer
    TheData = TheData + MsComm1.Input 'TheData will contain the data
  Loop Until MsComm1.CommEvent = comEvEOF
  MsComm1.PortOpen = False 'close the port
End Sub
```

Microsoft Masked Edit Control 6.0

The masked edit control can save you a lot of code work when you are trying to control the input to text boxes. For most purposes, this control will seem like an ordinary text box. The difference is that you can restrict the characters entered without having to write code in the Key events (see Chapter 7 for discussions of these events). Similarly, you can show certain characters in the control—to give users a visual cue that they should be entering a phone number or a social security number, for example. This control is data-aware. (See Chapter 22 for information on using data-aware controls.)

The most important property when working with the masked edit control is, naturally enough, the Mask property. You can set this property at both design time and run time. This property controls what the user sees and what he or she can enter. For example, if you wanted to allow only a standard U.S. phone number to be entered, you would set the Mask property to:

```
MaskEdBox1.Mask = "(###)-###-####"
```

This would result in a masked edit control that looks like this:

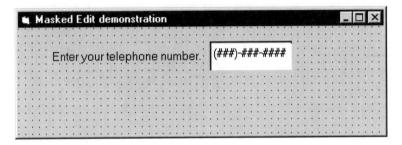

(At design time you would not use the quotes in the Properties window, of course.)

The masked edit control also has a Property Pages dialog box for its custom properties, as shown next:

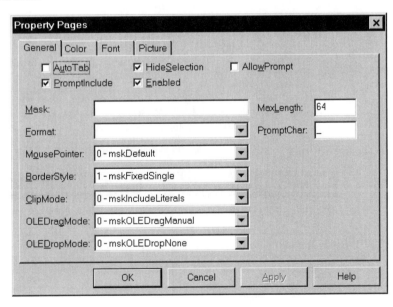

14

In general, the strings for the Mask property work much like format strings in the Format statement (see Chapter 6), so the # in the preceding example means a digit, and the hyphen (-) appears as a literal on the screen.

The following table summarizes the most common characters used in masks.

Mask Character	Description
#	Requires the user to enter a digit only.
.	Decimal placeholder. Which character the user sees depends on the current Windows settings.
,	Thousands separator. Again, which character the user sees depends on the current Windows settings.
:	Time separator.
/	Date separator.
?	Letter placeholder, for example: a-z or A-Z.
& (also C)	Allows the user to enter a single ANSI character in the ranges 32-126 and 128-255 only.
>	Converts all the characters that follow to uppercase.
<	Converts all the characters that follow to lowercase.
A	Requires that an alphanumeric character be entered.
a	Allows an alphanumeric character to be entered.
9	Allows a digit to be entered.

For example, a mask of "a9" would allow but not require the user to enter two characters. The first can be any alphanumeric character; the second would have to be a digit.

All other symbols are displayed as themselves. (If you want to have one of the special characters show up, precede it with a backslash (\). For example, using "\##" as a mask would show up as # followed by a blank where the user can enter a digit.

At design time you can use the following predefined masks:

Mask	Description
empty string (vbNullString in code)	(Default) No mask; makes the Masked Edit box work like a standard text box
##-???-##	Medium date (U.S.)
##-##-##	Short date (U.S.)
##:## ??	Medium time
##:##	Short time

The only unusual event in dealing with input to a Masked Edit box is the ValidationError event. This is triggered whenever a user tries to enter an invalid character. (The Masked Edit box prevents invalid characters from being entered—you might want to know if the user tried.)

Microsoft Multimedia Control

Multimedia devices, such as CD-ROM players, have become omnipresent on PCs. The idea of combining text, images, and sound on a computer is clearly the way of the future. The multimedia control lets users initiate what are called *media control interface* (MCI) commands. MCI commands are designed to be device independent and to control audiovisual peripherals. You use the multimedia device control to tell the multimedia device to start up, move forward, move back, pause, and so on. Since the multimedia control has about 60 properties, we can't cover it fully here, but roughly speaking, here's how it works. (Note that it does have a custom property page to make it easier to set properties at design time.)

To begin with, the multimedia control looks like this when you place it on a form:

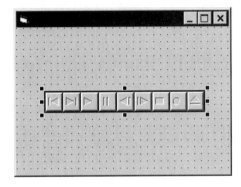

As you can see, it is a set of push buttons with the names: Prev, Next, Play, Pause, Back, Step, Stop, Record, and Eject.

Each time the user clicks on one of these buttons, you need to issue the correct MCI command. Before you can do this, though, you have to decide if you want to:

◆ Allow the user to control the action via clicks on the various buttons

◆ Control the multimedia action yourself

In the first situation, set the Visible and Enabled properties of the control to be True (usually this is done in the Form_Load event procedure). In the second situation, leave the control invisible and disabled.

14

For an example of the simplest use of the multimedia control—playing back a WAV (.wav) file without any checking about the nature of the file:

1. Add a text box for the name of the WAV file.

2. Add a command button to a blank form.

3. Add a multimedia control with the Visible and Enabled properties set to False.

4. Then use the following Form_Load to let the multimedia control do its job "in the background."

```
Private Sub Form_Load ()
  'Set the properties needed by the MCI control to work
  MMControl1.Notify = False
  MMControl1.Wait = True
  MMControl1.Shareable = False
  MMControl1.DeviceType = "WaveAudio"
End Sub
```

5. Now place the following lines in the Command1_Click procedure:

```
Sub Command1_Click()
  MMControl1.FileName = Text1.Text
  MMControl1.Command = "Open" 'play the file named in the
                             'textbox
End Sub
```

That's it!

Microsoft Picture Clip Control 6.0

The picture clip control gives you another way to store bitmaps in one control. Just as with animated buttons, this conserves Windows resources and speeds up access to the image. The obvious place to use this control is if you are adding a toolbox of controls to a Visual Basic project for the user to manipulate. Instead of loading each tool as a separate bitmap, you could use a picture clip to build them in all at once. The problem is that you need to build up the bitmap that contains the images first.

TIP: One way to build up multiple bitmaps into a single one is to use two copies of Windows Paint running at the same time. Cut and paste the bitmaps from one into the other, and repeat the process as often as necessary.

Because of the difficulty in building up a large bitmap from multiple files to use the PictureClip control, the ListImage control is usually much easier to use. Nonetheless, the sample picture clip program is a lot of fun to watch if you have it (look for Samples\comptool\Picclip\Redtop.vbp in the directory containing VB).

Microsoft Tabbed Dialog Control 6.0

The tabbed dialog control lets you add tabbed dialog boxes to your project—like the Tools|Options dialog box in Visual Basic, for example. The way this control works is that it provides a group of tabbed containers for other controls. Here's a picture of the default-sized tab control:

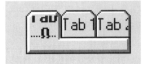

As you can see, the first thing you will want to do is expand the control so it is a reasonable size for displaying the information you want in each tab! Here's a picture of its very useful custom Property Pages dialog box:

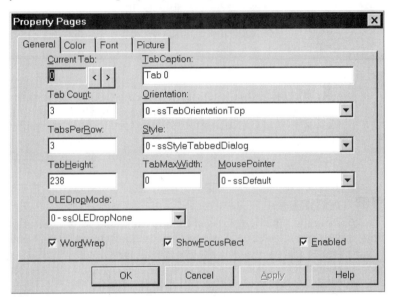

Example: Using the Tabbed Dialog Control

To work with this control at design time:

◆ Decide how many tabs you want.

◆ Decide what controls you want on each tab.

The number of tabs is the value of the Tabs property. (The default value is 3.) If you need more than one row of tabs, set the TabsPerRow property. Visual Basic then automatically adds the correct number of tabbed pages to your form. Set the Caption property of each tab to be what you want the user to see. (If you want to add a shortcut key, use the & before the shortcut character.) You can also add a picture to the tab via the Picture property. The TabHeight and TabWidth properties control how high and wide the tab appears to the user.

14

Next, you will want to design the actual tabbed pages. For this, select the tab you want to work with at design time by clicking on the tab. Since each tabbed page acts as a container control, you can add any ordinary controls to the page by using the customary techniques for working with container controls. (Remember *not* to use the double-click method—see the beginning of this chapter for more on working with container controls.)

NOTE: When your project is running, the tabbed dialog box works as the user expects. He or she can navigate by using *CTRL+TAB, CTRL+SHIFT+TAB,* or any shortcut key you define with the & character in the Caption property.

As with any custom dialog box, you will want to give users both an OK and a Cancel button.

TIP: Make the form that contains a tabbed dialog control into a custom dialog box by setting the BorderStyle property of the form appropriately. You may also want to add OK and Cancel buttons on the form outside the tabbed dialog control.

Menus

Designing the right kind of menus will make your applications much more user-friendly. Visual Basic lets you build up to six levels of menus. The screen in Figure 14-8 shows you a menu with four of the possible six levels. Menus that contain submenus are usually called *hierarchical menus*. Of course, using too many levels of menus can make the application confusing to the user. Four is almost certainly too many, and two or three levels are the most you will usually see. The user knows that a submenu lurks below a given menu item if there is a ▶ following the menu item.

Notice in the following illustration that each of the four items in the first level of menus in Figure 14-8 has the ▶ and so conceals a submenu.

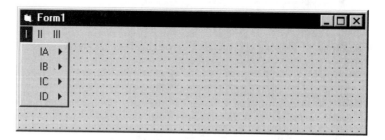

You can open a submenu by using the standard Windows conventions: press ENTER, click the item with the mouse, or press LEFT ARROW.

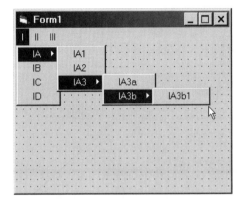

Menu Editor

You create menus in Visual Basic by using the Menu Editor window available by choosing Tools|Menu Editor (CTRL-E) whenever the form is showing. (You can also choose the Menu Editor tool from the toolbar, and Menu Editor is one of the options on the shortcut menu when the focus is in the form window.) The Menu Editor is shown in Figure 14-9. What follows is a short description of each of the components of this dialog box.

Caption Text Box What you type in the Caption text box is what the user sees. The caption also shows up in the text area inside the dialog box. Unlike other Visual Basic controls, menu items do not have default captions. ALT+P is the access key for the Caption text box in the Menu Editor window.

TIP: If the Caption property is set to a hyphen (-), Visual Basic inserts a separator bar between the items. Separator bars are a user friendly device to break long menus into groups of related items.

Name Text Box Each menu item must have a control name. Unless the menu items are part of a control array (see Chapter 11), they must have different control names. What you enter in the Name text box becomes the control name that is used by Visual Basic for the Click event procedure for the menu item. Visual Basic will not let you leave the Menu Editor window until you give each menu item a control name. The access key is ALT+M.

14

OK and Cancel Buttons Click the OK button when you are finished designing the menu. Click the Cancel button if you decide not to build the menu at all. Even after

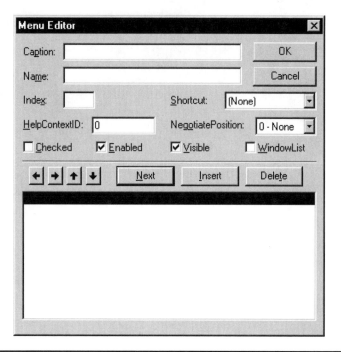

Menu Editor
window
Figure 14-9.

you've finished designing a menu and clicked on the Done button, you can return to
the Menu Editor window and make changes.

Index Box   Use the Index box if you want to make a menu item part of a control
array. As you saw in Chapter 11, control arrays let you add new instances of a control
at run time. In the case of menu items, this would let you have the menu enlarge or
shrink while the program is running. Once you've set a menu item to be part of a
control array at run time, you add new menu items with the Load method you saw in
Chapter 11. Similarly, you remove menu items from a control array by using the
Unload method. It is quite common to leave the Caption property blank for the first
menu item in a control array.

Shortcut Box   This box lets you add accelerator keys to your menu items. Recall
that accelerator keys are either function keys or CTRL+key combinations that activate a
menu item without the user's needing to open the menu at all. If you click the down
arrow to the right of the Shortcut box, a list box drops down with the choices for
accelerator keys. You need only click the key you want.

T IP: ALT+F4 is not an available shortcut. If you have an Exit item and want to remind people that ALT+F4 will exit the program, add ALT+F4 as part of the caption to the Exit item. (ALT+F4 triggers the QueryUnload event and closes the form if not canceled, which means there is functionality built into any form that has a control box.)

WindowList Check Box   Used when you have MDI windows. (See the section "MDI Forms" later in this chapter.)

HelpContextId Box   This is used when you are adding a Help system.

Checked Check Box   Determines whether a check mark shows up in front of the menu item. As you'd expect, this box controls the setting of the Checked property of the menu item. The default is off. It is much more common to switch the Checked property to True if a user selects the item while the program is running than to set it at design time.

Enabled Check Box   Determines the value of the Enabled property of the menu item. A menu item that is Enabled will respond to the Click event. An item that has been changed to False—either at design time by toggling the box off or at run time via code—shows up grayed.

Visible Check Box   Determines the value of the Visible property of the menu item. If a menu item is made invisible, all its submenus are also invisible.

Arrow Buttons   These buttons let you work with the current menu items. The menu item you're currently working with is highlighted in the large text window below the arrow buttons. Submenus are indicated by the indentation level in this text window, as you'll see in the next section. The left and right arrow buttons control the indentation level. Clicking on the left arrow button moves the highlighted item up one level; so a menu item would get promoted to the menu bar. Clicking on the right arrow button moves it one indentation level deeper, which makes it move to be a sub-menu of the item above it. You cannot indent an item more than one level deeper than the item above it. If you try, Visual Basic will not let you leave the Menu Editor window until you fix it.

Clicking on the up arrow button interchanges the highlighted menu item with the item above it; clicking on the down arrow button interchanges the highlighted item with the item below it. The up and down arrows do not change the indentation pattern of an item. See the section "Sample Menu Editor Window" for more on using the arrow buttons.

14

Next Button   Clicking the Next button moves you to the next menu item or inserts a new item if you are at the end of the menu. The indentation of the new item starts out the same as the indentation of the previous item. ALT+N is the access key. You can also use the mouse to move among items.

Insert Button   Clicking the Insert button inserts a menu item above the currently highlighted menu item. ALT+I is the access key.

Delete Button   Clicking the Delete button removes the currently highlighted item. The access key is ALT+T. You cannot use the DEL key to remove menu items.

Sample Menu Editor Window

The Menu Editor window that led to the hierarchical menu in Figure 14-8 began like the screen in Figure 14-10. Notice that the menu item that is not indented appears on the main menu bar. Menu items that are indented once (preceded by 4 dots) appear as a menu item below the main menu bar. Items indented twice (8 dots) are submenus, items indented three times (12 dots) are sub-submenus, and so on. You can always

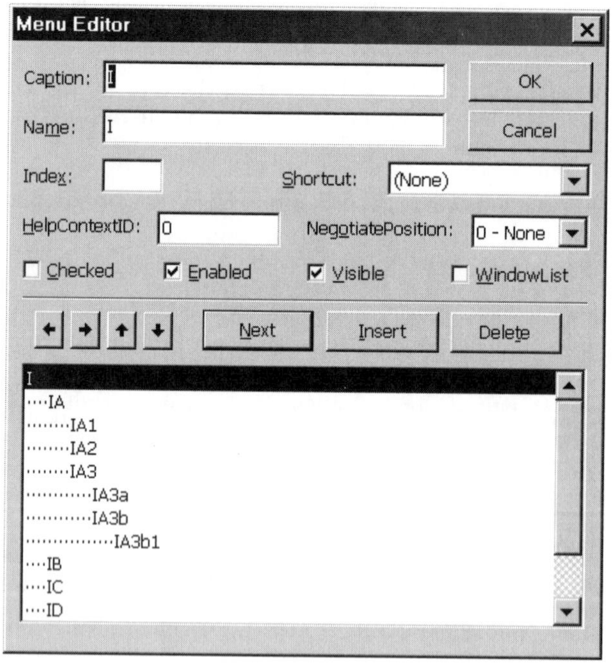

Beginning
of the
Menu Editor
window for
the menus in
Figure 14-8

Figure 14-10.

determine the main menu bar by looking for items that appear flush left in the Menu Editor text window.

Working with Menus at Run Time

Suppose you want to write a program that would help people convert between various kinds of units—for example, between inches, centimeters, meters, and feet. A form for this application might look like the one in Figure 14-11. Notice that this form has three items on the menu bar: Target, Source, and Quit. The Menu Editor window for this form looks like the one in Figure 14-12.

The control names and captions for the menu items and controls are given in the following table:

Control Name	Caption
txtSource	Source
txtTarget	Target
mnuFromInches	Inches
mnuFromFeet	Feet
mnuFromCentimeters	Centimeters
mnuFromMeters	Meters
mnuToInches	Inches
mnuToFeet	Feet
mnuToCentimeters	Centimeters
mnuToMeters	Meters
Label2	Source Units
Label3	Target Units

Notice that the Caption properties are the same for the items on the Target and Source menus; only the control names are different.

Whenever you write a conversion program, it's easiest to establish one unit as the basic unit and convert all the units using that as an intermediary. For this, set up the form-level variable

```
Dim BasicLength As Single
```

in the Declarations section of the form.

14

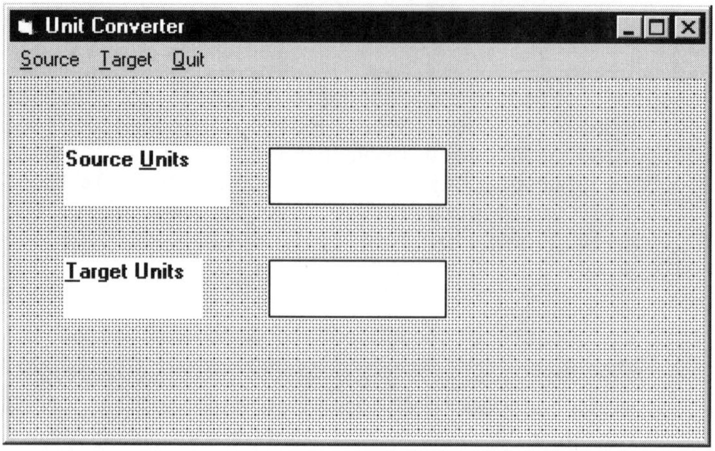

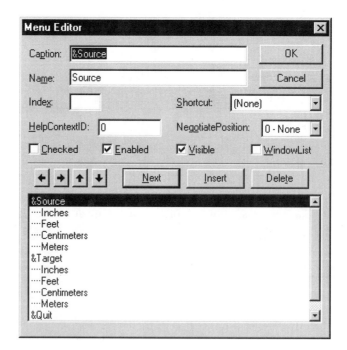

Form for
conversion
program
Figure 14-11.

Menu Editor
window for
conversion
program
Figure 14-12.

Now, suppose the user clicks the menu item marked Inches in the Source menu. The code should do the following:

◆   Put a check mark next to the Inches item and remove check marks from all other items.

◆   Disable the Inches item in the Target menu and enable all the other items.

Here's the code for the Click procedure that implements this outline for one of the menu items. (The others work the same.)

```
Sub mnuFromInches_Click()
  mnuFromInches.Checked = True
  mnuFromFeet.Checked = False
  mnuFromCentimeters.Checked = False
  mnuFromMeters.Checked = False
'change items on Target menu
  mnuToInches.Enabled = False
  mnuToFeet.Enabled = True
  mnuToCentimeters.Enabled = True
  mnuToMeters.Enabled = True
'set the caption for units
  Label2.Caption = "Inches"
End Sub
```

Now suppose the user clicks an item in the Target menu. You need to read the value from the text box, calculate the new value, and display the result in the first label. Suppose, for example, the user clicked the Meters item, indicating he or she wanted to convert from inches to meters. Here's the code that does this, using centimeters as the basic length:

```
Sub mnuToMeters_Click()
  Label3.Caption = "Meters"
  If mnuFromInches.Checked Then
    BasicLength = Val(Text1.Text)*2.54 '2.54 Centimeters/inch
  ElseIf mnuFromFeet.Checked Then
    BasicLength = Val(Text1.Text)*2.54*12
  ElseIf mnuFromCentimeters.Checked Then
    BasicLength = Val(Text1.Text)
  End If
  Label1.Caption = Str(BasicLength/100)
End Sub
```

This procedure uses the fact that clicking on an item in the Target menu changes the Checked property to False for all but the unit to be converted. If you add some directions to the Form_Load procedure, you can see the result shown in Figure 14-13.

14

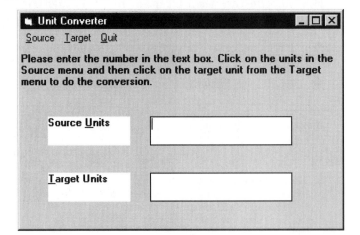

Results of
running the
conversion
program
Figure 14-13.

MDI Forms

MDI stands for *multiple document interface*, which is Microsoft's term for a windowing environment in which one window, usually called the *MDI container* or *MDI parent form*, contains many other windows, usually called *child forms*. For example, you can use an MDI parent form to allow a user to work with two separate windows in the same application. You can have only one MDI parent form to a project and that form must, naturally enough, be the startup form.

NOTE: Only controls with an alignment property, such as the picture box control, can be placed on an MDI form.

To make an MDI parent form, choose the New MDI Form option from the File menu. Next, create the additional forms (usually from the File menu as well). These will be the child forms to your newly created MDI form after you set the form's MDIChild property to True. (You can also turn an existing form into an MDI child form by adjusting this property.) At design time, child forms and the MDI parent form look alike—you can't see any differences between them.

When you run the project, on the other hand, all the child forms must be explicitly shown (with the Show method), and they are displayed within the MDI parent form's boundaries. Moreover, if the child form is minimized, its icon appears inside the MDI parent form, rather than in the Windows desktop. (If you maximize a child form, its caption replaces the caption of the parent form.) Finally, you can neither hide nor disable child forms.

One of the nicest features of Visual Basic's MDI forms is that the menus of the parent form change according to which child form has the focus. This lets you work with specific menus for each child form. What happens is that the menu for the child form that has the focus appears on the menu bar of the MDI parent form—replacing whatever menu was previously there. The user only sees the menu for the child form when that child form has the focus.

T IP: MDI child forms are easily generated using the New method (see Chapter 13). This is because you will often want all the child forms to be essentially the same. (A good example of this is when you use an MDI form to build an editor. If you want to allow multiple editing windows, the New keyword is ideal.) The Application Wizard will automatically add the necessary code for making child windows in this way if you choose the MDI option in it, and it is a great tool for helping to build the basics of an MDI application.

The Window Menu and the Arrange Method

Every MDI application should have a Window menu that allows the user to arrange or cascade the child windows—much like Windows itself does. The Window menu should also include a list of the MDI child windows. An example of such a menu is shown here:

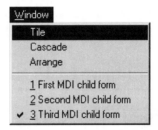

The list of MDI child windows is easy to put on the menu: set the WindowList check box on the Menu Editor window to be on. Visual Basic will automatically display the list of the MDI child form captions—and even put a check mark next to the one that most recently had the focus.

To activate the Tile, Cascade, and Arrange items on the Window menu, write code like this:

```
Sub mnuCascadeForms_Click()
  MDIParentForm.Arrange vbCascade
End Sub
```

This uses the vbCascade constant with the Arrange method. The other two constants are vbTileHorizontal and vbArrangeIcons.

14

Making Forms Independent of Resizing and Screen Resolution

As your projects have become more complicated, you have probably noticed that your carefully designed forms will easily go astray whenever the user changes the size of the form. Figures 14-14 and 14-15 show this dramatically. Figure 14-14 was designed with the form in the default size and the command button centered in the bottom of the form. Figure 14-15 is what happens when the user enlarges the form to maximum size. (Similar things will happen if you design your screen using 640 X 480 resolution. They will look strange on a 1024 X 780 screen—the proportions of the form and controls will change, and if the monitor is too small, they may be far too tiny.)

There are various ways around this problem:

◆ You can do what many professionals do—buy a custom container control like VideoSoft's VBElastic control that takes care of the details of adjusting control sizes for size and resolution changes. (If you do a lot of design work, this may be the best choice!)

◆ You can write the code yourself. (Even if you use a custom control that does this, it is a good idea to learn the trick for "rolling your own.")

If you choose to write the code yourself, the trick is to get out of the habit of thinking of controls as having a fixed size. Instead, think of them as having certain proportions relative to the form. Let's start with simple examples, the ones used in Figures 14-14 and 14-15. You want to write the code that will guarantee that the command button will always show up centered at the bottom of the form with the same proportions it had when you started out.

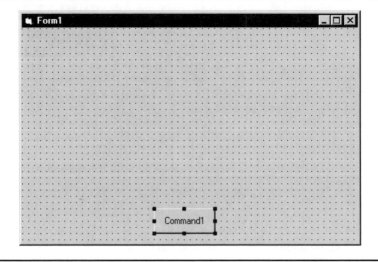

Form with a command button in default size

Figure 14-14.

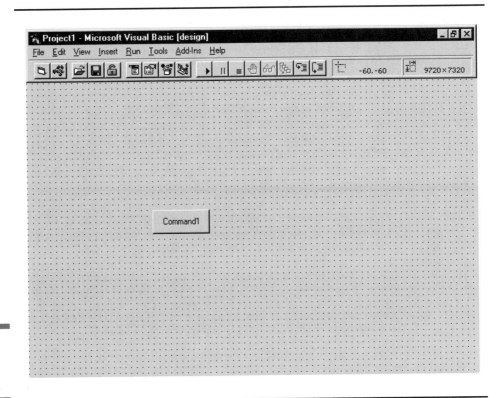

The form of
Figure 14-14
maximized
Figure 14-15.

Here are the relative dimensions on a 640 X 480 form. (Use the ScaleHeight and ScaleWidth properties to get at the dimensions of the interior of the form.)

Object	Height	Width
Command button	495	1215
Form	4140	6690

Thus the ratio of the heights is 495/4140 and that of the widths, 1215/6690. Given this information, you can use the Move method in the Form_Resize event to make sure the command is always centered on the bottom of the form and has the correct proportions. Recall that the Move method has the following syntax:

object.Move *left, top, width, height*

```
Sub Form_Resize()
Dim TheHeight As Single, TheWidth As Single
```

14

```
    TheHeight = (495/4140)*ScaleHeight
    TheWidth = (1215/6690)*ScaleWidth
    Command1.Move ScaleWidth/2 -(TheWidth/2), ScaleHeight -_
    TheHeight, TheWidth, TheHeight
End Sub
```

The key line

```
Command1.Move ScaleWidth/2 -(TheWidth/2), ScaleHeight -_
    TheHeight, TheWidth, TheHeight
```

moves the command button exactly where you want it whenever the size changes.

NOTE: If you haven't set AutoRedraw to True, you will want to have the Paint event procedure call the Resize event procedure.

Of course, this is rather cumbersome to do by hand if you have many controls on a form. However, it is not hard to see how to automate this process.

1. Set up a type called ControlProportions in the Declaration section of a code module:

   ```
   Type ControlProportions
      WidthProportions As Single
      HeightProportions as Single
      TopProportions As Single
      LeftProportions as Single
   End Type
   ```

2. Set up a form-level array of these records:

   ```
   Dim ArrayOfProportions() As ControlProportions
   ```

3. In the Form_Load event use the Controls.Count property to redimension the array you are using to hold the proportion information. (Every time you add a control by using a control array, you would have to update the information, of course.)

4. Fill the array with the correct values by iterating through the Controls collection to get the proportions of all the controls on the form.

5. Use the information now contained in the ArrayOfProportions in the Form_Resize procedure to resize all the controls on the form whenever the form is resized.

NOTE: The only thing to be aware of in writing the code is that you want to avoid checking the size of invisible controls, such as Timers or CommonDialog controls. One way to do this is simply to use the On Error Resume Next in this code as I did in the code below.

Here's the complete code for one version that will do this, assuming you have set up the type as I have just shown you.

```
Dim ArrayProportions() As ControlProportions
Private Sub Form_Load()
  ReDim ArrayProportions(0 To Controls.Count - 1)
  ArrayInitialize
End Sub

Sub ArrayInitialize()
  Dim I As Integer
  On Error Resume Next
  For I = 0 To Controls.Count - 1
    'take into account that some controls will be invisible!
    If TypeOf Controls(I) Is Timer Then
      'Do nothing
    ElseIf TypeOf Controls(I) Is CommonDialog Then
      'Do nothing
    Else
      With ArrayProportions(I)
        .WidthProportions = Controls(I).Width / ScaleWidth
        .HeightProportions = Controls(I).Height / ScaleHeight
        .LeftProportions = Controls(I).Left / ScaleWidth
        .TopProportions = Controls(I).Top / ScaleHeight
      End With
    End If
  Next I
End Sub

'the code for the Form_Resize then looks like this:
Sub Form_Resize()
  Dim I As Integer

  For I = 0 To Controls.Count - 1
    If TypeOf Controls(I) Is Timer Then
      'Do nothing
    ElseIf TypeOf Controls(I) Is CommonDialog Then
      'Do nothing
    Else
      'we will move the controls to where they should be
      'resizing them proportionally
```

14

```
      Controls(I).Move ArrayProportions(I).LeftProportions * _
ScaleWidth, _
      ArrayProportions(I).TopProportions * ScaleHeight, _
      ArrayProportions(I).WidthProportions * ScaleWidth, _
      ArrayProportions(I).HeightProportions * ScaleHeight
    End If
  Next I
End Sub
```

You may want to write additional code in the Form_Resize event to prevent the form from getting so small that the controls overlap or are no longer visible. (This is yet another reason not to crowd too many controls on a single form.)

Dealing with Screen Resolution Changes

When the screen resolution increases, your forms and controls become smaller relative to the whole screen. (They may also change their proportions.)

TIP: If you are running in a high resolution, the Form Layout Window will show you how the form will look at lower resolutions.

The methods for adjusting the size of the form are similar to those for adjusting controls—only this time you think of the form as having certain proportions relative to the Screen object. For example, if you add code like the following to the Form_Load, you will always get a centered form that has dimensions half that of the screen—regardless of the screen resolution.

```
Me.Height = Screen.Height / 2
Me.Width = Screen.Width / 2
Me.Top = (Screen.Height / 2) - (Me.Height) / 2
Me.Left = (Screen.Width / 2) - (Me.Left) / 2
```

In general, all you have to do is decide on where and what size you want your forms to be relative to the screen size, and code those values into the Form_Load (or Form_Resize if you want to prevent users from changing it).

TIP: If you use this method to initialize a form's size and also want to use the routine from the previous section to resize the controls, you may want to consider initializing the position of the controls before you initialize the array of proportions.

Help Systems

A professional Windows project needs a help system that does what Windows users expect. If your online help doesn't have the look and feel of a Windows help system, users will have to learn too much (and you'll probably be working too hard to teach them). The trouble is that Microsoft is in transition from the old Windows help system to an HTML-based help system and so it isn't clear which your users will expect! Luckily, as far as the VB programmer is concerned, you access the different kinds of help systems in exactly the same way.

NOTE: Fully explaining all the possible features of both kinds of Windows help systems would take a book almost the size of this one. This discussion concentrates on how you get a help system to interact with your Visual Basic application rather than on the mechanics of constructing the help system itself. The online help for both the Professional and Enterprise editions includes full documentation for building help systems.

TIP: Several third-party tools make writing both kinds of help files easier. The one I use all the time and highly recommend is "RoboHelp" from BlueSky Software. If you are building a sophisticated help system, RoboHelp is more than worth the cost.

Building In Context-Sensitive Help

The help file property is a global property of the App (application) object. You need to set this property to the name of the help file that you want to use for the application. You do this by working with the Project|Properties|General page. Simply enter the name of the compiled help file in the HelpFile text box. Give the full path name if it will not be in the same directory as the application. You can use either an HTML-based help (.chm) file or the older style WinHelp (.hlp) files.

Next, let's assume you have written (or someone has given you) a help file that is compiled and you need to attach it to your project. You will need to coordinate some of the features of the source code of the help file with your program before you can actually use context-sensitive help in your project.

◆ As far as the Visual Basic programmer is concerned, the key is setting the HelpContextID of the form or control appropriately. All controls—except line, shape, image, and label—have a HelpContextID property.

◆ As far as the writer of the help system is concerned, the key is to keep track of the HelpContextID numbers the programmer assigns to the various elements that will need context-sensitive help.

14

For example, if the programmer sets the HelpContextID property of the File menu to 5, the writer of the help system must know this. Then he or she must tell the help compiler how to *map* the HelpContextID property to specific topics. In this case, the FILE_MENU topic page has context number 5.

T **IP:** If you want to assign context-sensitive help to an image control that doesn't have a HelpContextID property, replace it with a picture box that does.

Accessing the Windows Help Engine

You can use the ShowHelp method of the common dialog control to access the Windows help engine. Follow these steps to use this method for the common dialog control:

1. Add a common dialog control to the project via Project|Components.
2. Add the control to the form where you want to use the Windows help engine.
3. Set the HelpFile and HelpCommand properties of the CommonDialog control to the appropriate constants or values.

For example, if you want to use the ShowHelp method to give context-sensitive help:

1. Set the HelpFile property to the name of the compiled help file.
2. Set the HelpCommand property to cdlHelpContext.
3. Set the HelpContext property to the context ID you want to display at the moment.
4. Finally, use the ShowHelp method to call the Windows help engine.

If you need or want to use the general Windows help engine (for example, to have a "Help on Help" option that would show the Windows "Help on Help" screen), you'll need to use the WinHelp API function instead. The next section shows you how to do this.

Example: Showing the Windows Help on Help Page Using the Windows API

To see how to do this:

1. Start up a new project and add a code module to it.
2. Add the appropriate declaration to a code module.

```
Declare Function WinHelp Lib "user32" Alias "WinHelpA"
(ByVal hWnd As Long, ByVal lpHelpFile As String,
ByVal wCommand As Long, ByVal dwData As Long) As Long
```

The hWnd ("window's handle") parameter will be the value of the form's hWnd property. The lpHelpFile parameter is the path name of the help file (if it is not in the same place as the .exe file).

You will also need to add the following constants to the code module; they are used for the wCommand parameter in the Help API.

```
Public Const HELP_CONTEXT = &H1 'Display topic by id number
Public Const HELP_QUIT = &H2          'Terminate help
Public Const HELP_INDEX = &H3         'Display index
Public Const HELP_HELPONHELP = &H4 'Display help on using help
Public Const HELP_SETINDEX = &H5      'Set an alternate Index
Public Const HELP_KEY = &H101         'Display topic for keyword in Data
Public Const HELP_MULTIKEY = &H201  'Look up keyword in alternate table
```

Next, to make it possible to call the general Windows "Help on Help" system, add this general procedure to the code module:

```
Public Sub DisplayHelp_On_Help(X As Form)
  Dim Foo As Long ' dummy variable
  Foo = WinHelp(X.hWnd,"C:\WINDOWS\HELP\WINDOWS.HLP", HELP_HELPONHELP,CLng(0))
End Sub
```

Finally, make the Form_Load for the form read:

```
Private Sub Form_Load()
  DisplayHelp_On_Help Me
End Sub
```

Then, immediately after this code is processed, Windows would pop up the Help on Help page. Which page you see depends on which operating system you are using. In Windows 95 you would get the older style help, in Windows 98 you'll see something like Figure 14-16.

NOTE: After you set the hCommand parameter to HELP_CONTEXT, use the dwData parameter for the context string ID number.

Finally, if you use the WinHelp API call to activate the help engine, you will probably want to call the WinHelp API function again to make sure that the extra help window is closed when your application ends. (The Windows help engine is a separate Windows application.) Since you want this to happen when your main

14

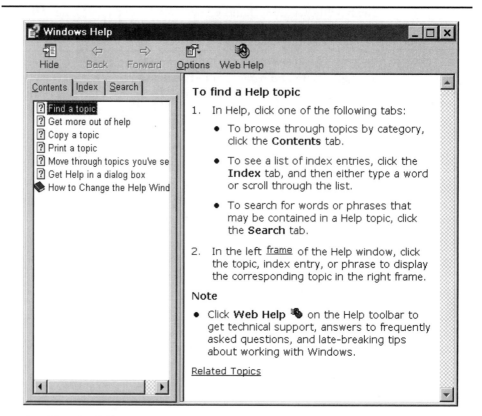

form closes down, this is usually done in the Form_Unload event by adding code like the following.

```
Sub Form_Unload(Cancel As Integer)
  Dim Foo As Integer, Bar As String   'dummy variables
  Foo = WinHelp(Me.hWnd, Bar, Help_Quit, CLng(0))
End Sub
```

(The variables Foo and Bar are "dummy" variables that you need to use in this API call: they must be of the right type (integer and string respectively) and must be used as in the example code above but they don't actually do anything and you can use any names for them that you want.)

Some Words on Windows Design

This short section cannot substitute for the official Microsoft publication *The Windows Interface Guidelines for Software Design* (ISBN 1-55615-679-0), but I hope a few words are not out of place. There's a temptation, especially for experienced DOS programmers, to force Visual Basic programs into a framework that is not Windows-oriented. I have been guilty of this myself on more than one occasion when porting DOS programs to Windows. But this temptation should be resisted. For example, having a sequence of input boxes to get data is very DOS—very linear—and not very Windows. Let the user stay in control; design input forms that the user can access from menus instead. Use DoEvents whenever your application is sitting around idle; don't hog resources. Just because Sub Main lets you write a standard old-fashioned linear (top to bottom) program doesn't mean you should. Windows is now multitasking, but use DoEvents when you are hogging CPU resources.

Make sure you are giving enough feedback to the user. Change the MousePointer to an hourglass when the user is going to have to wait. Don't monkey with what users have grown to expect. Leave control boxes on forms and have ALT+F4 close the form (use the QueryUnload event for any needed cleanup code). Allow users to resize forms and move them around unless there is some good reason not to do so. Scroll bars are helpful when users are going to have to work through lots of information. Don't crowd your forms with too many buttons; use menus instead. On the other hand, don't make menus too deep. Use custom or common dialog boxes as appropriate. Remember to set the ToolTipsText property if you want to use an icon on a button or other control so the user doesn't have to guess what the icon stands for.

Make the menus look like what users expect. Programs that handle files should have the standard order in the File menu, with the right captions and the right access keys (where appropriate). Users expect to see a File menu (with an ALT+F shortcut) that will have whatever subset of the following list is appropriate:

<u>N</u>ew
<u>O</u>pen...
<u>S</u>ave
Save <u>A</u>s...
<u>P</u>rint...
E<u>x</u>it

(You may need more items, of course, depending on your application.)

Similarly, the Help menu (ALT+H access key) would usually have at least these three items:

<u>C</u>ontents
<u>S</u>earch For Help On...
<u>A</u>bout

14

The best advice is: When in doubt, look to Visual Basic itself for how to design your menus and forms!

T IP: The Application Wizard will add these standard menus effortlessly to your application. Just be prepared to eliminate some of the extraneous code that the Application Wizard adds!

Here's a short table on the actions users expect:

Action	Function
Click left mouse button	Activates a control or selects an item from a list or combo box; in a text box, moves the insertion point
Double-click left mouse button	Performs the action
Click right mouse button	Pops up a context-sensitive menu
Drag with left button	Either encloses a specific area or moves an object
Press TAB key	Moves to the next control (watch your tab order!)

Of course, there are lots of keystroke combinations that should work automatically as users expect, because one of the nice things about Visual Basic is that the objects usually default to the expected response! For example, text boxes recognize the SHIFT+UP ARROW or DOWN ARROW keys to select and CTRL+C, CTRL+V to copy.

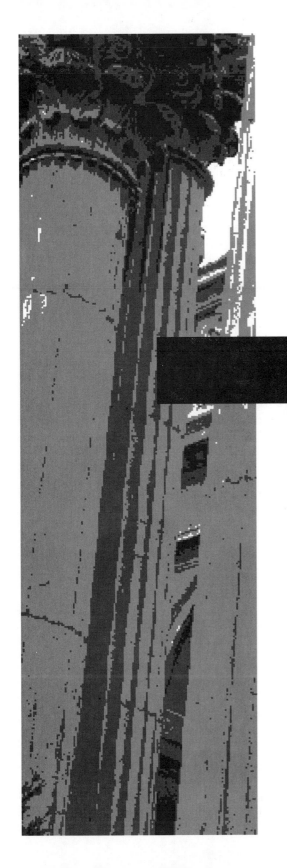

CHAPTER 15

Tools and Techniques for Testing, Debugging, and Optimization

563

This chapter shows you how to use the tools that Visual Basic offers for producing bug-free (well, at least less buggy) code. You'll also see some techniques for speeding up your programs that do the job and are unlikely to introduce new bugs (trying to over-optimize code is one of the most common sources of programming bugs). The chapter concludes with some words on good programming style.

Testing

Once a program becomes in any way complicated, no matter how carefully you outline your program or how carefully you plan it, it probably won't do what you expect—at first. This is one painful lesson programmers are forced to learn over and over again. It seems that no matter how robust you try to make a program, someone, somehow, will find a way to crash it. So after you write a program, you will need to test it for bugs. Once the testing process convinces you that there are bugs lurking, you need to find them and then eradicate them.

TIP: When I go to test and debug a program, I find it very helpful to have a hard copy of the program source code. You can get this by choosing File|Print and working with the dialog box that pops up. You might also want a copy of the specifications of the forms in text format (see Chapter 4) so you can quickly check whether the initial properties of a form and its controls match what you expect.

It is important to be realistic. You have to know when a product is "good enough to ship." (All shipping products that I have used for any length of time have bugs—I suspect your experience is no different.) A realistic goal is not a perfect program, but one that is as bulletproof (the buzzword is *robust*) as possible. This means that your program should not crash under normal circumstances, but if it does, it at least gives the user a chance to save his or her work before fading away. Obviously, your program can't ship if it has a bug that might corrupt files on the user's disk or, more generally, do *anything* that will make the user regret installing it. In sum, you might make it your goal to write programs that conform to a sign I once saw. Slightly paraphrased, it read,

---

Our goal is a program
THAT SPUTTERS OUT AND DOESN'T BLOW UP!

(The buzzword for "sputter out" is *degrade gracefully*.)

How to Test a Program?

Testing programs is the first step in the debugging process, because you cannot correct errors until you determine that errors exist. Some people's idea of testing a program consists of running the program a few times to see what happens, each time using slightly different input. This process can succeed when you have a short program, but it's not effective (or convincing) for a long program or even a short program that is in any way subtle. In any case, even for the simplest programs, the choice of test data (sometimes dignified with the fancy term *testing suite*) is all-important. A good testing suite is vital because you *must* test all possible execution paths inside your code in order to have any hope that it will be bug free.

Testing programs is an art, not a science. There's no prescription that always works. If your program is so long and complicated that you can't be sure that you are testing all the possibilities, you have to be content with testing the reasonable ones. (For example, Microsoft can't possibly test every possible combination of hardware before they release a new version of the operating system.)

The key to testing lies in the word *reasonable*, and the following story explains how subtle this concept can be. A utility company had a complicated but, they thought, carefully checked program to send out bills, follow-up bills, and finally, automatically cut off service if no response to a bill was received. One day, the story goes, someone went on vacation and shut off the electricity. The computer sent out a bill for $0.00, which, understandably, wasn't paid. After the requisite number of follow-up requests, the computer finally issued a termination notice saying that if this unfortunate person didn't pay $0.00 by Thursday, his electricity would be cut off.

A frantic call may have succeeded in stopping the shutoff; the story doesn't say. If this story is true, the programmer forgot to test what the program would do if the bill was $0.00 and the shutoff program only responded to an "unpaid bill." To the programmer, this wasn't a "reasonable" possibility. (Of course, all the programmer had to do was change a >= to a > somewhere in the program.)

One moral of this story is that you must always test your programs using the boundary values—the extreme values that mark the limits of the problem, like the $0.00 that the programmer in the story forgot. For example, for sorting routines, a completely ordered or reverse-ordered list is a good test case. In programs that require input, the empty string (or 0) is always a good test case.

Since errors are often caused by bugs, error trapping can help you isolate what portion of a procedure caused the bug. For example, you can add line numbers to your program and then use the Erl statement to find out which line of the program caused the error. You can even use a bisection process like the one described in Chapter 10 instead of putting line numbers everywhere. Place a line number in the middle of a program and find out which half of the program caused the error. Continue this bisection process until you isolate the line that caused the bug. (Of course, Visual Basic ordinarily stops a program at the line that causes an error, but you will often need to insert line numbers to debug a program with an error trap.)

TIP: Having an active error trap (On Error Goto) can prevent your tests from doing their job. You often will need to temporarily disable any active error traps before starting the testing process. To do this, go to the General tab of Tools|Options and set the "Break on All Errors" button on. (For more information on error traps, see Chapter 12.)

Designing Programs to Make Testing Easier

Long and complicated programs are never easy to test, but writing the programs in certain ways will make your job easier. (These methods also make programming easier in general.) You have two choices with Visual Basic 6:

◆ By breaking the program into manageable pieces (giving the program *modularity*, in the jargon), each of which ideally does one task alone, you can make testing your programs much, much easier.

◆ Use the techniques of object-oriented programming (described in Chapter 13). This involves breaking the program into manageable *objects*.

Most Visual Basic programmers at the present time seem to use a combination of the two techniques. They add class modules for the parts of their program that seem to use objects, and standard modules for the parts that don't seem particularly object oriented. (Of course, one should ideally use objects for everything—if one buys into the OOP paradigm.)

In many ways, the testing procedure doesn't change much whether you are using objects or a modular approach. The idea is still to have *manageable* pieces that you can test. Only then do you worry about the interactions of the various pieces. In particular:

◆ For a procedurally oriented approach, you need to check that each procedure or function can handle all possible parameters that may be passed to it. You also want to make sure that your procedures cause no undesired side effects by, for example, changing the parameters or global data incorrectly (which, of course, you should use rarely anyway!).

◆ For an object-oriented approach, you want to make sure each procedure behaves well for each possible message that it is sent.

NOTE: The members of your objects will need to be tested in the same way that individual procedures and functions are tested in the more traditional, modular approach.

Stub Programming

Many programmers find that if they insist that they always have a program that runs, regardless of whether all features are yet implemented, they produce less buggy code. In some cases, of course, a procedure, function, or member may need results from a piece not yet written in order to run. In this case, the best technique to use, called *stub programming* by academics, is that you substitute constants, where necessary, for the results of as-yet-unwritten procedures or functions. Define the Sub, Function, or Property procedure that you will eventually need, but fill them with constants instead of having them do anything. You can also use stub programming to test unimplemented functionality for your class modules. Simply add skeletons for the Sub, Function, and Property procedures in the class module. The procedure calls (or members of your objects) that use the unwritten code will still work, but they will receive only the constants from the stubs. You can then change the constants to vary the tests.

TIP: You can put a message box in the unwritten code that identifies what subprogram (or member) you are accessing, in addition to having the stub return the appropriate constant values.

Bugs

Now suppose you have eliminated the obvious syntax errors and can get the program to run—after a fashion. But testing the program has told you that it doesn't work as it's supposed to; it contains bugs that you need to isolate and eradicate. Don't be surprised or dismayed; bugs come with the territory. You have to find them and determine what kind they are.

There are essentially two kinds of bugs: grammatical and logical. An example of a grammatical error is a misspelled variable name, which leads to a default value that ruins the program. Surprisingly enough, they are often the most difficult kind of bug to detect. I can't stress strongly enough that the best way to deal with such bugs in Visual Basic is to prevent many of them from happening in the first place. You can do this by using the Option Explicit command (see Chapter 5), which forces you to declare all variables.

TIP: A useful tool for understanding how variables are used in your programs is a programmer's tool called a cross-reference (or XREF) program. This program works through the source code of a program and then lists the names of all variables and where they occur. A cross-reference program is especially useful for detecting the common error of an incorrect variable in an assignment statement. Although using meaningful variable names can help to a certain extent, the mistake of using the variable ThisWeeksSales when you really meant the variable ThisMonthsSales is still easy to make. The Option Explicit command doesn't help if the wrong variable was already dimensioned. (Some powerful commercial cross-reference programs are available—check out NuMega http://www.numega.com, for example.)

Logical bugs, on the other hand, form a vast family. These are usually errors that result from a misunderstanding of how a program works—for example, procedures that don't communicate properly, and internal logic errors inside code.

15

Finding and Dealing with Logical Bugs

To get rid of subtle logical bugs, you have to isolate them—that is, find the part of the program that's causing the problem. If you've followed the modular approach, and your modules and objects do as few things as possible (ideally, one thing), your task is a lot easier. The pieces are more manageable, so you'll be looking for your bug in a smaller haystack.

If you've been testing the program as you develop it, then you should already know in what procedure or function the problem lies. Pinpointing the problematic procedure or function is usually easier if you developed the program, mostly because you start off with a good idea of the logic of the program. If the program is not yours or you've waited until the program is "finished," you can use the following techniques to check the pieces one at a time.

Assume that you've chosen a faulty procedure or function (member) to test. There are only three possibilities:

◆ What's going in is wrong—what you've fed to the procedure or function is confusing it.

◆ What's going out is wrong—the procedure or function is sending incorrect information to other parts of the program (for example, it may be causing unplanned side effects).

◆ Something inside the procedure or function is wrong (for example, it's performing an operation too many times, or it's not clearing the screen at the right time).

In the first two cases, the fault can be traced to any or all of the following: the parameters you send to the procedure or function, what you've assigned to the parameters, or the form-level or global variables modified within the function or procedure. (Try not to use globals, of course.)

How do you decide which situation you're dealing with? First, it's hard to imagine a correctly written short procedure or function, whether it be part of a code module or part or a class module, that you can't analyze on a piece of paper to determine what should happen in most cases. Work through the procedure or function by hand, "playing computer" (this means don't make any assumptions other than what the computer would know at that point; don't assume variables have certain values unless you can convince yourself that they do). You now need to check that the functions and procedures are doing what they are supposed to do. This can be done using the Immediate window, which I'll take up next.

The Immediate Window

Most programming languages have a way to test program statements, procedures, and functions, and Visual Basic is no exception. Visual Basic uses the Immediate window shown in Figure 15-1 with the results of a simple calculation. You can use the Immediate window to test statements or to perform quick calculations when you are in break mode. If you type **Print 2 + 2** in the Immediate window and press ENTER, Visual Basic quickly responds with a 4.

The Immediate
window
Figure 15-1.

T IP: Almost every experienced Visual Basic programmer uses the ? shorthand for the Print command in the Immediate window. Thus, ? 2+2 works just as well as Print 2+2.

You can use the ordinary Microsoft Windows editing commands to modify the contents of a line in the Immediate window. You can also cut and paste between lines. Keep in mind, though, that the moment you press ENTER, Visual Basic attempts to process the line.

To bring the Immediate window to the foreground, use the View menu or click any part of the Immediate window that is visible. The Immediate window is movable or resizable by ordinary Windows techniques. (Move it while holding down the CTRL key in order to keep it form docking.) The Immediate window has its own shortcut menu that contains most of its common operations. Like any shortcut menu, a click on the right (non-primary) mouse button brings it up.

N OTE: Beginning with Visual Basic 5, the Immediate window can do a lot more than it could in earlier versions of Visual Basic. In particular, you no longer need to have Visual Basic in break mode to use the Immediate window.

Lines in the Immediate window can use the colon separator and the line continuation character. Because of these possibilities, you can write quite complicated code in the Immediate window, although it will look strange. For instance,

```
For I = 10 To 1 Step -1:Print = STR$(I)+vbtab _
: Next I
```

is a perfectly acceptable line of code for the Immediate window and would give you the string of the numerals from 10 through 1, separated by tab characters, in the Immediate window.

15

Keep in mind that you can always reexecute any lines that currently appear in the Immediate window by moving the cursor anywhere in the line and pressing ENTER. (If you have used the line continuation character, you must move to the last physical line before pressing ENTER.) Use the arrow keys or mouse to move around the Immediate window.

The Immediate window makes it easy to test an isolated procedure or function for its effects on certain values (for example, to see whether the results match with your hand calculations). You can test only procedures and functions that are attached to the form or module (anything in the scope).

Many debugging techniques use the Immediate window to examine the current value of variables or expressions based on the state of the program at the time you stopped it. The only expressions you can test are those whose variables are

◆   Local to the procedure where the execution is stopped

◆   Form-level variables for the current form (if you are stopped in a form)

◆   Module-level variables for the current module (if you are stopped in a module)

◆   Global variables

NOTE: The Immediate window used to be called the Debug window in early versions of VB—some old-timers still call it that, so don't be surprised if you hear this older terminology occasionally.

The Debug Object

You can also add lines of code to your program that print values directly to the Immediate window. For this, you use a predefined Visual Basic object called Debug in the following form:

```
Debug.Print NameOfVariable
Debug.Print Expression
```

Whenever Visual Basic encounters a Debug.Print statement, it sends the requested information to the Immediate window. It does not stop the program. You can then examine it at your leisure. Many programmers like to have these statements identify the variable, as shown here:

```
Debug.Print "The value of X is ";X
```

When you are through debugging your program, you'll want to remove all the Debug.Print statements, although theoretically you can leave them in a compiled .exe file without the user noticing.

TIP: You can change the values of variables that are in the current scope by making assignments in the Immediate window.

The Debugging Tools and What They Do

You can use the Debug menu to gain access to the tools needed for debugging, and most of the tools needed for testing and debugging can be found on the Debug toolbar as well (see Figure 15-2). Choose View|Toolbars|Debug if it isn't visible.

Usually, the debugging tools are used when the program is temporarily suspended (in *break mode* as it is usually called). I'll explain shortly the various ways of getting into break mode. Table 15-1 lists the debugging tools that you can use, in the order in which they appear on the toolbar.

The first three tools on the debug toolbar (also available on the Standard toolbar) are the most common way of switching from project design, or design mode, to break mode—where you'll be doing most of your debugging. You can always tell what mode you're in by looking at the title bar. For example, when you stop a program by switching to break mode, the title bar switches to:

> Project1 - Microsoft Visual Basic [break]   ▁□▓

Single Stepping

Often, when you have worked through a program by hand, you will want to have the computer walk through the same example, one line of code at a time. Visual Basic lets you execute one statement in your program at a time—*single stepping*—by repeatedly pressing F8 or the Single Step tool on the Debug toolbar. (Of course, if Visual Basic is waiting for an event to happen, there won't be any statements to execute.)

The first time you press F8 to start single stepping through your code, Visual Basic highlights the first executable statement of the program in the Code window and places a yellow arrow in the leftmost column (see Figure 15-3). Usually, the first

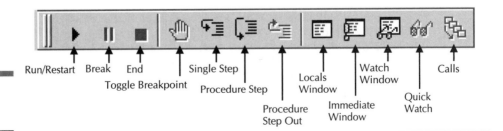

Run/Restart Break End Single Step Locals Window Watch Window Calls
Toggle Breakpoint Procedure Step Procedure Step Out Immediate Window Quick Watch

The Debug toolbar

Figure 15-2.

Tool	Keyboard Equivalent	Function
Run/Restart	F5/SHIFT+F5	Starts the program anew or restarts it
Break	CTRL+BREAK	Interrupts the program
End		Ends the program
Toggle Breakpoint	F9	Sets a line before which the program will stop
Single Step (Step into)	F8	Moves through the program one statement at a time
Procedure Step (Step over)	SHIFT+F8	Performs like the single-step tool, except procedure and function calls are treated as one step
Procedure Step Out	CTRL+SHIFT+F8	Executes whatever lines are remaining in the current procedure
Locals Window		Shows the Locals window (discussed later in this chapter)
Immediate Window		Shows the Immediate window (discussed previously in this chapter)
Watch Window		Brings up the Watch window (discussed later in this chapter)
Quick Watch	SHIFT+F9	Checks the value of the expression while the program is in break mode (discussed later in this chapter)
Calls	CTRL+L	Shows the procedure calls that got you to where you are in the order that they were executed

The Debugging
Tools and What
They Do
Table 15-1.

statement will be in the Form_Initialize procedure, or Form_Load procedure if there is no Form_Initialize. Each subsequent press of F8 or the Single Step tool executes the boxed statement and boxes the next statement to be executed. As you can imagine, single stepping through a program is ideal for tracing the logical flow of a program through decision structures and procedures.

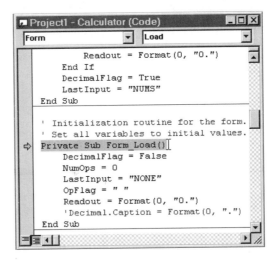

```
Readout = Format(0, "0.")
        End If
        DecimalFlag = True
        LastInput = "NUMS"
    End Sub

' Initialization routine for the form.
' Set all variables to initial values.
Private Sub Form_Load()
        DecimalFlag = False
        NumOps = 0
        LastInput = "NONE"
        OpFlag = " "
        Readout = Format(0, "0.")
        'Decimal.Caption = Format(0, ".")
    End Sub
```

Single stepping
Figure 15-3.

Whenever a procedure is called during single stepping, the procedure code fills the Code window. After its statements have been highlighted and executed (one at a time), the routine that called it reappears in the Code window.

Besides the F8 key or Single Step tool from the toolbar, you can also use SHIFT+F8 (or the Procedure Step tool) to single step through a program. With this method, each procedure is processed as if it were a single statement. In many cases, this is preferable to single stepping through a complex function that you already know works.

TIP: When you want to stop single stepping and run the program normally again, simply press F5 or the Run button.

Single stepping through a program will probably take you to the place where you know a problem lurks. Now you want to place a break at that point before continuing the debugging process. This can be done with the Stop statement or, more commonly, by using a breakpoint, one of the tools available from the Debug menu or Debug toolbar (and explained in the next section).

TIP: One of the niftiest features of VB is the ability to change the values of variables while a program is suspended and then have those new values be used when you continue stepping through or running the program. (This feature is usually called "edit and continue.") The trick is that any changes you make to a variable or a property in the Immediate window replace their current values in the program. You'll see an example of using edit and continue to debug a loop a little later on in this chapter.

15

Stopping Programs Temporarily

Debug.Print statements help you debug your program by printing values dynamically—while the program is running. (There are other methods for seeing what is happening dynamically—see the section on watchpoints a little later in the chapter.) More often than not, however, you'll need to stop your program temporarily and look at a snapshot of the values of many of its variables. The problem is that using CTRL+BREAK is a pretty crude tool to stop your program; you usually won't know exactly what procedure you are in when the program stops. For example, suppose you want to know why a variable seems not to have the value you want. You need to pinpoint the location where the value starts behaving strangely. Just printing the values to the Immediate window may not be enough.

There are three ways to stop a program temporarily. The least flexible is to use the Stop statement within your code. This method was inherited from GW-BASIC. Stop statements remain in your code until you remove them by hand, so many programmers avoid them.

Breakpoints, on the other hand, are toggled off or on by pressing F9 or using the "hand-up" tool from the toolbar. (You can also select Toggle Breakpoint from the Debug menu by pressing ALT+D, T.) Breakpoints are usually shown in red in your code and have a red dot next to the line in the code (see Figure 15-4).

When you run a program and Visual Basic encounters a breakpoint, Visual Basic stops the code just *before* executing the statement with the breakpoint. It then enters break mode. You can set multiple breakpoints. To remove a breakpoint, position the cursor on the breakpoint and press ALT+D, T (or press F9). To clear all breakpoints from a program, press ALT+D, C (or choose the Clear All Breakpoints option on the Run menu—CTRL+SHIFT+F9 is the shortcut).

Finally, Visual Basic 6 has the Assert statement to give you another way to stop a program. The idea is that at various places in your program you know certain

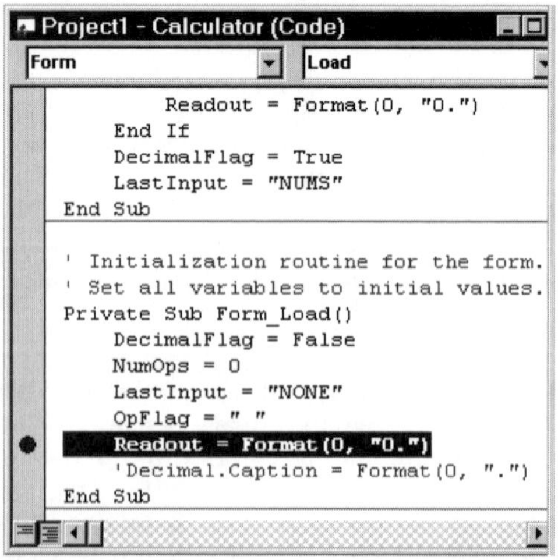

Line with a
breakpoint set

Figure 15-4.

expressions have certain values. (Well, at the debugging stage it is more correct to say that you think and hope the expression has certain values.) For example, suppose you are sure a Counter is between 1 and 10. Place the following statement in your code:

```
Debug.Assert (Counter >=1 And Counter <= 10)
```

From this point on, as long as you are in the development environment, Visual Basic will automatically put the program in break mode whenever this statement is processed and it is *False*. (Assert statements have no effect on compiled code, so they are really a nifty addition to your debugging toolbox.) In general, whenever Visual Basic encounters a statement in the development environment like,

Debug.Assert *Expression*

it will go into break mode if it processes this statement and discovers it is False.

Testing Programs in Break Mode

Once you have your program in break mode, you can use the Immediate window to examine the values of all your variables individually. As I said a moment ago, the edit and continue feature of VB even allows you to change the value of variables or properties. But even more is true: you can even make many changes directly into the Code window and then continue with your fixes added. (Visual Basic will warn you if a change you make means that it has to restart the program.)

However, it is sometimes helpful to see the values of all your local data at the same time. This can be done by opening the Locals window whenever you are in break mode. For example, Figure 15-5 shows the Locals window for the Calculator project supplied with Visual Basic when I placed a breakpoint at the end of one of the data-entry routines.

T ....
IP: Another form of edit and continue is that if you click on a value of a variable listed in the Value column of the Locals window, you can change the current value. Press ENTER to have the change go into effect. You can then continue the program using the new value.

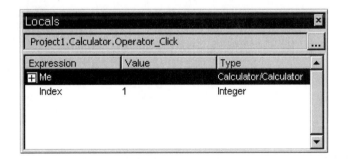

Locals window
for the
Calculator
project
Figure 15-5.

15

Now, suppose you want to test a procedure. Put a breakpoint (or Debug.Assert False statement) right before the call to the procedure or function you want to test, or at a place in the code where you will be calling it. Once the program stops at the breakpoint, open the Immediate window, if necessary, and write a driver program. A *driver* is a program fragment that calls a function or procedure with specific values. For example, suppose you know that with the parameter

```
Variable1 = 10
```

and the parameter

```
Variable2 = 20
```

the result of a procedure of two parameters is to make a form (a form-level variable named FormLevel1) have the value 97. When you want to test how this procedure or function behaves at a particular place in a program, add the breakpoint at the appropriate point and use the Immediate window to enter

```
WhateverYouAreTesting 10, 20
Print "The value of the variable FormLevel1 is: "; FormLevel1
```

See what happens. If the value of the variable FormLevel1 isn't right, you can begin to suspect that something inside this procedure is wrong. To confirm your suspicions, you'll need to check that no other form-level variable is causing the problem. You can add Print statements inside the Immediate window to check this, or use the Locals window. (Another possibility is to use watch variables—see the section on these that follows.) Examine the values of the relevant variables—the variables whose values affect the value of the variable FormLevel1. This check may quickly tell you whether something is wrong inside the procedure or function. If the value of the variable FormLevel1 is correct, then determine, again by hand, what happens for some other values. Always remember to try the boundary values (the strange values, like the $0.00 that the programmer in the story forgot). If the values always match your expectations, there's probably nothing wrong with the procedure or function.

Of course, in practice, you have to make sure your driver fragment sends all the information needed by the procedure or function—and that's not likely to be only the values of two variables. Before calling the procedure, you can make all the necessary assignments in the Immediate window while the program is stopped.

Assume that you've tested the procedure and know that the problem seems to be coming from outside it. Check each procedure that calls this procedure or function. Apply the same techniques to them: check what goes in and out of these procedures or functions. Of course, good documentation of a routine can help you by specifying the inputs and outputs.

TIP: Use SHIFT+F8 or the Procedure Step tool on the toolbar to treat a call to a Sub procedure or Function procedure as a single step. This way, you don't have to step through all the lines in all the functions and procedures in your program when you don't need to. Combine this with the View|Call Stack to see which procedure called the one you are in, or to look at the entire chain of procedure calls if need be.

Also, when you are in break mode, you can use the Step To Cursor item on the Run menu to process a group of statements in a procedure. (The shortcut is CTRL+F8.) Just move the cursor to where you want execution to stop and press CTRL+F8.

Quick Watch and Variable Watch

In every case, you eventually wind your way down to a procedure or function that just doesn't work. You now know that you have an error internal to a procedure or function. Although the Immediate window and the Locals window can be used to examine the values of expressions while single stepping through a program, using Visual Basic's Variable Watch and Quick Watch sometimes provides a more efficient mechanism.

The Variable Watch feature lets you see the current state of a variable when you are in break mode by simply holding the mouse over the variable. Your screen will look like this:

The Quick Watch item (SHIFT+F9) on the Debug menu lets you look at the value of any variable or expression. For example, you can look at the truth or falsity of an expression. To use Quick Watch:

1. Select the variable or expression you want to watch by moving the cursor to the item or highlighting the expression using SHIFT+arrow key combinations.

2. Choose Quick Watch from the Debug menu (SHIFT+F9) or use the Quick Watch button on the toolbar.

15

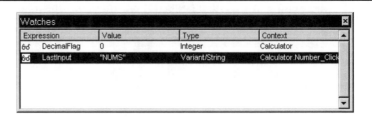

A dialog box like the one in Figure 15-6 (above) appears. If the value isn't currently available, Visual Basic will tell you. At this point, you can close the box with the ESC key or choose to add this variable as a watch item (described next).

Watch Items

Watch items are variables, expressions, or conditions that are displayed in a special window, called, naturally enough, the Watches window (see Figure 15-7).

You can choose the watch items you want to examine either before you start the program or while the program is running and is temporarily stopped. Any variable, expression, or condition can be entered into the dialog box that pops up when you choose Add Watch from the Debug menu. However, you can watch only global variables or variables attached to the current form or module. When you press ENTER, the item will appear in the Watches window with a little pair of eyeglasses as the icon at the far left (see Figure 15-7). As Visual Basic executes the program, the values of the watch items will be updated in the Watch pane of the Immediate window.

To create a watch item, use the Add Watch option on the Debug menu. A dialog box will appear, as shown in Figure 15-8. The Expression box initially uses whatever expression you highlighted. The Context option buttons are used to set the scope of the variables in the expression. You can restrict the scope to procedure-level, form-level, module, or global variables. The Watch Type option buttons offer two other ways of watching your program, covered in the next section.

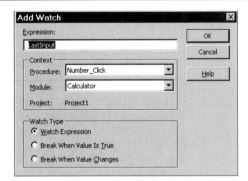

You have two ways to remove an item from the Watch window:

◆ Highlight the whole line in the Watch window and press DELETE.

◆ Choose Debug|Edit Watch. This opens a dialog box that looks similar to the Add Watch dialog box:

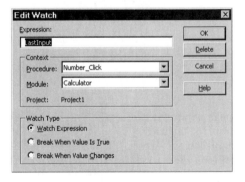

TIP: If you have to watch a string variable, use an expression like this:

"{" + NameOfStringVariable + "}"

Then you can quickly detect whether the string is the empty string, because if it is, all you'll see in the Immediate window are the brackets with nothing between them.

Watchpoints

As mentioned previously, sometimes the problem with a program appears to be tied to a variable or expression whose value falls outside some anticipated range, yet it is unclear in which line this occurs. In this case, setting a breakpoint at a specific line is

15

not appropriate, and watching the variable and single stepping may be too time-consuming. What is needed instead is the ability to suspend the program at the line that causes the variable or expression to reach or exceed some value. In Visual Basic, this debugging procedure can be done either by using the Assert method you saw earlier or by setting a *watchpoint*. Setting a watchpoint can be done from either the Add Watch item, the Edit Watch dialog box, or the Quick Watch dialog box.

If you choose the Break When Value Is True option button in Figure 15-8, Visual Basic stops the program as soon as the watched expression is True, and it highlights the line after the one that caused the expression to become True. The Break When Value Changes option button lets you stop execution when an expression has changed. The icons for these watch items in the Watches pane are a raised hand with an equal sign and a raised hand with a triangle.

TIP: Rather than using a watch statement and the Break When Value Is True option, consider using a Debug.Assert statement with the negative of the expression. Assert statements have the advantage of persisting between sessions.

Setting the Next Statement

Set Next Statement (CTRL+F9 is the shortcut) on the Run menu lets you bypass part of a program while you are stepping through it. Sometimes (especially when using the stub programming technique described earlier) you'll want to start a program somewhere other than at the beginning of a procedure or function; or you may, while single stepping, want to skip to another place in a procedure (you can't move to a different procedure). To use this option, you must be running a program in break mode (usually one you are stepping through). To set this option, while in the Code window, move the cursor to the line where you want to restart execution. Press CTRL+F9. When you tell Visual Basic to continue, Visual Basic starts executing at the line you just set. You can move both backward and forward within the procedure. You can also modify code at this point in order to test changes. Similarly, you can use the Show Next Statement item to have the cursor move to the line that Visual Basic intends to execute next.

Final Remarks on Debugging

Feeding a procedure or function specific numbers and using the debugging techniques described here are not cure-alls. No technique can help unless you have a good grip on what the procedure or function should be doing. If you are using an If-Then statement, are you testing for the right quantity? Should a >= be a >? Use watch items to check the value (True or False) of any Boolean relations that seem to be off (it is perfectly legal to enter X=19 as a watch value). Check any loops in the routine; loops are a common source of problems. Are counters initialized correctly; is there an off-by-one error? Are you testing your indeterminate loops at the top when you should be testing them at the bottom? The next few sections go through some hands-on examples that show off these techniques.

Example: Debugging a Buggy Loop

Recall that in Chapter 7, you saw a loop that looks like this:

```
Total = 0
PassNumber = 0
Do
  PassNumber = PassNumber + 1
  Total = Total + .1
Loop Until Total = 1
```

This loop would continue forever. Suppose you put a loop like this in a procedure, forgetting that you should never test single-precision or double-precision numbers for equality. How can you use debugging techniques and the Visual basic debugging tools to find and then fix this bug?

Whenever you have a loop that is running amok, you'll have a bunch of techniques available to you (most of the time you'll be combining them):

1. Watch the loop variable.
2. Set up a watchpoint involving the loop variable.
3. Use an Assert statement.
4. Use the edit and continue feature to bring the loop to the step right before you *think* it will end.

In the first technique, you will probably want to watch the value of Total. You would quickly discover that it is growing without bounds. Knowing this, you switch to the second technique and set a watchpoint with the expression:

```
PassNumber > 10
```

Once the program stops, you can examine the value of Total to discover that it isn't quite equal to 1—and that is the root of your problem.

How would you use the third technique, an Assert? Simply add the line

```
Debug.Assert(Total <10)
```

The moment the Total variable stopped being less than 10, you would be notified.

Finally, how could you use the "edit and continue" feature to help you debug this loop? Simply:

1. Put a breakpoint in the first line of the loop.
2. When the program stops, use the Immediate window to change the value of the Total variable to 9.9.
3. Run the program again (F5).

15

Regardless of which technique or combination of techniques you choose, you'll quickly rediscover the rule that says "don't use an equality test with floating point numbers!"

TIP: When a Do loop seems to be running too long, add a temporary counter to the Do loop. Then use the counter in a watchpoint at some (fairly) large value. When the program stops, examine the state of the expression tested in the loop to help determine why your loops are running too long.

Using the Watches Window with Objects

The VB Watches window has a wonderful ability to peer into the state of objects. This can be a very powerful tool for your transition to an Object Oriented approach to VB programming. I'll show you how this watch feature works by using it to peer into the innards of the second version of the DeckOfCards example from Chapter 13. So bring up this program. Now follow these steps:

1. Add the MyDeck object variable from the Form_Load routine as a watch variable.
2. Put a breakpoint at the start of the Loop.
3. Run the program.

Note that when Visual Basic hits the breakpoint, it will have stopped *after* the MyDeck object was created. This is because the MyDeck object was created by the line:

```
Dim MyDeck As New DeckOfCards
```

Waiting until the object we want to examine has been created is necessary. After all, how can we peer inside something that doesn't yet exist? After you rearrange your windows so that you can see the Watches window, your screen might look like Figure 15-9.

Notice that there is a little + sign next to the MyDeck object. As in many Windows windows, if you click on it, something will be revealed. Try it. The resulting Watches window will look something like Figure 15-10.

Now you can continue the process, peering inside the individual cards or the whole deck. For example, Figure 15-11 shows you what you will see if you continue the process a bit more. Notice that you can see the internal state of the object—that is, the value of its instance fields. As you can imagine, this ability can make what would otherwise be a very painful process of debugging an object (almost) fun.

Event-Driven Bugs and Problems

When you debug an event-driven program, you have to be aware of certain problems that could never come up in older programming languages. *Event cascades* are perhaps the most common. These are bugs caused by an infinite sequence of an event procedure calling itself or another event procedure, with no way to break the chain. The time such bugs are most likely to be introduced is when you make a change in

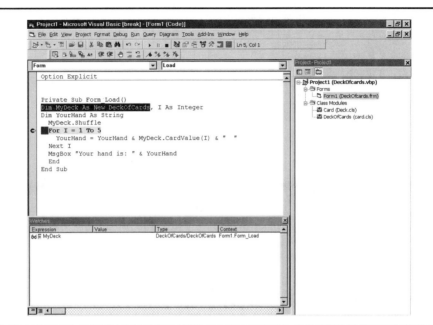

the Change event procedure for a control. The Change procedure is called again, which in turn is called again, and so on—theoretically forever, but in practice you'll get an "Out of Stack Space" error message. For example, add a text box to a new project and write the following (stupid) Text1_Change event procedure:

```
Sub Text1_Change()
  Text1.Text = Text1.Text & "Oops"
End Sub
```

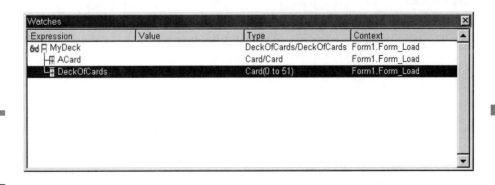

15

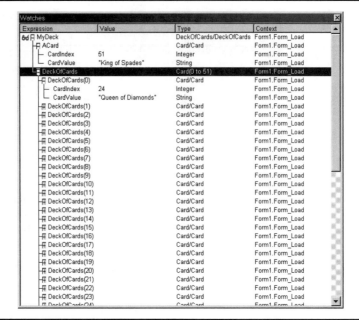

Peering inside
the state of the
objects that are
part of the
MyDeck object
Figure 15-11.

The moment you make a change in the Text box, the event cascade starts. The result will be an error message when VB reports that it has "run out of stack space."

Other special problems occur when you stop a program during a MouseDown or KeyDown event procedure. In both situations, during the debugging process you'll naturally release the mouse button or lift the key that invoked the event procedure. However, when Visual Basic resumes the program, it assumes the mouse button or the key is still down, and so the relevant MouseUp and KeyUp procedures will never be called. The usual solution is to call the MouseUp or KeyUp procedure from the Immediate window as needed.

Documentation and Program Style

Although you can remember the logic of a complicated program for a while, you can't remember it forever. Good documentation is the key that can open the lock. Some people include the pseudocode or an outline for the program as multiple Remark statements. Along with meaningful variable names, this is the best form of documentation. Set up conventions for global, form, or local variables and stick to them. Try to avoid tricky code; if you need to do something extraordinarily clever, make sure it's extensively commented. (Most of the time, you'll find that the clever piece of code wasn't really needed.) Nothing is harder to change six months down the line than "cute" code. Cute code often comes from a misplaced attempt to get a program to run more quickly. While this is sometimes necessary, Visual Basic 6 with its native code compilation ability is usually fast enough for most situations. I once saw a sign that made this point clearly:

Rules for program optimization:

1. Don't do it.

2. (For expert programmer's only) DON'T DO IT!

(Unless performance is unacceptable to the *user*.)

The point is that when you start thinking of tricks to speed up your programs, you can too easily lose sight of the fundamental issue: making sure your programs run robustly in the first place. In fact, dramatic speedups usually come from shifts in the algorithms in the program, not from little tweaks. Roughly speaking, an *algorithm* is the method you use to solve a problem. For example, in problems that involve sorting a list, the sort method you choose determines the speed of the sort. As you saw in Chapter 9, choosing the right sorting technique can speed up a program manyfold. This is more than any minor tweak can ever hope to accomplish. Discovering new (and, with luck, faster) algorithms is one of the main tasks of computer scientists and mathematicians.

This is not to say that after a program is running robustly, you might not want to consider ways of making it run faster. Here are some obvious, yet very useful, techniques that will likely never cause problems:

◆ Make sure that variables are integers whenever possible. (This is an obvious and not dangerous change.)

◆ Don't use variant variables unless you need their special properties. (Any statement using a variant that requires converting it to another type will run slower.)

◆ Use the simplest data type in loops. (For-Next loops with counters that are variants instead of integers may run half as fast; using single-precision counters can slow a loop down tenfold.)

◆ Never assign repeatedly to a property inside a loop unless you have to do interim updates; use a variable to accumulate the changes. (Property changes are much slower than variable assignments.)

The speedups from the last technique are so impressive that I suggest actually trying the following sample program. Add two command buttons and a text box to a new project. Have the MultiLine property of the text box be True. Add the following code to each command button's Click event procedure:

```
Private Sub Command1_Click()
'a test of how SLOW assigning to a property in a loop is
  Dim I As Integer
  For I = 1 To 10000
      Text1.Text =  Text1.Text & "  " & I
  Next I
End Sub
```

15

Now, for the second command button use a temporary variable to accumulate the growing string:

```
Private Sub Command2_Click()
'a test of how FAST using a temp variable instead of
'assigning to a property in a loop is
  Dim I As Integer, Temp As String
  For I = 1 To 10000
    Temp = Temp & "  " & I
  Next I
  Text1.Text = Temp
End Sub
```

The second one is about 35 times faster!

Here are a few additional techniques that can increase the speed of your program if the ones just given aren't sufficient:

◆ Preload the VB run-time code when the user starts Windows by putting a compiled Visual Basic program in the Windows Startup group. (This gives the appearance of speed but really doesn't speed up a program.)

◆ Use dynamic arrays whenever possible, and free up the space if it is not needed.

◆ Unload forms when they are no longer needed.

◆ Delete code if it is no longer used in your project.

◆ Use local variables whenever possible.

◆ Use a picture box for graphics rather than another form.

◆ Write a general-purpose error handler and pass the error code to it instead of having complicated error handlers in every procedure.

Finally, for advanced users:

◆ Use dynamic link library (DLL) routines; in particular, use API calls when appropriate.

(Obviously, it also helps to have as much RAM and as fast a hard disk as possible.)

CAUTION: Some ways known to make Visual Basic programs run faster (such as using global variables instead of parameters) are usually more dangerous than the minor speed improvement is worth.

One last point: there is sometimes a trade-off between speed and maintainable, readable code. For example, using the default property of a control is a little faster than giving the property explicitly, but I find it results in code that is harder to maintain. (And the difference is not even noticeable according to my tests!)

In any case, it's extremely difficult to modify or debug a program (even one that you, long ago, wrote yourself) that has few or no Remark statements, little accompanying documentation, and uninformative variable names. A procedure called MakeMartini(ShakenButNotStirred) should be in a program about James Bond (and perhaps not even there), not in a program about trigonometric functions. In addition, since Visual Basic allows long variable names, don't make your programs a morass of variables named X, X13, X17, X39, and so on. If you strive for clarity in your programs rather than worrying about efficiency at first, you'll be a lot better off.

Finally, if a procedure or function works well, remember to save it for reuse in other programs. Similarly, start accumulating a library of useful objects (class modules). Objects (or a modular program) will often have many procedures and functions. These procedures and functions may often have come up before in a slightly different context. This means that after you design the interface, sometimes all you have to do is modify and connect parts of a thoroughly debugged library of objects, or add some debugged subprograms and functions to the event procedures for the interface. (This is one reason why commercial toolkits for Visual Basic are so useful. The time saved is worth the small cost.)

CHAPTER 16

An Introduction to Graphics

This chapter introduces you to the techniques needed for building graphics into your Visual Basic applications. It starts by reviewing and extending the information on the Scale method you saw way back in Chapter 3. This is followed by a discussion of how the important AutoRedraw property works. Next, it's on to the Line and Shape controls. These let you easily draw lines and various shapes, such as circles and rectangles, on your form. (They work best if you have relatively few things to draw.) Then it's on to the graphical methods built into Visual Basic. Using the graphical methods can require writing a fair amount of code, but in return, these methods allow you to control every dot that appears on your screen or prints on your printer. Because Windows is a graphically based environment, the graphics powers of Visual Basic can be astonishing. The screen in Figure 16-1 shows you what a short program from this chapter can do.

The graphics methods in Visual Basic allow you to control each dot (usually called a *pixel* or *picture element*) that appears on the screen. If you take a magnifying glass to a monitor, you can see that each character is made up of many of these pixels. In fact, certain combinations of software, hardware, and monitors can divide the screen into more than 1,000,000 dots and theoretically choose from a palette of more than 16,777,216 (256 * 256 * 256) colors for each pixel. And the same graphics statements that work for the screen apply to the Printer object. This lets you control every dot your printer can put out; on a laser printer, this is at least 300 dots per inch.

In addition to drawing pretty pictures, the graphical methods and controls also allow you to embellish your Visual Basic projects, making them more professional. For example, as you'll see in this chapter, lines drawn around controls in special ways can dramatically change the look of your applications.

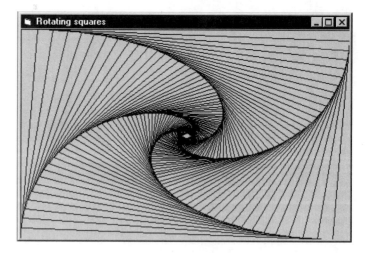

Rotating squares
Figure 16-1.

Computer graphics (especially three-dimensional drawings) is a subject in which mathematics must inevitably rear its head. However, this chapter uses nothing beyond a little trigonometry, and that only in the last few sections. Of course, you can just skip the math and use the programs; the results are pretty spectacular. Figure 16-2 shows an example of what you can do with polar coordinates.

Chapter 21 describes one other technique for creating graphics: using recursion to draw fractals. That chapter includes a short introduction to fractal graphics. Figure 16-3 is an example of what you can draw using those techniques.

You should be aware that in traditional programming languages, graphics are usually distinguished from text. This distinction is much less important with Windows and, therefore, with Visual Basic. With the exception of the various kinds of text boxes and labels, Visual Basic considers essentially everything placed on a form to be graphical. This is why forms can display text with such varied fonts and why you are able to use the CurrentX and CurrentY properties to position text accurately on the screen or in a picture box. Nonetheless, the graphics methods themselves work only on forms, picture boxes, and the printer. Since the ZOrder layer for controls (in particular, picture boxes and text boxes) is above that of the form, you can often get dramatic special effects by combining the two.

Finally, although this chapter shows you the techniques needed to do presentation-style graphs and charts, the Professional and Enterprise editions have a custom control to do this. If you need to make graphs and charts, you may want to upgrade to this version of Visual Basic rather than reprogramming all the tools yourself. The MSChart custom control supplied with the Professional and Enterprise editions makes it amazingly simple to build the most complex graphs.

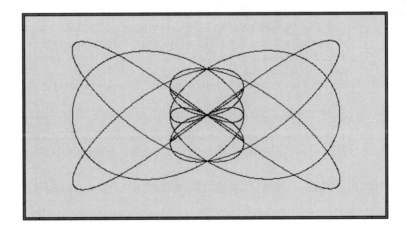

Polar
coordinates
demonstration
Figure 16-2.

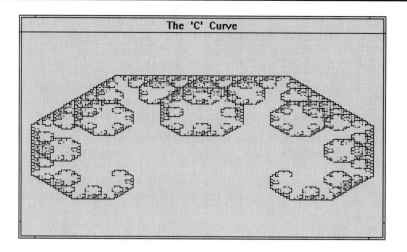

The 'C' Curve

Fractal drawing
Figure 16-3.

Fundamentals of Graphics

To draw on the screen, Visual Basic tells Windows what to display. Windows, in turn, tells the display adapter how to display the image. What this means is that what you can do with Visual Basic's graphics statements depends on the driver programs that Windows uses to control the screen and printer. However, using these driver programs is automatic. You do not have to worry about all the possible hardware combinations a user may have. This is different from what MS-DOS programmers are used to. When a program displays graphics under DOS, part of the program must check what kind of graphics board is installed (or whether any graphics board is installed), and then the program must be adjusted accordingly.

However, nothing comes for free. Windows has to do a lot to manage a graphics environment, and this forces trade-offs. For example, unless you set the AutoRedraw property to True so that Visual Basic saves a copy of the object in memory, you will have to manage the redrawing of graphics yourself. (Using jargon, you'd say that AutoRedraw controls whether graphics are *persistent* or not.)

NOTE: Images derived from setting the Picture property of a control and those that come from the Line and Shape controls are always persistent.

The effects of setting the AutoRedraw property to True are slightly different for forms and picture boxes:

◆ For a resizable form, Visual Basic saves a copy of the entire form. Thus, when you enlarge the form, no graphics information is lost. This option requires by far the most memory, but if your graphics do not currently fit on a form, but will when the form is enlarged, choose this option.

◆ For a picture box, Visual Basic saves an image only as large as the current size of the box. Nothing new will appear even if the box is enlarged later.

Thus, drawing to picture boxes requires less memory than drawing to forms, even if the picture box fills up the form.

How do you manage graphics yourself? The idea is that VB will trigger either the Paint event or the Resize event whenever you need to worry about redrawing the screen. To manage graphics yourself, therefore, simply put the code that will redraw the picture in a separate procedure, and call this procedure from both the Resize and Paint event procedures.

A Neat Feature of the AutoRedraw Property

There is one other interesting feature of AutoRedraw. Suppose you change AutoRedraw to False while a program is running. Then you clear the object by using the Cls method. Whatever you drew before you changed the AutoRedraw property will remain, but everything that was drawn after the switch will disappear. This feature can be very useful. To see how it works, start a new project and try the following demonstration program (recall that text is treated as graphics output on a form). For the Form_Load procedure, write

```
Private Sub Form_Load ()
  AutoRedraw = True
  Print "Please click to see a demonstration of AutoRedraw."
  Print "Notice that these two lines will stay on the screen after _
you double click."
End Sub
```

Now, for the Click procedure, add

```
Private Sub Form_Click ()
  AutoRedraw = False            'keeps old stuff
  Cls
  Print: Print: Print      'third line
  Print "But this line will disappear after you double click."
End Sub
```

Finally, the Double_Click procedure is simply:

```
Private Sub Form_DblClick ()
  Cls                      'Clears line from Click() procedure
End Sub
```

The ClipControls Property and the Paint Event

As long as AutoRedraw is off, Visual Basic activates the Paint event each time a part of the form is newly exposed. What happens within the Paint event in this case depends on how the ClipControls property is set at design time. If the ClipControls property is set to True (the default) and the AutoRedraw property is False, then Visual Basic repaints the entire object. If ClipControls is set to False, Visual Basic repaints only the newly exposed areas.

The ClipControls property has a few other features worth noting. Setting ClipControls to True also creates what Microsoft calls a *clipping region* around the nongraphical controls on the form or picture box. This means Visual Basic saves an extra outline of the form or picture box and the controls on it in memory. Windows can use this outline to speed up how painting the form works by not having to paint some parts, such as the background. Nor does it have to worry about information that is automatically persistent, such as the contents of a **TextBox** control.

Creating the clipping region does take time, so you have to balance whether the extra time (and memory) is worth it. Because Windows creates the clipping region and stores it in memory, setting this property to False can reduce the time needed to paint or repaint a form or picture box. The cost is that much more time is needed if the object is graphically complex with lots of controls on it. (Clipping regions exclude the Image, Label, Line, and Shape controls so these don't enter in the equation.)

 TIP: If the AutoRedraw property is True, you can speed up your program by setting ClipControls to False. Since VB is already maintaining the entire image, there's no need to spend even more time maintaining the clipping region!

More on the Paint Event

In any case, if you have set the AutoRedraw property to False, you will need to write (or call) the necessary code in the Resize and Paint procedure whenever you want to redraw part or all of a form or picture box. Therefore, the least memory-intensive way to handle the problem of text or graphics disappearing, because a user covered a form or picture box, is to redraw the image in the form or picture box in the Paint event procedure. Again, this solution involves a trade-off between memory-intensive and CPU-intensive programming activities. Setting AutoRedraw to True uses up memory, potentially speeding up the program. Using the Paint event procedure uses up time. You have to choose what's best for the application. At the extremes, the choice is easy: if the amount of drawing to be done is minimal, using the Paint event procedure is better. In any case, always remember that Visual Basic calls the Paint procedure for the object only if the AutoRedraw property of the object is set to False. If you inadvertently have set AutoRedraw to True and have code in the Paint event that you want to run anyway, you will be disappointed!

CAUTION: Be very careful about including in the Paint event procedure any commands that move or resize the object. If you include such commands, Visual Basic will just call the Paint procedure again, and you could be stuck in an infinite regression!

The Refresh Method

You will occasionally need to use the Refresh method when working with graphics. This method applies to both forms and controls. What calling this method does is *force* an immediate refresh of the form or control. Whenever Visual Basic processes an *Object*.Refresh statement, it will redraw the object immediately and generate the Paint event, if the object supports this feature. This, as mentioned previously, will let you see an image develop even when AutoRedraw is True. Note that when you call the Refresh method, Visual Basic will also call any Paint event procedure you have written for the object. The Refresh method is occasionally used in the Form_Resize procedure to redisplay any graphics that were calculated in the Paint event procedure. Also, while Visual Basic handles refreshing the screen during idle time, occasionally you will want to control this process yourself.

TIP: Don't overdo the Refresh method. If you use it too much, your application will slow to a crawl. (Imagine VB having to process a Refresh each time you work with an individual pixel!)

Saving Pictures

Visual Basic makes it easy to save the pictures you've drawn to a form or picture box. The SavePicture statement uses the following syntax:

SavePicture *ObjectName.Image, Filename*

The operating system uses the Image property to identify the picture in the form or picture box. If you leave off *ObjectName*, then, as usual, Visual Basic uses the current form. The syntax for this version of the method is

SavePicture *Image, Filename*

If you originally loaded the picture from a file by assigning an image to the Picture property of the form or picture box (see Chapter 3 for example), Visual Basic saves the picture in the same format as the original file. (For example, icon files stay icon files.) Otherwise, Visual Basic saves the picture as a bitmap (.bmp) file.

Example: Simple Animation

Although Visual Basic has many powerful tools to perform animation (see the sections "Animation and DrawMode" and "The PaintPicture Method" later in this chapter), you now have the tools to simulate one kind of animation: a so-called drunkard's walk (or, more technically, a random walk). All this means is that you imagine an object whose movements you can plot over time. If it seems to move randomly, you have a random walk. To simulate this, start with a form with a single command button, using the default settings. For this program, all you need to do is start a new project and double-click the command button. As you've seen, this puts the button at the default location in the middle of the screen. The Click event procedure will have the code for moving the button around. However, instead of moving the button a fixed amount, this project will move the button up and down and left and right 500 times. If you run the program, you'll see that the square will spend most of its time in a narrow range around the center. For this program, pixels seem to be the appropriate measurement choice (set ScaleMode = 3).

Here's the code. Notice that I have a Show in the Form_Load event so that you will see the directions. (Setting AutoRedraw to True will work as well, of course.)

```
Private Sub Form_Load()
  Dim M$
  Show
  M$ = "After you click on OK to make this " _
  & "box go away, click on the button " _
  "to see it move around the screen."
  MsgBox M$
End Sub
```

Here's the code for the Command1_Click procedure, which actually moves the button around "drunkenly" 500 times.

```
Private Sub Command1_Click()
  ' moving squares to imitate a random walk
  Dim X As Single, Y As Single
  Dim I As Integer

  Randomize
  frmRandomWalk.ScaleMode = 3               'pixel scale
  X = frmRandomWalk.ScaleWidth / 2          'start roughly in center
  Y = frmRandomWalk.ScaleHeight / 2

  For I = 0 To 500
    XMove = 3 * Rnd
    YMove = 2 * Rnd
    If Rnd < 0.5 Then
      X = X + XMove
    Else
      X = X - XMove
    End If
    If Rnd < 0.5 Then
      Y = Y + YMove
```

16

```
    Else
      Y = Y - YMove
    End If
    If X < 0 Or X > ScaleWidth Or Y < 0 Or Y > ScaleHeight Then
      ' DO NOTHING
    Else
      Command1.Move X, Y
    End If
  Next I
End Sub
```

The first two If-Then-Elses give the size of the random motion. The Else clause of the third If-Then-Else actually moves the command button up or down and left or right, depending on whether the random number generator delivers a number less than one-half or not. Later sections of this chapter show you how to add the code needed to give a trace of where the control has been. If you add the commands to change the background color of the command button (see the section "Colors" later in this chapter), the results are usually a quite attractive random pattern.

Screen Scales

The default scale for forms and picture boxes uses twips—that rather strange scale that is "1/20 of a printers point" (1/1440 of an inch). While this is a great scale for your printouts (since you are guaranteed the results), it can be less than ideal for displays. The default size for a form on an ordinary 14-inch VGA monitor running 640 X 480 is roughly 7,485 twips long by 4,425 twips wide. Since a twip is 1/1440 of an inch when printed, this default form size is roughly 5 inches by 3 inches if you use the PrintForm method on a screen of 640 X 480 resolution. Unfortunately, on a monitor running 1024 X 768 you get a default size of 3840 X 2880 twips or roughly 2.5 inches by 2 inches. (Thus confirming that a form that looks great at 640 X 480 *will* look like a postage stamp at a high resolution.) The following table gives you the coordinates in one column and the location of the point in the other, for a form on a monitor running 640 X 480.

Coordinates	Location
(0,0)	Top left corner
(7485,0)	Top right corner
(0,4425)	Bottom left corner
(7485,4425)	Bottom right corner
(3742,2212)	Roughly the center

Regardless of the resolution you are running, if two points have the same first coordinate, they're on the same vertical line; if they have the same second coordinate, they're on the same horizontal line.

Other Screen Scales

As I mentioned in Chapter 3, there are six other possible scales besides the default scale, as well as a totally flexible user-defined scale that you'll see in the next section. These scales are set by changing the ScaleMode property of the Form or Picture box at design or run time, as shown next:

ScaleMode	Units
1	Twips (the default)
2	Points (72 per inch)
3	Pixels (the number of dots as reported by Windows)
4	Characters (units default as 12 points high and 20 points wide)
5	Inches
6	Millimeters
7	Centimeters

Once you set the ScaleMode property to one of these new values, you can read off the size of the *drawing area*, which is the area inside the form (excluding the title bar and borders) or the picture box or the printable area on a piece of paper in your printer. This information is reported in the current units when you use the ScaleHeight and ScaleWidth properties. If you start up a new project and run the following little program, you'll see what the usable area is in different modes for your full screen:

```
Private Sub Form_Load()
Show
WindowState = vbMaximized
Dim I As Integer
For I = 1 To 7
  ScaleMode = I
  Print "The ScaleHeight dimension of the full screen in ScaleMode = " & I _
& " is " & ScaleHeight
  Print "The ScaleWidth dimension of the full screen in ScaleMode = " & I _
& " is " & ScaleWidth
  Print
Next I
End Sub
```

As you can see, all this program does is change the ScaleMode property inside a loop and report the size of a maximized form using that scale.

TIP: Since both ScaleHeight and ScaleWidth report their results using the units selected by ScaleMode, recalculating their values in the Form_Resize is a very convenient way for resetting form-level or global variables.

On the other hand, the Height and Width properties of a form are less useful for graphics. This is because these properties give you the area of the form, *including* the borders and title bar, if there are any. In graphics, you usually care more about the dimensions of the drawing area.

TIP: While the Height and Width properties of a form are less useful for graphics, the Height and Width properties of the Screen object are very useful. This is because they give you the usable area of the *whole* screen. Use form or global variables for the Height and Width properties of the Screen object and recalculate these in the Form_Resize event. Then you can use a percentage of these variables in your code in order to make it easier to have your code independent of the particular monitor and card. An example of this is may be found at the end of this chapter.

Custom Scales

The screen is normally numbered with (0,0) as the top left corner. This is obviously inconvenient for drawing tables, charts, graphs, and other mathematical shapes. In most of these situations, you want the coordinates to decrease as you move from top to bottom and increase as you move from left to right. For example, mathematics usually uses an X-Y (Cartesian) system, with X measuring how much across you are from a central point (the origin) and Y measuring how much up or down from the origin you are. Or, when you build graphs for your business, you'll probably want 0,0 to be on the left-hand boundary halfway down the screen.

For example, Figure 16-4 plots a few points on the X-Y plane with 0,0 in the center.

The Scale method sets up new coordinates for forms and picture boxes that you can use in any of the graphics methods. For example,

```
Scale (-320,240) - (320,-240)
```

sets up a new coordinate system with the coordinates of the top left corner being (-320,240) and the bottom right corner being (320,-240). After this method, the four corners are described in a clockwise order, starting from the top left:

```
(-320,240)
(320,240)
(320,-240)
(-320,-240)
```

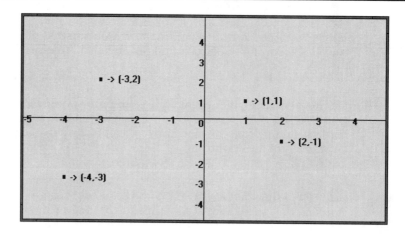

X-Y plane with
points
Figure 16-4.

Now 0,0 is roughly in the center of the screen. (This scale would be useful in converting a 640 X 480 screen to be used in making graphs where the center of the screen is supposed to be the origin.) This placement occurs because whenever Visual Basic processes a Scale method that changes to a custom scale, the program automatically finds the pixel that corresponds to your coordinates, rounding if necessary. On the other hand, code that defines a scale such as

```
Scale (0,0) - (640,480)
```

would give you roughly the same detail as the previous scale, but (0,0) would be the coordinates of the top left corner. In general, the Scale method looks like this,

```
    Scale (LeftX,TopY) - (RightX,BottomY)
```

where *LeftX* is a single-precision real number that will represent the smallest X coordinate (leftmost), *TopY* is a single-precision number for the largest Y (top), *RightX* is the right edge, and *BottomY* the bottom edge. For example,

```
Scale (-1E38,1E38) - (1E38,-1E38)
```

gives you the largest possible scale, which means the smallest amount of detail. Large X and Y changes are needed to light up adjacent pixels.

The statement

```
Scale (-1,1) - (1,-1)
```

gives you a relatively small scale. Regardless of your screen resolution, this scale lets you get very fine detail. Only tiny (less than 1) changes in X and Y are needed to light up adjacent pixels.

If you use the Scale method with no coordinates, Visual Basic will reset the coordinates back to the default scale of (0,0) for the top left corner and the units will be twips.

TIP: Some programmers prefer using a custom scale rather than percentages of the Screen.Height (ScaleHeight) and Screen.Width (ScaleWidth) properties in their code.

Another Way to Set Up Custom Scales

The Scale method is the simplest way to set up a custom scale, but there is one other way that occasionally may be useful. You simply specify the coordinates of the top left corner and how Visual Basic should measure the vertical and horizontal scales. You do all this by using combinations of the ScaleLeft, ScaleTop, ScaleWidth, and ScaleHeight properties. For example, after Visual Basic processes

```
Object.ScaleLeft = 1000
Object.ScaleTop = 500
```

then the coordinates of the top left corner of the object are (1000,500). After a statement like this one, all graphics methods for drawing within the object are calculated based on these new coordinates for the top left corner. For example, if you made these changes to a form, then to place an object at the top left corner now requires setting its Top property to 500 and its Left property to 1000.

The next thing you will do is set the ScaleHeight and ScaleWidth property. For example:

```
Object.ScaleLeft = 1000
Object.ScaleTop = 500
Object.ScaleHeight = 250
Object.ScaleWidth = 500
```

Then the bottom right corner would have coordinates 1500 (=ScaleLeft + ScaleWidth), 750 (=ScaleTop + ScaleHeight).

Just as with the Scale method, you can use any single-precision number to reset these four properties.

NOTE: When these properties have positive values, coordinates increase from top to bottom and left to right, respectively. If you set them to negative values, coordinates increase from bottom to top and right to left. This means that if you want a usual mathematical type scale where coordinates increase from left to right and decrease from top to bottom, you'll need to set ScaleHeight to be negative and ScaleWidth to positive. (You can see an example of this in Figure 16-5.)

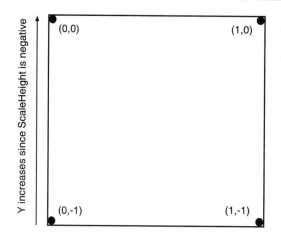

Setting a custom
scale using
ScaleHeight
with negative
values

Figure 16-5.

The Line and Shape Controls

You can quickly display simple lines and shapes or print them on a printer with the Line and Shape controls. They are different than most other controls because they do not respond to *any* events: they are for display or printing only. This lack of responsiveness means they are also quite sparing of Windows resources. The Shape control can be used to display rectangles, squares, ovals, or circles. You can also use it to display rounded rectangles and rounded squares. The icon for the Shape control is three overlapping shapes. The Line control can be used to display lines of varying thickness on a form. The icon for the Line control on the toolbox is a diagonal line. Figure 16-6 shows the various possibilities for lines and shapes.

The Shape Control

The Shape control has 20 properties. Usually, you change them dynamically with code while the application is running. The most important properties for the Shape control at design time are described in this section.

Shape   This determines the type of shape you get. There are six possible settings:

Setting of Shape Property	Effect
0	Rectangle (default)
1	Square
2	Oval
3	Circle
4	Rounded rectangle
5	Rounded square

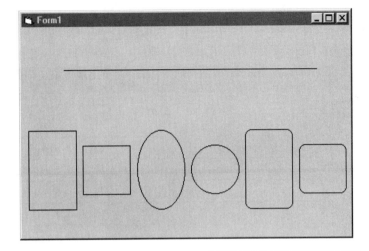

Possible Line
and Shape
controls
Figure 16-6.

To see the shapes for yourself, follow these steps:

1. Start up a new project.
2. Add a Shape control to a form.
3. Write the following code in the Form_Load and Form_Click procedures.

```
Private Sub Form_Click()
   Static CurrentShape As Integer
   Shape1.Shape = CurrentShape
   CurrentShape = CurrentShape + 1
   CurrentShape = CurrentShape Mod 6 'to prevent error
End Sub

Private Sub Form_Load()
   Dim M$
   M$ = "After you click on the OK button to make "
   M$ = M$ & "this button go away, each click on the form "
   M$ = M$ & "will change the shape of the Shape control."
   MsgBox M$
End Sub
```

BackStyle   This property determines whether the background of the shape is transparent. The default value is 1, which gives you an opaque border; BackColor fills the shape and obscures what is behind it. Set it to 0 (transparent) if you want to see through the shape to what is behind it.

BorderWidth   The BorderWidth property determines the thickness of the line. It is measured in pixels and can range from 0 to 8192 (rather too large to display on most forms).

BorderStyle   Unlike image controls, the BorderStyle property for Shape controls has six possible settings, as shown in the following table. Having no border (BorderStyle = 0) prevents the control from being visible, unless you modify the FillStyle and FillColor properties.

Setting of BorderStyle Property	Effect
0	No border
1	Solid (default)
2	Dashed line
3	Dotted line
4	Dash-dot line
5	Dash-dot-dot line

NOTE: If you set the BorderWidth property to greater than 1, resetting the BorderStyle property has no effect.

To see these border styles in effect, add the line Shape1.BorderStyle = CurrentShape to the previous demonstration program.

FillColor, FillStyle   FillColor determines the color used to fill the shape in the manner set by the FillStyle property. You can set the FillColor property in the same way as setting any color property, either directly via a hexadecimal code or by using the color palette.

The FillStyle property has eight possible settings:

Setting for FillStyle Property	Effect
0	Solid
1	Transparent (default)
2	Horizontal line
3	Vertical line
4	Upward diagonal
5	Downward diagonal
6	Cross
7	Diagonal cross

To see the various possibilities at work, start up a new project or modify the previous demonstration program so that your code reads as follows:

```
Private Sub Form_Click()
  Static CurrentStyle As Integer
  Shape1.FillStyle = CurrentStyle
  Cls
  CurrentStyle = CurrentStyle + 1
  CurrentStyle = CurrentStyle Mod 8 'to prevent error
  Print "This is in style # " & CurrentStyle
End Sub

Private Sub Form_Load()
  Show
  Print "Click on the form to see the different styles."
End Sub
```

This program uses rectangles, the default shape. If you want to see the effect of FillStyle on the other shapes, add the appropriate Shape1.Shape statement.

The Line Control

The Line control has 15 properties. Usually, you change them dynamically with code while the application is running. The most important properties for the Line control at design time are the BorderWidth property and the BorderStyle property. BorderWidth determines the thickness of the line. It is measured in pixels and can range from 0 to 8192 (too large to display on most forms). Like the Shape control, the BorderStyle property of the Line control has six possible settings, but as before, only the last five are really useful.

The most important properties at run time for the Line control are the X1, Y1, X2, and Y2 properties. These govern where the edges of the line appear. The X1 property sets (or tells you) the horizontal position of the left end of the line. The Y1 property sets (or tells you) the vertical position of the left-hand end point. The X2 and Y2 properties work similarly for the right end of the line.

NOTE: These properties use the underlying scale of the container for the line control.

Graphics via Code

If all you want to do is draw a few shapes on the screen, there is no need to use any of the graphical methods. On the other hand, once you master this material, you'll be able to take complete control of each dot that appears on the screen or that prints on the printer.

Colors

The first step is to decide what colors you want. If you do not specify a color, Visual Basic uses the foreground color of the object for all the graphics methods. There are four ways to specify colors. The first way is at design time using the palettes that show up in the Properties window. The second way is to work directly from the hexadecimal coding at design or run time (see Chapter 5).

The third way is to use the RGB function. The syntax for this function is

RGB(*AmountOfRed, AmountOfGreen, AmountOfBlue*)

where the amount of color is an integer between 0 (do not blend in any of that color) to 255 (maximum amount of that color blended in). Strangely enough, this is exactly the opposite order of that used in the &HBBGGRR& coding. (This is unfortunate because what this function does is return a long integer corresponding to the codes chosen, although you can still use this function in the Immediate window as another way to find the hex coding for a color.)

If you are comfortable with QuickBASIC and want to use the color scheme from there, use the fourth way, the QBColor function. The syntax for this function is

QBColor(*ColorCode*)

where *ColorCode* is an integer between 0 and 15. The colors this function gives are summarized in the following table:

Code	Color	Code	Color
0	Black	8	Gray
1	Blue	9	Light blue
2	Green	10	Light green
3	Cyan	11	Light cyan
4	Red	12	Light red
5	Magenta	13	Light magenta
6	Brown	14	Yellow
7	White	15	High-intensity white

For example, you can start up a new project and try the following demonstration program:

```
Private Sub Form_Load()
  Dim M$
  M$ = "After you click on the OK button to make "
  M$ = M$ & "this button go away, each click on the form "
  M$ = M$ & "will change the background color."
```

```
   MsgBox M$
End Sub
Private Sub Form_Click()
   Static ColorNumber As Integer
   Me.BackColor = QBColor(ColorNumber)
   ColorNumber = ColorNumber + 1
   ColorNumber = ColorNumber Mod 16    'recycle after 16 clicks
End Sub
```

Because ColorNumber is a static variable, each click on the form gives you the next color in the table as the background color.

Pixel Control

Now you know how colors are assigned, and you can change the scale of your screen as you see fit. How do you turn a pixel on? The syntax for this method is

> PSet(*Col, Row*) [, *ColorCode*]

(The PSet method doesn't support named arguments.)

Since the color code is optional (as indicated by the square brackets), all you need to do is replace the parameters with the values you want. The value of the first entry determines the column and the second determines the row. After Visual Basic processes this statement, the pixel defined by that point lights up. Obviously, where that point is depends on what scale you've chosen. For example, in the ordinary scale, using the default size for a form, the line

```
PSet(3722,2212)
```

would turn on the center pixel on a standard 14-inch VGA screen. After a ScaleMode=3 command, however, this would cause an overflow run-time error.

It is possible to use PSet outside the current limits of the form, but if you exceed the limits on the size of the screen, you'll almost certainly get an overflow run-time error. When you use PSet to turn on a point that is outside the form, Visual Basic records this information but doesn't plot any points. This is where the AutoRedraw property's being set to True can help. Suppose you ask Visual Basic to plot a point that is too large to fit the current size of the form and AutoRedraw is True for the form. Then the information isn't lost; set the WindowState property to 2 (maximized), and the point will show up.

For example, start up a new project and try the following simple Form_Click procedure. It uses PSet to draw a straight line down the center of the screen and a line across the bottom of the screen. Notice that the vertical line goes a little bit beyond the current size of the form because of the use of the ScaleHeight method in the line

```
For I = 0 To ScaleHeight + 1000
```

in the Form_Click procedure.

```
Private Sub Form_Load()
  Dim M$
  M$ = "After you click on the OK button to make "
  M$ = M$ & "this button go away, a click on the form "
  M$ = M$ & "will display a line via 'pixel control.'"
  MsgBox M$
End Sub
Private Sub Form_Click()
  ' line via PSet with a bit of 'clipping'
  Dim I As Integer
  AutoRedraw = True              'slows things down a bit
  For I = 0 To ScaleHeight + 1000
    PSet (ScaleWidth / 2, I)
  Next I
  For I = 0 To ScaleWidth
    PSet (I, ScaleHeight - 100)
  Next I
End Sub
```

The second For-Next loop gives you a horizontal line near the bottom of the screen. Figure 16-7 shows what you'll see. However, if you maximize the form, you can see that the graphics information wasn't lost, as shown in Figure 16-8.

Suppose you want to erase every other dot in this line. Although there are many ways to do this, at this point the simplest is to notice that redrawing a point in the background color erases it. For example, you might add another loop that reads

```
For I = 0 To ScaleHeight + 1000 Step 2
  PSet (ScaleWidth / 2, I) , BackColor
Next I
```

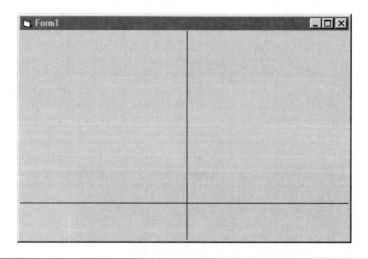

Line via PSet
(parts are
hidden)
Figure 16-7.

16

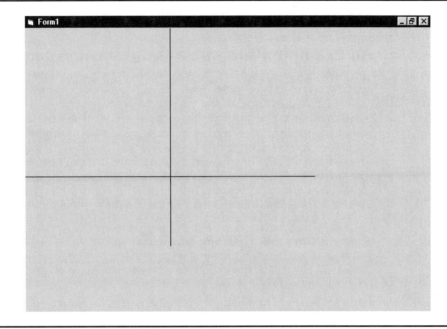

Parts
revealed from
Figure 16-7
Figure 16-8.

You might suppose that this fragment would make Visual Basic erase every other point. However, because of the way Visual Basic rounds off coordinates, this probably won't work on your monitor. In fact, adding this fragment to the previous program will probably accomplish nothing or too much. The coordinates of the points that are erased are so close to the ones that are turned on that either no changes show up or all the points are erased. This is because twips are a much finer scale than the actual screen resolution. For this reason, one possibility is to change the program to work in ScaleMode 3 (pixels) and modify the limits on the For-Next loop accordingly. Another possibility is to use a much larger Step size (50 seems to work well).

T IP: In a situation like this, where you need to know how many twips correspond to a single pixel, turn to Visual Basic's built-in TwipsPerPixelX and TwipsPerPixelY functions. (Since Windows API functions usually require pixels, these functions are often needed in using API graphics calls.)

You can use the Point method to determine the color code of any point on the screen. This returns a long integer using the &HRRGGBB& code you saw in Chapter 5. The syntax is

object.Point(*x*, *y*)

where *x, y* are single-precision values giving the X (left/right) and Y (up/down) coordinates of the point using the ScaleMode property of the form or picture box.

An Example Program: "Visual Basic A-Sketch"

The following program shows how powerful even a seemingly trivial method like PSet can be when combined with Visual Basic's event-driven nature. Many people find this program appealing because of its similarity to the popular Etch-A-Sketch™ toy. This program imitates that toy. For those who aren't familiar with this toy, the idea is that you can control the growth of a line by twisting and turning two knobs that control the up/down and left/right directions. The trick (and what makes the game so appealing) is that the line has to be continuous; you can't break it up. Nonetheless, you can draw what appear to be circles and other complicated shapes by carefully combining twists of the up/down and left/right controls. It obviously isn't nearly as sophisticated as the Paint program supplied with Windows, but it is a lot of fun.

The following program imitates this game by using the KeyDown event procedure to detect the arrow keys. Each time you press UP ARROW, the pixel directly up from where you were turns on. Each time you press LEFT ARROW, the pixel directly to the left is turned on, and so on. If you hold an arrow key down, you can draw multiple pixels in the same direction.

The program needs two forms, one for directions. Make this one the startup form and give it the name frmStartUp. The other form should be named frmSketch; that's the one we'll use for the drawing area. Note that the frmSketch form should have the AutoRedraw property set to True. The initial screen should look like the one in Figure 16-9. The two command buttons on the directions form should have control names: cmdDirections and cmdStart. We will also add a text box named txtDirections for the actual directions. The following summarizes the properties of the directions form set at design time.

Control	Properties and Settings
First command button	Default: size, shape, color
Control Name = cmdDirections	Caption = Directions
Location: left corner	
Second command button	Default: size, shape, color
Control Name = cmdStart	Caption = Start!
Location: right corner	
Text Box named txtDirections	Background color set to that of the form

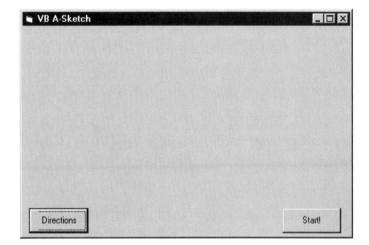

Here are the event procedures and what they do:

Event Procedure	Task
cmdDirections_Click (on frmStartUp)	Prints directions on startup form
cmdStart_Click (on frmStartUp)	Loads the form (frmSketch) for drawing
KeyDown (on frmSketch)	Interprets keystrokes, plots
QueryUnload (on frmSketch)	Unloads all the forms and ends the program

Here's the cmdDirections_Click procedure that is attached to the Directions button on frmStartUp:

```
Private Sub cmdDirections_Click()
   txtDirections.Text = "This program imitates the Etch-A-Sketch (TM) game." _
      & vbCrLf & vbCrLf & "As you hold down an arrow key a line will grow in " _
      & "that direction, starting from the center of the screen." _
      & " Press the End key to end." _
      & vbCrLf & vbCrLf & "Click on the Start button to start."
End Sub
```

For the cmdStart_Click procedure, which is attached to the Start button on frmStartUp, we'll load the form that contains the drawing area and hide the directions:

```
Private Sub cmdStart_Click()
  frmSketch.Show
  frmStartUp.Hide
End Sub
```

Now, the second form needs some form-level variables to contain information about how big the screen is.

```
Private fPixelHeight As Single, fPixelWidth As Single
Private fWhereX As Single, fWhereY As Single
```

The variables fPixelHeight and fPixelWidth hold the current size of the form. (Note the use of the "f" prefix to remind me that these are form-level variables.) The program uses these variables to make sure the user doesn't go off the form. The fWhereX and fWhereY variables give the current position on the screen.

The program sets all these variables, as well as the ScaleMode, in the Form_Load procedure for the form containing the drawing area (frmSketch).

```
Private Sub Form_Load() 'on frmSketch
  AutoRedraw = True
  ScaleMode = 3                    'Pixels
  fPixelHeight = ScaleHeight
  fPixelWidth = ScaleWidth
  fWhereX = fPixelWidth / 2
  fWhereY = fPixelHeight / 2
End Sub
```

Next, to allow a user to resize the form, the program uses the Resize event procedure. The Resize event procedure on frmSketch will be triggered by Visual Basic when the form is first displayed or if the user resizes it. This way you can change the allowable limits for drawing while the program is running.

```
Private Sub Form_Resize()
  fPixelHeight = ScaleHeight
  fPixelWidth = ScaleWidth
End Sub
```

Note that these methods are needed in both the Resize and Form_Load procedures of frmSketch in order to initialize the fWhereX and fWhereY variables in the Form_Load procedure. All the work is actually contained in the KeyDown event procedure attached to the second form. To make it easier to read the codes for the KeyDown procedure, this program uses the symbolic constants built into Visual Basic for the various keys.

```
Private Sub Form_KeyDown(KeyCode As Integer, Shift As Integer)
  Dim YesNo%
  Select Case KeyCode
    Case vbKeyLeft
      If fWhereX <= 0 Then        'don't go off drawing area
        fWhereX = 0                 'but round down may occur
      Else
        fWhereX = fWhereX - 1      'move left 1
      End If
    Case vbKeyRight
      If fWhereX >= fPixelWidth Then
        fWhereX = fPixelWidth
      Else
        fWhereX = fWhereX + 1          ' right 1
      End If
    Case vbKeyUp                     'up 1
      If fWhereY <= 0 Then
        fWhereY = 0
      Else
        fWhereY = fWhereY - 1
      End If
    Case vbKeyDown
      If fWhereY >= fPixelHeight Then
        fWhereY = fPixelHeight
      Else
        fWhereY = fWhereY + 1
      End If
    Case vbKeyEnd
      YesNo% = MsgBox("Are you sure you want to end?", vbYesNo)
      If YesNo% = vbYes Then End           '6 is Yes button click
    Case Else
      Beep
  End Select
  PSet (fWhereX, fWhereY)
End Sub
```

The message box uses Yes/No buttons and ends only if the user clicks the Yes button. Finally, the QueryUnload event makes sure that the program truly ends. (Remember, because of the way this was coded, the form used to hold the Directions is still in memory!)

```
Private Sub Form_QueryUnload(Cancel As Integer, UnloadMode As Integer)
Unload frmStartUp
Unload Me
End
End Sub
```

Lines and Boxes

Obviously, if you had to draw everything by plotting individual points, graphics programming would be too time-consuming to be practical. In addition to Line and

Shape controls, Visual Basic comes with a rich supply of graphics tools, usually called *graphics primitives*, that allow you to plot such geometric figures as lines, boxes, circles, ellipses, and wedges with single statements. The Line method takes the form

Line (*StartCol,StartRow*) - (*EndCol,EndRow*), ColorCode

which gives you a line connecting the two points with the given coordinates, using the color specified by ColorCode. (The Line method also doesn't support named arguments.)

For example, the following fragment replaces the two For-Next loops in our earlier PSet demonstration with the Line method:

```
Private Sub Form_Click()
  ' line via Line with a bit of `clipping'
  AutoRedraw = True                    'slows things down a bit
  Line (ScaleWidth/2,0) - (ScaleWidth/2,ScaleHeight + 1000)
  Line (0,ScaleHeight) - (ScaleWidth,ScaleHeight)
End Sub
```

As another example, the following program gives you a starburst by drawing random lines in random colors from the center of the screen. This program uses a custom scale so that (0,0) is the center of the screen. We will use a resolution of 640 X 480 for this demo, and to make the math work out easier, we will use the Scale command to adjust the top left-hand corner so that it has coordinates –320, 240. The body of the For-Next loop calculates a random point and color code on each pass. Another use of Rnd determines whether the coordinates are positive or negative. Next, the Line method tells Visual Basic to draw a line from the center of the screen to that point. We do all the work in a general procedure I called StarBurst, which will be called from the Form_Click procedure as well as by the Form_Load procedure. The screen in Figure 16-10 is an example of what you'll get.

```
Private Sub StarBurst()
  'random lines in random colors
  Dim I As Integer, CCode As Integer
  Dim Col As Single, Row As Single
  WindowState = 2
  Randomize

  Scale (-320, 240)-(320, -240)
  For I = 1 To 100
    Col = 320 * Rnd
    If Rnd < 0.5 Then Col = -Col
    Row = 240 * Rnd
    If Rnd < 0.5 Then Row = -Row
    CCode = 15 * Rnd
    Line (0, 0)-(Col, Row), QBColor(CCode)
  Next I
End Sub
```

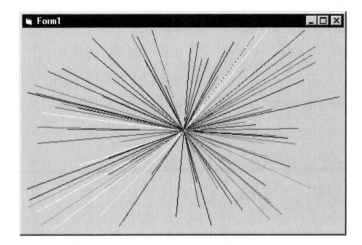

StarBurst
Figure 16-10.

The Form_Load sets AutoRedraw to be true but otherwise does nothing but display a message box with the directions. After the user clicks on OK to make the message box go away, the Form_Load calls the StarBurst routine.

```
Sub Form_Load()
  Dim M$
  AutoRedraw = True
  M$ = M$ & "After you click on OK to make this box go away "
  M$ = M$ & "you'll see the show. To make it more "
  M$ = M$ & "elaborate, click in the form again."
  MsgBox M$
  Show
  StarBurst
End Sub
```

Here's the Form_Click, which allows the picture to get more elaborate on each click of the form.

```
Private Sub Form_Click()
  StarBurst
End Sub
```

Last Point Referenced

Visual Basic keeps track of where it stopped plotting. This location is usually called the *last point referenced* (*LPR*), and the values of the CurrentX and CurrentY variables store this information. If you are continuing a line from the last point referenced, Visual Basic allows you to omit the LPR in the Line method.

For example,

```
Line - (160, 90)
```

draws a line from the last point referenced to the point with the coordinates (160, 90). When you start any graphics mode with a ScaleMode method or a custom scale, the LPR has the coordinates (0, 0) in that scale. For custom scales, this need not be the top left corner. After a Line method, the last point referenced is the end point of the line (the second coordinate pair).

Example: A Drawing Program

Suppose you wanted to have a program that would use the mouse to draw lines on the screen. To make it more powerful, you can let a click on the right mouse button start and stop drawing. Surprisingly enough, a program to do this takes one form-level Boolean variable (I'll call it fOKDraw) and just a few lines of code. You use the MouseDown event to determine whether the right mouse button has been clicked (see the next chapter for the details of the MouseDown event). If it has, you flip the form-level variable fOKDraw we are using as a "flag" and then reset the CurrentX and CurrentY properties. You do the actual drawing in the MouseMove event.

Here's the code:

```
Dim fOKDraw As Boolean  ' set as a form-level variable

Private Sub Form_MouseDown(Button As Integer, Shift As _
   Integer, X As Single, Y As Single)
   If Button = vbRightButton Then fOKDraw = Not (fOKDraw)
   CurrentX = X
   CurrentY = Y
End Sub

Private Sub Form_MouseMove(Button As Integer, Shift As _
   Integer, X As Single, Y As Single)
   If fOKDraw Then Line -(X, Y)
End Sub

Private Sub Form_Load()
   Dim M$
   M$ = "After you click on OK to make this "
   M$ = M$ & "box go away, you can draw on the form "
   M$ = M$ & "by right-clicking to start/stop mouse "
   M$ = M$ & "movements drawing."
   MsgBox M$
End Sub
```

16

Relative Coordinates

Up to now you've been using *absolute coordinates*. Each point is associated with a unique row and column. It's occasionally useful to use *relative coordinates*, where each point is defined by how far it is from the last point referenced. For example, if you write

```
PSet(12, 100)
```

which makes (12, 100) the last point referenced, then you can write

```
PSet Step(50, 10)
```

to turn on the point in column 62 (50 + 12) and row 110 (10 + 100). In general, when Visual Basic sees the statement

Step (*X*, *Y*)

in a graphics method, it uses the point whose coordinates are X units to the right or left and Y units up or down from the last point referenced (depending on whether X and Y are positive or negative).

Example: The X-Y Plane

Suppose you need to create an X-Y axis that allows numbers on the axes satisfying the following requirements:

-5 <= X, Y <= 5

Here's a fragment that will do this:

```
Scale (-5,5) - (5,-5)
Line (-5,0) - (5,0)                'X Axis
Line (0,5) - (0,-5)                'Y Axis
' Now to label the axes add:
LetterHeight = TextHeight("X")     'How high is a letter
LetterWidth  = TextWidth("X")      'How wide is a letter
CurrentX = -5 + LetterWidth
CurrentY = LetterHeight
Print "X - Axis";
For I = 1 To 6
  CurrentX = LetterWidth
  CurrentY = 5 + (I * LetterHeight)
  Print Mid$("Y Axis", I ,1)
Next I
```

This fragment calculates how high a letter is, using the TextHeight function, before resetting the CurrentX and CurrentY to allow a little space away from the axis. Since the CurrentX remains the same, all the letters are aligned, as shown in Figure 16-11. Finally, you might want to add numbers on the axes. You can do this by using the following fragment:

```
For I = -4 To 4
  CurrentX = I
  CurrentY = -LetterHeight/2
  If I <> 0 Then Print I
Next I
For I = -4 To 4
  CurrentX = -LetterWidth/2
  CurrentY = I-(LetterHeight/2)
  Print I
Next I
```

The result looks like the screen in Figure 16-12.

Grid Graphics

Suppose you want to draw a rocket ship, as shown in Figure 16-13. Since you can read off the coordinates from the diagram, it's easy (if a bit tedious) to write the following fragment.

```
Scale (0,0) - (25,20)
Line  (6,20) - (14,20)
Line  - (12,18)
Line  - (12,9)
Line  - (10,6)
Line  - (8,9)
Line  - (8,18)
Line  - (6,20)
```

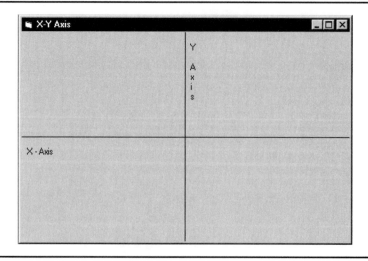

X-Y plane
Figure 16-11.

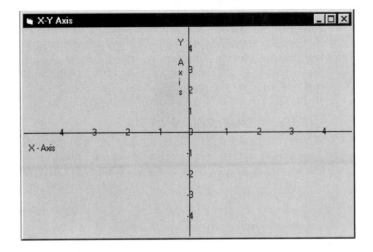

Labeled X-Y
plane
Figure 16-12.

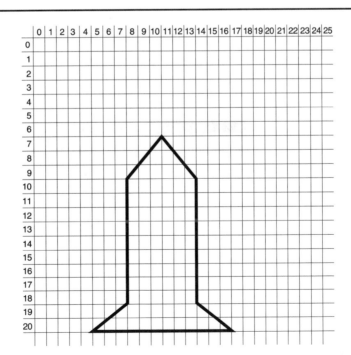

Rocket ship via
grid graphics
Figure 16-13.

It's at least theoretically possible to draw almost anything by outlining it using graph paper; just mimic the preceding example. However, as the object becomes more complicated, this method becomes less and less practical. One of the reasons that mathematics is needed for computer graphics is to give formulas for various complicated objects. The formulas then shorten the length of the program because they themselves incorporate an enormous amount of information. This makes it practical to write the program, whereas writing a few thousand PSet statements is not.

DrawWidth, DrawStyle

When you draw on the printer or the screen by using the PSet or Line method, Visual Basic uses dots that are normally drawn one pixel wide. (This is also true of circles. See the section "Circles, Ellipses, and Pie Charts" later in this chapter.) If you need to change the width of points or lines, use the DrawWidth property. The syntax for this method is

> *Object*.DrawWidth = *Size%*

The theoretical maximum size for DrawWidth is 32,767.

For example, Figure 16-14 shows what you'll get if you run the following Click procedure on a blank form:

```
Private Sub Form_Resize()
  Dim I As Integer
  For I = 1 To 10
    DrawWidth = I    ' Form is default
    Line (0, I * ScaleHeight / 12)-(ScaleWidth - _
(15 * TextWidth("X")) ,I * ScaleHeight / 12)
    CurrentY = I * ScaleHeight / 12
    CurrentX = ScaleWidth - 14 * TextWidth("X")
    Print " DrawWidth ="; I
  Next I
End Sub
```

The only tricky part of the above procedure is the use of the TextWidth method to decide where to display the caption. The Form_Load, as you can see, simply sets AutoRedraw to True and maximizes the Window.

```
Sub Form_Load()
  ' Demonstrates DrawWidth
  AutoRedraw = True
  WindowState = 2
End Sub
```

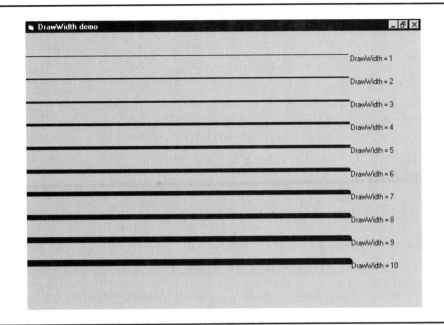

DrawWidth
demonstration
Figure 16-14.

If you do not want a solid line, all you need to do is change the DrawStyle property. You can see the effect of DrawStyle only when the DrawWidth is 1. There are seven possible settings when DrawWidth is 1:

Setting of DrawStyle Property	Effect
0 (default)	Solid
1	Dashed line
2	Dotted line
3	Dash-dot-dash-dot pattern
4	Dash-dot-dot pattern
5	Transparent (so you can't see it)
6	Inside solid (see the next section)

Figure 16-15 shows what you get if you run the following demonstration program and then enlarge the screen.

```
Private Sub Form_Resize()
  Dim I As Integer

  For I = 1 To 6
    DrawStyle = I
    Line (0, I * ScaleHeight / 8)-(ScaleWidth - _
        (15 * TextWidth("X")), _
        I * ScaleHeight / 8)
    CurrentY = I * ScaleHeight / 8
    CurrentX = ScaleWidth - 14 * TextWidth("X")
    Print " DrawStyle ="; I
  Next I
End Sub
```

Boxes

A modification of the Line method lets you draw a rectangle. The statement

Line (*FirstCol, FirstRow*) - (*SecCol, SecRow*), *CCode*, B

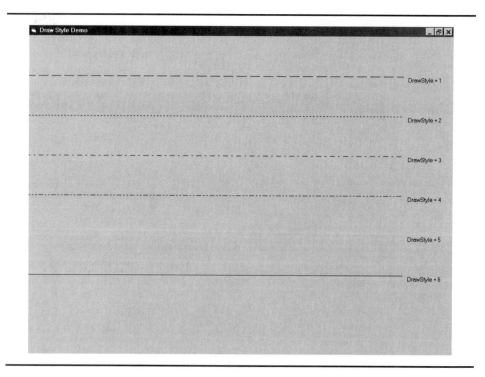

DrawStyle
demonstration
Figure 16-15.

draws a rectangle in the given color code (*CCode*) whose opposite corners are given by *FirstCol, FirstRow* and *SecCol, SecRow*. For example, the following fragment gives you nested boxes in a 640 X 480 scale.

```
Private Sub Form_Load()
  Show
  Dim I As Integer
  Scale (0, 0)-(639, 479)

  For I = 1 To 65 Step 5
    Line (5 * I, I)-(639 - 5 * I, 479 - I), , B
  Next I
End Sub
```

Notice that this program leaves off the color code but still keeps the comma to separate out the B. Without this comma, Visual Basic would think the B was the name of a variable rather than the Box command; Visual Basic would think you're asking for a line connecting

(5 * I, I)-(639 - 5 * I, 479 - I)

with color code the current value of B. (Since an uninitialized numeric variable has value 0, you probably would get a color code of 0.)

The width of the line defining the boundary of the box is determined by the current value of DrawWidth for the object on which you are drawing. When you have a fairly wide line for the boundary, you can see the effect of using the "inside solid" (DrawStyle = 6). As the following demonstration programs show, using the inside solid line makes for a boundary of the box that is half inside, half outside (see Figures 16-16 and 16-17).

Notice in Figure 16-16 the boundaries of the boxes merge, whereas in Figure 16-17 they don't. This is because the inside solid style puts half the boundary of the box inside itself, so there's less of a common boundary. Here is a program that doesn't use InsideLine:

```
Private Sub Form_Load()
  ' Demonstrates not using InsideLine
  Show
  DrawWidth = 10
  Line (0, 0)-(ScaleWidth / 2, ScaleHeight / 2), , B
  Line (ScaleWidth / 2, ScaleHeight / 2)-(ScaleWidth, _
      ScaleHeight), , B
End Sub
```

Now, to see InsideLine at work, run

```
Private Sub Form_Load()
  'Demonstrates using InsideLine
  Show
  DrawStyle = 6
  DrawWidth = 10
  Line (100, 100)-(ScaleWidth / 2, ScaleHeight / 2), , B
  Line (ScaleWidth / 2, ScaleHeight / 2)-(ScaleWidth - 100, _
  ScaleHeight - 100), , B
End Sub
```

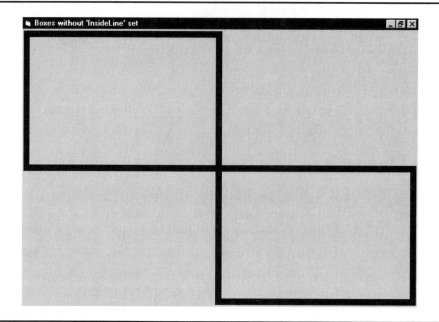

Boxes with
normal
boundary
Figure 16-16.

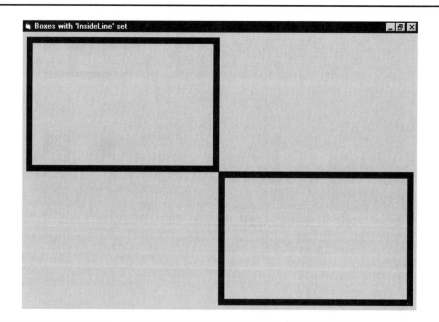

Boxes with
inside/outside
boundary
Figure 16-17.

16

Filled Boxes

You can arrange for the Line method to give a filled box as well. All you need to do is use BF rather than B, and you get a filled box. Therefore,

Line *(FirstCol, FirstRow)* - *(SecCol, SecRow)*, *CCode*, BF

will yield a solid rectangle whose opposite corners are given by *FirstCol, FirstRow* and *SecCol, SecRow*. For example, change the nested box program so the code looks like this:

```
Dim I As Integer
Scale (0, 0) - (639, 479)
For I = 1 To 64 Step 5
 CCode = QBColor(I Mod 16)
 Line (5*I, I) - (639 - 5*I, 479-I), CCode, BF
Next I
```

You get a rather dramatic nesting of colored frames, as shown with shades in Figure 16-18. This happens for two reasons. The first is that the Mod function lets you cycle through the QuickBASIC color codes in order, and the second is that when Visual Basic draws each smaller rectangle, it overdraws part of the previous one using the new color.

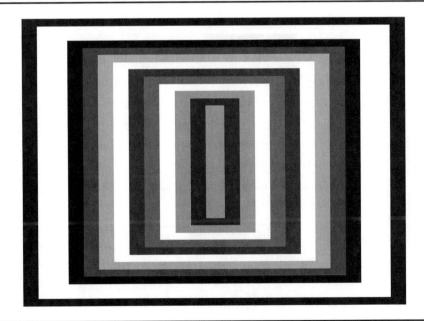

Demonstration of colored boxes

Figure 16-18.

FillStyle, FillColor

Boxes (and circles—see the next section) are usually empty or solid, but Visual Basic allows you seven different patterns to fill boxes. To do this, you need to change the FillStyle property of the form or picture box. Here are the FillStyle settings:

Setting of FillStyle Property	Effect
0	Solid
1 (default)	Empty
2	Horizontal line
3	Vertical line
4	Upward diagonal
5	Downward diagonal
6	Cross
7	Diagonal cross

Start up a new project and add the following code to the Form_Load. The screen in Figure 16-19 shows you the results of the following demonstration program.

```
Private Sub Form_Load()
  Show
  ' demonstrates FillStyle
  Dim I%
  Scale (0, 0)-(25, 25)
  For I% = 0 To 7
    FillStyle = I%
    Line (0, 3 * I%)-(4, 3 * (I% + 0.8)), , B
    CurrentX = 4.1: CurrentY = 3 * I% + 0.5
    Print "This is FillStyle # "; I%
  Next I%
End Sub
```

Once you have changed the FillStyle property from its transparent default (FillStyle = 1), you can use the FillColor property to set the color used for FillStyle. This property has the syntax

Object.FillColor = *ColorCode*

where, as usual, you can set the color code in any of the four ways mentioned previously.

Example: Framing a Control

There have been many visual improvements to Windows since release 3.0, but some of the little things have turned out to matter the most—one is the way controls look. For example, it was in Windows 3.1 that command buttons first gave the

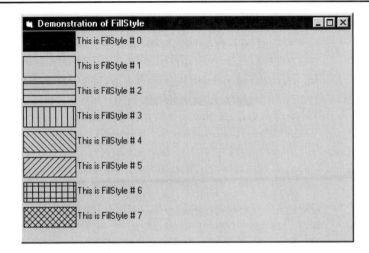

Fill patterns
Figure 16-19.

impression of being pressed when clicked. You control this 3-D effect with the Appearance property.

You can actually make your application much more visually appealing by framing controls in various ways other than by simply setting the Appearance property, using the frame control, or changing the BorderStyle property of the control. To do this, you need to draw different-colored lines of various thicknesses around the controls. If the colors you choose contrast with the background color of the form, you can get dramatic effects. Here's a routine that puts a frame around a single control:

```
Private Sub FrameControl(X As Control, CTop%, CRight%, CBot%, _
CLeft%, WidthOfFrame As Single)

   Dim LeftBoundary As Single
   Dim TopOfControl As Single
   Dim HeightOfControl As Single
   Dim WidthOfControl As Single

   DrawWidth = 1
   FillStyle = 1
   ScaleMode = 1

   LeftBoundary = X.Left
   TopOfControl = X.Top
   HeightOfControl = X.Height
   WidthOfControl = X.Width

   Line (LeftBoundary, TopOfControl - WidthOfFrame)-(LeftBoundary _
+ WidthOfControl + WidthOfFrame, TopOfControl + WidthOfFrame), _
QBColor(CTop%), BF
```

```
  Line -(LeftBoundary + WidthOfControl, TopOfControl + _
HeightOfControl + WidthOfFrame), QBColor(CRight%), BF
  Line -(LeftBoundary - WidthOfFrame, TopOfControl + _
HeightOfControl), QBColor(CBot%), BF
  Line -(LeftBoundary, TopOfControl - WidthOfFrame), _
QBColor(CLeft%), BF
End Sub
```

Although not short, the idea of this routine is simple. It draws four narrow filled boxes around the four sides of the controls. This version of the routine accepts a control, four color codes for the sides, and a width.

If you call this routine three times, first with a thicker width and one set of color codes, and then with successively narrower widths and different sets of color codes, the effects become even more dramatic. For example, if the BackColor of the form is light gray, try this routine with a black boundary around the box (QBColor(0)), a thick, light gray box, and then thin, white lines across the top and left (QBColor(15)), and dark gray across the bottom and right (QBColor(8)). Figure 16-20 was created using the following additional lines of code to surround a metafile that comes with the Professional and Enterprise editions.

```
Call FrameControl(Picture1, 0, 0, 0, 0, 100)
Call FrameControl(Picture1, 7, 7, 7, 7, 75)
Call FrameControl(Picture1, 15, 8, 8, 15, 25)
```

There are many other possibilities. Try reversing the white and gray lines; try leaving out the outer black lines. Experiment!

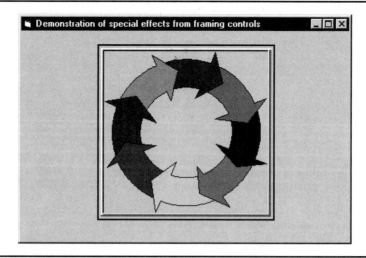

Demonstration
of special effects
from framing
controls
Figure 16-20.

TIP: For a routine that can frame many controls at once, replace the Control parameter in the above routine by four additional parameters that come from the leftmost control, the top control, the bottom control, and the rightmost control. Use these in place of the information provided by the control in the routine above. One way to obtain these parameters is to set up an array of the controls you want to frame. Next, write a routine to find out this information by passing the array to the routine and analyzing the position properties of the controls in the array.

Animation and DrawMode

The main problem with animation in Visual Basic is in redrawing what was there before the moving object obscured it. Redrawing the whole screen would take too long. Drawing the line in the background color wouldn't work because this would erase what was there before.

The key to successful animation is to use the analog for drawing of the Xor operator that you saw in Chapter 8. Recall that when you use this logical operator twice, it brings you back to where you started. When you set the DrawMode property to 7 for a form or picture box, then drawing a line restores the background exactly as it was before. The most dramatic way to see this is to run the following demonstration program, which combines the StarBurst demonstration given earlier with a box that moves randomly each time you click the form:

```
Private Sub StarBurst()
  'random lines in random colors
  Dim I As Integer, CCode As Integer
  Dim Col As Single, Row As Single
  WindowState = 2
  Randomize

  Scale (-320, 240)-(320, -240)
  For I = 1 To 100
    Col = 320 * Rnd
    If Rnd < 0.5 Then Col = -Col
    Row = 240 * Rnd
    If Rnd < 0.5 Then Row = -Row
    CCode = 15 * Rnd
    Line (0, 0)-(Col, Row), QBColor(CCode)
  Next I
End Sub
```

A Form_Resize procedure can simply call the StarBurst routine. Now, for the Form_Click procedure, try the following with the DrawMode line commented out and then with the line being executable:

```
Private Sub Form_Click()
  Static Col, Row As Single
  Static CCode As Integer
  DrawMode = 7
```

```
'This line erases the box and restores the background
Line (0, 0) - (Col, Row), QBColor(CCode), BF
'These lines move the box randomly
Col = 100*Rnd
If Rnd < .5 Then Col = -Col
Row = 50*Rnd
If Rnd < .5 Then Row = -Row
CCode = 15*Rnd
Line (0, 0) - (Col, Row), QBColor(CCode), BF
End Sub
```

(Use the Run menu or the CTRL+BREAK combination to stop the demonstration.)

There are 15 other possible settings for DrawMode. In all cases, Visual Basic compares the color code for each pixel in the object it is drawing with the color code of the pixel that was already there. This is done at the bit level by converting the color code to a bit pattern. For example, the DrawMode value of 7 that you've just seen applies the Xor operator to the color codes. A DrawMode property of 6 draws the new object by applying the Not operator to the color code of the original object. With a DrawMode of 4, Visual Basic applies the Not operator to the color code of the foreground and uses that code for drawing. You can find a complete list of the 16 possible settings for DrawMode in the online help, but 4, 6, and 7 are the most common values.

To see this at work, use the StarBurst fragment in the Form_Paint procedure and add the following Form_Click procedure:

```
Private Sub Form_Click()
  DrawWidth = 10
  DrawMode = 4
  Line (-245, 134) - (245, -134)
  DrawMode = 6
  Line (245, 134) - (-245, -134)
End Sub
```

Circles, Ellipses, and Pie Charts

Normally, to describe a circle in Visual Basic, you give its center and radius. The following fragment draws a circle of radius 0.5 units starting at the center of the screen:

```
Scale (-1,1) - (1,-1)
Circle (0,0), .5
```

The last point referenced (*CurrentX, CurrentY*) after a Circle method is always the center of the circle. You can also add a color code to the Circle method. For example,

```
Circle (0,0), .5, CCode
```

would draw a circle of radius 0.5 in the color code indicated here by the variable CCode. The following demonstration program shows off the Circle method, which produces the nested circles shown in Figure 16-21.

```
Private Sub Form_Load()
  Dim I As Single, CCode As Single
  WindowState = 2
  Show
  ' nested circles
  Scale (-1, 1)-(1, -1)
  For I = 0.1 To 0.7 Step 0.05
    CCode = 16 * Rnd
    Circle (0, 0), I, CCode
  Next I
End Sub
```

Next, you may be wondering what exactly the radius is. Is it measured in column units or row units, or is the measure the same in both the horizontal and vertical directions, as a mathematical radius would be? It turns out that the Circle method usually counts pixels by columns (horizontal units) to determine the radius. If you use the same horizontal units as vertical units, then the only problems will come from the aspect ratio of the screen (the aspect ratio is the ratio between the height and width of

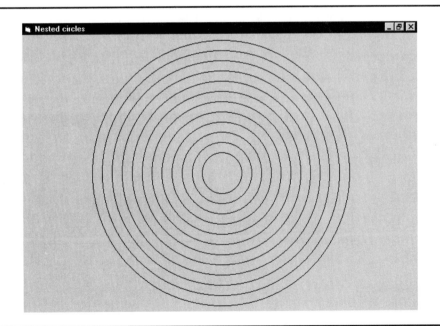

Circle
demonstration
Figure 16-21.

your screen). Usually Windows takes care of any aspect ratio problems automatically. In fact, the major screen resolutions (640 X 480, 800 X 600, and 1024 X 768) all have the same ratio. It's in the EGA area that you might have problems. You can take care of any aspect ratio problems with a variant on the Circle method, which will be discussed shortly.

You may have seen pie charts used to display data. Visual Basic sets up a pie chart with a modification of the Circle method. First, some terminology: a *sector* is a pie-shaped region of a circle, and an *arc* is the curved outer boundary of a sector, as shown in Figure 16-22.

To draw a sector or an arc, you have to tell Visual Basic at which angle to start and at which angle to finish. You do this using radian measure, which you may have learned about in school. (It is also used in the trigonometric functions in Visual Basic.) Radian measure isn't very difficult. It measures angles as percentages of the circumference of a circle of radius 1. For example, all the way around a circle of radius 1 is 2π units. It is also 360 degrees, so 360 degrees is equal to 2π radians. One-half of a circle of radius 1 is 180 degrees and is π units. Therefore, 180 degrees is π radians. Similarly, one-quarter of a circle (90 degrees) is $\frac{1}{2}\pi$ radians, and so on. To go from degrees to radians, multiply by $\pi/180$; to go back, multiply by $180/\pi$. (Since π is roughly 3.14159, 360 degrees is roughly 6.28 radians.) In any case, the statement

Circle (*XRad, YRad*), *Radius, CCode, StartAngle, EndAngle*

draws an arc of the circle starting at the angle given in radians by *StartAngle* and ending with *EndAngle*. (The Circle method does not, unfortunately, support named arguments.) To get a sector, use negative signs. Therefore, assuming you've set up Scale as (-1, 1) - (1, -1) and have set up a global variable called Pi = 3.14159 (or better yet, set Pi = 4*Atn(1)

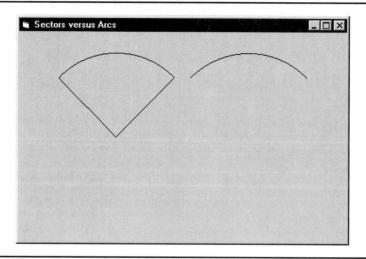

A sector and an
arc
Figure 16-22.

as a global variable), then the screen in Figure 16-22 may be obtained from the following code:

```
Scale (-1, 1) - (1, -1)
Circle (-.4, 0), .5, , -Pi/4, -3*Pi/4
' above line gives you the sector in Figure 16-22. And:
Circle (.4, 0), .5, , Pi/4, 3*Pi/4
' gives you the arc.
```

There are a few peculiarities of these methods that you should be aware of. The first is that although mathematics allows negative angles, Visual Basic does not. The negative sign only serves to indicate, "Draw a sector rather than an arc." The second peculiarity is that if you want your arc to start with a vertical line pointed due east (that is, 0 degrees = 0 radians), you shouldn't use -0 for the StartAngle or EndAngle. Instead, use $-2 * \pi$ (= -6.28 = -8*Atn(1)...). The final peculiarity is that angles in the Circle method can only have values between -2π (-6.28...) and 2π (6.28...).

Example: Pie Charts
Suppose you want to write a general pie chart program. This program takes a bunch of numbers (stored in an array) and sets up a pie chart using the numbers. Essentially, what you need to do is determine what percentage of the total each positive number is and set up an arc using that percentage. This should be a general procedure that is sent an array as a parameter:

```
Sub MakePie(A() As Single)
   ' This procedure takes an array of positive single
   ' precision entries and
   ' creates a pie chart using proportions determined by the
   ' array.

   ' LOCAL variables: I,First,Last,Total,StartAngle,EndAngle
   ' form level variable is assumed to be fTwoPi
   ' TWOPI should be 8*Atn(1)
   '

   Dim I As Integer, First As Integer, Last As Integer
   Dim Total As Single, StartAngle As Single
   Dim EndAngle As Single, LastAngle As Single

   First = LBound(A, 1)
   Last = UBound(A, 1)
   Total = 0
   For I = First To Last
     Total = Total + A(I)
   Next I
   Scale (-1, 1)-(1, -1)
   StartAngle = -TWOPI
   For I = First To Last
     EndAngle = ((A(I) / Total) * TWOPI) + StartAngle
     Circle (0, 0), 0.5, , StartAngle, EndAngle
     StartAngle = EndAngle
```

```
   Next I
End Sub
```

The key to this program is the statement determining the EndAngle. This statement determines what fraction of the total a particular entry is. Multiplying by TwoPi (roughly 2 * 3.14159=8*Atn(1)) gives you the radian equivalent. Since the StartAngle is -2 * π, adding this angle gives you the necessary negative number for the size of the sector starting due east and going counterclockwise.

You can add other parameters to control the size of the circle used and the scale used. You could also change the procedure to pass an array of strings that you could use to label the sectors.

How can you test this procedure? Simply create some random arrays of random sizes with random positive entries and call the procedure. Here's an example of the Form_Load you could use to test the procedure:

```
PublicTwoPieAs Single
Private Sub Form_Load()
   TwoPie = 8*Atn(1)
   Randomize
   Dim A(1 To 5) As Single
   Dim I As Integer
   For I = 1 To 5
     A(I) = 50 + 50 * Rnd
   Next I
   AutoRedraw = True
   Call MakePie(A)
End Sub
```

This is only a sample of the kind of business-related graphics you can produce with Visual Basic. It would be very easy to modify this program to produce bar charts if that was what you needed. However, if you are constantly using presentation-style graphs, you should consider getting the Visual Basic Professional edition. This product has almost all the graphing capabilities you'd ever want available via a custom control called MSChart (including 3-D bar and pie charts).

Ellipses and the Aspect Ratio

You convert the Circle drawing method to an Ellipse drawing command by adding one more option. This also lets you override Visual Basic's default settings if you need to adjust the aspect ratio for your monitor. The syntax for this method is

Circle [*Step*] (*XCenter, YCenter*), *radius, , , , aspect*

The four commas must be there, even if you are not using the color code and angle options that you saw earlier. (Step is optional, of course.) This version of the Circle method lets you change the default ratio of columns to rows. (It's really an Ellipse command.)

If the aspect parameter is less than 1, the radius is taken in the column direction and the ellipse is stretched in the horizontal direction. If the aspect parameter is greater than 1, the radius is taken in the row direction and the ellipse is stretched in the vertical direction. Start up a new project and then use the following code to demonstrate this, which increases the aspect ratio each time you click on the form:

```
Private Sub Form_Click()
   Scale (-2, 2)-(2, -2)
   Static I As Single
   Cls
   Circle (0, 0), 0.5, , , , I + 0.1
   CurrentX = -2: CurrentY = 2
   Print "This is aspect ratio "; Format$(I + 0.1, "#.#");
   Print ". Click to see the next size ellipse"
   I = I + 0.1
End Sub

Private Sub Form_Load()
   Dim M$
   M$ = "After you click on the OK button to make "
   M$ = M$ & "this button go away, each click on the form "
   M$ = M$ & "will change the shape of the ellipse."
   MsgBox M$
End Sub
```

Notice as the aspect ratio gets larger, the ellipse gets closer and closer to a vertical line.

Curves

This is where the real math starts. The first of the following sections uses the X-Y plane (Cartesian plane) and therefore a tiny bit of analytic geometry. The next section uses polar coordinates, and the last section uses some trigonometry.

The Scale method makes graphing any mathematical function trivial. The only problems come in deciding the maximum and minimum values to use for the Scale statement, which often takes calculus. However, as before, Visual Basic will clip any figure that is off the axis, so no problems result from setting the wrong scale, unless you are way out of line. In this case, you'll have to trap the overflow error that may result. You could have the error trap call a Resize procedure that would rescale the drawing area to allow the new information to be used. This might require recalculating all the points already drawn, however.

For an example, here's a program that draws a cosine graph, shown in Figure 16-23:

```
Private Sub Form_Click()
   Dim I As Single, TwoPi As Single
   TwoPi = 8 * Atn(1)
   Scale (-TwoPi, 1)-(TwoPi, -1)
```

```
   For I = -TwoPi To TwoPi Step 0.01
     PSet (I, Cos(I))
   Next I
End Sub

Private Sub Form_Load()
  Dim M$
  M$ = "After you click on the OK button to make "
  M$ = M$ & "this button go away, a click on the form "
  M$ = M$ & "will display the cosine wave."
  MsgBox M$
End Sub
```

You saw earlier in this chapter how to put in the axes and mark them. If you want to experiment with other functions, you'll need to change the scale accordingly.

Pictures Without Too Many Formulas

Now that you know about the Scale method, you can get to some serious picture drawing. The first method you'll see depends on the following simple idea. Imagine two points in the plane (say, with a tortoise at one and a hare at the other) chasing each other by having the hare move towards the tortoise on a direct line of sight. As the second point (the hare) moves, draw the line connecting the first point's (the tortoise's) old position to the new position of the hare (the second point). Now move the tortoise down this line a little bit (say, 10 percent of the way). Continue the process by drawing a new line between the new points. The screen shown in Figure 16-24 is what you get after a few stages if the second point (the hare) moves directly down five units and the tortoise always moves 10 percent of the way straight down the side of the form.

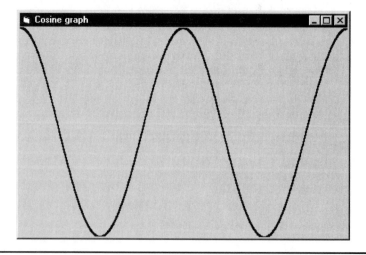

Cosine graph
Figure 16-23.

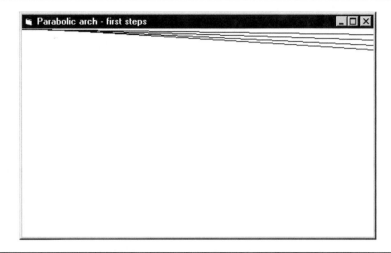

First steps in
tortoises and
hares
Figure 16-24.

To implement this idea, you need a formula that calculates the new coordinate of
where the tortoise is. Suppose first that you want the point halfway down on the line
connecting, say, 50,100 to 100,200. It's pretty obvious that it has to be 75,150.
Suppose, though, you wanted a point that was only 10 percent of the way along this
line. This turns out to be 55,110 (since, in a sense, you have 50 X units to move and
100 Y units to move). In general, the formula to move T percent of the way on a line
connecting *X1, Y1* to *X2, Y2* is

$$newX = (1-T) * X1 + T * X2$$
$$newY = (1-T) * Y1 + T * Y2$$

Here, *T* is the percentage moved, expressed as a decimal. (Some people like to think of
this as a weighing formula.) Here is the listing that implements this method, and the
result is shown in Figure 16-25.

```
Private Sub Form_Load()
  Show
  ' parabolic arch by tortoise and hare
  Dim PerCent As Single, X1 As Single, X2 As Single
  Dim Y1 As Single, Y2 As Single
  Scale (-300, 100)-(300, -100)
  PerCent = 0.1
  X1 = -300: X2 = 300
  Y1 = 100: Y2 = 100
  Do Until Y2 < -100
    Y2 = Y2 - 5                        'down five units
    Line (X1, Y1)-(X2, Y2)            'connect the points
    X1 = (1 - PerCent) * X1 + (PerCent * X2)    'move down line
    Y1 = (1 - PerCent) * Y1 + (PerCent * Y2)
  Loop
End Sub
```

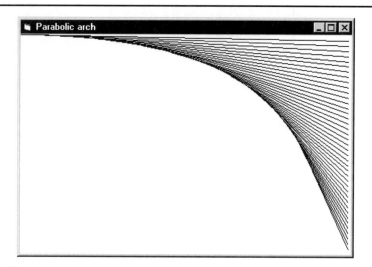

Parabolic arch
Figure 16-25.

Although this is not a bad start, you don't really begin getting results until you add more animals (points). Imagine that four animals start at the corners of a square. The first animal chases the second, the second chases the third, the third the fourth, and the fourth chases the first. The screen in Figure 16-26 shows you what you get after only four moves. Obviously, what is happening is that each square is both rotating and shrinking. If you continue this process, then you get what was shown back in Figure 16-1. Before you can work through the program, though, you'll need one more

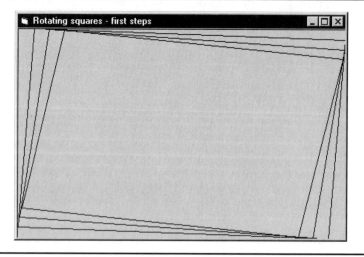

First steps in
rotating squares
Figure 16-26.

formula: the *distance formula* for points in the plane. This says that the distance between two points, *X1, Y1* and *X2, Y2*, in the plane is

$$\text{Sqr}((X2 - X1)^2 + (Y2 - Y1)^2)$$

where Sqr is the square root function. In Visual Basic, you'll want to make a function out of it:

```
Function Dist(X1, Y1, X2, Y2) As Single
   Dim A As Single, B As Single

   A = (X2 - X1)*(X2 - X1)
   B = (Y2 - Y1)*(Y2 - Y1)
   Dist = Sqr(A + B)
End Function
```

The purpose of the distance function is to tell the program when to stop—to know when the animals are "close enough." Next, you need a MoveIt procedure for the chase:

```
Sub MoveIt (A, B, T)
  A = (1 - T) * A + T * B
End Sub
```

Here's the Form_Click( ) procedure that does all the work:

```
Private Sub Form_Click()
  Dim T As Single, X1 As Single, Y1 As Single
  Dim X2 As Single, Y2 As Single, X3 As Single
  Dim Y3 As Single, X4 As Single, Y4 As Single

  Scale (-320, 240)-(320, -240)
  T = 0.05                          'Percentage moved if 5%
  X1 = -320: Y1 = 240
  X2 = 320: Y2 = 240
  X3 = 320: Y3 = -240
  X4 = -320: Y4 = -240
  Do Until Dist(X1, Y1, X2, Y2) < 10
    Line (X1, Y1)-(X2, Y2)
    Line -(X3, Y3)
    Line -(X4, Y4)
    Line -(X1, Y1)
    MoveIt X1, X2, T
    MoveIt Y1, Y2, T
    MoveIt X2, X3, T
    MoveIt Y2, Y3, T
    MoveIt X3, X4, T
    MoveIt Y3, Y4, T
    MoveIt X4, X1, T
    MoveIt Y4, Y1, T
  Loop
End Sub
```

The Do loop ends when the points get close enough—less than ten units from each other. Notice that you can't use the Box command because the square is rotated.

The block of repeated calls to the MoveIt function finds the new coordinates for each of the four points. By adding more parameters, you could have made the MoveIt subprogram make the changes one point at a time instead of one coordinate at a time. Finally, the following Form_Load procedure gives the directions:

```
Private Sub Form_Load()
   Dim M$
   M$ = "After you click on OK in order to make this "
   M$ = M$ & "message box go away, click anywhere in the form "
   M$ = M$ & "to see the picture!"
   MsgBox M$
   Show
End Sub
```

If you imagine the animals are moving independently along curves, then the kinds of pictures produced can be even more dramatic. The screen in Figure 16-27 shows one of the simplest ones. In this picture, you should imagine that one point is constantly moving around a circle around the origin while the other point chases it by moving along the line of sight. To write a program to do this or to construct one whose results are even more dramatic (chases along more complicated curves), you'll need formulas for the curves. That's the subject of the next section. That section shows you how to write the program that will draw what you see in Figure 16-27.

Polar Coordinates

Most complicated mathematical curves are more easily described by using polar coordinates. With polar coordinates, you describe the position of a point by saying

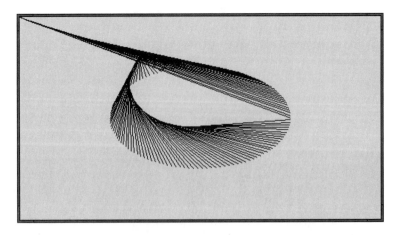

Circle chase
Figure 16-27.

how far it is from the origin and what angle a line connecting the origin to it makes with the positive X axis. Figure 16-28 shows this.

To go from polar coordinates to X-Y coordinates, use the formulas

$$X = R * Cos(Angle)$$

and

$$Y = R * Sin(Angle)$$

where *Angle* is the angle indicated in Figure 16-28. (These formulas come from dropping a perpendicular to the X axis and making a right triangle.)

To go from X-Y coordinates to polar coordinates, use

$$R = \sqrt{X^2 + Y^2} \text{ (in Visual Basic, Sqr(X*X + Y*Y))}$$

and the angle is Atn(Y/X) (unless X is zero).

The point of polar coordinates for computer graphics is that the equation of a curve may have a much simpler formula than in rectangular (X-Y) coordinates. For example, the equation of a circle of radius 0.5 around the origin is simply R = 0.5 (instead of $X^2 + Y^2 = 25$). This means the expressions

R * Cos(Theta)
R * Sin(Theta)

where the angle Theta runs from 0 to 2π radians are the X and Y coordinates of a circle in polar coordinates.

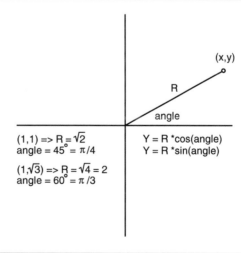

$(1,1) => R = \sqrt{2}$
$angle = 45° = \pi/4$

$(1,\sqrt{3}) => R = \sqrt{4} = 2$
$angle = 60° = \pi/3$

$Y = R * cos(angle)$
$Y = R * sin(angle)$

Polar
coordinates
Figure 16-28.

Here's the program that runs a chase around a circle, as was shown in Figure 16-27:

```
Private Sub Form_Click()
  Dim X1 As Single, Y1 As Single, X2 As Single
  Dim Y2 As Single, TwoPi As Single, I As Single

  Scale (-1, 1)-(1, -1)
  X1 = -1
  Y1 = 1
  TwoPi = 8 * Atn(1)
  For I = 0 To TwoPi Step 0.05
    X2 = 0.5 * Cos(I)
    Y2 = 0.5 * Sin(I)
    Line (X1, Y1)-(X2, Y2)
    X1 = (0.95 * X1) + (0.05 * X2)
    Y1 = (0.95 * Y1) + (0.05 * Y2)
  Next I
End Sub

Private Sub Form_Load()
  Dim M$
  M$ = "After you click on the OK button to make "
  M$ = M$ & "this button go away, a click on the form "
  M$ = M$ & "will display the picture."
  MsgBox M$
End Sub
```

Polar coordinates let you draw much more complicated figures. For example, you can easily draw objects like a four-leaf clover, as shown in Figure 16-29. The formula for the four-leaf clover curve is

Cos(2*Angle)

as the angle runs from 0 to 2π. (The rectangular X-Y version is very messy.) Combine this formula with the conversion formulas for X and Y given previously, and you have the following simple program that can draw a four-leaf clover:

```
Private Sub Form_Load()
  Dim X As Single, Y As Single
  Dim TwoPi As Single, I As Single, R As Single
  Show
  TwoPi = 8 * Atn(1)
  Scale (-2, 2)-(2, -2)
  For I = 0 To TwoPi Step 0.01
    R = Cos(2 * I)
    X = R * Cos(I)
    Y = R * Sin(I)
    PSet (X, Y)
  Next I
End Sub
```

16

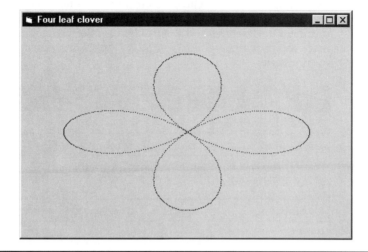

Four-leaf clover
Figure 16-29.

Don't be surprised if this takes a bit of time. After all, it requires a few thousand sine and cosine computations.

Combine this with a chase, and you get something like what is shown in Figure 16-30. (You can easily modify the "circle chase" program given previously to draw this.)

Four-leaf clover
chase
Figure 16-30.

Of course, you have to know the formula for whatever object you're trying to draw. Over the years, people have collected this information, and you can find books with massive lists of figures and their polar equations. Here's a short list of some of the more common ones where I am following the mathematical convention of using a "z" for the angle.

Polar Equation	Figure
$R = PositiveNumber$	Circle of that radius
$R = 1 + Sin(2*z)$	Infinity symbol on angle
$R = 1 + Cos(z)$	Cardioid (heart-shaped)
$R = 1 + 2*Cos(z)$	Limacon (Write a program to find out what this is!)
$R = Sin(n*z)$	Petaled rose—number of leaves depends on n>2
$R = z/c$	Spiral
$R = 1 + 2*Cos(2*z)$	Loop-the-loop
$R = Sec(z) + Tan(z)$	Strophoid (z <> 0, 90, 180...)
$R = Sec(z) + 1$	Conchoid
$R^2 = Cos(2*z)$	Lemniscate
$x = Cos(z)^3$	Astroid
$y = Sin(t)^3$	Also an astroid
$x = 3*Cos(z)-Cos(3*z)$	Nephroid
$y = 3*Sin(z)-Sin(3*z)$	Also a nephroid

It's easy to modify the four-leaf clover program to draw any one of these objects.

The PaintPicture Method

One problem with the earliest versions of Visual Basic (prior to VB4) was that there was no quick way within the program to paint a picture at a specific place on a form or picture box. (You had to use the BitBlt API call.) Visual Basic 4 added a version of this API call directly to VB. This new method is called *PaintPicture*. It has many uses—for example, it lets you do simple animation quite effectively solely within Visual Basic.

The simplest version of the syntax for PaintPicture looks like this:

object.PaintPicture *picture, x1, y1, width, height*

The object can refer to any form, picture box, or the printer. (If you leave it out, Visual Basic assumes you mean the form.) The picture parameter gives the source of the graphic to be drawn. (For example, it could be the Picture property of a picture box.) Finally, the *x1* and *y1* parameters give the coordinates of the top left corner of where you want the picture to appear (using the scale of the object parameter).

To see the PaintPicture method at work, add a picture box with the default size and width to the form. Assign the Picture property of the picture box to any of the bitmaps that come with Visual Basic (look in the subdirectories of the Bitmaps directory under the VB directory). Now try the following code in the Form_Resize procedure of a new project:

```
Private Sub Form_Resize()
Dim I As Integer, J As Integer
  Dim NumberOfCols As Integer, NumberOfRows As Integer
  pctMyPicture.Visible = False
  NumberOfRows = frmDrawBitmap.ScaleHeight / pctMyPicture.Height
  NumberOfCols = frmDrawBitmap.ScaleWidth / pctMyPicture.Width
  For I = 1 To NumberOfRows
    For J = 1 To NumberOfCols
        frmDrawBitmap.PaintPicture pctMyPicture.Picture, (J - 1) * _
        pctMyPicture.Width, (I - 1) * pctMyPicture.Height, _
        pctMyPicture.Width
    Next J
  Next I
End Sub
```

What this code first does is figure out the number of copies of the picture you can place on the form. For example, if the picture box is 400 twips high and the form is 4400 twips high, you can have 11 rows. A similar calculation is made for the columns. Next, comes the crucial line,

```
Form1.PaintPicture Picture1.Picture, (J - 1) * _
Picture1.Width, (I - 1)* Picture1.Height, Picture1.Width
```

which paints multiple copies of the picture on the form. Here's the Form_Load that gives the directions for the above code:

```
Private Sub Form_Load()
  Dim M$
  M$ = "After you click on the OK button to make "
  M$ = M$ & "this button go away, resizing the form "
  M$ = M$ & "will show you how neat the PaintPicture is!"
  MsgBox M$
End Sub
```

Finally, the full version of PaintPicture has the following syntax (it doesn't use named parameters, unfortunately):

> *object*.PaintPicture *picture, x1, y1, width1, height1, x2, y2, width2, height2, opcode*

The first three parameters you have already seen—they are all required. All the remaining parameters are optional. However, if you want to use an optional argument, you must specify all the optional arguments that would appear before it. (No empty commas allowed!)

The optional *width1* and *height1* parameters are single-precision values that let you set the width and height of the resulting picture. The optional *x2* and *y2* parameters let you specify single-precision values that give the left/right (X) and up/down (Y) coordinates of a clipping region within the original picture. The optional *width2* and *height2* parameters are single-precision values that give the coordinates of a clipping region within the original picture.

The optional *opcode* parameter is a long integer that is used only with bitmaps. This parameter will affect how the picture blends with whatever image was already at the location. Its uses are highly specialized, so please refer to the online help for the BitBlt API function call in Win32api.txt if you think you need to use this. (It uses the same values as the dwRop parameter in the BitBlt function.)

TIP: You can flip a bitmap horizontally or vertically by using negative values for the destination height (*height1*) or the destination width (*width1*).

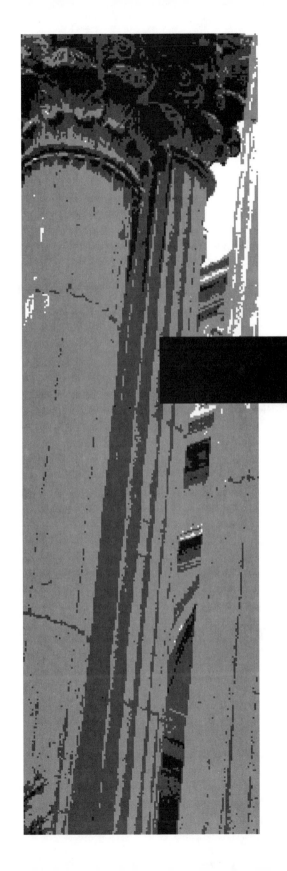

CHAPTER 17

Monitoring
Mouse Activity

Up to this point, all you have used are the Click and Double-click events. These detect whether the user clicked the mouse once or twice in a form or control. This chapter shows you how to obtain and use more subtle information. Was a mouse button pressed? Which button was it? Is the mouse pointer over a control? Did the user release a button, and if so, which one? Did the user move the mouse out of one form and into another? Exactly where inside the form is the mouse? Visual Basic can detect all these events. The reason is that Windows, and therefore Visual Basic, constantly monitors what the user is doing with the mouse. Of course, as with all Visual Basic operations, you must write the event procedures that determine how Visual Basic will respond to the event. For example, if you want to pop up a menu after a right mouse click, you'll need to write a bit of code.

NOTE: To allow the possibility of context-sensitive pop-up menus, all controls in Visual Basic 6 are mouse-sensitive.

Finally, just as designing a Visual Basic application involves dragging controls around a blank form, Visual Basic lets you write applications that let the user do things by moving controls around via dragging and dropping. The last section of this chapter shows you how.

NOTE: Remember that to get a "tooltip," a little label that pops up when the user holds the mouse over the control, requires nothing more than setting the ToolTipText property of the control. All controls where tooltips are needed in VB have this property.

 ## The Mouse Event Procedures

There are three fundamental mouse event procedures:

Name	Event That Caused It
MouseDown	User clicks one of the mouse buttons
MouseUp	User releases a mouse button
MouseMove	User moves the mouse pointer to a control or to a blank area of the form

In many ways, these procedures are analogous to the KeyUp and KeyDown event procedures that you saw in Chapter 8. For example, as with those event procedures, Visual Basic lets you use bit-masking techniques to determine if the user was holding down the SHIFT, ALT, or CTRL key at the same time he or she pressed or released a mouse button.

NOTE: Only forms and picture boxes return where the mouse pointer is in terms of their internal scales. For the other controls, it's necessary to calculate this information by using the scale of the surrounding container—a method that may or may not be practical.

17

Controls recognize a mouse event only when the mouse pointer is inside the control; the underlying form recognizes the mouse event in all other cases. However, if a mouse button is pressed *and held* while the mouse pointer is inside a control or form, that object *captures the mouse*. This means that no other Visual Basic object can react to mouse events until the user releases the mouse button, regardless of where the user moves the mouse.

All mouse event procedures take the same form and use the same parameters:

ObjectName_MouseEvent(*Button* As Integer, *Shift* As Integer, *X* As _
Single, *Y* As Single)

If the object were part of a control array, then, as usual, there is an optional first *Index* parameter:

ObjectInControlArray_MouseEvent(*Index* As Integer, *Button* As _
Integer, *Shift* As Integer, *X* As Single, *Y* As Single)

As the next sections show, bit masking lets you use the *Button* argument to determine which mouse button was pressed. Similarly, you can find out if the user was holding down any combination of the SHIFT, CTRL, and ALT keys by bit masking, using the *Shift* parameter. Finally, *X* and *Y* give you the information you need to determine the position of the mouse pointer, using the internal coordinates of the container object.

The MouseUp and MouseDown Events

To see the MouseDown and MouseUp event procedures at work, start up a new project. Double-click to open the Code window and move to the MouseDown event procedure for the form. Now enter the following code:

```
Private Sub Form_MouseDown(Button As Integer, Shift As _
Integer, X As Single, Y As Single)
  Circle (X,Y), 75
End Sub
```

This simple event procedure uses the positioning information passed by *X* and *Y*. Each time you click a mouse button, a small circle is centered exactly where you clicked—namely, at CurrentX = X and CurrentY = Y, of size 75 twips. If you add a MouseUp event procedure to the form that looks like this:

```
Private Sub Form_MouseUp(Button As Integer, Shift As Integer, _
X As Single, Y As Single)
  Dim CCode As Integer
  Randomize
```

```
    CCode = Int(15*Rnd)
    FillStyle = 0
    FillColor = QBColor(CCode)
    Circle (X,Y), 75
End Sub
```

then, each time you release the same button, Visual Basic fills the circle with a random color.

Keep in mind that even though you may have two or even three mouse buttons, Visual Basic will not generate another MouseDown event until you release the original mouse button. This prevents you from making some circles filled and others empty when using these two procedures.

T •••
  IP: To allow users to change their minds, make the action you take depend on the MouseUp event rather than the MouseDown event. The idea is that if you use the MouseUp event, users can simply move the mouse outside the control before releasing the mouse button to avoid a bad choice. (Which, of course is a very common Windows technique for avoiding bad choices on command buttons, for example.)

Finally, the MouseUp and MouseDown event procedures work similarly for picture boxes, the only difference being that, as you've seen, you must use the control name of the picture box (and the index, if the picture box is part of a control array). Here are what the headers for the event procedures look like:

Private Sub *CtrlName*_MouseDown(*Button* As Integer, *Shift* As Integer, _
X As Single, *Y* As Single)

Private Sub *CtrlNameInArray*_MouseDown(*Index* As Integer, _
Button As Integer, *Shift* As Integer, *X* As Single, *Y* As Single)

Using the Button Argument

Suppose, however, you wanted to make some circles filled and some empty. One way to do this is to use the added information given by the *Button* argument. For example, suppose the user has a two-button mouse. You can easily write code so that if the user presses the right mouse button, he or she gets a filled circle, and otherwise all he or she gets is a colored circular outline. The *Button* argument uses the lowest three bits of the value of the integer, as shown here:

Button	Constant	Value of Button Argument
Left	vbLeftButton	1
Right	vbRightButton	2
Middle	vbMiddleButton	4

Visual Basic will tell you about only one button for the MouseUp/MouseDown combination. You cannot detect if both the left and right buttons are down simultaneously, for example. Thus, you can rewrite the MouseUp event procedure to allow both filled and empty circles using the left and right buttons:

17

```
Private Sub Form_MouseUp(Button As Integer, Shift As Integer, _
X As Single, Y As Single)
  Dim CCode As Integer
  Randomize
  CCode = Int(15*Rnd)
  Select Case Button
    Case vbLeftButton
      Circle (X,Y), 75, QBColor(CCode)
      FillColor = &HFFFFFF&
    Case vbRightButton
      FillStyle = 0
      FillColor = QBColor(CCode)
      Circle (X,Y), 75
    Case Else
      'do nothing
  End Select
End Sub
```

Combining the Keyboard and the Mouse

You can also detect if the user presses one of the SHIFT, CTRL, and ALT keys while simultaneously working with the mouse. For example, you can have the SHIFT+right mouse button combination drop down a special pop-up menu as opposed to the standard one.

The trick to detect this user action is to use the *Shift* argument in the MouseUp or MouseDown event procedure.

NOTE: The name Microsoft chose for this parameter is a little bit confusing. Although it is the *Shift* parameter, it actually tells you whether the user has pressed one or more of the SHIFT/ALT/CTRL keys.

Here's a table of the possible values for the lower three bits of the *Shift* parameter that let you detect the special keys:

Action	Constant	Bit Set and Value
SHIFT key down	vbShiftMask	Bit 0: Value = 1
CTRL key down	vbCtrlMask	Bit 1: Value = 2
ALT key down	vbAltMask	Bit 2: Value = 4

Action	Constant	Bit Set and Value
SHIFT + CTRL keys down	vbShiftMask + vbCtrlMask	Bits 0 and 1: Value = 3
SHIFT + ALT keys down	vbShiftMask + vbAltMask	Bits 0 and 2: Value = 5
CTRL + ALT keys down	vbCtrlMask + vbAltMask	Bits 1 and 2: Value = 6
SHIFT + CTRL + ALT keys down	vbShiftMask + vbCtrlMask + vbAltMask	Bits 0, 1, and 2: Value = 7

At the present time, most people seem to be writing code for the SHIFT key by using a Select Case statement, as follows,

```
Select Case Shift 'this is the shift parameter in the mouse event
                  'procedure not the shift key!
  Case vbShiftMask '=1
    Print "You pressed the Shift key."
  Case vbCtrlMask '=2
    Print "You pressed the Ctrl key."
  Case vbShiftMask+vbAltMask '=3
    Print "You pressed the Shift + Alt keys."
  Case vbAltMask '=4
    Print "You pressed the Alt key."
End Select
```

and so on. Since you will see code like this very often, you have to be aware of it. However, Microsoft discourages this kind of code (though it certainly works in VB6) because they say they are reserving the possibility of using the higher order bits of the Shift parameter for something else. (They haven't used them for anything through the six versions of VB, of course.)

Anyway, on the off chance that in VB10 they will use them for something, it is probably preferable to do what they suggest—and what they suggest isn't that much harder. The idea is simple: use the And operator to isolate the first three bits before proceeding (see Chapter 5 for more on the And operator). As you saw with the KeyUp event procedure in Chapter 7, you can do this as follows:

```
Bits = Shift And 7  'only look at the last three bits
Select Case Bits
  Case vbShiftMask
    Print "You pressed the Shift key."
  Case vbCtrlMask
    Print "You pressed the Ctrl key."
  Case vbShiftMask+vbAltMask
    Print "You pressed the Shift + Alt keys."
  Case vbAltMask
    Print "You pressed the Alt key."
End Select
```

The idea is the same as you saw in the Bit Masking section in Chapter 5: by "Anding" with the number 7, which has a binary pattern of 111, you throw away any information that may be contained in bits 4 through 8. This lets your code concentrate on the information contained in the lowest three bits, which is where the SHIFT, ALT, and CTRL information is located.

TIP: You might also want to apply the same preventative against future problems when using the *Button* argument.

Making Pop-up Menus

First off, before I show you how to add a pop-up menu to a control, you have to be aware that certain Visual Basic controls have their own pop-up menus. For example, text boxes have pop-up menus that include normal cut and paste actions. Don't try to attach your own pop-up menu to a control that comes with its own because the original one will take precedence and you will confuse the user who will see two pop-up menus: first the built-in one and then the one you added. Thus, it is especially important when using a control for the first time to check whether it has a built-in pop-up menu; add it to a blank form and right-click on the control while the program is running.

Okay, let's assume you are working with a control (like a rich text box) that doesn't have a built-in pop-up menu. Here are the steps to add the pop-up capability. First you must build the menu. A pop-up menu is first and foremost an ordinary menu. As such, you must build it using the Menu Editor, as shown in Chapter 14. There are, however, some "gotchas" to keep in mind:

◆ The pop-up menu will not show the top level entry in the menu.

◆ If you don't want to see the pop-up menu on the main menu bar, you must set the Visible property of the top-level menu entry to False.

Once you take care of these gotchas, getting the pop-up menu to actually pop up in response to a right mouse-down action is a total triviality. Simply add code in the MouseDown event for the control's MouseDown event that follows the following template:

```
Private Sub TheControl_MouseDown(Button As Integer, Shift As Integer, _
X As Single, Y As Single)
   If Button = vbRightButton Then Me.PopUpMenu MenuName
End Sub
```

That's it. VB will pop up the menu whose top-level Name property is the same as the *MenuName* you give in the above code.

The MouseMove Event

Visual Basic calls the MouseMove event procedure whenever the user moves the mouse. This is the most powerful of the mouse event procedures because, unlike the MouseUp/MouseDown event pair, you can use it to analyze completely the state of the mouse buttons. For this event procedure, the *Button* argument tells you whether some, all, or none of the mouse buttons are down. (The Mouse Up/Mouse down pair can only detect if a single button is pressed.)

You should not get into the habit of thinking that the MouseMove event is generated continuously as the mouse pointer moves across objects. In fact, a combination of the user's software and hardware determines how often the MouseMove event is generated. To see the MouseMove event at work, start a new project and enter the following MouseMove event procedure:

```
Private Sub Form_MouseMove(Button As Integer, Shift As _
Integer, X As Single, Y As Single)
  DrawWidth = 3
  PSet (X,Y)
End Sub
```

Now run the project and move your mouse around the form at different speeds. Figure 17-1 shows an example of what is obtained as you decrease your speed, moving from left to right in a vaguely rectangular motion. As you can see, the dots are more tightly packed when you move the mouse slowly than when you move it rapidly. This happens because Visual Basic relies on the underlying operating system to report mouse events, and such events are generated frequently but not continuously.

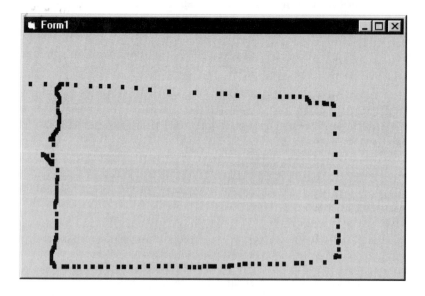

Demonstration
of MouseMove
response time

Figure 17-1.

17

Because the MouseMove event procedure is *not* called continuously, the dots are relatively sparse when the mouse is moved rapidly.

Nonetheless, since the MouseMove event procedure will be called relatively frequently, any code inside this event procedure will be executed often. For this reason, you will want to tighten the code inside the MouseMove event procedure as much as possible or provide a flag to prevent repetitive processing. For example, use integer variables for counters and do not recompute the value of variables inside this procedure unless the new value depends on the parameters of the event. Always remember that accessing object properties is *much* slower than using a variable.

As mentioned in the previous section, the MouseMove event uses the three lower bits of the value of the *Button* parameter to tell you the complete state of the mouse buttons, as shown here:

Button	Constant	Value
Left button	vbLeftButton	1
Right button	vbRightButton	2
Middle button	vbMiddleButton	4
Left + right	vbLeftButton + vbRightButton	3
Left + middle	vbLeftButton + vbMiddleButton	5
Right + middle	vbRightButton + vbMiddleButton	6
All three	vbLeftButton + vbMiddleButton + vbRightButton	7

Of course, if you don't have a three-button mouse, the third bit will always be zero. As with the *Shift* parameter in the MouseUp/MouseDown event procedures, you are safest masking out all but the lowest three bits before using this information:

```
Bits = Shift And 7
Select Case Bits
  Case vbLeftButton
    Print "The left mouse button is down."
  Case vbRightButton
    Print "The right mouse button is down."
  Case vbLeftButton + vbRightButton
    Print  "The left and right mouse buttons are down."
  Case vbMiddleButton
    Print  "The middle mouse button is down."
```

TIP: You can use the MouseMove event to add tooltips to a control that doesn't have a ToolTipText property. All you have to do is make an invisible label with the correct caption become visible in the correct location. When the mouse moves off the tool, set the label Visible property to False in the MouseMove event of all the other controls and of the form itself.

Dragging and Dropping Operations for Controls

To move a control as you are designing the interface in your Visual Basic project, you hold down a mouse button (the left one) and then move the mouse pointer to where you want the control to end up. A gray outline of the control moves with the mouse pointer. When you are happy with the location, you release the mouse button. The Microsoft Windows documentation calls moving an object with the mouse button depressed *dragging* and calls the release of the mouse button *dropping.* Visual Basic makes it easy to program this potential behavior into your projects. You can even drag and drop from one form to another if your project uses multiple forms.

Controls permit two types of dragging. These correspond to two different values of the DragMode property. The default is to not allow you to drag controls around, except under special circumstances. As always, you'll need to write the code for these special circumstances (see the section called "Manual Dragging" a little later on in this chapter). This is called *manual dragging,* and the DragMode property will have the value 0. Changing the value of this property to 1, *automatic dragging,* means that the user may drag the control around the project. Regardless of the setting for the DragMode property, the control will actually move only if you write the code using the Move method to reposition it, as shown in the next example.

For this example, start up a new project and add a single command button to it. Set the DragMode property of that command button to 1 (automatic). The event that recognizes dragging and dropping operations is called the DragDrop event, and it is associated with the control or form where the "drop" occurs. Thus, if you want to drag a control to a new location on a form, you write code for the form's DragDrop event procedure. For example, to allow dragging and dropping to move the single command button around the form in this example, use the following code:

```
Private Sub Form_DragDrop(Source As Control, X As Single, Y _
As Single)
   Source.Move X, Y
End Sub
```

Since the type of the *Source* parameter is a control, you can refer to its properties and methods by using the dot notation, as in the preceding example. If you need to know more information about what type of control is being dragged before applying a method or setting a property, use the

　　If TypeOf Control Is ...

or the

　　If TypeName (Control) =

statement. (You saw these satements in Chapter 8.)

If you run this example, you will notice that the object remains visible in its original location while the gray outline moves. You cannot use the DragDrop event to make a control invisible while the dragging/dropping operation takes place. This is because this event procedure is called only after the user drops the object. In fact, the DragDrop event need not move the control at all. You often use this event to allow the user just to initiate some action. This is especially common when dragging from one form to another.

If you want to change the gray outline that Visual Basic uses during a drag operation, you can. The easiest way to do this is to set the DragIcon property of the control at design time. To do this, select the DragIcon property from the Properties box, and then click the three dots to the left of the Settings box. This opens up the Load Icon dialog box for choosing icons. You can also assign the drag icon or icon property of one object to another. For example:

    FirstControl.DragIcon = *SecondControl*.DragIcon

The final possibility is to use the LoadPicture function. For example:

    Control.DragIcon = LoadPicture("C\VB\GRAPHICS\ICONS\MISC\CLOCK01.ICO")

If you design a custom icon, a common practice is to reverse the colors for the drag icon.

The following table summarizes the events, methods, and properties used for dragging and dropping:

Item	Description
DragMode property	Allows automatic dragging (value = 1) or manual dragging (value = 0)
DragIcon property	Set this to change from the gray rectangle to a custom icon when dragging
DragDrop event	Associated with the target of the operation; generated when the source is dropped on the target control
DragOver event	Associated with any control the source control passes over during dragging
Drag method	Starts or stops dragging when DragMode is set to manual

NOTE: There is another type of dragging called "OLE Drag and Drop" that you'll see in Chapter 20. Unlike the drag and drop methods that you just saw, OLE Drag and Drop actually drags around the data contained in an object. For example, as you will soon see, using OLE Drag and Drop you can do nifty things like drag files off of Windows Explorer and have their contents appear in a text box.

Manual Dragging

If you have left the value of the DragMode property at its default of 0, then you must use the Drag method to allow dragging of the control. The syntax for this method is

Control.Drag *TypeOfAction*

The *TypeOfAction* is an integer value from 0 to 2, as shown here:

Control.Drag 0	Cancel dragging
Control.Drag 1	Begin dragging
Control.Drag 2	Drop the control

If you omit the *TypeOfAction* argument, the method has the same effect as the statement *Control*.Drag 1. That is, Visual Basic initiates the dragging operation for the control.

One way to use the flexibility this method gives you is to allow expert users to drag and drop controls, but set the default for this not to happen. For example, use the CTRL+MouseDown combination to allow dragging to take place. You can do this by beginning the MouseDown event procedure with the following:

```
Private Sub CtrlName_MouseDown(Button As Integer, Shift As _
Integer, X As Single, Y As Single)
  If (Shift And 7) = 2 Then  'or vbCtrlMask
    CtrlName.DragMode = 1
  End If
.
.
End Sub
```

The DragOver Event

All Visual Basic objects except menus and timers will detect if a control is passing over them. You can use the DragOver event to allow even greater flexibility for your projects. This event lets you monitor the path a control takes while being dragged. You might consider changing the background color of the control being passed over. The event procedure template for forms is

Private Sub Form_DragOver(*Source* As Control, *X* As Single, *Y* As Single, *State* As _ Integer)

For controls, this event procedure template takes the form

Private Sub *CtrlName*_DragOver([*Index* As Integer,]*Source* As Control, *X* As Single, _ *Y* As Single, *State* As Integer)

As usual, the optional *Index* parameter is used if the control is part of a control array. The *Source* is the control being dragged, but the event procedure is associated with the control being passed over. The *X* and *Y* parameters give you the CurrentX and CurrentY values in terms of the scale of the object being passed over for forms and picture boxes and the underlying form for all other controls. The *State* parameter has three possible values:

Value of State Parameter	Description
0	Source is now inside target
1	Source is just left of target
2	Source moved inside target

17

T IP: You will want to test for the type of control being dragged by using the If Type Of statement or the TypeName function.

Example: Deleting Files via Drag/Drop

The idea behind the somewhat longer project in this section is to allow the user to drag one of the icons representing a file into a "disposal" unit, at which point (after a warning, of course) the file is deleted from the disk. Please be aware that since you haven't yet seen the file-handling controls from the toolbox (covered in Chapter 19), this project is a little less user-friendly than it could be. (We should be using the control that displays a directory rather than an input box.) Nonetheless, this project does demonstrate the techniques needed for handling dragging and dropping in one of its most common contexts.

Of course, the idea of letting the user drag an icon of a file to another icon representing a disposal unit has been around as long as graphical user interfaces. Apple's Macintosh uses a simple trash can; the now defunct NeXT computer used a black hole. Windows 95 and 98 use a more complicated icon of a trash can for the Recycle Bin since Apple has caused problems for those who use a simple trash can for this type of application. To avoid problems with Apple and Microsoft, this example uses a slightly different icon. After looking at all the icons supplied with VB (which VB owners can freely use), I settled on the Trash03 icon. (Although I didn't associate an appropriate sound file with the disposal process you are welcome to add this feature.)

Figure 17-2 shows an example of what the screen might look like. As you can see, the files are represented by a bunch of command buttons, which contain both a picture and the name of the file. (The actual command buttons are implemented as part of a control array in order to make the code cleaner.)

The screen you might see while using the Drag and Drop Demo

Figure 17-2.

NOTE: For an explanation of how to code another type of Drag and Drop (OLE Drag and Drop) see Chapter 20.

Most of the length of this project is caused (as is so often the case) by the needs of making it user-friendly. The real work is done in the following DragDrop event that is associated with the "Disposal Unit" (which I am naming imgGarbage). All this code does is:

1. Check which button was dropped by using the Source.Index method to get the index of the control array.

2. Extract the caption, which together with a previously saved form level variable that I named fCurrentPath will give the full path name of the file to be deleted.

3. Ask the user whether he or she really wants to delete the file.

4. If the answer is yes, the code deletes the file.

Notice that Step 1 in the list above is accomplished by the line

```
ControlIndex = Source.Index
```

in the code that follows. The next line makes the button temporarily invisible after the drop operation. The ControlIndex variable lets Visual Basic extract the caption (which, as I said, will be the name of the file) from the button. The message box that the code pops up is of type vbYesNo (4) so it's a Yes/No message box. (Its title, as you can see, is the natural: "Confirmation Box".) Next comes a line with the Kill command. The Kill command deletes a file from a disk. (You'll learn more about this command in Chapter 19.) Once the program deletes the file, the program unloads the button from the control array. If the user has made a mistake, and doesn't confirm by clicking on the No button, or the file can't be deleted, the code makes the button visible again.

```
Private Sub imgGarbage_DragDrop(Source As Control, X As _
Single, Y As Single)

  On Error GoTo Problems
  Dim Msg As String, ErrorMessage As String
  Dim ControlIndex As Integer, YesNo As Integer
  ControlIndex = Source.Index
  cmdFileName(ControlIndex).Visible = False
  Msg = "Do you really want to delete " & _
cmdFileName(ControlIndex).Caption & "?"
  YesNo = MsgBox(Msg, vbYesNo, "Confirmation Box")
  If YesNo = vbYes Then
    Kill (fCurrentPath & cmdFileName(ControlIndex).Caption)
    Unload cmdFileName(ControlIndex)
  Else
    cmdFileName(ControlIndex).Visible = True
  End If
  Exit Sub
Problems:
  ErrorMessage = "Sorry can't delete that file"
  cmdFileName(ControlIndex).Visible = True
  MsgBox ErrorMessage
End Sub
```

To follow the rest of the discussion, you will probably want to start up a new project and follow along. (The full code is at the end of the chapter and is, of course, available on the Net.) To get started, do the following:

1. Start up a new project with two forms.

2. Name the first one frmMain and the second frmDirections.

Building the UI: The Main Form

For the user interface of the main form, do the following:

1. Add an image control named imgGarbage to the lower-right corner of the startup form (frmMain).
2. Set the picture property of this control to the icon found in the Trash03.ico file. (This file may be found in the Computer subdirectory of the Icon library.)
3. Make sure the Stretch property of the imgGarbage control is false (the default).
4. Now, to finish the user interface on frmMain, set up a control array of command buttons that can hold pictures by:

    (a) Setting the Index property of the command button to 0

    (b) Setting the Style property to 1 (Graphical)

    (c) Making the Picture property be the Disk12 icon in the library of computer icons that comes with VB

    (d) Setting the DragMode property of the command button to 1 (Automatic)

    (e) Making the command button invisible by setting its Visible property to False

(As usual, all subsequent elements in these control arrays will inherit these properties.) Finally, add the following code to the Form_Load of the main form to calculate how many rows will fit on the form (storing the information in a form-level variable called fLastRow) and to load the form that holds the directions and calls the Directions routine that displays the information on that form:

```
Private Sub Form_Load()
  'rows are numbered from 0 to n-1 since static variables start at 0
  fLastRow = (ScaleHeight / (cmdFileName(0).Height + Spacing)) - 1
  Load frmDirections
  Me.Hide
  Directions
End Sub
```

Building the UI: The Directions Form

Next, let's worry about how we can give the user directions for what will happen. The first step is that we want the second form (the one named frmDirections) to have the following properties:

1. Set the BorderStyle property of the form to 3 (fixed single). This makes the Directions form, which we will use as a custom dialog box, as clean as possible.
2. Add a multiline text box with vertical scroll bars (named txtDirections) to the form. Make sure the background color of the text box is the same as the form. Set the BorderStyle property to 0 (no border).

3. Add the following code to the Form_Load of the Directions form in order to initialize the text box.

```
Private Sub Form_Load()
  Dim M$
  M$ = "This program illustrates dragging and dropping "
  M$ = M$ & "mouse operations. The user gives a file spec "
  M$ = M$ & "inside the message box. Then a form appears "
  M$ = M$ & "with buttons whose captions are the files "
  M$ = M$ & "whose names match that specification. You can then "
  M$ = M$ & "drag the button to 'flush' the file away, i.e., "
  M$ = M$ & "delete it. Also, if you right-click on a button "
  M$ = M$ & "you will get the standard information about that file."
  Me.txtDirections.Text = M$
End Sub
```

4. Now set the StartUpPosition property of this form to be CenterScreen.

Finally, be sure to add a command button named cmdOK to the Directions (frmDirections) form so that the user can hide the directions. Make the Click procedure for this button hide the form and display the main form as follows:

```
Private Sub cmdOK_Click()
  Me.Hide
  frmMain.Show
End Sub
```

Figure 17-3 shows you what the Directions form will look like. Notice how the multiline text box with no border makes it look like we have made a scrolling form.

Implementing the Menu Items
Now the question is how to fill up the form you saw in Figure 17-2. The buttons must not only have captions that are the names of the files that satisfy a given

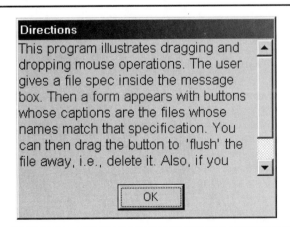

The Directions form

Figure 17-3.

specification, they have to be nicely spaced within the form. I did this by adding code that activates a New File Spec menu item. To do this, just add the following two menu items to a File menu attached to the original form (frmMain):

```
File
  New File Spec
  Exit
```

The idea is that clicking the New File Spec menu item will call a general procedure called mnuGetFile that reads the names of the files from the disk. (The Help item on the menu merely calls up the Directions form.)

Now the question is how to actually deal with a new file specification. The first time the user uses this application, Visual Basic needs to load a certain number of elements in the command-button control arrays. The program also needs to change the information contained in the captions, because these captions will ultimately contain the names of the files to delete.

Notice that we have to allow the process to be repeated, which means allowing for a way to load and unload the buttons. There are various ways of accomplishing this. The easiest is to simply unload all the existing elements in the control array of buttons. I did this with the following code in the mnuNewFileSpec_Click procedure:

```
On Error Resume Next 'for the error caused by unloading
                       'the intial control
Dim AControl As Control
For Each AControl In frmMain.Controls
  Unload AControl
Next
On Error GoTo 0  'stop error handling
```

The NewFileSpec routine must also reset the form-level variables we will use for positioning the controls so that we can start over at the top left with the new file specification. We also have to reset the form-level variable that gives us the current path:

```
fCurrentRow = 1
fCurrentWidth = 0
fCurrentHeight = 0
fCurrentPath = vbNullString
```

The GetFile general procedure is straightforward. It uses an InputBox to get a path name (with wild cards) and then uses InStrRev to find a backslash at the right end of the specification the user enters. It then pulls out the path name by disregarding the stuff after the last backslash. The code looks like this:

```
Private Sub mnuGetFile()
  'local variables
  Dim FileSpec As String
  Dim Message As String
  frmDirections.Hide
```

```
    FileSpec = InputBox$("File specification? (You can use wild cards of
course--C:\temp\*.tmp for example.)")
    fCurrentPath = Left(FileSpec, InStrRev(FileSpec, "\"))
    If fCurrentPath = vbNullString Then
      Message = FileSpec & " is NOT a valid file spec "
      Message = Message & "(did you forget the '\')? "
      Message = Message & "Remember file specs are things like "
      Message = Message & "C:\1temp\*.* or c:\*.tmp. "
      Message = Message & "Click on OK to reshow directions."
      MsgBox Message
      Directions
    Else
      frmMain.Show
      DisplayFiles (FileSpec)
    End If
End Sub
```

Finally, clicking the menu item marked Help calls the Directions general procedure:

```
Private Sub mnuHelp_Click ()
  Directions
End Sub
```

To finish the program, we only need to associate the simplest of event procedures with the Exit menu item in the file menu on the main form—unloading all the forms. Notice how this kind of code will automatically end the program since all forms will have been unloaded:

```
Private Sub mnuExit_Click ()
  Unload frmDirections
  Unload Me
End Sub
```

Displaying the Buttons with the File Names
The details of displaying the files on the startup form are conceptually quite easy but quite complex to carry out. We need to position the buttons along a row until there's no more room. We then have to move the next button to the beginning of the next row. When there is no more room on any of the rows, we stop and say that that is all the files we can display. We use the following form-level variables

```
fLastRow 'the number of possible rows
fCurrentRow 'the current row
fCurrentWidth 'where we are on a row
fCurrentHeight 'the height of a button (they're all the same)
```

to allow the positioning code to know where the last control was placed.

However, to make the code clearer, a lot of the work is shipped off to a function procedure that I called CanPosition. CanPosition will return True if we have room to position the control *and* position it properly. CanPosition will simply return False if the button will not fit. This function procedure needs to do some special processing for the first button, but after that it can simply check if there is room on the form for the next button.

```
Private Function CanPosition(TheIndex As Integer) As Boolean
   'take care of first button
   'assumes there is room for at least one control on each row!
   If TheIndex = 1 Then
       cmdFileName(TheIndex).Move 0, 0
       fCurrentWidth = cmdFileName(TheIndex).Width + _
fCurrentWidth + Spacing
       CanPosition = True
       Exit Function
   End If
   'now work with all other buttons
   Select Case fCurrentRow
      Case fLastRow
         If cmdFileName(TheIndex).Width + fCurrentWidth + _
Spacing + imgGarbage.Width <= ScaleWidth Then
            'have room on last row so add
            fCurrentWidth = fCurrentWidth + Spacing
            cmdFileName(TheIndex).Move fCurrentWidth, fCurrentHeight
            ' set new current width to add width of control
            fCurrentWidth = cmdFileName(TheIndex).Width + _
fCurrentWidth + Spacing
            CanPosition = True
         Else 'no room on last row so hosed
            CanPosition = False
            fCurrentRow = fCurrentRow + 1 'out of space
         End If
      Case Is < fLastRow 'not on last row
         If cmdFileName(TheIndex).Width + fCurrentWidth + _
Spacing >= ScaleWidth Then
            'need to move to next row
            fCurrentRow = fCurrentRow + 1
            fCurrentWidth = 0
            fCurrentHeight = fCurrentHeight + _
cmdFileName(TheIndex).Height + Spacing
            'have enough room so move the control
            cmdFileName(TheIndex).Move fCurrentWidth, fCurrentHeight
            ' set new current width to add width of control
            fCurrentWidth = cmdFileName(TheIndex).Width + _
fCurrentWidth
            CanPosition = True
         Else 'can put the control on current row
            fCurrentWidth = fCurrentWidth + Spacing
            cmdFileName(TheIndex).Move fCurrentWidth, fCurrentHeight
            fCurrentWidth = cmdFileName(TheIndex).Width + _
fCurrentWidth + Spacing
            CanPosition = True
         End If
      Case Else
         MsgBox "Oops shouldn't get to this case"
      End Select
End Function
```

The actual DisplayFiles routine uses repeated calls to the Dir function in order to get the file names. It then loads a new button in the control array and resizes the buttons to be a little (two characters) larger than the filename. It then simply calls the CanPosition routine, which does all the work.

```
Private Sub DisplayFiles(FileSpec As String)
  'local variables
  Dim I As Integer, Message As String
  Dim ControlIndex As Integer, NameOfFile As String
  On Error GoTo Problems

  NameOfFile = Dir$(FileSpec)
  If NameOfFile = vbNullString Then
    MsgBox "No Files found with that file specification!"
    Exit Sub
  End If

  Do Until NameOfFile = vbNullString Or fCurrentRow > fLastRow
    ControlIndex = ControlIndex + 1
    Load cmdFileName(ControlIndex)
    'make button 10% larger than width of caption
    'make the width of a control big enough to hold the text
    ' + two more characters
    cmdFileName(ControlIndex).Width = TextWidth(NameOfFile & "XX")
    cmdFileName(ControlIndex).Caption = NameOfFile
    If Not (CanPosition(ControlIndex)) Then
      Message = "Too many files with that specification. "
      Message = Message & "Will show only " & (ControlIndex - 1)
      Message = Message & " files with that specification."
      MsgBox Message
      Exit Sub
    Else
      cmdFileName(ControlIndex).Visible = True
    End If
    NameOfFile = Dir$
  Loop
  Exit Sub
Problems:
  MsgBox Err.Description
  End
End Sub
```

The Full Code for the Drag and Drop Example
Here is the code for the two .frm files that make up the whole drag and drop example:

```
Begin VB.Form frmDirections
    AutoRedraw      =   -1  'True
    BorderStyle     =   3   'Fixed Dialog
    Caption         =   "Directions"
    ClientHeight    =   2496
    ClientLeft      =   36
```

```
    ClientTop       =    324
    ClientWidth     =    3744
    ControlBox      =    0     'False
    LinkTopic       =    "Form2"
    MaxButton       =    0     'False
    MinButton       =    0     'False
    ScaleHeight     =    2496
    ScaleWidth      =    3744
    ShowInTaskbar   =    0     'False
    StartUpPosition =    2     'CenterScreen
    Begin VB.TextBox txtDirections
        BackColor       =    &H8000000F&
        BorderStyle     =    0     'None
        Height          =    1932
        Left            =    0
        MultiLine       =    -1    'True
        ScrollBars      =    2     'Vertical
        TabIndex        =    1
        Text            =    "DragDropExample.frx":0000
        Top             =    0
        Width           =    3732
    End
    Begin VB.CommandButton cmdOK
        Caption         =    "OK"
        Height          =    372
        Left            =    1440
        TabIndex        =    0
        Top             =    2040
        Width           =    972
    End
End
Attribute VB_Name = "frmDirections"
Attribute VB_GlobalNameSpace = False
Attribute VB_Creatable = False
Attribute VB_PredeclaredId = True
Attribute VB_Exposed = False
Private Sub Form_Load()
  Dim M$
  M$ = "This program illustrates dragging and dropping "
  M$ = M$ & "mouse operations. The user gives a file spec "
  M$ = M$ & "inside the message box. Then a form appears "
  M$ = M$ & "with buttons whose captions are the files "
  M$ = M$ & "whose names match that specification. You can then "
  M$ = M$ & "drag the button to 'flush' the file away, i.e., "
  M$ = M$ & "delete it. Also, if you right-click on a button "
  M$ = M$ & "you will get the standard information about that "
  M$ = M$ & "file
 Me.txtDirections.Text = M$
End Sub
Private Sub cmdOK_Click()
  Me.Hide
  frmMain.Show
End Sub
```

```
VERSION 5.00
Begin VB.Form frmMain
   Caption         =     "File Deletion via control drag and drop"
   ClientHeight    =     6300
   ClientLeft      =     132
   ClientTop       =     708
   ClientWidth     =     7380
   LinkTopic       =     "Form1"
   ScaleHeight     =     6300
   ScaleWidth      =     7380
   StartUpPosition =     3   'Windows Default
   Visible         =     0    'False
   Begin VB.CommandButton cmdFileName
      BackColor    =     &H00FFFFC0&
      Caption      =     "Command1"
      DragMode     =     1   'Automatic
      Height       =     612
      Index        =     0
      Left         =     120
      Picture      =     "Directions.frx":0000
      Style        =     1   'Graphical
      TabIndex     =     0
      Top          =     0
      Visible      =     0     'False
      Width        =     972
   End
   Begin VB.Image imgGarbage
      Height       =     384
      Left         =     6600
      Picture      =     "Directions.frx":0442
      Top          =     7080
      Width        =     384
   End
   Begin VB.Menu mnuFile
      Caption      =     "&File"
      Begin VB.Menu mnuNewFileSpec
         Caption          =     "New File Spec"
      End
      Begin VB.Menu mnuExit
         Caption          =     "E&xit"
      End
   End
   Begin VB.Menu mnuHelp
      Caption      =     "&Help"
   End
End
Attribute VB_Name = "frmMain"
Attribute VB_GlobalNameSpace = False
Attribute VB_Creatable = False
Attribute VB_PredeclaredId = True
Attribute VB_Exposed = False
```

```vb
Option Explicit
Const Spacing = 35
'USED FOR POSITIONING THE CONTROLS
Private fCurrentWidth As Integer
Private fCurrentRow As Integer
Private fCurrentHeight As Integer
Private fLastRow As Integer
Private fCurrentPath As String

Private Sub cmdFileName_MouseDown(Index As Integer, _
Button As Integer, Shift As Integer, X As Single, Y As Single)
If Button = vbRightButton Then
  Dim FileName  As String
  Dim Temp As String
  Dim Attrib As Integer

  FileName = fCurrentPath & cmdFileName(Index).Caption
  Attrib = GetAttr(FileName)
  Temp = FileName & vbCrLf & vbCrLf
  Temp = Temp & "Date/Time: " & FileDateTime(FileName) & vbCrLf
  Temp = Temp & "Size: " & FileLen(FileName) & " bytes" & vbCrLf
  If (Attrib And vbReadOnly) = vbReadOnly Then
    Temp = Temp & "ReadOnly: Yes" & vbCrLf
  End If
  If (Attrib And vbHidden) = vbHidden Then
    Temp = Temp & "Hidden: Yes" & vbCrLf
  End If
  If (Attrib And vbSystem) = vbSystem Then
    Temp = Temp & "System: Yes" & vbCrLf
  End If
  If (Attrib And vbArchive) = vbArchive Then
    Temp = Temp & "Archive: Yes" & vbCrLf
  End If
  MsgBox Temp
End If
End Sub

Private Sub Form_Load()
'rows are numbered from 0 to n-1 since static variables start at 0
  fLastRow = (ScaleHeight / (cmdFileName(0).Height + Spacing)) - 1
  Load frmDirections
  Me.Hide
  Directions
End Sub

Private Sub Form_QueryUnload(Cancel As Integer, UnloadMode _
As Integer)
  Unload frmDirections
  Unload Me
  End
End Sub

Private Sub Form_Resize()
  frmMain.imgGarbage.Move ScaleWidth - _
```

```
        imgGarbage.Width - Spacing, ScaleHeight - imgGarbage.Height
End Sub

Private Sub mnuExit_Click()
  Unload Me
End Sub

Private Sub mnuNewFileSpec_Click()
  On Error Resume Next
  Dim AControl As Control
  For Each AControl In frmMain.Controls
    Unload AControl
  Next
  On Error GoTo 0
  'reset form level variables for positioning
  fCurrentRow = 1
  fCurrentWidth = 0
  fCurrentHeight = 0
  fCurrentPath = vbNullString
  mnuGetFile
End Sub

Private Sub mnuHelp_Click()
  Directions  'display the directions form
End Sub

Private Sub mnuGetFile()
  'local variables
  Dim FileSpec As String
  Dim Message As String
  frmDirections.Hide
  FileSpec = InputBox$("File specification? (You can use wild cards of
course--C:\temp\*.tmp for example.)")
  fCurrentPath = Left(FileSpec, InStrRev(FileSpec, "\"))
  If fCurrentPath = vbNullString Then
    Message = FileSpec & " is NOT a valid file spec "
    Message = Message & "(did you forget the '\')? "
    Message = Message & "Remember file specs are things like "
    Message = Message & "C:\1temp\*.* or c:\*.tmp. "
    Message = Message & "Click on OK to reshow directions."
    MsgBox Message
    Directions
  Else
    frmMain.Show
    DisplayFiles (FileSpec)
  End If
End Sub

Private Sub imgGarbage_DragDrop(Source As Control, X As _
Single, Y As Single)

  On Error GoTo Problems
  Dim Msg As String, ErrorMessage As String
```

```
  Dim ControlIndex As Integer, YesNo As Integer
  ControlIndex = Source.Index
  cmdFileName(ControlIndex).Visible = False
  Msg = "Do you really want to delete " & _
cmdFileName(ControlIndex).Caption & "?"
  YesNo = MsgBox(Msg, vbYesNo, "Confirmation Box")
  If YesNo = vbYes Then
    Kill (fCurrentPath & cmdFileName(ControlIndex).Caption)
    Unload cmdFileName(ControlIndex)
  Else
    cmdFileName(ControlIndex).Visible = True
  End If
  Exit Sub
Problems:
  ErrorMessage = "Sorry can't delete that file"
  cmdFileName(ControlIndex).Visible = True
  MsgBox ErrorMessage
End Sub

Private Sub DisplayFiles(FileSpec As String)
  'local variables
  Dim I As Integer, Message As String
  Dim ControlIndex As Integer, NameOfFile As String
  On Error GoTo Problems

  NameOfFile = Dir$(FileSpec)
  If NameOfFile = vbNullString Then
    MsgBox "No Files found with that file specification!"
    Exit Sub
  End If

  Do Until NameOfFile = vbNullString Or fCurrentRow > fLastRow
    ControlIndex = ControlIndex + 1
    Load cmdFileName(ControlIndex)
    'make button 10% larger than width of caption
    'make the width of a control big enough to hold the text
    ' + two more characters
    cmdFileName(ControlIndex).Width = TextWidth(NameOfFile & "XX")
    cmdFileName(ControlIndex).Caption = NameOfFile
    If Not (CanPosition(ControlIndex)) Then
      Message = "Too many files with that specification. "
      Message = Message & "Will show only " & (ControlIndex - 1)
      Message = Message & " files with that specification."
      MsgBox Message
      Exit Sub
    Else
      cmdFileName(ControlIndex).Visible = True
    End If
    NameOfFile = Dir$
  Loop
  Exit Sub
Problems:
  MsgBox Err.Description
```

```
    End
  End Sub
Private Function CanPosition(TheIndex As Integer) As Boolean
  'take care of first button
  If TheIndex = 1 Then
      cmdFileName(TheIndex).Move 0, 0
      fCurrentWidth = cmdFileName(TheIndex).Width + _
fCurrentWidth + Spacing
      CanPosition = True
      Exit Function
  End If
  'now work with all other buttons
  Select Case fCurrentRow
    Case fLastRow
      If cmdFileName(TheIndex).Width + fCurrentWidth + _
Spacing + imgGarbage.Width <= ScaleWidth Then
          'have room on last row so add
          fCurrentWidth = fCurrentWidth + Spacing
          cmdFileName(TheIndex).Move fCurrentWidth, fCurrentHeight
          ' set new current width to add width of control
          fCurrentWidth = cmdFileName(TheIndex).Width + _
fCurrentWidth + Spacing
          CanPosition = True
      Else
          CanPosition = False
          fCurrentRow = fCurrentRow + 1 'out of space
      End If
    Case Is < fLastRow
        If cmdFileName(TheIndex).Width + fCurrentWidth + _
Spacing >= ScaleWidth Then
        'need to move to next row
          fCurrentRow = fCurrentRow + 1
          fCurrentWidth = 0
          fCurrentHeight = fCurrentHeight + _
cmdFileName(TheIndex).Height + Spacing
          cmdFileName(TheIndex).Move fCurrentWidth, fCurrentHeight
          ' set new current width to add width of control
          fCurrentWidth = cmdFileName(TheIndex).Width + _
fCurrentWidth
          CanPosition = True
      Else
          fCurrentWidth = fCurrentWidth + Spacing
          cmdFileName(TheIndex).Move fCurrentWidth, fCurrentHeight
          fCurrentWidth = cmdFileName(TheIndex).Width + _
fCurrentWidth + Spacing
          CanPosition = True
      End If
    Case Else
      MsgBox "Oops shouldn't get to this case"
    End Select
End Function
Private Sub Directions()
  frmDirections.Show
End Sub
```

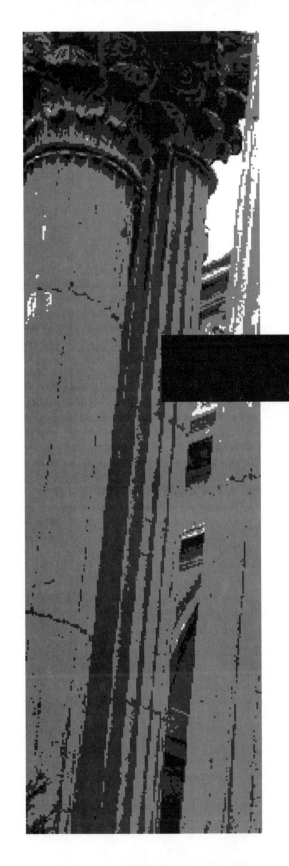

CHAPTER 18

Basic File Handling

This chapter and the next show you the basic ways of working with files in Visual Basic. The next chapter covers more advanced techniques, including the new file system objects that were added to VB6. The Professional and Enterprise editions of Visual Basic 6 have extraordinary power when it comes to handling corporate databases (see Chapter 22), but the ability to set up and work with files directly remains very important. For example, I'll show you how to write out any Visual Basic array so that it can be seen as a table on an HTML page. Also, random-access files are still useful for setting up certain kinds of databases, and binary file techniques are needed to work with files stored in non-ASCII format. In fact, the end of this chapter shows you some methods of keeping file information confidential by encrypting the information in files.

Before I show you the techniques for handling files, though, the first section of this chapter explains the Visual Basic commands that let you rename files, change the logged drive, or switch directories. Then you'll see the commands that make handling disk files easier. For example, you can copy files within a Visual Basic program with a single command.

CAUTION: (For people who are working with version 4 of Visual Basic, or lower.) Starting with version 5, Visual Basic changed the techniques for handling binary files. In order to have projects built with VB4 handle binary files correctly under VB6, you may need to change the source code. (See the section on binary files for the techniques that are now needed.)

Finally, keep in mind the common dialog boxes that you saw in Chapter 14. When users manipulate files in your programs, they will expect to see these boxes when appropriate.

File Commands

Visual Basic has six commands that interact directly with the underlying operating system, mimicking the usual operating system commands that handle files and drives on your machine. You already saw one of the commands in Chapter 17, the Kill command, which lets you delete a file. Table 18-1 summarizes these commands.

You use these commands by following them with a string or string variable. For example,

```
MkDir "TESTDIR"
```

would add a subdirectory called TESTDIR to the current directory. The line

```
MkDir "C:\TESTDIR"
```

would add the subdirectory to the root directory of the C drive.

Command	Function
ChDrive	Changes the logged drive for the underlying operating system
ChDir	Changes the default directory
MkDir	Makes a new directory
RmDir	Removes a directory
Name	Changes the name of a file or moves a file from one directory to another on the same drive
Kill	Deletes a file from a disk

Visual Basic's
File Handling
Commands
Table 18-1.

18

The commands that handle files also accept the normal file-handling wildcards. For example,

```
Kill "*.*"
```

deletes all the files in the current directory (not to be used casually!). As Table 18-1 indicates, the Name command can actually do a bit more than the old DOS REN command; it can move files from one directory in the current drive to another. To do this, give the full path names. For example,

```
Name "C:\VB\TEST.BAS" As "C:\EXAMPLES\TEST.BAS"
```

moves the TEST.BAS file from the VB directory to a directory named Examples.

In addition, the CurDir$ function returns a string that gives the path for the current drive. You can also specify a drive:

   CurDir$ (*Drive*)

The first character of *Drive* determines the drive. When used in this form, the function gives the path for the specified drive. (You can also use the CurDir function, which returns a variant rather than a string.)

As with any function that uses disk drives, you can generate a run-time error if the underlying operating system cannot perform the requested function. See the section "Making a File Program Robust: Error Trapping" later in this chapter for more on dealing with these types of errors.

Example: How to Reset the Logged Drive

Programs that are distributed to other users and that change the logged drive or path will often need to reset the drive to where it was when the program started. (It's the neighborly thing to do.) The original logged drive and path information are often stored in global variables in the Form_Load procedure of the startup form. If there is a chance that the Form_Load will be called more than once, you'll need to modify the code by introducing a static variable that tells you whether the form has already been loaded. Here's an example of the modifications needed:

```
Sub Form_Load ()
  'Global variables gOldDrive$ and gOldPath$
  Static AlreadyLoadedOnce As Boolean
  If Not (AlreadyLoadedOnce) Then
    gOldDrive$ = Left(CurDir, 2) 'get current drive
    gOldPath$ = CurDir     'and path so can reset at end
    AlreadyLoadedOnce = True
    'other code you want to use once goes here
    'Copyright notices, for example
  End If
End Sub
```

File-Handling Functions

Certain tasks are so common that the designers of Visual Basic decided to add them to the language itself, rather than make you use Windows API calls or requiring you to "shell" to one of the utility programs to access them. There are four of these functions: FileCopy, FileDateTime, GetAttr, and SetAttr. (Of course, you also have the power of the new File System Objects, as you'll see in the next chapter.)

The FileCopy Function

The FileCopy function copies a file from the source path to another path. It does not use the Shell command (see the next chapter) to activate the underlying operating system copy routine or call the File Manager. This function takes named arguments, and its syntax is

FileCopy *source, destination*

The FileCopy function does not allow wildcards.

The FileDateTime Function

The FileDateTime function returns the date and time a file was created or last modified. The syntax is

FileDateTime (*pathname*)

The GetAttr Function

The GetAttr function returns an integer. Using masking techniques to get at the individual bits, you can determine how the various attributes are set. The syntax for this function is

GetAttr (*pathname*) As Integer

Table 18-2 summarizes the values of these attributes as symbolic constants.

Attribute	Constant	Value
Normal	vbNormal	0
ReadOnly	vbReadOnly	1
Hidden	vbHidden	2
System	vbSystem	4
Volume	vbVolume	8
Directory	vbDirectory	16
Archive	vbArchive	32

Attribute
Constants
Table 18-2.

18

For example, if

GetAttr(*FileName*) = vbReadOnly + vbHidden

then the file is hidden and read-only. (You can also use: GetAttr(*FileName*) = 3 since vbReadOnly + vbHidden = 3.)

T IP: You can use this masking technique with the Dir (or its equivalent Dir$) function to find files that match both a file specification and a file attribute. The syntax for this version is Dir(*pathname, attributes*) where you add together the various symbolic constants (or their values) in order to specify the types of files to be looked for. For example,

```
Dir("C:\" , vbHidden + vbSystem + vbReadOnly)
```

would find files in the root directory that were simultaneously hidden, read-only, and of system type.

The SetAttr Function

The SetAttr function sets attribute information for files. Using the same bit values given in Table 18-2, you can change the various attributes. The syntax for this function is

SetAttr *Pathname, attributes*

Similarly, you can use the symbolic constants shown in Table 18-2. For example,

```
SetAttr FileName$, vbHidden + vbReadOnly
```

would hide the file and set it as read-only.

> **T** IP: Use the SetAttr function to hide files that you don't want casual users to know about. For example, putting an encrypted password in a hidden file and then examining that file is a common (and reasonably secure) method of making sure that a program is being used by the right person. (See the section "Adding Licensing Screens" later in this chapter.)

Example: A Function for Getting the Attributes of a File

Suppose you have a filename (including the full path); then, as I mentioned above, you can use bit masking on the results of the GetAttr function

```
Attributes = GetAttr(TheFileName)
```

in order to examine the nature of the file. This is so common that you should probably make a user-defined function out of it. The following function returns a string with the information (including the filename) separated by carriage returns.

```
Function GetFileInfo(FileName As String) As String
  Dim Temp As String
  Dim Attrib As Integer

  Attrib = GetAttr(FileName)
  Temp = FileName & vbCrLf & vbCrLf
  Temp = Temp & "Date/Time: " & FileDateTime(FileName) & vbCrLf
  Temp = Temp & "Size: " & FileLen(FileName) & " bytes" & vbCrLf
  If (Attrib And vbReadOnly) = vbReadOnly Then
    Temp = Temp & "ReadOnly: Yes" & vbCrLf
  End If
  If (Attrib And vbHidden) = vbHidden Then
    Temp = Temp & "Hidden: Yes" & vbCrLf
  End If
  If (Attrib And vbSystem) = vbSystem Then
    Temp = Temp & "System: Yes" & vbCrLf
  End If
  If (Attrib And vbArchive) = vbArchive Then
    Temp = Temp & "Archive: Yes" & vbCrLf
  End If
  GetFileInfo = Temp
End Function
```

To test this function, simply start up a new project and then call the function using the full path name of a file. For example, if you use

```
Private Sub Form_Load()
  MsgBox (GetFileInfo("C:\windows\calc.exe"))
  End
End Sub
```

you'll see this under my version of Windows 95:

Sequential Files

18

Sequential files are the most basic kinds of files—they basically hold human readable text. You can look at a sequential file in Notepad, for example, and expect to make sense out of it. Things like HTML pages are ultimately sequential files, for example, as are files such as the "ReadMe" files that are supplied with many programs.

One good analogy to keep in mind when dealing with sequential files is that of recording information on a cassette tape. The analogy is a particularly useful one because the operations on sequential files that are analogous to easy tasks for a cassette recorder, such as recording an album on a blank tape, will be easy. Those analogous to more difficult tasks, such as splicing tapes together or making a change within a tape, will be more difficult. To avoid unnecessary work, use a sequential file only when you know that you will:

◆   Rarely make changes within the file

◆   Process the file's information from start to finish, without needing to constantly jump around

◆   Add information to the file at the end of the file

It's not that you can't make changes within the file, jump around when processing information, or add to the file other than at the end; it's just that these procedures are a bit painful.

Here's a table of some common operations on a cassette tape and the analogous operations on a sequential text file called TEST in the currently active directory:

Operation	Visual Basic Equivalent
Rewind the tape, press Play and Pause	Open "TEST" For Input as #1
Rewind the tape, press Record and Pause	Open "TEST" For Output as #1
Press Stop	Close #1

Each time Visual Basic sees the Open command, it gets ready to write information to or read information from the file. (The jargon is that it "sets up a channel" to communicate with the file.) What follows the Open command is the name of the file you are working with. The filename must be a string variable or enclosed in quotation marks, and unless it is in the current directory, you need to provide enough information to identify its path. (The value of a string variable must be a legal filename.) Under Windows 95/98 and NT, of course, what constitutes a legal filename is much improved over the earlier versions of Windows. You can use up to 255 characters, and spaces are allowed. (You still can't use a \, ?, :, *, <, >, or |, however.)

On the other hand, if you want your files to be completely compatible with machines not running Windows 95/98 or Windows NT, you should follow the rules for filenames that DOS imposes:

◆ The filename can be at most eight characters with an optional three-character extension following the period.

◆ The characters you can use are the letters A–Z, numbers 0–9, and ( ) { } @ # $ % & ! - _ ' / ~

◆ Lowercase letters are automatically converted to uppercase.

In any case, you also need a file identifier. This is a number between 1 and 255 preceded by the # sign that is used to identify the file while it is open. Although you can't change this number until you close the file, the next time you open the file you can use a different ID number. The number of possible files you can have open at once is limited by operating system constraints.

When Visual Basic processes an Open command, it also reserves a file buffer in the computer's memory. Without a buffer, each piece of information sent to (or from) the disk would be recorded (or played back) separately. Since mechanical operations, such as writing to a disk, are much slower than writing to RAM, this would waste a lot of time. Instead, when a file buffer fills up, Visual Basic tells the underlying operating system to activate the appropriate drive, and a whole packet of information is sent in a continuous stream to the disk.

The Close command usually empties the buffer and tells the underlying operating system to update the FAT (file allocation table). But because of Windows' own buffering techniques, this may not happen precisely when Visual Basic processes the Close command. For this reason, a sudden power outage when you have a file open almost inevitably leads to lost information and occasionally even to having corrupted files on your hard disk if the FAT isn't written to properly. (The ScanDisk command is often necessary when this happens, and in order to fix the problem, Windows 95/98 will automatically run ScanDisk on staring up again.)

TIP: The Reset command, unlike the Close command, seems to force the underlying operating system to flush the buffers. Use this command in critical situations to make it more likely that the underlying operating system's file buffer is flushed.

The Print command sends information to a form. A slightly different command, Print #, provides one way to send information to a file. Here is an example of a fragment that sends one piece of information to a file named TEST:

```
' Writing to a file
Open "TEST" For Output As #1
Print #1, "TESTING 1, 2, 3"
Close #1
```

18

CAUTION: If a file in the current directory already exists with the name TEST, the Open For Output statement *erases* it. *Always* keep in mind that opening a file for sequential output starts a new file; the contents of a previous file with the same name are lost. (For details on appending information to an existing file, see the section on "Adding to an Existing File" a little later on in this chapter.)

After the usual Remark statement, the first executable statement in the preceding fragment tells Visual Basic that you are going to set up a file named TEST having file identifier #1. Next comes the statement that actually sends the information to the file. The comma after the file identifier number is necessary, but what follows the comma can be anything that might occur in an ordinary Print statement. And what appears in the file is the exact image of what would have occurred on the screen. For example, the file does not contain quotation marks. More precisely, the file will contain the word TESTING, followed by a comma, followed by a space, followed by the numeral 1, followed by another space, followed by the numeral 2, followed by a space, followed by the numeral 3, and then, although you may not have thought of it, the characters that define a carriage-return/line-feed combination—a CHR$(13) (carriage return) and a CHR$(10) (line feed).

It is extremely important that you keep in mind that the Print # command works exactly like the Print command. By now you know of the automatic carriage-return/line-feed combination that follows an ordinary Print statement. More precisely, if the line read

```
Print #1, "TESTING 1, 2, 3";
```

then the file would contain two fewer characters. The CHR$(13) and CHR$(10) would no longer be there because the semicolon suppresses the carriage-return/line-feed combination (just as for an ordinary Print statement). This is important because the cardinal rule of file handling is that you must know the exact structure of a file if you want to be able to efficiently reuse the information it contains.

As a third example, suppose you changed the line to read

```
Print #1, "TESTING", 1, 2, 3
```

Now the file contains many spaces (occurrences of CHR$(32)) that were not there before. To see why this must be true, just recall (Chapter 6) that a comma in a Print statement when you print to a form moves the cursor to the next print zone on your form by inserting spaces. Use a comma in a Print # statement, and the same spaces are placed in your file.

Finally, the Close command (followed by a file identifier) *flushes,* or moves, whatever is in the appropriate file buffer to the disk, but it may not necessarily move the actual data immediately, as I mentioned earlier. The Close command without a file ID flushes all open buffers—that is, it closes all open files.

The LOF Command

Once a file is open, you can use the Visual Basic "length of file" command LOF( ) to learn how large the file is, instead of using the FileLen command. To use LOF, place the appropriate file identifier number within the parentheses.

To see this command at work (and to confirm what was said earlier about the sizes of the various versions of the TEST file), try the following Form_Click procedure in a new project:

```
Sub Form_Click()
' a file tester
' demonstrates the 'exact' image property of Print #
  Open "Test1" For Output As #1
  Open "Test2" For Output As #2
  Open "Test3" For Output As #3
  Print #1, "TESTING 1, 2, 3"
  Print #2, "TESTING 1, 2, 3";
  Print #3, "TESTING", 1, 2, 3
  Print LOF(1)
  Print LOF(2)
  Print LOF(3)
  Close
End Sub
```

If you run this program, you'll see

```
17
15
47
```

As you can see, the first file does contain 2 more characters than the second (to account for the carriage-return/line-feed combination). And the third contains far more than the 14 characters in the phrase "TESTING, 1,2,3". The extra characters, as you'll soon see, are indeed spaces (CHR$(32)).

The FreeFile Command

If you are writing all of the code for the program, you can keep track of the file identifier numbers you are using for the various open files. Since you can't do this when you are part of a big project, it is better to let VB generate an unused file number for you.

The way to find an unused file identifier is with the command FreeFile. The value of FreeFile is always the next unused file ID number. Therefore, you merely need a statement like

18

```
FileNumber = FreeFile
```

at the appropriate point in your program, followed by

```
Open TheFileName For Output As #FileNumber
```

CAUTION: You must assign the results of the FreeFile function to a variable. Never use

```
Open TheFileName For Output as #FreeFile
```

Example: Writing a Visual Basic Array out to an HTML Page as an HTML Table

NOTE: This section, of course, assumes that you know basic HTML. If you don't, please consult any standard HTML reference for more on the HTML tags for tables.

With the Internet becoming more and more important, it is not uncommon to have to write out information generated in a VB program to HTML. (See Chapter 25 for other ways to work with HTML in VB6.) Probably the most common task you will want to automate is that of converting a VB two-dimensional array to an HTML table. To do this, all you need to do is write out a sequential file with the <TR>, <TD>, and <TB> tags. For example, lines like

```
Print #FileNumber, "<TD>"
Print #FileNumber, TheEntries(Row, Col)
Print #FileNumber, "</TD>"
```

will print the information in an element of the array named TheEntries into the file surrounded by the right HTML tags so that it will be the data in a cell in an HTML table.

Obviously one can make this kind of HTML table generation routine very elaborate (since tables in HTML have so many attributes). As an example of what you can do, I added two optional parameters to this procedure. These option parameters will control whether the table has a border as well as the alignment of data within a cell. You can see this in the header of the Sub procedure:

```
Sub MakeTable(TheEntries(), TheFileName As String, _
CellSpacing As Integer, CellPadding As Integer, _
Optional Border As Integer = 1, Optional Align As String = "RIGHT")
```

By using the Optional parameter with a default value, I set the defaults so that the table will have a 1 pixel border, and it will align the information in the cells on the right. In the actual code for the routine, I'll use the optional parameters in lines like:

```
If Border Then
    Temp = "<TABLE BORDER=" & Border & "" _
    & " CELLPADDING=" _
    & CellPadding & "CellSpacing= " & CellSpacing & " > "
  Else
    Temp = "<TABLE BORDER=0 CELLPADDING=" _
    & CellPadding & " CellSpacing= " & CellSpacing & ">"
  End If
Print #FileNumber, Temp
Print #FileNumber, "<TR Align=" & Align & ">"
```

The first Print # statement prints the HTML definition of the table with the indicated border size to the file, and the second sets the alignment of the cells in a row.

Here's the whole procedure:

```
Sub MakeTable(TheEntries(), TheFileName As String, _
CellSpacing As Integer, CellPadding As Integer, _
Optional Border As Integer = 1, Optional Align As String = "RIGHT")
  Dim Temp As String, FileNumber As Integer
  Dim Row As Integer, Col As Integer
  FileNumber = FreeFile
  Open TheFileName For Output As #FileNumber
  If Border Then
    Temp = "<TABLE BORDER=" & Border & "" _
    & " CELLPADDING=" _
    & CellPadding & "CellSpacing= " & CellSpacing & " > "
  Else
    Temp = "<TABLE BORDER=0 CELLPADDING=" _
    & CellPadding & " CellSpacing= " & CellSpacing & ">"
  End If
  Print #FileNumber, Temp
```

```
For Row = LBound(TheEntries, 1) To UBound(TheEntries, 1)
  Print #FileNumber, "<TR Align=" & Align & ">"
  For Col = LBound(TheEntries, 2) To UBound(TheEntries, 2)
    Print #FileNumber, "<TD>"
    Print #FileNumber, TheEntries(Row, Col)
    Print #FileNumber, "</TD>"
  Next Col
  Print #FileNumber, "</TR>"
Next Row
Print #FileNumber, "</TABLE>"
Close #FileNumber
End Sub
```

18

To test the routine, set up a new project and try the following code. It will generate a bunch of random currency amounts between 0 and $100 and then output the HTML so that the page displays a table with the data in the cells right-aligned—as one would probably want for currency amounts (see Figure 18-1). Note the use of named parameters in the procedure call, which I think are awfully convenient for these kinds of procedures!

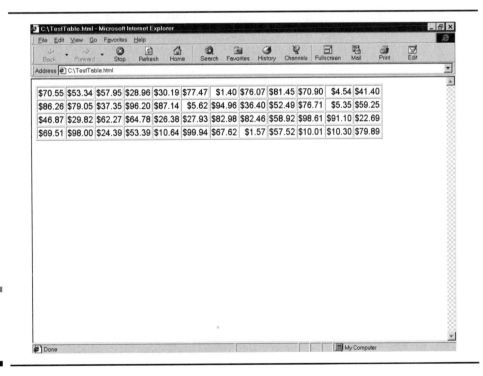

Outputting an
array as an
HTML table
Figure 18-1.

```
Private Sub Form_Load()
'Create an array
  Dim Row As Integer, Col As Integer
  ReDim A(1995 To 1998, 1 To 12) As Variant
    For Row = 1995 To 1998
      For Col = 1 To 12
        A(Row, Col) = Format(100 * Rnd, "Currency") & Space(2)
      Next Col
    Next Row
'now call the table generator routine
'using named parameters
  MakeTable TheEntries:=A, TheFileName:="C:\TestTable.html", _
  CellSpacing:=2, CellPadding:=2, Border:=1, Align:="RIGHT"
'now you should open your favorite browser and check the results
'by loading the file called C:\TestTable.html and looking
'at the results!
End
End Sub
```

Now you can open your favorite Web browser and look at the results by loading the file called C:\TestTable.html.

Reading Back Information from a File

To read information back from a file, you must open the file for Input using its name (again, the full path name if it's not in the currently active directory) and give it a file identifier that is not currently being used within the program. It doesn't have to be the same identifier that it was set up with originally, so you should simply use

```
FileNumber = FreeFile
Open FileName For Input As #FileNumber
```

It also is important that you know how the information was stored in the file. For example, is the information separated by commas, or is each piece of information on a different line? (The buzzword phrase is "how is it delimited?".) For example, the file I just named TEST1. contains the word TESTING, followed by a comma, followed by the three numbers, each separated from its successor by another comma. The file ends with the carriage-return/ line-feed combination.

Next, you use a variant on the old PC-BASIC "Input" command to retrieve the information. The idea is that the version of Input you choose to read back information from a file will read back either up to the next comma or a whole line, at which point you can use the nifty new Split function (see Chapter 10) to break up the line into useful pieces. You use the Line Input # statement to read information in a sequential file one line at a time and the Input# to read data up to the next comma. Here is a fragment that reads back and displays the contents of the file named TEST1:

```
' Reading back a file
'the Test1 file contains information on a single line
Open "TEST1" For Input As #1
Line Input #1, A$
```

18

```
Print A$
Close #1
```

As an alternative you could use

```
Open "TEST1" For Input As #1
Input #1, A$, B$, C$, D$
Print A$; " "; B$; " "; C$; " "; D$
Close #1
```

or

```
Open "TEST1" For Input As #1
Input #1, A$, B, C, D
Print A$; B; C; D
Close #1
```

The latter two options seem clumsier, though, and in any case yield slightly different results. For example, the last program has recovered the numbers as numbers (values of numeric variables) rather than as strings of numerals (part of a larger string). On the other hand, if you have stored numbers in a file, this is often the method to choose to retrieve them.

If you know how many entries there are in a file, a For-Next loop is often the easiest way to read the information back. For example, suppose you're a teacher with a class of 25 students. You know the currently active disk contains a file called CLASS that stores the information about the class in the following form:

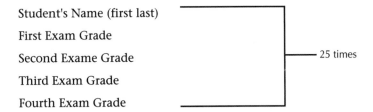

Student's Name (first last)

First Exam Grade

Second Exame Grade   25 times

Third Exam Grade

Fourth Exam Grade

Two useful terms that recur often in file handling are *fields* and *records*. Think of this file as being made up of 25 records and each record as consisting of 5 fields. Usually, a program that manipulates this file will read back the information by records—that is, 5 fields at a time. And each field can be picked up by a single Input # rather than needing the Line Input command. The similarity with user-defined records (see Chapter 10) is not a coincidence. You'll often find yourself filling in the components of a record from a file.

Knowing the exact format of this file means you can easily write a procedure that will retrieve this information. First, set up a record type:

```
Type StudentRecord
   Name As String
   FirstExam As Integer
   SecondExam As Integer
   ThirdExam As Integer
   FourthExam As Integer
End Type
```

Now make up an array of StudentRecords as a global variable,

```
Global StudentGrades() As StudentRecord
```

and then use the following general procedure:

```
Sub RetrieveGrade()
  Dim FileNum As Integer, I As Integer
  ReDim StudentGrades(1 To 25)
  FileNum = FreeFile
  Open "GRADES" For Input As #FileNum
  For I = 1 To 25
   Input #FileNum, StudentGrades(I).Name
   Input #FileNum, StudentGrades(I).FirstExam
   Input #FileNum, StudentGrades(I).SecondExam
   Input #FileNum, StudentGrades(I).ThirdExam
   Input #FileNum, StudentGrades(I).FourthExam
  Next I
  Close FileNum
End Sub
```

Now each row of the array StudentGrades contains a record with the name and grades of a student. You could easily incorporate this type of general Sub procedure into a program that analyzes the grades or places the information on a grid.

This file has a simple structure because the cardinal rule remains: You can't do anything with a file until you bring into memory the information you need from it.

The more complicated the structure of the file, the harder it is to work with. If you can keep the structure of your files simple, then filling up an array is often the method of choice. The reason is that once the information contained in the file is stored, massaging it is easy, usually requiring only a few For-Next loops to run through the array.

For example, suppose you want to write a procedure that can return the average grade and number of students absent for each exam. As always when dealing with an array of records, you could choose to store this information in two parallel arrays or in one string array. In this case, if you chose to store this information in an array of strings rather than in the array of records given earlier, you could write a Sub that would take a parameter for the exam number, as in the following listing:

18

```
Sub AnalysisOfExams(ExamNumber As Integer)
  Dim NumAbsent As Integer, Total As Integer, I As Integer
  ' StudentGrades() is a global string array
  NumAbsent = 0
  Total = 0
  For I = 1 To 25
    If StudentGrades(I, ExamNumber) = "absent" Then
      NumAbsent = NumAbsent + 1
    Else
      Total = Total + CInt(StudentGrades(I, ExamNumber))
    End If
  Next I
  Print "The number absent was"; NumAbsent
  Print "The class average was"; Total/(25 - NumAbsent)
End Sub
```

This procedure is straightforward. The parameter tells the procedure what exam number (column of the array) to look at, and the For-Next loop runs through each row. (The CInt command is needed because the exam grades are stored in a string array and we want to make Integers out of the exam grades.)

Adding to an Existing File

The GRADE file contains each student's name followed by a list of his or her grades. This is a bit unnatural. A different, more natural kind of file structure would occur if the teacher entered everything in steps: first the student's name and then, after a while, the results of the first exam, and so on. To write a program to do this, you need a command that lets you add information to the end of an already existing file. The statement

    Open *FileName* For Append As *File#*

causes three things to occur at once:

◆ Visual Basic opens the file (if the file doesn't exist, it creates it) and sets up the appropriate buffer.

◆ Visual Basic locates the end of the file on the disk.

◆ Visual Basic prepares to output to the file at its end.

CAUTION: Recall that if you open an existing file for Output, you erase it. *Only* by using the Append command can you add to an existing file.

If you are writing this type of program for yourself, then for a single class's records, you might want to update this file, using a short fragment that reads the students' names and stores them in an array before appending:

```
Dim I As Integer, StudentGrade$
ReDim StudentNames$(25)
Open "StudentGrades" For Input As #1
For I = 1 To 25
  Input #1, StudentNames$(I)
Next I
Close #1
Open "StudentGrades" For Append As #1
For I = 1 To 25
  M$ = "The grade for " + StudentNames$(I) + " is ?"
  StudentGrade$ = InputBox$(M$)
  Print #1, StudentGrade$
Next I
Close
```

This fragment assumes the file was already created and contains the names of the students. The point of the Close command is that to change a sequential file's status from reading to writing, it must first be closed. Once the file is closed, the Append command lets you add to it.

You will probably find yourself writing lots of these "quick and dirty" programs as you become more familiar with file-handling techniques. Although they're never very robust, they do get the job done. (You need special techniques to make file-handling programs robust; see "Making a File Program Robust: Error Trapping" later in this chapter.)

Suppose, however, you are teaching five classes, each with a different number of students. Then the "quick and dirty" approach is not worthwhile. It's possible to get the classes mixed up, leading to an error message or even to losing a student's grades. To prevent this kind of mishap, write a header to all your files. Use this header to put standard information about the file at the beginning of the file. You can then use this information to build a grid to allow data entry.

To write a usable grade book program, you can use the first few entries in the file for the name of the class, the semester, the number of exams, and the number of students. This kind of information isn't likely to change. (If you want to change it, see the section "Binary Files" later in this chapter.) Also, this has the added advantage that you can use this information to set up the bounds on the loops that will read and process the information contained in the file. The following table shows you the properties of the form that lets the user fill in this header information through various text boxes:

Type of Object	Control (Form) Name	Caption (Text)
Form	frmHeader	General Information
Label	Label1	File Name
Label	Label2	Class Name
Text box	txtNameOfFile	
Text box	txtNameOfClass	
Text box	txtNumberOfExams	
Text box	txtNumberOfStudents	
Command button	cmdSetUp	Set Up File

18

Now you can have the following general procedure that sets up a grade book on a disk in the currently active directory. (This procedure assumes you've checked that the filename is acceptable already, and it does not contain the error trap that is needed for any serious file-handling program.)

```
Sub cmdSetUp_Click()
' local variables
  Dim ExamNum As Integer, StuNum As Integer, FileNum As Integer

  FileNum = FreeFile
  Open txtNameOfFile.Text For Output As #FileNum
  Print #FileNum, txtNameOfClass.Text
  Print #FileNum, CInt(txtNumberOfExams.Text)
  Print #FileNum, CInt(txtNumberOfStudents.Text)
  Close #FileNum
End Sub
```

General Sequential Files

Although For-Next loops are a convenient way to read back information contained in a file, obviously there are times when they are not practical. There may be too much information in the file, or you don't know what limits to use. You need a way to implement the following outline:

```
While there's information left in the file
   Get next piece of Info
   Process it
Loop
```

To do this, you need a way to test when you're at the end of a file. The end-of-file statement in Visual Basic that lets you do this is mnemonic. It's

    EOF(FileIdentifier)

A quite general program to read back the information contained in a file set up with Print # statements looks like this:

```
FileNum = FreeFile
Open FileName$ For Input As #FileNum
Do Until EOF(FileNum)
  Line Input #FileNum, A$
  ' process line--this would probably be a procedure call or
  ' function call
Loop
Close #FileNum
```

You use a loop with the test at the top to take into account the unlikely possibility that the file exists but doesn't contain any information—that is, in case it was opened for output but nothing was actually sent to the file. This fragment is a more or less direct translation of the preceding outline. It picks up a line of data (that is, all the data up to a carriage-return/line-feed pair), and it continues doing this until it gets to the end of the file.

Use this kind of fragment to write a simple print formatter for text files. All you need to know is that you can enter each line (that is, that the lines are not too long or too short); then add the lines to the current value of a string variable. When you're done, make the lines the Text property of a multiline text box with vertical scroll bars.

TIP: Remember, it's always much faster in Visual Basic to first create the complete string by retrieving all the information, then using only one assignment to the Text property. Changing any property is one of the slowest operations you can perform in VB.

By the way, a lot of people use the Do While form of these loops, so you may see either of the following in code that you are asked to maintain:

```
Do While Not EOF(1)/Loop
```

or

```
While Not EOF(1)/WEnd
```

Since all three forms are equivalent, which one you choose is a matter of taste.

Reading Back Characters

One common use of the EOF statement is to read back the information contained in a file, character-by-character. The analogy to keep in mind, if you know PC-BASIC, is that you read a file as if it were the keyboard. The command that picks individual characters from the keyboard is Input$. In Visual Basic, you pick up individual characters from a file with the following statement

$StringVariableName$ = Input$(*NumberOfChars, FileIdentifier*)

where the first entry holds the number of characters and the second holds the file identifier. Therefore,

```
SixChar$ = Input$(6,#2)
```

picks up six characters from file #2 opened for input and assigns them to a string variable named SixChar$.

The following fragment reads the contents of a text file named FileName$ character-by-character and prints both the ASCII code and the character on the same line:

```
'A 'semi' master text file reader
FileNum = FreeFile
Open FileName$ For Input As #FileNum
Do Until EOF(FileNum)
  A$ = Input$(1,#FileNum)
  Print A$, ASC(A$)
Loop
Close FileNum
```

If you use this program on the files TEST1, TEST2, and TEST3 created earlier, you can easily check that the spaces and carriage-return/line-feed combinations the Print # statement sends to a file are, in fact, there (as stated earlier). Although the Input$(1 ,) statement lets you examine the structure of many text files character-by-character, it shouldn't be overused. For example, it's usually much slower than using the Line Input # or even the Input # function.

T IP: If all you want to do is suck up the whole contents of a file to manipulate it as one large string, then lines like

```
TheContents = Input(LOF(FileNumber), #FileNumber)
```

work like a charm. (Don't try this with multi-megabyte files, of course, or you may get an "out of memory" error.)

Keep in mind that the Input$ command may not be able to read files created by word processors or programs. This is because Visual Basic stops reading a sequential file when it encounters a CTRL+Z combination (CHR$(26)), the traditional end-of-file character. (Some files created by programs use the CHR$(26) character internally for purposes other than indicating the end of the file.) You can see this by trying to use the previous program to read back the file created with the following fragment:

```
'demonstrates CTRL+Z (=^Z=CHR$(26)) as EOF
Dim FileNum As Integer, I As Integer
FileNum = FreeFile
Open "TEST" For Output As #FileNum
Print #FileNum, CHR$(26)
For I = 1 To 10
  Print #FileNum, "The previous program can't ever read this"
Next I
Close #FileNum
```

T IP: Placing a CHR$(26) at the beginning of your file is a simple yet effective way to keep casual snoopers out of your files. They won't, for example, be able to look at them in Notepad.

Since it can be very important to massage non-ASCII files (such as spreadsheet files), Visual Basic has another method of reading back files that, among its other powers, gets around this CTRL+Z problem. (See the section "Binary Files" later in this chapter.)

In any case, even if a file can be read with the Input$ function, it's usually better to think of a file as being made up of fields, possibly grouped into records. Each field is separated from the next by a delimiter—that is, a comma or carriage-return/line-feed combination. The delimiter is what lets you use a single Input # to pick up the field in a way that lets you work with each group of data most easily. (For example, you might use Line Input to load the items in a list or combo box.)

Sending Special Characters to a Sequential File

Since you send information to a file as if it were the screen, you again have to solve the following problems:

◆   How do you send special characters (such as quotation marks) to the file?

◆   How do you nicely format a file?

Visual Basic uses the Write # statement, separated by commas and with quotes around strings, to send items to a file. For example,

```
Write #3, "Testing 1, 2, 3"
```

18

sends everything (including the quotes and the commas) to the output (or append) file with ID #3. This is similar to (and, of course, less cumbersome than) writing

```
Print #3, Chr$(34);
Print #3, "Testing";
Print #3, Chr$(34);
Print #3, "1, 2, 3"
```

(Note the three semicolons to prevent inadvertent carriage-return/line-feed combinations.)

As long as you send individual pieces of information to a file, the Print # and Write # commands can be used interchangeably. For example,

```
Print #FileNum, "Hello"
```

and

```
Write #FileNum, "Hello"
```

both put a single piece of information into a file. In either case, you can read back the information by using the Input # command. (The files won't be the same size, though, because the Write command adds two quotation marks (Chr$(34)) to the file.) It's only when you send more than one piece of information at a time that the differences really emerge. For example, to send three numbers to a file using

```
Print #FileNum, 1, 2, 3
```

sends a rather large number of superfluous spaces. The command

```
Write #FileNum, 1, 2, 3
```

sends the appropriate commas to the file, saving space and making it easier to read back the information. It's equivalent to the cumbersome

```
Print #FileNum, 1; ","; 2; ","; 3
```

Simply put, use Write # together with Input #, and use Print # with Line Input #.

Making Changes Inside a Sequential File

The information inside a sequential file is packed tight and is hard to change, but that doesn't mean you can't do it. If the changes you're making don't alter the size of the file, then the methods described in the "Binary Files" section of this chapter are your best bet. This section explains some other ways that do not use these techniques.

The Open FileName For Append As #FileNum command lets you add information to the end of a sequential file. Suppose you now want to add information to the beginning of a file. Proceed as follows:

1. Open a temporary file for output.
2. Use Print # or Write # to place the new information in the temporary file.
3. Close the temporary file.
4. Append the information from the original file onto the end of the temporary file. Two techniques are available to perform this task:

   ◆ The first technique involves reopening the temporary file For Append. The original file is then opened For Input, and information is read from the original file and appended to the temporary file. Finally, the temporary file is closed again.

   ◆ The second technique is much faster when the original file is large. Use Visual Basic's Shell command to execute the underlying operating system's COPY command. (See Chapter 20 for more on the Shell command.) As you probably know, the underlying operating system command

      COPY *file1+file2*

   appends the file named *file2* onto the file named *file1*. Thus, the Shell command would take the form

      Shell "COPY *TempFileName+OriginalFileName*"

   or

      Shell "COPY" + *TempFileName$* +"+" + *OriginalFileName$*

5. Delete the original file using the Kill command.
6. Rename the temporary file to the original file's name by using the Name command.

Now, suppose the new information does not go right at the beginning of the file, or you want to remove or replace information already in the file. To do this, imagine what you might do if you were to make these modifications on a cassette tape. First, you'd record the words to be added on a separate tape with a little bit of leader, which means you'd leave some blank tape so you can cut and paste. Then you'd find where on the tape the new information is to go and splice (or cut) the tapes.

For example, suppose you want to change all occurrences of the word "QuickBASIC" in a file to "Visual Basic" (or, more generally, to write your own search and replace function). Follow these steps:

1. Read the information in the file into a temporary file, stopping whenever you get to the string "QuickBASIC".
2. Write "Visual Basic" into the temporary file.

3. Move past the occurrence of the word "QuickBASIC" and continue repeating steps 1 and 2 until you reach the end of the file.

4. Now kill the original file and rename the temporary file with the original file's name.

Because you have to read the information back character-by-character, a program that implements this outline can run for a long time if done in this naive manner. Binary techniques can work much faster. (See the section on "Binary Files" for more on this.)

18

On the other hand, the program will run more quickly (and is also simpler to program) if you know that each occurrence of the string you're searching for is in a separate field. If this is true, you can use a loop that in pseudocode is:

```
OPEN Original File
OPEN Temp File
INPUT Field from Original File
DO UNTIL EOF(Original File)
   If field <>"QuickBASIC" THEN
      WRITE It To Temp File
   ELSE
      WRITE "Visual Basic" to Temp File
   END IF
   INPUT nextfield
LOOP
KILL Original File
RENAME Temp File as Original File
```

Finally, if you knew that each field contained the words you were searching for but wasn't necessarily equal to them, you could input the field and then write a little procedure to search through the field after it is in memory.

The RichTextBox Control and File Handling

If you are working with an edition of Visual Basic that has the RichTextBox control, you can use some properties of the RichTextBox control to make it easy to send its contents to a file (or conversely, to display the contents of a file inside of a RichTextBox control). Here are short descriptions of the properties and methods of the RichTextBox control that can be used in file handling.

LoadFile Method
The LoadFile method loads an .rtf file or text file into a RichTextBox control at one gulp. The syntax is

NameOfRichTextBox.LoadFile(*pathname*, *filetype*)

where *pathname* is a string expression defining the path and filename of the file you want to load into the control. The optional *filetype* parameter controls whether the file is loaded as an .rtf file. (The default is that it is, but you can use a value of 0 or the symbolic constant rtfRTF.) Use the value 1 (or the constant rtfText) to load a text file.

NOTE: The LoadFile method replaces whatever was in the RichTextBox control with the contents of the file.

SaveFile Method

The SaveFile method saves the contents of a RichTextBox control to a file in one swoop. The syntax is similar to that of LoadFile:

NameOfRichTextBox.SaveFile(*pathname, filetype*)

NOTE: You can also use ordinary file-handling techniques for working with a RichTextBox control. For example:

```
Open "FOO.RTF" For Input As 1
RichTextBox1.TextRTF = Input(LOF(1), 1)
```

but the above methods will actually read and write the file in the form that the control will automatically display.

Making a File Program Robust: Error Trapping

Usually, when you're testing a program, you don't care if you get a run-time error and your program crashes. However, when an open file is around, then after a crash, strange things may get written into your files, or information you need may never get there. Even if you've thoroughly debugged the program, someone may try to send information to a full disk or try to access a file that doesn't exist. To solve these problems, you must stop the program when, for example, it faces a full disk. The command that activates error trapping, as you saw in Chapter 12, is

On Error GoTo *label*

where *label* (line number) defines the error trap. (Recall that labels must be unique across a module or form.)

Now you need to transfer control to a part of the procedure that identifies the problem and, if possible, fixes it. If the error can be corrected, you can use the Resume statement to pick up where you left off. However, you can't correct an error if you don't know why it happened. Table 18-3 gives the error codes most common to file-handling programs and their likely causes. You would use this information as outlined in Chapter 12. For example, place the following statement somewhere in the program before the error can occur:

```
On Error GoTo DiskErrorHandler
```

Code	Message
52	Bad filename or number (Remember to use FreeFile correctly.)
53	File not found (This probably indicates a typo.)
54	Bad file mode (The code uses two types of file handling—without closing the file in between.)
55	File already open (You obviously can't open a file that is already open unless you use a different identification number.)
57	Device I/O error (Big problems! Your hardware is acting up. I/O stands for input/output, but check the disk drive anyway.)
58	File already exists
59	Bad record length
61	Disk full (There's not enough room to do what you want.)
62	Input past end of file (You put the test for EOF in the wrong place.)
63	Bad record number
64	Bad filename (You didn't follow the naming conventions for a filename.)
67	Too many files at the same time
68	Device unavailable
70	Permission denied (The disk you're writing to has the write-protect notch covered or the file is write protected.)
71	Disk not ready (The door is open, or where's the floppy?)
72	Disk media error (Time to throw out the floppy or start thinking about the state of your hard disk.)
74	Can't rename files across different drives
75	Path/File access error
76	Path not found (Probably a typo—you asked to open a file that doesn't exist.)

Common File-Handling Errors
Table 18-3.

Now add code, like the fragment given here, to your event procedure (or better, to a general procedure that processes the Err.Number code):

```
DiskErrorHandler:
Select Case Err.Number
  Case 53
    M$ = "Your file was not found. Please check on the "
    M$ = M$ + "spelling or call your operator for assistance."
  Case 57
    M$ = "Possibly big problems on your hardware. You should "
    M$ = M$ + "call your operator for assistance."
```

18

```
Case 61
  M$ = "The disk is full. Please replace with a slightly less "
  M$ = M$ + "used model." 'could Shell to FORMAT.COM here
Case 71
  M$ = "I think the drive door is open--please check."
Case 72
  M$ = "Possibly big problems on your hard disk. You"
  M$ = M$ + " definitely should call for help."
Case Else
  M$ = "Please tell the operator (= program author?) that"
  M$ = M$ & " error number " & Err.Number & " occurred. "
End Select
M$ = M$ + vbCrLf + vbCrLf + "If the error has been corrected, click on "
M$ = M$ + " retry, otherwise click on cancel."
WhatToDo% = MsgBox(M$, vbRetryCancel) 'retry/cancel message box
If WhatToDo% = vbRetry Then Resume Else End
```

The idea of this error trap is simple—the Select Case statement is ideal for handling the many possibilities. Each Case tries to give some indication of where the problem is and, if possible, how to correct it. If you reach the Case Else, the error number has to be reported. In any case, the final block gives you the option of continuing or not, using a Retry/Cancel message box.

NOTE: Only the most common errors are covered here—and, as mentioned in Chapter 12, you might want to consider a centralized error message handler that takes the error number property of the Err object.

Error trapping isn't a cure-all. Obviously, very little can be done about a hard disk crash. On the other hand, if you can "shell" to the Format command, then not having a formatted (empty) floppy around is not a crisis for the novice user. (Experienced Windows users can always use Windows' multitasking possibilities to leave the program in order to format a disk. See Chapter 20 for more on the Shell command.)

Adding a complete DiskCheck fragment to your file-handling programs is the only way to make them robust. You can merge the same module containing this kind of error trap into all your serious file-handling programs, using the Load Text option in the File menu or the clipboard.

On the other hand, as mentioned in Chapter 12, probably the simplest and cleanest way to put error trapping in your program is to write a function in a code module that analyzes the error code and gives the user the necessary feedback. A global function can do the work once the program passes the error code to it as a parameter. In any case, writing a serious file-handling program without an error trap is an awful idea.

Random-Access Files

Suppose you are tired of having to search through entire cassettes for certain songs. To avoid this, you decide to put songs that you want instant access to on individual cassettes. The advantages of doing this are obvious, but there are disadvantages as well. First, to gain more or less instant access to an individual song, you're going to waste a considerable amount of blank tape on each cassette. If, to prevent this, you decide to create a standard-sized tape—one that holds, say, four minutes—you're sure to have at least a couple of songs that run more than four minutes. It's clear that no matter what you do, you'll either waste space or have a few songs that won't fit. Also, if you single out too many songs for separate tapes, you increase the number of cassettes you have to store. If you have hundreds of tapes, each containing an individual song, then you're almost back where you started. It can't possibly be easy to find an individual song if you have to search through a hundred tapes. At this point you would probably choose to alphabetize the tapes by some key feature (such as singer or title), set up an index, or both.

18

Random-access files are stored on a disk in such a way that they have much the same advantages and disadvantages as the song collector's tapes. You gain instant access to individual pieces of information, but only at some cost. You must standardize the packets of information involved, which means that some things may not fit or that space is not efficiently used, and if the file grows too big—with too many pieces of information—you'll have to set up another file to index the first.

NOTE: The data-handling features of Visual Basic (see Chapter 22) make random-access files somewhat less important. But the amount of overhead involved with using data access sometimes makes setting up your own random-access files the right choice. This is especially true for small files.

When setting up a sequential file, it's occasionally useful to think of a group of fields as forming a single record. For example, in the grade book program, grouping the fields by fives (the student name and four exam scores) gave a logical and convenient way to read back the information in the file. It's worth stressing, however, that this particular grouping was not intrinsic to the file—it's only the way the program looks at the file. The only intrinsic divisions within a sequential file are those created by the delimiters (commas or carriage-return/line-feed combinations). When you read back information, you read it field by field, with the delimiters acting as barriers.

In a random-access file, however, the notion of a record is built in. A *random-access file* is a special disk file arranged by records. This lets you immediately move to the 15th record without having to pass through the 14 before it, which saves a considerable amount of time.

When you first set up a random-access file, you specify the maximum length for each record. When you enter data for an individual record, you can, of course, put in less information than this preset limit, but you can never put in more. So just like the song collector, you might need to prepare for the worst possible situation.

The command that sets up a random-access file is analogous to the one for opening a sequential file. For example,

```
Open "SAMPLE.RND" As #5 Len = 100
```

opens a random-access file called SAMPLE.RND on the current directory with a file ID of 5 and with each record being able to hold 100 characters. Note that, unlike the situation for sequential files, you don't have to specify whether you're opening the file for input, output, or appending. As you'll soon see, this distinction is taken care of in the commands that manipulate a random-access file; an open random-access file can be read from and written to essentially simultaneously. You can have any mixture of random-access and sequential files open at the same time. The only restrictions are set by the underlying operating system. To prevent confusion between file types, many programmers use an extension like .rnd for all random-access files, as in the preceding example.

Similarly, you close a file opened for random access by using the Close command followed by the file ID number. As before, the Close command without a file ID number closes all open files, regardless of whether they were opened for sequential or random access. This is especially useful because a sophisticated program for random files often has many files open simultaneously—both sequential and random.

Suppose you want to write a random-access file that would keep track of someone's library. You start by designing the form. You decide on five categories—Author, Title, Subject, Publisher, and Miscellaneous, and after looking over your library, you decide on the following limits for the categories:

Category	Size
Author	20
Title	30
Subject	15
Publisher	20
Miscellaneous	13

Therefore, the total for each record is 98. You set up a random-access file to fit this form (via FileNum = FreeFile, as always):

```
Open "MYLIB.RND" As FileNum Len = 98
```

Just as each file has an ID number, each record within a random-access file has a record number. A single random-access file can hold from 1 to 16,777,216 records. Moreover, you don't have to fill the records in order. As you'll see, you can place information in the 15th record without ever having touched the first 14. The disadvantage of doing this, however, is that Visual Basic would automatically set aside enough space for the first 14 records on the disk, even if nothing is in them.

The word "record" has been used frequently in this chapter. This is no coincidence. One of the reasons QuickBASIC and then Visual Basic implemented record types was to simplify working with random-access files. First, set up a user-defined type (record):

```
Type Bookinfo
  Author As String*20
  Title As String*30
  Subject As String*15
  Publisher As String*20
  Miscellaneous As String*13
End Type
```

18

You must use fixed-length strings in order to work within the limitations of a random-access file because of the record length.

Next, suppose ExampleOfBook has been previously dimensioned as being of type Bookinfo. Then the command

```
Get FileNum, 10, ExampleOfBook
```

would transfer the contents of the 10th record from the random-access file into the record variable ExampleOfBook, automatically filling in the correct components of ExampleOfBook.

The command

```
Put FileNum, 37, ExampleOfBook
```

would send the components of ExampleOfBook to the 37th record of file #FileNum.

This method of sending information to a random-access file is unique to QuickBASIC and Visual Basic, and it's a valuable improvement over the older PC-BASIC. Visual Basic does not allow you to use the older (and much clumsier) method, which requires what are called field variables.

The record types you create determine the size of the random-access file. Since records can hold numbers as well as text, it's a bit messy to compute the length of a record variable of a given record type. (Remember that an integer takes 2 bytes, a long integer 4, and so on.) Visual Basic makes it simple, however, because the Len command not only gives the length of a string, it gives you the length of a record as well. Take any variable of the given type—for example,

```
Dim ExampleOfRecord As ThisType
LenOfRecord = Len(ExampleOfRecord)
```

and use this to set the length for the Open command used to create the random-access file.

Headers and Indexes for Random-Access Files

If you have the information you want to transfer to a newly created random-access file stored in an array of records, you can use a loop to send the information there. The loop counter determines where to put the record. Usually, however, you set up a variable whose value is the number of the next record you want to read from or write to.

Similarly, you can read back all the information in a random-access file by using the EOF flag after making the dimensions of the array records sufficiently large:

```
Dim I As Integer
Do Until EOF(FileNum)
  I = I + 1
  Get FileNum, I, Records(I)
Loop
```

There are many problems with doing this. For one, you're unlikely to want all the information contained in the file at once, and it may not fit, anyway— suppose you have 1,000,000 records. Also, go back to square one: how do you even know what length to use to open the random-access file? While there are many ways to determine this, a common practice is to set up another file that contains this (and other) vital information about the random-access file. At the very least, this sequential file will contain information about the sizes and types of the fields, possibly names for the fields, and the number of records stored to date. In fact, it may even contain an index of certain keys (like the keys for a collection object, a key is a way to identify a specific item) and the numbers of the records that contain those keys.

Indexes are vital to a random-access file. Some database managers are nothing more than elaborate programs to manage random-access files. Their speed depends on how the program finds the record containing keyed information. This can only be done effectively through indexes. (The alternative is to examine the relevant component of each record, one by one.)

An index can be as simple as a sequential file containing a list of keys followed by a record number, or it can be a more elaborately ordered one.

NOTE: Given the database-handling features of Visual Basic, you are unlikely to go to the trouble of creating a random-access file if it needs an elaborate index. If you do need an index for a random-access file, then a good choice for the index is to simply make a new Collection object to store the index. For example, if the index is stored in a sequential file in the form—record number, key—you can simply read this information directly in a Collection object each time you need it. If the index is too large (say more than 20,000 records) to fit comfortably into a Collection object, you should be using VB's database features directly (see Chapter 22).

Binary Files

Binary files are not a new type of file but a new way of manipulating any kind of file. Binary file techniques let you read or change any byte of a file. They are extraordinarily powerful tools but, like any powerful tool, they must be used with care.

CAUTION: (For early users of Visual Basic and QuickBASIC programmers especially.) Binary file-handling techniques have changed from Visual Basic 3, so be sure to read the next few sections carefully. Depending on what you are doing, you may have to change your code in order to make it work with the 32-bit version of Visual Basic.

18

Among other features, binary file techniques do not care about any embedded EOFs (CTRL+Z = CHR$(26)) that the file may have. (Recall that it was impossible to read back the file created earlier in the chapter using sequential file techniques because of the CTRL+Z sequences in the file.)

The command

Open *FileName* For Binary As # *FileNum*

sets up a file to be read with these new techniques. And, just as with random-access files, you can now both read and write to the file.

Now, as long as you are reading back information you are sure was stored as strings, then the easiest way to pick up the information from a text file open in binary file mode is with the Input$(,) function you saw earlier. Because of the automatic conversions that the 32-bit version of Visual Basic makes between Unicode and ANSI strings, this will work transparently for you. (Visual Basic automatically converts ANSI strings to Unicode when data is read back to your application, and back to ANSI when strings are written to a file.)

The first slot of the Input$ function still holds the number of characters and the second the file ID number. For example, the following listing gives a module that prints the contents of any file, regardless of any embedded control characters:

```
Sub PrintAFile(A$)
' example of binary input
  Dim I As Integer, FileNum As Integer, Char$
  FileNum = FreeFile          ' get free file ID
  Open A$ For Binary As #FileNum

  For I = 1 To LOF(FileNum)
    Char$ = Input$(1,#FileNum)
    Print Char$;
  Next I
  Close #FileNum
End Sub
```

More often than not, however, you'll want to modify this module by adding some filtering lines—for example, to make it strip out the control characters or those with ASCII codes greater than 127. Once you strip such a file, it can be displayed with the underlying operating system's Type command or be more easily sent by a modem.

For example, suppose you are confronted with converting a program from the archaic (but at the time very popular) WordStar word processing program. It turns out that this program normally stores a file in such a way that if you try to import it as a text file, you will have trouble reading the file. Stated simply, here's what WordStar does:

◆   It uses certain control codes inside the file (such as CTRL+B for bold).

◆   Each word-wrapped line ends with CHR$(141) + CHR$(10). Note that 141 = 13 + 128. Thus, 141 corresponds to a carriage return with the high-order bit set. Also, the first letter of each word in a word-wrapped line may have its high-order bit set.

◆   WordStar uses the carriage-return/line-feed combination (CHR$(13) + CHR$(10)) for hard returns. This indicates that someone pressed ENTER rather than that the program performed word wrapping.

It's easy to modify the earlier procedure to strip out all formatting (control) codes and then convert characters with their high-order bits set. (For those who do use WordStar, the procedure will not strip out dot commands; the changes needed for that are left to you.) Here's how to modify the procedure:

```
Sub WordStarStripper (A$)
  Dim FileNum As Integer, I As Integer
  Dim Char$

' Example Of Binary Input for a text file!
  FileNum = FreeFile                    ' get free file ID
  Open A$ For Binary As #FileNum
  For I = 1 To LOF(FileNum)
    Char$ = Input$(1, #FileNum)
    ' strip high-order bit, if any
    If Asc(Char$) > 127 Then
      CharCode = Asc(Char$)
      Char$ = Chr$(CharCode - 128)
    End If
    ' Ignore All Control Codes Except Line Feed
    If Char$ >= Chr$(32) Then
      Print Char$
    ElseIf Char$ = Chr$(10) Then
      'Issue A Chr$(13) And A Chr$(10)
      Print
    End If
  Next I
End Sub
```

Of course, in a more general program, you'd probably want to do something more than print the character.

Of course, this routine reads the information from the file one byte at a time. This is inefficient. You should consider reading in the information in larger chunks—if the file isn't too large, you should simply read the whole contents into a string variable and then use Mid to analyze the individual characters, as in the following version of the above procedure:

18

```
Sub FasterWordStarStripper (A$)
  Dim FileNum As Integer, I As Integer
  Dim TheText As String

' Example Of Binary Input for a text file!
  FileNum = FreeFile                        ' get free file ID
  Open A$ For Binary As #FileNum
  For I = 1 To LOF(FileNum)
    TheText = Input$(LOF(FileNum), #FileNum)
    ' strip high-order bit, if any
    Chr$ = Mid$(TheText, I, 1)
    If Asc(Char$) > 127 Then
      CharCode = Asc(Char$)
      Char$ = Chr$(CharCode - 128)
    End If
    ' Ignore All Control Codes Except Line Feed
    If Char$ >= Chr$(32) Then
      Print Char$
    ElseIf Char$ = Chr$(10) Then
      'Issue A Chr$(13) And A Chr$(10)
      Print
    End If
  Next I
End Sub
```

NOTE: If the file is too large for this routine, at the very least you should consider bringing in a few thousand characters of the text at a time! (Use a power of 2, such as 4096.)

Using Binary Access in More General (Non-Text) Situations

The big change (and one that will break a lot of previous code, unfortunately!) is that you can no longer use the Input$(,) for picking up individual bytes from a non-text file, such as a .tif or .jpg file. Instead, you must use the Get statement with an array of bytes. The problem is that because of Unicode, a character no longer takes up a single byte. Thus, because of Unicode, the procedure is a lot more cumbersome than it was in earlier versions of Visual Basic.

NOTE: In a Unicode 2-byte encoding of an ordinary ANSI string, the first byte will be the ANSI code; the second is used only for the language. Visual Basic is smart enough to recognize text files where the characters take up only one byte. This is why it doesn't automatically pick up two bytes for each use of Input$(1,).

The first step in reading back a file using Binary file techniques is easy: Get the bytes out of the file into a byte array using the Get function. The syntax is

    Get file#, position, ByteArray

The number of characters this statement picks up is equal to the size of the byte array given as the last parameter. The second parameter is needed because Visual Basic maintains a file pointer within a file opened for binary access. Each time you pick up a byte, the file pointer moves one position farther within the file.

Here's an example of how to use Get for a binary file that is small enough to fit in memory:

```
Sub BinaryPickUp (A$)
  Dim FileNum As Integer, I As Integer
' Example Of Binary Input for a general file!
  FileNum = FreeFile                  ' get free file ID
  Open A$ For Binary As #FileNum
  ReDim ArrayOfBytes(1 To LOF(FileNum)) As Byte
  Get #FileNum,1, ArrayOfBytes
```

(Theoretically this would let you store up to 2^{31} characters, but I suspect memory constraints would prevent this in the vast bulk of machines.)

Once you have the bytes in memory, you will have to decide how you want to manipulate the raw byte information. One possibility is that you can leave the bytes in the array and then work with them using ordinary array-handling techniques. Another possibility is to:

◆   Assign the byte array to a string. (This will not do any translations.)

◆   Use the appropriate B character function, as given in Table 18-4, to work with the byte string. (B character functions work similarly to their ordinary namesakes that you saw in Chapter 8, except that they work with byte strings.)

Function	Purpose
AscB	Returns the value given by the first byte in a string of binary data
InStrB	Finds the first occurrence of a byte in a binary string
MidB	Returns the specified number of bytes from a binary string
LeftB, RightB	Takes the specified number of bytes from the left or right end of a binary string
ChrB	Takes a byte and returns a binary string with that byte

Binary Array
Equivalents of
the String
Functions
Table 18-4.

The Seek Command

The Seek command is a fast-forward command and a rewind command combined into one. More precisely,

Seek *filenum, position*

moves the file pointer for the file with ID #*filenum* directly to the byte in that *position*. Any following Input$ statement would start picking up characters from this location.

Seek has another use. Seek(*filenum*) tells you the position number for the last byte read for either a binary or sequential file. You can also use the Seek function with random-access files. Now it will return the record number of the next record.

18

The Put Command

To place information within a file opened for binary access, use a modification of the Put command. For example,

```
Put #1, 100, ByteArray()
```

would place the contents of the byte array directly into the file with file ID #1 starting at the 100th byte. The number of characters sent to this file is, of course, given by the size of the byte array. The Put command overwrites whatever was there. If you leave a space for the byte position but don't specify it in the Put command, like this,

```
Put #1, , ByteArray()
```

then the information is placed wherever the file pointer is currently located.

NOTE: You can also use Put with string variables by replacing the *ByteArray* parameter with a string variable. However, to avoid problems that come from mixing bytes and strings in the same file when using binary access, you are best off doing this only for text files. Also, if you choose to do this, you should initialize a string to be the correct size, using the Space$ command.

Final Remarks on Binary File Handling

Now that you know the commands for manipulating files on the byte level, you're in a position to write any file utility you like. (If you need to massage the output of an application program, you will need to know the internal file format of the program.)

For example, the features of the Seek command make it easy to write a function to search through a text file for a string and replace it, as well (see the next section). To find a string, read the file back in chunks. Use the InStr function to search for the string inside the chunk. If the string is found, exit the function and report success. If the string is not found in a specific chunk, reset the Seek pointer back by one less than the length of the string searched for and repeat until the file is processed. (You have to reset the file pointer back to allow for the string being only partially digested by the Input$ command.)

If you want to allow for replacement, combine the above technique with a temporary file, as you saw in the section "Making Changes Inside a Sequential File." If the replacement string is exactly the same size, you can use the Put command instead of a temporary file.

For example, the following procedure takes any text file and replaces all occurrences of one string inside of it by another. It adjusts the size of the replacement string by padding or truncating to match the original string.

NOTE: If you want to modify this program to work with any binary file, replace the Input$ command by the appropriate Get command with a binary array and the various string functions by their "B" equivalent as listed in Table 18-4.

Here's the procedure that uses a chunk size of 4096, which seems to work well in most situations:

```
Const ChunkSize = 4096

Sub ChangeFile(FName$, IdString$, NString$)
  Dim PosString As Integer, WhereString As Integer
  Dim FileNumber As Integer, A$, NewString$
  Dim AString As String*ChunkSize

  FileNumber = FreeFile
  PosString = 1
  WhereString = 0
  AString = Space$(ChunkSize)

  'Make sure strings have same size
  If Len(IdString$) > Len(NString$) Then
    NewString$ = NString$ + Space$(Len(IdString$) - Len(NString$))
  Else
    NewString$ = Left$(NString$, Len(IdString$))
  End If

  Open FName$ For Binary As FileNumber
  If LOF(FileNumber) < ChunkSize Then
    A$ = Space$(LOF(FileNumber))
    Get #FileNumber, 1, A$
    WhereString = InStr(1, A$, IdString$)
  Else
    Get #FileNumber, 1, AString
    WhereString = InStr(1, AString, IdString$)
  End If
```

18

```
      If WhereString <> 0 Then
        Put #FileNumber, WhereString, NewString$
      End If
      PosString = ChunkSize + PosString - Len(IdString$)

      Do Until EOF(FileNumber) Or PosString > LOF(FileNumber)
        If PosString + ChunkSize > LOF(FileNumber) Then
          A$ = Space$(LOF(FileNumber) - PosString)
          Get #FileNumber, PosString, A$
          WhereString = InStr(FileNumber, A$, IdString$)
        Else
          Get #FileNumber, PosString, AString
          WhereString = InStr(FileNumber, AString, IdString$)
        End If
        If WhereString <> Then
          Put #FileNumber, PosString + WhereString - 1, NewString$
        End If
          PosString = ChunkSize + PosString - Len(IdString$)
      Loop
      Close
End Sub

Problems:
  ' error trap goes here
End Sub
```

This procedure is fairly subtle, so let's go over it carefully. First, it sets up a constant for the size of each chunk. As mentioned earlier, 4096 seems to give good performance on my machine, but your experience may vary.

Next come the declarations for the various counters used in this program. In particular, there is a fixed-length string equal in size to the chunk size. Since binary file techniques for text files require that the strings replaced be exactly the same size, the first If-Then-Else takes care of this by setting up a correctly sized local variable NewString$ to hold the replacement string.

The procedure then starts picking up pieces of the file. Because you are reading the file in chunks, you have to be careful not to go past the boundaries of the file. You use a temporary value A$ in case the file is smaller than the size of the chunks. Because Get only reads as many characters as are currently stored in the file, you need to initialize A$ properly. (Remember that we are assuming the file contains only ordinary ASCII/ANSI strings.)

Next, you use the InStr command to search for the IdString$. If you find it, you put the NewString$ in its place. Next comes the Loop that looks through the rest of the file. This allows you to do multiple replacements. At each step you have to adjust the pointer back slightly because of the possibility that you have picked up part of the target string in a chunk. Notice, as well, that the chunk size again requires you to monitor the remaining characters in the file inside the loop. Finally, this procedure indicates where the error trap would go, although to save space, one hasn't been included.

NOTE: You can easily modify this procedure to change it into a function that returns True or False depending on whether the string is found or not. You can also modify it to allow changes in individual bytes in a file by using a byte array instead of the string for picking up the data.

Sharing Files

As more files are available only off networks, it becomes more important to prevent someone from inadvertently working with a file while you are working with it. Visual Basic's file-handling functions can easily be adapted to a networking environment by using the keywords described in the following table:

Keyword	Function
Lock	Prevents access to all or part of an open file
Unlock	Allows access to a file previously locked

You can use these functions after you have opened the file, in which case the syntax takes the form

Lock [#]*filenumber*[, *WhatToLock*]

for the Lock command and

Unlock [#]*filenumber*[, *WhatToUnlock*]

for the Unlock command. Both commands use the file number with which the program opened the file. The *WhatToLock* (*WhatToUnlock*) parameter specifies what portion of the file to lock or unlock. You use it by giving the Start and End values, where they denote the first record (for random-access files) or first byte (for binary access). For example,

```
Open "FOO" For Binary As #1
Lock #1, 1 To 100
```

locks the first 100 bytes of the file FOO. If you leave off the optional parameter, then Lock locks the whole file. (For sequential files, Lock and Unlock affect the entire file, regardless of the range specified by the *WhatToLock* parameter.)

CAUTION: Be sure to remove all locks with the corresponding Unlock statement before closing a file or quitting your program. (The arguments must match exactly.) Not doing this may foul up the files from that point on!

General Form of the Open Command

You can also control file sharing at the time you open the file by using the most general form of the Open statement. Its full syntax looks like this:

Open *pathname* [For *mode*] [Access *access*] [lock] As [#] *filenumber* [Len=*reclength*]

What follows are short descriptions of the syntax elements.

18

Pathname
This string expression specifies the filename. It may include both directory and drive information.

Mode
This keyword specifies the file mode you have already seen: Append, Binary, Input, Output, or Random.

Access
You specify what operations are permitted on the open file with *access*. There are three: Read, Write, and Read Write. You use one as in the following example:

```
Open FOO For Binary Access Read As #1
```

This will let you read the file but not make any changes to it.

Lock
This parameter specifies the operations permitted on the open file by other processes (unlike the Access parameter, which controls how your program can access the file). There are four possibilities: Shared, Lock Read, Lock Write, and Lock Read Write, as described in the following table:

Keyword	Description
Shared	Other processes can both read and write to the file, even while your program is working with it.
Lock Read	No other program can open the file to read it while your program is working with it.
Lock Write	No other program can open the file to write to it while your program is working with it.
Lock Read Write	No other program can work with the file at all while you are working with it.

The following example lets you read the file and prevents everyone else from using it while you are using it:

```
Open FOO For Binary Access Read Lock Read As #1
```

Filenumber

A valid file number must be in the range 1 to 511, inclusive. (As you have seen, it's best to use the FreeFile function to find the next available file number.)

Reclength

This is an integer from 1 to 32,767. For files opened for random access, this number gives the record length. For sequential files, this value is the number of characters buffered by the operating system.

NOTE: In binary, input, and random file modes, you can open a file using a different file number without first closing the file. For sequential append and output, you must close a file before you can use it.

Adding Licensing Screens

If you are going to distribute your program, you'll probably want to add a startup licensing screen. This section describes one simple technique for doing this completely in Visual Basic.

TIP: In prior versions of Visual Basic, you used to be able to modify a global variable in the .exe file directly; this has not worked since Visual Basic 5.

This technique ultimately depends on using binary file techniques to carefully examine and make some subtle changes in a file. The routine in the previous section is a general purpose procedure for doing this for text files.

First, though, you'll need to use information derived from the App object. This is a very useful Visual Basic object for this situation because it can tell you the full path name of the Application (App.Path) or the root name of the .exe file (App.ExeName), as well as the Help file associated with the application, the Title, or whether another copy of it is running at the present time.

Now that you have the procedure to make changes inside any text file, and the necessary properties of the App object, you can move on to my favorite of the techniques for adding licensing screens. By far the easiest way to do this is to have the Form_Initialize (or Sub_Main) look for a hidden file in the same directory as the application. Install this hidden file at the same time as the program. During the installation procedure, open this hidden file and modify a string so as to give the licensee's name. (If you also want to encrypt this information inside the file, see the next section in this chapter.) You can use the Path property of the App object to determine which directory to examine. If you can't find the required information inside the hidden file, or can't find the hidden file, do not permit the program to proceed.

To modify the hidden file, you can use a Form_Initialize procedure in the installation program for the startup form (or Sub Main if there is no startup form) that uses the ChangeFile program you saw earlier. The procedure might look something like this.

```
Form_Initialize ()
On Error GoTo Problems
Dim InstallTries As Integer, Install$, Person$

Person$ = ""
Do Until Person$ <> "" Or InstallTries > 2
  Person$ = InputBox$("Please enter your name.")
  InstallTries = InstallTries + 1
Loop
If InstallTries > 3 Then
  MsgBox "Installation Failure--no name supplied "
  End
End If
User$ = "Program licensed by " + Person$
IdString$ = "This program has not been licensed to anybody. "
Call ChangeFile(HiddenFileName$, IdString$, Person$)
```

This program assumes you would supply the hidden file name as the value of the HiddenFileName$ variable and that the IdString$ to search for (and change) is, "This program has not been licensed to anybody."

Once you modify the hidden file, the Form_Load of the .exe file can use the function variation on the ChangeFile mentioned in the previous section to ensure that the string "This program has not been licensed to anybody" no longer occurs.

Keeping File Information Secret

Since a simple utility program using binary file techniques can read back the information contained in any file, the data contained in your files is readily available to anyone with a compatible computer, a little programming skill, and a copy of your disk. In the next few sections you'll see how to encode a file so that only people having the right key can easily read your file. These methods work very well with the hidden file technique just described for handling licensing screens. Of course, the methods here aren't perfect, but considering how easy they are to implement, they are surprisingly secure.

First, a little history. All the earliest ciphers that we know about use simple substitutions. For example, Julius Caesar kept his messages secret by taking each letter in the message and replacing it with the one three letters further on; the letter A is replaced by D, B by E, and so on, until you get to the letters after X. Since X is the 24th letter of the alphabet, you have to wrap around to the beginning of the alphabet, and X becomes A, Y becomes B, and Z becomes C. Here is a normal alphabet and below it a complete Caesar alphabet:

ABCDEFGHIJKLMNOPQRSTUVWXYZ
DEFGHIJKLMNOPQRSTUVWXYZABC

(Actually, in Caesar's time, the alphabet had fewer letters—23 instead of 26. For example, U and V developed out of V around 1,000 years ago, and J came around 500 years after that.) For example, the sentence, "Can you read this", becomes

FDQ BRX UHDG WKLV

Shift ciphers go back further than Caesar; one occurs in the Bible. In Jeremiah 25–26, the prophet conceals his prophecy by changing the name of Babylon using a cipher that splits the Hebrew alphabet in half and replaces the first letter with the middle letter, the second by the middle + 1, and so on.

Here is a general procedure that shifts any character by any number of characters, wrapping around if necessary.

```
Sub CaesarShift(A$, Shift%)
  Dim CharNum As Integer
  CharNum = (Asc(A$) + Shift%) Mod(256)
  A$ = Chr$(CharNum)
End Sub
```

It wouldn't be hard to incorporate this procedure into a file encrypter; just pass the contents of the file to the procedure, character by character. The trouble is that a shift cipher is easy to break; you can even do it by hand. Look at the coded message and run back down the alphabet by steps, shifting the letters back step by step. After, at most, 25 steps, you're done. Here's what you get at each step in the example:

FDQ	BRX	UHDG	WKLV
ECP	AQW	TGCF	VJKU
DBO	ZPV	SFBE	UIJT
CAN	YOU	READ	THIS

Note that it's better to work with the whole message than with individual words because occasionally English words (*clear text*) show up by mistake. For example, the word "HTQI" backs up to the word "FROG" on the second try and to the word "COLD" on the fifth.

Decoding a Caesar cipher, simple as it is, stresses the usefulness of the computer and its limitations. It can do the drudgery, but you have to recognize when to stop. For the more complicated ciphers described in what follows, this division of labor is essential.

More Complicated Ciphers

Since a shift cipher provides virtually no security, the next step is to change the letters in a more random manner. Write down the alphabet, and below it, write all the letters in some arbitrary order:

ABCDEFGHIJKLMNOPQRSTUVWXYZ
QAZXSWEDCVFRBGTYHNUJMIKOPL

Now, every time you see an A in your original message, replace it with a Q, replace each B with an A, each C with a Z, and so on. This cipher can't be broken by the techniques used for shift ciphers, but it's extremely hard to remember the random alphabet used for the code. Around 1600, in an attempt to combine the virtues of this method with the ease of shift codes, people began to use a *keyword cipher*. The idea is to replace the letters of the alphabet with the letters in the key phrase, using the order in which they occur there. For example, suppose the key is THE RAY GUN ZAPPED ME QUICKLY. Now look at the following:

18

```
ABCDEFGHIJKLMNOPQRSTUVWXYZ
THERAYGUNZPDMQICKLBFJOSVWX
```

What this does is take the individual letters from the key phrase, avoiding duplicates as needed, and places them below the normal alphabet. Since the phrase contains only 18 different letters, the unused letters go at the end. To encipher a message using this code, replace the letters in the original message with the ones directly below them—A with T, B with H, and so on.

Here's one possible outline for a procedure that takes a key phrase and creates the code:

```
Get keyphrase
    Run through each letter in keyphrase
    Check if already used
    if not used:
        store in next place in 'cipher list
        mark that letter as used
    Until no more letters are in the keyphrase
Now store unused letters from normal alphabet into key
```

However, this outline turns out to be not quite the best way of proceeding. For example, suppose you want to decipher a message enciphered this way. Say you see an A in the coded message; then, because an A is below an E in the alphabets just given, the original letter must have been an E.

To set up the two lists to be used for encoding and decoding, start with two ordinary alphabets. Now, since T replaces A, you swap the A in the first alphabet with the T in the second. Next, you swap the B and the H. How can you tell if a letter is already used? Just look at that letter's position in the second alphabet. If the letter is still in its original position, that letter has not been used. When you are done with the letters in the key phrase, any remaining letters should be swapped out of the first alphabet into the second one.

To actually write this program, set up two lists. To make life easier, use two global arrays of integers dimensioned to run from 65 to 90 (the ASCII codes for A to Z):

```
Global Dim EncodeAlph() As Integer, DecodeAlph() As Integer
```

Now call an Initialize procedure from the Form_Load procedure:

```
Sub Initialize( )
  Dim I As Integer
  ReDim EncodeAlph(65 To 90) As Integer
```

```
    ReDim DecodeAlph(65 To 90) As Integer
    For I = 65 To 90
     EncodeAlph(I) = I
     DecodeAlph(I) = I
    Next I
End Sub
```

Now you can write the Sub that creates both lists by translating the preceding outline. To do this, you need to keep track of where you are in the original alphabet because that determines where the letter will go. Suppose you call this variable PosOfLetUsed. Each time you use a letter from the key, swap the letter determined by this position number with its counterpart in the other alphabet, determined from the key, and increase PosOfLetUsed by one. The tricky part comes when you've used up all the letters in the key. Then you have to decide where to put the letters remaining from the first alphabet. The problem occurs because there is no convenient pointer to the unused letters in the second alphabet. To take care of this, set the letters you use to the negative of their ASCII values. For example, if X, Y, and Z were the only letters not used in the key, then they would be the only ones that were still positive in the Decode alphabet.

```
Sub Makelists (Key$)
    'Uses Global Variables EncodeAlph(), DecodeAlph()
    'Local Variables
    Dim LenKey As Integer, PosOfLetUsed As Integer
    Dim I As Integer, A As Integer
    Dim A1$

    LenKey = Len(Key$)
    PosOfLetUsed = 65                       'start with Asc("A")

    For I = 1 To LenKey
      A1$ = Mid$(Key$, I, 1): A$ = UCase$(A1$)
      Select Case A$
      Case "A" To "Z"
        A = Asc(A$)
        If DecodeAlph(A) = A Then        'Character Not Yet _ Used
          EncodeAlph(PosOfLetUsed) = A
          DecodeAlph(A) = -PosOfLetUsed      'Swap The _
Encode/Decode And Flag A Used Char
          PosOfLetUsed = PosOfLetUsed + 1
        End If
      Case Else
        ' Not A Letter - Of Course You Can
        ' Do Something With These Too
      End Select
    Next I
    ' Now Throw In Unused Letters
    ' This Loop Should End If You've Used Up All 26 Letters Or
    ' You Can't Find Any New Letters To Swap
    For I = 65 To 90                 ' Start Looking In Second Alph
                                     ' Here.

      If DecodeAlph(I) = I Then
```

```
      EncodeAlph(PosOfLetUsed) = I
      DecodeAlph(I) = -PosOfLetUsed    'Swap The Encode / Decode
      PosOfLetUsed = PosOfLetUsed + 1
    End If
  Next I
End Sub
```

Now encoding or decoding a letter is almost a trivial task. Suppose you want to encode a C (ASCII code 67). You just look at the value of Encode(67) to find the ASCII value for the coded version. Similarly (and this is the nice part), to decode a C, you just have to look at the absolute value of the entry in Decode(67). Thus, you can pass the appropriate array as a parameter and use the following listing:

18

```
Sub EncodeDecode(A(),X$)
  Dim X1 As Integer
  X1 = Asc (UCase$(X$))
  X$ = Chr$(Abs(A(X1)))
End Sub
```

A More Secure Cipher

Having spent all of the previous section on a fairly subtle program to create a keyword cipher, you might expect it to be secure—or at least difficult to break. Unfortunately, though it does work quickly, any substitution cipher can be broken, given enough text. In fact, assuming the encoded text was originally written in standard, everyday English, it's pretty easy to find the encoding algorithm if you have, say, a thousand words of encoded text. The key to breaking a substitution code is that letters do not exist in isolation. The letter E is almost certainly the most common letter, T is likely to be the next most common, and A is likely to be third highest. Over the years, cryptographers have examined thousands of pages of texts to determine the frequency of letters in standard English. The problem with a simple substitution cipher is that if you always replace a letter with the same symbol, someone can break it by using frequency analysis.

One way to avoid this method of breaking a code is to change the substitution. Instead of always replacing, say, an E with the letter T, use a T the first time and a Z the next. This way, each time an E occurs, it is replaced with another letter. This method is called a *multi-alphabet substitution cipher.* It's much more difficult to break this cipher, but it's also much more difficult to set up. After all, you have to devise a way of getting these multiple alphabets.

However, you can use the built-in random number generator in Visual Basic to generate the alphabets. Recall that the command X = Rnd or X = Rnd(1) gives you a random number between 0 and 1. However—and this is the key to breaking the cipher—given enough data, a professional cryptographer (or a good amateur) can find out the next number in the sequence. Cryptographers would say the random number generator in Visual Basic isn't "cryptographically secure." Finding (and then proving that you have) a cryptographically secure random number generator is probably the most important problem in cryptography.

The idea for the cipher that follows is that you scale this number and use it to determine the "Caesar shift." Now, instead of always using the same shift for the next letter, use the random number generator to get a different shift for each letter. Each time you encode a letter, it's transformed differently.

Unfortunately, this method won't quite work. Since the patterns don't obviously repeat (that's what is meant by random), there isn't any reasonable method of decoding the message. You would never know what to shift back by. You have to modify this approach slightly. The first idea that might come to mind is that the Rnd function, when given a negative number as an argument, is supposed to give a repeatable sequence. Thus, if you precede all other uses of Rnd with a statement of the form

Randomize *Seed*

where *Seed* is a negative number, then Visual Basic is always supposed to give you the same sequence of random numbers. Each seed is *supposed* to yield a different, repeatable sequence of random numbers. *Unfortunately, in the current version of Visual Basic 6 available to me, this feature won't work as it is supposed to.* You need to modify the procedure slightly. To get a repeatable sequence of random numbers, you must have Visual Basic process the following statement before generating the next random number in the sequence:

Rnd(*the negative number*)

(This should always work regardless of the version of VB you are using.)

Now, to use random Caesar shifts, you need only ask the user for a key—say, a four-digit positive number. Use this to reseed the random number generator:

```
X = Rnd(-Key)
```

Now you can generate a list of shifts, one for each character in the file:

```
NextShift = Int(256 * Rnd)
```

Use these shifts just as in a Caesar cipher—call this shift generator for each letter in the message.

Now the question is how to decode. The whole point of repeatability is that if you process the command

```
X = Rnd(-Key)
```

again, then when you generate Caesar shifts, you get the same series of numbers as you did before. As before, if you know what the original shift was, you can reverse it just as easily.

However, rather than using this procedure as presented, you can use a more elegant and faster approach. Recall from the bit twiddling section of Chapter 8 that the Xor operator has a convenient property: If

```
B = A Xor Shift
```

and you enter

```
C = B Xor Shift
```

18

then the value of C is the same as the original value of A. Thus, by Xoring twice, you get back to where you started. Thus, you can use the same procedure to both encode and decode. Here's the procedure to do that:

```
Sub EncodeDecode (FileName$, KeyValue)
  ' local variables:
  Dim FileNum As Integer, X As Single, I As Integer
  Dim CharNum As Integer, RandomInteger As Integer

  Dim SingleChar As String * 1        'for use in GET and PUT

  X = Rnd(-KeyValue)
  FileNum = FreeFile
  Open FileName$ For Binary As #FileNum
  For I = 1 To LOF(FileNum)
    Get #FileNum, I, SingleChar
    CharNum = Asc(SingleChar)
    RandomInteger = Int(256 * Rnd)
    CharNum = CharNum Xor RandomInteger 'this is it
    SingleChar = Chr$(CharNum)
    Put #FileNum, I, SingleChar
  Next I
  Close FileNum
End Sub
```

As mentioned before, you will find that the program works faster if you read the information from the file in larger (at least 4096 byte-character) chunks. You can also choose the improved version of the random number generator presented in Chapter 10 to make this approach even more secure.

NOTE: You should be aware that a quick but insecure way to encrypt a file is to Xor the contents of the file with a single password. This is quick and does take advantage of the fact that Xoring twice gets you back to where you started. What it *isn't* is secure enough from any but the most basic hacking.

CHAPTER 19

File System Controls and File System Objects

The last chapter showed you how to manipulate the files using the traditional file-handling code that has, in one form or another, been around since the dawn of BASIC on the PC. This chapter moves to more modern methods. Here, I'll show you how to use the File System Controls that complement the common dialog boxes you saw in Chapter 14, as well as how to use the new, exciting, and powerful *File System Objects* that have been added to VB6. These are amazingly neat and powerful—VB programmers have long desired easy and efficient access to this kind of functionality. (Earlier versions of VB needed long chains of indecipherable API calls to obtain it.)

NOTE: The File System Objects are currently supplied in the form of a separate DLL that you'll need to add via the Tools|References dialog box. Microsoft has said that future versions of VB will have more and more of its file handling features wrapped into these objects. Presumably, therefore, the next version of VB will not require you to go to Tools|References and manually add a reference to the necessary library.

File System Controls

The file system controls in Visual Basic allow users to select a new drive, see the hierarchical directory structure of a disk, or see the names of the files in a given directory. As with all Visual Basic controls, you need to write code to take full advantage of the power of the file system controls. In addition, if you want to tell the underlying operating system to change drives or directories as the result of a mouse click by a user, you'll need to write code using the commands you saw in the previous chapter.

Figure 19-1 shows a version of the toolbox with the file system controls marked (your toolbox may look a little different). The file system controls are designed to work together. Your code checks what the user has done to the drive list box and passes this information on to the directory list box. The changes in the directory list box are passed on to the file list box. (See the section "Tying All the File Controls Together" a little later in this chapter.) As you can imagine, the file system controls complement the common dialog boxes you saw in Chapter 14.

File List Boxes

A file list box defaults to displaying the files in the current directory. (Microsoft's suggested prefix for the Name property is "fil".) As with any list box, you can control the position, size, color, and font characteristics at design time or via code. Most of the properties of a file list box are identical to those of ordinary list boxes. For example, as with all list boxes, when the number of items can't fit the current size of the control, Visual Basic automatically adds vertical scroll bars. This lets the user move through the list of files using the scroll bars. You can set the size, position, or font properties of file list boxes via the Properties window or via code, as needed. Similarly, file list boxes can respond to all the events that list boxes can detect. For example, you

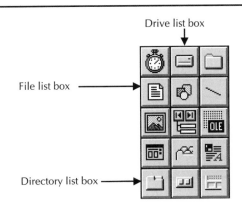

Drive list box

File list box

Directory list box

File system
controls in the
toolbox
Figure 19-1.

19

can write event procedures for a keypress or a mouse movement. One point is worth
remembering, though: the Windows convention is that double-clicking a file, not
single-clicking, chooses the file. This is especially important when using a file list box,
because using an arrow key to move through a file list box would call any Click
procedure that you have written. (Recall that, for list boxes, arrow movements are
functionally equivalent to single mouse clicks.)

It is quite common to use the List, ListCount, and ListIndex properties to analyze
the information contained in a file list box rather than using the Dir command.
For example, suppose the file list box has the default name of File1 and you have
already set up a string array for the information contained in the box. Then a
fragment such as

```
For I% = 0 To File1.ListCount -1
  FileNames$(I%) = File1.List(I%)
Next I%
```

would fill a string array with the information contained in the file list box named File1.
If you need to find out the name of the file that a user selects, you can use
File1.List(ListIndex) or the FileName property, which, when read, has the same function.

You can have a file list box display only files that are read-only (good for novice users)
or those that have the Archive bit turned on or off (that is, to indicate whether or not
the files have been backed up since the last change). There are five Boolean properties
(True/False values) that control what type of files are shown in a file list box: Archive,
Hidden, Normal, ReadOnly, and System. The default setting is True for Archive,
Normal, and ReadOnly, and it is False for Hidden and System.

As an example of this, consider the code that activates the form shown in Figure 19-2,
which has a single file list box and five check boxes to specify the type of files the file
list box shows. For example, if the file list box is named File1 and one of the check
boxes is named chkShowHidden, a line of code like

```
File1.Hidden = chkShowHidden.Value
```

would tell the file list box to display (or not display) hidden files, depending on whether or not the box was checked.

Pattern and Path

The most important properties for file list boxes are Pattern and Path. The Pattern property determines which files are displayed in the file list box. The Pattern property accepts the ordinary file wildcards—the asterisk (*), which will match any character, and the question mark (?), which will match a single character. The default pattern is set to *.* to display all files. (Of course, the Pattern property works in combination with the attribute properties discussed previously.) When you change the Pattern property, Visual Basic looks to see if you have written a PatternChange event procedure for the file list box and, if so, activates it.

T IP: Multiple patterns can be used; just separate them with semicolons.

The Path property sets or returns the current path for the file list box, but not for the underlying operating system. To tell the underlying operating system to change the current path from Visual Basic, you need the ChDir command that you saw in the last

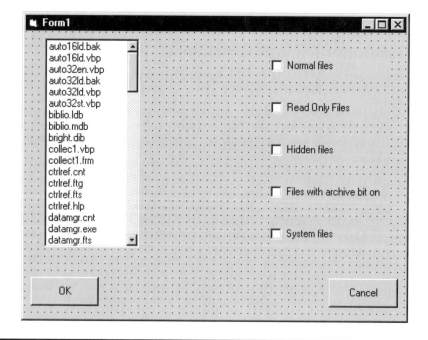

Form with a single file box and five check boxes for file properties

Figure 19-2.

chapter. On the other hand, you may just need to accumulate this information for use by your program without disturbing the default path. When you change the Path property, Visual Basic looks to see whether you have written a PathChange event procedure for the file list box and, if so, activates it.

Changing the FileName property activates the PathChange event or the PatternChange event (or both), depending on how you change the FileName property. For example, suppose you are in the C:\ root directory. Setting

```
File1.Filename ="C:\WINDOWS\COMMAND\*.COM"
```

activates both the PathChange and PatternChange events.

Directory List Boxes

A directory list box displays the directory structure of the current drive. (Microsoft's naming convention is to use a "dir" prefix for the Name property.) The current directory shows up as an open file folder. Subdirectories of the current directory are shown as closed folders, and directories above the current directory are shown as non-shaded open folders.

NOTE: When the user clicks on an item or moves through the list, that item is highlighted. When he or she double-clicks, Visual Basic automatically updates the directory list box.

The List property for a directory list box works a little differently than it does for file list boxes. While subdirectories of the current directory are numbered from 0 to ListCount-1, Visual Basic uses negative indexes for the current directory and its parent and grandparent directories. For example, -1 is the index for the current directory, -2 for its parent directory, and so on. Unfortunately, you cannot use the LBound function to determine the number of directories above a given directory; you must either count the number of backslashes in the Path property or move backward through the items in the directory list box.

As an example of how powerful the file system controls can be when they begin to work together, put a directory list box and a file list box together on a new project, as shown in Figure 19-3. Now suppose you want a change by the user in a directory list box named dirBox to tell Visual Basic to update the file list box immediately. All you have to do is enter one line of code in the Change event procedure:

```
Sub dirBox_Change()
  File1.Path = dirBox.Path
End Sub
```

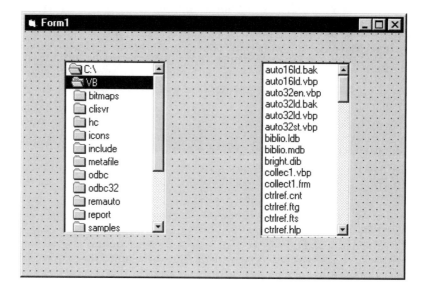

Project with a
directory list box
and file list box
Figure 19-3.

This is all it takes to update the file list box whenever a user changes the current directory. To activate this event procedure, the user must double-click a new directory in the directory list box, which I've named dirBox.

NOTE: Directory list boxes do not recognize the DoubleClick event; instead they call the Change procedure in response to a double-click and reassign the Path property.

Again, Visual Basic cannot use a single click to activate the Change event because then users could not use the arrow keys to move through the list box. If you want users to be able to press ENTER to update the file list box as well, use the directory list box's KeyPress event procedure as follows:

```
Sub dirBox_KeyPress(KeyAscii As Integer)
  If KeyAscii = 13 Then    'Or vbKeyReturn
    dirBox.Path = dirBox.List(dirBox.ListIndex)
  End If
End Sub
```

You can also write a procedure that calls the previous event procedure when the user presses ENTER.

Again, this procedure doesn't change the Path property directly because doing so is superfluous. Visual Basic calls the Change event procedure for a directory list box whenever you change the value of the Path property.

Finally, it's important to keep in mind that while the meaning of the Path property for file list boxes and directory list boxes is similar, it is not identical. For directory list boxes, the Path property specifies which directory was selected; for file list boxes, the Path property specifies where to look for files to display.

Drive List Boxes

Unlike file and directory list boxes, drive list boxes are pull-down boxes. (Microsoft's naming convention suggests "drv" as the prefix for the Name property.) Drive list boxes begin by displaying the current drive, and then when the user clicks on the arrow, Visual Basic pulls down a list of all valid drives.

19

The key property for a drive list box is the Drive property, which can be used to return or reset the current drive. For example, to synchronize a drive list box with a directory list box, all you need is code that looks like this:

```
Sub drvBox_Change()
  dirBox.Path = drvBox.Drive
End Sub
```

On the other hand, if you also want to change the logged drive that the underlying operating system is using, enter this code:

```
Sub drvBox_Change()
  dirBox.Path = drvBox.Drive
  ChDrive drvBox.Drive
End Sub
```

Tying All the File Controls Together

When you have all three file system controls on a form like the one shown in Figure 19-4, you have to communicate the changes among the controls in order to have Visual Basic show what the user wants to see.

For example, if the user selects a new drive, Visual Basic activates the Change event procedure for the drive box. Then the following occurs:

1. The Change event procedure for the drive box assigns the Drive property to the directory box's Path property.
2. This changes the display in the directory list box by triggering the Change event procedure for the directory list box.
3. Inside the Change event procedure, you assign the Path property to the file list box's Path property. This updates the File list box.

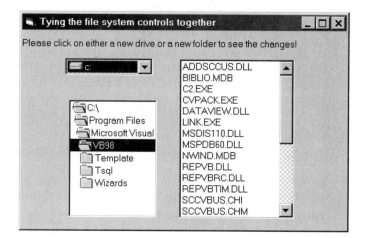

Here's the .frm file that creates and activates the form shown in Figure 19-4. It
contains simple code that follows the preceding steps and is all that is needed to
activate this form.

```
VERSION 5.00
Begin VB.Form Form1
    Caption         =   "Tying the file system controls together"
    ClientHeight    =   3408
    ClientLeft      =   48
    ClientTop       =   336
    ClientWidth     =   5772
    LinkTopic       =   "Form1"
    ScaleHeight     =   3408
    ScaleWidth      =   5772
    StartUpPosition =   3   'Windows Default
    Begin VB.FileListBox File1
        Height          =   2760
        Left            =   2808
        TabIndex        =   2
        Top             =   480
        Width           =   2052
    End
    Begin VB.DirListBox Dir1
        Height          =   2016
        Left            =   840
        TabIndex        =   1
        Top             =   1200
        Width           =   1572
    End
    Begin VB.DriveListBox Drive1
        Height          =   288
        Left            =   768
```

```
        TabIndex        =   0
        Top             =   480
        Width           =   1572
      End
      Begin VB.Label Label1
        Caption         =   "Please click on either a new drive or a
                             new folder to see the changes!"
        Height          =   372
        Left            =   0
        TabIndex        =   3
        Top             =   120
        Width           =   5652
      End
End
End
Attribute VB_Name = "Form1"
Attribute VB_GlobalNameSpace = False
Attribute VB_Creatable = False
Attribute VB_PredeclaredId = True
Attribute VB_Exposed = False
Private Sub Dir1_Change()
  File1.Path = Dir1.Path
End Sub

Private Sub Drive1_Change()
  Dir1.Path = Drive1.Drive
End Sub
```

It is easy to add a text box for a file pattern to this example. All we need to do is assign the contents of a text box to the file list box's Pattern property. Similarly, we could have check boxes that would allow the user to choose what type of files to view in the file list box by changing the Archive, Hidden, ReadOnly, and other properties of the file list box. Including all this information gives you something that looks like the usual Microsoft Windows file control box that you saw in Chapter 14, but one that is potentially far more flexible. Occasionally you will need the extra flexibility that using file controls provides.

 CAUTION: Often you will combine the path name obtained from the Path property with the filename taken from the FileName property to get the full path name of a file. Unfortunately, if you are in the root directory, there is a "\" at the end of the path name property that would lead to two backslashes in a row if you naively combined the two properties. Instead, use code such as the following:

```
If Right(File1.Path, 1) <> "\" Then
  NameOfFile = File1.Path + "\" + File1.FileName
Else
  NameOfFile = File1.Path + File1.FileName
End If
```

19

The File System Objects

By now I hope you are convinced that the idea of working with the properties and methods of objects is a really flexible way of programming. Ironically, it took 6 (!) versions of VB before Microsoft decided to follow this model and *start* giving you this flexibility in working with files. (There's still more work needed.) These file programming capabilities are supplied with VB6 as the Microsoft Scripting Runtime library of objects, in a file called SCRRUN.DLL. Since this is a precompiled library, you'll need to go to Tools|References to add it, as shown in Figure 19-5.

Although the FileSystemObject (that is the name you use when programming with it) has rather a lot of built-in properties (some of which themselves are objects) and many methods associated with it, the basic idea of how to use it is pretty simple.

◆ You will always need to add the reference to the scripting library, as shown in Figure 19-5.

◆ You will always need to make a new "FileSystemObject" as your first step.

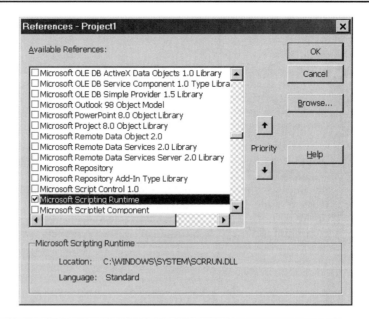

Adding the File
System Library
(SCRRUN.DLL)
Figure 19-5.

◆ Once you have a new FileSystemObject, it has a "Drives" collection that tells you about the individual drives on the user machines.

◆ The Drives collection can give you a 'Folders" collection that tells you about the Folders on a drive.

◆ The Folders collection can have another Folders collection inside of it for its subfolders and a Files collection for the files in the folder.

And finally:

◆ You will have many ways of getting at individual drives, folders, or files, and of reading off their properties.

19

If all this seems too abstract, look at the following code. What it will do *after* you add the reference to the scripting runtime is tell you the total space and the free space you have available on each drive the program runs on. As you can see by looking at the code, the names of the methods you use to get this information are pretty mnemonic, but, just to make sure all the pieces are in place, I'll go over it line by line after you have had a chance to read it through:

```
Private Sub Form_Load()
Dim MyFileSystem As New FileSystemObject
Dim ADrive As Drive
Show ' so that we can see the results of the Print statements!
For Each ADrive In MyFileSystem.Drives
  If ADrive.IsReady Then
    Print "Drive " & ADrive.DriveLetter & _
    " has "; FormatNumber(ADrive.AvailableSpace, 0) & _
    " bytes available from " & _
    FormatNumber(ADrive.TotalSize, 0)
  End If
  Print
Next
End Sub
```

The first declaration makes a new file system object, since we use the New keyword in the Dim statement.

```
Dim MyFileSystem As New FileSystemObject
```

In a more complicated program you might want to make this a form or global variable. For a form level variable, you can do this by rewriting the code (new lines in bold):

```
Private MyFileSystem As FileSystemObject
Private Sub Form_Load()
Set MyFileSystem = New FileSystemObject
Dim ADrive As Drive
Show ' so that we can see the results of the Print statements!
For Each ADrive In MyFileSystem.Drives
  If ADrive.IsReady Then
```

```
      Print "Drive " & ADrive.DriveLetter & _
        " has "; FormatNumber(ADrive.AvailableSpace, 0) & _
        " bytes available from " & _
        FormatNumber(ADrive.TotalSize, 0)
    End If
    Print
  Next
End Sub
```

NOTE: When scripting the operating system (see Chapter 25 and http://www.microsoft.com/scripting) you'll need to use the CreateObject function to make a FileSystemObject. This code would take the form:

```
Set fso = CreateObject("Scripting.FileSystemObject")
```

where I called the file system object I created "fso."

Next, we have the line that declares an object variable to be of Drive type.

```
Dim ADrive As Drive
```

From that point on, the variable ADrive can refer only to Drive objects. As you might expect, the statement

```
MyFileSystem.Drives
```

is necessary in the For-Each loop because the Drives property of a file system object gives you a *collection* of the drives on the user's machine. The For-Each statement allows us to iterate through the elements (which are the individual drives) in this Drives collection. *In other words, Drives is the collection of individual Drive objects.*

Once we have an individual drive object, we start banging on it using the methods of the Drive object. As you can imagine, the IsReady method tells you whether the drive is ready. This is a very useful check to make before you work with a drive; if the drive is a floppy or a zip drive, there might not be any media in the drive. If the drive is ready (that is, the IsReady method gave us True), we use two more properties of the Drive to get the amount of total space available. The results are shown in Figure 19-6.

NOTE: You may be wondering why the numbers shown in Figure 19-6 for my C and D drives are the same. Unfortunately, the first shipping version of the scripting library that came with VB6 seems to have a bug. If you have more than 2 gigabytes free or in total space, it will only report that much space free or available. You should check the Microsoft Web site (http://www.microsoft.com/scripting) for updates to this library! (I know I am—frequently.)

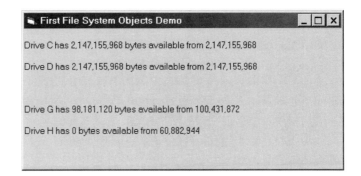

Using the Drives collection
Figure 19-6.

The next thing you may have noticed is that I didn't use the Format function, but its cousin, FormatNumber, which gives me the usual comma-delimited format for numbers. I did this so that you can easily modify this code to use with VBScript (see Chapter 25), which doesn't have the full Format function.

TIP: The reason you'll want to be able to use the File System objects with VBScript is that the necessary scripting DLL comes with Windows 98 and can be downloaded from Microsoft's Web site for Windows 95 and NT 4. This means that, for the first time, you can stop using klutzy batch files to automate system tasks. For example, PC Magazine will be having a regular column on how to use the File System objects and other parts of the scripting DLL to automate boring tasks. (I wrote one of the first columns for them in fact.) I'll show you some examples of this kind of automation later on in this chapter and also in Chapter 21.

Here's a list of the main properties of a Drive object. As you can see, the names are quite mnemonic.

◆ AvailableSpace
◆ DriveLetter
◆ DriveType
◆ FileSystem
◆ FreeSpace
◆ IsReady
◆ Path
◆ RootFolder
◆ SerialNumber

♦ ShareName
♦ TotalSize
♦ VolumeName

The Most Common Methods of the FileSystemObject

In this section, Table 19-1 lists some of the most important of the methods of the FileSystemObject. (Full documentation on the FileSystemObject is available from the http://www.microsoft.com/scripting Web site.) I'll be using these methods in some of the examples that follow (after we cover the most important properties of the Drive, Folder, and File objects).

Name and Signature of the Method	Description
CopyFile *source, destination*[, overwrite]	Another way to copy a file. The overwrite (True/False) flag allows you to choose to overwrite an existing file with that name or not.
CopyFolder *source, destination*[, overwrite]	A way to copy a folder or directory that will automatically copy all subdirectories and sub-subdirectories as well!
CreateFolder(*foldername*)	Creates a folder by name.
DeleteFile *filespec*[, force]	Another way to delete a file. If the optional force parameter is true, this will delete read-only files.
DeleteFolder *folderspec*[, force]	A way to delete a folder or directory. Caution: this will not check if the folder is empty and will automatically delete all subdirectories and sub-subdirectories as well!
DriveExists (*drivespec*)	Returns true if a drive exists with that specification.
FileExists (*filespec*)	Returns true if a drive exists with that specification. Looks in the current folder only, unless you give it a path name.
FolderExists (*folderspec*)	Returns true if a folder (directory) exists with that specification. Looks in the current folder only, unless you give it a path name.
GetAbsolutePathName (*pathspec*)	Returns the complete and unambiguous path from the path specification given; you can use this on a folder to get the full path.
GetBaseName (*path*)	Returns a string that gives the base name of the file (everything before the ".") or folder.

The Methods of the FileSystemObject
Table 19-1.

Name and Signature of the Method	Description
GetDrive *drivespec*	This important method returns a Drive object corresponding to the specification. The *drivespec* parameter can be a drive letter (c), a drive letter with a colon (c:), a drive letter with a colon and path separator (c:\), or any network share specification (\\OurNet\share1).
GetDriveName (*path*)	Returns a string containing the name of the drive for a specified path.
GetExtensionName(*path*)	Returns a string that gives the extension of the file (everything after the ".") or folder.
GetFile(*filespec*)	This important method returns a File object corresponding to the path specification given (or uses the current drive and folder).
GetFolder(*folderspec*)	Returns a Folder object corresponding to the path specification given (or uses the current drive and folder).
GetParentFolderName(*folderspec*)	This method returns a string (and not a Folder object) corresponding to the specification given. Returns a zero-length string ("") if there is no parent folder because you are at the root of a drive.
GetSpecialFolder(*folderspec*)	Returns a Folder object corresponding to either the Windows folder (use a 0 or a constant called WindowsFolder), the System folder (use a 1 or the constant called SystemFolder), or the Temp folder set aside by Windows (use a 2 or the constant called TemporaryFolder).
GetTempName	Returns a randomly generated temporary file or folder name.
MoveFile *source, destination*	Moves a file from the source to the destination.
MoveFolder *source, destination*	Moves a folder from the source to the destination.

19

The Methods of the FileSystemObject (*continued*)

Table 19-1.

Working with Folder and File Objects

You get a specific folder object by working with the GetFolder method of the FileSystemObject or the GetSpecialFolder method. Also, every Folder object has a SubFolders property that gives you a collection of all the folders inside of it. Similarly, you can get at all the files in a given folder by using the Files collection, which is a property of a Folder object. You can get at a specific File object by working with the GetFile method.

For example, suppose you wanted to store a list of the names of all the non-hidden folders in a given folder in an array. You would simply need to check if the Attributes property of the Folder objects was equal to Hidden or not before adding it to the array.

The following code, which assumes you have a global FileSystemObject named FSO, gives you a function that does this. (Notice how I use VB6's neat new feature of being able to return an array as the value of a function.)

```
Function GetFolderList(folderspec) As String()
  Dim I As Integer, AnArray() As String
  Dim AFolder As Folder, TempFolder As Folder
  Set AFolder = FSO.GetFolder(folderspec)
  For Each TempFolder In AFolder.SubFolders
    If TempFolder.Attributes <> Hidden Then
      I = I + 1
      ReDim Preserve AnArray(1 To I)
      AnArray(I) = TempFolder.Name
    End If
  Next
  GetFolderList = AnArray
End Function
```

To test this function, start up a new project and add the following code to it:

```
Private FSO As FileSystemObject
Private Sub Form_Load()
  Set FSO = New FileSystemObject
  Dim TheList() As String, I As Integer
  TheList = GetFolderList("C:\")
  Show
  For I = LBound(TheList) To UBound(TheList)
    Print TheList(I)
  Next
End Sub
```

Working with Folder and File Objects

Once you have a File or Folder object, you will most commonly be using the following methods, which work exactly the same as the similarly named versions do for the parent FileSystemObject (see Table 19-1).

◆ Copy *destination*[, *overwrite*]

◆ Delete [force]

◆ Move *destination*

For example, if FSO is a file system object, you could use code such as the following:

```
Set TheFile = FSO.GetFile("c:\test.txt")
TheFile.Move "c:\windows\desktop\"
Set TheFile = FSO.GetFile("c:\tempstuff.txt")
TheFile.Delete
```

Table 19-2 describes the properties of both Folder and File objects. Notice how the GetParentFolder property of the Folder object gives you another Folder object and not a string identifying the parent folder.

As an example, this little program uses some of these properties to pop up a message box to tell you some information about my \Program Files\Microsoft Visual Studio directory, as shown here:

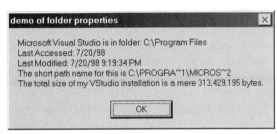

19

```
Private FSO As FileSystemObject
Private Sub Form_Load()
  Set FSO = New FileSystemObject
  MsgBox ShowFolderInfo("\Program Files\Microsoft Visual Studio")
  End
End Sub
'OK because there is a form level FSO variable for the FileSystemObject
Function ShowFolderInfo(FolderSpec As String) As String
  Dim AFolder As Folder, S As String
  Set AFolder = FSO.GetFolder(FolderSpec)
  S = AFolder.Name & " is in folder: " & AFolder.ParentFolder & vbCrLf
  S = S & "Last Accessed: " & AFolder.DateLastAccessed & vbCrLf
  S = S & "Last Modified: " & AFolder.DateLastModified & vbCrLf
  S = S & "The short path name for this is " & AFolder.ShortPath & vbCrLf
  S = S & "The total size of my VStudio installation is a mere "
  S = S & FormatNumber(AFolder.Size, 0) & " bytes."
  ShowFolderInfo = S
End Function
```

(The reason it is only 300 or so megabytes is I didn't install VC++—that alone would have added another 300 or so megabytes!)

Example: Deleting Files with a Given Extension in a Given Folder

Suppose we wanted to write a function that would delete all the .tmp (temp) files with a given extension in a given folder. We could use code like this:

```
Sub KillTmpFilesIn(FolderSpec As String)
  Dim AFile As File, TheFiles As Files
  Set AFolder = FSO.GetFolder(FolderSpec)
  On Error Resume Next 'in case we try to delete a file that is locked
  Set TheFiles = AFolder.Files
  For Each AFile In TheFiles
    If Right(AFile.Name, 3) = "tmp" Then AFile.Delete
  Next
End Sub
```

Property	Description
Attributes	Allows you to check or change the attributes of the given file or folder. The possible constants are Archive, Normal, ReadOnly, Hidden, and System, all of which are read/write, and Volume, Directory, and Compressed, which are read only.
DateCreated	Returns the date and time the file or folder was created (read only).
DateLastAccessed	Returns the date and time the file or folder was last accessed (read only).
DateLastModified	Returns the date and time the file or folder was created (read only).
Drive	Returns the drive letter where the file or folder lives.
Files	This important property returns a collection of File objects that are in the Folder.
IsRootFolder	Returns True if the folder is a root folder, such as C:\.
Name	Returns a string that gives the name of the file or folder.
ParentFolder	Returns a Folder object (not a string) of the parent folder of a given folder or returns the Folder object containing the file.
Path	Returns the path for the file or folder.
ShortName	Returns the short (8+3) name of the file or folder.
ShortPath	Returns the short (8+3) path of the file or folder.
Size	Returns the size in bytes of the file or the size in bytes of everything inside the folder (including subfolders and sub-subfolders, etc.).
SubFolders	This important property returns a collection of Folder objects for all the subfolders of the given folder.

Properties of
Folder and File
Objects
Table 19-2.

Although this kind of code works fine, the trouble with it is that it is too limiting. Extensions are no longer restricted to just three letters anymore; you need to write code that takes this into account! Luckily, by using the GetExtensionName method of the FileSystemObject that was described in Table 19-1, you can easily modify the preceding code so that it's useful for serious Windows 95/98 and NT development. Here's the modified code:

```
Sub KillFilesWithExtensionIn(AFolder As Folder, TheExtension As String)
    Dim AFile As File, TheFiles As Files
    On Error Resume Next
    Set TheFiles = AFolder.Files
    For Each AFile In TheFiles
        If UCase(FSO.GetExtensionName(AFile.Path)) = TheExtension Then
```

```
        AFile.Delete
      End If
   Next
End Sub
```

NOTE:　The next step is to have this code work on the subfolders and the sub-subfolders and so on. This requires a new programming technique called *recursion* that is covered in Chapter 21.

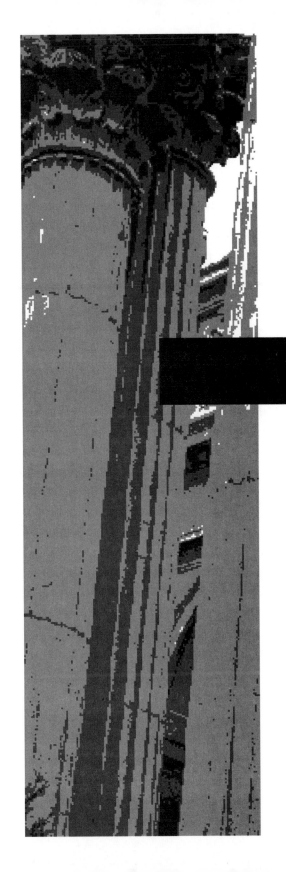

CHAPTER 20

Communicating with Other Windows Applications

The various versions of Windows 95/98 and NT can *multitask,* or run several applications at once. (How effective this will be depends on how the applications were written. Modern Windows applications can be multitasked by the operating system alone; applications designed for Windows 3.1 must cooperate by relinquishing control for multitasking to work.) As you'll soon see, Visual Basic lets you take advantage of Windows' multitasking powers by writing code that activates any Windows application or that sends commands directly to the active application from a Visual Basic project.

Multitasking becomes even more powerful if the various applications can work with each other. Suppose you could write a Visual Basic program that monitors what a spreadsheet, such as Excel, is doing. This would make it possible to use Visual Basic to add a feature that isn't built into the spreadsheet. For example, you might want to notify the user if a crucial quantity has changed or reached a target. Perhaps you want to write a program that analyzes, in real time, a document being written in a Windows word processor, such as Word for Windows, notifying the user when he or she has written a certain number of words. All this and more are possible through Visual Basic for Applications (built into Excel) and *object linking and embedding* (built into VB and most Windows applications).

NOTE: Object linking and embedding is usually called OLE for short— although, as you will see, OLE does a lot more now than its original acronym would have us believe.

The simplest way to exchange information between applications is with the Windows clipboard, so the first section of this chapter covers the clipboard. If you haven't spent much time using the clipboard, you'll see that it is much more than a passive place to store objects for cutting and pasting. Next, we move on to the useful Shell command, which lets you start up another Windows application directly from VB. Then it is on to the amazing SendKeys statement, which allows you to send keystrokes to another Windows application or even to the running VB program. (A great tool for self-running demos!)

Finally, it's on to what should be called ActiveX/COM/OLE, since all three technologies are essentially one. (I usually call them COM/OLE technologies, but everyone seems to pick their own name for the three. In fact, every few months it seems the marketing people at Microsoft announce a name change for these technologies: first it was OLE, then it was ActiveX, now it is COM, soon it will be enlarged and called COM+ and then it will be further enlarged to be called "DNA" (http://www.microsoft.com/dna/).)

Regardless of its current name, this technology lets you build your own integrated Windows applications using Visual Basic as the "glue" that binds together the disparate objects and applications. (The objects can even be accessed through the Internet and not even be on your machine!) COM/OLE is also the basis of writing ActiveX controls in Visual Basic (see Chapter 23) and is the way you can turn the classes you build in VB (Chapter 13) into reusable objects for use by other programs (usually called ActiveX servers or OLE servers—see the last section of this chapter). People will be able to use your classes for their Windows programming—even those writing in other languages, such as C++ or J++. I'll introduce you to this ability at the end of this chapter. COM/OLE is also the basis for what is usually called "OLE Drag and Drop," which lets you drag files from the Windows Explorer to your application and have the information processed in them effortlessly. Still, I'll be honest: COM/OLE is an immense topic—the standard books on it run many hundreds of pages. Thus, the sections on COM/OLE in this chapter are more a survey of what you are able to do with it.

NOTE: Besides the white papers available at Microsoft's web site, the book to read to get an overview of COM/OLE is David Chapell's *Understanding ActiveX and OLE* (Microsoft Press, 1996).

20

The Clipboard

The Windows clipboard lets you exchange both graphics and text between Windows applications, and it is often used for cut-and-paste operations inside a specific Windows application. In particular, Visual Basic uses the clipboard for its cut-and-paste editing feature, and you can use the clipboard together with the properties given in the section "Selecting Text in Visual Basic" to implement similar features in your projects.

The clipboard can hold only one piece of the same kind of data at a time. If you send new information of the same format to the clipboard, you wipe out what was there before. (You can use the Clipboard Viewer program supplied with Windows to examine the current contents of the clipboard.)

Sometimes, however, you will want to make sure that the clipboard is completely free before working with it. To do this, add a line of code inside your project that looks like this:

```
Clipboard.Clear
```

As you might expect, this applies the Clear method to the predefined Clipboard object. If you need to send text to and from the clipboard, use the two additional methods described next.

Clipboard.SetText   The SetText method is normally used in the following form:

    Clipboard.SetText *StringData*

This sends the string information contained in the variable or string expression *StringData* to the clipboard, wiping out whatever text was there.

Clipboard.GetText   The GetText method takes a copy of the text currently stored in the clipboard. Because the text contents of the clipboard remain intact until you explicitly clear the clipboard or send new text to it, you can do multiple pasting operations.

You use this method like a function. The usual form is

> *Destination* = Clipboard.GetText

You can also add an optional parameter; for example, GetText (vbCFRTF) to get RTF-formatted text.

Selecting Text in Visual Basic

When you use a text box or a combo box on a Visual Basic form, users can select text following the usual Windows convention: press SHIFT and use an arrow key, PAGE UP, or PAGE DOWN. Sending selected text to other Windows applications is quite common. Moreover, you will often want to add cut-and-paste editing functions that work with selected text to your project, especially for multiline text boxes. To do this within Visual Basic, you refer to selected text by three properties, two of which have long integer values and the third of which is a string.

 NOTE: These properties work the same as those we used in Chapter 6 for working with selected text in the rich text box control.

SelStart   The SelStart long integer gives you the place where the selected text starts. If the value is 0, the user has started selecting text from the beginning of the text or combo box. If the value is equal to the length of the text string—Len (Text1.Text), for example—the user wants the code to start working after all the text that's currently in the box. You can specify where selected text starts (for example, in a demonstration program) by setting the value of this property from code. For example, for a text box named Text1, a line of code like this starts the selected text in midstream:

```
Text1.SelStart = Len(Text1.Text)/2
```

SelLength   This property gives you the number of characters the user has selected. If SelLength equals 0, no text was selected. If SelLength is equal to the length of the text string, all the characters in the control were selected. To highlight the first half of the contents of a text box, you would use code like this:

```
Text1.SelStart = 0
Text1.SelLength = Len(Text1.Text)/2
```

SelText   The SelText property is the actual string the user has selected. If the user hasn't selected any text, this is the empty (null) string. If you add the following line of code to the fragment just given,

```
FirstHalfOfText$ = Text1.SelText
```

then the value of the string variable FirstHalfOfText$ is the selected string.

If you assign a new string value to the SelText property, Visual Basic replaces the selected string with the new value. To allow users to copy selected text, combine these properties with the SetText method. For a menu item named Copy and a text box named Text1, all you need to do is use

```
Private Sub Copy_Click()
  Clipboard.SetText Text1.SelText
End Sub
```

To change this to a procedure that cuts out the selected text, use the following code:

```
Private Sub Cut_Click()
  Clipboard.SetText Text1.SelText
  Text1.SelText = ""
End Sub
```

20

By adding the line that resets the value of SelText to the empty string, you have cut the selected text out of the text box.

To implement a Paste_Click procedure at the place where the user has set the insertion point inside a text box named Text1, use the following code:

```
Private Sub Paste_Click()
  Text1.Text = Clipboard.GetText
End Sub
```

Notice that if the user hasn't selected any text, this acts as an insertion method. Otherwise, it replaces the selected text.

Clipboard Formats and Graphics Transfers

To retrieve graphical images from the clipboard, Visual Basic must know what type of image is stored there. Similarly, to transfer images to the clipboard, the program must tell the clipboard what type of graphics it is sending. The following table summarizes this information. The first column of the table gives the name of the most useful of these predefined constants.

Symbolic Constant	Value	Format
vbCFLink	&HBF00	DDE conversation information
vbCFText	1	Text (.txt)
vbCFBitmap	2	Ordinary bitmap (.bmp)
vbCFMetafile	3	Windows metafile (.wmf)
vbCFDIB	8	Device-independent bitmap (.dib)
vbCFPalette	9	Color palette

You ask the clipboard what type of image it is currently storing by using the GetFormat method. The syntax for this method is

Clipboard.GetFormat(*Format%*)

where *Format%* is one of the values or constants given in the previous table. This method returns True if the image in the clipboard has the right format, for example:

```
If Clipboard.GetFormat(2) Then MsgBox "Clipboard has a bitmap"
```

To retrieve an image from the clipboard, you use the GetData method. The syntax for this method looks like this,

Clipboard.GetData(*Format%*)

where *Format%* has the value 2, 3, 8, or the symbolic equivalent, as in the preceding table. (Remember, you use the GetText method to retrieve text data from the clipboard.)

Clipboard Example Program

As an example of how to use the clipboard methods, start a new project and add a picture box and a multilevel text box with vertical scroll bars and four command buttons. The screen in Figure 20-1 shows you what the form might look like. Suppose you give the command buttons the following control names: cmdTextCopy,

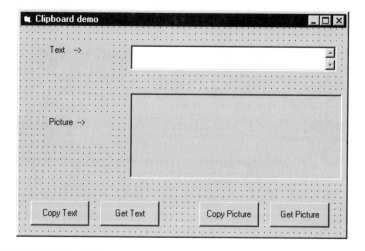

Clipboard
example
program
Figure 20-1.

cmdTextGet, cmdPictureCopy, and cmdPictureGet. Then the code that activates the Click procedures for these four buttons looks like this:

```
Private Sub cmdTextCopy_Click ()
  If Text1.Text = "" Then
    MsgBox ("No text to copy")
  Else
    Clipboard.Clear
    Clipboard.SetText Text1.Text
  End If
End Sub
```

This code checks the contents of the Text1 text box. If there is nothing there, it tells Visual Basic to inform the user. Otherwise, it clears the clipboard and sends the text contained in the box to the clipboard. (Strictly speaking, the Clear method isn't needed except in unusual circumstances; sending new text to the clipboard wipes out whatever text was there.)

20

To retrieve text from the clipboard, you first have to make sure the clipboard contains text. The If clause in the following procedure does this, using the GetFormat statement:

```
Private Sub cmdTextGet_Click ()
  If Clipboard.GetFormat(vbCFText) Then
    Text1.Text = Clipboard.GetText
  Else
    MsgBox ("No text in Clipboard")
  End If
End Sub
```

Retrieving a graphical image requires checking the format by using GetFormat and then modifying the parameter for the GetData method accordingly. Here's the procedure:

```
Private Sub cmdPictureGet_Click ()
  If Clipboard.GetFormat(vbCFText) Then
    MsgBox ("Only text in Clipboard")
  ElseIf Clipboard.GetFormat(vbCFBitmap) Then
    Picture1.Picture = Clipboard.GetData(vbCFBitmap)
  ElseIf Clipboard.GetFormat(vbCFMetafile) Then
    Picture1.Picture = Clipboard.GetData(vbCFMetafile)
  ElseIf Clipboard.GetFormat(vbCFDIB) Then
    Picture1.Picture = Clipboard.GetData(vbCFDIB)
  Else
    MsgBox "No recognizable picture in clipboard"
  End If
End Sub
```

To copy images from the picture box to the clipboard as a bitmap, use

```
Private Sub cmdPictureCopy_Click ()
  ' As BITMAP
  Clipboard.Clear
  Clipboard.SetData Picture1.Picture, 2
End Sub
```

Finally, you might want to consider using menus rather than command buttons. The control names can remain the same. The Menu Design window would look like the screen shown in Figure 20-2.

Running Another Windows Program from Within Visual Basic: The Shell Function

Although a few file-handling utility-type programs are built into Visual Basic commands—usually with slightly different names, such as Kill for Del—or are part of the Windows Scripting Host (Chapter 19), most are not. Experienced users can move to the Windows desktop and use the Explorer or the Start button to format disks, copy multiple files, or run another program. On the other hand, inexperienced users might not be comfortable doing this. For this reason, you may want to build in the ability to start other programs from your Visual Basic programs.

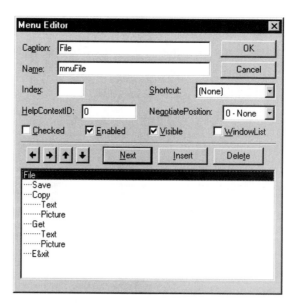

Menu Design window for the clipboard example

Figure 20-2.

You can use the Shell function to run any .com, .exe, .bat, or .pif file from a Visual Basic program. For example, you can call the Format.com program under Windows 95 with a line like this:

```
Shell "C:\WINDOWS\COMMAND\FORMAT.COM A:"
```

In general, the operating system must know where the file you are running is located. It can know this if the file you are shelling to is located in a directory in the path or in the current directory. If you give the full path name of the application, then you can use files not in these directories.

When Visual Basic shells to a program, it generates a new iconized window and gives it the focus. In many situations this is not ideal. For example, the user has to actually press ENTER for formatting to occur. You can change this behavior with the general form of the Shell function, as follows:

20

Shell(*Pathname, WindowStyle*)

Here, *Pathname* contains the full path name of the stand-alone program (or batch file) that you want to execute, along with any information needed by the program; WindowStyle sets the type of window the program runs in. The possible values for WindowStyle are as follows:

Symbolic Constant	Value	Type of Window
vbHide	0	Window is hidden but has the focus
vbNormalFocus	1	Normal with the focus
vbMinimizedFocus	2	Iconized with the focus
vbMaximizedFocus	3	Maximized with the focus
vbNormalNoFocus	4	Normal without the focus
vbMinimizedNoFocus	6	Iconized without the focus

NOTE: The Shell function takes named arguments, so you can use it in the form:

Shell PathName:= , WindowStyle:=

Use the Shell function with care, especially while you're developing the program within Visual Basic. Ideally, you should have enough memory to keep Windows, Visual Basic, the programs currently running, and the program to which you are "shelling" all simultaneously in memory. Otherwise, you have to rely on Windows to manage the memory for you by swapping to disk, and things will slow down dramatically.

Sending Keystrokes to the Active Windows Application

One nifty feature built into VB is the ability to send any keystrokes you want to the active Windows applications. You can even have a running Visual Basic application send keystrokes to itself—the obvious key to a self-running demo.

The AppActivate statement moves the focus to another application currently running on the Windows desktop; it does not start a program, nor does it change whether the application is minimized or maximized. The syntax for this statement (it takes named arguments) is

AppActivate *title*[, *wait*]

The *title* argument is a string expression that matches the one in the title bar of the application you want to activate. It is not case-sensitive. The optional *wait* parameter is either True or False. Usually you will leave it at the default value of False. (If you set it to True, then whichever application is doing the calling waits until it has the focus before it activates the new application.)

If the title parameter doesn't make a match with the whole title bar of an active application, Windows looks for any application whose title string begins with that title and activates it—you cannot control which one gets activated in this case. For example, AppActivate "Exploring" will usually start an instance of the Windows Explorer, even though its title bar might be something weird like "Exploring - HardDisk1_(C:)."

Sending Keystrokes to an Application

Once you've activated another Windows application by using AppActivate, you use the SendKeys statement to send keystrokes to the active window. SendKeys cannot send keystrokes to a non-Windows application that happens to be running under Windows in a virtual DOS window. If no other window is active, the keystrokes go to the Visual Basic project itself. (This is useful in testing programs and self-running demos.) The syntax for this statement (it takes named arguments) is

SendKeys *string*[, *wait*]

If the *wait* Boolean expression is True (nonzero), Visual Basic will not continue processing code until the other application processes the keystrokes contained in *string*. If the expression is False (0, the default), Visual Basic continues with the procedure immediately after it sends the keystrokes to the other application. The *wait* parameter matters only when you are sending keystrokes to applications other than your Visual Basic application itself. If you send keystrokes to your Visual Basic application and you need to wait for those keys to be processed, use the DoEvents function (see Chapter 12).

The value of the *string* parameter is the keystrokes you want to send. For keyboard characters, use the characters. For example,

```
SendKeys "Foo is not Bar", False
```

sends the keystrokes "F", "o", "o", and so on, to the active application, exactly as if the user had typed them. Since the *wait* parameter is False, Visual Basic does not wait for these keystrokes to be processed by the active application.

The only exceptions to sending keystrokes are the plus sign (+), caret (^), percent sign (%), brackets ([ ]), tilde (~), parentheses (( )), and braces ({ }). As you'll soon see, these have special uses in the SendKeys statement. If you need to send these keys, enclose them in braces. For example, to send "2+2" to the active application, use this:

```
SendKeys "2{+}2"
```

You'll often need to send control key combinations, function keys, and so on, in addition to the ordinary alphanumeric keys (A-Z, 0-9). To send a function key, use F1 for the first function key, F2 for the second, and so on. For other keys, such as BACKSPACE, use the following codes:

20

Key	Code
BACKSPACE	{BACKSPACE} or {BS} or {BKSP}
BREAK	{BREAK}
CAPS LOCK	{CAPSLOCK}
CLEAR	{CLEAR}
DEL	{DELETE} or {DEL}
DOWN ARROW	{DOWN}
END	{END}
ENTER	{ENTER} or ~
ESC	{ESCAPE} or {ESC}
Help	{HELP}
HOME	{HOME}
INS	{INSERT}
LEFT ARROW	{LEFT}
NUM LOCK	{NUMLOCK}
PAGE DOWN	{PGDN}
PAGE UP	{PGUP}
PRINT SCREEN	{PRTSC}
RIGHT ARROW	{RIGHT}
SCROLL LOCK	{SCROLLOCK}
TAB	{TAB}
UP ARROW	{UP}

For combinations of the SHIFT, CTRL, and ALT keys, use the codes just given, but place one or more of these codes first:

Key	Code
SHIFT	+
CTRL	^
ALT	%

To indicate that one (or all) of the SHIFT, CTRL, and ALT keys should be used with a key combination, enclose the keys in parentheses. For example, to hold down CTRL while pressing A and then B (that is, what this book would symbolize as CTRL+A+B), use "^(AB)". The string "^AB" would give you the three keystrokes individually.

You can also send repeated keys more easily by using the string in the form *Keystrokes$ Number%*. There must be a space between the keystrokes and the number. For example, SendKeys "UP 10" sends ten presses of the UP ARROW to the active application.

As an example of putting all this together, the following fragment activates the Windows Explorer and maximizes the window in which it is running by sending the keystrokes needed to open the control box and then choosing the Maximize item on its control box menu:

```
AppActivate "Exploring"
SendKeys "% {Down 4}{Enter}", -1
```

The SendKeys statement sends the ALT key followed by a press of the SPACEBAR (because the quotes enclose a space). These keystrokes open the control menu. The next strokes move you to the Maximize menu item and choose that item.

NOTE: This technique (using cursor keys instead of the accelerator letters) also works in the international version of Visual Basic, or any application where the words on a menu may differ but the order of the items remains the same.

As another example, if your current Visual Basic application is active, and a text box has the focus, you can send an "Undo" command to the text box via SendKeys:

```
SendKeys("^Z")
```

(In fact, this will send an Undo command to any application that follows standard Windows conventions.)

Overview of COM/OLE

OLE, which originally stood for *object linking and embedding,* started out as a technology that complemented and extended dynamic data exchange, which in turn was a technology that essentially automated clipboard transfers. It has gone far beyond its origins now. It's just another one of those acronyms that has passed into standing for itself.

One way OLE goes beyond simply using the clipboard is that, instead of information being merely transferred, information passed with OLE is presented in the same way it would appear in the originating application. Spreadsheets appear as spreadsheets, word-processed documents appear as they would in the word processor, and so on. When you add an OLE container control to your Visual Basic project, you give the user a bridge to another Windows application, and what they see *will look to them like that other application.*

When working with OLE, first and foremost come the *objects.* This is the data supplied by the Windows applications that support OLE—for example, an Excel worksheet (or, more likely, part of an Excel worksheet). You use Object variables (Chapter 13) for dealing with OLE objects, and you normally use the Variant data type when communicating information to these objects.

To understand *linking,* imagine that you are part of the group working on this book. Besides the author, there are a technical editor, a copyeditor, a proofreader, and others involved. The most efficient way for your group to work would be to maintain a single copy of the document and have each person link to it and make changes. *There should still be only one copy of the document involved* (on a central server); that way your group doesn't have to worry about important changes being missed. (In the jargon, this allows the group to work in a parallel rather than a serial way.) With a linked object, the data stays in the application that created it. Think of linking as attaching a chain to preexisting data—like any chained objects, you can effect changes by jerking on the chain. Technically, when you use linking in a VB application, linking inserts a placeholder into the Visual Basic application, and an image of the data is stored in the OLE control.

The idea of the *embedding* part of OLE is that you create documents that integrate various Windows applications under one roof. Embedding in OLE allows the custom control to maintain the object's data inside itself. When Visual Basic activates the OLE control, control switches back to the application that created the data, and you can use that application's power to modify the data in place.

One of the main ideas behind the introduction of OLE was that Microsoft wanted to get users away from thinking of applications as being paramount. Instead, you think of the document itself as central. For example, suppose you are preparing a complicated report that uses spreadsheet data and a graphics package. You want parts of the document to be under the control of the word processor and parts to be under the control of the spreadsheet. In OLE, the other application temporarily takes over to work with the data embedded in the control. When you embed an object in an OLE client control, no other application can access the data (as opposed to linking it, where they can). Moreover, the application that created the embedded data is automatically started whenever the user works with the embedded data.

Another part of OLE, called OLE Automation, allows you to take control of other applications. In fact, your own Visual Basic applications can be controlled by other applications. For example, from Visual Basic you can control Excel by using *its* version of Visual Basic, or you can control Word using *its* version of Visual Basic. (Office 97 unifies the languages for all its components so that they are all based on Visual Basic for Applications, which is also built into VB.)

Finally, it is worth noting that OLE is really now part of a technology that most people call COM/OLE. (COM stands for the *component object model*.) The idea is based on the importance of objects for modern computing. In the 1990s it has become clear that more and more people will simply be sending objects across the Net—the rallying cry is "objects everywhere." COM/OLE has become a subtle technology that allows objects to be used across the Net—and even, soon, across platforms.

Using the OLE Client Control

When you add an OLE client control to your Visual Basic project, you create what Microsoft calls an *OLE compound document.* (In fact, the moment you add a client control, Visual Basic pops up a dialog box asking you for the name of the application it should hook into. See the section "Using the OLE Client Control at Design Time" a little later in the chapter for more on this dialog box.) The OLE client control comes with all versions of Visual Basic. The icon is usually at the bottom of the toolbox and has a grid and an "OLE" in a box inside of it.

With OLE, your Visual Basic project can be the client (or *container*) application that receives the information, or the server (*source*) application that sends it out. In most cases with OLE, your Visual Basic project receives the information and serves as the client. (The OLE control supplied with Visual Basic is an OLE client control and does not allow a Visual Basic application to become an OLE server. Visual Basic does allow you to do this, though. You just need to use a class module or a custom control in order to create an OLE server—see the section on "Building COM/OLE DLL Servers" later in this chapter.)

Creating OLE Objects

As mentioned earlier, an OLE object is any data the OLE control can work with. It can be a single graph, a range of cells in a spreadsheet, a whole spreadsheet, or part or all of a word-processed document. An application that supports OLE will have an *object library* that it can *expose.* (Expose is jargon for "here are the things you can work with. You can work with them in the following ways.") The Object Browser is usually the best way of getting information about these object libraries.

Next, before moving on with OLE, there is one phrase that will frequently recur, the *OLE class.* This is the application that produces the OLE object. Any application that supports OLE has a unique OLE class name, for example, "WordDocument" or "ExcelWorksheet." (Class names can be case-sensitive.) You can get a list of the available class names by clicking on the ellipsis for the Class property in the Properties window for the OLE control.

There are four ways you can create OLE objects. The simplest is to embed or link the object within an OLE container control. This enables you to change objects on the form at run time and create linked objects.

Descriptions of the more sophisticated methods follow.

Creating OLE Objects via the Toolbox
To add an OLE object to the toolbox:

1. Choose Project|Components and go to the Insertable Objects tab.
2. Check off the box for the object you want to work with in the dialog box that pops up.

For example, you can add an Excel Worksheet object to the toolbox by filling in the Insertable Objects dialog box as shown here:

20

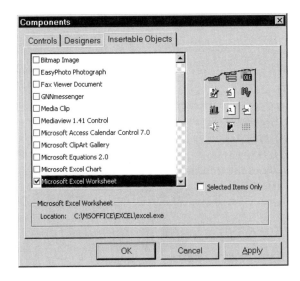

Now, when you use this tool to draw the object directly on a form, you automatically embed the object in your application. Figure 20-3 shows what your form looks like if you embed an Excel object this way. (Notice the Excel object in the toolbox on the left side of Figure 20-3.)

Objects via the Project | References Item
The most modern OLE-compliant applications are available from the dialog box that pops up when you choose Project|References. This is how we added the File System Objects to our project in the last chapter. As you saw there, these object libraries are particularly nice because they contain definitions of all the objects, methods, and properties the object supplies that you can access via the Object Browser. Moreover, help is usually available from the Object Browser for the command syntax. For example, if you add the Excel object library to Visual Basic this way and then use the Object Browser to study this library, you can see at a glance what the syntax is. Figure 20-4 is an example of this.

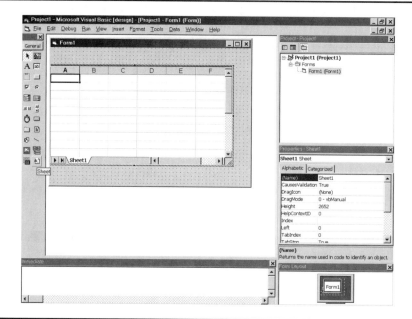

An Excel
embedded
object
Figure 20-3.

Once you have set a reference to the object library via the Project|References dialog
box, you can use the New method to create the object in code—just as you did for the

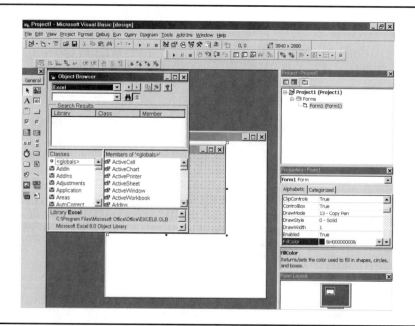

Using the
Object Browser
to study the
Excel object
library
Figure 20-4.

File System objects. For example, Application is the top-level Excel object, so you can use

```
Dim MyExcelApp As New Excel.Application
```

to make one. Notice how the IntelliSense shows you all the possible objects you can make when you type the dot after Excel! Once VB has processed this, you can access the parts of an Excel application using the methods and properties of MyExcelApp.

You can also use the CreateObject method introduced in Chapter 19 that takes a string (analogous to the programmatic id that you saw in Chapter 13). Here's an example of the code for an Excel worksheet using CreateObject:

```
Dim objExcel As Object
Set objExcel = CreateObject("EXCEL.SHEET")
```

These two lines of code create an object variable (named objExcel in this case). This object variable can also be used to control Excel. (See the section on "OLE Automation" a little later in the chapter.)

CAUTION: Always set the object variable to Nothing when you are finished with it (otherwise the memory and resources it takes up will not be freed).

Creating Objects When the Object Does Not Supply an Object Library

An object library is not supplied for some objects (such as Word 95 or Word 6.0), which, although they are OLE-aware, do not have all the behavior the user would like (Word 97 is fully OLE-aware). In particular, applications that do not expose an object library make you dig out their objects, methods, and properties from their documentation (or in some cases, from a cry on the Internet). For this situation you can't use New and must use the CreateObject function to refer to the object. Here's an example:

```
Dim objWordBasic As Object ' for use in older version of Word
Set objWordBasic = CreateObject("Word.Basic")
```

(As before, remember to set the object variables to Nothing when you are done.)

Using the OLE Client Control at Design Time

Creating links or embeddings with OLE at design time is easy. Essentially, you need only work with the dialog boxes that will be described in this section.

If you have added an OLE client control to a form, you will almost immediately get a dialog box like Figure 20-5. (The more applications you have, the more items will appear.) This gives you the names of all the Windows applications you can hook into. As Figure 20-5 indicates, you can have the object show up as an icon or with the data visible in the OLE control by clicking on the Display As Icon check box on the right.

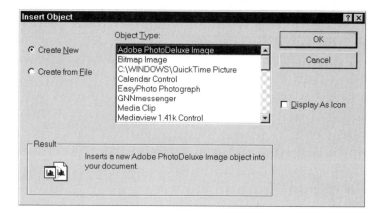

Insert Object
dialog box
Figure 20-5.

The two radio buttons on the far left determine whether you will work with an existing file created by the application (a linked object—Create from File) or whether you want the other application to create one anew (an embedded object—Create New). If you choose to link the control by selecting the Create from File option, the dialog box changes to Figure 20-6. You can click on the Browse button to open a dialog box that lets you pick the file. When you have done that, check the Link box in Figure 20-6.

NOTE: You can click on Cancel if you want to set the OLE properties via code. You do not need to use this dialog box in order to work with OLE. In fact, if you create an executable file with an OLE connection made at design time, the file will be much larger than if you create the connection at run time with code.

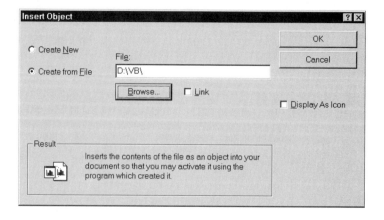

Insert Object
dialog box for
Create from File
Figure 20-6.

Paste Special

Sometimes you want to create linked or embedded objects by using information stored in the Windows clipboard to determine the SourceDoc and SourceItem properties. To do this, you first need to copy the data from the source application to the clipboard by using the Copy command in that application. You then need to use the Paste Special dialog box, which is available at design time by clicking the right mouse button when the focus is in the OLE control and choosing Paste Special from the pop-up menu that results. This dialog box automatically examines the contents of the clipboard to determine the needed OLE properties.

T IP:　The context menu for the OLE container control contains many useful shortcuts that are worth checking out.

20

OLE Properties

As you might expect, the dialog box only makes it simpler to set the properties of the OLE control. You can always change them via the Properties window or code (and, of course, you will have to do this to enable OLE at run time).

For example, the Display as Icon check box in Figure 20-6 actually sets the DisplayType property. The SizeMode property allows you to change how the control looks at run time. If the value is 0 (vbOLESizeClip), the control clips the data displayed at run time. If you want to stretch the image to fit the current size of the OLE control, set the value of this property to 1 (vbOLESizeStretch). Finally, you can have the control automatically resize itself by setting the property to a value of 2 (vbOLESizeAutoSize).

The dialog box that pops up also sets the crucial Class property, which specifies the application containing the data. The OLEType property determines what type of object you have created. Is it linked, embedded, or either? The SourceDoc property gives the name of the linked object or the file to be used as a template for an embedded object. The SourceItem property is used for linked objects to specify what portion of the linked document the Visual Basic application can work with. (For example, a spreadsheet range might be indicated by setting this property to "R1C1:R1C10.")

Common OLE Container Control Methods

Finally, there are the very important methods that apply to the OLE container control, which specifies exactly what should be done to the OLE object. Do you want to update the object, create it, delete it, save the information in the object to a file, retrieve it from a file, and so on? What follows is a short discussion of the most common methods.

CreateEmbed Method　　This creates an embedded OLE object. To do this, you must first set (via the OLE dialog box or code) both the Class and OLETypeAllowed properties. The OLETypeAllowed property possible values are 0 for Linked, 1 for Embedded, or 2 for Either, and the Class property determines the type of OLE object. (Class names are available from the OLE dialog box or the Properties window. You can use the OLEType property to determine what kind of link you have at run time.) When you create a new embedded OLE object, the application must either be active (use AppActivate), or it must be in the system's path.

CreateLink Method   This creates a linked OLE object from an existing file. To do this, first set the OLETypeAllowed and SourceDoc properties. In this case the OLETypeAllowed is 0 (linked) or 2 (either).

The SourceDoc property gives the name of the file for the linked object. If you want to restrict yourself to working with a portion of the linked object, set the SourceItem property too.

Just as with embedding a document, the application must either be active or in the path.

Copy Method   This sends all the data and linking properties of the object to the Windows clipboard. Both embedded and linked information can be copied to the clipboard.

Paste Method   This copies data from the clipboard to an OLE control. You'll need to check the PasteOK property of the control.

Update Method   This is a very important action because it pulls the current data from the application and gives you a view of it in the OLE control.

DoVerb Method   This activates an OLE object. To use this action, you will need to set the Verb parameter of this method, which specifies what operation you want performed.

NOTE: If you set the AutoActivate property of the control to double-click (value = 2), the OLE control will automatically activate the current object when the user double-clicks in the control. If the application supports "In Place Activation," you can arrange it so that the application is activated whenever the OLE control gets the focus (set AutoActivate to 1).

Close Method for OLE Objects   This is used only for embedded objects, since it closes the OLE object and cancels the connection with the application that controlled the object.

Delete Method   Use this if you want to delete the object. OLE objects are automatically deleted when a form is closed.

SaveToFile Method   If the OLE object is embedded, this method is vital. Because the OLE control data is maintained by the OLE control, it will be lost unless you specifically save it. You do this by writing the necessary code using the SaveToFile method to this value.

ReadFromFile Method   If you use the SaveToFile method just discussed, the ReadFromFile method reloads an OLE object from the data file created using the SaveToFile method. The code needed for this action is similar to that for saving data, except, of course, this time you'll be reading the data back.

InsertObjDlg Method   This pops up the same Insert Object dialog box that Visual Basic uses when you put an OLE control on a form. At run time, use this method to allow the user a friendly way to create a linked or embedded object.

PasteSpecialDlg Method   This displays the Paste Special dialog box. At run time, you display this dialog box to allow the user to paste an object from the clipboard.

FetchVerbs Method   This gets the list of verbs supported by the application.

SaveToOLE1File Method   Use this if you need backward compatibility with the earlier version of OLE.

OLE Automation

Visual Basic is extendable—that's one of its greatest strengths. However, you may not want to spend your time creating custom controls or DLLs that duplicate functionality found in other applications, such as Excel or Word. The key to tapping other (OLE-compliant) applications is OLE Automation. You can use Visual Basic (technically the part of VB called Visual Basic for Applications = VBA in the Object Browser) in order to write programs that let you manipulate the data and the objects in these applications.

Some objects that support OLE Automation also support linking and embedding. If an object in an OLE container control supports OLE Automation, you can access its properties and methods using the Object property. If you draw the object directly on a form or create it in code, you can directly access the properties and methods of the object. A full discussion of OLE Automation is beyond the scope of this section. If what you read here whets your appetite, refer to your Visual Basic manuals for more information.

Using OLE Automation

As you have seen earlier, you can create a reference to objects in code if you can set a reference to the object with the New keyword, CreateObject, or GetObject from outside the OLE server that created it. Microsoft Excel's and Word's Application objects are examples of these types of objects. Some subsidiary objects, such as a cell in Excel, can only be accessed by a method of a higher-level object.

For example, go to Project|References, and select the Excel object library in order to make Visual Basic aware of Excel's objects. Now add a text box to a form. Then use the following OLE Automation code to fill a bunch of cells in the second column of an Excel worksheet with consecutive values, sum them, and then place the sum into a text box in Visual Basic:

```
Private Sub Form_Click()
  Dim objExcel As Object
  Set objExcel = CreateObject("EXCEL.SHEET")
  objExcel.Application.Visible = True
  For I = 1 To 10
    objExcel.Cells(I, 2).Value = I
  Next I
  objExcel.Cells(11, 2).Formula = "=sum(B1:B10)"
  Text1.Text = objExcel.Cells(11, 2)
  objExcel.Application.Quit
  Set objExcel = Nothing
End Sub
```

A few points worth noting:

◆ OLE Automation requires being familiar with the object you want to program. The syntax is always going to be tricky. (The Object Browser can be a real time-saver here!)

◆ On a Pentium 90 with 16MB of RAM, this simple code took a bit of time to run (roughly 0.6 seconds). On a Pentium 200 with 80MB of RAM, it was essentially immediate. The moral is, a fast processor and lots of RAM are needed to make OLE really successful.

◆ The previous point shows that although OLE may be a great technology, incredibly fast it ain't. You should think long and hard before using OLE Automation in an application that is destined to run on slower legacy machines with limited RAM.

◆ You can use Windows API calls to detect the kind of hardware a user has. The amount of RAM seems to be even more important than the speed of the CPU. Don't try to use OLE Automation if your user has 8MB of RAM. OLE will start getting usable when you have 16MB of RAM, but 32MB or more seems to be the "sweet spot."

Building COM/OLE DLL Servers

In this section I want to show you the basics of how you can turn a class module into a dynamic link library (DLL). (Think of these as being like ActiveX controls but having no visual component.) People will be able to use your DLLs the same way they use libraries supplied for Excel or by a commercial vendor.

The first step in making a DLL is to tell VB you want to build one. This can be done from the New Project dialog box (choose ActiveX DLL). In this case VB automatically adds a class module to the Project Explorer. Notice that there is now an Instancing Property for this class module. Here are short descriptions of the various settings for this useful property of your DLLs.

Private This is the default value. When people make an object from your DLL, these instances can only be created by the project that they are a part of. This is the only possible setting for classes in a standard EXE. At least one of the classes in your DLL can't be private, or nobody will be able to use the code!

PublicNotCreatable   This setting lets other applications use instances of your class but doesn't let the other applications create them. This is the ideal setting for data structures where you may have a utility class that you want exposed, but only the controlling class should be able to create the utility class.

MultiUse   This setting allows somebody to create as many objects of your class as they would like. Although you don't have to actually set it, a user control is obviously a MultiUse object factory—having a control on the toolbox that could be used only once would be sort of funny.

GlobalMultiUse   This is occasionally a very useful setting. Like MultiUse it allows someone to create as many instances of your class as they want. The neat feature of this setting is that if someone is working in their copy of VB, after they add a reference to an ActiveX DLL that has its instancing property set to GlobalMultiUse, they won't have to create an instance of the class using New in order to use your code. They can use the functionality of your class as if those functions were built into VB.

20

CAUTION: Since the names of the methods and properties of a GlobalMultiUse class module in a DLL become part of the "name space" used by VB, you have to be careful not to have any conflicts with names reserved by VB.

An Example of Using a Globalmultiuse Class
For this example, do the following:

1. Start up an ActiveX DLL.
2. Select the Project in the Project Explorer and change its name to GlobalMultiUseDemo.
3. Set the Instancing property of the class in the DLL project to 6—GlobalMultiUse.
4. Add the following code to the class:

```
Public Sub Hello(YourName as String)
  MsgBox "Hello " & YourName & "!"
End Sub
```

This will give us a public method of the class that takes a string.

Now we need to add another project to VB in order to test our DLL. For this:

1. Choose File|Add Project and choose Standard Exe.
2. Go To Project|References and you should see an item marked GlobalMultiUseDemo (below the highlight in Figure 20-7). Check it off.
3. Make the Form_Load for Project1 look like this:

```
Private Sub Form_Load()
  Hello "Gary Cornell"
End Sub
```

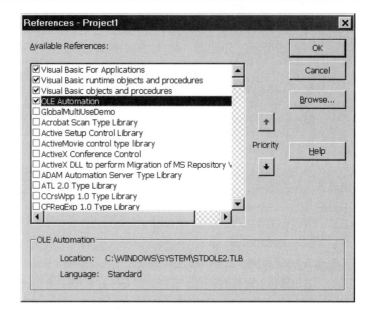

Don't hit the Run button yet. (If you do, nothing will seem to happen). There is one last step to take in testing a DLL project when you build it this way. The problem is that we started with a DLL project, so Visual Basic uses it as the startup project.

T IP: You can always tell the startup project because it is highlighted in the Project Explorer.

We need to make the test project the startup project. For this:

1. Right click on the line that says Project1 in the Project Explorer.
2. Choose "Set As Start Up" from the context menu that pops up.
3. Run the project.

That's it. You should see a message box like this one,

thus proving that the keyword "Hello" is now as much a part of VB as is the keyword Print. (Well, it is until you uncheck the line in Project|References that refers to the GlobalMultiUseDemo DLL.)

How to Permanently Register ActiveX DLL Projects

When we made a project group to test our DLL by adding another project to VB's IDE, VB temporarily added the needed information to the registry on your machine so that you could see the DLL in the Project|References dialog box. If you want to use (or have someone be able to use) a DLL you build with VB permanently, you must follow these steps:

1. First, compile your DLL by choosing File|Compile.
2. Then, run a program called regsvr32 to *register* it (write information about it to the registry) on your or their machine.

20

The regsvr32 program can be found in the \Tools\RegUtils directory on the VB CD or you can download the latest version from the Microsoft's MSDN web site http://www.microsoft.com/msdn.) You can run regsvr32 from the DOS prompt or the Run box off the Start menu. Assuming you copy the regsvr32 program to the \Windows directory, you simply put a line like this in the Run box available off the Start menu.

```
regsvr32 PathNameOf/GlobalMultiUseDemo.dll
```

TIP: To unregister a DLL, use the /U switch. For example:

```
regsvr32 /U PathNameOf/GlobalMultiUseDemo.dll
```

OLE Drag and Drop

Unlike the standard drag and drop you saw in Chapter 17, *OLE drag and drop* lets you drag an object that contains the data from one place to another. For example, you can almost certainly drag a file from Windows Explorer to your e-mail program in order to attach it.

OLE drag and drop often seems like magic, for example:

1. Create a document using WordPad—the supplied mini word processor that comes with Windows. Be sure to add lots of fonts and font size changes.
2. When you choose Save, make sure you save it in "rich text format." It should be saved with an .rtf extension.
3. Start up a new VB project, go to Project|Components, and add the RichTextBox to your toolbox. (See Chapter 6 for more on this control.)

4. Add a rich text box to a form, making it big enough to see.

Now:

5. Start the VB project that has the rich text box control and leave it running.
6. Go into Windows Explorer to the directory where you saved the file you created in step 1 above, and then drag the file you created from Windows Explorer to the RTF control in the running form.

Pretty amazing, isn't it?

T IP: If you don't see the embellished text show up in the rich text box, go back to VB and make sure that OLEDragMode and OLEDropMode for the rich text box are both set to automatic.

As you just saw, automatic OLE drag and drop is trivial in VB. Many controls (like rich text boxes) know how to handle certain data inside a file and will do so without you writing any code.

Manual OLE drag and drop is a totally different story. I can only get you started on the road to mastering the very powerful but complicated techniques involved. First off, as you might expect, many of the OLE drag and drop methods, events, and properties are similar to those you saw in Chapter 17 for ordinary mouse drag and drop. Thus, the fundamental idea of how you code manual OLE drag and drop isn't hard: you need to write code in one or more of the OLE drag and drop events in order to get things to work the way you want.

T IP: To see if a control supports OLE drag and drop, check the Properties window to see if it shows OLEDragMode and OLEDropMode properties. Essentially all Visual Basic components (including forms) support manual OLE drag and drop.

Working with OLE Drag and Drop

The main subtleties about OLE drag and drop result from the fact that in OLE drag and drop you are moving data around and not objects. It should come as no surprise, given VB's increasing object orientation, that the data being dragged around in OLE drag and drop is stored as a predefined Visual Basic object called the DataObject. The DataObject works a lot like the Clipboard object. For example, the DataObject has Clear, GetData, GetFormat, and SetData methods that work much as they did for the Clipboard object.

The example I want to show you is a simple yet typical example of coding OLE drag and drop. We will let the user drag a set of filenames from Windows Explorer to a

Visual Basic list box. The list box will then display the full path names. To make this happen, all we will need to do is write code in the OLEDragDrop event. VB triggers this event when data is dropped onto the target control. *It is an event of the target control and not of the source control.*

For our sample application:

1. Add a list box to a new Visual Basic project.
2. Set the OLEDropMode property of the list box to 1—Manual.
3. Write the following OLEDragDrop event procedure for the list box:

```
Private Sub List1_OLEDragDrop(Data As DataObject, Effect As Long, _
  Button
As Integer, Shift As Integer, X As Single, Y As Single)
  Dim TheFileName
  If Data.GetFormat(vbCFFiles) Then
    For Each TheFileName In Data.Files
       List1.AddItem (TheFileName)
    Next TheFileName
  Else
    MsgBox "Not a list of file names, sorry!"
  End If
End Sub
```

I want to go through this procedure line by line, since it illustrates so well the ideas you'll need to master for coding OLE drag and drop. First off, I needed to check the type of the data being dragged to the list box. This is done exactly as we did when working with the Clipboard object: use the GetFormat method. The next line uses the GetFormat(vbCFFiles) method, which returns True if and only if the data contains a bunch of filenames (for example, filenames that were selected in Windows Explorer). Now here's where the magic of OLE drag and drop comes into place. If the user did select a bunch of filenames, the *Files* property of the DataObject gives us a collection of the full path names for the files that the user had selected. Once we have it in a collection, we simply use the standard For-Each loop to run through the items in a collection, using the For-Each statement and adding the path name of each filename to the list box.

Okay, to see the program at work simply:

1. Run the VB program.
2. Open Windows Explorer.
3. Select a bunch of files (using SHIFT+click or CTRL+click) in Explorer.
4. Drag the files to the list box in the running VB project.

That's it, Figure 20-8 shows you what your desktop will look like. (I minimized VB in order to have room for both the running VB project and Explorer.)

20

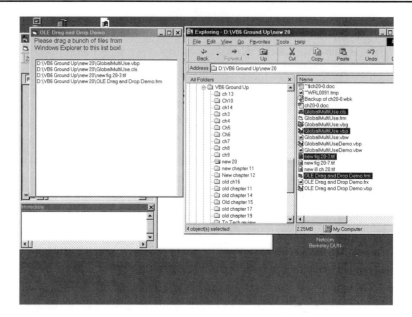

OLE drag and
drop at work
Figure 20-8.

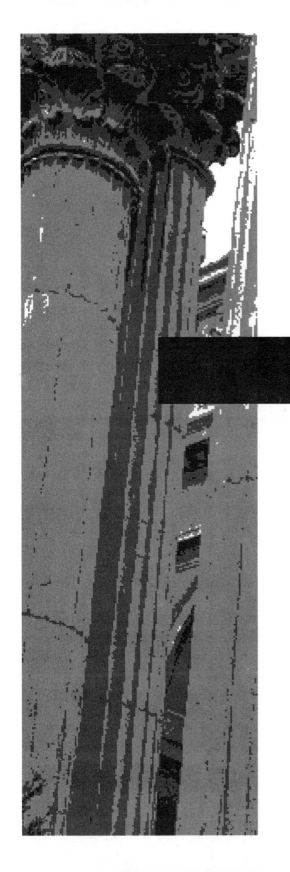

CHAPTER 21

Recursion

Recursion is a general method of solving problems by reducing them to simpler problems of a similar type. For the experienced programmer, thinking recursively presents a unique perspective on certain problems, often leading to particularly elegant solutions and, therefore, equally elegant programs. In Visual Basic, you usually use recursion in general procedures to make event procedures or the whole project run more smoothly or quickly. For example, this chapter shows you how to use recursion to build one of the fastest sorting routines—it's called, naturally enough, Quicksort.

However, the most common use of recursion for a Visual Basic programmer is in dealing with the hierarchical file structure on your machine. I'll show you how recursion makes it almost trivial to write routines that do common tasks like deleting all your .tmp files that may be hanging around. Finally, this chapter has a section that introduces you to recursive graphics. These are usually called *fractals*. The screen in Figure 21-1 shows an example of the Koch Snowflake. This is just one of the figures that can be drawn using the programs in this section.

NOTE: Recursion is a technique often avoided even by experienced programmers. One reason is that recursion is sometimes thought of as a mysterious, even mystical, process, but this reputation is undeserved. (See, for example, the Pulitzer prize-winning book, *Gödel, Escher, Bach,* by Douglas Hofstadter (New York: Basic Books, 1979). It's a book some people swear by and others swear at.) The real reason that many programmers tend to avoid recursion after they understand it is because they have had bad experiences with it—unless you are careful, recursive programs crash easily. And, even if they don't crash, they may run much slower than programs that use other techniques to solve the problem at hand.
Thus recursion, like many powerful tools, can be overused. At the end of this chapter, you will find a short section on when *not* to use recursion.

A fractal
drawing
Figure 21-1.

Getting Started with Recursion

Before this chapter shows you how to program recursive procedures and functions, let's look at some typical examples of recursive problem solving. Discovering a recursive solution to at least one problem seems innate—at least with children. Have you ever met a three-year-old who didn't intuitively know how to solve the following problem with the solution given here:

PROBLEM:	How do I deal with my parents?
SOLUTION:	Deal with father first, then deal with mother (or vice versa).

This method of solving a problem is, naturally enough, called *divide and conquer,* and it clearly has a long history.

For a more serious example of divide and conquer but one still away from the programming arena, consider the following old problem: You have seven balls and a balance scale. One ball is heavier than the other six. Find the heaviest ball in just two weighings. To solve this, first try a simpler case—three balls. Notice that if you try to balance two balls, there are only two possibilities:

21

◆ They balance (in which case the remaining ball is the heaviest).

◆ They don't balance (in which case the heaviest one is obvious).

Now, to do the seven-ball problem, divide the balls into two groups of three with one left over. If they balance, then, as before, the heaviest one is the one left over. If they don't balance, then whichever side is heavier is also obvious. This reduces the problem to the previous case. (Similarly, you can do 15 balls in three weighings, 31 in four, and so forth.)

As a final example of divide and conquer, here's an outline of a recursive method for sorting (called merge sort) that you'll see soon. Merge sort follows this outline:

```
To SORT a LIST
   If a list has one entry stop
Otherwise:
   SORT(the first half)
   SORT(the second half)
   Combine (merge) the two halves
```

As long as the operation of combining the two takes substantially less time than the sorting process, you have a viable method of sorting. As you'll soon see, it does and we do.

Any operation on a directory that is supposed to work similarly on subdirectories will need recursion when the operation is programmed. For example, when you use

XCOPY *.* *NewPath* /S

to copy files in all subdirectories to a new place, you are using recursion. The XCOPY routine constantly calls itself on lower and lower subdirectories until it finishes.

You will soon see a procedure that deletes all files with a given extension on a disk. The outline for this is:

1. Delete all files with the given extension in the folder passed to the routine using the techniques you learned in Chapter 19.
2. Next find all the subfolders of the given folder using the SubFolders property of the Folder object. (This gives us a collection of Folder objects.)
3. Then delete all files with the given extension in each subfolder by calling the previous routine on each subfolder in the collection of Folders returned by the SubFolders property.
4. Finally, call the routine again using the object that represents each subfolder.
5. Stop the process when there are no more subfolders to work with.

As you can see, a recursive solution to a problem will always follow this outline:

Solve recursively (problem)
  If the problem is trivial, do the obvious
  Simplify the problem
Solve recursively (simpler problem)
  (Possibly) combine the solution to the simpler problem(s)
  into a solution of the original problem

The point always is that a recursive procedure constantly calls itself, each time in a simpler situation, until it gets to a trivial case, at which point it does whatever it needs to do and then exits.

NOTE: There's also indirect recursion, where a function or procedure calls itself via an intermediary. For example, function A calls function B, which in turn calls function C, which calls function A, and so on. Unlike languages such as Pascal, you can use indirect recursion in VB in the same way that you use direct recursion.

Recursive Functions and Procedures

You know a function can call another function or a procedure can call a function. All these calls will show up in the Call Window. Recursion occurs when a function eventually calls itself. Before looking at an example of a recursive program in Visual Basic, stop and think for a second what Visual Basic must do when one function or procedure calls another. Obviously, Visual Basic has to communicate the current value or location of all the parameter variables to the new function or procedure. To do this, Visual Basic places the locations of the variables (or the location of a copy of the values, if you are passing by value) to a reserved area in its memory called the *stack*. Now suppose this second function needs the results from a third function. This requires yet another storing of the locations of variables, and so on. However, this process can take place regardless of the nature of the other functions. It is this that makes recursion possible.

Here's an example. The factorial of a positive integer is the product of the numbers from 1 up to the integer and the custom is to use an exclamation mark (!) to symbolize it. For example:

2! = 2*1	(= 2)
3! = 3*2*1	(= 6)
4! = 4*3*2*1	(= 4*3! = 24)
5! = 5*4*3*2*1	(= 5*4! = 120)

As you can see, the factorial of an integer can be written using the factorial of the previous integer and a multiplication. Using this idea, here's a recursive definition of the factorial:

21

```
Function Factorial (N As Integer) As Long
   If N <= 1 Then
      Factorial = 1                        'factorial not usually
   Else                                    'defined for N<0
      Factorial = N * Factorial(N - 1)     'note the call to
   End If                                  'itself in a simpler
End Function                               'situation
```

Suppose you now write Print Factorial(4). Then Visual Basic does the following:

1. It calls the function with N = 4. The first statement processed is the If-Then test. Since the If clause is False, it processes the Else clause.
2. This says compute 4*Factorial(3).
3. It tries to compute Factorial(3). And so it now has to start building up its stack. The stack will hold partial results—those obtained to date. Think of what gets pushed onto the stack as a little card containing the status, location, and values of all the variables, as well as what is still left "up in the air." In this case, the card would say

    N = 3. Need to compute 4 * (an as yet unknown number = Factorial(3))

4. Now Visual Basic repeats the process, calling the factorial function with a variable now having the value 3. And so another card gets pushed onto the stack:

    N = 2. Need to compute 3 * (an as yet unknown number = Factorial(2))

5. Repeat the process again so the stack contains three cards:

    N = 1. Need to compute 2 * (an as yet unknown number = Factorial(1))

Now Visual Basic does one final call, with the variable N having the value 1, and sets up a fourth card. But at this point the process can stop—the top card no longer contains an unknown quantity. By the first clause, Factorial(1) is 1, so Visual Basic can start "popping the stack." The results of the top card (the number 1) feed into the second card. Now Visual Basic can figure out what the second card stands for (the number 2), and so Visual Basic can pop the stack one more time and feed the information accumulated to the third card (the number 6). Finally, Visual Basic feeds the results to the bottom card and comes out with 4! = 24. Since the stack is empty, this is the answer. Figure 21-2 shows you one way of imagining the stack.

The explanation of the process, of course, takes much longer than the actual solution via Visual Basic. Visual Basic keeps track of the partial results of any recursive operation via its stack. You don't need to be aware of the stack—most of the time. The only time you do worry about the stack is when it "overflows" and your program crashes or behaves erratically. The disastrous error message you'll see is number 28, "Out of stack space." This is not usually a problem, however, as the stack has more than enough space for normal needs. (The number of recursive calls you can make varies with how much information the stack needs to keep track of. The limit in the VB6 version is many thousands. Heavy use of the stack, where many variables are being passed, could cut this down by a factor of 2.)

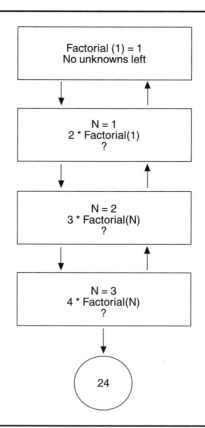

Picture of the
stack
Figure 21-2.

There are many other examples of recursive functions. For example, the Fibonacci numbers are defined as follows:

◆ The first Fibonacci number is 1 (in symbols, Fib(1) = 1).

◆ The second Fibonacci number is also 1 (in symbols, Fib(2) = 1).

◆ From that point on, the next Fibonacci number is the sum of the two preceding ones (in symbols, Fib(n) = Fib(n–1) + Fib(n–2)).

For example:

    Fib(3) = Fib(2) + Fib(1)   (= 1 + 1 = 2)
    Fib(4) = Fib(3) + Fib(2)   (= 2 + 1 = 3)
    Fib(5) = Fib(4) + Fib(3)   (= 3 + 2 = 5)

and so on. The recursive definition of the Fibonacci numbers is almost simple:

```
Function Fib (N As Integer) As Integer
  If N <= 2 Then
    Fib = 1                'Making negative Fibonacci numbers = 1
  Else
    Fib = Fib(N - 1) + Fib(N - 2)
  End If
End Function
```

21

Note the pattern. The simple case is taken care of first. This is followed by reducing the calculation to a simpler case. Finally, the results of the simpler case or cases are combined to finish the definition. (Also, the Fibonacci numbers were arbitrarily defined at negative N to be 1.)

However elegant this may seem, it turns out to be an incredibly inefficient way to calculate these numbers. See the section "When Not to Use Recursion" later in this chapter for why this is so.

As a final example of a recursive function, consider the calculation of the greatest common divisor (GCD) of two numbers. (For those who have forgotten their high school mathematics, this is defined as the largest number that evenly divides both of them. It's used when you need to add fractions.) Therefore,

◆ GCD(4,6) = 2 (because 2 is the largest number that divides both 4 and 6)

◆ GCD(12,7) = 1 (because no integer greater than 1 divides them both; 1 is the largest "common divisor")

Around 2,000 years ago, Euclid gave the following method of computing the GCD of two integers, a and b:

    If b divides a, then the GCD is b. Otherwise,
        GCD(a,b) = GCD(b, a Mod b)

NOTE: This is usually called the Euclidean algorithm. Algorithms are what programming is ultimately about. More precisely, an algorithm is a method of solving a problem that is both precise (no ambiguity allowed) and finite (the method must not go on forever). In the case of the Euclidean algorithm, since the Mod operation shrinks the integer each time, the process must stop.

Recall that the Mod function gives the remainder you get by dividing *b* into *a*; it's obviously less than *b*. If *a* Mod *b* is zero, then *b* divides *a*. Here is this recursive outline translated into a Visual Basic function:

```
Function GCD (P As Long, Q As Long) As Long
  If Q Mod P = 0 Then
    GCD = P
  Else
    GCD = GCD(Q, P Mod Q)
  End If
End Function
```

Here, the pattern is a trivial case followed by a reduction to a simpler case, with no need to combine results. (Since the Mod function is not restricted to long integers, it's easy enough to change the function to work with short integers as well. The advantage of this is that you can use the preceding code for both kinds of integers by converting the integer to a long integer before calling the function.)

Simple Recursive Procedures

Just as you can have recursive functions, you can have, through the magic of the stack, recursive procedures. A good example of this is a rewritten version of the binary search method for looking through an ordered list:

> If list has length 1
> > then check directly (the simple case)
>
> Else
> > look at the middle of the list
>
> If middle entry is too big Then
> > search the first half
>
> Else
> > search the second half

Note that this outline for a recursive solution is quite close to one's intuitive notion of how to search an ordered list. Here is this outline translated to a procedure:

```
Sub RecursiveBinSearch (X$, A$(), Low as Integer, High As _
Integer)
'LOCAL variable is: Middle
  Dim Middle As Integer
```

```
   If Low >= High Then       'If list is empty or has 1 item
     If A$(Low) = X$ Then
       MsgBox ("Target found at entry " + Str$(Low))
     Else MsgBox ("Target not found!")
     End If
     Exit Sub
   End If

   Middle = (Low + High) \ 2
   If A$(Middle) = X$ Then
     MsgBox ("Target found at entry " + Str$(Middle))
     Exit Sub
   ElseIf A$(Middle) > X$ Then
     RecursiveBinSearch X$, A$(), Low, Middle - 1
   Else
     RecursiveBinSearch X$, A$(), Middle, High
   End If
End Sub
```

To test this, you can use the same techniques as for testing the nonrecursive binary search mentioned in Chapter 10.

Whenever you're trying to understand a recursive program, it's a good idea to think about what is on the stack and what happens when the stack is finally popped. In this case, each "card" on the stack contains

◆ The address of the array

◆ The current values (actually the addresses) of the variables Low and High and the location of a new copy of the local variable Middle

Knowing what is on the stack is also essential when you are debugging a recursive procedure. After all, watching the variables on the stack is useless if you don't know what values they're supposed to have.

Example: Recursive Deletion of Files with a Given Extension
The new File System Objects make it almost trivial to write a program that recursively handles the subdirectories on your disk. For example, as you saw in Chapter 19, the following code deletes all files in a folder that have the extension stored in a variable named TheExtension.

```
Sub DeleteFilesWithExtension(AFolder, TheExtension)
  Dim AFile, TheFiles
  On Error Resume Next
  Set TheFiles = AFolder.Files
  For Each AFile In TheFiles
    If UCase(FSO.GetExtensionName(AFile.Path)) = TheExtension Then
      AFile.Delete
    End If
  Next
End Sub
```

Now we need to make this routine part of a recursive process by applying this routine to all the subfolders of a given directory until we have moved through all the sub-sub-sub-subfolders of a given folder.

Here's the basic code for the recursive routine:

```
Sub MoveToSubFolders(ByVal AFolder, ByVal TheExtension)
  Dim MoreFolders, TempFolder
  DeleteFilesWithExtension AFolder, TheExtension
  Set MoreFolders = AFolder.SubFolders
  For Each TempFolder In MoreFolders
    MoveToSubFolders TempFolder, TheExtension
  Next
End Sub
```

Note the line inside the routine that calls itself:

```
MoveToSubFolders TempFolder, TheExtension
```

This line makes the routine recursive. What happens is VB gives the routine the current folder object (named TempFolder) and then starts the process again. And, of course, it does all the stack management needed for unwinding the chain of calls to the subfolders of subfolders of subfolders without you needing to worry about what is going on under the hood. Here's the code for a project that adds a few input boxes to start the process and converts the main form into a dialog box that displays a count of the folders processed so far. (I'll leave it to you to convert this project to a version that uses the common dialog control to show a File Dialog box instead of input boxes for the user's choice of folders.) (Again the full code may be downloaded from http://www.osborne.com if you don't want to type in all this code!)

```
Begin VB.Form Form1
    BorderStyle     =   3  'Fixed Dialog
    Caption         =   "Recursive File Deletion Demo"
    ClientHeight    =   2496
    ClientLeft      =   36
    ClientTop       =   324
    ClientWidth     =   3744
    ControlBox      =   0    'False
    LinkTopic       =   "Form1"
    MaxButton       =   0    'False
    MinButton       =   0    'False
    ScaleHeight     =   2496
    ScaleWidth      =   3744
    ShowInTaskbar   =   0    'False
    StartUpPosition =   2    'CenterScreen
End
Attribute VB_Name = "Form1"
Attribute VB_GlobalNameSpace = False
Attribute VB_Creatable = False
Attribute VB_PredeclaredId = True
Attribute VB_Exposed = False
```

```
Private FSO As FileSystemObject

Private Sub Form_Load()
Dim TheExtension As String, TheFolder As Folder
Dim WhereToStart As String, YesNo As Integer

  Set FSO = New FileSystemObject

  WhereToStart = InputBox("Please enter the folder or drive to work with--use _
                         C:\ for example")
  Set TheFolder = FSO.GetFolder(WhereToStart)

  TheExtension = InputBox("What extension to delete--don't use a '.', _
                         example: tmp")
  TheExtension = UCase(TheExtension)

  Message = "Are you sure you want to delete ALL files in ALL subdirectories "
  Message = Message & "of " & WhereToStart & " with the extension " & vbCrLf
  Message = Message & vbCrLf & vbTab & vbTab & vbTab & TheExtension
  YesNo = MsgBox(Message, vbYesNo)
  If YesNo = vbYes Then
    Message = "Press Enter or click on OK to start the process. "
    Message = Message & "Note, this can take some time. An information "
    Message = Message & "box will be updated as each directory is processed."
    MsgBox Message
    Show
    Me.MousePointer = vbHourglass
    WorkWithSubFolders TheFolder, TheExtension
  Else
    End
  End If
  MsgBox "Done! Click on OK or press Enter to end."
  End
End Sub

Sub WorkWithSubFolders(ByVal AFolder As Folder, ByVal TheExtension As String)
  Dim MoreFolders As Folders, TempFolder As Folder
  Static TheCount As Integer
  TheCount = TheCount + 1
  Message = "Have worked so far with " & TheCount _
    & " folders."
  Me.Cls
  Me.CurrentX = (ScaleWidth / 2) - (TextWidth(Message) / 2)
  Me.CurrentY = (ScaleHeight / 2) - (TextHeight(Message) / 2)
  Me.Print Message
  KillFilesWithExtensionIn AFolder, TheExtension
  Set MoreFolders = AFolder.SubFolders
  For Each TempFolder In MoreFolders
    WorkWithSubFolders TempFolder, TheExtension
  Next
End Sub

Sub KillFilesWithExtensionIn(AFolder As Folder, TheExtension As String)
  Dim AFile As File, TheFiles As Files
```

```
On Error Resume Next
Set TheFiles = AFolder.Files
For Each AFile In TheFiles
  If UCase(FSO.GetExtensionName(AFile.Path)) = TheExtension Then
    AFile.Delete
  End If
Next
End Sub
```

Example: The Tower of Hanoi

By now you may be thinking that recursion is just a fancy way of avoiding loops. There's some truth to this (see "When Not to Use Recursion" later in this chapter), but there are many problems for which it would be hard to find the loop equivalent. Perhaps the most famous example of this is the "Tower of Hanoi" problem. (As the quote that follows indicates, it was originally called the "Tower of Brahma.") Here's the problem, extracted from *Mathematical Recreations and Essays* by W. W. Rouse Ball and H. S. M. Coxeter (New York: Dover, 1987):

> In the great temple at Benares, says he, beneath the dome which marks the center of the world, rests a brass plate in which are fixed three diamond needles, each a cubit high and as thick as the body of a bee. On one of these needles, at the creation, God placed sixty-four discs of pure gold, the largest disc resting on the brass plate, and the others getting smaller and smaller up to the top one. This is the Tower of Brahma. Day and night unceasingly the priests transfer the discs from one diamond needle to another according to the fixed and immutable laws of Brahma, which require that the priest on duty must not move more than one disc at a time and that he must place this disc on a needle so that there is no smaller disc below it. When the sixty-four discs shall have been thus transferred from the needle on which at the creation God placed them to one of the other needles, tower, temple and Brahmins alike will crumble into dust, and with a thunderclap the world will vanish.

(There's also a famous Arthur C. Clarke story, called "The Nine Billion Names of God," on a similar theme.)

The idea, then, is to transfer the disks one at a time, taking care to never put a larger disk on a smaller one. The explanation that follows continues to use 64 disks, but solving this problem with this many disks would take the priests (or a super computer, for that matter) more time than scientists say the universe has been around or is likely to be around. For n disks, the solution takes $2^n - 1$ steps; for 64 disks, this has 19 digits (approximately 1.844674E+19, according to Visual Basic). The graphically based solution found in the next section limits you to 15 disks, and with that many disks the problem takes about two minutes to solve on a reasonably fast Pentium.

To solve this problem recursively, you need to decide on the "trivial" case—the one that the recursion stops on. Obviously, when the tower is down to 1 disk (height 1), you can just move that disk. Next, you have to find a way to simplify the problem while retaining the same form (and making sure that this process does eventually lead to the trivial case). The key is to note that the bottom disk is irrelevant when you move the first 63 disks from the first tower to any other tower. Since it's larger than any disk, you can just as well regard a peg with it at the bottom as being empty when it comes to moving disks around. Next, note that you can change the destination temporarily if this helps to simplify the problem. Given all this, here's an outline of a solution to the Tower of Hanoi:

> Move the top 63 disks to tower 3 using tower 2 (a simpler case)
> Move the bottom disk to its destination (tower 2)
> Move the top 62 disks to tower 1 using tower 2

(Of course, to move 62 disks is a problem of smaller size. And similar to before, the bottom *two* disks will now if left alone also be irrelevant. So we now move the bottom 61 disks to tower 3 and are left with the 62 disk on tower 1. We then move it to tower 2 so tower 2 has the largest two disks and there are 61 disks to move around.)

Here is procedure code that implements this outline. This procedure only gives directions for a solution:

21

```
Sub SolveTowerOfHanoi (Height As Integer, FromTower As _
Integer, ToTower As Integer, UsingTower As Integer)

  If Height = 1 Then
    Print "Move a disk from tower #"; FromTower; _
"to tower #"; ToTower
  Else
    SolveTowerOfHanoi Height - 1, FromTower, UsingTower, ToTower
    Print "Move a disk from tower #"; FromTower; "to tower
#"; ToTower
    SolveTowerOfHanoi Height - 1, UsingTower, ToTower, FromTower
  End If
End Sub
```

If you've set up a global variable called NumberOfDisks, then to actually see the directions for solving the problem, all you have to do is write

```
SolveTowerOfHanoi NumberOfDisks, 1, 2, 3
```

As mentioned in the outline, the key to this solution is the switch in the destinations between the two procedure calls:

```
SolveTowerOfHanoi Height-1, FromTower, UsingTower, ToTower
```

and

```
SolveTowerOfHanoi Height-1, UsingTower, ToTower, FromTower
```

If this is confusing, try analyzing the stack for the simple case of three disks by "playing computer." Work through this case using the outline and the procedure.

Next, get a printout of the steps by changing the Print statements to Printer.Print statements. Finally, compare your hand solution to the solution that Visual Basic will print out using the preceding program.

A Visual Version of the Towers

While the preceding section gives the directions for solving the problem, it would be much more interesting to have Visual Basic move disks around. The initial screen might look like the one in Figure 21-3.

If you use two forms, you can use the second form for directions and the first for the solution. To follow this discussion, you need to start up a new project and add another form. The second form will need to have the Caption property set to Directions but otherwise needs no special treatment. The directions form would just tell the user about the problem and ask him or her to click a command button to start the project. To get to the screen in Figure 21-3, the first form should have the following properties:

Property	Setting
Caption	Tower of Hanoi/Brahma
BorderStyle	Fixed single (=1)
ControlBox	False
MaxButton	False
MinButton	False
Auto Redraw	True

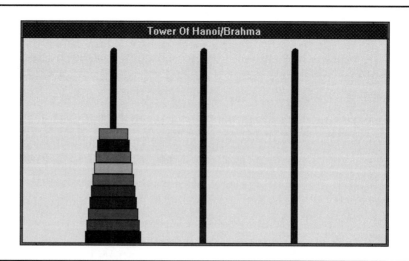

Initial screen for
Tower of
Hanoi/Brahma
Figure 21-3.

Next, add a text box called Disk and set the Index property to zero for this control, thus setting up a control array. Change the Height property to 285 to make the text boxes flatter and make the Text property the empty string. Now, the code to initialize the first form in order to get the screen in Figure 21-3 uses the following in a code module:

```
Sub Init ()
  Dim I As Integer

  HowWide = Form1.ScaleWidth       'global variable
  HowHigh = Form1.ScaleHeight      'ditto
  Form1.Show
  Form1.Cls
  DrawWidth = 9
  For I = 1 To 3
    Line ((I / 4) * HowWide, HowHigh)-((I / 4) * _
HowWide,ScaleTop - 250)
  Next I
  M$ = InputBox$("Number of disks--15 or less?")
  NumberOfDisks = Val(M$)
  Do Until NumberOfDisks > 0 And NumberOfDisks < 16
    M$ = InputBox$("Number of disks--15 or less?")
    NumberOfDisks = Val(M$)
  Loop

  ReDim DiskInfo(NumberOfDisks, 3)
  ' Put Picture boxes

  For I = 1 To NumberOfDisks
    DiskInfo(I, 1) = NumberOfDisks + 1 - I
    Disk(I).Move (HowWide / 4) - 600 + 30 * I, HowHigh - (285 * _
I), 1200 - (65 * I), 285
    Disk(I).BackColor = QBColor(I)
    Disk(I).Visible = True
    Form1.Refresh
  Next I
  DiskInfo(0, 1) = NumberOfDisks
  DiskInfo(0, 2) = 0
  DiskInfo(0, 3) = 0
End Sub
```

The DiskInfo global array will hold the information as to which disks are on which towers. The zeroth position holds the number of disks. Because of the previous For-Next loop, DiskInfo(1,1) holds the number of the bottom disk, DiskInfo(2,1) the number of the second disk, and so on. The Move method is used to stack the disks in the right place.

As the initialization routine showed, you'll need the following global variables in a code module:

```
Global DiskInfo() As Integer
Global HowWide, HowHigh As Single
Global NumberOfDisks As Integer
```

The Form_Load procedure hides the original text box (disk), sets the AutoRedraw property to True, and loads 15 new disks (text boxes) but keeps them invisible. When Visual Basic finishes loading the text boxes (disks), you call a procedure to display the second form with directions:

```
Private Sub Form_Load()
  Disk(0).Visible = 0 : AutoRedraw = True
  For I% = 1 To 15
    Load Disk(I%)
  Next I%
  GiveDirections        'should give the directions
End Sub
```

The Directions form tells the user to click the first form to start the process.

The procedure to actually solve the puzzle replaces the Print statements by a call to a procedure that will move the disks around using the information contained in the DiskInfo( ) array:

```
Sub SolveTowerOfHanoi (Disks As Integer, FromTower As Integer,
ToTower As Integer, UsingTower As Integer)

  If Disks = 1 Then
    MoveADisk FromTower, ToTower
  Else
    SolveTowerOfHanoi (Disks - 1), FromTower, UsingTower, ToTower
    MoveADisk FromTower, ToTower
    SolveTowerOfHanoi (Disks - 1), UsingTower, ToTower, FromTower
  End If
End Sub
```

Now the key MoveADisk procedure replaces the simple Print statement in the solution from the previous section:

```
Sub MoveADisk (FromTower As Integer, ToTower As Integer)
  DiskNumber = DiskInfo(0, FromTower)
  DiskIndex = DiskInfo(DiskNumber, FromTower)
  DiskInfo(DiskNumber, FromTower) = 0
  DiskInfo(0, FromTower) = DiskInfo(0, FromTower) -1
  DiskInfo(0, ToTower) = DiskInfo(0, ToTower) +1
  DiskNumber = DiskInfo(0, ToTower)
  If DiskNumber > NumberOfDisks Then
    Exit Sub
  Else
    DiskInfo(DiskNumber, ToTower) = DiskIndex
  End If

  NewLeft = (HowWide * ToTower / 4) - Disk(NumberOfDisks + 1 - _
  DiskIndex).Width / 2
  NewTop = HowHigh - (DiskNumber * 285)
  Disk(NumberOfDisks + 1 - DiskIndex).Move NewLeft, NewTop
  Form1.Refresh
End Sub
```

The click procedure that starts the process is now pretty simple:

```
Private Sub Form_Click()
   Init
   Form1.Enabled = 0   'no user input needed
   SolveTowerOfHanoi NumberOfDisks, 1, 2, 3
End Sub
```

Recursive Sorts

In Chapter 10, you saw three ways to sort: insertion, ripple, and Shell sorts. Insertion and ripple sorts are good for short lists, and Shell sort is good for moderately sized lists. The sorts you'll see in this section are among the fastest known; they are the sorts of choice for most very large lists.

Merge Sort

The first sort, called merge sort, has the easiest outline. You saw it in the first section of this chapter:

21

> To SORT a LIST
>   If a list has one entry stop
> Otherwise:
>   SORT(the first half)
>   SORT(the second half)
>   Combine (merge) the two

Once you write the merge procedure, the procedure to sort a list is easy. Here's the sort procedure:

```
Sub MergeSort (A$(), Start As Integer, Finish As Integer)

 'LOCAL  Variable is Middle
  Dim Middle As Integer

  If Start < Finish Then
    Middle = (Start + Finish) 2
    MergeSort A$(), Start, Middle
    MergeSort A$(), Middle + 1, Finish
    Merge A$(), Start, Middle, Finish
  End If
End Sub
```

This procedure keeps on splitting the list. When it gets to *n* lists of size 1, the merge procedure combines them into *n*/2 ordered lists of size 2, *n*/4 ordered lists of size 4, *n*/8 ordered lists of size 8, and so on. (At this point, the details have been swept under the rug by moving them to the as-yet-unwritten merge procedure.)

Merging two ordered files (or ordered parts of the same file) is intuitively obvious but a bit tricky to program. What you have to do is set up a temporary array and work your way slowly through the lists, filling up the temporary array with the appropriate entry from one of the two lists. When you're done, you have to write the temporary array back to the original array.

Here's the Merge procedure:

```
Sub Merge (A$(), Start As Integer, Middle As Integer, Finish _
As Integer)
   'local variables are:
   'Temp$(), Begin1, End1, Begin2, End2, TempLocation, I

   ReDim Temp$(Start To Finish)
   Dim  Begin1 As Integer, End1 As Integer, Begin2 As Integer
   Dim  End2 As Integer, TempLocation As Integer, I As Integer
   Begin1 = Start
   End1 = Middle
   Begin2 = End1 + 1
   End2 = Finish
   TempLocation = Start
   Do While Begin1 <= End1 And Begin2 <= End2
     If A$(Begin1) <= A$(Begin2) Then
       Temp$(TempLocation) = A$(Begin1)
       TempLocation = TempLocation + 1
       Begin1 = Begin1 + 1
     Else
       Temp$(TempLocation) = A$(Begin2)
       TempLocation = TempLocation + 1
       Begin2 = Begin2 + 1
     End If
   Loop
   If Begin1 <= End1 Then
     For I = Begin1 To End1
       Temp$(TempLocation) = A$(I)
       TempLocation = TempLocation + 1
     Next I
   ElseIf Begin2 <= End2 Then
     For I = Begin2 To End2
       Temp$(TempLocation) = A$(I)
       TempLocation = TempLocation + 1
     Next I
   End If

   For I = Start To Finish
     A$(I) = Temp$(I)
   Next I
End Sub
```

The Do loop runs through the list that is passed to the procedure. It systematically compares entries in the two parts of the list and moves the smaller one to the temporary list. After every move, it shifts a pointer (TempLocation) that moves one step forward within the temporary list. Similarly, it moves a pointer within a given sublist (either Begin1 or Begin2) whenever it does a swap. The loop constantly checks the status of these pointers to avoid going past the boundaries of the individual sublists.

You get to the If statement following the Do loop when one of the sublists is "used up." This block copies the remainder of the other list to the temporary array.

The final For-Next loop copies the temporary array back to the original array. Without this, the recursion would fail.

Although merge sort is theoretically one of the fastest sorts, in practice the simple formulation just given is not very fast for small or moderate-sized lists. A list of 300 random four-letter strings takes about the same amount of time for insertion sort and merge sort, and both are far slower than Shell sort. However, unlike insertion and ripple sort, doubling the size of the list no longer quadruples the time; it only slightly more than doubles it. Therefore, even this simple formulation of merge sort will be much faster than insertion sort for a list of 1000 items. Shell sort still remains much faster.

TIP: One problem is that copying the temporary array back to the original list takes too much time. If you stick to dynamic arrays, you can speed the program up considerably by using the new assignment feature for dynamic arrays in VB6 (see Chapter 10).

21

The procedure also spends too much time (and stack space) on the trivial cases of lists of sizes one and two. You can dramatically speed up merge sort (and save a lot of stack space) by modifying what the procedure regards as the "trivial case." For example, suppose you directly sort all lists of length one or two by swapping entries as needed. Change the original procedure to the following:

```
Sub MergeSort(A$(),Start As Integer, Finish As Integer)
  'local variables
  Dim Middle As Integer

  If  Finish - Start <= 1 Then
    If A$(Finish) < A$(Start) Then
      'SWAP A$(Finish),A$(Start)
      Temp$ = A$(Finish)
      A$(Finish) = A$(Start)
      A$(Start) = Temp$
    End If
  Else
    Middle = (Start + Finish) \ 2
    MergeSort A$(),Start,Middle
    MergeSort A$(),Middle+1,Finish
    Merge A$(),Start,Middle,Finish
  End If
End Sub
```

Now you are directly swapping the entries when the lists are tiny. The savings are dramatic. For a sort of a few thousand random four-letter combinations, which take 8 seconds for insertion sort and approximately 2.9 seconds for the original version of merge sort, this tweaked version of merge sort takes approximately 2.25 seconds—

around a 20 percent improvement. (Shell sort is still the fastest; it takes approximately 0.6 second.)

Slightly more savings result from modifying the "trivial case" even further. Recall that insertion (or ripple) sort is very fast for small lists (say, lists of size 64 or less). Modify insertion sort's procedure to allow a start and a finish location within the array. Then modify the procedure for the merge sort by rewriting the fundamental procedure, as in the following:

```
Sub MergeSort (A$(), Start As Integer, Finish As Integer)
  If Finish - Start <= 7 Then
    InsertionSort A$(),Start,Finish
  Else
    Middle = (Start + Finish)
    MergeSort A$(),Start,Middle
    MergeSort A$(),Middle+1,Finish
    Merge A$(),Start,Middle,Finish
  End If
End Sub
```

In any case, all these tweaks preserve the essential advantage of the original merge sort—doubling the list still only slightly more than doubles the time needed. Unfortunately, all the versions of merge sort do have one big disadvantage, and ironically this disadvantage shows up only for the very large lists on which merge sort should shine: you need twice as much memory space as is needed for Shell sort because of the temporary array or variant used in the merge procedure. This means that you're likely to run out of memory space for very large lists. It turns out that merge sort is of more theoretical than practical interest in most situations, but see the section "Making Sorts Stable" for these exceptional situations.

Quicksort

As many people have remarked, finding a better general-purpose sort is the "better mousetrap" of computer science. Unfortunately, the best general-purpose sort currently known, usually called Quicksort, unlike the various modifications of merge sort, is not guaranteed to work quickly. In very unlikely situations, it can be the slowest sort of all.

If the merge sort is a "divide-and-conquer" recursion, then Quicksort can be thought of as a "conquer-by-dividing" recursion. To understand this, consider this list of numbers:

5,12,4,9,17,21,19,41,39

The number 17 is in an enviable place: all the numbers to the left of it are smaller than it and all the numbers to the right of it are greater than it. This means that 17 is in the correct position for when this list is sorted. It *partitions* the list and will not have to be moved by any sort. The idea of Quicksort is to create these "splitters" artificially, on smaller and smaller lists. Here's the basic outline:

1. Take the middle entry of a list.
2. By swapping elements within the list, make this element into a splitter. (Note that this element may need to move, and this is the most difficult part to program.)
3. Divide the list into two at the splitter and repeat steps 1 and 2.
4. Continue until all the lists created by making more and more splitters have a size of at most one.

The following code translates this outline into a procedure.

```
Sub QuickSort (A$(), Start As Integer, Finish As Integer)
  'Local variable PosOfSplitter
  Dim PosOfSplitter As Integer

  If finish > Start Then
     Partition A$(), Start, Finish, PosOfSplitter
     QuickSort A$(), Start, PosOfSplitter - 1
     QuickSort A$(), PosOfSplitter + 1, Finish
  End If
End Sub
```

Now you need to write the procedure that forces the splitter. This procedure is subtle and makes Quicksort harder to program than merge sort. Luckily, there are many ways to do this. The one shown here is inspired by insertion sort. You move the splitter "out of the way" first. Next, you start from the left end of the list and look for any entries that are smaller than the splitter. Whenever you find one, you move it, keeping track of how many elements you've moved. When you get to the end of the list, this marker will tell you where to put back the splitter. Here is that procedure. (It assumes you've written a Swap procedure to interchange two elements in the array, fixing the gap in Visual Basic.)

```
Sub Partition (A$(), Start As Integer, Finish As Integer, _
LocOfSplitter As Integer)
   ' LOCAL variables are: SplitPos, NewStart, I, Splitter$
   Dim SplitPos As Integer, NewStart As Integer
   Dim I As Integer, Splitter$

   SplitPos = (start + finish) \ 2
   Splitter$ = A$(SplitPos)
   Swap A$(SplitPos), A$(start)        'get it out of the way
   LeftPos = start                     'needs to be written!
     For I = start + 1 To finish
       If A$(i) < Splitter$ Then
         LeftPos = LeftPos + 1
          Swap A$(LeftPos), A$(i)
       End If
     Next i
   Swap A$(start), A$(LeftPos)         ' LeftPos marks the hole
   LocOfSplitter = LeftPos             ' This gets passed
End Sub                                'to the original procedure
```

Quicksort is usually quite fast. (It will actually be a bit faster if you write the Swap routine inside the module instead of using another procedure.) For example, sorting a list of 2,000 random four-letter strings is roughly on a par with Shell sort. Note that Quicksort is usually faster than Shell sort for larger lists.

However, how fast Quicksort works depends completely on how much the splitter splits; the ideal is when it splits the list in two. If each time you sort the smaller list, the element you are trying to make into a splitter is the smallest (or largest) in the list, then in one of the recursive calls, too little work is done, and in the other, too much is done. This makes Quicksort slow down; for all practical purposes, it becomes a complicated version of insertion sort. If this unfortunate situation should come to pass, you may end up waiting a long time to sort a list of a few thousand entries. Luckily, this worst case is quite unlikely, but it can happen.

To prevent this situation, computer scientists offer some suggestions. The first is that you use an insertion or ripple sort for small lists, much like the tweaked version of the merge sort. (This appears to work best when you use insertion sort or ripple sort on lists of size eight or smaller.) Using an insertion or ripple sort for small lists speeds up the program by around 10 percent. It also saves stack space.

Second, and most important, to eliminate the chance of the worst case happening, don't use the middle element as the potential splitter. One idea is to use the random number generator to find a "random" element on the list. Change the lines

```
SplitPos = (Start + Finish) \ 2
Splitter$ = A$(SplitPos)
```

to

```
SplitPos = Start + Int((Finish - Start+1)*Rnd)
```

Doing this makes it almost inconceivable that you'll end up with the worst case. The problem is that using the random number generator takes time. While it makes the worst case almost inconceivable, it does appear to slow down the average case around 25 percent. On the other hand, if you use this idea in the tweaked version described earlier, the deterioration is much less. This combination seems to cause only a 10 percent reduction, and it's still faster than the original version of Quicksort. Far fewer calls to the random number generator are necessary because Visual Basic is not dealing recursively with small lists. (This is my favorite version of Quicksort.)

Another possibility that many people prefer is to keep on using insertion or ripple sort for small lists but, instead of calling the random number generator to find a candidate for the splitter, use the median of the start of the list, the middle term, and the end of the list. The code for finding the median of three items is simple (and doesn't take very much time).

Making Sorts Stable

Finally, why so many sorts? One reason for presenting them is that they illustrate programming techniques so well, but there's a more serious reason. Although Quicksort and Shell sort are fast, they do have one disadvantage that insertion, ripple, and merge sorts do not have. They are not *stable.* To understand what stability means, suppose you have a list of names and addresses that is already ordered alphabetically by name. Suppose now that you want to re-sort the list by city and state. Obviously, you want the list to be ordered alphabetically by name within each state. Unfortunately, if you use Quicksort or Shell sort, the alphabetical order of the names will disappear. With merge sort, you can preserve the old order within the new.

There is one other way to deal with the problem of making your sorts stable. You can set up an integer array and fill the entries with consecutive integers. These entries serve as pointers to the items in the list you want to re-sort. Next, sort the pointer array using the entries in the original list, but leave the original list intact. This solution requires a lot more programming to print the list in the new order because you have to check both lists at the end. In addition, this solution adds to the space requirement since you need to maintain two arrays instead of one, but it can be faster if you need to move many large entries in an array around.

Fractals

This section depends on an understanding of recursion and trigonometry. The mathematician Benoit Mandelbrot, who coined the term "fractal" and is doing much to show how useful the idea is, begins his book *The Fractal Geometry of Nature* (San Francisco: W. H. Freeman, 1982) with the following:

21

> Why is geometry often described as "cold" and "dry"? One reason lies in its inability to describe the shape of a cloud, a mountain, a coastline, or a tree. Clouds are not spheres, mountains are not cones, coastlines are not circles, and bark is not smooth, nor does lightning travel in a straight line.

A little bit later he goes on to say that these objects are most often "identical at all scales." This is the simplest way to understand fractals; they are objects that, no matter how powerful the magnifying glass, remain essentially the same. The large-scale structure is repeated ad infinitum in the small structure. One of Mandelbrot's standard examples is a coastline: from an airplane, from afoot, or using a magnifying glass, you get the same pattern on an ever-smaller scale. A pseudocode description of a general fractal is

Draw the object in the large
Replace pieces of the large object with smaller versions of itself

This is obviously a description of a recursive process. Before you get to any of the classic fractals, look at Figure 21-4. As you can see, this figure consists of squares, the corners of which are replaced by still smaller squares. The pseudocode for this program might be something like:

Sub Draw A Square
    At each corner of the square
    Draw a square of smaller size,
        Draw a square unless the squares are already too small
End Sub

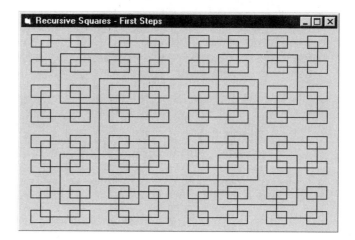

Beginning of
recursive
squares
Figure 21-4.

Here's a Form_Click procedure that implements this outline:

```
Sub Form_Click()
  ' recursive squares
  Scale (-2000, 2000)-(2000, -2000)
  Square -1000, 1000, 2000
End Sub

Sub Square (x, y, Size)
  'To end recursion
  If Size < 50 Then Exit Sub
  Line (x, y)-(x + Size, y - Size), , B    'Draws the large
                                           'square

    Square x - Size / 4, y + Size / 4, Size / 2    'Recursive
                                                   'call
    Square x + Size - Size / 4, y + Size / 4, Size / 2
    Square x - Size / 4, y - Size + Size / 4, Size / 2
    Square x + Size - Size / 4, y - Size + Size / 4, Size / 2
End Sub
```

On each recursion, there are four new corners. Each one is moved one-quarter of the size of the previous one in or out from the previous one and is half as big.

Figure 21-5 is a screen dump of the start of one of the first fractals to be discovered. It's the beginning of a fractal called the Koch Snowflake that you saw in Figure 21-1. As you can see, this consists of a star repeated on an ever-smaller scale. The key to

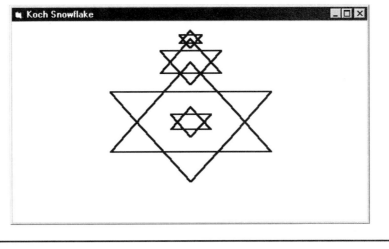

Start of the Koch
Snowflake
Figure 21-5.

programming this is to notice that if you start from the center of the star of, say, size eight, then each vertex has a one-, two-, or four-unit shift in the X or Y level.

Once you understand this, then writing the program only requires setting up an array that, on each call, holds the current values for the 12 vertexes. Here's a fragment that does this:

```
Sub Koch (Xpos, Ypos, size)
' The Koch Snowflake
 'local variables are X(),Y(), shift, i, column
  ReDim x(12), y(12)
  Dim shift As Single, I As Integer
  If size < 4 Then Exit Sub
  shift = size / 8
  x(1) = Xpos: y(1) = Ypos + 4 * shift
  x(2) = Xpos + shift: y(2) = Ypos + 2 * shift
  x(3) = Xpos + 3 * shift: y(3) = y(2)
  x(4) = Xpos + 2 * shift: y(4) = Ypos
  x(5) = x(3): y(5) = Ypos - 2 * shift
  x(6) = x(2): y(6) = y(5)
  x(7) = Xpos: y(7) = Ypos - 4 * shift
  x(8) = Xpos - shift: y(8) = y(5)
  x(9) = Xpos - 3 * shift: y(9) = y(5)
  x(10) = Xpos - 2 * shift: y(10) = Ypos
  x(11) = x(9): y(11) = y(2)
  x(12) = x(8): y(12) = y(2)
  Line (x(1), y(1))-(x(5), y(5))
```

```
      Line -(x(9), y(9))
      Line -(x(1), y(1))
      Line (x(3), y(3))-(x(7), y(7))
      Line -(x(11), y(11))
      Line -(x(3), y(3))
      Koch Xpos, Ypos, 2 * shift
      For I = 1 To 12
        Koch x(i), y(i), 3 * shift
      Next I
    End If
End Sub
```

You might want to experiment by adding color to the routine by changing the ForeColor property. The results can be fascinating.

To actually use this procedure, you need to put this fragment in the event procedure that will start the process:

```
Scale (-100,100) -(100,-100)
Koch 0, 0, 120
```

Other Fractal Curves

To better understand the fractal curves described in this section, observe that there's another way to think of the Koch Snowflake. What you're doing is replacing each straight line segment with a line segment that looks like this:

This idea of continually replacing a straight line with a "bent" line is the key to the next two curves. In the first, usually called a C-curve, you replace each straight line with a bend, like this:

This eventually gives you a figure that looks like the one in Figure 21-6. You can modify the C-curve for the next fractal, called the Dragon curve, by putting the bends on opposite sides. The replacement parts alternately go out and in. The screen in Figure 21-7 shows a picture of what you get. The pseudocode for both these programs is the same:

```
    Sub DrawAFractal with MakeABend
      If the line isn't too small
      Replace the line with the bent one.
        Sub for the smaller line
    End Sub
```

The only point remaining is to describe, mathematically, "making a bend." This is where trigonometry comes in. What you need is a formula that, given a line

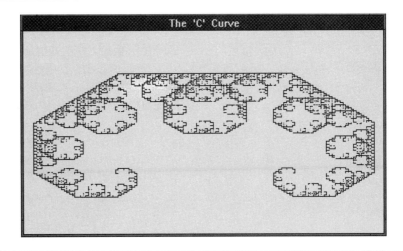

The C-curve
Figure 21-6.

connecting any two points and an angle, finds the coordinates of the new point that gives the bent line. Look at Figure 21-8. Notice that if the angle is 45 degrees, as it is in the C- and Dragon curves, then the size of the spike is

$$COS(45)*D= (SQR(2)/2)*D$$

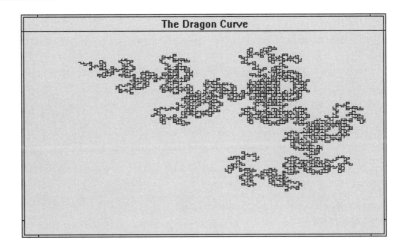

The Dragon
curve
Figure 21-7.

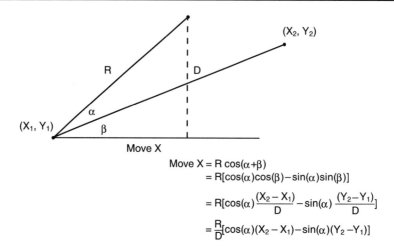

$$\text{Move X} = R\cos(\alpha+\beta)$$
$$= R[\cos(\alpha)\cos(\beta)-\sin(\alpha)\sin(\beta)]$$
$$= R[\cos(\alpha)\frac{(X_2-X_1)}{D}-\sin(\alpha)\frac{(Y_2-Y_1)}{D}]$$
$$= \frac{R}{D}[\cos(\alpha)(X_2-X_1)-\sin(\alpha)(Y_2-Y_1)]$$

The trigonometry of finding a new point
Figure 21-8.

because the triangle is a 45-45-90 right triangle. Using this, the keys to a program for the C-curve are the following MoveX and MoveY functions:

```
Function MoveX (X1!, Y1!, X2!, Y2!) As Single
   ' local variables: Angle(in radians), D, XShift, YShift
   Dim Angle As Single, D As Single
   Dim XShift As Single, YShift As Single
   Angle = Radians(45)
   D = Dist(X1!, Y1!, X2!, Y2!)
   R = (SQR(2) / 2) * D
   XShift = Cos(Angle) * (X2! - X1!)
   YShift = Sin(Angle) * (Y2! - Y1!)

   MoveX = R / D * (XShift - YShift)
End Function

Function MoveY (X1!, Y1!, X2!, Y2!) As Single
   ' local variables: Angle(in radians), D, XShift, YShift
   Dim Angle As Single, D As Single
   Dim XShift As Single, YShift As Single
   Angle = Radians(45)
   D = Dist(X1!, Y1!, X2!, Y2!)
   R = (SQR(2) / 2) * D
   XShift = Sin(Angle) * (X2! - X1!)
   YShift = Cos(Angle) * (Y2! - Y1!)

   MoveY = (R / D) * (XShift + YShift)
End Function
```

Before you can get to the main recursive procedure, you need the distance function and a function to convert to radian measure:

```
Function Dist (X1!, Y1!, X2!, Y2!) As Single
  ' finds the distance between points
  ' local variables are: X, Y
  Dim X As Single, Y As Single
  X = (X2! - X1!) * (X2! - X1!)
  Y = (Y2! - Y1!) * (Y2! - Y1!)
  Dist = SQR(X + Y)
End Function

Function Radians! (X!)
  ' converts degrees to radians
  ' Needs global variable PI = 4*Atn(1)
  Radians! = X! * PI / 180
End Function
```

Next, you have the main (recursive) Sub:

```
Sub Curve (X1!, Y1!, X2!, Y2!)
  Dim DistPt As Single, NX1 As Single, NY1 As Single
  DistPt = Dist(X1!, Y1!, X2!, Y2!)
  If DistPt < 10 Then
    Exit Sub
  End If
  NX1 = X1 + MoveX(X1!, Y1!, X2!, Y2!)        'find the coord for
  NY1 = Y1 + MoveY(X1!, Y1!, X2!, Y2!)        'the spike
  ' If these are in a module, replace Line with FormName.Line
    Line (X1!, Y1!)-(X2!, Y2!), BackColor     'erase previous line
    Line (X1!, Y1!)-(NX1, NY1)                'make the spike
    Line -(X2!, Y2!)
  Curve X1!, Y1!, NX1, NY1                     'now recurse on the
  Curve NX1, NY1, X2!, Y2!                     'spikes
End Sub
```

Here's the rest of the program for the C-curve. First, as commented in the Radians function, you need a form-level variable, Pi, for the value of π. Then all you have to do is set Pi = 4*Atn(1) in the Form_Load procedure and do the following:

```
Private Sub Form_Click()
  Dim X1!, X2!, Y1!, Y2!
  Scale (-500, 500)-(500, -500)
  X1! = -250: Y1! = -200
  X2! = 250: Y2! = -200
  Curve X1!, Y1!, X2!, Y2!
End Sub
```

The nice thing about these kinds of fractals is that all you ever have to do is change the MoveX and MoveY functions. For the Dragon curve, you need to modify them so they alternate sides each time—a perfect situation for static variables. For example, here's what you need to do to modify the MoveX function—the MoveY function is similar and left to you.

```
Function MoveX (X1!, Y1!, X2!, Y2!) As Single
  ' modified mover for Dragon curve
  ' local variables: Angle(in radians), D, XShift, YShift
  Dim D As Single, XShift As Single, YShift As Single
  Static J As Integer
  J = J + 1
  Angle = Radians!(45)
  If J Mod 2 = 0 Then Angle = -Angle:J=0    'alternate on each
                                            'call!
  D = Dist(X1!, Y1!, X2!, Y2!)
  R = (SQR(2) / 2) * D
  XShift = Cos(Angle) * (X2! - X1!)
  YShift = Sin(Angle) * (Y2! - Y1!)
  MoveX = R / D * (XShift - YShift)
End Function
```

The screen in Figure 21-9 shows the result of a program to draw a model of a landscape. Modification of this program can give extremely realistic three-dimensional pictures. Even clicking twice gives a more three-dimensional effect, as you can also see in Figure 21-9. (For example, fractal techniques were used to create the Genesis sequence in the Star Trek movie *The Wrath of Khan.*) The only difference between this and the two preceding curves is that this time the angle is to be random, as is the size of each "spike." To do this, you have to change the Move functions by incorporating a random factor for the angle (instead of 45 degrees) and for the size of the spike (instead of Cos(45*D)). For example, the following listing does this for MoveX:

```
Function MoveX (X1!, Y1!, X2!, Y2!) As Single
  ' local variables: Angle(in radians), D, XShift, YShift
  Dim Angle As Single, D As Single, R As Single
  Dim XShift As Single, YShift As Single
  Angle = Radians!(15 + 60 * Rnd)
  If Rnd(1) > .5 Then Angle = -Angle
  D = Dist(X1!, Y1!, X2!, Y2!)
  R = (.15 + (.6 * RND(1))) * D
  XShift = Cos(Angle) * (X2! - X1!)
  YShift = Sin(Angle) * (Y2! - Y1!)
  MoveX = (R / D) * (XShift - YShift)
End Function
```

Finally, instead of one call that acts recursively on a single line, this time you'll build the shoreline out of three recursive calls to three lines that form a triangle. The following fragment will do this if you add it to the Click routine given above:

```
Scale (-500!, 500!)-(500!, -500!)
X1! = -250: Y1! = 200
X2! = 250: Y2! = 200
Curve X1!, Y1!, X2!, Y2!
Curve X2!, Y2!, 0, -Y2!
Curve 0, -Y2!, X1!, Y1!
```

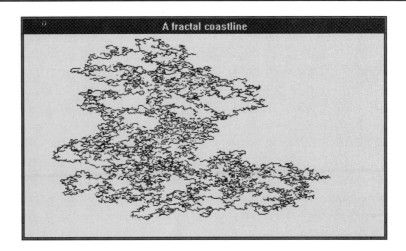

A fractal coastline

A fractal
landscape
Figure 21-9.

21

When Not to Use Recursion

Many of the example programs given in this chapter could have been solved by iteration (writing a loop). To quote Niklaus Wirth, the inventor of Pascal, from his book, *Algorithms + Data Structures = Programs* (Englewood Cliffs, NJ: Prentice Hall, 1976), "...the lesson to be drawn is to avoid the use of recursion when there is an *obvious* solution by iteration" [italics in original].

The reason is that although a recursive procedure is often shorter to write, it almost inevitably takes longer and uses much more memory to run. (You may counter that memory is cheap, but no matter what you do in Visual Basic, the stack is limited to what Visual Basic provides.)

In fact, as Wirth and others have pointed out, what should be the standard examples of when not to use recursion are also the examples most commonly given of recursion: the factorial and the Fibonacci numbers. (They're used as they were in this chapter because they illustrate the techniques well.)

Both the factorial and Fibonacci numbers can be computed more easily and quickly (and using much less memory) by using loops. The factorial is obvious, the Fibonacci numbers only slightly less so. You need to keep track of the previous two Fibonacci numbers, as in the following listing:

```
Function Fib% (n as Integer)
' LOCAL variables are: I, First, Sec, CurrentFib
  Dim First As Integer, Sec As Integer
  Dim I As Integer, CurrentFib As Integer
  If N <= 1 Then
    Fib% = N
    Exit Function
```

```
     Else
        First = 0
        Sec = 1
        For I = 2 To N
           CurrentFib = First + Sec
           First = Sec
           Sec = CurrentFib
        Next I
        Fib% = CurrentFib
     End If
End Function
```

Although you can use the Timer command to demonstrate the difference between the two versions, a more graphic demonstration is obtained by drawing a diagram of how much wasted effort there is in the recursive version of Fibonacci, as shown in Figure 21-10.

Note that to compute Fib(5) recursively, a program has to compute Fib(3) twice, Fib(2) three times, and get to the trivial case (Fib(1)) five times. It never saves the information it so laboriously computes—it just recomputes it constantly.

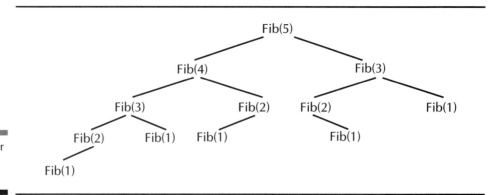

Calls needed for
recursive Fib

Figure 21-10.

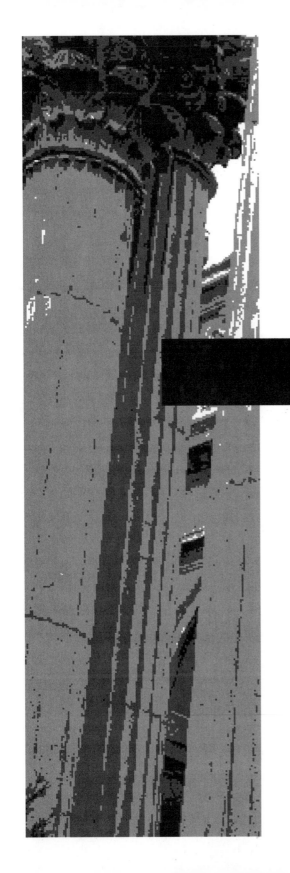

CHAPTER 22

A Survey of Database Development Using Visual Basic

This chapter introduces you to some of VB's database features. The reason I can only give you a survey of VB's power in the database arena in this chapter is that a full treatment of VB's database powers would require a book at least as thick as this one (actually, even thicker would be my guess). Certainly, as you read this chapter, keep in mind that VB6 has much more powerful database-handling features than did earlier versions of VB. And so, even though I can't fully explain these new powers of VB6, it is fair to say that, finally, VB is almost as good at handling giant corporate databases as it has always been at handling smaller "Access-style" databases.

NOTE: In this chapter I'll concentrate on the techniques needed to handle these smaller Access-style databases and so I won't have much to say about the special problems inherent in accessing large corporate databases—databases that are based on SQL Server, ORACLE, or similar server-based databases. In fact, I'll be using the sample Access database stored in the file named Biblio.mdb (found in the \VB directory of most versions of Visual Basic) as the sample database for all the discussions in this chapter.

First, I'll give you a quick look at the ideas behind modern databases. I'll introduce you to the control-based methods for examining data. Then I'll give you a "ten-minute tour" of SQL, the structured query language that is built into most modern databases. I'll show you how to combine basic SQL with various VB controls in order to allow the user to see the results of querying a database. None of this will require much code; almost all the power needed for these tasks can be released by setting a few properties at design or run time. Then, I'll give you a brief introduction to how to use code with databases.

TIP: The source code for the Visual Data Manager add-in, which was written completely in VB, is supplied with many versions of VB. Among its other features, this program lets you build databases easily without having to own a tool like Access. Running this project (or using the add-in) will whet your appetite for what Visual Basic can do. The program is a superb example of the kind of database development you can do with the higher-end versions of Visual Basic. And, after you read this chapter and the appropriate sections of the Programmer's Guide, studying it will teach you a lot about how to program databases using VB.

Finally, a quick search on the Web showed me that there were more than 25 books on database development with VB6 planned or in print. Most of them are (or will be) almost as thick as this book—some will be even thicker. One of the best books for readers who have gotten to this point will certainly be the revision of Jeff McManus' earlier book called *Database Access with Visual Basic* (Ziff-Davis Press).

Some General Words on Modern Databases

Before you start working with database development using VB, it is a good idea to get a feel for what modern databases are all about. Without getting too technical, this section explains what is usually called the *relational model* for a database. This is the model used by Visual Basic, Microsoft Access, and many other programmable PC databases such as FoxPro, as well as the giant corporate databases like ORACLE or SQL Server.

However, let's start with the ideas behind the simpler databases before getting into the more sophisticated relational model of a database. A Rolodex is a good analog for this kind of simpler database, often called a *flat file* database. A flat file database is merely an indexed set of "cards" and can easily be created using the techniques you saw in Chapter 18. Random-access files are ideal in building such databases because they are easy to set up and manipulate and don't require massive resources. Notice that in these databases the data exists in a set form. Indexes are added as a way of quickly getting to specific records, but they are not essential—especially for small sets of data.

The trouble with using only (indexed) random-access files for all database applications is that they are too limited. Suppose, for example, you are running a business. This business maintains a list of customers in one indexed system and a list of bills in another. Someone's address changes; ideally, you would want the address to change in both places automatically. This is impossible without a lot of work, as long as data for each situation is kept in separate databases.

More sophisticated *relational* databases, like the ones you can build with the Visual Data Manager supplied as an add-in to VB or build using code completely with Microsoft Access or Visual Basic's Professional and Enterprise editions, aren't limited to the indexed card model. This makes it easy to avoid the update problem mentioned in the previous paragraph. These databases have many other advantages as well, although the extra power comes at a cost. The extra cost usually will be the need for more powerful computers and more code.

There really is no easy way to describe the underlying structure of the databases that you build using the relational database model. This is true even if it is as simple an example of using a relational database engine as the "Jet" (Access) engine supplied with all versions of Visual Basic. By this I mean you cannot get "under the hood" to see what actually lies on the user's hard disk. In fact, for now, it is best to think of a relational database as a large amount of data that exists in no fixed form; it is merely "out there" in some sort of nebulous glob. (Database vendors use lots of tricks in order to make this blob of data manageable.)

A nebulous blob of data wouldn't be very useful except that you should also think of this data as controlled by an oracle with great powers. These powers let the oracle bring order out of chaos. For example, suppose the database is all the computer books published (or even all books published). You want to ask this oracle a specific question about computer books. There are a lot of computer books out there, many covering the same subject with the same title (as authors well know). There are also a

22

lot of authors out there (as publishers well know). So there is a lot of information out there. The oracle, being very powerful and having lots of storage space, has all possible information about computer books stored away in some form or other—the authors, the titles, the page counts, the publishers, and lots more. The information kept by the oracle could be used in many ways. You might need all books by a specific author, all books with a specific string in the title, all books by a specific publisher, or all books that satisfy the three conditions.

Now, imagine that you ask the oracle a question such as, "Present me with all books published by Osborne/McGraw-Hill in 1998. Show me the title, the author, and the page count." The oracle works through all its data and then presents you with a gridlike arrangement of the books satisfying the question you just asked. Notice that you neither know nor care how the oracle does this—how the information was actually stored and processed. You are satisfied with a grid containing the results that you can easily manipulate.

Next, notice that a random-access file really can't handle this type of situation. For example, suppose you had a single record associated to each author. You would simply have no way of knowing how many fields to add to allow for all of the books by that one author. He or she may continue to write and write. Of course, you could have a separate record for each book, but this forces a lot of duplication—the vital statistics of the author would need to be repeated in the record for each book, for example.

However, if the data is simply out there in some vague formless mass, the oracle can use lots of internal bookkeeping tricks to avoid redundancies, to compress the data, to search through the data, and so on.

In the version of modern database terminology used with VB, the questions you ask are called *queries,* and the grid you are presented with displays the contents of a *recordset*. There are three types of recordsets: *tables, dynasets,* or *snapshots*. The latter two possibilities are sometimes called *views*. The difference between a table and a view is that a table is built into the database structure (which is typically made up of many tables), and a view is the result of a query. The following table lists the three types of recordsets and their characteristics. By knowing these differences you can select the correct type of recordset for the task at hand.

Recordset Type	Contents	Seek/Find	Writable
Table	All rows from a specific table	Seek available with an Index. Find always available	Yes
Dynaset	The rows returned from the query	Find is available	Depends on the query
Snapshot	The rows returned from the query	Find is available	No

NOTE: Seek is virtually instantaneous while the various Find methods (FindFirst, FindNext, FindPrevious, FindLast—see the section on them later in this chapter) may take a while, depending on the number of rows in the recordset. For this reason, using the Table type recordset is the best choice when only one table is represented in the recordset and instant searching is needed. (Of course you will have to index the particular column you will be searching through.)

Okay, back to the oracle: the oracle will respond to different queries with different tables or different views, although there is still only one (potentially huge) database out there made up of many tables. The usual language for asking queries of a relational database is called *SQL* (usually pronounced "es que el" or "sequel"), which stands for *structured query language*. Essentially all of SQL is built into Visual Basic Professional and Enterprise editions, and a very large subset of SQL is built into the Learning edition.

When you make a query, the database engine either sends you a subset of one of the tables that already exists or temporarily creates a new grid (view) in memory by combining data from all the tables it has already stored. Since the grid is made up of a set of records extracted from the database, the object that Visual Basic builds based on your query is called, naturally enough, a RecordSet. Working with the properties and methods of the RecordSet object is how you manipulate the database.

22

How Tables Are Organized and Related

Now, in real life, oracles don't exist and data can't be nebulous. So, as you'll soon see, the data in a database is essentially stored in overlapping tables (grids) that are joined together as needed by the database engine. The columns of these tables are called *fields* and the rows are called *records*. For example, the Biblio.mdb database that we will use in this chapter is designed to maintain information about books. It stores each book's publisher in four tables: There's a table of publishers, and each book's information (which includes the publisher) is in a Titles table, and so on.

To avoid redundancy, the Publishers table gives each publisher a unique ID number. That way, for example, the Titles database can refer to a publisher by the ID number and have that publisher's information stored in only one place in the table of publishers. A field like the publishers' ID number is an example of what is called a *primary key*.

NOTE: Keys are how you relate tables, and it is the ability to relate tables by keys that gave relational databases their name.

Every table should have at least one primary key that is unique. For example, because it is possible for two publishes to share the same name, the designers of the Biblio.mdb database had to come up with a "PubID" field which would artificially associate a unique number with a publisher to identify it.

If you look at Figure 22-1 (a screenshot taken in Access—which is full of great tools for looking at databases), you can see the complete structure of the Biblio.mdb database. As you can see there are actually four tables: Publishers, Titles, Title Authors, and Authors.

In order to avoid redundancy each table is linked to the next table by a primary key as you can see in Figure 22-1. For example, the PubID key field lets us relate the publisher information in the Publisher and Titles tables. This way if we are in the Titles table we can look up the publisher by ID number without having to repeat all the publisher information for each title.

NOTE: Learning how to design databases to avoid redundancy is partially an art and partially a science. Tools that come with databases like Access can help you with this task but you might also want to check out a book called *Database Design For Mere Mortals: A Hands-On Guide to Relational Database Design* by Michael J. Hernandez (Addison Wesley, 1996). Though it is not specific to VB database development, it is full of useful information for a novice database programmer.

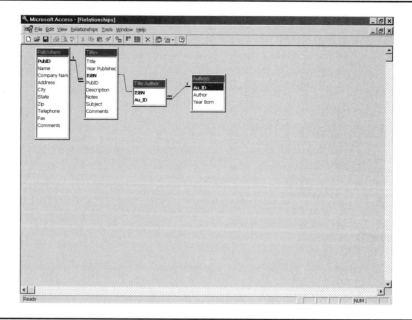

The structure of the Biblio.mdb database

Figure 22-1.

Using the Data Control

There are actually three different versions of the data control supplied with Visual Basic. The intrinsic data control that comes on the standard toolbox uses the Microsoft "Jet" (Access) Database engine. This is the control we will use in this chapter since it works very well with smaller PC based databases, such as those built with Access.

NOTE: The other two data controls are custom controls and would need to be added to your toolbox through the Project|Components dialog box before you can use them. They're called the Remote Data Control and the ADO Data Control. The Remote Data Control is included with VB6 solely for backward compatibility with VB5. The new ADO Data Control is what you would use to talk to large server-based databases. It uses Microsoft's new ActiveX Data Objects (ADO) model. The Data Form Wizard add-in uses ADO.

Luckily, using the basic method of accessing a database, all three data controls work in a similar fashion (they even look the same on your form). So, if you learn how to use the intrinsic data control by reading this chapter, you won't have any trouble moving on to one of the other two data controls.

22

Roughly speaking, here's how a data control works (the next two sections give you some hands-on examples). First, by setting properties of the data control, you hook the data control to a specific database. You can then set a property of the control to grab a table or a view from the database. The data control itself displays no data. Think of the data control as simply conducting the flow of information back and forth between your project and the database. In fact, all the data controls have a set of four buttons that would allow the user to go forward by one, forward to the end, backwards by one, or backwards to the beginning of the recordset.

You can have many data controls in a single project, each of which can be connected to a different database or a different table in the same database or to a query about a database (and so to a recordset). The properties that control this are easy to set at design time but can be set (or reset) at run time as well.

Once you have set up a data control as the conductor, you can then use many of the ordinary Visual Basic controls to display the data. Controls that can work with the data control to access data are said to be *data aware* or *data bound,* and the process of tying a data-aware control to a data control is called *binding* the data-aware control. Many Visual Basic controls are data aware; the way to tell if a specific control is data aware is to see if it has a DataSource property. The DataSource property of the bound control must be set to the name of the data control for each data-aware control. You will therefore need to have added the data control before you set the DataSource property. Only after you set the DataSource property to the name of the data control can the data-aware control display data from the database.

After you have set up the data controls to hook up to the database, it's time to add the data-aware controls to the form and bind them to the data control. Choose the kind of control that best suits the information to be picked up. Use a Picture or Image control if it is a graphical image, or a check box if it is a Boolean. You could use a label or a locked text box if you don't want someone to be able to update it, or an unlocked text box if you do. If you want to get tabular information, use one of the grid controls. If you need to see a whole column use the DataList or DataCombo controls, and so on.

Next, you have to tell the newly data-aware control what table, recordset, or part of a table to get the information from. If it is one of the grid controls, this is done automatically when you set the DataSource property to the data control. If it is a control like the DataList control that can display only one column from a table, this is done by setting the DataField property of the data-aware control to the column's name. If Visual Basic can access the database at design time, then clicking on the down arrow for the DataField property will give you a list of the columns in the RecordSource that are connected by the DataSource property.

Most of the standard controls are data aware. Here's the list of data-aware controls supplied with all versions of Visual Basic. Of the intrinsic controls, the following are data aware:

◆ CheckBox
◆ ComboBox
◆ Image
◆ Label
◆ ListBox
◆ PictureBox
◆ TextBox

Of the custom controls supplied with all versions of Visual Basic, the following are data aware:

◆ DataList
◆ DataCombo
◆ DataGrid
◆ Microsoft Flex Grid
◆ Microsoft Hierarchical FlexGrid
◆ RichTextBox
◆ Microsoft Chart
◆ DateTimePicker
◆ ImageCombo
◆ MonthView

NOTE: The difference between the two flex grid controls and the DataGrid control is that both versions of the flex grid control only allow you to peer into the database—they give snapshots rather than dynasets. The DataGrid control not only allows you to peer into the database, it allows you build up grids and make changes to the database by changing the information displayed in the grid.

Example: Using the MSFlexGrid Control with the Data Control to Look at a Table

About the simplest example of using the data control is to grab a whole table and display the results in the MSFlexGrid control. Since this control gives you a read-only view of a database, you are never in danger of inadvertently changing the contents of the database.

To see an example of this control, start up a new project and then:

1. Add the data control to the form and enlarge it so you can see it a little better.
2. Choose Project|Components and add the MSFlexGrid control to your toolbox.
3. Add an instance of the MSFlexGrid control to your form.
4. Enlarge the MSFlexGrid control and change the Rows and Col properties and the FixedCol and FixedRows properties both to 0. In Figure 22-2, I used 15 rows and 8 columns.

22

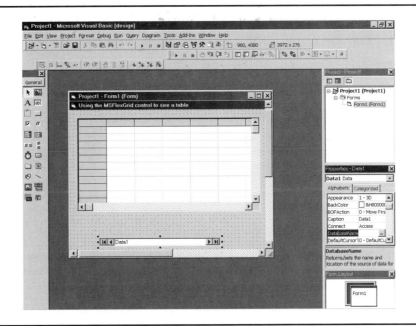

First steps in designing the MSFlexGrid Data View project

Figure 22-2.

Okay. Now we have to hook up the data control to the Biblio.mdb database and then the MSFlexGrid control to a table in the Biblio.mdb database (I'll use the Titles table). The DataBaseName property of the data control determines which database the data control will (try to) connect to. If you go to the Properties window and click the ellipses for the DataBaseName property of the data control, you are presented with a common dialog box to select the database, as shown in Figure 22-3. Notice that you can use the Type list box on the left to change the kind of extensions that are shown. The default is to show only .mdb extensions. For example, if you double-click on the Biblio.mdb file, you will attach this database to the data control (which is what we are trying to do).

Next, you need to set the RecordSource property of the Data control to the specific table or query in the database. You can only do this after you have hooked up the database to the data control by setting the DataBaseName property. For example, using the Biblio.mdb database, you have the choices shown here:

In general, if Visual Basic can find the database determined by the DataBaseName property, it will list the tables and queries in the database when you click the down arrow for the RecordSource property. We want to set this property to Titles so that the MSFlexGrid control will show all the titles in the Biblio.mdb database.

NOTE: You can also set the RecordSource property to an SQL query and so get a view from your database. Please see the section on SQL later in this chapter for an explanation of how to do this.

Finally, we need to hook up the MSFlexGrid control to the data control. For this, set its DataSource property to be the Data1 data control.

That's it. If you run the program, you can see the Titles table in the Biblio.mdb database as shown in Figure 22-4. (Of course, we should have changed the width of the first column so it could show more of the name of the book—but that is easy enough to do using the properties of the MSFlexGrid control you saw in Chapter 11.)

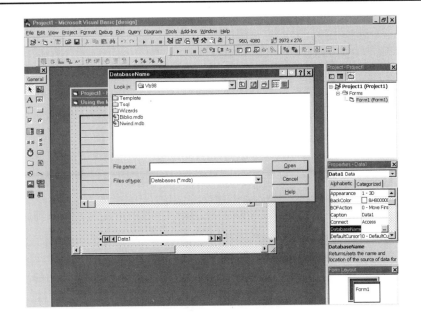

Setting the
DataBaseName
property
Figure 22-3.

22

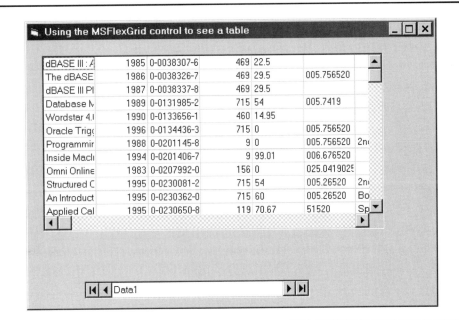

The MSFlexGrid
control
combined with
the data control
Figure 22-4.

Example: Moving Through Records with the Data Control

The data control has the ability to automatically move through the records in the table or recordset that it is connected to. This wasn't necessary in the previous example because we were taking a whole table from the database in one fell swoop. As you can see in Figure 22-2, when you stretch out a data control, there are buttons that resemble the controls on a VCR. As noted in the illustration here, the various arrows move to the beginning of the table, back one record, forward one record, and to the end of the table.

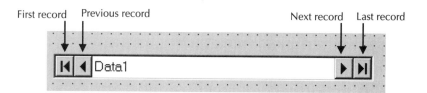

Each time you press one of these arrow keys, any controls on your form that are bound to this data control will be automatically updated. You do not have to write any code for this to take place. In other words, once you set things up properly, a click on one of these buttons would move you to a new record in the database. Note that the same techniques can be used to bind the DataList or DataCombo control to display a specific column extracted from a table.

To see this power of the data control, start up a new project and add a couple of labels and text boxes (text boxes are data aware). Make sure the properties of these controls are as described in the following table. The form should look something like Figure 22-5.

Control	Needed Properties	Settings
Data1	DataBaseName	Biblio.mdb
	RecordSource	Publisher
Text1	DataSource	Data1
	DataField	Name
	Locked	True
Text2	DataSource	Data1
	DataField	Address
	Multiline	True
	Scroll Bars	Vertical
	Locked	True
Label1	Caption	Name
Label2	Caption	Address

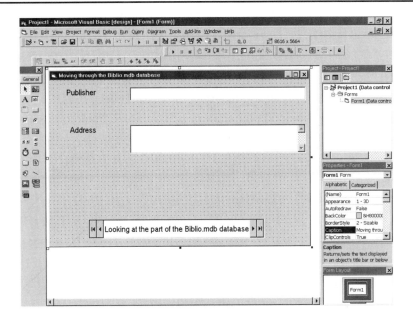

Form for
demonstrating
the move
buttons on the
data control
Figure 22-5.

22

The nice thing is that once you have set this up as indicated in the table, the user can move through the records merely by clicking the arrow keys on the data control. The data control automatically gets the needed information from the database and passes it on to the bound controls. Each click of one of the buttons changes the current record as shown in Figure 22-6. (Think of the current record as being the row that Visual Basic is currently looking at.)

NOTE: Using SQL (see the SQL section later in this chapter), you can even extract specific information from one or more tables and only present those titles.

CAUTION: If data is changed in a bound control and you click an arrow key in the data control to move to a new record, Visual Basic will update the database with this new information. This is why I set the Locked property of the text boxes to be True. Since they are locked you can't change their contents and hence change the Biblio.mdb database. (See the section "Monitoring Changes to the Database," later in this chapter, for more on how to work with updating a database from VB.)

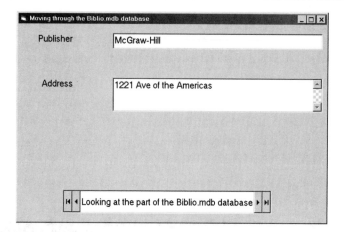

Navigating
through the
database using
the data control

Figure 22-6.

Other Properties of the Data Control Commonly Set at Design Time (for Access-Style Databases)

There are a few properties of the data control that you will commonly set at design time when working with an Access-style database. (Of course, you are just as likely to reset them as needed at run time.) Here are short descriptions of them.

Connect This property specifies the type of database. You do not need to set this property if you are working with a database in Microsoft Access format. The Connect value is usually the name of the data file type (the program), as shown here:

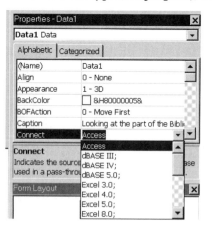

RecordSetType This property determines if what you will get for the recordset is a table, dynaset, or snapshot. Obviously, if you set this to be a snapshot you never have to worry about the user changing the database.

Exclusive Set this True/False property to True and no one else will be able to gain access to the database until you relinquish it by closing the database. The default is False.

BOFAction, EOFAction These two properties (BOF stands for "beginning of file" and EOF is, of course, "end of file") determine what happens when the data control has taken you to the beginning and end of the database. The choices you have are to stay at the beginning (end), move to the first (last) record, or actually add a new record when you are at the end.

DefaultType This property specifies whether the JET engine (Access) or the much more sophisticated ODBC (open database connectivity) model is used. For Access-style databases like the Biblio.mdb you shouldn't change this property!

Setting Properties at Run Time

Setting the various startup properties of the data control is often easier at design time, but this is not always possible. You may not know the name of the database, for example. Here is an example of the code needed to connect to a FoxPro 6.0 database at run time:

```
Data1.DataBaseName = "C:\FOXPRO\DATA\Business"
Data1.Exclusive = True
Data1.ReadOnly = False
Data1.Connect = "FoxPro 6.0"
```

22

Although the Options property can be set at design time, the Options property of the Data control is often set in the Form_Load and reset whenever you access a new table or recordset. This property controls how the data from that table or recordset will be handled. For example, you can deny other users the ability to write or read from the tables that are the sources of the data contained in the table you created. The reason for this parameter is that you must have the ability to control what is happening to the source of your information if, for example, you are going to change it. (Imagine the problems if everyone is changing the same data at the same time!)

There are nine possible options. You can combine the options by adding the relevant constants together. The following table summarizes what will happen if you set a specific option.

Data Constant	Effect
dbDenyWrite	Prohibits users from writing to the source tables.
dbDenyRead	Prohibits other users in a multiuser environment from reading from the source tables.
dbReadOnly	Determines whether users can write to the dynaset created (and so to the tables in the database).
dbAppendOnly	Allows only additions to the RecordSet, not modification of existing records.

Data Constant	Effect
dbInconsistent	A change in one field can affect many rows—even in the join rows.
dbConsistent	(Default.) A change in one field cannot affect the join rows, only one row.
dbSQLPassThrough	When using data controls with a SQL statement in the RecordSource property, sends the SQL statement to an ODBC database, such as a SQL Server or ORACLE database, for processing.
dbForwardOnly	The RecordSet scrolls forward only. The only move method allowed is MoveNext. This option cannot be used on RecordSet objects manipulated with the data control.
dbSeeChanges	Generates a trappable error if another user is changing data you are editing.

Programming with the Data Control

Although you can do many things with the data control without code, only code lets you take full advantage of its powers. However, for the data control in particular, there is no need to go overboard on setting properties at run time with code. This is because although the data control properties *can* be set at run time, it is often easier to set properties such as RecordSource, DataSource, and DataField at design time when the Properties window can help you find the needed information.

To give you an idea of what code for working with the data control will look like, suppose you want to check whether you can update the RecordSet. This is done with code that looks like this:

```
If Data1.RecordSet.Updatable Then
    'RecordSet will be updatable  by  the  user
Else
    'RecordSet is viewable only
End If
```

As you can see, code for working with a data control looks like the code for working with any Visual Basic object. The only difference is that you are actually using a property of the RecordSet object associated with the data control rather than a property of the data control.

Similarly, to determine whether you are before the first or after the last record, you need to use the BOF (beginning of file) and EOF (end of file) properties of the RecordSet. The code might look like this:

```
If Data1.Recordset.BOF Then ….
If Data1.Recordset.EOF Then ….
```

NOTE: In most cases you will be working with properties of the RecordSet object associated with the data control rather than with properties of the data control itself.

In particular, the standard edition of Visual Basic does not allow you to create the necessary database objects such as a RecordSet object independently of the data control. The Professional and Enterprise editions of Visual Basic do allow database objects to be created independently. Think of the RecordSet object as pointing to the underlying table, dynaset, or snapshot that is created by the data control by following a SQL query or by getting a table in the database.

Every click on a button of the data control at run time has a corresponding method of the RecordSet object at run time. The following table summarizes this correspondence for a data control named Data1 using the current RecordSet. (All of these methods change the current record.)

22

Control Action	Data1.Method
Click the ◄	Data1.RecordSet.MoveFirst
Click the ◄	Data1.RecordSet.MovePrevious
Click the ►	Data1.RecordSet.MoveLast
Click the ►	Data1.RecordSet.MoveNext

Structured Query Language (SQL) Basics

There are literally hundreds of books that have hundreds of pages on using SQL. They range from the expected *SQL For Dummies* to one (I kid you not) titled *SQL for Smarties*. This short section can only give you a feel for SQL; experienced users of SQL should just skim it to see how to hook SQL queries up to RecordSet objects.

The idea behind SQL, though, is very simple. The SQL language consists of English-like statements designed to select records from one or more tables in a relational database according to criteria that you give in that SQL statement. Most commonly, SQL criteria use the SQL keyword SELECT followed by one of these keywords: WHERE, SELECT, FROM, HAVING, GROUP BY, or ORDER BY. (By convention, SQL statements are written in all caps, although this is not necessary.) For example, suppose you wanted to work with the table named Publishers in the Biblio.mdb database. This table has four fields: Name, Address, State, and Phone Number.

If a data control (named Data1, for example) had its DataBase property set to Biblio.mdb, you could use the following statement (called a *SQL query*) to set the RecordSource property at *design* or *run time* in order to create a dynaset or snapshot at design time that consists only of the names contained in the Publishers table. (Which you get depends on the RecordSet property.) Here's what it would look like at design time:

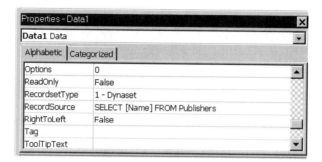

Notice that you don't use the double quotes. If you wanted to do this at run time you could use code like this that would include the quotes (SQL queries are ultimately strings):

```
Data1.RecordSource = "SELECT [Name] FROM Publishers"
```

The FROM statement is required in every SQL SELECT statement. The FROM clause tells Visual Basic which table(s) or query(s) to examine to find the data.

CAUTION: After any query you make at run time you must use the Refresh method to actually get the records you want from the database.

More on SELECT Statements

The SELECT statement usually occurs first in a SQL statement. It is almost inevitably followed by the field names. You can have multiple field names by using a comma between them:

```
Data1.RecordSource = "SELECT [Name], [State] FROM Publishers
```

(Strictly speaking, the brackets around field names are only necessary if the field names have spaces in them. Most people use them all the time because it makes it easier to read the SQL statement.)

When you use a FROM clause to select data from more than one table or query simultaneously, you run the risk of having the same field name occur in two different places. In this case you use a variant on the dot notation that you've already seen for Visual Basic properties to specify which field. For example, if you had a database containing customer IDs (field name CuID) in both the Addresses table and the Orders table and wanted to extract this information from the Addresses table only, you would use

```
Data1.RecordSource = "SELECT [Addresses.CuID] FROM ...Addresses, Orders
```

Finally, you can use an asterisk (*) to say you want all fields from the table:

```
Data1.RecordSource = "SELECT * FROM Publishers"
```

Now suppose you wanted to create a dynaset with even more restrictions, for example, the list of publishers located in New York. This can be done by adding a Where clause to the previous SQL query. It might look like this:

```
Data1.RecordSource = "SELECT [Name] FROM Publishers WHERE State = 'NY'"
```

Notice the single quotes inside the SQL statement. This is how you identify a string inside a SQL statement (which is itself a string).

NOTE: SQL statements must occur on a single line or be a single string.

One way around the problem is to build the string up using the & operator and then assign the RecordSource properties:

```
TheQuery = "SELECT [Name] FROM Publishers "& _
" WHERE State = 'NY'"
Data1.RecordSource = TheQuery
```

22

The WHERE clause can use pattern matching using the LIKE operator:

```
TheQuery = "SELECT [Name] FROM Publishers "& _
"WHERE [State] LIKE 'N*'"
Data1.RecordSource = TheQuery
```

This statement builds a view consisting of all publishers' names from states beginning with the letter "N" (states like Nevada, Nebraska...New Hampshire...New York).

The ORDER BY SQL statement lets you decide how to display the results. For example,

```
TheQuery = "SELECT [Name] FROM Publishers "& _
" WHERE [State] Like 'N*' ORDER BY Name"
Data1.RecordSource = TheQuery
```

would display the publishers alphabetically by Name.

One of the most common tasks with SQL is to take information from two tables and display the results. For this you can also use the FROM and WHERE statements (although Access, and therefore VB, has a non-standard method built into their version of SQL called an Inner Join). For example, the following SQL query along with a little code built up the view in the MSFlexGrid control shown in Figure 22-7 that gives you the publisher's name next to the title.

```
TheQuery = "SELECT Titles.[Title], Publishers.[Name] " & _
 "FROM Publishers, Titles  WHERE Titles.[PubId] = Publishers.[PubID] ORDER
BY Titles.[Title]"
 Data1.RecordSource = TheQuery
```

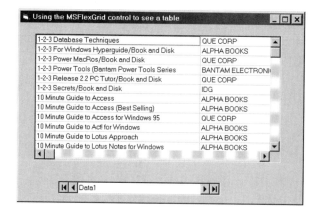

Using the SQL
FROM and
WHERE
statements
together
Figure 22-7.

Here's the .frm file that will activate Figure 22-7:

```
VERSION 5.00
Object = "{5E9E78A0-531B-11CF-91F6-C2863C385E30}#1.0#0"; "MSFLXGRD.OCX"
Begin VB.Form Form1
    Caption         =   "Using the MSFlexGrid control to see a table "
    ClientHeight    =   2496
    ClientLeft      =   48
    ClientTop       =   336
    ClientWidth     =   3744
    LinkTopic       =   "Form1"
    ScaleHeight     =   2496
    ScaleWidth      =   3744
    StartUpPosition =   3   'Windows Default
    Begin VB.Data Data1
        Caption         =   "Data1"
        Connect         =   "Access"
        DatabaseName    =   "C:\Program Files\Microsoft Visual
                            Studio\VB98\Biblio.mdb"
        DefaultCursorType=  0   'DefaultCursor
        DefaultType     =   2   'UseODBC
        Exclusive       =   0    'False
        Height          =   324
        Left            =   960
        Options         =   0
        ReadOnly        =   0    'False
        RecordsetType   =   1    'Dynaset
        RecordSource    =   "SELECT [Name] FROM Publishers"
        Top             =   3720
        Width           =   3972
    End
    Begin MSFlexGridLib.MSFlexGrid MSFlexGrid1
        Bindings        =   "FROM-WHERE demo.frx":0000
        Height          =   3012
```

```
         Left          =    360
         TabIndex      =    0
         Top           =    240
         Width         =    6012
         _ExtentX      =    10605
         _ExtentY      =    5313
         _Version      =    393216
         Rows          =    15
         FixedRows     =    0
         FixedCols     =    0
         AllowUserResizing=   1
    End
End
Attribute VB_Name = "Form1"
Attribute VB_GlobalNameSpace = False
Attribute VB_Creatable = False
Attribute VB_PredeclaredId = True
Attribute VB_Exposed = False
Private Sub Form_Load()
 MSFlexGrid1.ColWidth(0) = 2 * MSFlexGrid1.Width / 3
 MSFlexGrid1.ColWidth(1) = MSFlexGrid1.Width / 3

 TheQuery = "SELECT Titles.[Title], Publishers.[Name] " & _
  "FROM Publishers, Titles  WHERE Titles.[PubId] = Publishers.[PubID] _
 ORDER BY Titles.[Title]"
 Data1.RecordSource = TheQuery
End Sub
```

Finding Records Using SQL

You can use the four SQL Find methods combined with a SQL statement to examine the contents of a current RecordSet attached to a data control. These functions are FindFirst to find the first record, FindLast to find the last record, FindNext to find the next record, and FindPrevious to find the previous record. Here's an example of what this syntax looks like:

DataControlName.RecordSet.FindFirst SQL criterion

NOTE: The standard edition requires you to use this syntax. Only the Professional and Enterprise editions allow you to dimension objects as RecordSet objects that exist independently of the data control.

The SQL criterion for the Find method is what would follow the Where clause in a SQL SELECT statement. For example:

```
Data1.RecordSet.FindFirst "State = 'CA'"
```

Use the NoMatch property of the RecordSet object to determine if a match was found.

22

Modifying a Table's Data Through SQL

To this point you have only seen SQL statements that look through the tables in a database and extract information from them. It is also possible to write *action queries* that actually change data to match the conditions given in a SQL statement. For example, suppose you have a store with a table named Items and fields named Current Price and Placed On Shelf. You want to reduce the current price of all items that have not sold by 10 percent if they have been on the shelf since January 1, 1998. This is the kind of situation for which action queries are ideal. Using an action query is much faster than examining each record to see if it matches the necessary condition. The SQL keywords you need to perform an action query like this are UPDATE and SET combined with the Execute method of the DataBase object. UPDATE tells the Access engine that changes should be made, and the SET keyword tells it which field should be changed and how. The Execute property actually carries out the change (although you could be running a transaction control to buffer this change for possible cancellation, of course).

Here's what the action query for this situation might look like:

```
Dim ActionQuery As String
ActionQuery = "UPDATE [Items] "
ActionQuery = ActionQuery & "SET [Current Price] =
[Current Price]*.9
ActionQuery = ActionQuery & " WHERE [Placed On Shelf] <= 1998"
Data1.Database.Execute ActionQuery
```

Similarly, you can change several fields at the same time by separating them with commas. You can use many other SQL keywords in an action query. Probably the most important, besides UPDATE, is DELETE, which allows the query to delete those records that satisfy certain criteria.

TIP: SQL comes with built-in functions for taking averages, finding maximums and minimums in a field, and a lot more. Consult the online help or a book on SQL for more about what you can do with action queries.

An Introduction to Programming with Database Objects

When Visual Basic works with a database, it does so through the creation of special Visual Basic objects and collections associated with the database. You have already seen the RecordSet object. Analyzing properties of these objects and collections can give you much finer information about the database you are working with. For example, as you know, every Visual Basic collection has the Count property associated with it. You can use the Count property to find out how many tables there are in the database or how many fields there are in a table. You can then write a loop to analyze this information. What follows is a short discussion of the other important Visual Basic objects and collections associated with a RecordSet object.

NOTE: Visual Basic's Professional and Enterprise editions let you create your own objects for working with databases without going through the data control. Even more is true: You will no longer be restricted to using only the collections and other database objects that Visual Basic supplies. In particular, you can write code (like the one in the VisData add-in supplied with VB) that lets you build and manipulate databases to your heart's content. For example, in the Professional and Enterprise editions you can use a statement like

```
Dim Foo As Database
Dim Bar As RecordSet
```

and then use the Set operator together with the OpenDatabase method to tie these object variables to a database or SQL query:

```
Set Foo = OpenDatabase("C:\VB\BIBLIO.MDB").
```

The other point to keep in mind is that VB6 can use Microsoft's new ADO (active data objects) programming model. ADO programming is potentially incredibly powerful, but for Access programmers it is certainly overkill.

22

Regardless of which version of VB you have, however, you can still use the Set command to assign a Database object to a RecordSet object through the medium of the data control. For example:

```
Dim TheBooks as Database
Set TheBooks = Data1.Database
```

or

```
Dim CurrentRecordSet As RecordSet
Set CurrentRecordSet = Data1.RecordSet
```

To store the name of the database, for example, you can use

```
NameOfDBase$ = Data1.Database.Name
```

Similarly, to find out if the database supports transaction control, you can use

```
Dim TransacFlas As Boolean
TransacFlag = Data1.Database.Transactions
```

Or, to find out if the database is updatable (before trying to update a record), you can use

```
Dim UpdateFlag As Boolean
UpdateFlag = Data1.DataBase.Updatable
```

There are a couple of other properties, such as CollatingOrder, which are less important—consult the online help for information on them.

The TableDef Object and TableDefs Collection

Think of a TableDef object as giving the framework of the grid for one of the tables in your database. You can use the DateCreated property of a Table object to find out when it was created and the LastUpdated property to find out when it was last changed. The TableDefs collection, on the other hand, is a property of the Database object and collects all the TableDef objects in the database into a single group.

For example, to print all the names of all the tables in the database on the form and when they were last updated, you can use:

```
Dim I As Integer
For I = 0 To Data1.Database.TableDefs.Count - 1
  Print Data1.Database.TableDefs(I).Name
  Print Data1.Database.TableDefs(I).LastUpdated
Next I
```

The Field Object

The most important object associated with the RecordSet object is the Field object. Think of this as giving you the name and properties of a single column in the grid. By reading or resetting the value of this object you can analyze or update information in the current record of the database. For example, the following line of code might be used to print the name of the author in the current record:

```
Print Data1.RecordSet.Fields("Author")
```

T IP: The default property of the RecordSet object is the Field property. This means you could also use the following line of code:

```
Print Data1.RecordSet("Author")
```

The following table summarizes the most common properties of the Field object. (Check the online help for more information.) To understand this table, you might want to imagine you are at a specific row (the current record) in the database. Also, keep in mind that the Field object refers to a specific column.

Property	What It Tells You
Attributes	What characteristics the field has; for example, is it updatable?
Size	How large the field can be.
Type	What type of data is contained in the field.
Value	What is actually in the row and column.

You can analyze other properties of the data control, RecordSet, or Field object to analyze the database's structural properties. This lets you find out lots of information about the database or RecordSet.

Field objects are also associated with each TableDef object. (In practice, there really isn't that much difference if all you are doing is checking the names of the fields. The main difference is that the Value property of a Field object is only available when a table is bound to a data control, thus creating a RecordSet.)

The Fields collection is the set of all Fields associated with a given TableDef. For example, you can nest the previous loop together with another loop to analyze the fields belonging to all the TableDefs in the database:

```
Dim I As Integer
For I = 0 To Data1.Database.TableDefs.Count - 1
  Print Data1.Database.TableDefs(I).Name
  For J = 0 To Data1.Database.TableDefs(I).Fields.Count - 1
    Print Data1.Database.TableDefs(I).Fields(J).Name
    Print Data1.Database.TableDefs(I).Fields(J).Type
    Print Data1.Database.TableDefs(I).Fields(J).Size
    Print Data1.Database.TableDefs(I).Fields(J).Attributes
  Next J
Next I
```

22

The Index Object and the Indexes Collection

A specific table may have many indexes or it may not be indexed at all. The Name property of the Index object tells you the name used by the database for this object. The Indexes collection is all the indexes for a specific table. Using loops similar to ones you have seen in the previous section, you can map out the Index collection as well.

Other Useful Methods and Events for the Data Control

This section discusses most other methods that you will need to go beyond what the data control can do on its own.

Refresh   The Refresh method, when applied to a data control, opens a database. If you have changed either the DataBaseName, ReadOnly, RecordSet, Exclusive, or Connect properties, you must have Visual Basic process a line of code containing this method. The syntax looks like this:

DataControlName.Refresh

The Refresh method also resets the current record back to the first record (row) in the table or view, and it even refetches the data in case changes were made by other users.

AddNew   The Access database engine maintains a buffer (called the *copy buffer*) where it keeps pending data that it will be writing to the database. The AddNew method clears the copy buffer and moves the current record to the end. (Think of this as potentially adding a new row to the grid.)

Since the copy buffer is empty, you will be able to send new information to the table (and so to the database). The syntax is

DataControlName.RecordSet.AddNew

The AddNew method doesn't actually add the information to the database. This is the function of the Update method discussed next.

TIP: Always make the default that users must confirm that they want the data added (you can let them change this default, of course). Since the AddNew method lets you clear out the information in the copy buffer without actually copying it, use this method if the user doesn't confirm the update operation.

Update   This method actually sends the contents of the copy buffer to the table or dynaset. (You cannot use Update on a snapshot, of course.) The syntax is

DataControlName.RecordSet.Update

Suppose you have a table attached to the Data1 control and want to add a record. You have an Author and a Title field only in this table. The code to add this record might look like this:

```
Data1.RecordSet.AddNew
Data1.RecordSet.Fields("Author") = "Homer"
Data1.RecordSet.Fields("Title") = "Iliad"
Data1.RecordSet.Update
```

If the Update is unsuccessful, Visual Basic generates a trappable error.

NOTE: Any method that moves the current record will cause an automatic update. If the data control is available, pressing any of the arrow buttons will do this.

UpdateControls   Suppose the current record sent data to the bound control and someone changed this data. Since the current record is still current, there ought to be a quick way to have Visual Basic, for instance, refresh the data without needing to actually move forward and backward. This is exactly what the UpdateControls method does.

T IP: Use the UpdateControls method to reset the contents of bound controls to their original values when the user clicks on a Cancel button. (Always provide some method of canceling a database transaction.)

22

Edit   Visual Basic always maintains a pointer into the current table or dynaset. The Edit method copies the current record into the copy buffer for editing. (Just moving to the record doesn't do this.) If the database or RecordSet is read-only or the current record is not updatable, then trying to use this method gives a trappable error.

Suppose you have a table attached to the Data1 control and want to edit the Author field in the current record. Suppose the procedure to allow changes to a specific field (via a custom dialog box, for example) is called ChangeField. Then code to use this method might look like this:

```
Data1.RecordSet.Edit
AuthorName = Data1.RecordSet.Fields("Author")
Call ChangeField(AuthorName)
Data1.RecordSet.Fields("Author") = AuthorName
Data1.RecordSet.Update
```

This code assumes the procedure displays the old name and then, since you are passing by reference (see Chapter 9), you can use the same variable to pass on the new information.

UpdateRecord   If you want to quickly save the contents of the bound controls to the current record, use this method. It is exactly the same as using the Edit method, moving to a different record, and clearing the copy buffer with the Update method, except that this is a little more dangerous because UpdateRecord does not activate the Validate event (see the section of this chapter "Monitoring Changes to the Database").

Delete   This method deletes the current record in the RecordSet. If the RecordSet is read-only, Visual Basic returns a trappable error. This method deletes one record at a time. The syntax is

   DataControlName.RecordSet.Delete

After you delete a record, you must move the record pointer away from the deleted record by a Move method (MoveNext, MoveFirst, and so on). For example, the following code will delete all the records in a table:

```
Data1.RecordSet.MoveFirst
Do While Not Data1.RecordSet.EOF
  Data1.RecordSet.Delete
  Data1.RecordSet.MoveNext
Loop
```

NOTE: The preceding code is probably overkill. You can use SQL statements to delete all records that satisfy specific criteria.

Closing a RecordSet or Database

If you need to close an open database object attached to a data control or close the specific RecordSet currently attached to the control, use the following syntax:

   ObjectName.Close

The ObjectName can be any open database, RecordSet, workspace, dynaset, snapshot, or Table object, or an object variable that refers to one of these objects.

You must use the Update method (if there are changes to the database pending) before you use the Close method. This must be done on all open RecordSet objects before you close the database itself. If you are using the Professional or Enterprise edition and leave a procedure that created a RecordSet or database object, then after the database is closed:

◆   All pending transactions are rolled back.

◆   Any pending changes to the database are lost.

In particular, any unsaved changes are lost.

Putting Bookmarks in a Table

Generally you should not think of a table as being made up of records in a fixed order, because the order can change depending on what index you are using. Nonetheless, there are times when you will want to tag a specific record for quick access at a later time. This is done using the BookMark property of the RecordSet. The idea is that when you are at the record you want to tag, you have Visual Basic process code that looks like this:

```
Dim ABookMark As Variant
ABookMark = Data1.RecordSet.BookMark
```

Now, if you need to get to that record quickly, have Visual Basic process a line of code that looks like this:

```
Data1.Recordset.BookMark = ABookmark
```

Once the preceding line of code is processed, the record specified by the bookmark immediately becomes the current record.

TIP: One common use for a bookmark is to monitor the record that was last modified. You can do this with a line of code that looks like this:

```
Data1.RecordSet.BookMark = Data1.RecordSet.LastModified
```

Example: Cycling Through a Query from a Database Automatically

You now have enough of the methods and properties of the data control to write many useful routines. A good example of tying together all the methods and properties that you have seen is a slide-show routine—a program that cycles through all the records in a table or RecordSet without user intervention. The Timer control makes it easy to do this—just set the Interval property to the space between slides that you desire. Every time the Timer wakes up, the program moves to the next record from the Table or RecordSet. The data control automatically updates the information to a data-bound control. Start up a new project and add a data control, a command button, and two labeled text boxes as shown in Figure 22-8. Set the visible property of all but the command button to be False. (We might as well make the data control invisible since we want the movement through the database to be completely controlled by the timer. The other controls will be made visible in the Click routine.)

22

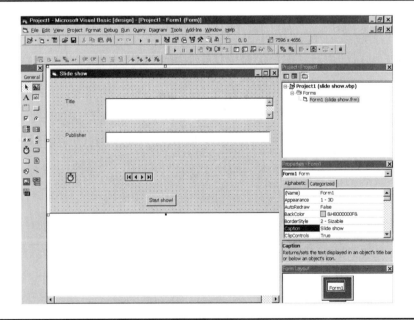

Cycling through the database

Figure 22-8.

A click on the command button activates the Timer control and makes the controls visible. Here's the code for this:

```
Private Sub cmdStartShow_Click()
   Label1.Visible = True
   Label2.Visible = True
   txtPublisher.Visible = True
   txtTitle.Visible = True
   Timer1.Enabled = True
End Sub
```

The code inside the Timer event is

```
Private Sub Timer1_Timer()
   If Data1.Recordset.EOF Then
     Data1.Recordset.MoveFirst
   Else
     Data1.Recordset.MoveNext
   End If
End Sub
```

Finally, the Form_Load sets up the RecordSet and uses the Refresh methods to grab the result of a SQL query.

```
Private Sub Form_Load()
   Dim TheQuery As String
   TheQuery = "SELECT Titles.[Title], Publishers.[Name] " & _
   "FROM Publishers, Titles  WHERE Titles.[PubId] = Publishers.[PubID]"
   Data1.RecordSource = TheQuery
   Data1.Refresh
   txtTitle.DataField = "Title"
   txtPublisher.DataField = "Name"
End Sub
```

T IP: If you use a database that contains graphical images, adding a bound picture box to a form and using the preceding code gives you an easy and efficient method of creating true automatic slide-show demonstrations.

Here's the entire .frm file for this example.

```
VERSION 5.00
Begin VB.Form Form1
   Caption         =    "Slide show "
   ClientHeight    =    4272
   ClientLeft      =    48
   ClientTop       =    336
   ClientWidth     =    7500
   LinkTopic       =    "Form1"
```

```
ScaleHeight      =    4272
ScaleWidth       =    7500
StartUpPosition =    3   'Windows Default
Begin VB.CommandButton cmdStartShow
    Caption          =   "Start show!"
    Height           =   372
    Left             =   3120
    TabIndex         =   4
    Top              =   3720
    Width            =   972
End
Begin VB.Data Data1
    Caption          =   "Data1"
    Connect          =   "Access"
    DatabaseName     =   "C:\Program Files\Microsoft Visual
                         Studio\VB98\Biblio.mdb"
    DefaultCursorType=   0   'DefaultCursor
    DefaultType      =   2   'UseODBC
    Exclusive        =   0   'False
    Height           =   324
    Left             =   2400
    Options          =   0
    ReadOnly         =   0   'False
    RecordsetType    =   2   'Snapshot
    RecordSource     =   ""
    Top              =   3000
    Visible          =   0   'False
    Width            =   972
End
Begin VB.Timer Timer1
    Interval         =   1000
    Left             =   480
    Top              =   3000
End
Begin VB.TextBox txtPublisher
    DataSource       =   "Data1"
    Height           =   372
    Left             =   1800
    TabIndex         =   1
    Top              =   1716
    Visible          =   0   'False
    Width            =   5412
End
Begin VB.TextBox txtTitle
    DataSource       =   "Data1"
    Height           =   696
    Left             =   1800
    MultiLine        =   -1  'True
    ScrollBars       =   2   'Vertical
    TabIndex         =   0
    Top              =   636
    Visible          =   0   'False
    Width            =   5532
End
```

22

Visual Basic 6 from the Ground Up

```
      Begin VB.Label Label2
         Caption         =       "Publisher"
         Height          =       372
         Left            =       480
         TabIndex        =       3
         Top             =       1716
         Visible         =       0       'False
         Width           =       972
      End
      Begin VB.Label Label1
         Caption         =       "Title"
         Height          =       372
         Left            =       480
         TabIndex        =       2
         Top             =       636
         Visible         =       0       'False
         Width           =       972
      End
   End
End
Attribute VB_Name = "Form1"
Attribute VB_GlobalNameSpace = False
Attribute VB_Creatable = False
Attribute VB_PredeclaredId = True
Attribute VB_Exposed = False
Private Sub cmdStartShow_Click()
  Label1.Visible = True
  Label2.Visible = True
  txtPublisher.Visible = True
  txtTitle.Visible = True
  Timer1.Enabled = True
End Sub

Private Sub Form_Load()
 Dim TheQuey As String
 TheQuery = "SELECT Titles.[Title], Publishers.[Name] " & _
 "FROM Publishers, Titles  WHERE Titles.[PubId] = Publishers.[PubID]"
 Data1.RecordSource = TheQuery
 Data1.Refresh
 txtTitle.DataField = "Title"
 txtPublisher.DataField = "Name"
End Sub

Private Sub Timer1_Timer()
  If Data1.Recordset.EOF Then
    Data1.Recordset.MoveFirst
  Else
    Data1.Recordset.MoveNext
  End If
End Sub
```

Monitoring Changes to the Database

To this point all the examples have prevented the user from making changes to any of the bound controls. We did this either by

1. Using locked text boxes.
2. Using the MSFlexGrid control, which only gives snapshots.
3. Explicitly setting the RecordSet property to be a snapshot.

The point, of course, is that any changes you make to bound controls other than the flex grid controls have the potential to ruin the database. All the user has to do is make a change to a bound control and hit one of the Move buttons to move to a new record. The changes they made will then automatically be sent by the data control to the database.

Thus, you will want to *validate* the changes before you let the data control tell the database to make them. Luckily, VB6 has a very easy way to validate the contents of any control when the user leaves that control that is a lot more flexible than using the LostFocus event that you saw way back in Chapter 4.

The Validate event and its associated CausesValidation property are now a part of every control supplied with VB. The idea is that these are triggered *before* the user can shift focus away from that control. For example, you can put validation code in the Validate event of a (unlocked) text box and thereby prevent the user from shifting the focus until the criteria for the shape of the data that you set are satisfied. The framework for a validate event looks like this:

22

> Private Sub *ControlName*_Validate(Cancel As Boolean)
> End Sub

If you set cancel to be True, the user will not be able to leave the control until he or she gets the data right. For example, a simple routine might be:

```
Private Sub Text1_Validate(Cancel As Boolean)
If Len(Text1.Text) = 0 Then
  MsgBox "You forgot to fill in this box"
  cancel = True
End If
End Sub
```

Actually, VB gives you one more line of defense: VB also generate a Validate event for the data control whenever the current record is going to change—for example, by a MoveFirst method or before it processes the Update, Delete, or Close method. The syntax for this event procedure is as follows:

> Sub *DataControlName*_Validate ([Index As Integer,] Action As Integer, _
> *Save* As Integer)

CAUTION: Do not put any method in the Validate event that changes the current record. The result would be an infinite event cascade. The only data-access methods you should put into this event are UpdateRecord and UpdateControls, because neither one generates the Validate event. This gives you a way of updating the database or bound controls in this event procedure.

As always, the optional Index parameter is used if the data control is part of a control array. The Action parameter is sent by Visual Basic to the event procedure and tells what actually caused the Validate event to be generated. Here is a list of the possible values using the symbolic constants built into Visual Basic:

Constant	Cause of Validate Event
vbDataActionMoveFirst	The MoveFirst method.
vbDataActionMovePrevious	The MovePrevious method.
vbDataActionMoveNext	The MoveNext method.
vbDataActionMoveLast	The MoveLast method.
vbDataActionAddNew	The AddNew method.
vbDataActionUpdate	The Update method.
vbDataActionDelete	The Delete method.
vbDataActionFind	The Find method.
vbDataActionBookMark	The Bookmark property was set.
vbDataActionClose	The Close method.
vbDataActionUnload	The form is about to be unloaded.

If you change the Action parameter to

    vbDataActionCancel

then Visual Basic will cancel the operation after it leaves the Sub procedure. In addition, if you change the Action parameter to one of the other values, Visual Basic will actually perform that operation instead of the original operation when the procedure is over. For example, if the Validate event procedure was caused by a MoveFirstMethod and in the course of the Sub procedure you have a line like

```
Action = vbDataActionMoveLast
```

then Visual Basic will actually move the current record to the end of the table. You can only use this possibility if the actions are compatible. For example, you cannot change a MoveFirst action parameter to a vbDataActionUnload parameter without an error.

The Save parameter is either True or False. If any information in the bound data-aware controls has been changed, this parameter is True. This gives you a way of analyzing the information contained in the bound control before updating the database. To determine which data-aware controls were changed, use the DataChanged property of the control. This will be True if the contents of the control were changed and False otherwise.

TIP: To make it easier to determine which controls were changed, set up an array for the data-aware controls on the form in the Form_Load event. That way you can use a loop to run through all the data-aware controls, checking the DataChanged property of each.

Transaction Control

Even if you allow a change to be made to a database, the changes made by Visual Basic need not be irrevocable. You have the ability to keep track of any changes you have made and cancel them if necessary, provided, of course, that the database is sophisticated enough to handle this—Microsoft Access databases certainly can. Consult the documentation of your database to see if it supports *transaction processing,* as this capability is usually called. Transaction processing is among the most sophisticated features you will want to control in your databases.

22

Technically, a *transaction* in database terminology is a sequence of alterations made to a table in the database. What you need to do is tell Visual Basic to store all the transactions it is making so that it can undo them. This is done using the BeginTrans statement discussed next.

BeginTrans   This statement tells Visual Basic to start logging the changes for possible cancellation later on. Once Visual Basic processes this statement, it must process one of the two statements described next in order to continue working with the database.

NOTE: It is possible to nest transactions. This way you can undo small portions of the changes without undoing them all. You can have up to five transaction logs going at the same time.

CommitTrans   This statement tells Visual Basic to go ahead and make the changes. If you are nesting transactions, this closes the innermost transaction log. However, no changes would be made to the actual database until Visual Basic closes all transaction logs.

RollBack   This is the statement you need to undo all the changes made once transaction logging has started (by processing a BeginTrans statement). If you are nesting transactions, this statement closes the innermost log.

The Data Form Wizard

In keeping with its new emphasis on supplying wizards to help you with routine coding, VB comes with a Data Form Wizard that is available as an add-in (it is not available in the New Project dialog box for some reason). You'll need to use the Add-In manager in order to make it available to your existing project. Note that the Data Form Wizard requires that you have an open project.

Using the Wizard should be utterly straightforward *except* that it uses the newer and more complicated ADO (active data objects) programming model for its automatically generated code. It also uses the Microsoft Hierarchical FlexGrid (MSHFlexGrid) control instead of the simpler MSFlexGrid control that I used. Still, programming with ADO and the MSHFlexGrid control is close enough to the programming model you have just seen (for Access style databases with the MSFlexGrid control) that you should be able to understand most of the code generated automatically by the Wizard. In fact, studying the code generated by the Wizard is actually a good way to break into ADO programming. (Although you'll probably also want a book like the one by Jeff McManus that I recommended at the beginning of this chapter.) Figure 22-9 is an example of what you get when you use the Data Form Wizard to generate a database front end.

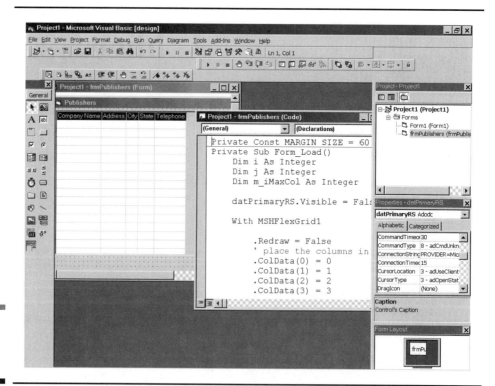

The Result of using the Data Form Wizard
Figure 22-9.

CHAPTER 23

Building Your Own ActiveX Controls

The idea of powerful, reusable controls that are easy to "glue" together with code is the foundation for Visual Basic's success. However, and somewhat ironically, while Visual Basic is the most popular and effective way to use controls, until now Visual Basic couldn't *make* controls. Visual Basic programmers had to rely on C++ programmers for their flour to make their daily bread. No more! Ever since Visual Basic 5 (in all its versions), Visual Basic that can build reusable controls. (In fact, the free Control Creation edition was explicitly designed to allow you to do no more than make controls and test them.)

The controls that you can build follow the new ActiveX specification that Microsoft has made central to its strategy for the desktop, the Internet, and even the intranets that more and more companies are deploying. These controls must be used in Windows 95/98 or Windows NT 3.5 or later; they cannot be used in Windows 3.1 nor in versions of Visual Basic before VB4. However, the controls you build with any version of VB6 are usable in both the 32-bit version of Visual Basic and any version of Visual Basic 5 or 6. Even more is possible: the controls you build can also be used in:

◆   Internet Explorer 3.0 for Windows 95/NT (or later versions)

◆   Microsoft Office 97 components, such as Access 97

◆   Any program that can serve as a container for ActiveX components

(Your controls can even be used in Netscape Navigator once you install the ncompass labs (http://www.ncompasslabs.com) plug-in for Navigator's Windows 95 or NT version.)

In this chapter you'll see how to build a special-purpose text box—one that accepts only numbers. This is an example of the most common kind of control that you can build. Generally, you add more properties and often (as in this case) more events to an existing control. The idea is that the builder of the new *user control* will add new features to an existing control in order to make it more useful. Since there are more than 3,000 ActiveX controls already available, you have lots of controls to extend!

Building a control is a little different from building an application; it requires a different mind-set. For this reason, this chapter is organized a bit differently than the other chapters in this book. What I'll do is lead you through a step-by-step process of building a numeric text box. At each step you *will* have a functioning control—it will just need (lots of) further tweaking in order to make it work the way we want a numeric text box to work.

NOTE: Although the control we build in this chapter consists of only a single text box, you can also build a new control by combining many controls into a single larger control.

Finally, remember that what we do in this chapter covers the most typical way to build a user control. However, you can do a *lot* more; we will only scratch the surface of what is a fairly complex topic. For more information, please consult one of the many books on control creation using Visual Basic. I do want to point out that Visual Basic comes with a couple of wizards that make the next steps easier to perform.

First Steps

Before you start writing code, you need to design the control first. For example, you have to decide what properties, events, and methods your control should expose to its users. Our numeric text box will ultimately have the following properties:

◆ The current value

◆ A minimum acceptable value

◆ A maximum acceptable value

◆ A range value that allows you to easily set a symmetric range (for example -10 to 10)

The text box will have two custom events that the user of the control can use:

◆ BadKey for when the user tries to type something like a letter in the box

◆ BadValue for when the user exceeds the range or copies a non-number into the text box

There will be no methods to this control.

By the way, the methods, events, and properties of your user control are often called its *members*. I will use the "member" shorthand for these elements as well. The members of your control can be public, private, or friend (visible to everything in the same project). The visibility is controlled by your use of the Public, Private, or Friend access specifier in the relevant code.

Start Visual Basic 6 if it is not already running. (All editions of Visual Basic can build user controls.) Choose ActiveX Control from the New Project dialog box. The result looks like Figure 23-1. It should look familiar—it looks like the ordinary Visual Basic environment, except that the title bar for the form in the center of the IDE reads:

Project1 – [UserControl1 (User Control)]

The terminology people use is that we are now working in the *user control designer,* and the form in the middle of the screen is now called a *user control form.* It is the control or controls you place on the user control form and how they interact and react that determine how powerful and useful your user control will be. (The controls you place inside your user control form that give the user control its functionality are often called its *constituent controls,* by the way.)

You manipulate the user control form and its constituent controls the same way that you are now familiar with: simply drop controls from the toolbox, set properties in the Properties window, and then write code in the associated Code window.

23

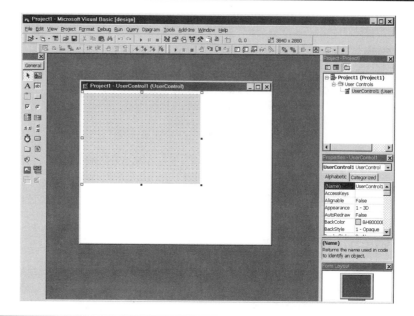

Since UserControl1 is not a very good name for a numeric text box, let's change it to better reflect the object's functionality. For this:

1. Go to the Properties window.
2. Change the name to be NumericTextBox.

As you would expect, the title bar has changed to reflect the new name, as shown here:

Now add a text box to the user control form. This will be the place where users enter the numbers (and after we add some code, they will only be able to enter numbers—that is, after all, the point of the control). Your user control form now looks like this:

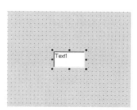

If you want, you can try to adjust the size of the form and the size and position of the text box so that they fit together perfectly like this:

As you will soon see, this is the *wrong* way to proceed in order to make the text box fill up the user control form. But the best way to be convinced of the importance of the resize code that I will soon show you is to try this naive method of making the user control look right.

Testing the Control

The usual way to test a control you have built is to start another project within the Visual Basic environment. This gives you what is usually called a *project group*. For this:

1. Choose File|Add Project.
2. When you see the Project dialog box, choose Standard EXE and click on Open.

At this point, your Project Explorer window in the top right corner should contain two projects, as shown here:

23

NOTE: You could also compile the control into an ocx by choosing File | Make ocx (see Chapter 26). Then you could start another program to test it—even start another copy of Visual Basic. Doing this is usually not necessary except in final testing when you might need to see how the control works in, say, Office. (The reason that you will do this only for final testing is that it is usually much easier to use Visual Basic's new project group feature mentioned earlier.)

Now double-click on Form1 in the Forms folder in the Project Explorer to bring up the test form in this project. Look at where the arrow is pointing in Figure 23-2 (the bottom right corner of the toolbox). You should see a grayed outline of the default icon for a custom control along with a ToolTip that gives its name. (The ToolTip is added automatically by Visual Basic, using the name you gave the user control.) You will see how to add meaningful icons for your custom controls in the next section.

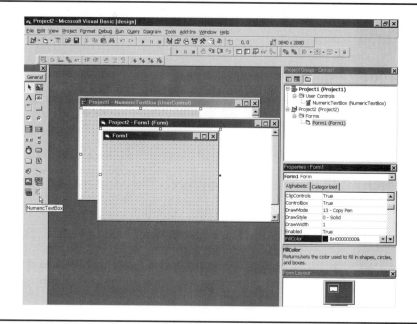

Test form
designer with
inactive control
Figure 23-2.

Suppose you want to use this control now. If you double-click on this control in order to use it, Visual Basic pops up this message box:

This message box sums up the problem: our custom control is currently inactive. This is because the user control designer is still active and, so to speak, it has control of the control. To activate the control:

1. Double-click on the NumericTextBox line in the Project Explorer to make the NumericTextBox designer active.
2. Close the control designer by clicking on the X button in the menu bar (not on the X button in the title bar).

That's it. As soon as you close the ActiveX designer for the user control, Visual Basic brings up the form designer. However, as you can see, the NumericTextBox is now an active icon on the toolbox—the default icon for the user control is no longer grayed.

To use this control, you can simply double-click on its icon in the bottom right corner of the toolbox—this will place the control on Form1. Of course, this control accepts anything, and so it is hardly a numeric text box—yet.

Also note that if you look at the Properties window, this control has no custom properties nor, if you look at the Code window, does it have any custom events. Adding these kinds of features will require a fair amount of code that we will add over the course of the rest of this chapter.

Polishing the Presentation of Your Control

First let's take care of setting the bitmap for the icon for our control. There are lots of tools for creating icons available as shareware or even freeware (http://www.hotfiles.com). Some versions of Visual Basic even come with an icon editor for creating and modifying icons, and most versions of Visual Basic come with hundreds of icons for your use. In any case, once you have created the icon for your control, simply set the ToolboxBitmap property of the user control form to the icon file you want to use. Once you assign this property and compile the control into an ocx, the bitmap is made part of the ocx file, so you don't have to supply it separately to the user of your control.

Although a professional-looking control certainly needs a reasonable icon, the most important issue you need to deal with in a user control is ensuring the proper sizing of your control form with respect to its constituent controls. If you don't make the constituent controls that are inside the form behave properly, your control will look unprofessional. To see the problem at work:

1. Go back to the user control form.
2. Set the background color of the user control form to black (but don't change the color of the text box that is on the user control form).
3. Add your new user control to a test form as described previously.
4. Stretch the user control on the test form.

23

The result is shown in Figure 23-3—pretty ugly isn't it?

The problem is that the constituent TextBox control inside the user control is not resizing itself properly in response to changes in the size of the user control form that contains it *at design time*. Once you reset the background color of the user control form to black, this becomes obvious.

The way to fix the bad behavior shown in Figure 23-3 is in the UserControl_Resize event. This event is triggered whenever the user of your control resizes the control (that is, the user control form) at design time. For example, to fix up the display shown in Figure 23-3 requires adding only two lines of code to the event (the lines shown in bold):

```
Private Sub UserControl_Resize()
  'stretch to width and height of the control
  Picture1.Width = Width
  Picture1.Height = Height
End Sub
```

Now the constituent picture box will always be as wide and as high as its container.

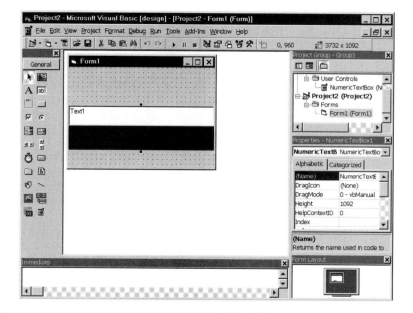

User control at
work with no
resize code
Figure 23-3.

NOTE: For an ordinary form, you would use ScaleHeight and ScaleWidth in similar code. The reason is that ScaleHeight and ScaleWidth give the internal area of an ordinary form—without the title bar and such. Height and Width give the actual height and width, including the title bar. Since user control forms do not have a title bar, it doesn't matter which you choose.

TIP: It is easy to adapt the generic resize code given in Chapter 14 for your user controls that have many constituent controls.

Adding the Functionality

Try typing in the text box. Notice that you can type anything in it. This is not the behavior we expect in a numeric text box! What we need to do is restrict the keys the user can press, as well as what he or she can paste into it. To restrict what the user can type, we write code in the KeyPress event for the text box that is inside the user control. Before we do that, though, we want to add some instance fields to the code of our user control object for bookkeeping.

Here's what I did: first I set up an Enum (enumerated type—see Chapter 10) for the various bad things the user can do, such as try to enter a number that is too large or a non-numeric entry. These will become important when we add custom events and properties.

```
Enum BadThing
  OutOfRange = 1
  NotNumeric
End Enum
```

Then, I set up some default initial values:

```
'Default Values for the property
Const mOriginalValue = 0
Const mOriginalMinValue = -1000
Const mOriginalMaxValue = 1000
Const mOriginalRange = 1000
```

Finally, I set up variables for the instance fields of the user control object:

```
'Private Instance Field Variables:
Dim mValue As Double
Dim mMinValue As Double
Dim mMaxValue As Double
Dim mRange As Variant 'to allow for no range at all
```

23

Restricting Keypresses

Now we need to write the code to restrict keypresses. It is pretty straightforward except for the somewhat complex code needed to check that we have only one decimal point and that the minus sign is at the beginning. Here's what the first pass in the code in this event procedure needs to look like. (We will need to add some more code when we want to add custom events.)

```
Private Sub txtValue_KeyPress(KeyAscii As Integer)
  Static bDecimalPointUsedUp As Boolean
  Static bMinusSignAlready As Boolean
  Select Case KeyAscii
  Case vbKeyBack, vbKeyRight, vbKeyLeft
    'do nothing
  Case Asc("0") To Asc("9")
    ' do nothing
  Case Asc("-")
    If txtValue.SelStart <> 0 Or bMinusSignAlready Then
      KeyAscii = 0
    Else
      bMinusSignAlready = True
    End If
  Case Asc(".")
    If bDecimalPointUsedUp Then
```

```
      KeyAscii = 0
    Else
      bDecimalPointUsedUp = True
    End If
  Case Else
    KeyAscii = 0
  End Select
End Sub
```

Ultimately, the idea of this code is pretty simple: we make sure that the user enters at most one decimal point and the minus sign goes at the beginning.

Restricting Paste Operations

To take into account that the user might paste information from another Windows object into our text box, we put some code in the Change event of the text box as follows (we will modify this event a lot later, when we add custom properties to our control):

```
Private Sub txtValue_Change()
  'check the current value for being a number
  If Not IsNumeric(txtValue.Text) Then
    txtValue.Text = mValue
  Else
    'set the instance variable directly
    mValue = Val(txtValue.Text)
  End If
End Sub
```

Notice that if the value is a number, we store it in the mValue instance fields. (Later on we will add the code to check that the value entered is in the correct range.)

Adding Custom Events

If you have added the code described in the last two sections, you'll see that the control will now only accept numbers. But a control should also raise custom events. For example, I mentioned in the first section of this chapter that I want the control to tell the user of the control when someone types a bad key or puts a non-numeric value into the box. For this we need to add declarations to the user control code that tell Visual Basic that we want to raise custom events. For this:

1. End the program that is using the user control, if it is still running.
2. Move to the Code window for the numeric text box by highlighting the line with NumericTextBox in the Project Explorer and choosing View|Code.
3. Add the following declarations to the (General) section of the user control form.

   ```
   Public Event BadValue(WhatsWrong As Integer)
   Public Event BadKey()
   ```

Note that Public is the default, but you can also have Private or Friend events by using those modifiers. In general, the distinction is as follows:

◆ Public events give the developer using your control the opportunity to react to something.

◆ Private events give your control the opportunity to react to something.

◆ Friend events give the other components of your user control project, but not the user of your control, the opportunity to react to something (relatively rare).

Making the Custom Event Happen

Once we have the declaration for the custom event, we need to modify the code for the KeyPress, Change, and LostFocus events to *raise* the event when the user makes a mistake. For example, here's how the LostFocus event looks:

```
Private Sub txtValue_LostFocus()
  If Not (IsNumeric(txtValue.Text)) Then
    RaiseEvent BadValue(NotNumeric)
  End If
End Sub
```

Notice that we also pass a parameter to the BadValue event that tells the user of our control what kind of BadValue we had, using the enumerated type described earlier. (This is because we will soon add a Range property, and we will want to pass this information to the custom event as well.)

23

Here's how the code in the KeyPress event might look now, with the lines that need to be added in bold:

```
Private Sub txtValue_KeyPress(KeyAscii As Integer)
  Static bDecimalPointUsedUp As Boolean
  Static bMinusSignAlready As Boolean
  Select Case KeyAscii
  Case vbKeyBack, vbKeyRight, vbKeyLeft
    'do nothing
  Case Asc("0") To Asc("9")
    ' do nothing
  Case Asc("-")
    If txtValue.SelStart <> 0 Or bMinusSignAlready Then
      KeyAscii = 0
      RaiseEvent BadKey
    Else
      bMinusSignAlready = True
    End If
  Case Asc(".")
    If bDecimalPointUsedUp Then
      KeyAscii = 0
      RaiseEvent BadKey
    Else
      bDecimalPointUsedUp = True
    End If
```

```
Case Else
   KeyAscii = 0
   RaiseEvent BadKey
End Select
End Sub
```

That's it. We have added the code to *raise* an event whenever the user enters a bad character. To test it, we need to go back to Form1:

1. Close down the user control designer.
2. Go back to the Form1 that contains the user control by double-clicking in the Form1 line of the Project Explorer.
3. Remove the previous instance of the numeric text box and add another one. (Strictly speaking, this isn't necessary, but I find VB sometimes gets confused, so it is worth doing as a safety measure. You only have to remove an instance of an user control when it shows up with cross-hatching in the test form.)
4. Add a new instance of the numeric text box.
5. Choose the control and then choose View Code.
6. Drop down the event list for the numeric text box, as shown here. Notice that there is an event procedure for the BadKey event.

7. Type the following line of code inside the event procedure template.

```
MsgBox "Please enter only integers!"
```

That's it! If you run the program, you'll see that any attempt to make a bad keypress shows in the message box (proving that our control does indeed respond to a custom event).

Adding Custom Properties

Just as the events your user control can raise are those declared with the Public keyword (or no keyword, since Public is the default for a user control), the properties of your control come from the Property procedures you write. The Public Property procedures become the properties of your user control that can be used by the user of your control. The Private Property procedures are for those properties you don't want the user or the other parts of the project to be able to manipulate. The Friend properties are those you do want other parts of your project to manipulate. More precisely, a Public Property Get/Property Let or Public Property Set/Property Let combination becomes a property that the user of your control can both read and write to. Unless you change the Visual Basic defaults, the Public properties are the same properties of your user control that are visible in the Properties window of the IDE when the user of your control adds an instance of that control to his or her form.

Similarly, when you use a Public Property Get procedure without the corresponding Property Set/Let procedure in the code for your control, you have a user-readable read-only property. (It is also possible, as you will soon see, to create read/write properties that can be set only at design time or only at run time.)

NOTE: Although our numeric text box has no methods, the methods that a user of your user control can call are exactly the same Public functions and procedures you write. Any Private functions and procedures you write will never be seen by the user of your control. This lets you hide whatever code was needed to carry out the tasks of the control and furthers encapsulation. And perhaps more important, if you come up with a better way to carry out an internal task, you probably won't break any existing code. The user of the control never sees what you did inside the private code you placed in your user control.

Adding the Properties

As mentioned in the first section of this chapter, I wanted the numeric text box to have a Value property, along with MinValue, MaxValue, and Range properties. Here, for example, is the Property Get/Let pair that gives us a MinValue property. (The MaxValue code is similar.)

```
Public Property Get MinValue() As Double
  MinValue = mMinValue
End Property

Public Property Let MinValue(ByVal New_MinValue As Double)
  If New_MinValue > mMaxValue Then
    MsgBox "Minimum cannot exceed Maximum!"
  Else
    mMinValue = New_MinValue
    PropertyChanged "MinValue"
  End If
End Property
```

Notice how we use the instance variable named mMinValue to maintain the current state of the property. Next, notice in the Property Let, there is one statement that you haven't seen before: a PropertyChanged statement. This kind of statement is absolutely essential when writing any Property Let procedure. If you leave it off, Visual Basic will not be able to keep the Properties window and the property value in sync.

CAUTION: Every Property Let procedure needs a call to the PropertyChanged method.

23

There are actually two ways to change a property via code. The most common is the one you have just seen—indirectly via a change to one or more of the instance variables in your control. This works because the Property procedures themselves have code that reads off the current state of the instance variables that they are concerned with inside themselves. Thus, whenever the Property procedure code is processed, you would see the change. Occasionally, you need to make sure that changes are made directly to a property without waiting for the Property Let to be called at some future time. You would want to do this if changing one property affected other properties that were showing in the Properties window.

An example of this is the Range property of this control. The Range property would let you automatically set up a symmetrical range. If you set the Range to be 50, the MinValue would automatically be –50 and the MaxValue would automatically be +50. We obviously want any change in the Range property to be immediately reflected in what shows in the Properties window for the MinValue and MaxValue properties. The first step in doing this is to directly change the MinValue and MaxValue properties, as in the following code:

```
Public Property Let Range(ByVal vNewValue As Variant)
  If vNewValue = "" Then
    mRange = ""
  ElseIf Not (IsNumeric(vNewValue)) Or vNewValue < 0 Then
    MsgBox "Value must be a positive number!"
  Else
    MinValue = -vNewValue
    MaxValue = vNewValue
    mRange = vNewValue
  End If
  PropertyChanged "Range"
End Property
```

Notice the lines like this:

```
MaxValue = vNewValue
```

This directly changes the value of an associated property and is the best way to keep things in sync.

Finally, once you have created the Property procedures that define your custom properties, changes to the properties are done when the CCE (Control Creation edition) processes the code in your Property Lets and Property Sets.

 TIP: One way to see this at work is to use the debugging techniques described in Chapter 15 to stop execution whenever your version of Visual Basic is processing code inside a Property Let. Then change that property via the Properties window. You would see that Visual Basic really does go to the Property Let any time you change a property.

The Life Cycle of a Control

When you change a property of a user control on a form, you certainly want this information to be preserved in the .frm file. Similarly, if a user loads a .frm file, you need to have your user control use the information about its properties that were preserved in the .frm file. Or, to take it from another angle, we certainly want the Properties window to reflect any changes we make to the properties in the various Property procedures. The key to all this is putting the right code in the "life cycle" events of your user control. Since the details of the life cycle for a user control are a bit strange, we will concentrate on what you need in order to get your controls up and running. First, though, here are the life cycle events for a user control in the order in which they occur:

◆ At birth: Initialize, InitProperties, ReadProperties, Resize

◆ At death: WriteProperties, Terminate

You would most likely use the InitProperties event to read off data from the instance variables to set the initial state of your control. For example, here's the InitProperties procedure for our numeric text box:

```
'Initialize Properties
Private Sub UserControl_InitProperties()
  mValue = mOriginalValue
  mMinValue = mOriginalMinValue
  mMaxValue = mOriginalMaxValue
  mRange = mOriginalRange
End Sub
```

(Since mOriginalRange is a variant, I am allowing for the possibility that the range is not set, by allowing mOriginalRange to be the empty string.)

Next, we need the code that allows us to read and write back the information about the state of the control. For example, we need to read back the information contained in the .frm file for any form that uses our control. This code is placed in the ReadProperties/WriteProperties pair event. The way this works is that Visual Basic uses a gadget called a "PropertyBag" to hold the state of your properties. You don't have to worry about how PropertyBags are implemented; just make sure you always have code like this:

```
'Load property values from storage
Private Sub UserControl_ReadProperties(PropBag As PropertyBag)
  On Error Resume Next
  mMinValue = PropBag.ReadProperty("MinValue", mOriginalMinValue)
  mMaxValue = PropBag.ReadProperty("MaxValue", mOriginalMaxValue)
  Value = PropBag.ReadProperty("Value", mOriginalValue)
End Sub
```

23

```
'Write property values to storage
Private Sub UserControl_WriteProperties(PropBag As PropertyBag)
  On Error Resume Next
  Call PropBag.WriteProperty("MinValue", mMinValue, _
mOriginalMinValue)
  Call PropBag.WriteProperty("MaxValue", mMaxValue, _
mOriginalMaxValue)
  Call PropBag.WriteProperty("Value", mValue, mOriginalValue)
End Sub
```

At the risk of seeming tiresome, I want to emphasize:

> *Every control you create must have code that looks like this.*

In general, you will have one PropBag.WriteProperty and one PropBag.ReadProperty statement for each public property in your control. (The reason you need the On Error Resume Next statement is to take into account that your control may be used in a situation where there is no way to save the current state locally.)

The Full Code for the Numeric Text Box

Here's the full code for the numeric text box so you can see how all the pieces that we have discussed fit together:

```
VERSION 5.00
Begin VB.UserControl NumericTextBox
    ClientHeight    =    336
    ClientLeft      =    0
    ClientTop       =    0
    ClientWidth     =    4800
    ScaleHeight     =    336
    ScaleWidth      =    4800
    Begin VB.TextBox txtValue
        Height          =    330
        Left            =    0
        TabIndex        =    0
        Text            =    "0"
        Top             =    0
        Width           =    1710
    End
End
Attribute VB_Name = "NumericTextBox"
Attribute VB_GlobalNameSpace = False
Attribute VB_Creatable = True
Attribute VB_PredeclaredId = False
Attribute VB_Exposed = True
Option Explicit
Enum BadThing
  OutOfRange = 1
  NotNumeric
End Enum
```

```
Public Event BadValue(WhatsWrong As Integer)
Public Event BadKey()
'Default  Values for the property
Const mOriginalValue = 0
Const mOriginalMinValue = -1000
Const mOriginalMaxValue = 1000
Const mOriginalRange = 1000
'Private Instance Field Variables:
Dim mValue As Double
Dim mMinValue As Double
Dim mMaxValue As Double
Dim mRange As Variant 'to allow for no range at all


Private Sub txtValue_Change()
  'check the current value for being a number
  If Not IsNumeric(txtValue.Text) Then
    RaiseEvent BadValue(NotNumeric)
    txtValue.Text = mValue
    'check the current value for proper range
  ElseIf Val(txtValue.Text) < mMinValue Then
    'raise the BadValue event
    RaiseEvent BadValue(OutOfRange)
    If OutOfRange Then
      'reset to the min value
      txtValue.Text = mMinValue
    Else
      'reset to previous value
      txtValue.Text = mValue
    End If
  ElseIf Val(txtValue.Text) > mMaxValue Then
    'raise the event
    RaiseEvent BadValue(OutOfRange)
    If OutOfRange Then
      'reset to the max value
      txtValue.Text = mMaxValue
    Else
      'reset to previous value
      txtValue.Text = mValue
    End If
  End If
  'set the instance variable directly
  mValue = Val(txtValue.Text)
End Sub

Private Sub txtValue_KeyPress(KeyAscii As Integer)
  Static bDecimalPointUsedUp As Boolean
  Static bMinusSignAlready As Boolean
  Select Case KeyAscii
  Case vbKeyBack, vbKeyRight, vbKeyLeft
    'do nothing
  Case Asc("0") To Asc("9")
    ' do nothing
  Case Asc("-")
```

```
      If txtValue.SelStart <> 0 Or bMinusSignAlready Then
        KeyAscii = 0
        RaiseEvent BadKey
      Else
        bMinusSignAlready = True
      End If
    Case Asc(".")
      If bDecimalPointUsedUp Then
        KeyAscii = 0
        RaiseEvent BadKey
      Else
        bDecimalPointUsedUp = True
      End If
    Case Else
      KeyAscii = 0
      RaiseEvent BadKey
    End Select
End Sub


Private Sub txtValue_LostFocus()
  If Not (IsNumeric(txtValue.Text)) Then
    RaiseEvent BadValue(NotNumeric)
  End If
End Sub

Private Sub UserControl_Resize()
  'stretch to width and height of control
  txtValue.Width = Width
  txtValue.Height = Height
End Sub

Public Property Get Value() As Double
  Value = mValue
End Property

Public Property Let Value(ByVal New_Value As Double)
  If New_Value < mMinValue Then
    MsgBox "Minimum Limit Exceeded!"
    mValue = mMinValue
  ElseIf New_Value > mMaxValue Then
    MsgBox "Maximum Limit Exceeded!"
    mValue = mMaxValue
  Else
    mValue = New_Value
  End If
  txtValue.Text = mValue
  PropertyChanged "Value"
End Property

Public Property Get MinValue() As Double
  MinValue = mMinValue
End Property
```

```vb
Public Property Let MinValue(ByVal New_MinValue As Double)
  If New_MinValue > mMaxValue Then
    MsgBox "Minimum cannot exceed Maximum!"
  Else
    mMinValue = New_MinValue
    PropertyChanged "MinValue"
  End If
End Property

Public Property Get MaxValue() As Double
  MaxValue = mMaxValue
End Property

Public Property Let MaxValue(ByVal New_MaxValue As Double)
  If New_MaxValue < mMinValue Then
    MsgBox "Maximum cannot be less than Minimum!"
  Else
    mMaxValue = New_MaxValue
    PropertyChanged "MaxValue"
  End If
  PropertyChanged "Range"
End Property

Public Property Get Range() As Variant
  Range = mRange
End Property


'Initialize Properties
Private Sub UserControl_InitProperties()
  mValue = mOriginalValue
  mMinValue = mOriginalMinValue
  mMaxValue = mOriginalMaxValue
  mRange = mOriginalRange
End Sub

'Load property values from storage
Private Sub UserControl_ReadProperties(PropBag As PropertyBag)
  On Error Resume Next
  mMinValue = PropBag.ReadProperty("MinValue", mOriginalMinValue)
  mMaxValue = PropBag.ReadProperty("MaxValue", mOriginalMaxValue)
  Value = PropBag.ReadProperty("Value", mOriginalValue)
End Sub

'Write property values to storage
Private Sub UserControl_WriteProperties(PropBag As PropertyBag)
  On Error Resume Next
  Call PropBag.WriteProperty("MinValue", mMinValue, _
mOriginalMinValue)
  Call PropBag.WriteProperty("MaxValue", mMaxValue, _
mOriginalMaxValue)
  Call PropBag.WriteProperty("Value", mValue, mOriginalValue)
End Sub
```

Sample Code for Using the Control

Here's the code for a simple example that uses the control:

```
VERSION 5.00
Begin VB.Form Form1
    Caption         =   "Form1"
    ClientHeight    =   2496
    ClientLeft      =   48
    ClientTop       =   336
    ClientWidth     =   3744
    LinkTopic       =   "Form1"
    ScaleHeight     =   2496
    ScaleWidth      =   3744
    StartUpPosition =   3   'Windows Default
    Begin NumericTest.NumericTextBox NumericTextBox1
        Height      =   372
        Left        =   0
        TabIndex    =   0
        Top         =   1080
        Width       =   3732
        _ExtentX    =   6583
        _ExtentY    =   656
    End
End
Attribute VB_Name = "Form1"
Attribute VB_GlobalNameSpace = False
Attribute VB_Creatable = False
Attribute VB_PredeclaredId = True
Attribute VB_Exposed = False

Enum BadThing
  OutOfRange = 1
  NotNumeric
End Enum

Private Sub NumericTextBox1_BadKey()
  MsgBox "Bad key entry"
End Sub

Private Sub NumericTextBox1_BadValue(b As Integer)
  If b = OutOfRange Then
    MsgBox "Out of permitted range."
  ElseIf b = NotNumeric Then
    MsgBox "Not a number in text box."
  End If
End Sub
```

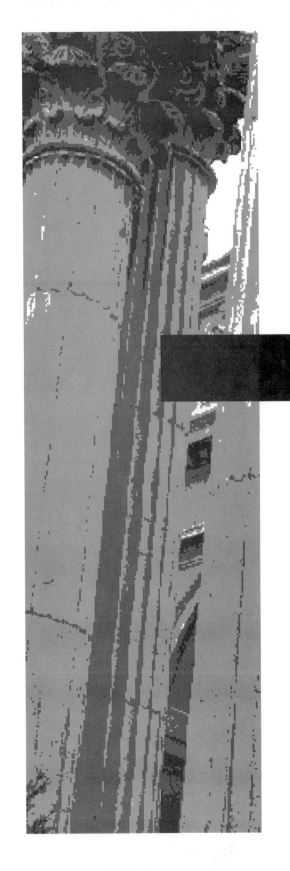

CHAPTER 24

Visual Basic and the Internet: Building a Special-Purpose Browser

Internet Explorer is a capable World Wide Web browser, as is Netscape Navigator. Nonetheless, there are times when it is convenient to have your own special-purpose browser. For example, you might want to disallow people from cruising outside a specific domain, or perhaps you don't want your children looking at http://www.playboy.com. You might want to have the browser be an MDI application rather than the SDI version built into Internet Explorer. The purpose of this chapter is to show you what you need to know about Microsoft's incredibly powerful WebBrowser control so that you will be able to code a special-purpose browser.

Getting Started with the WebBrowser Control

The Web Browser is a custom control so you'll need to go to Project | Components in order to add it to your project. It's the item listed as the Microsoft Internet Controls in this dialog box. To actually use the WebBrowser control, you will need a connection to the Internet using the Internet capabilities of Windows 95/98 or Windows NT. This could be done through a dial-up ISP (Internet Service Provider) using a modem, or via a network at work or school that is directly connected to the Internet. (Actually, having a direct network connection simplifies the procedure for connecting to the Internet considerably.) For example, if you are at work, you probably go through a specialized machine called a Proxy Server. By using special software, the Proxy Server controls what you can download—or even what sites you can connect to. There is also likely to be a specialized piece of hardware called a *router* that manages the communication between the machines on your local net and the Internet. For a dial-up connection, you must have a special program called a WinSock, which comes with modern versions of Windows, to manage the connection.

However, the magic of the WebBrowser control and the Internet is such that all this should be transparent to users once they have connected to the Net. If you or the people using your program are on the Net (or know how to get on the Net), you can almost certainly use the WebBrowser control.

NOTE: I find it easier to be connected to the Internet before starting to run a program that uses the WebBrowser control, although the WebBrowser control will try to connect to the Internet when it starts running.

The WebBrowser control does the following:

1. Take a location you give it
2. Pick up the HTML document there in the form of raw HTML codes
3. Translate the raw HTML document codes into the usual HTML-based Web pages that we have all grown accustomed to seeing

(HTML stands for Hypertext Markup Language—the language in which Web pages are written. Check out one of the hundreds of books on HTML at your local bookstore if you are curious as to how the raw codes work. Tools like Front Page do a pretty good job at hiding the raw HTML from you.)

In its simplest use, think of the WebBrowser control as a special-purpose container control that automatically translates the HTML document that you receive over the Internet or your company's Intranet into the usual visual Web pages that have become so familiar to us all. However, as you will soon see, the WebBrowser control can do a lot more than give you a way to look at Web pages. You can use it to add downloading capability to an application, for example. The WebBrowser control even maintains a history list with the data cached. This means that with a few lines of code, you can let users browse backward and forward almost instantly through pages and sites they have visited in that session. (One could make a good case that most of Internet Explorer is simply this control wrapped in a fancy user interface!)

As you might expect, all this is done by setting properties and using the methods of the WebBrowser control, so we will take up the most important of them next.

 NOTE: The WebBrowser control is necessary for viewing the online help that comes with VB6, so you certainly will have it if you did a standard installation.

Using the WebBrowser Control

The most important method for the WebBrowser control is the Navigate method. This takes a string that is the URL (uniform resource locator) that you want the WebBrowser to display. For example,

24

```
Private Sub Form_Load()
  On Error Resume Next
  WebBrowser.Navigate ("www.microsoft.com")
End Sub
```

would take you to the Microsoft site when a form containing the WebBrowser control was first loaded. (Notice that you don't need the "http://www.microsoft.com" form of the address—the WebBrowser control is smart enough to add this automatically!)

 NOTE: Though usually it is not a good idea to use the On Error Resume Next in your code, the code that manipulates the WebBrowser control (like the user controls from the last chapter) is an exception. This is because many of the WebBrowser control's methods could return an error when there is no error in your code. (For example, the site you want to visit could be down.) For this reason, most programmers use the On Error Resume Next liberally with the WebBrowser control in lieu of trapping all the possible browser errors explicitly.

You can also browse a location on a local disk by giving the full path name for the file in the form of "file://pathname." By including a text box for the URL in your application, you can let the user specify where to go. For example, suppose you had a text box named txtAddress and a command button named cmdGo; then you could use code like this

```
Private Sub cmdGo_Click()
  On Error Resume Next
  WebBrowser.Navigate txtAddress.Text
End Sub
```

to pick up the location to browse to, and then this code will pass this location to the Navigate method. Here's the full code for the Navigate method (of course, you could check whether you want the person to visit that site):

```
Private Sub cmdGo_Click()
  On Error Resume Next
  If InStr("playboy.com", txtAddress.Text) Then
    MsgBox "Sorry that is not a site I want you to visit."
  Else
    WebBrowser.Navigate txtAddress.Text
  End If
End Sub
```

NOTE: By default, the WebBrowser control is hidden when it is first created. Visual Basic reveals it either when you have set the Visible property to True or when you call the Navigate method (or the GoSearch method—see the section "Where Are You?" later in this chapter).

TIP: You can use the Busy property (which returns True or False) to check whether the WebBrowser control is in the process of navigating to a new location or downloading a file. If it is taking too long (or if the user clicks a cancel or stop button), you can use the Stop method to cancel the operation.

Here's the general syntax for the Navigate method:

> *WebBrowserControlName*.Navigate *URL* [*Flags,*] [*TargetFrameName,*] [*PostData,*]
> [*Headers*]

(You could also use an object variable that was set to an instance of the WebBrowser control, of course, in order to shorten the amount of typing you have to do.)

NOTE: There is also a Navigate2 method that not only allows you to visit an URL and a file identified by a full path but also lets you browse special folders, such as Desktop and My Computer.

URL This is the string expression whose value is the address—the "URL" (uniform resource locator) in Internet speak—of the location you want to display. It can also be the full path name of the local HTML file you want to display.

Flags As the brackets indicate, this is an optional parameter. This parameter controls whether you want to keep the location cached or stored in the history list (or both). It also lets you pop up a new browser window with that location displayed. The possible flags are given in the following table, and you add them together to set multiple flags.

Symbolic Constant	Value	Meaning
navOpenInNewWindow	1	Open the location or file in a new window.
navNoHistory	2	Do not add the location to the history list maintained by the control. (The new page replaces the current page in the list.)
navNoReadFromCache	4	Do not try to see if there is a cached copy.
navNoWriteToCache	8	Don't write the HTML page to the local cache.

24

TargetFrameName This optional parameter allows you display the HTML page in a new frame.

PostData This optional parameter is used when you work with HTML forms. For those familiar with HTML forms, if you leave this parameter off, the Navigate method uses the HTML GET method. This parameter is ignored if the URL is not a Web page.

Headers This optional parameter allows you to send additional information to the HTML server that contains the page you are going to download. You could use this if the server you are visiting allows other actions that are specified with the URL request.

Where Are You?

If you are writing a special-purpose browser, it would certainly be convenient to be able to give the user feedback as to where he or she is. You can use the LocationName and LocationURL properties of the WebBrowser control for this. The difference is that if the WebBrowser control is currently displaying an HTML page from the World Wide Web, the LocationName gives the title of that page, and the LocationURL gives the URL. If you are viewing a local HTML page, then LocationName and LocationURL both retrieve the full path name of the folder or file.

For example, the special-purpose browser that you will see at the end of this chapter contains the following code to update the status bar control that displays useful pieces of information.

```
StatusBar1.SimpleText = WebBrowser.LocationURL
```

After a Visit

The WebBrowser control, like Internet Explorer itself, uses part of your RAM and part of your hard disk to store recently visited places. This allows you (unless you set the Flag property in the Navigate method as described in the previous section) to speed up revisiting previously visited locations. The methods used to go backward and forward are easy to remember: they are GoBack and GoForward.

NOTE: You can also use the GoHome method to make the WebBrowser control return to the user's home or start page and the GoSearch method to go to the user's Web searching page. (The WebBrowser control actually uses the information set in the Internet Explorer Preferences dialog box to determine the location of these sites.)

You can also force the WebBrowser control to refresh the page without using the cached version—which is useful for information that changes frequently. This is done with two methods called, naturally enough, Refresh and Refresh2. The difference is that Refresh simply reloads the page that the WebBrowser control is currently displaying, but Refresh2 allows you to send information back to the Web page on the *level* that the Web server should use. The syntax is

   fWebControlReference.Refresh2 *Level*

where the Level parameter can be any one of the symbolic constants described in the following table.

Symbolic Constant	Value	Meaning
REFRESH_NORMAL	0	This is the default.
REFRESH_IFEXPIRED	1	Refresh only if the page has expired.
REFRESH_COMPLETELY	3	This essentially tells the Web server to send the page as if it was the first time. (Technically, this sends a special "header" to the Web server called a "pragma:nocache".)

WebBrowser Events

As with all Visual Basic controls, the WebBrowser control triggers various events at crucial times. You can write code in the associated event procedures to give the user feedback as to what is happening. For example, right before the WebBrowser moves to a new location, it triggers the BeforeNavigate event, whose syntax looks like this:

Private Sub *WebBrowserReference*_BeforeNavigate(ByVal *URL* As String, ByVal *Flags_* As Long, ByVal *TargetFrameName* As String, *PostData* As Variant, ByVal *Headers* As_ String, *Cancel* As Boolean)

The parameters are described in the following table.

Parameter	Meaning
WebBrowserReference	The name of the WebBrowser control or an object variable that is set to it.
URL	The string expression whose value is the URL.
Flags	Not currently used.
TargetFrameName	Used if you are going to display the information in an HTML frame.
PostData	Used for posting data to the Web server.
Headers	These are various headers you can use in advanced HTML programming to send information to the server about you or what you want done.
Cancel	A True/False option. Use True to stop the operation or False to allow it to proceed.

You can monitor progress using the ProgressChange event that is triggered periodically as the downloading continues. Here is the syntax for this event:

Private Sub *WebBrowserControl*_ProgressChange(ByVal *Progress* As Long, _ ByVal *ProgressMax* As Long)

TIP: If the Progress parameter is -1, the operation is over, or you can multiply the value of the Progress parameter by 100 and then divide by the value of ProgressMax to get a percentage of the download completed so far.

DownloadComplete Event

When the download is completed, the DownloadComplete event occurs. It would usually occur because the operation was finished, but it also occurs when you halt the download or when a download fails. This event is always triggered *after* the control

24

starts to go to a URL. (This is different from what happens with the NavigateComplete event, which is triggered only when the Browser successfully navigates to a URL.)

TIP: Any animation or hourglass-like "busy" indicator should be coded in this event.

Putting It All Together

Figure 24-1 shows the form I put together for the special-purpose browser. As you can see, the icons have a similar look as in Internet Explorer. To keep the code short, I didn't add the expected menus, nor did I add any filtering capability (like the filter for http://www.playboy.com described earlier). I'll leave you to customize this project for yourself. As Table 24-1 shows, Figure 24-1 is made up of a bunch of image controls, a status bar on the bottom, a picture box to contain the image buttons, the text box, and the command button.

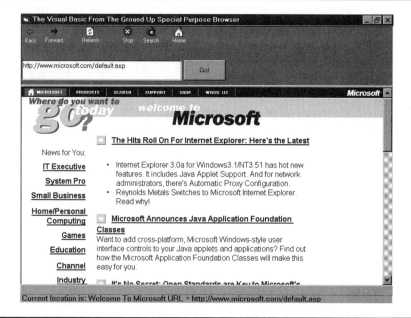

The form window for our special-purpose browser

Figure 24-1.

Type of Control	Name	Container
Web Browser	WebBrowser	
PictureBox	Picture1	
CommandButton	cmdGo	Picture1
TextBox	txtAddress	Picture1
Image	imgRefresh	Picture1
Image	imgStop	Picture1
Image	imgForward	Picture1
Image	imgBack	Picture1
Image	imgPrint	Picture1
Image	imgSearch	Picture1
Image	imgHome	Picture1
StatusBar	StatusBar1	

Controls in our
Special-Purpose
Browser
Table 24-1.

TIP: If you use the Application Wizard to build a WebBrowser application, you get all the standard Internet Explorer icons automatically.

The Full Code for Our Special-Purpose Browser

Here is the .frm file for the special-purpose browser that corresponds to Figure 24-1.

```
VERSION 5.00
Object = "{EAB22AC0-30C1-11CF-A7EB-0000C05BAE0B}#1.0#0"; "SHDOCVW.DLL"
Object = "{6B7E6392-850A-101B-AFC0-4210102A8DA7}#1.1#0"; "COMCTL32.OCX"
Begin VB.Form frmMain
   Caption         =   "The Visual Basic From The Ground Up Special _
Purpose Browser"
   ClientHeight    =   6990
   ClientLeft      =   1890
   ClientTop       =   510
   ClientWidth     =   8475
   LinkTopic       =   "Form1"
   PaletteMode     =   1  'UseZOrder
   ScaleHeight     =   6990
   ScaleWidth      =   8475
   Begin SHDocVwCtl.WebBrowser WebBrowser
      Height       =   3735
      Left         =   0
      TabIndex     =   3
      Top          =   1440
      Width        =   8535
```

24

```
      Object.Height            =    249
      Object.Width             =    569
   AutoSize          =    0
   ViewMode          =    1
   AutoSizePercentage=    0
   AutoArrange       =    -1   'True
   NoClientEdge      =    -1   'True
   AlignLeft         =    0    'False
End
Begin ComctlLib.StatusBar StatusBar1
   Align             =    2    'Align Bottom
   Height            =    615
   Left              =    0
   TabIndex          =    4
   Top               =    6375
   Width             =    8475
   _ExtentX          =    14949
   _ExtentY          =    1085
   Style             =    1
   SimpleText        =    ""
   _Version          =    327680
   BeginProperty Panels {0713E89E-850A-101B-AFC0-4210102A8DA7}
      NumPanels      =    1
      BeginProperty Panel1 {0713E89F-850A-101B-AFC0-4210102A8DA7}
         AutoSize       =    1
         Object.Width          =    14446
         TextSave       =    ""
         Key            =    ""
         Object.Tag            =    ""
      EndProperty
   EndProperty
   BeginProperty Font {0BE35203-8F91-11CE-9DE3-00AA004BB851}
      Name           =    "MS Sans Serif"
      Size           =    9.75
      Charset        =    0
      Weight         =    400
      Underline      =    0    'False
      Italic         =    0    'False
      Strikethrough  =    0    'False
   EndProperty
   MouseIcon         =    "frmBrowser.frx":0000
End
Begin VB.PictureBox Picture1
   Align             =    1    'Align Top
   AutoSize          =    -1   'True
   BackColor         =    &H00808080&
   Height            =    1500
   Left              =    0
   ScaleHeight       =    1440
   ScaleWidth        =    8415
   TabIndex          =    0
   Top               =    0
   Width             =    8475
   Begin VB.CommandButton cmdGo
```

```
        Caption         =     "Go!"
        Default         =     -1    'True
        Height          =     500
        Left            =     4440
        TabIndex        =     1
        Top             =     840
        Width           =     1050
   End
   Begin VB.TextBox txtAddress
        Height          =     500
        Left            =     0
        TabIndex        =     2
        Top             =     840
        Width           =     4140
   End
   Begin VB.Image imgRefresh
        Height          =     525
        Left            =     1560
        Picture         =     "frmBrowser.frx":001C
        Top             =     0
        Width           =     585
   End
   Begin VB.Image imgStop
        Height          =     525
        Left            =     2520
        Picture         =     "frmBrowser.frx":035A
        Top             =     0
        Width           =     585
   End
   Begin VB.Image imgForward
        Height          =     525
        Left            =     600
        Picture         =     "frmBrowser.frx":0698
        Top             =     0
        Width           =     585
   End
   Begin VB.Image imgBack
        Height          =     525
        Left            =     0
        Picture         =     "frmBrowser.frx":09D6
        Top             =     15
        Width           =     585
   End
   Begin VB.Image imgPrint
        Height          =     525
        Left            =     0
        Picture         =     "frmBrowser.frx":0D14
        Top             =     1920
        Width           =     585
   End
   Begin VB.Image imgSearch
        Height          =     525
        Left            =     3120
        Picture         =     "frmBrowser.frx":1052
```

24

```
            Top           =    0
            Width         =    585
        End
        Begin VB.Image imgHome
            Height        =    525
            Left          =    3840
            Picture       =    "frmBrowser.frx":1390
            Top           =    0
            Width         =    585
        End
    End
End
Attribute VB_Name = "frmMain"
Attribute VB_GlobalNameSpace = False
Attribute VB_Creatable = False
Attribute VB_PredeclaredId = True
Attribute VB_Exposed = False
Option Explicit

Private Sub cmdGo_Click()
  On Error Resume Next
  WebBrowser.Navigate txtAddress.Text
End Sub

Private Sub Form_Load()
  On Error Resume Next
  WebBrowser.Navigate ("www.microsoft.com")
End Sub

Private Sub Form_Resize()
  StatusBar1.Height = 1.2 * TextHeight("I")
  WebBrowser.Left = 0
  WebBrowser.Top = Picture1.Height + 25
  WebBrowser.Width = frmMain.ScaleWidth
  WebBrowser.Height = frmMain.ScaleHeight - Picture1.Height - 2 * _
StatusBar1.Height
  cmdGo.Left = txtAddress.Left + txtAddress.Width + 60
  cmdGo.Top = txtAddress.Top
End Sub

Private Sub imgBack_Click()
  On Error Resume Next
  'Navigate backward through the user's history list
  WebBrowser.GoBack
End Sub

Private Sub imgForward_Click()
  On Error Resume Next
  'Navigate forward through the user's history list
  WebBrowser.GoForward
End Sub

Private Sub imgPrint_Click()
  On Error Resume Next
```

```
      WebBrowser.PrintOut
   End Sub

   Private Sub imgRefresh_Click()
      On Error Resume Next
      'Reload the currently displayed URL
      WebBrowser.Refresh
   End Sub

   Private Sub imgSearch_Click()
      'use altavista
      On Error Resume Next
      WebBrowser.Navigate "www.altavista.digital.com"
   End Sub

   Private Sub imgStop_Click()
      On Error Resume Next
      WebBrowser.Stop
   End Sub


   Private Sub webBrowser_BeforeNavigate(ByVal URL As String, ByVal Flags As _
   Long, ByVal TargetFrameName As String, PostData As Variant, ByVal Headers As _
   String, Cancel As Boolean)
      On Error Resume Next
      StatusBar1.SimpleText = "Opening... " & URL
      MousePointer = vbHourglass
   End Sub

   Private Sub webBrowser_DownloadBegin()
      On Error Resume Next
      StatusBar1.SimpleText = "Downloading..."
   End Sub

   Private Sub webBrowser_DownloadComplete()
      On Error Resume Next
      StatusBar1.SimpleText = "Current location is: " & _
   WebBrowser.LocationName & "URL = " & WebBrowser.LocationURL
      MousePointer = vbDefault
   End Sub

   Private Sub webBrowser_FrameBeforeNavigate(ByVal URL As String, ByVal Flags _
   As Long, ByVal TargetFrameName As String, PostData As Variant, ByVal _
   Headers As String, Cancel As Boolean)
      On Error Resume Next
      MousePointer = vbHourglass
      StatusBar1.SimpleText = "Navigating Frame: " & TargetFrameName & " URL -> _
      " & URL
   End Sub

   Private Sub webBrowser_FrameNavigateComplete(ByVal URL As String)
      On Error Resume Next
      MousePointer = vbDefault
      StatusBar1.SimpleText = "Ready"
```

24

```
End Sub

Private Sub webBrowser_FrameNewWindow(ByVal URL As String, ByVal Flags _
As Long, ByVal TargetFrameName As String, PostData As Variant, ByVal _
Headers As String, Processed As Boolean)
  On Error Resume Next
  StatusBar1.SimpleText = "Opening New Frame: " & TargetFrameName & " URL _
  -> " & URL
End Sub

Private Sub webBrowser_NavigateComplete(ByVal URL As String)
  On Error Resume Next
  StatusBar1.SimpleText = WebBrowser.LocationURL
  txtAddress.Text = URL
End Sub
```

Possible Improvements for Our Browser

The next step in enhancing this special-purpose browser would be to not only vet the URLs for improper sites but also to check the *content* of the page—and all this should occur *before* you ask the WebBrowser control to display the page. You can do this with the Internet Transfer control (MSINET.ocx). This is a custom control, so you will need to go to Project Components in order to add it. This control can automatically handle the two most common protocols used in the Internet:

◆ FTP (file transfer protocol)—used for sending files across the Net

◆ HTTP (hypertext transfer protocol)—used for sending hypertext files across the Net

◆ The basic way to use this control is trivial; simply use the OpenURL method of this control along with a string that identifies a valid URL in order to get the information on that page *in the form of raw HTML*.

To see this control at work, try the following:

1. Add a multiline text box to a blank form in a new project.
2. Make sure the Internet Transfer has been added to your Toolbox via Project | Components.
3. Add the Internet Transfer control to the form.

Now make the Form_Load read:

```
Sub Form_Load()
  Show
  WindowState = 2
  Text1.Font.Size = 12
  Text1.Width = ScaleWidth
  Text1.Height = ScaleHeight
  Text1.Text = Inet1.OpenURL("http://www.yahoo.com")
End Sub
```

Using the
Internet Transfer
control to see
the raw HTML
of a Web site
Figure 24-2.

Then, as you can see in Figure 24-2, you will see the raw HTML for the main page at Yahoo's Web site (in 12 point type in order to make it easier to see).

Why is getting the raw HTML useful? How do you combine the power of the Internet Transfer control with the power of our special-purpose browser? The answer is that you can simply store the HTML in an invisible text box and then use InStr and Fuzzy searching in order to determine if the page contains information that you might prefer a child not to see, for example. If the page does contain words and phrases that you are monitoring for, and you therefore want to prevent the child from seeing that site, then simply don't display the page in the browser.

Here's an example of how to do this: suppose you call the function to do the checking ContentOK, and the invisible text box to "hold" the text txtContent; then you can use code like the following to work in tandem with the Navigate method.

```
Private Sub cmdGo_Click()
  On Error Resume Next
  txtContent = Inet1.OpenURL(txtAddress.Text)
  If Not ContentOK(txtContent.Text) Then
    MsgBox "Sorry, that is not a site I want you to visit."
  Else
    WebBrowser.Navigate txtAddress.Text
  End If
End Sub
```

24

Here's a very simple example of a ContentOK function. It returns false if the page contains the word "breast" but *not if the page contains the words "breast cancer."*

```
Function ContentOK(TheText As String) As Boolean
  Dim Temp As String
  Temp = UCase(TheText)
  If InStr(Temp, "BREAST CANCER") Then
    ContentOK = True
    Exit Function
  ElseIf InStr(Temp, "BREAST") Then
    ContentOK = False
  End If
End Function
```

Finally, the Internet Transfer control has one other nifty power: if you give the URL a file name, then the Internet Transfer control will actually grab the file (note the following example uses a dummy filename):

FileData$ = Inet1.OpenURL("ftp://ftp.osborne.com/catalogue")

Now, of course, you can use the usual file handling techniques (Chapter 18) in order to save the information to a file on the user's hard disk.

NOTE: The OpenURL method uses what is often called *synchronous* methods to get its data. This means that the control must finish grabbing the data before any other code can be executed. If you want to allow other activities to go on in your Visual Basic program, you'll need to replace the OpenURL method with a method of the Internet Transfer control called the Execute method. This method allows what is called *asynchronous* transmission. If you use the Execute method, you will also need to monitor what is happening in the StateChanged event procedure of the Internet Transfer control. (Consult the online help for more on this event.)

CHAPTER 25

Visual Basic and the Internet: VBScript and Dynamic HTML

What I want to do in this short chapter is to explain VBScript to you, concentrating on its use in activating Web pages. VBScript (its official name is "Visual Basic Scripting Edition") is a lightweight, simplified offshoot of Visual Basic—as a result it should take almost no time for you to master it.

NOTE: I am assuming that you have a basic knowledge of the Web and HTML, including using HTML controls, such as text boxes and buttons, as well as the basics of HTML forms.

VBScript is currently completely supported only in Internet Explorer, but a plug-in makes it usable in Netscape and, in any case, VBScript is the default language for Microsoft's Internet Information Server Active Server Pages. It can also be used to automate basic repetitive operating system tasks via the Windows Scripting Host that was introduced in Chapter 19.

TIP: As I mentioned in Chapter 19, the trick to operating system automation with VBScript is to use the CreateObject function rather than the New keyword to create your file system objects.

One advantage to using VBScript over JavaScript in working with HTML is that like Visual Basic itself and like HTML, VBScript is *not* case sensitive. Bitter experience has shown that since HTML is not case sensitive, a Webmaster's eyes are often less sensitive to bugs in their scripts that are really case problems for variables. Using a variable named *Cost* when what you meant was a variable named *cost* can lead to a painful bug-detecting session if you are using a case-sensitive scripting language like JavaScript.

Finally, as you will see later in this chapter, event-driven Dynamic HTML programming with VBScript follows Visual Basic's way of dealing with event-driven programming for its objects. As a result, you won't have any trouble mastering using VBScript for Dynamic HTML either.

NOTE: VB6 does have the ability to add Visual Basic code to an HTML page. The trouble is that, in my opinion, this feature requires adding way too much overhead to the process, such as the VB runtime. Working with what the designers of VB6 named a Dynamic HTML project means creating a separate DLL for the communication between VB and the Web page. You can find a description of this technology (and a related technology called ActiveX Documents) in the supplied documentation for VB6. VBScript, since it is part of the Web page, is much more lightweight. I would suggest using the Dynamic HTML project technology only if you need to keep your code secret or have need of some feature of VB that can't be achieved by combining VBScript and Dynamic HTML. (Remember, your script code is readily available to anyone who chooses View|Source from Internet Explorer.)

Basic Syntax of VBScript

If you think of VBScript as being Visual Basic where all variables are automatically variants, you are well on your way toward mastering it! VBScript is a typeless language based on VB's variant type, which means it does automatic (usually relatively smart) conversions between basic types, such as strings and the various kinds of numbers. For example, if you concatenate the data in a string variable and a number then VBScript will automatically convert the number to a string. For example,

```
Dim TheQueen
TheQueen = "Elizabeth "
Dim WhichOne
WhichOne  = 2
TheTitle = TheQueen & WhichOne
```

gives you, as in VB itself, "Queen Elizabeth 2" with no error messages. As in VB, variables need not be declared in VBScript (as I did with the Dim statement above), although by using Option Explicit (which VBScript also supports) at the beginning of your script, you can prevent the all-too-common error of a misspelled variable name.

The If-Then and Do-Loop control structures are the same as in Visual Basic itself.

```
If Salary > 290000 Then
  TaxRate = .39
ElseIf Salary > 150000
  TaxRate = .32
Else
  TaxRate = .28
End If
```

The For-Next loop has one limitation: the For-Next loop doesn't (and can't) use the counter variable:

25

```
For I = 10 to 1 Step -1
  MsgBox "It's t minus " & I & " counting."
Next
MsgBox "Blastoff"
```

Finally, the Select statement in VBScript is not as powerful as in VB itself. You can only test for equality and not a range of values.

```
Select Case TheLetter
  Case "A", "E", "I", "O", "U"
    MsgBox "Vowel"
  Case "Y"
    MsgBox "Sometimes a vowel"
  Case Else
   MsgBox "Consonant"
End Select
```

VBScript comes with a complete supply of functions for string manipulation, including the neat Split and Join and Replace functions you saw in Chapters 8 and 10. It also allows you to use user-defined procedures and functions that follow the same syntax as you saw in Chapter 9.

TIP: If you put your VBScript functions and procedures in a code module and set Sub Main as the startup, you can easily use VB's powerful debugging facilities to debug your VB code.

The following tables summarize VBScript's entire language. As you can see, it is definitely a lightweight subset of VB, so you can use any VBScript code in VB itself.

NOTE: The special Format functions (FormatNumber, FormatCurrency, FormatPercent, FormatDateTime) are all you have in VBScript, rather than VB's more powerful Format function.

Of course, all these functions are also available in VB6 to maintain compatibility with VBScript. For VB code, however, I only use them occasionally such as in writing code like the code in Chapter 19. Why bother using them when you have the far more powerful Format function available to you?

Category	Features
Array handling	Array Dim ReDim IsArray Erase LBound UBound
Assignments	= Set
Comments	Comments using ' or REM
Constants, procedures, and variables	Const Dim ReDim ByRef ByVal Call Function Sub Private Supplied Intrinsic constants

Category	Features
Control flow	Do...Loop For...Next For Each...Next If...Then...Else Select Case (restricted functionality) While...Wend
Conversions	CBool CByte CCur CDate CDbl CInt CLng CSng CStr
Dates/Times	Date Time DateAdd DateDiff DatePart DateSerial TimeSerial DateValue TimeValue Day Month Year Hour Minute Second Now Timer Weekday
Formatting strings	FormatNumber FormatCurrency FormatPercent FormatDateTime Hex MonthName Oct WeekdayName Error Handling On Error Resume Next Err Object

25

Category	Features
Input/Output	InputBox LoadPicture MsgBox Literals Empty Nothing Null True False
Math	Atn Cos Exp Sin Tan Log Sqr Randomize Rnd
Objects	CreateObject (non-browser based VBScript only) Dictionary (non-browser based VBScript only) GetObject (non-browser based VBScript only) FileSystemObject (non-browser based VBScript only) TextStream (non-browser based VBScript only)
Operators	Addition (+) Subtraction (-) Exponentiation (^) Modulus arithmetic (Mod) Multiplication (*) Division (/) Integer Division (\) Negation (-) String concatenation (&) Equality (=) Inequality (<>) Less Than (<) Less Than or Equal To (<=) Greater Than (>) Greater Than or Equal To (>=) Is And Or Xor Eqv Imp
Options	Option Explicit

Category	Features
Rounding	Abs Fix Int Round Sgn
Script engine identification	ScriptEngine ScriptEngineBuildVersion ScriptEngineMajorVersion ScriptEngineMinorVersion
Strings	Asc AscB AscW Chr ChrB ChrW Filter InStr InStrB InStrRev Join Len LenB LCase UCase Left LeftB Mid MidB Replace Right RightB Space Split StrComp String StrReverse LTrim RTrim Trim
Variants	IsArray IsDate IsEmpty IsNull IsNumeric IsObject TypeName VarType

25

Features of VB Not in VBScript

The following table summarizes the features of VB not in VBScript. If you need to port code that was written in pure VB to VBScript you'll need to make sure that you don't use any of the features shown in Table 25-1.

Category	Omitted Feature/Keyword
Array Handling	Option Base No ranges in array indices (lower bound must be 0)
Collection	Add, Count, Item, Remove Access to collections using ! character (e.g., MyCollection!Foo)
Conditional Compilation	#Const #If...Then...#Else
Control Flow	DoEvents GoSub...Return, GoTo On Error GoTo On...GoSub, On...GoTo Line numbers, Line labels With...End With
Conversion	CVar, CVDate Str, Val
Data Types	All intrinsic data types except the Variant data type No user-defined types via Type...End Type
Date/Time	Date statement, Time statement Timer
DDE	LinkExecute, LinkPoke, LinkRequest, LinkSend
Debugging	Debug.Print End, Stop
Declaration	Declare (for declaring and using DLLs) New (to make new objects) Optional arguments in procedures ParamArray in procedures Property Get, Property Let, Property Set Static
Error Handling	Erl Error On Error...Resume Resume, Resume Next
File Input/Output	All traditional file I/O
Financial	All financial functions

Features of VB
not in VBScript
Table 25-1.

Category	Omitted Feature/Keyword
Object Manipulation	TypeOf
Objects	Clipboard Collection Collection access using !
Operators	Like (fuzzy searching)
Options	Def*type* Option Base Option Compare
Select Case	Expressions containing the Is keyword or any comparison operators Expressions containing a range of values by using the To keyword
Strings	Fixed-length strings LSet, RSet Mid as a statement (use Replace) StrConv

Features of VB
not in VBScript
(*continued*)
Table 25-2.

Form Design and Validation with VBScript

One of the most common uses for script code on a Web page is to allow for client-side form validation. There are actually two ways to do form submission with VBScript. The first follows the traditional HTML-based form approach. The second (only recommended where security is not an issue, like within a corporate intranet) is to use the Internet Transfer or Winsock ActiveX controls that come standard with VB. The former has the advantage of being instantly familiar; the latter has the greatest flexibility. In this chapter I'll only talk about HTML form-based submission.

25

The key to doing form validation with VBScript is the On_Submit event, which is triggered whenever the user clicks on the Submit button in the HTML form. You write the code in the associated OnSubmit function to return True as the value of this function if the information should be sent and False if not. For example, if you had a form identified with the ID AddressForm than you would have VBScript code like this:

```
Function AddressForm_OnSubmit()
  Dim BadData
  If AddressForm.YourName.Value = "" Then BadData = True
  If AddressForm.YourAddress.Value = "" Then BadData = True
  If BadData Then
    MsgBox "Bad data"
    AddressForm_OnSubmit = False
  Else
    MsgBox "Thanks for submitting correct data"
    AddressForm_OnSubmit = True
  End If
End Function
```

All this can be done without involving ActiveX controls at all—just standard HTML intrinsic controls.

How to Use ActiveX Controls on a Web Page

Suppose you wanted to use the MaskEdit control supplied with VB6 on your Web page in order to make it easier for the user to enter correct data. The necessary HTML code to use a masked edit control (or any ActiveX control, for that matter) on a Web page is rather weird. For a masked edit control that will accept only phone numbers, the needed HTML looks something like this (note how it is all embedded in an <OBJECT> tag):

```
<OBJECT ID="MaskEditBox1" WIDTH=100 HEIGHT=50
 CLASSID="CLSID:C932BA85-4374-101B-A56C-00AA003668DC">
    <PARAM NAME="_ExtentX" VALUE="2117">
    <PARAM NAME="_ExtentY" VALUE="1058">
    <PARAM NAME="_Version" VALUE="327680">
    <PARAM NAME="MaxLength" VALUE="12">
    <PARAM NAME="Mask" VALUE="###-###-####">
    <PARAM NAME="PromptChar" VALUE="_">
</OBJECT>
```

Look this HTML code over and it should be clear that the main problem for using an ActiveX control is the totally inscrutable CLASSID that identifies the Masked Edit ActiveX control "uniquely across time and space." Because of the CLASSID, you can always be sure that your users will be using a compatible version of the control, but because of its complexity you will either go nuts cutting and pasting entries from the Windows registry or you will turn to a tool. There are only a few tools that handle ActiveX controls and VBScript gracefully. The free ActiveX Control Pad, downloadable from Microsoft, is probably the most popular. FrontPage 98, Dreamweaver, and most professional HTML editors all can handle inserting the CLASSID for you as well. (My favorite tool for scripting is NetObjects ScriptBuilder (http://www.netobjects.com). All these tools also allow you to easily set the properties of the ActiveX control.

 NOTE: Properties are usually called parameters in HTML, and they are given by the PARAM tag as in the above code.

Once you decide to introduce an ActiveX control, there are two added complications. The first one is that the dynamic HTML model in Internet Explorer requires you to refer to the properties of all ActiveX controls on the page using the following syntax:

Document.*NameOfControl.NameOfProperty*

For example, to refer to the text in the masked edit control given previously, you would use

Document.MaskEditBox1.Text

The more serious problem is that the information stored by the user in the masked edit control is not automatically packaged up with the rest of the information stored in the HTML intrinsic controls when he or she clicks on the Submit button. The trick for this and similar situations is to use a *hidden* HTML control to "mirror" the current state of any ActiveX control. Then, you must make sure that the value of the ActiveX control is copied to the appropriate hidden control in the On_Submit event function. (This extra step isn't needed if you are using the ActiveX Transfer or Winsock control.)

For example, suppose we added two masked edit controls—one for the person's zip code and one for the phone number—to an HTML form. We would then have to add two hidden controls so our HTML might look like this:

```
<HTML>
<HEAD>
<TITLE>Demo of Form Submission in HTML Combined with ActiveX Controls</TITLE>
</HEAD>
<BODY>
<FORM NAME=AddressForm>
  Enter your name please.
  <BR>
<INPUT TYPE = TEXT
  Name=TheName SIZE=30>
  <BR>
  Enter your address please.
  <BR>
  <TEXTAREA NAME=TheAddress
  ROW=2 COL = 30></TEXTAREA>
  <BR>
  Enter your zip code please.
  <BR>
<OBJECT ID="TheZipCode" WIDTH=100 HEIGHT=25
 CLASSID="CLSID:C932BA85-4374-101B-A56C-00AA003668DC">
    <PARAM NAME="_ExtentX" VALUE="2117">
    <PARAM NAME="_ExtentY" VALUE="1058">
    <PARAM NAME="_Version" VALUE="327680">
    <PARAM NAME="MaxLength" VALUE="12">
    <PARAM NAME="Mask" VALUE="#####-####">
    <PARAM NAME="PromptChar" VALUE="_">
</OBJECT>
<BR>
Enter your phone number please.
<BR>
<OBJECT ID="ThePhoneNumber" WIDTH=100 HEIGHT=25
 CLASSID="CLSID:C932BA85-4374-101B-A56C-00AA003668DC">
    <PARAM NAME="_ExtentX" VALUE="2117">
    <PARAM NAME="_ExtentY" VALUE="1058">
    <PARAM NAME="_Version" VALUE="327680">
    <PARAM NAME="MaxLength" VALUE="12">
    <PARAM NAME="Mask" VALUE="###-###-####">
    <PARAM NAME="PromptChar" VALUE="_">
</OBJECT>
<BR><BR>
```

25

```
<INPUT TYPE = HIDDEN Id= PhoneNumber>
<INPUT TYPE = HIDDEN Id= ZipCode>
<INPUT TYPE = SUBMIT Value = "Submit data">
</FORM>
</BODY>
</HTML>
```

Now the key is to add lines like the following in the AddressForm_OnSubmit( ) function.

```
PhoneNumber.Value = Document.ThePhoneNumber.Text
ZipCode.Value = Document.TheZipCode.Text
```

(As you saw in Chapter 14, the Text property of a masked edit control corresponds to the Value property of an HTML intrinsic control, i.e., to the actual contents.)

The Full HTML Source for the Form Validation Example
Here's a full HTML page that you can use in Internet Explorer to test the concepts that we covered in the previous section. (I am leaving out the code that would activate the server's processing of the form—I am simply using message boxes to give you some feedback as to the results of the data entry.)

```
<HTML>
<HEAD>
<TITLE>Demo of Form Submission in HTML combined with ActiveX Controls</TITLE>
<SCRIPT LANGUAGE="VBSCRIPT">
  <!--
    Function AddressForm_OnSubmit
      Dim BadData
      'copy data to hidden HTML objects
    AddressForm.PhoneNumber.Value = Document.ThePhoneNumber.Text
    AddressForm.ZipCode.Value = Document.TheZipCode.Text
    If AddressForm.TheName.Value = "" Then BadData = True
    If AddressForm.TheAddress.Value = "" Then BadData = True
    If AddressForm.PhoneNumber.Value = "" Then BadData = True
    If AddressForm.ZipCode.Value = "" Then BadData = True
    If BadData Then
        MsgBox "Bad data"
        AddressForm_OnSubmit = False
    Else
        MsgBox "Good data"
        AddressForm_OnSubmit = True
    End If
    End Function
  -->
  </SCRIPT>
</HEAD>
<BODY>
<FORM NAME=AddressForm>
```

```
   Enter your name please:
   <INPUT TYPE=TEXT NAME=TheName SIZE=30>
   <BR>
   Enter your address please:
   <TEXTAREA NAME=TheAddress ROW=2 COL=30></TEXTAREA>
   <BR>
   Enter your zip code please.
   <BR>
<OBJECT ID="TheZipCode" WIDTH=125 HEIGHT=25
CLASSID="CLSID:C932BA85-4374-101B-A56C-00AA003668DC">
    <PARAM NAME="_ExtentX" VALUE="2117">
    <PARAM NAME="_ExtentY" VALUE="1058">
    <PARAM NAME="_Version" VALUE="327680">
    <PARAM NAME="MaxLength" VALUE="12">
    <PARAM NAME="Mask" VALUE="#####-####">
    <PARAM NAME="PromptChar" VALUE="_">
</OBJECT>
   <BR>
   Enter your phone number please.
   <BR>
<OBJECT ID="ThePhoneNumber" WIDTH=125 HEIGHT=25
   CLASSID="CLSID:C932BA85-4374-101B-A56C-00AA003668DC">
    <PARAM NAME="_ExtentX" VALUE="2117">
    <PARAM NAME="_ExtentY" VALUE="1058">
    <PARAM NAME="_Version" VALUE="327680">
    <PARAM NAME="MaxLength" VALUE="12">
    <PARAM NAME="Mask" VALUE="###-###-####">
    <PARAM NAME="PromptChar" VALUE="_">
</OBJECT>
   <BR><BR>
   <INPUT TYPE=HIDDEN Name= PhoneNumber>
   <INPUT TYPE=HIDDEN Name= ZipCode>
   <INPUT TYPE=submit Value = "Submit data to server">
</FORM>
</BODY>
</HTML>
```

25

VBScript and Dynamic HTML

The key to understanding Dynamic HTML (regardless of whether you choose VBScript or JavaScript to control it) is this:

> *Essentially every item on your Web page is an object that you can script.*

All you need to do is give the HTML tag an ID and set its properties using code.

What makes the combination of VBScript and Dynamic HTML so appealing to experienced VB programmers is that what you then need to do for event handling also follows the VB event model very closely. For example, suppose you want to detect and do something whenever the mouse clicks in a certain <H1> head. Here's what you need to do:

Expand the tag for the head so that it includes an ID—the equivalent of a VB control's Name property. For example:

```
<H1 ID=AResponsiveHead>Please click me!</H1>
```

Then you program the OnClick event for this head in a way completely analogous to what you would do for the OnClick event of any control. For example:

```
Sub AResponsiveHead_OnClick()
  MsgBox "Hello—welcome to Dynamic HTML!"
End Sub
```

So Dynamic HTML, when combined with VBScript, uses exactly the same framework used so successfully in VB:

> Sub *NameOfObject_NameOfEvent(parameters)*
> ' lines of code
> End Sub

Here's the full HTML code for this example:

```
<HTML>
<HEAD>
<TITLE>A Simple Dynamic HTML Demo with VBScript</Title>
<SCRIPT LANGUAGE = VBScript>
<!--
Sub AResponsiveHead_OnClick()
  MsgBox "Hello—welcome to Dynamic HTML!"
End Sub
-->
</SCRIPT>
</HEAD>
<BODY>
<H1>This is a plain old H1 head. Clicking does nothing.</H1>
<H1 ID=AResponsiveHead>This is a dynamic H1 head-click me and see!</H1>
</BODY>
</HTML>
```

T IP: If you add VB controls to a form and make their Name properties the same as the Names of the form controls inside an HTML form, you can usually come up with a pretty good facsimile of your HTML page for testing in the VB IDE.

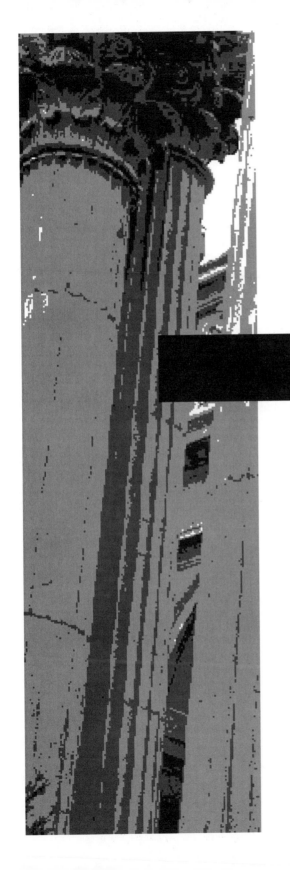

CHAPTER 26

Distributing Your Application: The Package and Deployment Wizard

This short chapter covers the basics of distributing a Visual Basic executable that you create. In most cases, the Package and Deployment Wizard supplied with all the editions of Visual Basic makes this a snap. You fill in various dialog boxes as you move through the wizard's screens, then the wizard goes off and does what needs to be done!

Getting Started

Everything you write with Visual Basic that you want to be run outside the Visual Basic integrated development environment needs a file called Msvbvm60.dll. (The name stands for Microsoft Visual Basic Virtual Machine.) This file contains all the support routines and intrinsic controls that are needed for Visual Basic to do *anything*. It is a pretty big file (around 1,400K). Luckily, no matter how many Visual Basic applications a person is running at the same time, he or she needs only one copy of this file in memory and only one copy stored on the hard disk (usually in /Windows/System).

You aren't done yet: You will need the custom control file for each custom control that is in your application or that is part of your control. These are the files that end in .ocx and they are relatively small—often less than 30K each. Still, when combined with the need for the Msvbvm60.dll file, the result is that the number of floppy disks needed to install a Visual Basic executable or control built with VB can be quite large. If none of the needed files are available on the target machine, the simplest Visual Basic will require at least two floppy disks—even with the compression done by the Package and Deployment Wizard. Most of the time, therefore, you will want to choose a CD as your distribution medium!

Luckily, while you do have to make sure the users of your Visual Basic project or control have the Msvbvm60.dll file and any other supporting files, many users of Windows 95/98 and Windows NT will already have the Visual Basic Virtual Machine dll file installed on their systems. If you are working in a corporate environment where you know what is on people's machines, your job is much simpler, of course, and you may be able to use floppies as the distribution medium. For example, most users of Internet Explorer will have the file already, and I expect that soon Microsoft will set the Msvbvm60.dll file to install at the same time someone installs the operating system files. This will greatly reduce the minimum footprint (size of the resulting file) needed to distribute a Visual Basic project.

Finally, when someone runs an executable file that contains a custom control, the .ocx file for the custom control must be in the system's path or in the same directory as the .exe file. The Package and Deployment Wizard automatically puts the files in the appropriate place. (If the appropriate .ocx can't be found, the Visual Basic Virtual Machine generates an error message and dies.)

Building the Executable

Early versions of Visual Basic did not have the ability to make true executables. Since version 5.0 this is no longer the case. But what does "a true executable" mean and why should you care?

First off, earlier versions of Visual Basic always translated the Visual Basic code into something called *p-code*. This is an intermediate language that is different from the machine language for the Intel chip. The resulting p-code was then interpreted by the Visual Basic run-time engine essentially line by line into Intel machine code. This is inefficient. For a loop, it is obviously easier to do the translation into machine language once and not retranslate the code for each pass through the loop! On the other hand, p-code gives you the smallest possible files.

Only the Professional and Enterprise editions of Visual Basic have the ability to make true executables. This is controlled by choosing File|Make Exe or File|Make Ocx and then clicking on the Options button in the Make Project dialog box shown in Figure 26-1.

What you see is shown in Figure 26-2. The Make tab lets you add version control and copyright information. You also set the project icon that the user will see in the executable and set command line information if you choose to allow this.

If you have the Professional or Enterprise edition, click on the Compile tab. This takes you to a screen like the one shown in Figure 26-3. I want to go over the options in this important dialog box one by one.

Compile to P-Code   This lets you compile your project into p-code. Although slower to execute, this option allows a significantly smaller "footprint" than code compiled into Intel machine code. (It is often one-half to two-thirds the size.)

Compile to Native Code   This is the default and, as I mentioned, it allows you to compile a project using native code with the optimizations you select via the remaining buttons, which are described in Table 26-1.

26

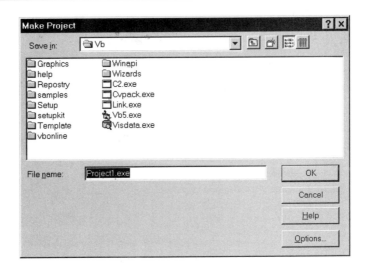

The Make
Project
dialog box
Figure 26-1.

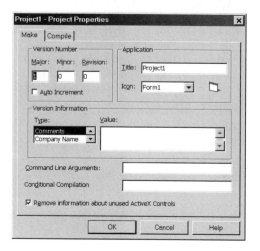

NOTE: A program that makes heavy use of loops, such as some of the standard benchmarks, will show a dramatic improvement—often a tenfold increase over the comparable program built with VB versions earlier than VB5. In practice though, the speedup is likely to be much, much less (often less than 50 percent, sometimes as little as 20 percent) since the user interface code doesn't benefit much from the native code compilation process.

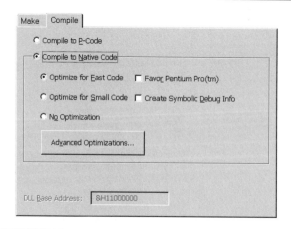

Button	Description
Optimize for Fast Code	Maximizes the speed.
Optimize for Small Code	Minimizes the size. You probably do not get much advantage over simply using the p-code option.
No Optimization	Compiles without optimizations.
Favor Pentium Pro	Optimizes the code created so it works best with the Pentium Pro chip (as well as the Pentium II chip since they share the same architecture). Code generated with this option checked will still run on earlier processors but will run slower on 486s and Pentiums (even those with MMX) than it would if you left this unchecked.
Create Symbolic Debug Info	Used when you want to run your VB code through a stand-alone debugger such as the ones from NuMega or those supplied with Microsoft's Visual Studio components.

Buttons for
Compiling to
Native Code
Table 26-1.

Advanced Optimizations   Clicking this button brings up the Advanced Optimizations dialog box shown here. The default is to have no options checked. I do not recommend changing any of the defaults here—they are for VB gurus only.

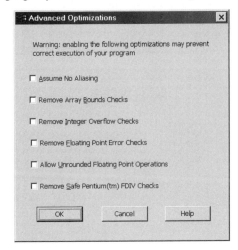

26

The Package and Deployment Wizard

The Package and Deployment Wizard is a really nifty tool that lets you distribute your application or a control almost effortlessly. You can start it as an add-in to the VB environment or use it as a stand-alone program that gets installed when you install VB. To use it as an add-in:

1. Select Tools|Add-Ins|Add-In Manager.
2. Choose the Package and Deployment Wizard.
3. Click on the Loaded/Unloaded check box.

The wizard will then appear on the Add-Ins menu and you only have to click on it in order to start the wizard.

As a stand-alone program, you can get to it via the submenu of the Visual Basic 6 item on the Start menu, or from the Microsoft Visual Studio Tools item if you have Visual Studio. Assuming you used the standard installation, the Package and Deployment Wizard program will be in a directory called \Wizards\PDWizard below where your product was installed.

NOTE: Regardless of which method you choose to get to the wizard, you must have saved the project file at least once before you can use the Package and Deployment Wizard.

When you start the Package and Deployment Wizard, you are taken to the initial setup screen, which looks like Figure 26-4.

Let's go over the items in the main screen. First, there is a Help button that takes you to the (short) online help file for the wizard and a Cancel button to end the wizard. (There's also an Exit button in the top right-hand corner to close the wizard.) If you are not using it in the IDE, you'll have to fill in the text box with the name of the project. Luckily, there is a Browse button that opens up a standard File dialog box so

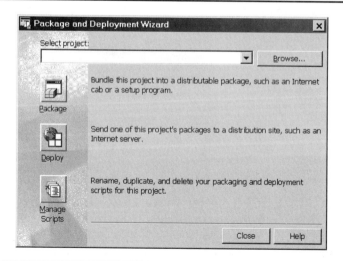

Initial screen in the wizard

Figure 26-4.

that you can easily find the project (which means finding the .vbp file I talked about in Chapter 12).

There are three different ways to use the wizard depending on which of the buttons you click in the left-hand side of Figure 26-4, as shown here:

Package	This is the option you would choose if you want to distribute your application via floppy disks or by downloading it from a Web site in the form of a self-extracting file. In the latter case, you will work with the next option after you make the package.
Deploy	This option only becomes active after you have made a package for your project via the first button.
Manage Scripts	This option is for experts only. It lets you modify what the wizard does, which has never been necessary for the times I have used it!

Building the Package

Once you fill in the text box with the name of the project (if you are using the wizard as an add-in, it's filled in for you automatically), click on the Package button. You may see a dialog box like this since the wizard needs to have a compiled version of your project to work with.

I always find it best to have the wizard do the compile. This ensures I have the latest version of the compiled code in my package. After a short delay while the wizard compiles the project, you are taken to a screen like Figure 26-5.

26

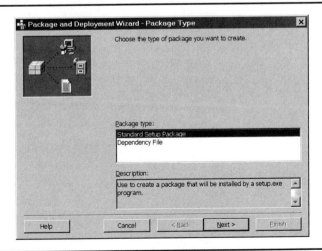

Choosing the type of package in the wizard

Figure 26-5.

As you can see in Figure 26-5, you have two choices. The first item is the one you want. The second item simply gives you a file that lists everything you would need to make a package (such as the names of the .ocx controls you used).

A Hands-On Session

For illustration purposes, let's suppose you want to distribute the OLE Drag and Drop application from Chapter 20. This project is a good one to have the wizard work with because, simple as it is, it uses some of the most sophisticated features built into VB and therefore the package will need a lot of support files. (Remember the source code for this project is available from Osborne's Web site.)

I'll assume you are using the wizard as an add-in and have loaded the OLE Drag and Drop project into the VB IDE and moved through the wizard screen shown in Figure 26-5. When you hit the Next button, you are taken to a screen like Figure 26-6.

This screen is where you tell the wizard where you want the files stored while the package is being assembled. The convention is to store the package in a directory called Package below the directory holding the project as shown here:

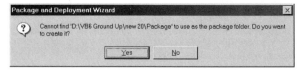

After you create the directory for the package, you are taken to a screen like the one shown in Figure 26-7 that lists all the files you need to deploy this package. As you can see in Figure 26-7, there are many of them for the OLE Drag and Drop project!

Click Next. The resulting screen shown in Figure 26-8 is the crucial one. "Cab files" is the name Microsoft gives to the compressed "cabinet" files it uses to deploy all its

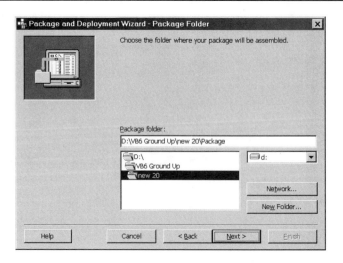

Choosing the location for the package screen

Figure 26-6.

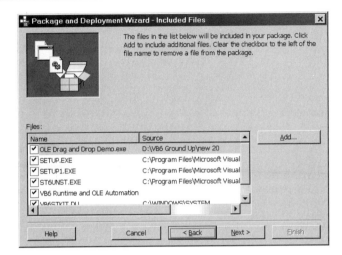

The Included
Files screen
Figure 26-7.

application. If you are using the Web or a CD, you can have one large Cab file. If you are using floppies to distribute your application, click on the Multiple Cabs button in Figure 26-8.

After a short delay you are taken to a screen like Figure 26-9 where you can give a name to be displayed when the Setup program is run by the user. As you can see in Figure 26-9, I am calling this the OLE Drag and Drop Project.

The next screen, shown in Figure 26-10, lets you add your application to the user's Start menu—a really nifty feature that would otherwise be quite painful to program!

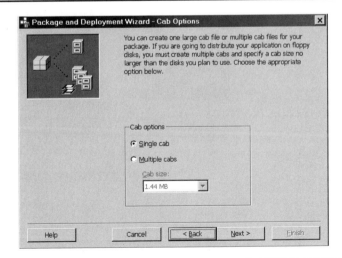

26

Cab options
screen
Figure 26-8.

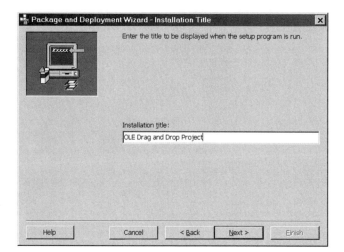

Entering a title
for the Setup
program
Figure 26-9.

If you don't like the default location (Program Files\Name Of Project), you can work with the buttons shown on the right of Figure 26-10 in order to add them to a new location on the Program menu that will automatically be created.

I don't recommend changing the defaults for the next screen, shown in Figure 26-11. You will make people very unhappy with you if you install your program in one of the options shown in Figure 26-12, unless it is a control you are packaging.

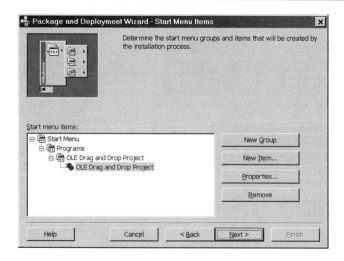

Adjusting the
location of the
installed
program on the
Start menu
Figure 26-10.

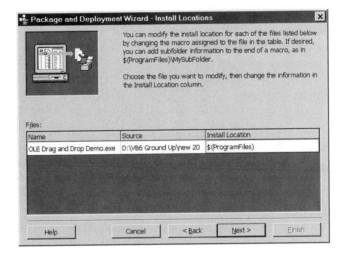

Install location screen

Figure 26-11.

The next screen, shown in Figure 26-13, allows you to enable people to share your files. This option would generally be chosen only if you were making an OLE server using the techniques from Chapter 20. Since the OLE Drag and Drop program is a separate executable, don't do anything in this screen except click the Next button!

The next screen is the Finished screen shown in Figure 26-14. As you can see here, you can give a name to the options you chose in the wizard so that you can reuse them. In this case, I didn't make any strange choices so I won't bother changing the name suggested by the wizard.

26

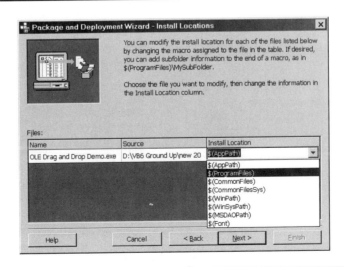

List of possible install locations

Figure 26-12.

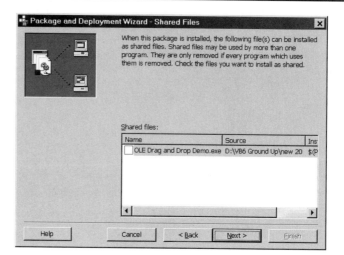

Making shared
files
Figure 26-13.

After the wizard does its work, it gives you a report screen like the one shown in
Figure 26-15. As you will see, the package for this simple project is a mere 4.3MB or
about three floppies.

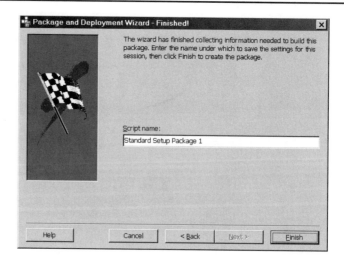

The Finished
screen
Figure 26-14.

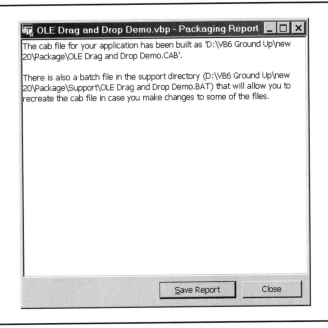

The report
screen
Figure 26-15.

Here's the directory substructure of the \Package directory for this example. It is pretty typical of what you will get from the wizard when you show all the hidden files.

```
D:\VB6 Ground Up\new 20\Package\setup.exe
D:\VB6 Ground Up\new 20\Package\OLE Drag and Drop Demo.CAB
D:\VB6 Ground Up\new 20\Package\SETUP.LST
D:\VB6 Ground Up\new 20\Package\Support
D:\VB6 Ground Up\new 20\Package\Support\Project1.DDF
D:\VB6 Ground Up\new 20\Package\Support\COMCAT.DLL
D:\VB6 Ground Up\new 20\Package\Support\MSVBVM60.DLL
D:\VB6 Ground Up\new 20\Package\Support\OLE Drag and Drop Demo.BAT
D:\VB6 Ground Up\new 20\Package\Support\OLE Drag and Drop Demo.exe
D:\VB6 Ground Up\new 20\Package\Support\OLEAUT32.DLL
D:\VB6 Ground Up\new 20\Package\Support\OLEPRO32.DLL
D:\VB6 Ground Up\new 20\Package\Support\ASYCFILT.DLL
D:\VB6 Ground Up\new 20\Package\Support\SETUP.EXE
D:\VB6 Ground Up\new 20\Package\Support\Setup.Lst
D:\VB6 Ground Up\new 20\Package\Support\SETUP1.EXE
D:\VB6 Ground Up\new 20\Package\Support\ST6UNST.EXE
D:\VB6 Ground Up\new 20\Package\Support\STDOLE2.TLB
D:\VB6 Ground Up\new 20\Package\Support\VB6STKIT.DLL
```

26

If you were to distribute this application, you would simply copy everything in the \Package directory to the CD or the Web.

CAUTION: It is the Setup program in the Package directory you have to run, not the one in the \Support directory.

For example, if you ran the Setup program, you'll soon be in a usual Windows Setup program as shown in Figure 26-16.

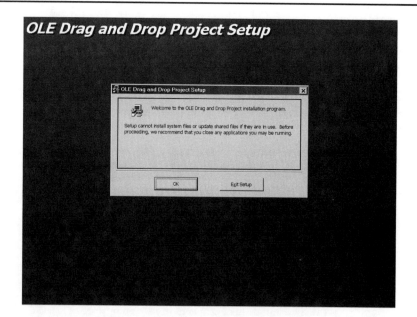

Running the Setup program created by the wizard

Figure 26-16.

Index